College
Third Edition
Majors
HANDBOOK

with Real Career Paths and Payoffs

The Actual Jobs, Earnings, and Trends for Graduates of 50 College Majors

Neeta P. Fogg, Ph.D.

Thomas F. Harrington, Ph.D.

Paul E. Harrington, Ed.D.

Laurence Shatkin, Ph.D.

jist Works

America's Career Publisher®

College Majors Handbook with Real Career Paths and Payoffs, *Third Edition*

© 2012 by JIST Publishing

Published by JIST Works, an imprint of JIST Publishing
875 Montreal Way
St. Paul, MN 55102
E-mail: info@jist.com   Website: www.jist.com

> Visit www.jist.com for information on JIST, free job search tips, tables of contents, sample pages, and ordering information on our many products.

Acquisitions and Development Editor: Susan Pines
Production Editor: Jeanne Clark
Cover Designer: Aleata Halbig
Interior Layout: Jack Ross
Proofreader: Charles Hutchinson
Indexer: Cheryl Ann Lenser

Library of Congress Cataloging-in-Publication data is on file with the Library of Congress.

Printed in the United States of America

18 17 16 15 14 13 12   9 8 7 6 5 4 3 2 1

ISBN 978-1-59357-771-1

Table of Contents

Introduction

"What's your major?" Every first-year student entering a college or university is asked that question. A *major* is a concentration of specialized courses, usually a minimum of 24 credit hours (such as eight 3-hour courses), taken during a student's third and fourth years in a 4-year program.

Some colleges and universities require students to declare a major immediately upon entering their freshman year, most often in specialized technical areas such as electrical engineering, nursing, or computer science. In a liberal arts college or university, students are exposed to a spectrum of courses from different academic disciplines during the first 2 years for a general education. At the beginning of the third, or junior, year, most colleges require students to concentrate their studies in a particular field, such as psychology, journalism, or chemistry, as preparation for a career after graduation.

Some first-year students know exactly what they want to major in and what career they want to pursue after graduation. At the other extreme, some freshmen enter college without having made any decision about either a major or a career. Between the two extremes are most students, who have tentative or—at best provisional—ideas about possible majors and subsequent careers. Decisions for choosing one major above another are sometimes made for superficial yet practical, short-term reasons, such as which courses are less difficult and which departments have professors who give better grades. We believe that the choice of major field of study should be based on long-term career and lifestyle goals and informed by sound information.

Most of the publications offering guidance for enrolling in college contain little more than a description of the more than 3,500 colleges and universities across the nation. They provide a sketch of each college in terms of the types of students enrolled and the nature of the educational process at each college, including class sizes, student-faculty ratios, and proportion of faculty with a doctoral degree. They also provide some information on the types of programs offered. In recent years, this type of publication has provided a quality ranking of the colleges based on the admissions competitiveness of the school.

Although these publications can provide a thumbnail sketch of a large number of colleges across the country, they don't provide much insight into perhaps the most important decision that a college student will make—a decision that is even more important than the actual college selection—the choice of a major.

This book provides substantive information on long-term career alternatives for bachelor's degree holders in 58 major fields of study. The basic tenet of this book is that the cost of a college or university education is an investment that can yield payoffs in the form of economically rewarding and personally fulfilling careers. Fifty-eight chapters—each devoted to a single major—detail the economic rewards and employment experiences of graduates in each field. The chapters also discuss training opportunities at work, the types of duties performed at work, and the most common occupations in which the graduates from each of the 58 major fields of study are employed.

To be sure, salary is not the only form of payoff from a college education. Interests, values, and abilities are personal goals for job satisfaction. This book responds to this need by integrating the work of psychology and economics into a single comprehensive volume. You receive information about the personality and labor market implications of undergraduate majors. We have tried to cross the boundaries of a single academic discipline to provide new and more meaningful information to those confronted with making a college investment decision.

For those inclined toward graduate education, this book discusses the role of graduate education in career advancement. It also presents the actual postgraduate schooling experiences of bachelor's degree holders in each of the 58 major fields, including the types of postgraduate degrees earned and the major field of study in which a degree was received.

This informative book should help you replace superficial, short-term assessments about a major with long-term considerations of several economic, personal, and psychological dimensions of your choice of major that should have a positive impact on your future employment and lead to a professionally rewarding career.

This book enables you to easily compare the payoffs of each of the 58 majors on the basis of a survey of 170,000 bachelor's degree holders. For parents, students, career counselors, and anyone involved in the choice or use of a college major, this book is an enlightening and indispensable resource for choosing one major above another.

Organization of the Book

Chapter 1 starts out with the relationship between pre-college decisions on college and career choice. This chapter describes the importance of decisions made during high school on college and career outcomes. Chapters 2 and 3 provide a discussion of the psychology and economics involved in the choice of major field of study. Psychologist Thomas Harrington writes about the role that personal values, interests, personality, and abilities play in the selection of majors and career fields. Economists Neeta Fogg and Paul Harrington examine the economics of the college investment decision. We focus on the economic benefits and costs of a college diploma and the impact that the choice of a major has on long-term labor market success.

The remainder of the book provides specific information on 58 major fields of study. The profile of each undergraduate major begins with a definition of the major and the various subfields that it includes. Next, a discussion of the skills required to enter the field successfully and the types of values, interests, personalities, and abilities that persons in the field generally possess is included.

For each major field of study, different kinds of data are provided on the employment and earnings outcomes as well as on graduates' educational pathways. Information is provided on the kinds of jobs held by graduates with a bachelor's degree in each major, the activities that they undertake at work, and the sector in which they are employed. An extensive discussion of the earnings of graduates by major—including their long-term earnings experiences—is provided. The level of company-supported training and the future educational activities of graduates are presented as well.

Finally, we provide data on the employment outlook—developed by the U.S. Bureau of Labor Statistics—for each of the most commonly held jobs by graduates in every major field of study. All the data and analysis included for the majors pertain to college graduates who have earned a bachelor's degree only (with a few exceptions that are noted). The outcomes for persons with an earned graduate degree are not included, although information on the likelihood of earning a graduate degree of some type and the kinds of advanced degrees earned is included for each major.

Sources of Information

Many of the findings and analyses in this book are based on the results of the National Survey of College Graduates (NSCG). The NSCG is a sample of more than 170,000 respondents in the United States who completed a comprehensive questionnaire designed to gather information on the educational, employment, and earnings experiences of a cross section of college graduates. The NSCG represents the largest and most comprehensive study of college graduates ever conducted.

The NSCG allowed us to produce statistically reliable and detailed data for post-graduation outcomes of graduates in alternative major fields of study. For the first time, we have a systematic perspective on the long-term outcomes associated with choosing a particular undergraduate major. Ironically, the results on which this book is based are simply a by-product of a more ambitious data collection program undertaken by the U.S. Bureau of the Census for the National Science Foundation. This larger study provides longitudinal information on college graduates in scientific, engineering, and technical fields of study.

Some information in this book was taken from U.S. Department of Labor publications and various college and university catalogs. Other materials used include *Ability Explorer* by Joan and Thomas Harrington (JIST Publishing, 2006), *The Career Decision-Making System* by Thomas Harrington and Arthur O'Shea (American Guidance Service, 1992), and *A Guide to the Development and Use of Myers-Briggs Type Indicator* by Isabel Briggs Myers and Mary H. McCaulley (Consulting Psychologist Press, 1995).

The employment projections are derived from a computer data file containing the occupational projections of the Bureau of Labor Statistics. These projections can be found at the website of the Employment Projections Program (www.bls.gov/emp). The analysis that accompanies the projections is mostly derived from the *Occupational Outlook Handbook*, by the U.S. Department of Labor, available from JIST Publishing.

Timeliness of the Information

Information about education and careers is a lot like the food that you buy: It has a limited shelf life before it gets stale. This is inevitable because the American educational system and economy are evolving continuously. Nevertheless, the authors have tried to make the information in this third edition as timely as possible.

The data from the National Survey of College Graduates was gathered in 2003 and is the most recent data from that survey that could be used for a book of this kind. The NSCG conducted a more recent survey in 2006, but that year's survey focused only on people who had degrees in science, technology, engineering, and mathematics.

Here are some guidelines to keep in mind regarding the timeliness of the data in the descriptions of college majors:

▶ Educational requirements for some careers have become more rigorous in recent years. For example, a bachelor's in pharmacy used to be sufficient schooling for licensure as a pharmacist, whereas nowadays a Pharm.D. degree is almost always required. This book notes those majors for which requirements have changed since the 2003 survey was conducted and adjusts the descriptions accordingly.

▶ Earnings figures for graduates of the majors, although based on the 2003 survey, have been inflated to 2010 dollars. They apply to full-time workers only.

▶ Figures related to the employment status of graduates can lose accuracy because of ups and downs in the economy. A recession can cause the percentage of unemployed workers to increase or cause some graduates to drop out of the workforce. On the other hand, boom times can boost the percentage of employed workers. The figures in this book are based on the situation of graduates at the time of the survey, 2003. That year, the unemployment rate for the nation was 6 percent, a somewhat high rate historically but much lower than what we are experiencing as this book goes to press. If the figures for the various majors do not closely match current conditions in the labor market, they are still useful for comparing one major to another.

▶ Statements about the employment outlook for occupations are based on the most recently available projections from the Department of Labor and apply to the years 2008–2018.

▶ The ratio of male and female graduates of majors is likely to have changed somewhat since the 2003 survey, in most cases trending toward increased female presence. Note that this figure describes graduates in the population, not students enrolled in the major, so even though the ratio of new female degree recipients is increasing for many majors, the proportion of female grads in the population is changing much more slowly. Nevertheless, instances where the trend has changed markedly in recent years are noted in the text. Trends for some other topics of information also receive comments in cases where conditions have changed greatly since 2003.

▶ Probably the most important trend in workplace activities since 2003 has been toward increased use of computer applications. The actual amount of this usage is probably considerably higher than what is indicated by the figures in the descriptions. However, these figures are still useful for comparing one major to another.

Credits and acknowledgments: The task of writing this volume was indeed daunting. The computer programming and data analysis required to accurately portray the career options and earnings experiences of college graduates for individual major fields of study required sophisticated skills and great attention to detail. Two data analysis and extraction programs were invaluable aids for sorting through the massive databases on which this book was based: the SESTAT program on the website of the National Science Foundation (http://sestat.nsf.gov/sestat/sestat.html) and the DataFerrett program on the website of the Census Bureau (http://dataferrett.census.gov). While the authors created this book, it is based on the work of many others. The occupational and educational information is based on data obtained from the U.S. Department of Labor, the U.S. Census Bureau, and the National Science Foundation. These sources provide the most authoritative occupational and educational information available. Some of the skills information is from the O*NET database, which was developed by researchers and developers under the direction of the U.S. Department of Labor. They, in turn, were assisted by thousands of employers who provided details on the nature of work in the many thousands of job samplings used in the database's development. We used the most recent version of the O*NET database, release 16.0. We appreciate and thank the staff of the U.S. Department of Labor for their efforts and expertise in providing such a rich source of data. Please consider that the academic and occupational information in this book has its limitations. It should not be used in legal settings as a basis for academic or occupational injuries or other matters. This is because the information in this book reflects jobs as they have been found to occur in general, but they may not coincide in every respect with the compensation for and the content of jobs as performed in particular establishments or at certain localities. Users of this information demanding specific job requirements should supplement this data with local information detailing jobs in their community.

PART 1

What You Need to Know About the College Investment Decision, College Success, and Career Choice

CHAPTER 1

What Pays Off in High School:
Pre-College Decisions and College and Career Choices

Today's high school students, and even children leaving middle school and entering high school, are confronted with a bewildering set of choices requiring decisions that can affect their future personal well-being. The choices that young teens must make are far more complex than those made by their parents at the same age. Moreover, the ramifications of making the wrong choice at an early age can be much more severe than was the case even a few decades ago. As the rewards for making the right decision have become greater, the adversity associated with making the wrong decision has also become more severe. As a result, the gap between those who succeed and those who struggle has increased considerably in the past two decades.

Middle and high school students today make decisions about schooling, sexual behavior, and drugs and alcohol use (among other things) that will shape a good part of their pathway to adulthood. While a misstep at an early age may not necessarily be fatal to long-term success, it will certainly divert a youngster from that pathway. Bearing a child while in high school does not automatically mean that a young female's chances of long-term employment and earnings success fall to zero, but it does mean that the likelihood of achieving such success will decline sharply. Similarly, a young male abusing drugs and alcohol will likely experience a sharp reduction in his chances for life success. In both instances, a set of obstacles to personal development is created by the youth based on some bad decisions at an early age.

Certainly, all of this is unfair. Youngsters aged 13 or 14, or even 17 or 18, shouldn't have their life chances reduced because of decisions made in ignorance, on whim and caprice, or because of the teen torment of peer pressure. Yet the clear fact is that life has become increasingly unforgiving and certainly more risky for youth than has been the case in the recent past. Powerful economic and social forces have dramatically altered the outcomes associated with the decisions that parents and children make regarding the way the adolescent develops.

Technological change and economic growth have combined to dramatically increase the economic payoff to basic skills development, educational attainment, early work experience, and occupational proficiency. As Chapter 3 shows, today's economy offers the biggest payoff, in terms of earnings and likelihood of being hired, to people who have the kinds of skills that are learned in college.

This chapter examines the set of decisions that high school students must make about the following four key issues:

▶ Developing basic skills—reading, writing, and mathematics

▶ Establishing educational goals

▶ Mixing work and school

▶ Developing occupational skills

It also provides a brief review of some of the key economic behaviors of colleges and universities when recruiting their entering undergraduate classes—including college pricing and financial aid strategies—along with a discussion of their meaning for students and parents.

Before we get into the specific questions that adolescents and parents need to consider, let's first spend a bit of time discussing the nature of the education decision-making process.

Understanding the Investment Characteristics of the Education Decision and the Need for Parental Involvement in Decision Making

Most day-to-day decisions that youngsters make are what economists think of as decisions about *consumption*. Consumption can be thought of as simply paying the cost for a good or service and receiving all of the benefits for that good or service immediately. There is no time difference between when the costs are paid and the benefits received. A good example might be the purchase of an ice cream cone. On a hot summer afternoon we might buy a double Rocky Road. When we purchase our cone from the vendor, we pay the costs at the same time that we receive the benefits of the purchase. An important implication of this is that we know with a high degree of certainty what the benefits of the ice cream cone are when we make the purchase. This means that there is relatively little risk associated with a well-informed consumption decision. When we buy the cone, we are pretty certain of what we will receive in return.

A second key category of household spending is *investment goods or services*. These differ from consumption goods and services in many important ways. The critical distinguishing factor between consumption and investment is time. Unlike with consumption spending, the costs and benefits of investment spending are not closely connected in time or even necessarily in space.

Investment occurs when current consumption is sacrificed toward the purchase of a good or service that is expected to yield a higher level of benefits in the future, which frequently accrue in the form of higher future income and therefore higher levels of future consumption. While many adults understand the idea of deferring current consumption for higher future consumption, it may not be an idea with which most adolescents are familiar. An 18th-century economist noted that current consumption confronts our senses, while future consumption can only be imagined. Because of their limited life experiences, adolescents may have a more limited ability than their parents to imagine the gains from delaying the gratification of their current consumption desires. This is one reason why parental involvement in schooling is so important. Middle and young high school students may have less understanding than their parents of how the abilities they develop in school will make a difference in the long run. Fundamentally, adolescents seem to have limited ability to look into the future, at least compared to parents.

Perhaps the reasons that parents better understand the difference between consumption and investment is that investment, by its very nature, involves a degree of uncertainty and therefore risk. Because the benefits of investment, by definition, occur in the future, it is not certain that they will occur at all or that all of the anticipated benefits will be produced by the investment activity. There is only a chance or a probability that the expected benefits of an investment will actually materialize. Parents, largely through observation and experience, have a better notion than children of the uncertainty and risk associated with an investment activity, thus placing them in a better position to make investment decisions, which are usually more sophisticated than consumption decisions. For most people, especially adolescents, the preference is for current consumption. Part of being a responsible parent means pushing children to forgo current consumption (such as watching television or playing video games) to engage in activities that are investment-like in nature (for example, studying and doing extra work at school), as they are expected to yield gains in the

future that exceed the value of forgone current consumption.

When individuals invest, they are in a very real sense gambling—betting that forgoing current consumption will yield higher future consumption. An individual investor's willingness to give up current consumption is in part dependent on his perception of stability and certainty of receiving the expected benefits. The more stable the investment environment, the more certain the investment will result in the expected gains or benefits. Reducing uncertainty about the future justifies placing greater weight on future benefits versus present benefits. If the future looks very uncertain, then we will not invest. For example, students with more stability in their home lives have better basic skills proficiencies than do those with less stability, so family and social stability play an important role in the investment decision. Stability in the labor market also will alter investment decisions in the labor market. If students and parents have a great degree of uncertainty about future prospects in alternative career areas, then the benefits of investing in a given field become more risky.

The problem for many students, and even parents, is that they fail to think of high school education as an investment good. For too many students, high school is a place to hang out and meet friends but not a place to develop skills and abilities and prepare for the future. Part of the reason that students and parents treat high school matriculation somewhat cavalierly is that, in economic terms, it is often a "free good." For most students (and their parents) there are no direct out-of-pocket costs associated with a high school education. Most transactions follow the simple economic dictum that those who pay the costs receive the benefits. Transactions that are based on this rule are more likely to follow a certain sort of price discipline. Extending our ice cream example, if I pay for the ice cream, I won't throw it out because I paid for it directly with the expectation to receive some kind of benefit for the cost incurred. But in the case of a free good, a third party pays the cost, and the beneficiaries usually undervalue the free good and waste it because they did not pay for it. A "free" good such as public high school education can frequently be badly abused by the consumer.

High school students are educational investors, and a third party—taxpayers—pays the dollar costs of their investment activity. Students make critical investment decisions over the course of the 4 years in school but often are unaware that they are engaged in an investment activity. The proof of this is clear. Less than 70 percent of this year's entering freshman class will graduate with a regular high school diploma 4 years from now. The reading, writing, and math skills of these dropouts will be markedly below those of students who complete school and earn a diploma. Those who drop out will find a labor market that is very unwelcoming to them. They will have limited employment chances, and when employed they will be more likely to find low-wage jobs with few benefits. Their long-term employment and earnings prospects are bleak. The gap in labor market success between those who choose to finish high school and those who drop out is large and has risen sharply over time.

The chances of welfare dependency, incarceration, disability, and experiencing a whole range of other social pathologies are much greater among school dropouts than among those youth who complete their high school education with a diploma. Sadly, most of the adolescents who drop out have little understanding of this. Indeed, they have very unrealistic expectations for their future and thus make a bad decision that will be quite difficult to recover from in the future. It is the role of parents to provide both the stability and knowledge for students to make solid choices when making high school education investment decisions.

Despite the fact that they can receive a free high school education that will cost taxpayers an average of about $40,000 over 4 years, nearly one in three students won't graduate. No second chance to access this $40,000 for schooling will come later in life. It is a cost that is unrecoverable. These dropouts have chosen current consumption, often in the form of personally and socially destructive behavior, over the uncertainty and risk associated with higher future consumption. In less technical jargon, they failed to see how education could help them. Perhaps because of unstable families or a lack of guidance, they saw little chance of future success by completing high school compared to the current gains of quitting school before completing.

Basic Skills and Economic Success

In the early 1980s a group of elected officials, educators, and business leaders published a study of elementary and secondary education titled *A Nation at Risk,* which recast the discussion of the role of education in American society. From this small volume the education reform movement was born. Reformers advocated for back-to-basics curriculum changes that emphasized reading, writing, and mathematics skills development. This emphasis was designed to correct the drift toward the "general track" course of study that increased neither students' basic skills nor occupational skills proficiencies.

The changing nature of employment opportunities in the nation has dramatically changed the role of basic skills in determining economic success. As late as 1950 almost one-half of all the workers in the best-educated state in the nation (Massachusetts) were high school dropouts. Most employment at that time was concentrated in manufacturing and other blue-collar-dominated industries, where skills (sometimes very complex ones) were learned almost exclusively on the job. Indeed, even into the 1970s some high schools in New England held "leaving ceremonies" for students (mostly boys) who dropped out at age 16 to begin their apprenticeship in trades such as machinist, tool and die maker, and many construction-related trade areas. By developing their skills on the job over the next 6 or 7 years, those who completed their apprenticeship could have access to a very solid middle-class standard of living.

However, dramatic changes in the nature of employment since the 1970s have meant that the economic opportunities for high school dropouts have all but disappeared. In 2010, the unemployment rate of high school dropouts was almost 15 percent, and that counts only those who have not yet given up on finding work. When dropouts do work, it is seldom in a full-time year-round job and almost never in a formal apprenticeship program or a job that provides substantial on-the-job learning opportunities. Instead, dropout employment is largely relegated to very low-level service jobs, such as parking-lot attendant or kitchen helper in restaurants. Worse still for high school dropouts, the large influx of illegal immigrants into the United States (many of whom are dropouts themselves) has pushed high school dropouts out of even these very low-level jobs. Many employers say that they favor these immigrant workers (more often in their early to mid-20s) because they have better work attitudes than native-born dropouts.

Access to employment has become very strongly connected with basic skills levels. During the 1990s a large-scale study of the basic skills levels of the American workforce was sponsored by the U.S. Department of Education. This study measured the prose, document, and quantitative skills of adults and connected the results of these tests to the employment and earnings experiences of these individuals. The results of the study unequivocally demonstrated the importance of basic skills in the labor market. Basic skills affect labor market outcomes in two distinct ways—directly in the labor market and somewhat more indirectly by exerting a strong influence on the level of educational attainment completed and the kinds of labor market skills developed in school.

The effect of basic skills on labor market outcomes surpasses the effect of education. Even for job seekers with the same amount of schooling, the chance that an adult will have a job is very closely connected to his or her basic skills level. Employers utilize signals of wages and unemployment in the labor market to assess the basic skills of workers quite accurately and reward those with strong basic skills. Even after accounting for the level of educational attainment, we find that those with higher basic skills have better outcomes in the job market than those with weak basic skills. Employers readily identify the considerable differences in reading, writing, and math skills that exist even among 4-year college graduates. Firms are more likely to employ and try to retain and pay a higher annual salary to those college graduates with the strongest basic skills than to those graduates with the same degree level but lower basic skill proficiencies. Bachelor's degree holders with the strongest basic skills have the best employment and earnings outcomes. Those with weaker basic skills lag behind, despite holding a college degree. This kind of basic skill gap translates into labor market outcome gaps at every level of educational attainment—even among dropouts. While most dropouts have poor basic skills, dropouts with stronger basic skills have better employment and earnings outcomes than their counterparts with weak basic skills. The labor market is very good at identifying and rewarding workers with stronger basic skills with employment and higher wages—and also good at relegating those with weaker skills to either no employment or to lower-paying jobs. The rewards for basic skills in the labor market are manifested in a variety of ways, including

- Increased chance of being hired
- More hours of work over the year
- Higher hourly earnings
- Higher annual earnings
- Increased benefits offerings, such as health insurance

- Greater employment stability
- Better upward mobility
- Increased chances of employer-supported training

The lesson of the last two decades is that basic skills—reading, writing, and mathematics—are the essential ingredients for labor market success. In the absence of strong basic skills, the chances of labor market success in 21st-century America are dramatically diminished. Projections of employment growth in the future suggest that the role of basic skills in determining long-term labor market success will gain even greater importance in the future. (Chapter 3 identifies the specific transferable skills associated with the fastest-growing occupations.)

Basic skills not only influence the overall employment and earnings experiences of workers but also play a critical role in influencing access to career pathways across industries and occupations. The data provided in Table 1 examines the average literacy level of workers employed in various sectors of the U.S. economy. The average American worker achieved a score of 863 on this measure of prose, document, and quantitative skill. A closer look at the table reveals very large differences in average literacy scores across both industry sectors of the U.S. economy and major occupation groups within each of these industries. For example, the data reveals that workers employed in the manufacturing industry had an average literacy score of 840—modestly below the national industry average score of 863. However, the manufacturing score was nearly one standard deviation lower than that of the average worker employed in the finance, insurance and real estate, and professional services industries. Most of the difference in industry basic skills is associated with differences in the kinds of workers

Table 1

Mean Combined Prose, Document, and Quantitative Proficiencies of Employed Adults in the U.S.

Major Occupations	Manufacturing	Retail Trade	Finance, Insurance, and Real Estate	Professional Services	All Workers
Executive, Managerial	971	906	956	997	963
Professional Specialty	995	957	1,048	986	988
Technicians	926	—	—	918	925
High-Level Sales	914	885	—	—	914
Low-Level Sales	—	839	906	816	839
Clerical	881	864	686	903	890
Services	—	793	753	779	787
Craft, Precision Production	828	825	—	833	818
Operatives, Fabricators	741	808	—	788	758
Laborers and Handlers	724	794	—	—	733
All Workers	840	836	926	917	863

employed in that industry. The manufacturing sector is dominated by blue-collar jobs that have low literacy requirements. For example, routine operative, fabrication, and assembly jobs have a mean literacy score of just 741, placing the average worker in those occupations in the bottom one-sixth of the basic skills distribution of all workers. In contrast, professional specialties—such as engineering, finance, and accounting jobs—in the manufacturing industry have very high literacy requirements, with an average score among workers in those occupations of 995, placing these workers at the very highest end of the literacy proficiency distribution. Within the manufacturing industry sector, the basic skills gulf between professional workers and blue-collar workers employed in routine fabrication and operative jobs is enormous.

Over the past three decades, technological change and foreign competition have caused enormous worker dislocation (permanent job loss) and employment reorganization within the nation's manufacturing sector. Employment of workers in the professional specialties in manufacturing firms has actually increased as the remaining U.S. producers employ increasingly sophisticated production methods and organizational strategies that require high levels of professional skill. This is, in essence, replacing a large number of blue-collar workers with a new technology and a smaller, but much more productive, cadre of increasingly professional workers to produce and distribute these goods and services. Despite the fact that blue-collar workers may have many years of work experience in the manufacturing sector, they lack the basic skills needed to work in the higher-growth professional fields within the industry.

Blue-collar workers dislocated from manufacturing find few alternatives in the rapidly expanding financial and professional industry sectors of the economy. First of all, these white-collar industries employ almost no workers in production occupations, so skills learned by dislocated blue-collar workers from past work experiences are not transferable. The literacy skills needed to work in the high-end managerial and professional jobs that dominate those industries essentially preclude employment in these industry sectors for those with even average basic skill levels.

The most rapidly expanding industries in the U.S. are dominated by occupations that require strong basic skills. If students fail to develop these skills by the end of high school, they will essentially be locked out of access to the best employment opportunities. This is a powerful underlying factor in understanding the role of education as an investment good. Those high school students who take rigorous courses that develop their reading and analytical skills, their ability to write effectively, and their math proficiency will have much greater access to a variety of career fields. The lower a given individual's basic skills, the fewer life and career options he or she will have. A major part of life's story is written while in high school. Course selections that help develop basic skills will lead to a much wider and better set of choices after school. Failure to develop basic skills by the end of high school means many fewer options in a world that rewards those with the greatest set of alternatives.

Basic skills play a very important role in providing access to a college degree. Often when college admissions staff and high school counselors discuss access to college, the conversation turns quickly to financial aid. When elected officials talk about increasing access to college for students from various race-ethnic groups, they most often talk of increasing financial aid or reducing tuition. Two of the authors of this book are economists, and so of course we believe that money plays an important role in access to a college degree. Yet our analysis of a variety of data has led us to conclude that money is not the greatest barrier to a college degree, even for minority students. The greatest barrier to earning a college degree is poor basic skills. We find that students with high basic skills can often overcome money problems and complete a college degree. But students with low basic skills cannot overcome the barriers created by these deficiencies even if they do not have money problems.

The findings in Figure 1 compare the proportion of high school students who earned a college degree within 12 years of high school by their relative position in the basic skills distribution and the family income distribution. Unsurprisingly, students from high-income families with high basic skills (that is, family income in the highest fifth of the family income distribution and basic skills scores in the top fifth of the skills distribution) are very likely to earn a 4-year college degree within 12 years after high school. The chart reveals that more than three-quarters of those from the highest-income families who also have the strongest basic skills will earn a college degree. At the other extreme, the data reveals that students from the lowest-income backgrounds who also have poor basic skills will almost never

earn a college degree. Only about 1 out of 100 high school students from the lowest-income families who have basic skill scores at the bottom of the distribution will earn a bachelor's degree.

More interesting than these very predictable results are the findings about students from low-income backgrounds who have strong basic skills, as well as about their opposites—high-income students with poor basic skills. The data reveals that high-income, poor-basic-skills students are very unlikely to earn a college degree. Fewer than 3 in 100 will graduate from college within 12 years of high school. High family income seems to do little to compensate for the low basic skills of these students. In contrast, strong basic skills partially overcome low family income. Of the low-income, high-basic-skills students, more than one-third earned a college degree.

FIGURE 1

Percentage of the 14- to 17-Year-Old High School Students Who Earned a 4-Year College Degree Within 12 Years, by Their Position in the Basic Skills Distribution and Their Family's Position in the Family Income Distribution

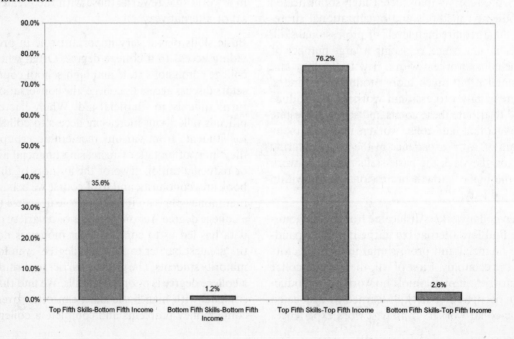

High family income in the absence of basic skills does little to enhance a student's chances of earning a 4-year college degree. Yet strong basic skills substantially reduce the impact of low family income on the ability of students to earn a college degree. Of course, developing strong basic skills does not fully offset the disadvantages from growing up in a low-income family—because money does matter. However, having basic skills plays a much more important role than money does in gaining access to a college degree. It is best to have both strong basic skills and high family income, but if you can have only one, then basic skills are by far the more important.

Having poor basic skills does not just mean a lack of educational and employment opportunities for high school students. Low basic skills sharply increase the chances that high school students will suffer from a number of social pathologies by the time they enter their early twenties. The best evidence reveals that young adults with low basic skills are at much greater risk of joblessness, poverty, welfare dependence, and a host of accompanying problems. Figure 2 provides data on the mean percentile basic skill ranking of 19- to 23-year-olds who have experienced one or more of a variety of social pathologies. The typical young adult who has been arrested scores at the 32nd percentile of the basic skills distribution. Those who were jobless scored at the 26th percentile. A young adult who had a child out of wedlock scored at the 21st percentile of the basic skills distribution, while those who were poor and welfare-dependent had a mean score that placed them at the 16th percentile. Clearly, poor basic skills mean more than diminished economic opportunity. All too often the lack of reading, writing, and math skills can result in a life pathway of dependency and criminal behavior. The choices high school students make

FIGURE 2

Mean Percentile in the Basic Skills Distribution of 19- to 23-Year-Old Young Adults, All and Subgroups with Various Social Pathologies

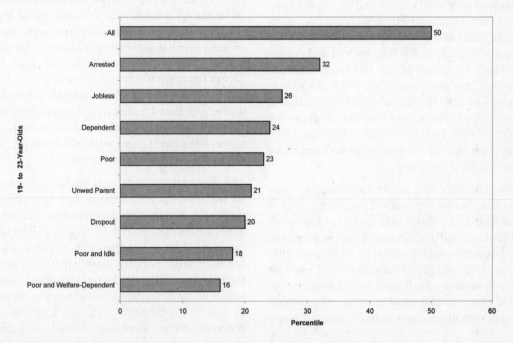

have effects—both positive and negative—that last a lifetime.

The level and kinds of courses students take while in school have important impacts on basic skills development and on educational and labor market outcomes. Students who take courses that help develop basic skills, such as sciences, mathematics, language arts, history, and social studies, substantially increase their basic skills. Strong academic courses of study exercise reading, writing, and math skills at a high level and therefore yield strong basic skills outcomes.

Academic and college courses of study are not the only pathway to positive outcomes for high school students. High school graduates who had enrolled in focused and intensive vocational-technical programs of study that are tied to local labor demand have much better post–high school labor market experiences than those non-college-bound high school graduates who have no vocational or technical preparation. These gains are tied to finding employment in an occupation closely connected to the vocational area of specialization. More intensive vocational-technical education closely tied to the needs of local employers results in substantial long-term employment and earnings advantages. However, vocational study that is intermittent and not intensive or that is not closely tied to the needs of the local employer community yields few advantages. Thus, the quality of vocational-technical programs of local school districts, measured by their intensity and connection to the local labor market, is an essential element in the decision to enroll in these programs.

Some students may prefer to choose a "general track" course of study. The general track is dominated by courses that do little to improve either basic skills or occupational proficiencies. Consequently, such a course of study does little to improve students' educational and employment options in the future. State education reform efforts have worked to reduce the number of students in general-track courses, but many secondary programs still offer these low-quality alternatives. Courses that fail to increase educational and employment options either through emphasis on basic skills or through vocational preparation are simply a bad investment and should be avoided.

The best courses of study emphasize math and science along with strong reading and writing skills. Not only does the number of such courses taken increase basic skill levels, but also taking courses in a sequence of increasing difficulty generates higher payoffs to students, even if taking tougher courses means lower grades.

Investing in Work Experience

Frequently, one thinks of high school students who work part-time—after school, on weekends, or perhaps in a summer job—as simply earning extra money for personal consumption or perhaps, in some instances, to help support their families. Certainly, the employment of high school students provides them with the benefits of increased income, and the earnings of high school students alleviate the poverty problems of some families. But does it make sense for high school students to work while they are in school? Doesn't mixing work and schooling activities mean that students will have less time for studies and school-based extracurricular activities? If a bit more disposable income for teen consumption is the only benefit from work, then is it really a worthwhile activity for students?

The gains to students working in high school go well beyond the earnings they generate for themselves and their families. Working at an early age is a developmental activity akin to developing basic skills or occupational proficiencies in a school setting. Early work experience helps further enhance the productive abilities of young adults along dimensions that are not addressed by classroom-based educational activities. In economic terms, work experience during high school is an investment in developing human capital that has similar impacts as investments in education. For example, students who work more frequently during high school tend to participate in the labor market more intensively as adults, are less likely to experience a bout of unemployment as adults, and, if they become unemployed, become reemployed more quickly than those with little or no work experience while in high school. Research has estimated that high school seniors who worked 20 hours per week had annual earnings as young adults that were 25 to 30 percent higher than seniors who didn't work.

Work experience while in high school can have powerful impacts on long-term labor market outcomes. Through on-the-job learning, it provides teens and even young adults with the opportunity to develop a whole set of behavioral characteristics that are highly prized by employers. Indeed, while employers place great emphasis on basic skills and occupational knowledge and ability, these behavioral traits, sometimes known as *soft skills*, are their top priority when hiring and retaining workers. Willingness to learn, respectfulness for other workers and supervisors, strong work ethic, capability to communicate effectively, and ability to follow simple work rules such as punctuality are essential to employers. Employers simply avoid those who lack these soft skills, even if they possess strong math and literacy abilities or a special sort of occupational skill.

It is no coincidence that virtually every resume submitted to employers describes the educational and work experiences of the applicant, along with a set of references. Employers use the information on the resume to assess a job applicant's strengths and weaknesses in regard to behavioral skills based on his or her record of work experience. When references are contacted, most of the conversation centers on the applicant's soft skills. Often the primary purpose of the job interview is to personally assess an individual's work attitudes, ethics, and ability to work with others.

Work experience among high school students does not seem to come at the price of less study time or fewer extracurricular activities. Our analysis of the work activities of high school students in Massachusetts found that students who worked simply watched less television than those who did not work. We found that those who worked spent about the same amount of time on homework as those who did not work at all. Virtually all researchers who have studied the connection between in-school work experiences and academic performance have concluded that working up to 20 hours per week has no adverse impacts on the academic performance of high school students.

The evidence suggests that early work experience of most kinds has a positive impact on the long-term labor market experiences of teens. However, the quality of work experience also has a positive impact on labor market outcomes. Jobs that provide the chance for students to engage in reading, writing, mathematics, and technical skills bolster long-term employment and earnings prospects, as do jobs that provide students with the chance to learn a new skill. Jobs with these characteristics are hard to find because they are often available in industries that hire few teens, such as health, finance, insurance, and professional services. However, both parents and school systems should try hard to find employment for students in these industries because of the quality of work experience that they can provide to students and because of the career exposure that working in "adult" labor markets can provide teens.

High school students too often have little awareness of the array of career opportunities that exist in a particular industry. For example, many young people are attracted to the "helping" fields in the health arena but have little understanding of the variety of careers available in these fields or of the education and training pathways into these fields. Working in a hospital gives students exposure not only to a wide variety of health profession careers, but also to health professionals, who themselves can offer advice and information about health careers and in some instances serve as professional role models.

Work experience is a valuable form of human capital that is quite different from human capital developed in formal academic or occupational education settings. Work experience reduces dropout rates of students—especially among low-income and minority youth. Reductions in dropout rates can be particularly strong when work experiences are tied directly to the schooling activities of teens. Work-based learning increases the students' perception of the relevance of school-based learning. Indeed, we find high rates of enrollment in postsecondary education when work experience programs are run directly through the high schools in low-income communities. High school students engaged in the labor market see firsthand how the labor market distinguishes between those with a college degree and those with fewer years of schooling. Among students who choose not to enroll in college, prior work experience smoothes their transition into the full-time labor market after high school. Students with work experience while in school avoid long-term idleness that often characterizes the first few years after high school of non-college-bound high school graduates with no work experience.

Interestingly, there is a strong connection between the level of family income and the likelihood that a teen will be employed, but not in the way that we might expect. Most people assume that because of family income needs, students from low-income families work at higher rates than do students from higher-income backgrounds. Yet the opposite is true. The employment rate of teens rises sharply with family income. Students who live in high-poverty neighborhoods and students from low-income families are very unlikely to work, while those residing in higher-income communities or from higher-income families are more likely to be employed. Part of the difference is due to higher-income students growing up in a culture where

the major activity of adults is work. The gains of work experience are clear to both parents and students, and so the children work at higher rates. Moreover, employed parents encourage their children to work and can often help their children find employment. Teens who live in high-poverty neighborhoods live in areas where the majority of adults are not employed. With adults cut off from employment, a nonworking culture takes root. Teens have fewer role models to indicate the importance of employment and have fewer resources to help them find employment. Thus, large work experience gaps are created between students from high-poverty neighborhoods and those who live in communities where work is the primary activity of adults.

It is clear that work experience produces a variety of positive outcomes for teens. Teens who do not work find themselves disadvantaged not only because of the gap in the positive outcomes associated with working, but also because of negative outcomes that are associated with not working. The facts are that teen girls who do not work are much more likely to become pregnant during their teenage years. Among boys, criminal behavior is closely associated with limited work experience. A high rate of male teen idleness makes criminal activity, especially the sale of street drugs, more attractive.

The Educational Attainment Decision

High school students must make decisions about how much education they will complete through their early adult years. A more detailed analysis of the underlying role of educational attainment on labor market outcomes is provided in the following chapters. Yet it is important to note that high school students make a set of choices about how much schooling they will undertake in their lives. The educational attainment decision is not usually made all at once. Rare is the high school student who decides that he or she will earn a doctoral degree in a particular field of study. Most often decisions to continue in school are made incrementally or, in economic terms, at the margin. For example, teens decide to finish high school or to drop out, but often the decision to finish or drop out is made on an even more incremental basis than this. Often, dropping out of high school occurs almost in a subconscious fashion, with little thought given to quitting school. Students drop out of school simply by choosing to be absent from school with increasing frequency. So the decision to drop out isn't made all at once. Instead it is often made by the choice made each morning to either stay in bed or get up and go to school.

The decision to drop out has strong adverse economic outcomes for students in terms of poor employment and earnings prospects and increasing risk of antisocial behavior. Those students who drop out are most often those with the poorest basic skills. It is obvious that poor basic skills are one effect of dropping out of school. However, it is important to understand that poor basic skills also are a key cause of dropping out. Too often students lack the reading, writing, and math skills to effectively master high-school-level material. These students are more likely to quit school than are students with stronger basic skills. The act of quitting school is much more than simply failing to complete high school; it is a way of dropping out of mainstream society and limiting life choices, resulting all too often in an existence at the margins of a community.

Students who finish high school have many more educational and employment options than do dropouts. High school graduates have much higher employment rates, are much less likely to be jobless, and have much higher annual and lifetime earnings than dropouts. Each year a large proportion of high school seniors choose to enroll in some type of postsecondary educational program. Last year a little more than 70 percent of all graduating seniors were enrolled in school during the fall after graduation. These students enrolled in educational institutions

ranging from short-term (just a few months) occupational training programs run by private, for-profit organizations to those who enrolled in full-time undergraduate programs at the nation's most prestigious educational institutions. The amount of schooling that students complete after high school has important impacts on their long-term labor market experiences. Those with more years of schooling have higher earnings than those with less. Young graduates of 2-year degree programs earn 22 percent more per year than high school graduates with no degree. Young bachelor's degree holders earn about 66 percent more per year than their high-school-graduate counterparts. Large earning gaps also exist between those with advanced degrees and those with a bachelor's degree only.

Not only do those with more years of schooling achieve large employment and earnings advantages compared to those with only a high school diploma, but the size of these advantages grows larger over time. The earnings of college graduates grow more rapidly for more years than the earnings of high school dropouts. The higher growth in annual earnings over the working lives of better-educated workers is in part the product of greater chances for advancement for college graduates and because firms make much greater education and training investments in their college-educated staff than they do in their high-school-graduate staff. College grads have proved they can learn, so employers make their human capital investments in those staff that they believe will give them the greatest return on their investment.

Investing in Occupational Skills

The nature of employment growth in the U.S. over the past two decades has had the effect of shifting education and training costs away from firms and directly upon households and families. Colleges and universities have increasingly become a key source of labor supply for firms seeking high-level occupational skills. Indeed, whole new fields of study have been created in health, information technology, engineering, business, communications, and the arts. These new majors and degree fields were organized to meet newly emerging high-end skill demands in the American labor market.

This book provides information on the nature of expected labor market outcomes associated with earning a bachelor's degree in alternative fields of study. Our findings reveal very large employment and earnings differences for bachelor's degree holders depending on their undergraduate major field of study. These differences also are quite large at the level of master's and doctoral degrees.

The choice that students make about their major field of study is a key component of developing their career plan. Too many students opt into major fields of study by default, without giving much consideration to their choice, at least with respect to the kinds of career options this choice will both create and eliminate. The choice undergraduates make about their major will have widely varying impacts on the kinds of careers they can pursue after graduation. For example, students who choose one of the very demanding engineering majors will find they have a much broader array of employment as well as educational options than, say, a student who chooses a social science or humanities field. Engineering graduates have much better access to degrees in nontechnical or scientific fields, while graduates from social sciences and humanities are much less likely to earn a degree in a technical or scientific field. Engineers also have a somewhat wider array of employment options at the undergraduate level, including finance, insurance, and health-care areas. Engineering majors simply have better employment and earnings experiences across a wide variety of occupations than do majors in other fields.

The choice of major field of study is complex and one that will heavily influence the professional career experiences that graduates will have in the future. The chapters immediately following this one explore the nature of this choice in greater detail. Before we examine this choice, however, it is useful to at least briefly discuss the last major component of the college investment decision—the cost.

College Prices and College Finance

Four-year college tuition and fees have risen at a very rapid pace since the early 1980s, and high tuition is often viewed as a major barrier to college access for many in American society. Congress has conducted a number of hearings related to rising college costs, and many within the higher education system itself worry that access to a 4-year degree is declining for race-ethnic minorities in the nation because of skyrocketing tuition.

Clearly understanding the potential benefits of a college education is a key element of the college investment decision. However, benefits represent only one-half of the investment equation. Parents and students need to have a clear understanding not only of the gains from a college degree, but also of the costs of earning such a degree in economic terms. The cost of college is made up of two key components:

- Tuition and fees, as well as other out-of-pocket costs
- Potential earnings that students would have earned had they not attended college

Putting aside forgone earnings for the moment, parents and students need to fully understand the costs of earning a college degree. Unfortunately, parents and students too often have a poor understanding of actual college tuition or financial aid availability, sometimes erroneously concluding that the costs at a given college are too high for their family circumstances.

A recent survey of the parents of 1,600 high school students found that parents and students were making decisions about the affordability of college costs without accurate or complete information about what those costs were likely to be. Among students who planned to attend college, more than half ruled out colleges on the basis of the "sticker price" alone. Only about one-third of students or their parents used one of the handy financial aid calculators that can be found on the Web.

That high school parents and students have a limited understanding of college costs and financial aid availability is not surprising, given the degree of complexity of college finance. This complexity is in part a consequence of the very nature of colleges and universities. One highly regarded economist who has studied higher education remarked that colleges act like a cross between churches and used-car dealers. Most colleges are nonprofit organizations and as such are in fact charities of a sort. While tuition may be high, virtually every college student receives a subsidy of some type in the sense that the total of student payments never covers the cost of running a college. Other sources of income—from federal, state, and local government; alumni; the business community; and other sources—pay the balance of costs of operating 4-year colleges and universities. In this sense colleges are like churches in that they are the conduit through which society promotes a desired set of values, in this instance the values of knowledge, literacy, educational achievement, and the support of a wide array of social, cultural, and economic activities and objectives.

Colleges are like car dealers in the way that they operate in college enrollment markets (as well as in their growing commercial activities in sports and the commercialization of faculty research, to name just two), engaging in what college enrollment managers call "strategic packaging." Colleges and universities produce a product that is unique in that its perceived quality is largely judged by the characteristics of those who enroll in it. Rankings of college quality are largely determined by several measures of the quality of the entering freshman class each year. Applicant SAT or ACT scores, high school class rank, and fraction of applicants admitted are frequently used measures of college quality. These measures tell us a lot about who attends a given school but reveal nothing about the quality of education these students receive once enrolled. Certainly, the most common measures of college quality now used fall far short of the rigorous measures of elementary and secondary student learning gains now required in each state under No Child Left Behind.

The level of demand for enrollment in a given college is closely connected to its perceived quality, and the quality of a college is determined by its ability to recruit a freshman class composed of the best and the brightest. So enrollment managers engage in a set of activities in the enrollment market that are designed to maximize market position by enrolling the best high school seniors possible while at the same time meeting key revenue goals for the college. One way that colleges are able to do this is to try to engage in a tuition discounting strategy whereby financial aid is used to attract those students with the best student profile as determined by the basic college quality measures. Enrollment managers try to use financial aid to entice the best and brightest students to their school while being constrained by the need to meet specific revenue targets.

The result of all of this is that the official college tuition information provided to counselors, parents, and students is really little more than a "sticker price," much like a buyer would find on the window of a car for sale. Large differences exist between the sticker price of college tuitions published by colleges and the net tuition that an average student at a given college will actually end up paying. Some analysts have found that the gap between the sticker price and the net tuition students pay in their first year may be as high as 30 to 40 percent for the average student in private, nonprofit institutions. There also are large differences between sticker prices and net tuition costs in public 4-year schools, especially among those with high tuition levels.

Colleges offer tuition discounts to those students who best meet their goals for their entering freshman class student profile. Students with high class rankings, strong basic skills as measured by the SAT or ACT, and other characteristics that suggest they will complete their degree program will receive substantial discounts, sometimes in the form of full-tuition scholarships and in some cases the inclusion of room and board. Top students thus have a certain amount of bargaining power in establishing what their net tuition level might be. Most often college enrollment managers develop a set of criteria, based on sophisticated data analysis, to determine how much aid a student with desirable characteristics will receive. In some cases enrollment management staff will actually negotiate net tuition, much like a car salesman will negotiate a net price from a car's sticker. The sticker is a place where the tuition discussion can begin, not where it ends.

Decisions made by parents and students on college affordability need to be based on the net tuition price, not on the sticker price. Students and parents who have multiple acceptance offers and aid packages may be in a position to negotiate larger merit aid packages (read: tuition discounts).

College enrollment managers spend a lot of time thinking through their discounting strategy and determining who among their applicants should receive financial aid, what type of aid they should receive, and how much tuition should be discounted. Top enrollment managers are able to produce high-quality entering freshman classes that further bolster the quality assessment of the institution in the enrollment market and set the stage for further gains in the near future—all the while meeting their tuition revenue objectives. This question remains (as it does for car dealers): Why don't colleges just charge the net tuition price to all students and

stop this strategic packaging and hidden net tuition discounting? Much of the answer to this question is associated with the fact that a college degree has some of the characteristics of what economists refer to as a "snob good." A key feature of a snob good is that little is known about its real qualities, so consumers often use its price level as a measure of quality. Examples of this sort of good or service abound in liquor, fashion, retail, automobile, and many other industries, as well as in higher education. Indeed, it is one of the reasons that firms spend so much time, energy, and resources in developing a name brand—a brand that identifies certain qualities with products or services offered by that brand. Many in the higher education system believe that a high tuition sticker sends a signal of exclusivity and therefore quality.

A college degree not only has some of the characteristics of a snob good, but it is also what economists describe as a positional good. The quality of a college is not judged on the basis of its absolute level of academic excellence. Rather, parents judge colleges and universities by their position in rankings of all colleges. A good education is one that is defined by most in a relative way. So when we say we want a good education for our children, we in fact mean we want a better education than that received by other students. This puts parents and students in an educational "arms race" to enroll in elite, exclusive, or the best colleges and universities. By definition, the number of top "elite" schools is limited, and these schools are careful not to raise enrollment levels in response to rising demand. Parents and students are playing a game that as a group they cannot win. There will always be a limited supply of top 100 colleges, no matter how much parents and students strive for access to the "best." In an effort to gain access to a seat at an elite school, families send their children to exclusive preschools and grammar schools at great expense, donate extra funds to elite colleges in excess of tuition, and often try to use political and business connections to gain admission to the limited supply of seats at the top of the college pecking order. But even as more and more families try to crack into the best colleges, the number of seats at the top 100 schools remains the same. Rising demand for quality education cannot coax out additional supply, as in the case of most goods. Instead, it means a growing frenzy of parents struggling against worsening odds to get their children enrolled in an elite school.

Interestingly, little evidence supports the view that earning a degree from an elite college markedly improves long-term employment and earnings outcomes. After accounting for basic skills proficiency and undergraduate major, graduates from elite colleges earn only 2 to 3 percent more over their working lives than graduates from nonelite colleges. While parents judge colleges by their relative rankings, the labor market largely judges college graduates on the basis of their work experiences; their proficiency in reading, writing, and mathematics; and their specific occupational knowledge and skill. Chapter 3 examines the connection between the choice of college and the selection of a major field of study and provides the costs and benefits of the college investment decision.

CHAPTER 2

The Psychology of Career Choice
Assessing Abilities, Interests, and Values

This chapter is about making informed choices. Because many of us do not allow enough time for making choices, we create stress and pressure in our lives. In this chapter, you will learn what information is important to know about yourself. You will also learn how to find this information and then organize it to make decisions that are thorough and comfortable for you. By the end of the chapter, we hope you can say, "This is my choice and my plan."

Most people think that the task of choosing a major is based simply on information and facts; therefore, the choice should be easy and straight-forward. Wrong! Choosing a major—like choosing the college you will attend—takes time. You should take the time to make an informed choice about your major for the following reasons:

▶ Parents or other authority figures may have imposed their goals or wants on you. Families sometimes disapprove of a student's plans and believe they have a "say," especially when they are paying some of the tuition. This attitude complicates the student's choices because it

creates uncertainty and risks by making the parents part of the decision process. In this case, some negotiations need to occur.

▶ Several stumbling blocks may exist. These have to be dealt with first, before a decision is finalized. Consider some of these examples:

"I don't have enough money for the specific education or major I want."

"I have to work now."

"According to published information, my test scores are not good enough for the field."

"There are not many of my gender in the major."

"No colleges are in my geographic region, so I will have to leave home. This is obviously an additional cost factor."

If any of these scenarios are true for you, they will involve additional decisions. Many people, because of their youthful inexperience, get overwhelmed. An eerie feeling emerges around choosing a major—it is a monstrous choice! "What if I pick wrong? Then I have failed." Do not subscribe to this attitude. The system forces everyone to decide, and they survive.

▶ In the process of making decisions, students may discover that they lack the perceived self-awareness that their friends have. Some people are not accustomed to being self-initiating and self-directing, so making a decision independently is a new challenge and very difficult. Some find they lack the support of others who will respect their views without imposing their judgments. Still others lack self-esteem and question whether they are good enough to be successful in a preferred career field. Thus, self-doubts and emotional immaturity surface to complicate the decision-making process more than was initially expected.

▶ If it is any consolation, the largest major in many colleges is "undecided," which shows that making this life-changing decision is a complex step. The choice involves work in order to complete the task correctly. Don't be afraid to take a chance or to make a decision, even if the decision may not be correct. The decision may be "incorrect" not because of what you thought would be the case, but for reasons you haven't thought about. Remember that the task of making the decision itself moves you along in a series of choices that you will be making. Take your time, check out your options, and try to make a reasonable attempt.

Knowing Yourself

The first step for you to review is your knowledge of yourself. Learning how to self-assess is a lifelong skill that will serve you well as you develop into the person you are meant to be. In this section, we will focus on three areas for self-assessing: your abilities, interests, and values.

Abilities

Abilities are skills, talents, or things you can do. Ability represents a degree of mastery. Occasionally the term *ability* is used interchangeably with *aptitude*. In other words, *aptitude* is the ability to do schoolwork or to reason verbally and quantitatively. Ability is not intelligence.

One last distinction: Abilities constitute broad categories of skills; that is, ability is a *macro* concept, while a skill involves doing something at a more specific *micro* level. For example, *artistic ability* is the macro term that involves *skills* of color discrimination, eye-hand coordination, and depth perception at the micro level. One person may be better at landscapes while another has portrait skills. Many people think of taking tests to learn about their abilities. We will be introducing a different methodology here: asking you to self-report your abilities.

Before proceeding, you need to know why abilities are important. Work and life satisfaction both depend on the extent to which individuals find adequate outlets for abilities, needs, values, interests, personality characteristics, and self-concepts. Ability is part of your self-concept, according to career-development experts.

The major work-related abilities include artistic, clerical, interpersonal, language, leadership, manual, musical/dramatic, numerical/mathematical, organizational, persuasive, scientific, social, spatial, and technical/mechanical. What about athletic and dancing abilities? While athletes and dancers are very much in evidence in the media, they, in fact, do not involve large numbers of people in the workforce. However, these two abilities are included under the manual and musical/dramatic categories. Reading is a basic skill and ability that is foundational to the development of many other abilities and general learning. The 14 major career-related abilities are briefly defined in the following list:

▶ **Artistic:** Involves principles and techniques in drawing, painting, photography, sculpting, decorating, or designing.

▶ **Clerical:** Involves eye-hand-finger coordination to enter numbers into a computer or a form, knowledge of the operation of office and business machines, and proficiency on a computer keyboard. The skills require accuracy and attention to detail.

▶ **Interpersonal:** Involves the abilities to communicate well with many kinds of people; to contribute ideas and suggestions; to work cooperatively; and to demonstrate understanding, friendliness, adaptability, and politeness in a variety of settings.

▶ **Language:** Involves speaking clearly; understanding and responding to feedback; asking questions appropriately; and using correct grammar, spelling, and punctuation in letters and reports.

▶ **Leadership:** Involves making decisions that affect others; reacting quickly in emergency situations; and motivating others to work by communicating thoughts, feelings, and ideas well enough to justify a viewpoint.

▶ **Manual:** Involves the abilities to coordinate hands, fingers, and eyes to operate a piece of equipment, to adjust controls on machines, to manipulate hand tools, or to assemble something that requires reading and following directions.

▶ **Musical or Dramatic:** Involves playing instruments; singing; reading and writing music; or interpreting roles and expressing ideas and emotions through gestures and facial expressions in comedy, plays, or movies.

▶ **Numerical or Mathematical:** Involves the abilities to do basic arithmetic computations or to use mathematical reasoning and concepts to solve difficult mathematics problems.

▶ **Organizational:** Involves maintaining written or computerized records and other forms of information in a systematic method and setting priorities that determine how to get the most important tasks completed first and on time.

▶ **Persuasive:** Involves the abilities to convince or motivate an individual or group of people to take a certain action, such as buying something, or to influence someone to a certain viewpoint.

▶ **Scientific:** Involves understanding and using scientific principles and logic to deal with different types of problems (possibly done in a technical or scientific laboratory), diagnosing and treating human and animal injuries and diseases, or studying various life forms.

▶ **Social:** Involves gathering, studying, and analyzing information by using logical thinking to help other people define and solve personal problems; it can include teaching others.

▶ **Spatial:** Involves the abilities to see differences in size, form, and shape and to visualize relationships between objects.

▶ **Technical or Mechanical:** Involves the abilities to understand technical or mechanical terms or language, to follow the proper procedures in setting up or operating equipment, to operate machines, and to understand why machines don't work and to have the capability to fix or repair them.

Self-Assessing Abilities

Each term in the preceding section defines a specific ability. Decide whether you perform the activity well, above average, below average, or not well at all. The level of mastery is important because it may communicate a positive self-esteem or low self-efficacy or low self-perception to perform in a specific area. Creating a table like the one in Table 1 may be helpful. Try to be honest with yourself as you do the rating. If all your abilities are high or average or low, you may find it difficult to assess yourself.

By saying, "I'm good at this task but not so good at that one," you can identify possible sources of self-esteem. You may find yourself saying, "Gee, look at that. Each ability is weak (average or great). No wonder I have trouble doing this task." Self-insights are powerful sources of self-information. Most of us are good at some things and not as good in other matters.

Reality testing—or obtaining feedback on your performance—is an important part of self-assessment. A requirement for accurate reality testing is that you know your work and have experience in the ability area to make an objective rating. Sources of reality testing are available to you, but frequently you must seek them. Some useful sources of reality testing are schoolwork, part-time jobs, internships, extracurricular activities, and volunteer work. Grades for schoolwork are one indication of your skills, and you can also make your own judgments about how well you performed at tasks in these settings.

However, self-evaluations are subjective, so getting feedback from a respected, qualified person is helpful. Consider getting feedback about your performance from acquaintances, friends, and

Table 1
Worksheet for Reality Testing Each Ability

Ability	Self-Rating (High, Above Average, Below Average, Not Well)	Grades	Work Experience	Activities/ Experiences
Artistic				
Clerical				
Interpersonal				
Language				
Leadership				
Manual				
Musical/Dramatic				
Numerical/ Mathematical				
Organizational				
Persuasive				
Scientific				
Social				
Spatial				
Technical/Mechanical				

family members. Keep in mind that these people often do not want to alienate you, so the way you solicit feedback from them or the format you use to collect information is most important. One format that people can use is to rate you in comparison to others they know in a specific ability area. For example, are you equal to the best, better than most, about the same as most, or not as good as others?

Increasingly, some schools and organizations are implementing a portfolio method of assessment. A *portfolio* involves samples of your best work, including English papers, science projects, letters of recommendation for performing an activity, or pictures showing how you are using a specific machine or how you are being recognized for a special achievement. A concluding observation is that performing a self-assessment can identify areas in which you may want to pursue further developmental work. The self-assessment and its documentation also provide potential information for a functional resume; that is, they help to specify those activities you can do.

An additional resource for assessing abilities is the Skills Profiler at the U.S. Department of Labor's CareerOneStop website (www.careerinfonet. org/skills). Or, if you have had some work experience, you may find insights at another Department of Labor site, My Skills My Future (www. myskillsmyfuture.org). The *Ability Explorer* is an assessment from JIST Publishing (www. jist.com) that a school counselor can give you. Finally, Chapters 4 through 61 provide information about abilities that are required in the most popular jobs associated with each field of study.

Interests

Interests indicate the direction of a person's preferences; that is, your liking or disliking of an activity. Interests are important. Can you imagine working for a long time at a job that you dislike? Remember that *ability* answers the question, "What do I know and what can I do?" *Interest*

answers the inquiry, "Do I like and want to do it?" Generally these are two separate questions.

An assumption of one of the major career-development theorists is that each of us can be classified according to a limited number of personality types. Work settings or work environments also can be described as uniquely accommodating to the same personality types. According to this theory, each personality type will seek out its corresponding occupational environment or job. People have a combination of personality types, so jobs also accommodate a variety of personality types. These personality types are assessed by people's interests and are described with corresponding jobs that require postsecondary education as follows:

▶ **Artistic:** These people prize independence and seek opportunities for self-expression. Some prefer lifestyles that enjoy such creative activities as art, entertainment, music, and writing.

Sample jobs: actor/actress, advertising manager, art teacher, composer, copy writer, dancer, fashion designer, graphics designer, musician, painter, public relations specialist, radio/TV announcer, radio/TV producer, reporter, translator

▶ **Business (also known as Enterprising):** These people seek careers where they can lead others. They usually have good communications skills. They can persuade others to buy their products or ideas, and they gain satisfaction by convincing others to think the way they do.

Sample jobs: bank manager, buyer, farm manager, financial planner, government administrator, health-care manager, hotel/food service manager, human resources manager, insurance salesperson, lawyer, marketing personnel, property manager, retail store manager, sales manager, transportation manager

▶ **Crafts (also known as Realistic):** These people prefer to work with tools and things rather than with people and words. They like to build something, and they want to see practical results. They enjoy mechanical work and physical activity.

Sample jobs: airline pilot, electronics technician, forest and conservation technician, drafter, medical lab technician, ship's captain, technical illustrator

▶ **Office Operations (also known as Conventional):** These people seek financial success and status with a preference for jobs that have clearly defined duties. They tend to be orderly and systematic, and they like to work with words and numbers.

Sample jobs: accountant, auditor, bank loan officer, budget analyst, insurance underwriter, market research analyst

▶ **Scientific (also known as Investigative):** These people enjoy mathematics and science. They are studious, curious, and creative, and they often work with theories and unproven ideas. They may prefer to work alone.

Sample jobs: actuary, agricultural scientist, architect, biologist, chemist, computer programmer, dentist, engineer, geologist, mathematician, physician, physicist, optometrist, software engineer, statistician, surgeon, systems analyst

▶ **Social:** These people provide services for others and care about the well-being of others. They have good verbal skills and get along well with people.

Sample jobs: clergy member, college administrator, counselor, dental hygienist, elementary or preschool teacher, historian, librarian, museum curator, nurse, occupational therapist, political scientist, recreation leader, school principal, secondary or vocational/technical teacher, social worker, sociologist, surgical technician

A person most often is a combination of personality types and rarely exemplifies a single personality type. For example, a common combination is social/artistic; these personality types frequently find employment in human service careers. If you feel that two types describe you, then also consider reversing the types, such as artistic/social. By making this simple switch, you can expand the number of career options that are deemed appropriate for you.

Some of the common combinations of personality types are listed in Table 2 with corresponding occupations. If you notice that some combinations are missing, it may be because some combinations are not typically found among occupations requiring postsecondary education and training.

As you can see, adding the second personality type brings better clarification, and the focus for a major's selection becomes more distinctive. For example, people who are primarily scientific must decide whether they prefer to relate to people as a physician would or to data and things as a physicist would. Being aware of and sensitive to your personal characteristics are factors in determining your satisfaction in picking a major.

An additional resource for a comprehensive interest assessment is the *Harrington-O'Shea Career Decision-Making System Revised (CDM-R)*, available from Pearson Assessments (www.pearsonassessments.com). This instrument assesses and integrates a person's interests, abilities, and values and provides information about personality type and related occupations.

Another approach to assessing your interests is to use the O*NET Interest Profiler, developed by the U.S. Department of Labor. The resource is available free at the My Next Move website. (Click under "Tell us what you like to do" at www.mynextmove.org.)

Finally, you may want to consider the career cluster scheme developed by the U.S. Department of Education, which organizes all jobs in the United

Table 2
Employment Opportunities with Personality Type Combinations

Common Personality Type Cominations	Jobs
Artistic/Business	comedian, motion picture camera operator, photojournalist
Artistic/Social	art teacher, copy writer, fashion designer
Business/Crafts	park superintendent, wine maker
Business/Social	insurance sales agent, director of student affairs, legislative assistant
Crafts/Scientific	mining engineer, airline pilot
Office Operations/Business	tax auditor, customs inspector
Scientific/Business	industrial-organizational psychologist, pharmacist
Scientific/Crafts	veterinarian, civil engineer
Scientific/Social	physician assistant, psychiatrist, pediatrician
Social/Artistic	music therapist, speech pathologist, clergy member
Social/Business	employment relations specialist, director of special education
Social/Scientific	dietitian, clinical psychologist

States into 16 interest categories. The following checklist is based on this scheme. If you place a check mark in front of sample occupations to indicate whether you like the job, the results may help to indicate a career direction.

Several words of caution: The 16 career clusters do not contain the same number of occupations—either as examples listed here or in the reality of the job market. For example, the artistic and scientific categories include fewer jobs than the mechanical category. Also, because this method covers all jobs in the United States, many of the jobs do not require postsecondary education. And lastly, remember that no activity or occupation is only for men or only for women.

Place a check mark in front of the jobs you think you might like to do.

Agriculture, Food, and Natural Resources

___ Farm Manager

___ Geological Test Technician

___ Animal Scientist

___ Oil and Gas Derrick Operator

___ Nursery/Greenhouse Worker

___ Forest and Conservation Worker

___ Park Naturalist

Architecture and Construction

____ Construction Manager

____ Construction Worker

____ Architectural Drafter

____ Surveying Technician

____ Landscape Architect

____ Construction and Building Inspector

Arts, Audio/Video Technology, and Communications

____ Editor

____ News Reporter

____ Painter

____ Actor

____ Sculptor

____ Graphic Artist

____ TV Broadcast Technician

____ Desktop Publisher

____ Musician

____ Singer

____ Dancer

Business, Management, and Administration

____ Public Relations Manager

____ Labor Relations Specialist

____ Wholesale and Retail Buyer

____ Accountant

____ Purchasing Manager

____ Human Resources Manager

Education and Training

____ Principal

____ Interpreter

____ Industrial Trainer

____ Recreation Worker

____ Teacher

____ Professor

____ Librarian

Finance

____ Financial Analyst

____ Bill and Account Collector

____ New Accounts Clerk

____ Loan Officer

____ Budget Analyst

____ Personal Financial Advisor

Government and Public Administration

____ Environmental Compliance Inspector

____ Urban Planner

____ Tax Examiner

____ Emergency Management Director

Health Science

___ Occupational Therapist	___ Medical Lab Technologist
___ Physician	___ Radiologic Technologist
___ Surgeon	___ Veterinarian
___ Pharmacist	___ Dietitian/Nutritionist
___ Dentist	___ Athletic Trainer
___ Optometrist	

Hospitality and Tourism

___ Hotel Manager	___ Flight Attendant
___ Travel Guide	___ Travel Agent
___ Concierge	

Human Services

___ Clergy	___ Social Worker
___ Psychologist	___ Mental Health Counselor
___ Health Educator	___ Marriage and Family Therapist

Information Technology

___ Computer Hardware Engineer	___ Video Game Designer
___ Web Administrator	___ Computer Systems Analyst
___ Computer User Support Specialist	___ Search Marketing Strategist

Law, Public Safety, Corrections, and Security

___ Lawyer	___ Fire Investigator
___ Police Officer	___ Military Service
___ Immigration and Customs Inspector	___ Court Reporters

Manufacturing

___ Telecommunications Line Installer	___ Automotive Master Mechanic
___ Printing Press Operator	___ Welder
___ Team Assembler	___ Machinist

Sales and Marketing

___ Marketing Manager	___ Securities Salesworker
___ Advertising Salesworker	___ Real Estate Broker

Science, Technology, Engineering, and Mathematics

___ Survey Researcher

___ Physicist

___ Chemist

___ Biologist

___ Economist

___ Historian

___ Political Scientist

___ Computer Systems Analyst

___ Mathematician

___ Engineer

___ Engineering Technician

Transportation, Distribution, and Logistics

___ Transportation Manager

___ Air Traffic Controller

___ Airplane Pilot

___ Ship's Pilot

___ Truck Driver

This survey can be helpful when all the check marks are clustered together; however, the check marks are often scattered throughout the clusters, so no clear pattern emerges. This result is a problem with this kind of survey and shows the advantage of an interest survey. Interest surveys have scales that summarize the results and indicate a focus unique to the person.

However, if a substantial number of check marks fall under one of the 16 career clusters, this preference can provide valuable clues and meaning. For example, the survey can show that working in an office may be torture for people wanting to work with plants and animals; an office job may lack the excitement of physical work or the action that law enforcement work may offer. Physical activity may offer the opportunity to publicly perform in highly competitive events, such as an athletic event.

In summary, sometimes we are good at doing a job, but we don't enjoy doing the activities that go with the job. Other times we like or enjoy an activity, but we don't do the activity well. While a relationship exists between abilities and interests, each has unique elements. Therefore, all your interests demand examination. Don't prematurely write off or ignore a major without giving it consideration. In each description of the 58 majors

in this book, you will find information about the typical interests that people in the field possess.

Values

Job values, as distinguished from personal values, represent what people want to get out of work. Values bring job satisfaction. They are very personal; therefore, the same job can satisfy different values in different people. Values are viewed as cognitive representations of personal needs and are considered basic to a person's belief system. Values are fairly change-resistant. People learn values from their parents, significant others, and daily living experiences. Several examples of values are independence, working with your mind, and altruism.

A well-known expert on value clarification stated that if a belief is to be considered a value, all seven of the following standards must be met: it must be chosen freely, chosen from alternatives, chosen after due reflection, prized and cherished, publicly affirmed, acted upon, and part of a pattern of behavior that is a repeated action. Therefore, if you want to work with your mind, you should pursue a pathway of intellectual curiosity. You should wonder about the "whys" of facts rather than work with your hands. If you pursue this learning style over time, however, you may have to accept that you may be perceived by others as a little "nerdy" or "techy."

People should identify personal values, study their relative importance, and tentatively prioritize them. Consider the following example of how values may help in career planning: A person expresses an interest in farming but finds this career blocked because of the large capital investment required to purchase land and equipment. If the person's attraction is understood in terms of valuing autonomy, alternative jobs will become immediately evident. (For example, most managerial jobs offer a lot of autonomy.) In the current economy—where companies are downsizing, merging, outsourcing, and going out of business—transition to other work can more easily be accomplished if individuals have identified their work values. These economic realities are another reason why self-assessment of abilities, strengths, and weaknesses is viewed as a lifelong process.

Assessing job values and benefits is approached a little differently than assessing abilities and interests. You should consider the job values and benefits as options and weigh their importance to you in the jobs you are pursuing. You need to determine the values and benefits that are the most important to you. Use the following list from *The Career Decision-Making System Revised* to help you determine those values. Circle your four most important values in the following list:

- **Creativity:** Have a job where you can use your imagination and be inventive.

- **Good salary:** Be well paid for your work.

- **High achievement:** Be able to do things of importance or to succeed in a job that is difficult.

- **Independence:** Do work that lets you be your own boss and do the job the way you want without someone watching over you.

- **Job security:** Have a steady job from which you are unlikely to be fired.

- **Leadership:** Direct the work of others and make decisions affecting others.

- **Outdoor work:** Work outside most of the time.

- **Physical activity:** Do work that calls for moving about and using physical strength.

- **Prestige:** Have a job where you get respect and feel important.

- **Risk:** Work in a job that requires you to take physical risks.

- **Variety:** Do many different and interesting tasks.

- **Work with hands:** Have a job where you can use your hands, machines, or tools to make or repair things.

- **Work with people:** Work in close contact with people and be able to comfort and help others.

- **Work with mind:** Do work that requires a high level of mental ability.

What do you do now that you have indicated your four preferred values? In each description of the 58 majors in this book, you will read about values and benefits that you may receive in that field. Thus you will be able to use the information gained from rating your most desired values as you seek work satisfaction within each major you explore.

In closing, you may be interested in knowing about the different work values that adolescents, college students, and workers have about their jobs. A high priority for adolescents is a good salary. This value decreases for many workers as they come to value the following more: being involved in setting policy, getting recognition for work, and improving their working conditions. Also, compared to adolescents, experienced workers are less likely to perceive their workplaces as sources of socialization. Additional studies have noted that the values of adolescents are remarkably the same from one country to another. If you accept the idea that values are representative of needs, then many of us around the world have the same basic needs.

Collecting Information

Effective career decision making requires a multidimensional approach that involves the three domains we have already examined—abilities, interests, and values—as well as factual information about career fields. Achievement demonstrated in course work or work experience related to a specific field is obviously a source of helpful information.

While each chapter in this book describes a major's uniqueness, the psychological characteristics of career fields are often very similar. Many career fields have an affinity to other fields, so the abilities, interests, and values associated with them may overlap. In other words, people with a certain profile of skills, likes, and desires usually have several equally rewarding career options. Thus identifying alternative options is also an important task.

Each chapter has been written to answer the following questions about a major field of study:

▶ What is the nature of the career?

▶ What kind of work is performed by typical graduates so that I can match my abilities to the work?

▶ How is the field described so that I can assess my interest in the major?

▶ What are the major values and benefits that may emerge in this type of occupation?

▶ What are the personality characteristics of workers in this major?

▶ What kinds of work activities are in each major?

▶ Is further graduate or professional education likely to be required in this major?

▶ Will I get a job? Will it be in my major? In what part of the economy will it be? (A very valuable table will show the top five occupations that employ graduates with a bachelor's degree in this major. The data also considers gender. With this information, you can easily determine—either through government publications, job postings on the Web, or the campus career-placement office—the viability of finding employment in the major when you graduate.)

▶ What kind of on-the-job learning will there be, and what will it entail? (Most college graduates ignore the fact that once they are employed, their employer will demand more learning on the job.)

▶ What will I be paid, and how much can I make if I remain in this field?

▶ How does the salary in this field compare with that of other college graduates?

With the information collected from these questions, you are ready to integrate the occupational information with your personal desires into a structure that will permit further analysis. The decision-making process is different for each person. Some will find the major simply by focusing on which one will make them the most money and will result in the best lifestyle. For others, this process will sound like too much work, and they will drift along and take what life dishes out.

Others will plan more and will want to have more control of their lives. For these people, such concepts as short-term goals, long-term goals, and maximizing opportunities will become a part of their formal decision-making process, which the next section discusses.

For anyone who desires more detailed information about career areas not covered by the 58 majors in this book, excellent resources from the U.S. Department of Labor are the O*NET database (http://online.onetcenter.org) and the *Occupational Outlook Handbook* (www.bls.gov/oco/home.htm). The *Handbook* is updated every 2 years, so it is the most current source readily available. Print versions of these two resources, with additional print-only content, are available from JIST Publishing and can be obtained at virtually every library or career resource center.

Organizing the Information

The following five steps sum up the decision-making process that students must go through to determine their future work lives:

1. Set the goals.

2. Know what is most important.

3. Examine the options.

4. Assess the risks involved.

5. Establish an implementation plan.

All too frequently a solution for identifying goals is to administer a battery of tests. Presto! The results identify a person's goals and skills by offering a career cluster or occupational titles. However, using this approach exclusively misses the following important areas:

▶ Faulty assumptions, beliefs, and implications

▶ Self-improvement goals

▶ Activities that one does well and that provide personal satisfaction

▶ Future considerations of life roles and their compatibility with goals

While you can use this book as a complete self-help text, many people will find it valuable to run their ideas by others to receive feedback. At some time, almost 70 percent of students have discussed their future plans with at least one of their parents by their junior year in college. It is very valuable to dialogue about your dreams and aspirations in the past, present, and future.

Step 1: Setting Goals

Once you have identified your goals, the logical next step is to set goals. Identifying goals often requires someone to cajole, nurture, and draw out a person's ideas and feelings. Goal setting requires organizational and planning skills to develop a plan of action. The first step in goal setting is to sum up the issues that were raised about your job future and major area of study. Be sure to clarify this information with people you respect, because we all know people who change their mind each time you ask.

After you sum up the issues, you need to prioritize them. This process sets up an agenda for future steps that you have to take. This prioritizing can be tricky because you have to consider motivational factors to achieve success. In other words, goal setting is based on the reinforcement theory that success is the best motivator for the student.

You need to put your goals in a certain order: The goals that are the easiest to achieve and require the least time should be your first objectives to pursue. When you achieve success by accomplishing these easy goals, you can then go on to the more difficult ones that may require prerequisite learning or experiences. Goal setting establishes a structure. If you have found people—friends, parents, high school counselors, or college staff members—to assist you, they may suggest some experiences to increase the likelihood that a goal can be successfully achieved.

You should give yourself enough time so that the decision-making process is less stressful. Take a look at the following true example: A high school senior knew that he was good in science and got good grades; however, he didn't know whether to major in chemistry or engineering. He talked with some people in the respective fields and chose to enter college as a chemical engineering major. He was not as lucky as his high school classmate who went to a university that did not allow freshmen to declare a specific field of engineering to study. Our person chose chemical engineering according to the college's procedures for freshmen. Despite doing well academically, he struggled for three semesters until he decided that he needed a time-out—almost 2 years—before he chose to return to college in the same major. He later obtained work as a chemical engineer and returned for postgraduate study in the same area. What he truly needed was time for self-examination, clarification, and reconfirmation.

You should write down each goal you want. Think of the written list as a contract, a statement that includes the following points: what you anticipate doing, how long each task should take, and what outcomes you expect from the activities you pursue. You should evaluate your progress based on the satisfaction you get from the outcome of your achievements.

It would be a major oversight not to mention inappropriate goals. Other people can often recognize unrealistic expectations or inappropriate goals in you because the goals are often incompatible with data from achievement, ability, personality, or interest domains. These people can use the following ways to help you determine unrealistic goals: They can tell you that you cannot reach the stated goal, they can suggest information for you to read or a person to whom you can talk, or they can tell you to come to them for more advice. Some people don't want advice; these people may learn best by failing.

However, experience suggests that creative helpers can work with clients to make apparent mismatches actually work. For example, the introvert who wants to be a salesperson may master the computer to mount direct sales campaigns through the Web. And a disabled person who wants to be a professional mountain climber may design a unique piece of equipment that wins the acclaim of climbers. If helpers respond to seemingly inappropriate goals without acknowledging the individual's personal needs, outcomes may be jeopardized. An individual's goal may reflect a desire for a personal need to triumph over adverse forces that seem overwhelming.

Step 2: Knowing What Is Most Important

In this section, the values you prioritized earlier are considered in relation to other information. Frequently we like to know and compare ourselves to what other people say or to what others select as their top choices. What follows is a summary of more than 10,000 U.S. high school students' job values grouped into their top five choices, their second five choices, and the four choices least frequently chosen. The top five values include getting a good salary, having job security, holding down a job with variety, working with people, and earning high achievements. You may be interested to know that Canadian, Australian, and French youth selected these same five values in the same order as Japanese, Norwegian, and Portuguese youth.

The second tier of values includes being independent, working with your hands, gaining prestige, being creative, and working with your mind. Some variability did occur among these values in the six countries studied. The values least chosen include physical activity, leadership, outdoor work, and (physical) risk. Among the American youth, several gender differences were noted, following traditional male/female patterns. Females ranked higher than males on working with people, gaining prestige, and working with their mind; they ranked lower than males, however, on working with their hands, participating in physical activity, and being independent.

The two most frequently chosen values are good salary and job security. Often when students initially choose a good income as the most important value, they will adjust their thinking in the course of their work experiences. What they will end up saying is "I want the money I feel my work deserves. I don't want to be taken advantage of." In recent years, job security has become more important to young adults as they see that this goal has become harder to obtain in today's work market. These studies and their results also worry employers from around the world when they see that the values of working with the mind and exhibiting leadership are ranked in the 10th and 12th places, respectively, out of 14 values.

Research, however, shows that the popularity of the adolescent values described changes with age. A study of one-half million employees cited 11 reasons that were more important than pay in staying with their current employer: career opportunity, challenge, feeling of making a contribution, coworkers, teamwork, a good boss, recognition, fun on the job, autonomy, and flexible hours and dress code (B. Kaye and S. Jordan-Evans, *Love 'Em or Lose 'Em: Getting Good People to Stay.* San Francisco: Berrett-Koehler Publishers, Inc., 1999, p. 6).

Realistically, job values will eventually compete with personal values. You have to be prepared to think about how the conflict between these two priorities will affect your family life and your work life as you integrate them. The following list includes some personal values.

▶ **Family:** Raising a family or caring for aged parents.

▶ **Leisure:** Having time and money for leisure.

▶ **Community:** Taking an active part in community affairs.

▶ **Personal growth:** Working on self-improvement.

▶ **Helping others:** Improving the quality of the lives of others.

▶ **Environment:** Conserving or restoring the environment.

▶ **Spiritual:** Doing things that follow one's personal beliefs.

▶ **A good life:** Achieving a comfortable and high standard of living.

Values can change as you get older and enter relationships where people come from different backgrounds. New priorities will emerge, and prior values will be replaced. Although values are important, interests may have greater influence on you when you are younger. As you develop, however, values definitely play an influential role in your life.

Step 3: Examining the Options

You can use Table 3 to consolidate the information about your education alternatives. To assess a major, record your evaluations of the 10 areas in the corresponding rows of Table 3. Indicate in the first row any major(s) you are considering.

1. Excellent, good, fair, or poor match of your abilities with those required by the major.

2. Good, fair, or poor match of your interests with those activities and opportunities that the major can provide.

3. Very compatible, compatible, or conflicting values with people in the occupations that this major prepares you for.

4. Good, fair, or poor fit of your personality characteristics with people who enter occupations from this major.

5. Very acceptable, acceptable, or not acceptable salary.

6. Agree, do not agree, or in a quandary about whether you are willing to go

Table 3
Evaluating Your Majors

Name of Major			
Abilities (1)			
Interests (2)			
Values (3)			
Personality Characteristics (4)			
Salary (5)			
Requires More Education (6)			
Relocation (7)			
Employment Outlook (8)			
Job Readiness (9)			
Industry Attractiveness (10)			

back for additional schooling. Additionally, place an *X* on the line if you believe a source of funding is available to pay some postgraduate tuition costs.

7. Will relocate or will not relocate to find employment or to go to school in this major.

8. Excellent, good, fair, or poor outlook for jobs with this major. Additionally, put a *C* on the line if this is a very competitive field.

9. Yes or no that you will be fully qualified for employment with this major when you receive your bachelor's degree.

10. Attractive, fairly attractive, or not attractive, depending on whether you like the industry in which the job is or its growth potential.

The reason for using visual aids, such as Table 3, is to identify areas that are restraining you from making a decision. You must know which areas need to be addressed if most of the other factors are valued positively. By examining the options, you can weigh the pros and cons of the consequences of a decision. Also, if some of the descriptive words from the list don't appeal to you, you can use this test as a signal to stop and question the original goal(s) set in Step 1.

There is fluidity to this decision-making process. Maybe you have chosen incorrect goals originally. By examining the options in Step 3, for example, you may come to the realization that you have established goals based on what your brother or sister has advised you, not your own personal goals. Or you may have been influenced by people who have said that you should be in a certain profession just because they like that profession. After assessing your own abilities, you may finally come to your own conclusion about what you like to do and how well you do it. It is okay to go back to Step 1 and select a new goal. You will be surprised how fast the process goes the second or even the third time you go through it because you have already done a lot of the work.

Step 4: Assessing the Risks

The decision model is based on the concepts of value and probability. *Value* refers to the desirability of something or to an outcome, which can be either positive or negative. A negative value means that the outcome or event is undesirable. This concept of value closely resembles the behavioral concepts of positive and negative reinforcement. In examining and evaluating the options in Step 3, you are determining the values that appear the most or least desirable.

Probability refers to the likelihood that an event or outcome will happen. Probability is related to risk, which has the following ranges:

- **No risk:** The outcome is known and certain.

- **Risky:** The outcome is known but has a specified probability factor; for example, 80 percent of people applying are accepted.

- **Uncertain:** The chances of the outcome occurring are unknown.

Many states have lotteries, which are examples of probabilities in action. For example, you buy a ticket for $1 or $2 with a probability of 1 million to 1 that you may win a big prize. The outcome is like a dream. On the other hand, because employers want to hire female engineers to satisfy governmental nondiscrimination laws, the probability is very high that the opportunities for employment will be excellent, because relatively few women are studying engineering.

Probabilities are not totally controlled by the person. For example, when the economies of Southeast Asia, Japan, and Korea are in difficulty, this situation affects the world economy, with results trickling down to the individual. You encounter risk daily in driving a car or in meeting people—after all, other people may not like you!

The values you indicated while examining your options are your *expectations*—the possible outcomes that you expect to gain from each of the criteria, such as utilizing your abilities, liking the activities of the occupation, and so on. Assessing the risks is really determining the probability (high, medium, or low) that each criterion will result in the expected outcome. For example, if you get good grades in the introductory subjects, you can expect to do well in that major. If you take an internship in an area and you like what you are doing, you can expect to like the work in the future. As you can see, making a decision involves data collection. After reviewing your answers to multiple questions, you can finally make an informed choice.

Risk taking is learned. Some people avoid taking risks, while others are more comfortable taking risks. Comfort with risk taking is not a universal quality. Some people will take many chances, including participating in such physical activity as rock climbing, which involves potential danger. Other people will take a risk in making money or in maintaining relationships or in being assertive. And others will take risks simply by expressing themselves, moving to take a new job, or traveling alone on a motorcycle across the country. Developing your talents or gifts always involves some kind of risk. Remember that each individual may have different risk-taking tendencies, depending on the situation. For this reason, you need to understand a bit about motivation.

An instructor of a college career planning course once wrote, "The most common cause of failure in college is not the lack of ability; it is the failure to establish a reason for being there." When you first establish your goals, you address this issue;

however, you may not understand your motivation for going to college or choosing a major. You may not understand that college is an opportunity—both a time and a place to identify, search out, and develop your talents and gifts. Maybe you need some perspective to see that selecting a major is an opportunity in itself and can often be a motivational force.

Motivation is an internal process that drives a person to act in a purposeful manner. An individual's needs, drives, and actions are included in his motivational forces. Motives develop from needs, which are related to goals, which reflect what the individual wants. Wondering about an opportunity or a dream can be a goal and can be articulated. Motives are *inner drives* that cannot be seen. Only inferences can be made about a person's motives. However, goal statements and actions that are movements toward a goal are observable and can serve as the means by which the strength and understanding of the drive can be measured.

Motivation is the energy or the fuel that drives the self-development process. Motivation is the internalization of a person's drive for goal attainment. We hope that as a young adult, you have started questioning who you are, what you want, and what your talents are, because now is the time to do these things. So goal identification and goal attainment are parts of motivation, but the creation of excitement is also part of motivation. Dreaming or envisioning yourself in a certain major can be fun. A noted career researcher said, "An individual's future is limited only by the imagination of those involved in the planning." Although thinking about the future may be scary, anxiety is also the energy that drives a person to change and to learn.

Find someone to listen to you as you describe or act out how you will perform in a specific occupation. In fact, do this exercise for several different occupations, because it may indicate adequate or inadequate job knowledge. For example, this exercise will take you from the point of saying,

"I want to be a TV producer" to "This is what I would do as a TV producer." How you fill in the details about the job and how you describe the advancement opportunities for the job are critical to your success in that field.

Take a look at the following job history as it relates to being a TV producer. This example shows the detail that you must have as you act out each occupation that you are considering. To be a TV producer, you often have to start at the bottom as a gofer, a person who runs errands for others. You probably will have to do part-time work, which is usually in the evenings for a very low salary. This low salary will prevent you from participating in many activities that your friends are doing, so you may have to get a second job just to keep up with them. After several years of this kind of work, you may get a chance at full-time work, but you will still work weekends and evenings. You will see your social life impaired in comparison with others because you finish work at midnight and leave for work at 2 p.m.

One way to learn the realities that come with holding a particular job is to talk to people in the occupation. Get a variety of opinions to balance out biases. You may also benefit from visiting the worksite. Find out what it looks like, sounds like, and smells like. Doing part-time or volunteer work in the same setting can be even more revealing.

After examining a job in this real-world detail, you are ready to answer the question about whether you have the motivation to pursue this career. A person's motivation is often embedded in his or her self-portrayal of actually doing the job. Only you can determine the sacrifices and compromises you are willing to make to work in the kind of job you want.

In closing, this step in the development of dreams or talents can involve risks. Remember that motivation is definitely part of goal attainment.

Step 5: Establishing a Plan

You may consider this step a "no-brainer" because it is simply the mechanical process of writing down a schedule of events to do. However, it is critical to the implementation and the culmination of earlier steps.

Perhaps all that your choice of major involves is checking off a box on a class registration form. Great! Other institutions may require you to apply to be admitted and to wait for a decision—ideally, to be invited to come aboard. But what about the other issues that you raised as you explored your choice of major? How did you decide to resolve them?

Take a look at Table 4. You can use this table as a guide to plan your future. In column 1, you should list the actions to be completed—those ideas, concerns, and issues that you want to explore further. In column 2, you should list the steps you have to take to answer the questions posed in the first column. Some sample steps could include the following questions: With whom do you speak, where do you get the information or resources,

where do you go or whom do you see to obtain the hands-on experience you want, and where do you take a prerequisite course? In column 3, you list your estimation of the time the activity will take and the date that you propose to do the activity.

Prolonging the completion of the action steps is not motivational; therefore, it is critical to examine your time frames for completing all your tasks. You may be able to do some of the tasks concurrently so that you can move along in your goal to choose a career.

In this chapter, you have been exposed to the challenge of seeking self-knowledge, which some people only minimally achieve during their lifetime. Learning about yourself is a hard task and usually takes considerable time. Self-estimates of abilities are expressions of self-perceptions. Remember that people tend to behave in a manner consistent with their image of themselves. You have also been studying how to make a decision. Remember that *not* making a decision is also a choice. We all have choices, and choosing to act on them is empowering. Selecting a major is one way that you can empower yourself.

Table 4
A Sample List of Headings for an Action Plan

Goals/Activities/Issues	What Needs to Be Done and Resources to Obtain or People to Contact	Time Estimate and Date to Be Completed

CHAPTER 3

The Economics of Career Choice

Enrolling in a college or university after graduation is widely prevalent among American high school graduates. A sizable majority of students graduating from high school choose to pursue postsecondary education. During the fall of 2010, out of 3.2 million members of that year's high school graduating class, 2.2 million, or more than 68 percent, were enrolled in colleges and universities. Year after year, many high school graduates and their families make one of the most important decisions of their lives—the decision to enroll in college.

A college education is one of the costliest purchases that you will ever make, and completing a college education with a degree can have a life-long impact on your economic and psychological well-being and on your social status. Despite well-intentioned messages—from high school graduation speakers—that college is a journey to be experienced and explored, the reality is that college is a demanding, time-consuming, and expensive investment. Its status as an investment gives it special properties, chief among which is that it is expected to lead to benefits or desirable outcomes in the future in return for costs incurred today.

College requires such a great expenditure of money, time, and effort that you should give considerable thought to whether you will go to college. The quality of your decision is partly determined by the quality of the information on which you base the decision—information about your interests, aptitudes, and abilities balanced against the costs and expected benefits of attending college at specific institutions and in specific academic fields.

Unfortunately, for many high school graduates whose college investment decision is not made with sufficient information, preparation, and thought, college will prove to be a failure in this regard. A substantial proportion of those entering college will fail to earn an associate or a bachelor's degree. They will withdraw from college and try to find an alternative path through life. Others will graduate from college, but they will be unable to find meaningful work or to gain access to a lifestyle that meets their basic values. For these individuals, the college investment has not worked because they failed to reach a destination with value and meaning for them. Indeed, college is a journey, but as with all journeys, it has meaning only when the journey ends at the right destination.

Investment in a college education can be very lucrative. As you will learn later in this chapter, the average rate of economic return for a bachelor's degree measured by annual earnings and total earnings over a lifetime is quite high. But before we discuss the returns for a college investment, let us explore the college investment decision and compare it with other investment activities.

39

The Costs and Benefits of Investment in Higher Education

Investment is an activity in which you sacrifice something today in the expectation of some greater benefit in the future. Attending college is akin to investment since college has costs that are incurred today in the expectation of benefits that will accrue in the future. If you plan to invest in a college education, you need to weigh the total costs of attending college with the total expected future benefits from a college education. Although many potential college enrollees are generally aware of the costs of a college education, particularly out-of-pocket costs, they are not as cognizant of the stream of future monetary benefits that will accrue to them after completing a college education. You will incur two major types of costs when you enroll in college. The first is the out-of-pocket costs of tuition and fees that you pay to finance your education. Although these costs are large and rising, they are only a part of the total cost that you and your family pay for a college education.

A second major cost for college is the earnings you forgo while enrolled in school. Most college students do not hold full-time jobs while they are in school. Many students hold part-time jobs for a limited number of weeks over the year, while others choose not to work. This reduced work effort represents "lost" earnings that college students could have had if they opted to work full-time instead of enrolling in college. Thus, the true cost for enrolling in college includes both your out-of-pocket costs, such as tuition and fees, and your lost earnings. (Most economists do not include dormitory and boarding costs in calculating the total cost of college because you would have to pay these costs even if you were not in college.)

In the 2011–2012 academic year, average tuition and fee costs at private American 4-year nonprofit colleges were approximately $28,500 per year. At public colleges nationwide, in-state tuition and fee costs were nearly $8,250 per year (according to *Trends in College Pricing,* The College Board, Washington, DC, 2011). These costs are the average costs for attending a 4-year college, and they vary considerably by state and by type of college. Added to these costs are the lost earnings of students who give up full-time work. In 2011, the average young adult who obtained a high school diploma but did not enroll in postsecondary school earned about $16,800. If we assume that the typical college freshman could have had a job that paid this amount, then the average student enrolled in college gave up about $16,800 in earnings during the first year of college.

Thus, the cost for a young adult entering a private college was about $45,300, which included the average tuition plus the lost earnings for the year—exclusive of room, board, and ancillary expenses. If we assume that students complete their education in 4 years, then a conservative estimate for a bachelor's degree from a private college in the 2014–2015 academic year will be $181,200. This amount is sufficient to purchase a single-family home in many parts of the country or to put toward a down payment for a home in the most expensive areas. Clearly such high costs require that substantial returns be generated to justify the expense!

A college education does, in fact, provide substantial benefits that, on average, justify the costs. Moreover, at least the monetary benefits of a bachelor's degree have increased over time. Table 1 presents a comparison of the earnings of young college graduates with a bachelor's degree with those of young adults who have earned only a high school diploma. The comparison is presented over the 1967 to 2011 period, and annual earnings are expressed in inflation-adjusted 2011 dollars. From the late 1960s through the early 1970s, the average young adult with a college degree earned between 22 percent and 25 percent more than high school graduates. For a brief period in the early 1970s, the earnings advantage of college graduates actually declined to the 17 percent range. This decline in the earnings advantage of college graduates was considered to be evidence of an oversupply of college graduates.

Table 1
Mean Annual Earnings of Employed College Graduates and High School Graduates Aged 20 to 29, 1967–2011

Year	High School Graduates	College Graduates with a Bachelor's Degree	Absolute Difference	Relative Difference
1967	$27,822	$34,704	$6,882	24.7%
1968	$28,147	$34,950	$6,803	24.2%
1969	$29,221	$35,933	$6,712	23.0%
1970	$28,589	$35,395	$6,805	23.8%
1971	$28,175	$34,452	$6,277	22.3%
1972	$29,619	$34,249	$4,631	15.6%
1973	$29,348	$35,701	$6,353	21.6%
1974	$27,789	$32,566	$4,777	17.2%
1975	$26,523	$33,744	$7,221	27.2%
1976	$27,211	$33,898	$6,687	24.6%
1977	$26,900	$34,263	$7,363	27.4%
1978	$27,845	$34,292	$6,447	23.2%
1979	$27,666	$34,157	$6,492	23.5%
1980	$25,854	$32,508	$6,654	25.7%
1981	$24,478	$31,970	$7,492	30.6%
1983	$23,620	$33,100	$9,480	40.1%
1984	$24,406	$34,835	$10,429	42.7%
1985	$24,226	$36,745	$12,519	51.7%
1986	$24,489	$37,700	$13,211	53.9%
1987	$25,011	$37,842	$12,831	51.3%
1988	$25,337	$38,221	$12,884	50.8%
1989	$25,008	$38,880	$13,871	55.5%
1990	$24,047	$36,632	$12,585	52.3%
1991	$23,228	$34,986	$11,758	50.6%
1992	$22,787	$34,474	$11,687	51.3%
1993	$22,061	$33,614	$11,553	52.4%
1994	$22,935	$34,503	$11,568	50.4%
1995	$22,720	$35,376	$12,655	55.7%

(continued)

Table 1 (continued)
Mean Annual Earnings of Employed College Graduates and High School Graduates Aged 20 to 29, 1967–2011

1996	$22,671	$36,842	$14,171	62.5%
1997	$23,552	$38,333	$14,781	62.8%
1998	$24,943	$40,443	$15,501	62.1%
1999	$24,069	$40,877	$16,808	69.8%
2000	$25,838	$43,585	$17,747	68.7%
2001	$25,249	$42,061	$16,812	66.6%
2002	$28,933	$43,509	$14,576	50.4%
2003	$27,076	$42,786	$15,709	58.0%
2004	$26,976	$42,833	$15,857	58.8%
2005	$26,088	$42,938	$16,850	64.6%
2006	$27,062	$41,392	$14,330	53.0%
2007	$27,432	$43,186	$15,754	57.4%
2008	$26,688	$42,000	$15,312	57.4%
2009	$27,144	$44,390	$17,246	63.5%
2010	$25,461	$41,075	$15,614	61.3%
2011	$25,484	$39,705	$14,221	55.8%

Source: U.S. Bureau of the Census, Current Population Surveys, March Supplement, 1968–2011. Tabulations produced by the authors.

However, since the end of the 1970s, the size of the earnings advantage for college graduates has increased at a fairly steady rate. By 1981, young college graduates earned 31 percent more each year than high school graduates with no postsecondary schooling. The economic boom of the 1980s provided further advantages for college graduates. By 1990, the average young adult with a college degree earned 52 percent more per year than high school graduates.

The 1990s saw another increment in the college earnings premium. In 1999, young college graduates earned nearly 70 percent more, on average, than young adults with only a high school diploma. The onset of the recession at the start of the new millennium resulted in a slight reduction of the earnings advantage of employed young college graduates. This recession saw an increase in underemployment among college graduates who were forced to shift down the employment queue and take jobs that did not fully utilize their skills and were typically filled by less-educated youth. The less-educated youth in turn were pushed further down the employment queue, leaving many of them jobless. However, even during the recession the mean annual earnings of employed young college graduates were two-thirds higher than those of young employed high school graduates. Moreover, the deeper recession that set in at the end of the first decade of the new century reversed the slight decline in the earnings advantage of the college degree. The layoffs and decline in hiring that accompanied this recession had their biggest impact on young people without a degree.

Over time, the size of the earnings advantage of college graduates relative to high school graduates has increased among young adults. But what happens to the earnings of college graduates as they age? Are college graduates able to maintain their earnings advantage relative to high school graduates over their entire working lives, or is the earnings advantage transitory, disappearing as both college graduates and high school graduates age?

To answer these questions, we need to examine the earnings experience of college graduates relative to high school graduates at different ages by constructing an age-earnings profile for each group. The age-earnings profiles presented in

Figure 1 trace the earnings of college graduates by age, relative to the earnings of high school graduates of the same age.

Three observations are readily apparent from Figure 1. First, at every age level except the very lowest, college graduates earn more than high school graduates. Second, the earnings for high school graduates peak much earlier than those of college graduates. Third, the relative size of the earnings advantage for college graduates increases with age, on average. This increase indicates that the earnings advantage of a college degree increases over the life of the college graduate.

FIGURE 1

Mean Annual Earnings of Employed Persons 25 to 64 Years Old, by Educational Attainment, by Age, 2011

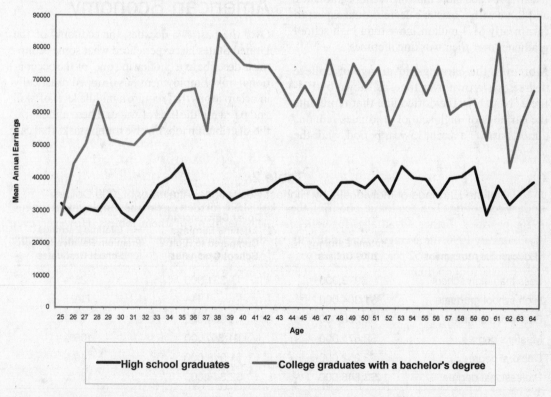

Source: U.S. Bureau of the Census, Current Population Survey Public Use Micro-data Samples (PUMS) Data Files, 2011. Tabulations produced by the authors.

These earnings advantages of a college degree accumulate to a substantial amount over the working lifetime of these graduates. Table 2 is a comparison of the lifetime earnings of individuals with different levels of schooling. On average, individuals with a bachelor's degree earn almost an additional three-quarters as much as those with just a high school diploma over their working lifetime. A master's degree is expected to roughly double one's lifetime earnings (relative to a high school diploma). This means that for every dollar earned by a high school graduate, individuals with a bachelor's degree earned $1.74, and individuals with a master's degree earned $2.05 over their lifetimes. Even higher earnings premiums can be projected for those who hold a doctoral or professional degree. These earnings premiums result in sizable aggregate dollar amounts. In 2009, individuals with a bachelor's degree could expect to earn $964,000 more than high school graduates, and those with a master's degree could expect to earn nearly $1.4 million more than high school graduates over their working lifetimes.

Moreover, the earnings advantage of college degrees has grown over time, as shown by Figure 2. Note how the dotted line that represents the earnings of high school graduates remains almost flat over a recent 15-year period, while the

dashed line representing the bachelor's degree and the solid line for advanced degrees both slope upward. As the cost of living has gone up, especially the cost of health care, wage-earners whose income has remained flat are losing ground.

What underlies these divergent trends in the economic fortunes of college graduates and their poorly educated counterparts? The next section describes the American economy that has emerged with the dawning of the 21st century and examines the relationship between the current American economic environment and the employment and earnings prospects of individuals with different levels of formal education.

Skills, Wages, and Employment in the American Economy

Over the past two decades, the economy of the United States has experienced what some economists describe as a "hollowing out" of the occupational mix: Employment has dropped drastically in occupations that require a middle level of skill and pay a middle level of wages. These middle-of-the-distribution jobs involve routine tasks that can

Table 2
Lifetime Earnings of Individuals, by Highest Educational Attainment, 2009 Dollars

Educational Attainment	Lifetime Earnings, 2009 Dollars	Dollar Difference in Lifetime Earnings Compared to High School Graduates	Lifetime Earnings Premium Relative to High School Graduates
Less than high school	$973,000	−331,000	−25%
High school graduate	$1,304,000	NA	NA
Bachelor's degree	$2,268,000	$964,000	74%
Master's degree	$2,671,000	$1,367,000	105%
Doctoral degree	$3,252,000	$1,948,000	149%
Professional degree	$3,648,000	$2,344,000	180%

Source: Anthony P. Carnevale, Stephen J. Rose, and Ban Cheah, The College Payoff: Education, Occupations, Lifetime Earnings, Washington, The Georgetown University Center on Education and the Workforce, 2011.

FIGURE 2

Mean Annual Earnings of Wage and Salary Earners 16 Years and Older, by Educational Attainment, 1996–2011

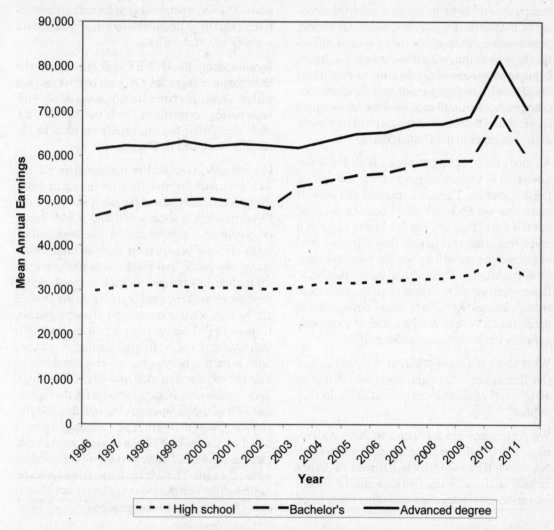

Source: Bureau of Labor Statistics, Usual Weekly Earnings of Wage and Salary Workers, 1996–2011. Tabulations produced by the authors.

be either automated or shipped overseas. Many of these are manufacturing jobs that a robot or a worker in China can do much more cheaply. At the same time, there have been workforce increases at the high and low ends of the skill and wage distributions. At the high end, you can find high-paying nonroutine jobs that require a high level of skill, such as physicians, lawyers, and managers. At the low end are the low-paying nonroutine jobs that require low skills, such as truck drivers, security guards, and landscaping workers. Many low-skill jobs are not threatened by automation because they demand recognition of language or some other kind of low-level decision making that cannot yet be automated. For example, proofreaders in the publishing industry must make judgments that are too subtle for a computer to make because they involve the meaning of the words, not just the spelling. Of course, proofreading can be offshored to other English-speaking countries where the wages are lower, but many other low-skill jobs must be performed on-site and therefore cannot be offshored. For example, home health care workers, landscaping laborers, and hotel housekeepers must be present at the worksites in the United States.

Anyone who is reading this book is probably not interested in the occupations at the low end of the distribution. These occupations will provide numerous job openings in the coming decades, but the wages they pay are too low to support a middle-class lifestyle. In fact, they provide a level of income that would leave you one paycheck away from bankruptcy. Even with a steady paycheck, these wages would not permit you to accumulate enough savings to be able to escape devastation in the event of a workplace injury, a fire at your living quarters, or some other random mishap.

What about the occupations at the other end of the distribution—the nonroutine jobs requiring a high level of skill? Exactly what skills do they require?

We Americans are fortunate to have a database, the O*NET (Occupational Information Network), that the U.S. Department of Labor created to describe occupations and rate them on various characteristics, including the level of

skill that they require. The Department of Labor also surveys employers on a regular basis to learn what wages are paid to people in various occupations. The Occupational Employment Statistics (OES) survey is updated every year and covers roughly 800 occupations.

By comparing the O*NET skill ratings and the dollar figures from the OES survey, we can see which skills are consistently associated with high-paying occupations. (Note that the O*NET skills are similar but not totally identical to the abilities discussed in Chapter 2.)

For example, take skill in mathematics. Of the 747 occupations that are included in both the O*NET database and the salary surveys of the Department of Labor, you'll find a wide range of occupations represented. At the high end of math skill are occupations such as mathematicians, physicists, and mechanical engineers. In the middle are occupations such as travel agents, driver/sales workers, and librarians. At the low end are bailiffs, telemarketers, and crossing guards. If this range of occupations is broken down into skill-level zones with an equal number of occupations in each zone, you can observe the relationship between level of skill and level of earnings. Table 3 shows the average earnings for the highest one-fifth of the occupations, the middle one-fifth, and the lowest one-fifth. Each earnings figure is based on the average of the median wages (half earn more and half earn less) for all occupations within the zone. The average is a weighted average, meaning that occupations with larger workforces count for more in the computation.

Table 3

Average Annual Earnings for Occupations at Three Levels of Skill with Mathematics

Zone of Skill	Examples of Occupations	Average Annual Earnings
Very High	mathematicians, physicists, mechanical engineers	$68,511
Medium	travel agents, driver/sales workers, librarians	$40,657
Very Low	bailiffs, telemarketers, crossing guards	$27,470

*Sources: O*NET database, release 16.0; May 2010 Occupational Employment Statistics survey. Tabulations produced by the authors.*

Of course, mathematics is not the only skill associated with earnings, and it may not be a skill that you are interested in developing. Table 4 uses the same approach as Table 3 for six other skills.

Tables 3 and 4 cover seven skills, but the O*NET database covers 35 in all. You may wonder which have the best payoff in dollar terms. To determine this, the best method is not the zone approach of Tables 3 and 4 but rather a statistical method called *correlation*. This calculation looks at how much a variation in one factor is accompanied by variation in another.

For example, when cigarette smoking first became popular, doctors noticed that heavy smokers

Table 4
Average Annual Earnings for Occupations at Three Levels of Various Skills

Skill and Level	Examples of Occupations	Average Annual Earnings
Complex Problem Solving		
Very High	foresters, economists, sales managers	$80,276
Medium	chefs and head cooks, radiation therapists, roofers	$41,671
Very Low	floral designers, file clerks, cashiers	$23,393
Critical Thinking		
Very High	judicial law clerks, microbiologists, logisticians	$77,882
Medium	upholsterers, insurance sales agents, tellers	$35,661
Very Low	models, floor sanders and finishers, bartenders	$23,914
Management of Financial Resources		
Very High	lodging managers, civil engineers, curators	$64,519
Medium	athletic trainers, motorboat operators, concierges	$34,881
Very Low	photographers, court reporters, telemarketers	$27,596
Negotiating		
Very High	lawyers, marketing managers, instructional coordinators	$60,148
Medium	optometrists, budget analysts, new accounts clerks	$39,478
Very Low	paperhangers, biological technicians, pharmacy aides	$26,749
Reading Comprehension		
Very High	surgeons, editors, mental health counselors	$82,452
Medium	art directors, broadcast technicians, commercial pilots	$35,491
Very Low	parking lot attendants, funeral attendants, shampooers	$23,307
Social Perceptiveness		
Very High	physician assistants, fashion designers, credit counselors	$67,627
Medium	flight attendants, surveyors, technical writers	$37,151
Very Low	etchers and engravers, tire builders, file clerks	$26,376

*Sources: O*NET database, release 16.0; May 2010 Occupational Employment Statistics survey. Tabulations produced by the authors.*

were more often afflicted with certain diseases. Long before researchers were able to pinpoint the mechanisms by which the smoke caused harmful biological processes, they were able to demonstrate a statistical correlation between these two factors. To be sure, sometimes correlations are misleading. Some doctors once believed that there was a connection between polio and ice cream because the disease struck most often during the summer, when the most ice cream was eaten. Eventually the polio virus was discovered, and swimming was found to be an excellent way to acquire it.

Nevertheless, correlations often indicate a cause-and-effect relationship. And when it comes to the relationship between skills and earnings, any employer can tell you that this is a real relationship, not like polio and ice cream. Employers look for highly skilled workers and pay them premium salaries.

So computing the correlations between the 35 O*NET skills and the occupations in the American workforce can be a useful indication of which skills have the highest value in the job market. A perfect correlation would be 1.0, meaning that any difference in skill levels between any two occupations is accompanied by a commensurate increase in the wages paid by those occupations. It would also mean that the difference goes in the same direction: higher pay when there's higher skill. If skill increases were linked to wage *decreases,* the correlation would be a negative number. If no relationship existed between the two factors, just random variation, the correlation would be zero.

Table 5 shows, from highest to lowest, the correlations between each of the 35 O*NET skills and the median wages paid in the 747 occupations that are included in both the O*NET database and the salary surveys of the Department of Labor.

You can see from Table 5 that some skills have a much closer association with high pay than others. Seven skills have a negative correlation; these skills are used at a high level in many blue-collar jobs

Table 5
Correlations Between O*NET Skills and Occupational Wages

Skill	Definition	Correlation
Judgment and Decision Making	Weighing the relative costs and benefits of a potential action.	0.8
Complex Problem Solving	Identifying complex problems, reviewing the options, and implementing solutions.	0.7
Active Learning	Working with new material or information to grasp its implications.	0.7
Reading Comprehension	Understanding written sentences and paragraphs in work-related documents.	0.7
Critical Thinking	Using logic and analysis to identify the strengths and weaknesses of different approaches.	0.7
Time Management	Managing one's own time and the time of others.	0.7
Systems Evaluation	Looking at many indicators of system performance and taking into account their accuracy.	0.7
Monitoring	Assessing how well one is doing when learning or doing something.	0.7
Active Listening	Listening to what other people are saying and asking questions as appropriate.	0.6

Skill	Definition	Correlation
Writing	Communicating effectively with others in writing as indicated by the needs of the audience.	0.6
Systems Analysis	Determining how a system should work and how changes will affect outcomes.	0.6
Operations Analysis	Analyzing needs and product requirements to create a design.	0.6
Speaking	Talking to others to effectively convey information.	0.6
Science	Using scientific methods to solve problems.	0.6
Instructing	Teaching others how to do something.	0.6
Management of Personnel Resources	Motivating, developing, and directing people as they work; identifying the best people for the job.	0.6
Persuasion	Persuading others to approach things differently.	0.6
Coordination	Adjusting actions in relation to others' actions.	0.6
Learning Strategies	Using multiple approaches when learning or teaching new things.	0.6
Social Perceptiveness	Being aware of others' reactions and understanding why they react the way they do.	0.5
Mathematics	Using mathematics to solve problems.	0.5
Negotiation	Bringing others together and trying to reconcile differences.	0.5
Management of Financial Resources	Determining how money will be spent to get the work done and accounting for these expenditures.	0.5
Management of Material Resources	Obtaining and seeing to the appropriate use of equipment, facilities, and materials needed to do certain work.	0.4
Service Orientation	Actively looking for ways to help people.	0.4
Programming	Writing computer programs for various purposes.	0.4
Technology Design	Generating or adapting equipment and technology to serve user needs.	0.3
Quality Control Analysis	Evaluating the quality or performance of products, services, or processes.	0.0
Operation Monitoring	Watching gauges, dials, or other indicators to make sure a machine is working properly.	−0.1
Installation	Installing equipment, machines, wiring, or programs to meet specifications.	−0.1
Troubleshooting	Determining what is causing an operating error and deciding what to do about it.	−0.1
Equipment Selection	Determining the kinds of tools and equipment needed to do a job.	−0.1
Operation and Control	Controlling operations of equipment or systems.	−0.2
Repairing	Repairing machines or systems, using the needed tools.	−0.2
Equipment Maintenance	Performing routine maintenance and determining when and what kind of maintenance is needed.	−0.2

Sources: O*NET database, release 16.0; May 2010 Occupational Employment Statistics survey. Tabulations produced by the authors.

that do not pay well. (This is not to say that *every* occupation that uses them at a high level has low pay; elevator installers and repairers, for example, use many of these negatively correlated skills at a high level and average almost $71,000 per year.)

Of course, money is not the only issue you need to consider when you plan your career. You won't earn any wages if you aren't hired, so the future availability of jobs in various careers is another key issue.

Here again, we can benefit from figures supplied by the Department of Labor. Every 2 years, the Office of Occupational Statistics and Employment Projections publishes the 10-year employment outlook for about 800 occupations: the percentage by which they expect the workforce will expand, plus how many job openings they expect will be created each year over that decade. These projections are not guarantees. A catastrophic economic downturn, war, or technological breakthrough could change the outcome. The projections are also averages over a 10-year period. During economic slowdowns, job growth and openings will be lower; during recoveries, both will be higher. But these projections are the best available data about future job opportunities.

Therefore, it also makes sense to examine the correlations between the 35 skills and the outlook for occupations. This information can help answer this question: Which skills are likely to be in greatest demand in the near future?

Table 6 shows, from highest to lowest, the correlation between each of the 35 O*NET skills and the percentage growth that the Department of Labor projects for the 735 occupations that are included in both the O*NET database and the growth-projections database of the Department of Labor.

Table 6
Correlations Between O*NET Skills and Occupational Growth Projections

Skill	Definition	Correlation
Service Orientation	Actively looking for ways to help people.	0.5
Active Listening	Listening to what other people are saying and asking questions as appropriate.	0.4
Active Learning	Working with new material or information to grasp its implications.	0.4
Speaking	Talking to others to effectively convey information.	0.4
Social Perceptiveness	Being aware of others' reactions and understanding why they react the way they do.	0.4
Writing	Communicating effectively with others in writing as indicated by the needs of the audience.	0.4
Critical Thinking	Using logic and analysis to identify the strengths and weaknesses of different approaches.	0.4
Learning Strategies	Using multiple approaches when learning or teaching new things.	0.4
Reading Comprehension	Understanding written sentences and paragraphs in work-related documents.	0.4
Science	Using scientific methods to solve problems.	0.4
Judgment and Decision Making	Weighing the relative costs and benefits of a potential action.	0.4

Skill	Definition	Correlation
Instructing	Teaching others how to do something.	0.4
Persuasion	Persuading others to approach things differently.	0.4
Systems Evaluation	Looking at many indicators of system performance and taking into account their accuracy.	0.4
Systems Analysis	Determining how a system should work and how changes will affect outcomes.	0.4
Complex Problem Solving	Identifying complex problems, reviewing the options, and implementing solutions.	0.4
Coordination	Adjusting actions in relation to others' actions.	0.4
Monitoring	Assessing how well one is doing when learning or doing something.	0.3
Negotiation	Bringing others together and trying to reconcile differences.	0.3
Time Management	Managing one's own time and the time of others.	0.3
Management of Personnel Resources	Motivating, developing, and directing people as they work; identifying the best people for the job.	0.3
Operations Analysis	Analyzing needs and product requirements to create a design.	0.3
Mathematics	Using mathematics to solve problems.	0.2
Programming	Writing computer programs for various purposes.	0.2
Management of Material Resources	Obtaining and seeing to the appropriate use of equipment, facilities, and materials needed to do certain work.	0.2
Management of Financial Resources	Determining how money will be spent to get the work done and accounting for these expenditures.	0.2
Technology Design	Generating or adapting equipment and technology to serve user needs.	0.2
Installation	Installing equipment, machines, wiring, or programs to meet specifications.	−0.1
Quality Control Analysis	Evaluating the quality or performance of products, services, or processes.	−0.2
Equipment Selection	Determining the kinds of tools and equipment needed to do a job.	−0.2
Troubleshooting	Determining what is causing an operating error and deciding what to do about it.	−0.2
Operation Monitoring	Watching gauges, dials, or other indicators to make sure a machine is working properly.	−0.2
Repairing	Repairing machines or systems, using the needed tools.	−0.3
Equipment Maintenance	Performing routine maintenance and determining when and what kind of maintenance is needed.	−0.3
Operation and Control	Controlling operations of equipment or systems.	−0.3

Sources: O*NET database, release 16.0; U.S. Department of Labor, Office of Occupational Statistics and Employment Projections, Occupational Projections and Training Data, 2008–2018. Tabulations produced by the authors.

Table 7
Skills That Ranked High on Both Tables 5 and 6

Skill	Position by Pay	Position by Growth
Active Learning	3	3
Active Listening	9	2
Critical Thinking	5	7
Judgment and Decision Making	1	11
Reading Comprehension	4	9
Writing	10	6
Speaking	13	4
Complex Problem Solving	2	16

If you compare Table 6 with Table 5, you'll notice that the ordering of the skills shows many differences. For example, the most lucrative skill in Table 5, judgment and decision making, is found in only eleventh place in Table 6. Complex problem solving, second-ranked in Table 5, appears in the middle of the pack in Table 6. The lesson here is that no single skill dominates all others in promising success.

But it's still possible to identify several skills that have relatively prominent placement in both lists, as you can see in Table 7.

Because these skills are clearly valuable to bring to the job market, the next question is how to acquire these skills. Keep in mind that a skill is not something you are born with. You may have an inborn talent that makes it easier for you to acquire a skill—for example, playing the trumpet—but you will not become skilled unless you make the effort to learn the skill.

How much effort is required to learn these eight skills? Consider the occupations in which these skills are at especially high levels. It is possible to make a list of the occupations that have the highest combined rating on these skills and then determine what level of education or training is necessary to qualify for these jobs.

Table 8 lists seven education levels that are commonly required for entrance to various

Table 8
Postsecondary Education and Training Normally Required for Occupations Rated Highest on the Eight Top Skills

Level of Education/Training	Number of Occupations
Doctoral degree	39
Bachelor's degree	20
Master's degree	17
First professional degree	14
Bachelor's or higher degree, plus work experience	8
Associate degree	1
Long-term on-the-job training	1

occupations. The table shows, out of the 100 occupations with the highest combined rating on the eight high-ranking skills, how many occupations require each level of education.

The lesson to take away from Table 8 is that **college is the place** to acquire the skills needed for the high-paying, high-growth occupations of the near future.

Keep in mind that up to this point we have been considering only *transferable* skills, the skills that are needed in many occupations and can be carried from one occupation to another. Workers also need *occupation-specific* skills. For example, physicians need transferable skills such as complex problem solving and critical thinking, but they also need highly specific medical skills such as being able to recognize the signs of pneumonia. Accountants need occupation-specific skills such as being able to evaluate a balance sheet. And, again, postsecondary education is the place to acquire these occupation-specific skills.

So, investing in a college degree is likely to lead to substantial returns. However, it is important to note that these returns on the investment vary enormously by the type of college education you get. To maximize the returns within the context of your interests, abilities, aptitudes, and values, you must answer some key questions: What type of college should I attend? Should I attend a 2-year or a 4-year school, a public or private school, a local or long-distance school?

In addition, you must decide on the type of degree you want and whether you want to earn just a bachelor's degree or pursue postgraduate education and an advanced degree. To decide, you must choose from dozens, if not hundreds, of alternatives. This enormous menu of choices is a major strength of American higher education. Yet this enormous array of options adds layers of complexity to your college investment decision and may seem daunting to you and your parents. To better understand the degree of this complexity, it is useful to compare the nature of the investment decisions made by stock market investors to that of college investors like you.

Information Requirements of the College Investment Decision

The hallmark of successful Wall Street traders is their ability to obtain and process information. They know where on the Web to find up-to-the-minute information on the performance of companies and stock prices. They know which newspapers and magazines publish in-depth stories about the products and future plans of a wide range of businesses. Armed with this and other information and a familiarity with the market, the Wall Street trader is in a better position to assess the benefits and costs of investment alternatives.

College investors also have some general knowledge about the economic returns of their college investment. Yet the similarity ends here. While Wall Street traders have detailed information on the performance of specific companies, prospective students have little information on the stream of benefits that they can expect from a specific college investment. Students know little about the outcomes of graduates from any individual college. What they do know is derived directly from the college admissions or public relations office—hardly the sort of objective source of information on which the Wall Street trader relies. Instead, prospective students rely on perceptions of college status as judged by friends, classmates, high school teachers, and counselors and such publications as *U.S. News & World Report* and *Barron's*. These perceptions may have little relationship to the advantages that the college may, in fact, offer.

Limited information often forces students, parents, and counselors to rely on less-than-systematic assessments of the career pathways associated with alternative fields of study. In fact, many career counselors advise students to avoid picking specific major fields of study. Instead, they recommend students major in the humanities and social sciences: fields that keep career options open and make students more flexible in responding to the changing needs of the workplace.

Yet opinion surveys have shown that parents and students tend to believe that the acquisition of specialized skills in a university setting will make a college graduate more employable in a labor market that is hungry for specific occupational and technical proficiencies.

Thus, college investors are torn between two views of the field-of-study decision. One view suggests that narrow vocational fields will lead to skills that will become increasingly obsolete and that the emphasis of a college education should be on transferable skills. The other view suggests that the best careers will be built on developing the occupation-specific skills required in engineering, health, computer software, and finance—the growth sectors of the American economy. Clearly the college investor is faced with a shortage of information about investment alternatives.

One way to deal with poor information and uncertainty in making an investment decision is to adopt a hedging strategy. Many casual investors on Wall Street do not have the time to gather the information to make specific stock purchases. These investors want to tap into the earnings generated by Wall Street, but they do not have the resources to gather and analyze information on costs and performance of specific companies. These investors often purchase a mutual fund that is composed of a portfolio of a cross section of firms selling shares in the market. By purchasing shares in a variety of firms, the investor hedges against the failure of any single company to generate positive earnings. Despite the lack of information, the Wall Street investor hopes to minimize the risk of substantial loss while capturing some benefits.

The educational investor, however, does not have access to the array of hedging strategies that are available to the Wall Street investor. It is not possible to construct an educational investment portfolio that contains a mix of alternatives—each carefully balanced to provide a high rate of return while minimizing risk. The closest that an educational investor comes to adopting a hedging strategy is by choosing to major in a broad liberal arts field. Many college counselors, college educators, and even some business leaders contend that this approach will help hedge against the "wrong" field-of-study choice. The proponents of this strategy believe that the labor market demands a broad set of skills that provides students with a high degree of flexibility to respond to changes in the demand for skills. Moreover, proponents of this view believe that choosing a major in a professional field—such as health, technology, or business—results in a degree of specialization that inhibits the very flexibility that is in demand.

Evidence of earnings of individuals who graduated in different majors does not support this perspective. A large and persistent earnings advantage accrues to college graduates who have degrees in professional fields. A study prepared by one of the authors reveals large differences in the earnings of college graduates by major—after accounting for other variables known to influence earnings. Graduates with degrees in such fields as engineering, computer science, health, and business have large earnings advantages compared to liberal arts graduates. These advantages persist over the working lives of the graduates. The study also found that the average earnings advantage of graduates from these professional fields declines sharply if they work in a job that is unrelated to the major.

Enrollment trends of the past few decades show that many young people are recognizing the advantages of choosing a professional field of study that prepares them for a career in a specific field rather than following the "educational hedging" strategy of choosing a broad liberal arts major. Over the past 40 years, the share of undergraduate degrees awarded in professional fields such as business, health, engineering, and computer science has grown dramatically, and the share of degrees awarded in the traditional liberal arts fields has declined. Earnings of graduates from these professionally oriented fields strongly suggest that the specific skills that the graduates acquire while in college contribute substantially to their postgraduation earnings premiums. These findings clearly illustrate that the educational investor is not in a position to capture the benefits of a bull education market by adopting a hedging strategy. Instead, the educational investor must make a series of all-or-nothing decisions.

Another all-or-nothing decision that an educational investor must make is college choice. As with the choice of a college major, college choice is not an irreversible decision. However, changing colleges or major fields imposes high costs on the educational investor. If students enroll in a college that isn't right for them, the cost can be high in several ways: lost time, loss of credits that don't transfer, and the psychological cost of matriculating at an institution that does not reflect their values or meet their educational, social, and psychological needs.

How should a potential enrollee select a college? Proponents of selecting a college by status believe that the status of the college signals to employers something about the skills and abilities that the graduates possess. Thus, an Ivy League degree in the humanities signals to employers that the individual with such a degree possesses stronger intellectual skills than the average college graduate. This is not because Ivy League colleges necessarily instill these traits into their graduates, but because Ivy League colleges screen out students who do not possess these characteristics. These schools accept only those students who are at the very top of the nation's high school classes. Knowing this, firms that desire to hire persons of high ability hire graduates from these colleges.

Research reveals that the earnings of students who graduate from elite colleges (many of which offer only a liberal arts education) are substantially higher than the earnings of graduates from the mainstream of higher education.

However, research that examined the underlying causes of these differences reveals that after one takes account of the differences between the pre-enrollment literacy skills of students of elite colleges relative to those of mainstream college students, the earnings advantage of elite students is no greater than 1 to 2 percent per year. These findings suggest that the independent effect of enrolling in an elite college is quite small and that a large part of the positive outcomes of graduates of elite colleges is attributable to the preexisting ability of students who enroll at these institutions.

In other words, students with strong academic proficiencies have a high degree of labor market success regardless of where they attend college. Thus, the earnings advantage of graduates of elite institutions is much more closely associated with their selection of only those students with above-average academic ability. Because the labor market provides substantial earnings rewards for these abilities, the average pay of graduates from these colleges is also well above average within a given field of study.

The earnings premiums of college graduates come about through a combination of solid intellectual skills, development of specific professional skills desired by employers, and access to a job that utilizes the skills learned in school. In addition to choosing the appropriate major field of study, choosing a college that has a strong record of placing its graduates in good-quality jobs is an important factor in the college investment decision.

The Educational and Labor Market Experiences of College Graduates

Depending on the choice of major, the college investment decision for many graduates does not end with the receipt of the bachelor's degree.

College graduates engage in a wide array of activities after they complete their undergraduate education. Although many graduates immediately enter career fields that become their life's work, others seek more schooling, frequently in fields other than that of their undergraduate specialty. Still others devote their lives to endeavors outside the paid labor market. The people in this last group often decide to meet the challenges of family life on a full-time basis.

Graduate Study

People frequently pursue graduate education after earning an undergraduate degree. More than 35 percent of those who earn a bachelor's degree go on to earn an advanced degree. Table 9 reveals that a little more than one-quarter of all college graduates earn a master's degree; almost 5 percent earn a doctorate; and almost 5 percent earn a professional degree, most often in law or medicine.

Approximately 24 percent of men and 27 percent of women with a bachelor's degree go on to earn a master's degree. For degrees higher than the master's, larger gender gaps appear, but in the opposite direction. Men are almost twice as likely as women to have earned a doctorate or professional degree. This gap seems likely to end or even reverse in a few years, because currently women

outnumber men in graduate and professional school enrollments by approximately 3 to 2.

Table 10 presents the proportion of bachelor's degree recipients in various major fields of study who eventually earn an advanced degree. The likelihood of earning a graduate degree is closely related to the undergraduate major field of study. For example, bachelor's degree holders who major in a physical science are very likely to earn an advanced degree. Only 59 percent of the graduates in this field end their schooling at the bachelor's degree level. The remaining 41 percent go on to earn some type of advanced degree, often a doctoral degree in the physical sciences. Although Table 10 is based on 2003 data, the relative differences among the majors have probably changed little since then.

Those who earn an undergraduate degree in education are even more likely to earn an advanced degree, although they earn a master's degree much more frequently than a professional degree. In contrast, students who complete an undergraduate degree in business-related fields are less likely to earn any graduate degree. Most of the graduates in these majors head directly into the labor market after graduation. Similarly, engineering majors are much less likely to earn a graduate degree. Strong labor demand and high wages make graduate school less attractive to majors from these fields.

Table 9
Percentage of Bachelor's Degree Recipients Who Earned an
Advanced Degree, by Type of Advanced Degree, by Gender

Gender	Percentage of Bachelor's Degree Holders with an Advanced Degree	Type of Advanced Degree		
		Master's	Doctoral	Professional
Total	35.2%	25.7%	4.6%	4.9%
Men	36.1%	23.7%	6.1%	6.3%
Women	34.4%	27.5%	3.3%	3.6%

Source: U.S. Bureau of the Census, Current Population Survey Public Use Micro-Data File, 2011. Tabulations produced by the authors.

Table 10

Percentage Distribution of All College Graduates (with a Bachelor's Degree or
More) in Each Broad Undergraduate Major, by Highest Degree Earned

Broad Undergraduate Major Field of Study	Bachelor's	Master's	Doctoral	Professional
Agricultural sciences	81.3%	9.7%	9.0%	0.0%
Biological sciences	71.9%	14.5%	13.6%	0.0%
Business	72.8%	26.4%	0.8%	0.0%
Computer science	65.8%	32.0%	2.2%	0.0%
Education	63.7%	35.0%	1.1%	0.2%
Engineering	73.7%	22.2%	4.2%	0.0%
Health professions	74.5%	21.3%	1.8%	2.4%
Humanities	59.5%	16.3%	4.0%	20.2%
Mathematics	71.0%	21.1%	7.9%	0.0%
Physical sciences	58.7%	19.0%	22.2%	0.0%
Social sciences	71.6%	21.2%	6.6%	0.6%

Source: National Science Foundation, National Survey of College Graduates, Public Use Micro-Data File, 2003. Tabulations produced by the authors.

In what fields of study are these advanced degrees earned? A look at the distribution of advanced degrees by major field of study reveals that graduate study among baccalaureate degree holders is concentrated in certain fields. Most often, persons who earn a master's degree choose business as their major field of study. Thirty percent of all master's degree holders in the country earn their degree in a field of business (see Table 11). The choice of major at the advanced degree level varies greatly by gender. Men are twice as likely as women to earn a master's degree in business. Forty-one percent of all men with a master's degree majored in business.

About one-fifth of all master's degree holders earn their degree in the field of education; again, the gender differences are quite large. More than one-third of all master's degrees earned by women are in education. Together, social sciences and humanities account for a little less than one-quarter of all master's degrees earned in the country. About the same proportion of men and women earned their master's degrees in humanities, but a much larger share of women earned the degree in a social science.

Table 11
Distribution of Master's Degrees Received, by Broad Major Field of Study, by Gender

	(A)	(B)	(C)	(D)
				Ratio of Male Major Concentration and Female Major
Broad Major Field of Study	**All**	**Men**	**Women**	**Concentration (B) / (C)**
Total	100%	100%	100%	—
Agricultural sciences	0.2%	0.3%	0.1%	2.7
Biological sciences	2.6%	2.8%	2.4%	1.2
Business	30.5%	40.9%	19.7%	2.1
Computer science	4.0%	5.3%	2.8%	1.9
Education	21.4%	9.2%	34.0%	0.3
Engineering	8.2%	13.7%	2.5%	5.5
Health professions	6.3%	1.9%	10.8%	0.2
Humanities	13.4%	13.2%	13.7%	1.0
Mathematics	1.6%	2.0%	1.2%	1.6
Physical sciences	1.9%	2.7%	1.0%	2.7
Social sciences	9.0%	6.6%	11.4%	0.6
Other	0.9%	1.4%	0.4%	3.0

Source: National Science Foundation, National Survey of College Graduates, Public Use Micro-Data File, 2003. Tabulations produced by the authors.

The choice of major field of study among graduates with a doctoral degree differs sharply from the choice of major of individuals with a master's degree. At the doctoral level, the largest share of degrees is earned in the social sciences and humanities fields. Almost 4 out of 10 doctoral degrees held in the United States are earned in these two specialties (see Table 12, also based on 2003 data). Women are more likely than men to earn their doctorates in social sciences, and both gender groups are roughly equally likely to earn their doctoral degree in the humanities fields. Only about 4 percent of all doctorates in the nation are in the education fields. The gender gap persists at the doctoral level, with women more than twice as likely as men to hold degrees in this field.

Mathematics and the physical sciences together account for 18 percent of doctoral degrees in the nation. In these specialties, men are roughly twice as likely to earn degrees as women. Men who receive doctoral degrees are more than four times as likely as women to receive their degrees in engineering (13 percent of men versus 3 percent of women). Although business is the most common degree at the bachelor's degree level, few doctoral degrees are awarded in this field.

Table 12
Distribution of Doctoral Degrees Received, by Broad Major Field, by Gender

	(A)	(B)	(C)	(D)
Broad Major Field of Study	All	Men	Women	Ratio of Male Major Concentration and Female Major Concentration (B) / (C)
Total	100%	100%	100%	—
Agricultural sciences	1.4%	1.6%	1.0%	1.6
Biological sciences	15.8%	15.7%	16.0%	1.0
Business	6.0%	6.4%	5.1%	1.2
Computer science	1.8%	2.1%	1.0%	2.0
Education	4.2%	2.8%	7.1%	0.4
Engineering	9.8%	13.1%	2.7%	4.9
Health professions	3.4%	2.0%	6.4%	0.3
Humanities	21.2%	20.4%	23.1%	0.9
Mathematics	3.8%	4.2%	2.9%	1.5
Physical sciences	14.1%	17.5%	6.5%	2.7
Social sciences	18.1%	13.6%	27.9%	0.5
Other	0.5%	0.6%	0.4%	1.5

Source: National Science Foundation, National Survey of College Graduates, Public Use Micro-Data File, 2003. Tabulations produced by the authors.

Labor Market Participation of College Graduates

Surveys of freshman classes at American colleges and universities consistently reveal that improved career opportunities and job access are the most important reasons for earning a bachelor's degree. For most college graduates, the economic and social rewards of a college degree are found in their work.

As noted previously, about 36 percent of all college graduates go on to earn an advanced degree of some type, but the remaining 64 percent conclude their formal schooling at the bachelor's degree level. For the graduates in the latter group, the transition into the career labor market begins at the conclusion of their undergraduate education.

Economists have developed key measures of labor force activity to assess and compare labor force behavior of different groups. Household surveys similar to the National Survey of College Graduates are administered to gather information on the labor market activity of the working-age population, defined as individuals who are 16 years or older. Each working-age individual is assigned to one of the following three mutually exclusive labor force categories:

▶ **Employed:** Persons who worked for 1 or more hours for pay or profit during the survey reference week or who worked 20 or more hours in an unpaid position in a family business

▶ **Unemployed:** Persons who were jobless during the survey reference week but who had actively sought a job within the prior four weeks and were immediately available to take a position

▶ **Out of the labor force:** All persons not classified as either employed or unemployed within the scope of the survey

The first measure that economists often use to examine labor market activity is the labor force participation rate. This measure is calculated by dividing the number of persons classified as active members of the labor force (the sum of employed and unemployed persons) by the total working-age population (16 years of age and older). The labor force participation rate is thus

FIGURE 3

Labor Force Participation Rates Among Persons 16 to 64 Years Old, by Educational Attainment, 2011

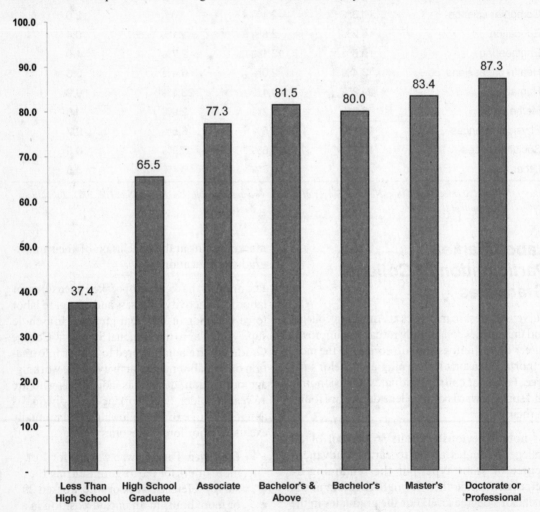

Source: U.S. Bureau of the Census, Current Population Surveys Public Use Micro-data Samples (PUMS) Data Files, 2011. Tabulations produced by the authors.

a measure of the proportion of any group of working-age persons who are active in the labor market at a point in time.

The labor force participation rates of 16- to 64-year-old individuals classified by their highest level of education are presented in Figure 3. Findings reveal that college graduates are much more likely to participate in the job market than persons with fewer years of schooling. The participation rate is about 65 percent for those with a high school diploma but no postsecondary schooling and 37 percent among adults who have not completed high school.

In contrast, college graduates have an overall labor force participation rate of 81 percent, a level that is 16 percentage points higher than the level among high school graduates with no postsecondary schooling. Moreover, the labor force participation rates among college graduates are highest for those with advanced degrees. The participation rate for bachelor's degree holders is 80 percent, which means that 80 out of 100 persons with only a bachelor's degree are active partici-

pants in the labor force. At the master's degree level, the participation rate is about 83 percent, while 87 percent of persons with a doctorate or a professional degree participate in the job market.

The probability that a college graduate will actively participate in the labor market is influenced by a number of key factors, including expected salary, gender, marital status, presence of children in the household, and level of educational attainment. The major field of study also has some influence over the likelihood of labor market participation, in part because of the relationship of major fields to the expected level of annual salary.

The data provided in Table 13 reveals that the participation rates of persons vary systematically by major field of study as well as by the highest degree earned. For example, at the bachelor's degree level, only about 72 percent of all persons who earned a degree in education are actively engaged in the labor market. In contrast, the participation rate of persons with a bachelor's degree in computer science is 93 percent, which means

Table 13
Labor Force Participation Rates (as Percentages), by Major Field of Study and Educational Attainment

Broad Major Field of Study	Bachelor's	Master's	Doctoral or Professional
Agricultural sciences	89.0%	83.4%	83.4%
Biological sciences	83.4%	82.4%	82.4%
Business	85.6%	88.0%	88.0%
Computer science	93.0%	94.5%	94.5%
Education	72.1%	75.9%	75.9%
Engineering	85.9%	88.3%	88.3%
Health professions	82.1%	87.2%	87.2%
Humanities	80.8%	84.2%	84.2%
Mathematics	79.9%	82.7%	82.7%
Physical sciences	80.2%	84.1%	84.1%
Social sciences	80.8%	82.9%	82.9%

Source: National Science Foundation, National Survey of College Graduates, Public Use Micro-Data File, 2003. Tabulations produced by the authors.

that only 7 out of 100 persons with a degree in the latter field are not actively participating in the labor market, compared to more than one-quarter of persons with a bachelor's degree in education.

Part of this low labor force participation rate may be because education majors are more likely to be women who may withdraw from the labor market for family reasons. Additionally, education majors have among the lowest annual salaries of all college graduates, while computer science majors work in considerably higher-paying jobs. These differences in salary expectations of graduates from the two fields also underlie the differences in their labor force participation. The choice of major field of study is closely associated with the decision to work at any given time. High rates of participation in the labor force, intensive employment, and the resultant accumulation of work experience significantly improve the long-term earnings prospects of college graduates.

The Employment Experiences of College Graduates

Individuals who participate in the labor market do so to obtain employment. Those who participate in the labor market and fail to obtain employment are considered to be unemployed. In the case of college graduates, most who participate in the labor market secure employment. In 2010, almost 95 out of 100 labor force participants with a bachelor's degree were either employed or out of the workforce—the unemployment rate among this group was only 5.4 percent. The unemployment rate of individuals with a master's was 4 percent, 2.4 percent with a professional degree, and 1.9 percent with a doctoral degree. This data clearly indicates that most college graduates actively participate in the labor market and are almost always successful in securing employment.

In this section, we will examine various attributes of the jobs in which college graduates are em-

ployed. These attributes shed light on the quality of jobs held by employed college graduates across different major fields of study. The job attributes that we will examine include the full-time versus part-time status of the job, the relationship of the job to undergraduate major field, and the occupation in which the graduate is employed.

The vast majority of college graduates work in full-time positions. More than 9 out of 10 college graduates with a bachelor's hold full-time jobs, with only about 9 percent of them working in part-time jobs. Part-time employment status varies considerably by gender. Among men, only about 4 percent hold part-time jobs, while about 18 percent of women with a bachelor's degree work in part-time positions. Persons employed in part-time positions either choose to work part-time because they prefer part-time work or are forced to work part-time because they could not obtain full-time employment. Most women who work part-time do so voluntarily for the flexibility of part-time schedules. This flexibility helps them meet other demands in their family lives. Only about 8 percent of women holding part-time jobs do so because they cannot get access to full-time positions.

The likelihood of a woman with a college degree holding a part-time position varies considerably by major field of study. For example, only about 15 percent of women with a bachelor's degree in computer science work in part-time jobs (see Figure 4). In contrast, almost one-quarter of women with a degree in the health professions work in part-time jobs. Given the large share of women employed in the health fields, businesses such as hospitals and other employers of health professionals often will organize work to accommodate the work desires of women who possess the skills they need. In contrast, in fields such as computer science, engineering, and business, where a large fraction of all graduates are men, employers are much more likely to organize work schedules on a full-time basis.

FIGURE 4

Percentage of Employed Women Working in Part-Time Positions, by Major Field of Study

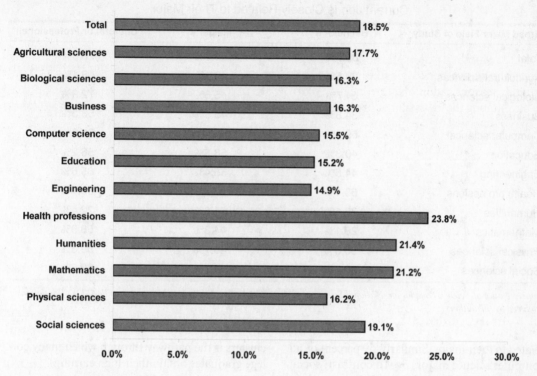

Source: National Science Foundation, National Survey of College Graduates, Public Use Micro-Data File, 2003. Tabulations produced by the authors.

A key factor influencing the earnings experience of college graduates is the relationship between their major fields and their jobs. Graduates employed in jobs that are closely related to their major generally earn much higher annual salaries than graduates employed in jobs that are unrelated to their major. Those working in jobs that are somewhat related to their major generally have salaries that are lower than those employed in jobs closely related to the major but higher than the salaries of those working in jobs unrelated to their undergraduate field of study.

The median annual earnings of all bachelor's degree holders employed full-time in jobs that were closely related to their undergraduate major field of study are $53,700 (in 2010 dollars), or 24

percent higher than the $43,300 median annual earnings of their counterparts employed in jobs unrelated to their major. Access to jobs that utilize the skills learned in school has a strong positive impact on the earnings experience of college graduates, particularly among graduates who major in a professional field.

More than one-fifth of all employed college graduates with a bachelor's degree work in a job that is not related to their undergraduate major. The likelihood of college graduates working in a job closely related to their major varies sharply depending on their major and highest degree level earned. According to data in Table 14, at the bachelor's degree level, 58 percent of all health professions majors work in jobs that are closely

Table 14

Percentage of Respondents Who Said Their
Current Job Is Closely Related to Their Major

Broad Major Field of Study	Bachelor's	Master's	Doctoral or Professional
Total	35.7%	54.1%	73.6%
Agricultural sciences	39.5%	43.1%	58.1%
Biological sciences	31.7%	45.6%	72.9%
Business	34.8%	46.5%	58.3%
Computer science	59.1%	65.7%	68.0%
Education	40.3%	58.3%	56.2%
Engineering	44.5%	55.4%	65.6%
Health professions	58.1%	67.4%	83.1%
Humanities	26.1%	54.8%	72.4%
Mathematics	28.1%	44.3%	68.9%
Physical sciences	30.3%	46.7%	59.3%
Social sciences	20.2%	47.1%	69.5%

Source: National Science Foundation, National Survey of College Graduates, Public Use Micro-Data File, 2003. Tabulations produced by the authors.

related to their major. Similarly, 59 percent of all computer science majors do. In contrast, social science majors are much less likely to work in jobs that are closely related to their major (20 percent), as are humanities majors (26 percent).

At the advanced degree level, the likelihood of graduates finding work in a job closely related to their major increases substantially. Increased specialization that accompanies advanced studies appears to increase the likelihood of finding major-field-related employment. Even in the social sciences and in humanities, those with master's degrees, doctoral degrees, and professional degrees are much more likely to be working in a job related to their major than those with only an undergraduate degree.

College graduates find work in a wide variety of occupational areas. The annual earnings in certain occupational areas—including professional, managerial, and high-level sales occupations—are substantially above the average earnings for all occupations. Access to jobs in these key occupational clusters is the pathway through which many college graduates obtain their high earnings.

The data provided in Table 15 reveals that almost 20 percent of those with a bachelor's degree work as financial specialists, such as accountants and auditors; 10.4 percent are employed in sales and sales management positions; and about 10 percent are employed in art and design positions. These three occupational areas account for more than 40 percent of all employment for those with only a bachelor's degree. An additional 3.3 percent of all bachelor's degree holders are employed in the teaching profession.

Most occupations listed in Table 15 constitute what economists term the *college labor market,* which consists of professional, technical, managerial, and high-level sales jobs that employ a large share of college graduates. However, not all persons with a bachelor's degree work in the college labor market. Administrative support workers, service workers and supervisors, and some other occupations are excluded from the definition of

Table 15

Percentage Distribution of Employed College Graduates, by Major Occupational Category of Their Job (All Graduates and Graduates in Each Degree Category)

Occupation	All Graduates	Bachelor's	Master's	Doctoral	Professional
<u>College Labor Market Occupations</u>					
Financial Specialists	19.8%	20.4%	5.1%	2.6%	18.1%
Art and Design Workers	10.1%	8.7%	10.5%	1.1%	9.0%
Health Diagnosing and Treating Practitioners	3.7%	4.1%	7.7%	60.6%	8.9%
Salesworkers and Supervisors	10.4%	7.1%	5.2%	1.4%	8.8%
Entertainers and Performers, Sports and Related Workers	5.5%	4.7%	5.6%	0.6%	4.9%
Business Operations Specialists	5.6%	3.4%	2.2%	0.8%	4.6%
Other Management Occupations	3.9%	6.7%	11.1%	0.9%	4.4%
Protective Service Workers and Supervisors	4.7%	2.6%	0.5%	0.7%	3.8%
Media and Communication Workers	3.9%	3.4%	4.0%	0.4%	3.5%
Preschool and K–12 Teachers	2.8%	6.9%	1.9%	0.2%	3.5%
Counselors, Social Workers, and Social Service Specialists	2.0%	7.7%	2.6%	0.4%	3.2%
Lawyers, Judges, and Related Workers	0.3%	0.2%	0.7%	25.4%	2.4%
Operations Specialties Managers	2.1%	2.3%	1.5%	0.3%	2.0%
Health Technologists and Technicians	2.4%	0.9%	1.5%	0.6%	1.9%
Computer Occupations	1.6%	2.1%	2.2%	0.1%	1.6%
Advertising, Marketing, and Sales Managers	1.6%	1.8%	1.1%	0.2%	1.5%
Top Executives	1.3%	2.0%	2.9%	0.5%	1.4%
Engineering and Science Technicians	1.0%	0.5%	1.1%	0.0%	0.8%
Librarians, Curators, and Archivists	0.3%	2.1%	0.9%	0.3%	0.7%
Engineers	0.7%	1.0%	2.1%	0.0%	0.7%
Religious Workers	0.3%	1.4%	3.0%	0.5%	0.7%
Life Scientists	0.4%	0.6%	9.1%	0.3%	0.6%
Other Health-Care Practitioners and Technical Occupations	0.6%	0.6%	0.8%	0.3%	0.6%
Other Teachers	0.5%	1.1%	0.7%	0.1%	0.6%
Social Scientists and Related Workers	0.1%	1.0%	7.2%	0.3%	0.5%
Physical Scientists	0.2%	0.3%	3.1%	0.0%	0.3%

(continued)

Table 15 (continued)
Percentage Distribution of Employed College Graduates, by Major Occupational Category of Their Job (All Graduates and Graduates in Each Degree Category)

Occupation	All Graduates	Bachelor's	Master's	Doctoral	Professional
Architects, Surveyors, and Cartographers	0.3%	0.3%	0.1%	0.0%	0.2%
Postsecondary Teachers	0.0%	0.1%	0.9%	0.3%	0.1%
Mathematical Science Occupations	0.0%	0.1%	0.3%	0.0%	0.1%
Non-College Labor Market Occupations					
Administrative Support Workers	4.2%	1.7%	0.8%	0.5%	3.2%
Service Workers and Supervisors	3.9%	1.1%	0.6%	0.2%	2.8%
Transportation Workers	2.5%	1.1%	1.4%	0.2%	2.0%
Mechanics, Installers, and Repairers	2.4%	1.1%	0.5%	0.1%	1.9%
Health-Care Assistants, Aides, and Support Workers	0.6%	0.6%	0.8%	0.3%	0.6%
Construction and Forestry Workers	0.4%	0.2%	0.2%	0.0%	0.3%
Total	100%	100%	100%	100%	100%

Source: National Science Foundation, National Survey of College Graduates, Public Use Micro-Data File, 2003. Tabulations produced by the authors.

the college labor market because people in these positions usually have less than a 4-year college degree. The bachelor's degree holders who work in jobs outside the college labor market usually have much lower salaries than those graduates who work in the college labor market sector, even those graduates whose job is not related to their major.

A key element of success for college graduates is access to jobs in the college labor market. Graduates unable to gain access to work that utilizes their academic skills find themselves employed in occupations outside the college labor market. These graduates are working for employers who are unwilling to pay a premium to acquire workers who possess skills that will not be utilized on the job. A college education has an impact on earnings only when the academic and professional skills that a college graduate possesses are utilized on the job. Failure to find a job that uses at least some of these skills translates into less advantageous

long-term employment and earnings experiences, despite having earned a college diploma.

College graduates are employed in a variety of industrial settings that also influence the nature of their work and the level of their earnings. While we commonly think of the American economy as dominated by employment in private, for-profit firms, less than one-half of college graduates with a bachelor's degree work as employees of for-profit business organizations. Large shares of college graduates work for educational organizations, government agencies, and nonprofit foundations. While 47 percent of all graduates are employed by for-profit businesses, 16 percent work in education; 11 percent work for federal, state, or local governments or the military; and 7 percent are employed in the nonprofit sector (see Figure 5).

Interestingly, college graduates as a group are quite entrepreneurial in nature. Almost one-fifth of college graduates with a bachelor's degree are

FIGURE 5

Distribution of Employed College Graduates with a Bachelor's Degree, by Sector of Employment

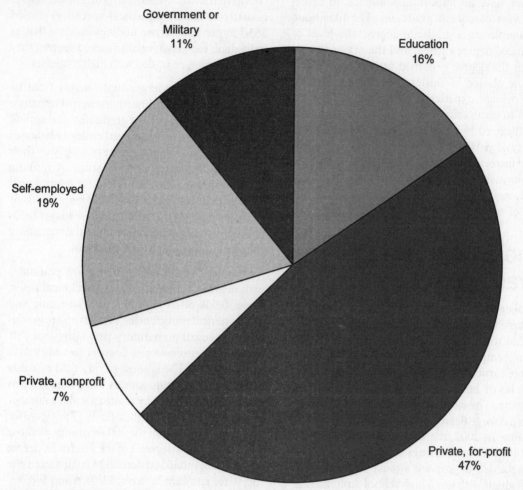

Source: National Science Foundation, National Survey of College Graduates, Public Use Micro-Data File, 2003. Tabulations produced by the authors.

self-employed; either they own and operate a business or they provide consulting services. The earnings of college graduates are substantially influenced by the industry sector in which they work. Even within the same major field of study, graduates working in private, for-profit businesses usually have salaries that are substantially higher than those of their counterparts who work in non-profit organizations or educational institutions.

As may be expected, access to employment in various sectors of the economy varies sharply by major field of study. For example, private, for-profit firms employ more than 70 percent of computer science majors. In contrast, only 18 percent of those with a degree in education work in the for-profit sector of the economy. Social science majors are almost twice as likely as graduates with a degree in business to hold a job in a government agency.

The preceding data and analyses clearly indicate that the choice of undergraduate major does, in fact, have an important influence on career pathways of college graduates. The likelihood of completing a graduate degree, the level of advanced degree earned, and the major field in which the degree is earned are all conditional on the choice of undergraduate major. The employment experience of graduates with respect to occupation and sector of employment is influenced by the major field, as is the probability of participating in the labor force. All of these factors combine to influence the long-term employment and earnings experience of college graduates. The next section presents an examination of earnings outcomes of college graduates.

The Earnings of College Graduates

A college degree provides a strong earnings advantage to those willing to make the sacrifices needed to earn it. As you saw in Figure 2, the average employed young person with a bachelor's degree earned 81 percent more per year in 2011 than his or her counterpart with a high school diploma. The earnings premium of individuals with a college degree persists over their working lifetime. In 2002, the Census Bureau estimated that the lifetime earnings of an individual with a bachelor's degree are almost twice those of individuals with just a high school diploma ($2.7 million versus $1.5 million in 2009 dollars). Researchers at Georgetown University estimate that the earnings advantage grew from 75 percent to 84 percent between 2002 and 2009.

Furthermore, the earnings advantage of college education continues beyond the bachelor's degree. The Bureau of Labor Statistics estimates that bachelor's degree holders earned an average of almost $54,000 in 2010, while their counterparts whose highest degree was a master's degree earned $64,144 per year (see Figure 6). The earnings advantage from obtaining a doctorate or a professional degree

is also quite high. Those with a doctoral degree had median annual salaries of $80,600, while their counterparts who possess a professional degree (usually in law or a medical specialty) earned $83,720 per year. These findings indicate that as individuals earn additional advanced degrees, they are, on average, rewarded with higher salaries.

The choice of undergraduate major field of study has an extraordinarily powerful influence on the earnings of college graduates. The annual salaries of full-time employed college graduates with a baccalaureate degree vary widely by their undergraduate major field of study. A ranking of the annual salaries of full-time employed bachelor's degree recipients for 58 major fields of study is provided in Table 16. These major fields of study are described in detail in the remaining chapters (4 through 61) of this book.

At the very top of the ranking are graduates with degrees in health-care and technical fields. These fields often require strong scientific and mathematical proficiencies. At the top are graduates of medical preparatory programs, many of whom have professional degrees in addition to the bachelor's. The highest-paying field of study at the undergraduate level is computer systems engineering, followed by pharmacy and a number of engineering and scientific fields. (The figure for pharmacy is based on the 2003 earnings of those with a bachelor's degree, but the Pharm.D. degree is now the standard credential.) Graduates of the top 10 majors earn between $20,000 and $48,000 more—or 29 percent to 43 percent more—per year than all full-time employed bachelor's degree graduates. The only social science or humanities field to make the top 15 is economics, and even in this major, strong mathematics proficiencies play a key role in successfully completing an undergraduate program. Economics graduates earn $19,300 more, or 44 percent more, per year than graduates who major in English.

At the bottom of the earnings distribution among persons with a bachelor's degree are individuals with undergraduate degrees in the humanities and

FIGURE 6

Median Annual Earnings of College Graduates 2010, by Highest Degree Earned

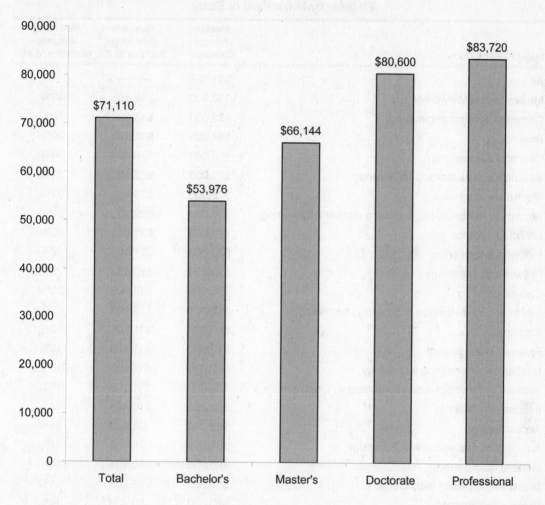

Source: "Education Pays," U.S. Bureau of Labor Statistics, U.S. Bureau of the Census, Current Population Survey.

in education. For example, persons with degrees in philosophy earn 34 percent less per year than all full-time employed bachelor's degree graduates.

Clearly, the choice of undergraduate major has a powerful impact on the earnings and, ultimately, the living standards of college graduates. Analysis in this chapter has also revealed a strong relationship between the college major field of study and several labor market outcomes, including labor force participation, access to employment in certain high-level occupations, and access to full-time jobs. Graduates from certain majors, such as computer science and business, are less likely to pursue postgraduate studies and more likely to enter the labor market after earning a baccalaureate degree. In contrast, graduates

Table 16

Annual Earnings of Full-Time Employed College Graduates with Only a Bachelor's Degree, by Major Field of Study

Major Field of Study	Median Annual Earnings	Absolute Difference Relative to All	Percentage Difference Relative to All
All	$51,597	———	———
Medical preparatory programs	$100,000	$48,403	43%
Computer systems engineering	$85,000	$33,403	39%
Pharmacy	$84,000	$32,403	39%
Chemical engineering	$80,000	$28,403	36%
Electrical and electronics engineering	$75,000	$23,403	31%
Mechanical engineering	$75,000	$23,403	31%
Aerospace, aeronautical, and astronautical engineering	$74,000	$22,403	30%
Computer science	$73,400	$21,803	30%
Industrial engineering	$73,000	$21,403	29%
Physics and astronomy	$72,200	$20,603	29%
Civil engineering	$70,000	$18,403	26%
Electrical and electronics engineering technology	$65,000	$13,403	21%
Economics	$63,300	$11,703	18%
Financial management	$63,000	$11,403	18%
Mechanical engineering technology	$63,000	$11,403	18%
Applied mathematics, operations research, and statistics	$62,800	$11,203	18%
Information systems	$62,000	$10,403	17%
Accounting	$60,000	$8,403	14%
Architecture and environmental design	$60,000	$8,403	14%
General mathematics	$60,000	$8,403	14%
Industrial production technology	$60,000	$8,403	14%
Public administration	$60,000	$8,403	14%
Marketing	$59,800	$8,203	14%
Political science, government, and international relations	$57,800	$6,203	11%
Legal studies and pre-law	$56,800	$5,203	9%
Chemistry	$56,000	$4,403	8%
Physical therapy	$53,000	$1,403	3%
General business	$52,200	$603	1%
Geology and geophysics	$51,600	$3	———
Journalism	$50,000	−$1,597	−3%
Nursing	$50,000	−$1,597	−3%

Major Field of Study	Median Annual Earnings	Absolute Difference Relative to All	Percentage Difference Relative to All
Communications	$48,000	−$3,597	−7%
Health and medical technology	$48,000	−$3,597	−7%
History	$48,000	−$3,597	−7%
Forestry and environmental science	$47,200	−$4,397	−9%
Biology and life sciences	$46,400	−$5,197	−11%
Microbiology and biochemistry	$45,600	−$5,997	−13%
Liberal arts and general studies	$45,000	−$6,597	−15%
English language, literature, and letters	$44,000	−$7,597	−17%
Plant science	$44,000	−$7,597	−17%
Foreign languages and literature	$43,700	−$7,897	−18%
Anthropology and archaeology	$42,000	−$9,597	−23%
Geography	$42,000	−$9,597	−23%
Physical education and coaching	$42,000	−$9,597	−23%
Psychology	$42,000	−$9,597	−23%
Sociology	$41,000	−$10,597	−26%
Music and dance	$40,000	−$11,597	−29%
Secondary teacher education	$40,000	−$11,597	−29%
Visual arts	$40,000	−$11,597	−29%
Family and consumer sciences	$38,500	−$13,097	−34%
Animal science	$38,000	−$13,597	−36%
Mathematics and science teacher education	$37,800	−$13,797	−37%
Parks, recreation, fitness, and leisure studies	$37,000	−$14,597	−39%
Special education	$37,000	−$14,597	−39%
Elementary teacher education	$36,000	−$15,597	−43%
Philosophy and religion	$35,700	−$15,897	−45%
Dramatic arts	$35,000	−$16,597	−47%
Preschool/kindergarten/early childhood teacher education	$33,000	−$18,597	−56%

*Earnings figures for **legal studies and pre-law** and **medical preparatory programs** are for graduates with at least a bachelor's. Average earnings for all graduates with at least a bachelor's are $56,757. Source: National Science Foundation, National Survey of College Graduates, Public Use Micro-Data File, 2003. Tabulations produced by the authors.*

who major in physical sciences or mathematics are more likely to pursue postgraduate studies.

These close associations of the undergraduate major field of study with several important labor market and educational outcomes make a compelling case that you should exercise care in selecting your major. The idea that the choice of major field of study will have little influence on your postgraduate employment and earnings is *wrong*. Your choice of major will strongly influence your experiences after you graduate and transition to the adult career labor market. The skills and abilities you acquire in college will have lasting and even lifetime influences on your labor market outcomes, your status in the community, your happiness on the job, and your standard of living.

We do not believe that you should choose your undergraduate major solely or even primarily on the basis of your earnings prospects in a given field. In fact, on the nonmonetary issue of overall job satisfaction, 4 liberal arts or social science majors ranked among the top 10 majors in the survey. However, because enrolling in college is a costly investment decision, you need to be well informed about important aspects of the investment alternatives available to you. The rest of this book contains accurate, up-to-date, and detailed information on 58 undergraduate fields of study that cover well over 100 study areas and careers. It is our hope that you will become better informed about what you want out of college and about the opportunities available to you after graduation.

PART 2

Behavioral and Medical Sciences

CHAPTER 4

Family and Consumer Sciences

This major covers several specializations, including consumer economics, child development, consumer marketing, and apparel and textile studies. But the most popular specialization is dietetics, food, and nutrition, so the following discussion focuses on this aspect of the major.

This specialization within the major studies the promotion of healthy eating habits to foster good health and to prevent illness. Dietitians and nutritionists plan nutrition programs and supervise the preparation and serving of meals. They help treat illness by evaluating clients' diets and suggest diet modifications on the intake of fat, salt, and sugar and other carbohydrates.

In nursing homes and hospitals, dietitians and nutritionists can function in clinical roles and also manage the food service department. In their clinical capacity, they may offer special group programs for diabetic or overweight patients. In public health clinics and home health agencies, they take an educational role. For food manufacturers, they can perform food analyses, prepare reports for public dissemination, and serve as nutritional resources for marketing food products. Some function in specialized roles in wellness centers or for sport teams or perform nutritional screening—for example, monitoring cholesterol levels.

To become a dietitian or nutritionist, two preparation routes are available: a bachelor's degree with a major in family and consumer sciences with a specialization in dietetics, foods, and nutrition; or a major in food service management plus supervised practice experience. Students take courses in foods, nutrition, institutional management, chemistry, biology, microbiology, and physiology, as well as other courses such as statistics, business, and computer science.

The abilities required for this major cover a broad span and can vary in emphasis depending on whether the worker applies scientific principles to research and development, does hands-on work directing and training food service workers, or makes plans and possibly budgets and purchases food for an institution. Scientific abilities are necessary for the required science course work. Computer skills are helpful in the scientific area and also are invaluable for the business dimensions of the field. Language and communication abilities are essential. Also, manual and finger coordination skills are used in laboratory work, applied food and nutrition courses, and supervised practice experience.

Dietitians and nutritionists enjoy working with people in a helping capacity and like science, food, and health. The scientific interest suggests that these majors like high school courses in mathematics, biology, and chemistry. Dietitians and nutritionists enjoy leadership roles, assuming responsibility for directing others and working to accomplish organizational goals.

The benefits for people in this field are influenced by their interpersonal orientation. They value providing services to persons with nutritional and health problems.

Note that the term *family and consumer sciences* has largely replaced another title that used to be common for this major, *home economics*.

Where Do Family and Consumer Sciences Majors Work?

One-third of employed family and consumer sciences graduates with only a bachelor's degree work for businesses and corporations in the private, for-profit sector. Twenty-eight percent work at educational institutions, primarily as kindergarten, elementary, and secondary school teachers. Almost one-fifth work in the private, for-profit sector as self-employed workers in their own business or practice. About 11 percent of the grads work in tax-exempt or charitable organizations such as health clinics, nonprofit home health agencies, and wellness centers. Among employed family and consumer science graduates, about 16 percent work part-time schedules.

Almost two-thirds of family and consumer sciences graduates are employed in jobs that are closely related or somewhat related to their undergraduate major. This is not surprising, given the applied nature of this major. Dietitians and nutritional scientists can apply their classroom knowledge in a clinical capacity or as health and nutrition scientists in various settings, such as health clinics, food manufacturers, wellness centers, and sports teams. A little more than one-third of all employed family and consumer sciences graduates work in jobs that are not related to their undergraduate major.

Eighty-one percent of economics graduates under the age of 65 are employed. Only 2 percent are not employed and are actively seeking

Table 1
Percentage Distribution of Employed Persons with Only a Bachelor's Degree, by Economic Sector, Size, and New Business Status of Employer

	Family and Consumer Sciences	All
Economic Sector		
Private for-profit	32.7	47.3
Self-employed	18.9	18.5
Government/Military	9.3	11.0
Education	28.4	15.6
Nonprofit	10.8	7.5
Employer Size		
Small (Fewer than 100 employees)	16.6	28.5
Medium (100–999)	10.3	22.4
Large (1,000–24,999)	12.3	29.6
Very large (25,000 or more)	6.6	19.5
Percent working in new business established within past 5 years	2.4	5.6

Table 2
Percentage Distribution of Employed Persons with Only a Bachelor's Degree in Family and Consumer Sciences, by the Relationship Between Their Job and College Major

Relationship of Job to Major	Percent
Closely related	41.3
Somewhat related	24.5
Not related	34.2

Percent who report the following as the most important reasons for working in a job that was not related to major:

Family-related reasons	24.8
Working conditions (hours, equipment, environment)	18.0
Pay, promotion opportunities	17.3
Change in career or professional interests	16.7
Job in highest degree field not available	12.1

work. Of the remaining 17 percent, about one-third are out of the workforce because they have retired. About 30 percent cite family commitments. Another one-quarter say they have no need to work.

Occupations

The top 5 occupations in Table 3 employ nearly one-third of all working family and consumer sciences graduates. Nearly 9 percent of the graduates work in unspecified administrative occupations. More than 7 percent are employed in

Table 3
Top 5 Occupations Employing Persons with Only a Bachelor's Degree in Family and Consumer Sciences, by Percentage

Top 5 Occupations	All	Men	Women
Other Administrative Occupations	8.7	5.0	9.3
Registered Nurses, Pharmacists, Dietitians, Therapists, Physician Assistants	7.5	2.2	8.4
Teachers—Secondary, Other Subjects	5.8	3.2	6.3
Other Marketing and Sales Occupations	4.9	2.3	5.4
Teachers—Elementary School	4.4	2.4	4.8
Total, Top 5 Occupations	31.3	15.1	34.2
Balance of Employed	68.7	84.9	65.8
All Employed	100.0	100.0	100.0

health occupations; many of these are probably working as clinical dietitians and nutritionists. About 6 percent teach in secondary school and another 4 percent in elementary school. Almost 5 percent work in marketing and sales occupations.

Almost 9 out of 10 family and consumer sciences graduates are women. Among the small number of male graduates, 9 percent work in various management occupations; of these, many may be employed as food service managers.

Work Activities

▶ More than one-fifth of the graduates consider teaching duties to be the major part of their job, and 38 percent spend at least 10 hours of their workweek teaching.

▶ These graduates are more high-tech than you may expect. Fully 88 percent regularly engage in working with computer applications, although only 4 percent spend most of their time during a typical workweek performing these duties.

▶ Another 48 percent of all employed family and consumer sciences grads spend at least 10 hours of the workweek managing or supervising people or projects, and 14 percent report that these duties consume most of their time at work.

▶ Fifteen percent of family and consumer sciences graduates spend most of their time at work on sales, purchasing, or marketing, and 42 percent engage in this for at least 10 hours out of their typical week.

▶ Thirty percent regularly deal with tasks related to accounting, finance, or contracts, and 8 percent spend most of their time at work in these activities.

▶ Only 2 percent of family and consumer sciences graduates spend most of their work time engaged in employee relations,

but almost one-third spend a significant amount of time on these tasks.

Workplace Training and Other Work-Related Experiences

The career potential of a job is closely associated with the amount of work-related training. Work-related training is regarded as an investment by firms because it makes workers more productive. The incidence of work-related training among family and consumer sciences graduates is significantly lower than the rate of participation in work-related training among all college graduates. While 61 percent of all college graduates acquire some kind of work-related training during a year, 55 percent of family and consumer sciences majors annually engage in work-related training.

▶ Of those family and consumer sciences graduates who receive some training during the year, 47 percent receive technical training in the occupation in which they are employed.

▶ Sixteen percent of the training recipients receive management or supervisory training.

▶ Twenty-one percent receive training to improve their general professional skills, such as public speaking and business writing.

Although family and consumer sciences graduates decide to participate in work-related training activities, workshops, or seminars for numerous reasons, the dominant reason is a desire to improve skills and knowledge in the occupational area of their employment. Almost one-third of the grads cite this as the most important reason. Nine percent get training primarily because their employer requires it. Qualifying for licensure or certification is most important among almost

7 percent of all family and consumer sciences graduates who receive work-related training. (Teachers typically get in-service training to maintain licensure.) Five percent cite the need to learn skills for a newly acquired position as the key factor that underlies their decision to engage in training.

Salaries

The median annual salary of family and consumer sciences graduates with only a bachelor's degree is $38,500, a level that is 34 percent lower than the median annual salary of all employed college graduates. On average, employed family and consumer sciences graduates work for 38 hours per week and for 49 weeks per year, resulting in 1,862

hours of employment per year. The level of work effort among family and consumer science graduates is 13 percent lower than the average among all college graduates (which is 43 hours per week and 50 weeks per year, resulting in 2,150 hours per year).

The average annual salary of family and consumer sciences graduates who work in all types of jobs closely related to their major field of study is $44,500, considerably higher than the $37,200 averaged by those who are employed in jobs that are somewhat related to their major. The average salary of graduates employed full-time in a job that is not related to their field of study is $40,300.

The average annual salary of family and consumer sciences graduates employed by the private,

FIGURE 1

Age/Earnings Profile of Persons with Only a Bachelor's Degree in Family and Consumer Sciences (Full-Time Workers, in 2010 Dollars)

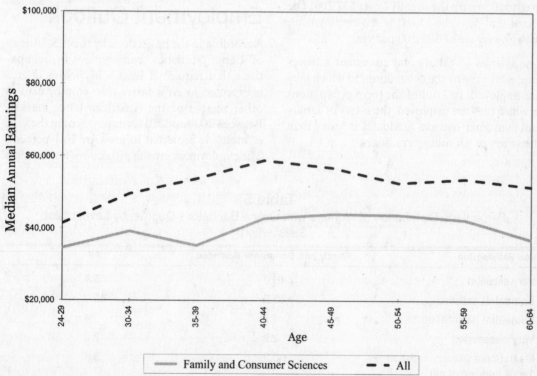

Table 4
Annual Salary of Workers with Only a Bachelor's Degree, Top 5 Occupations (in 2010 Dollars)

Earnings in Top 5 Occupations	All	Family and Consumer Sciences
Total	$38,500	$40,800
Other Administrative Occupations	$38,200	$37,200
Registered Nurses, Pharmacists, Dietitians, Therapists, Physician Assistants	$55,700	$45,700
Teachers—Secondary, Other Subjects	$39,200	$40,200
Other Marketing and Sales Occupations	$54,700	$42,800
Teachers—Elementary School	$37,200	$40,200

for-profit sector at corporations and businesses is $43,100. The second-highest salary, $40,800, is reported for graduates working in the government sector. Family and consumer sciences majors who are employed in the private, nonprofit sector earn $38,500 per year, and those working in education earn the slightly lower $37,200. The sector that pays the lowest is self-employment, with an average of $29,500 per year.

The salaries of family and consumer sciences graduates vary by the occupations in which they are employed. In 3 out of the top 5 occupations in which they are employed, the salary of family and consumer sciences graduates is lower than the salary of all college graduates.

Job Satisfaction

The overall level of job satisfaction of family and consumer sciences majors is about the same as the average for all graduates.

Employment Outlook

According to the projections by the U.S. Bureau of Labor Statistics, employment in occupations that require at least a bachelor's degree is expected to grow faster than employment in other sectors of the American labor market. Between 2008 and 2018, employment in the U.S. economy is projected to grow by 10.1 percent. The employment growth projections for the top 5

Table 5
Percentage Distribution of Workers with Only a Bachelor's Degree, by Level of Job Satisfaction

Job Satisfaction	Family and Consumer Sciences	All
Very satisfied	46.0	45.4
Somewhat satisfied	43.5	45.0
Somewhat dissatisfied	7.7	7.4
Very dissatisfied	2.9	2.2
Mean Score (4=very satisfied, 1=not satisfied at all)	3.3	3.3

occupations that are most likely to employ family and consumer sciences graduates are presented in Table 6.

▶ The total employment in miscellaneous administrative occupations is projected to grow about as fast as average, an expansion of 10.8 percent, despite technological advances such as fast computers, faxes, e-mail, and voice mail. Employee turnover will create many job openings.

▶ The health-care occupations that are the second-largest employer of family and consumer sciences grads are projected to grow at a rate of almost 22 percent, much faster than average.

▶ Secondary and primary teaching occupations are each projected to increase by about 15 percent between 2008 and 2018, a faster-than-average rate. Job prospects should be better in inner cities and rural areas than in suburban districts.

▶ The miscellaneous marketing and sales occupations that employ about 5 percent of family and consumer sciences grads are projected to grow a little more slowly than average, 7.3 percent.

Pathways Beyond the Bachelor's Degree

A bit more than one-quarter of family and consumer sciences graduates with a bachelor's degree proceed to earn a postgraduate degree: 24 percent earn a master's degree, 2 percent graduate with a doctoral degree, and only 1 percent earn a professional degree.

▶ Only 9 percent of the master's degrees are earned in family and consumer sciences. A larger share, 10 percent, earn the degree in special education. Another 8 percent get some other kind of M.Ed. degree.

▶ One-fifth of the doctoral degrees earned by family and consumer sciences grads are in nutritional sciences. Sixteen percent are in family and consumer sciences. Eleven percent are in food sciences and technology.

▶ Of the few family and consumer sciences grads who go on to professional degrees, about one-quarter go into the medical professions, such as medicine, dentistry, optometry, osteopathy, podiatry, and veterinary. Thirteen percent earn the degree in physical therapy or other rehabilitation or therapeutic services.

Table 6
Projected Growth and Job Openings in the Top 5 Occupations Employing Persons with Only a Bachelor's Degree in Family and Consumer Sciences

Top 5 Occupations	Projected Growth 2008–2018	Projected Annual Job Openings
All top 5	13.9%	435,410
Other Administrative Occupations	10.8%	166,130
Registered Nurses, Pharmacists, Dietitians, Therapists, Physician Assistants	21.5%	119,640
Teachers—Secondary, Other Subjects	15.3%	25,110
Other Marketing and Sales Occupations	7.3%	64,880
Teachers—Elementary School	15.8%	59,650

CHAPTER 5

Health and Medical Technology

This major involves the study of tissues and cells and the analysis of body fluids with the goal of detection, diagnosis, and treatment of disease. The major prepares students for the roles of medical technologist and technician and for the performance of clinical laboratory tests.

Depending on the specialization area, health and medical technologists may have different titles. For example, clinical chemistry technologists prepare specimens and analyze the chemical and hormonal contents of body fluids. Microbiological technologists examine and identify bacteria, parasites, and other microorganisms. Blood bank technologists collect, type, and match blood for transfusions. Immunology technologists examine elements and responses of the human immune system to foreign bodies that can show how a patient is responding to treatment. Cytotechnologists prepare slides of body cells and microscopically examine the cells for abnormalities that can indicate the beginning of a cancerous growth. Whatever focus the health/medical technologists have, after analyzing and evaluating their results, they all communicate the outcomes to physicians.

Technicians usually perform less-complex tests and procedures than technologists. For histology technicians, common jobs are cutting and staining tissue specimens for microscopic examination by pathologists, and for phlebotomists, common jobs are drawing and testing blood.

Overall, however, the whole health and medical technology area is being affected by the development and use of new, sophisticated laboratory equipment. Another factor is the development of new kinds of tests.

Course work includes chemistry, biology, microbiology, mathematics, and specialized courses in the clinical laboratory areas. In addition, computer applications, business, and management courses are also taken.

The abilities needed in these clinical laboratory technologies are scientific analytical judgment, problem-solving skills, and the ability to obtain measurable and verifiable information. It must not be forgotten that medical technologists work with infectious specimens. Paying attention to following detailed procedures is critical because small differences or changes in test substances or numerical results can be crucial for patient care. Technologists often work under pressure. Manual and finger dexterity plus color vision are needed to use delicate and sensitive equipment. Computer skills are important because automated laboratory equipment is increasingly used.

The interests of those in this field are definitely scientific, including both the chemistry and biology areas. Because of the laboratory work involved and the hands-on approach to work, medical technologists enjoy working with their hands and machines.

Where Do Health and Medical Technology Majors Work?

About 38 percent of health and medical technology graduates are employed by businesses and corporations in the private, for-profit sector. Many research laboratories, including medical testing firms, are in this sector. Twenty-six percent of these graduates are employed in the private, nonprofit sector. About 17 percent work for educational institutions. Only 10 percent are self-employed in their own business or practice, and about 9 percent work in the government sector. About one-fifth of employed health and medical technology graduates work part-time.

The skills and knowledge that health and medical technology graduates acquire during their schooling are directly applicable in the labor market. The extent of practical application of the skills of health and medical technology graduates enables many graduates to find jobs in their field. Three-quarters are employed in jobs that are closely related to their undergraduate major field of study. The remaining share of graduates is divided equally between those who are employed in jobs that are somewhat related to their undergraduate major and those in jobs that are not related to their major.

Out of all health and medical technology graduates under the age of 65, almost 88 percent are employed. Less than 2 percent are officially unemployed; that is, they are not employed and are actively seeking employment. The remaining 10 percent are out of the labor force; that is, they are not employed and are not seeking employment. Two main reasons underlying the labor force withdrawal of health and medical technology graduates are family responsibilities, accounting for 36 percent of those out of the workforce, and retirement, accounting for another 33 percent.

Table 1
Percentage Distribution of Employed Persons with Only a Bachelor's Degree, by Economic Sector, Size, and New Business Status of Employer

	Health and Medical Technology	All
Economic Sector		
Private for-profit	38.2	47.3
Self-employed	10.0	18.5
Government/Military	8.7	11.0
Education	16.7	15.6
Nonprofit	26.3	7.5
Employer Size		
Small (Fewer than 100 employees)	7.1	28.5
Medium (100–999)	17.0	22.4
Large (1,000–24,999)	31.2	29.6
Very large (25,000 or more)	9.3	19.5
Percent working in new business established within past 5 years	1.2	5.6

Table 2

Percentage Distribution of Employed Persons with Only a
Bachelor's Degree in Health and Medical Technology, by the
Relationship Between Their Job and College Major

Relationship of Job to Major	Percent
Closely related	78.9
Somewhat related	12.2
Not related	8.9

Percent who report the following as the most important
reasons for working in a job that was not related to major:

Family-related reasons	33.1
Pay, promotion opportunities	19.1
Working conditions (hours, equipment, environment)	16.9
Change in career or professional interests	11.6
Other reason	11.5

Occupations

The employment of health and medical technology graduates is concentrated in only a few occupational fields. Almost two-thirds of all employed graduates work as health technologists and technicians. This field includes a wide variety of specializations, such as licensed practical and licensed vocational nurses; pharmacy technicians; radiologic technologists and technicians; emergency medical technicians and paramedics; dental hygienists; medical records and health information technicians; and medical and clinical laboratory technologists.

Four percent work as technicians in the biological sciences. Slightly less than 4 percent are employed as medical scientists, and the same percentage manage medical or health services.

A bit more than 4 out of 5 health and medical technology graduates are women. The occupational employment patterns of male and female graduates are roughly similar, with the exception of the clerical jobs that employ a small number of female grads and virtually no male grads.

Work Activities

▶ Sixty-one percent of employed health and medical technology graduates spend at least 10 hours during a typical workweek providing professional services, and 36 percent spend most of their time during a typical week performing these duties.

▶ Forty-one percent of the graduates spend at least 10 hours of the workweek performing production, operations, or maintenance duties, and 19 percent consider these duties a major part of their job.

▶ Another 41 percent of all employed health and medical technology graduates spend at least 10 hours per workweek performing management and administration tasks, and 13 percent report that these duties consume most of their time at work.

Table 3
Top 5 Occupations Employing Persons with Only a
Bachelor's Degree in Health and Medical Technology, by Percentage

Top 5 Occupations	All	Men	Women
Health Technologists and Technicians	60.9	53.2	62.9
Technologists and Technicians in the Biological/Life Sciences	4.0	3.2	4.2
Medical Scientists, Except Practitioners	3.6	7.1	2.7
Medical and Health Services Managers	3.6	7.5	2.6
Secretaries, Receptionists, and Typists	3.3	–	4.1
Total, Top 5 Occupations	75.4	71.0	76.5
Balance of Employed	24.6	29.0	23.5
All Employed	100.0	100.0	100.0

▶ Thirty-two percent engage regularly in employee relations during a major portion of their typical workweek, but less than 2 percent spend most of their time at these tasks.

▶ Eighty-eight percent of health and medical technology grads spend a significant part of the workweek on computer applications, although only 4 percent consider this their major task.

Workplace Training and Other Work-Related Experiences

The career potential of a job is closely associated with the amount of work-related training on the job. Work-related training is regarded as an investment by firms because it makes workers more productive. The incidence of work-related training among health and medical technology graduates is higher than the rate of participation in work-related training among all college graduates. While 61 percent of all college graduates acquire some kind of work-related training during a year, 66 percent of health and medical

technology graduates annually engage in work-related training.

▶ Of those health and medical technology graduates who receive some training during a year, 58 percent receive technical training in the occupation in which they are employed.

▶ Fourteen percent of the training recipients participate in management or supervisory training.

▶ Sixteen percent receive training to improve their general professional skills, such as public speaking and business writing.

When asked to select the most important reason to acquire training, 41 percent of health and medical technology graduates who undergo training identify the need to improve their occupational skills and knowledge. One-tenth of grads report mandatory training requirements by the employer as the most important factor underlying their involvement in work-related training. Seven percent rank the need to obtain a professional license or certificate as the number one reason to participate in work-related training. Three percent get training to learn skills for the sake of a salary increase or promotion.

Salaries

The median annual salary of health and medical technology graduates with only a bachelor's degree is $48,000, a level that is 7 percent lower than the median annual salary of all employed college graduates. On average, employed health and medical technology graduates work for 37 hours per week and for 50 weeks per year, resulting in 1,850 hours of employment per year. The level of work effort among health and medical technology graduates is 14 percent lower than the average among all college graduates (which is 43 hours per week and 50 weeks per year, resulting in 2,150 hours per year).

The average annual salary of health and medical technology graduates who work in jobs that are related to their undergraduate major field of study is higher than those who work in jobs that are not related to their major field of study. Closely related jobs pay full-time employed health and medical technology graduates $49,500 annually. The same average earnings are reported by graduates employed in jobs that are somewhat related to their major. However, those in jobs unrelated to their undergraduate field of study earn only $33,000 per year.

With an average salary of $50,600 annually, health and medical technology graduates who work in the private, for-profit sector earn a higher salary than those who are employed in other sectors. The pay for health and medical technology graduates in the education sector is $50,200 per year. The government sector pays

FIGURE 1

Age/Earnings Profile of Persons with Only a Bachelor's Degree in Health and Medical Technology (Full-Time Workers, in 2010 Dollars)

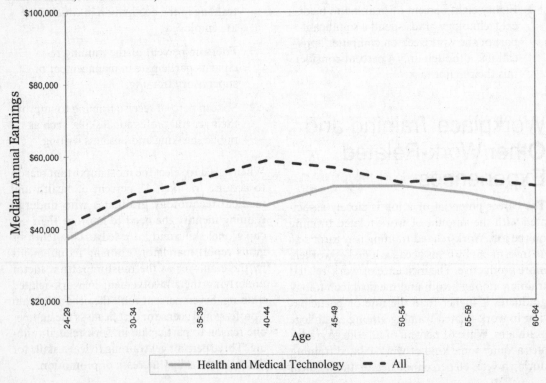

Table 4
Annual Salary of Workers with Only a Bachelor's Degree, Top 5 Occupations (in 2010 Dollars)

Earnings in Top 5 Occupations	All	Health and Medical Technology
Total	$48,000	$49,200
Health Technologists and Technicians	$42,300	$48,500
Technologists and Technicians in the Biological/Life Sciences	$44,400	$48,500
Medical Scientists, Except Practitioners	$47,500	$51,600
Medical and Health Services Managers	$74,300	$64,000
Secretaries, Receptionists, and Typists	$31,000	$31,000

these graduates $46,900 per year; those employed by not-for-profit businesses earn $49,500 annually. Self-employed grads earn the lowest annual average, $30,100.

▶ Almost two-thirds of the graduates are employed as health technologists and technicians, with average earnings of $48,500 per year.

▶ Health and medical technology graduates employed in medical and health services management occupations earn an average annual salary of $64,000, but this occupation employs less than 4 percent of the grads.

▶ Health and medical technology graduates who are working as medical scientists earn $51,600 per year.

▶ Those working as technologists and technicians in the life sciences also average $48,500 annually.

Job Satisfaction

The level of job satisfaction of health and medical technology majors is slightly higher than the average for all graduates.

Table 5
Percentage Distribution of Workers with Only a Bachelor's Degree, by Level of Job Satisfaction

Job Satisfaction	Health and Medical Technology	All
Very satisfied	39.0	45.4
Somewhat satisfied	54.8	45.0
Somewhat dissatisfied	5.2	7.4
Very dissatisfied	1.1	2.2
Mean Score (4=very satisfied, 1=not satisfied at all)	3.4	3.3

Table 6
Projected Growth and Job Openings in the Top 5 Occupations Employing Persons with Only a Bachelor's Degree in Health and Medical Technology

Top 5 Occupations	Projected Growth 2008–2018	Projected Annual Job Openings
All top 5	18.3%	66,180
Health Technologists and Technicians	20.1%	35,070
Technologists and Technicians in the Biological/Life Sciences	14.8%	8,790
Medical Scientists, Except Practitioners	39.3%	6,790
Medical and Health Services Managers	16.0%	9,940
Secretaries, Receptionists, and Typists	4.0%	5,590

Employment Outlook

According to the projections by the U.S. Bureau of Labor Statistics, employment in occupations that require a bachelor's degree is expected to grow faster than employment in other sectors of the American labor market. Between 2008 and 2018, the U.S. workforce is projected to grow by 10.1 percent, creating an average of 15.2 million job openings per year. The bachelor's-level jobs are expected to increase by 17.7 percent over the same time.

▶ The health technologist and technician occupations that employ 6 out of 10 health and medical technology graduates are expected to grow rapidly over the decade. Employment in these fields is projected to increase by 20.1 percent, a rate double that projected for the nation's workforce as a whole. New technologies and the aging of the U.S. population are expected to fuel much of this increase in demand. Although hospitals are expected to continue to be the major employer of clinical laboratory workers, employment is expected also to grow rapidly in medical and diagnostic laboratories, offices of physicians, and all other ambulatory health-care services. The large workforce of this occupation ensures many job openings from turnover as well as from occupational growth.

▶ Even higher rates of job growth—39.3 percent—are projected for medical scientists, although that represents an increase on a base of workers that is much smaller than the number working in health technologist and technician occupations. Those with both a Ph.D. and M.D. are likely to experience the best opportunities.

▶ About 15 percent employment growth is projected for technologists and technicians in the biological sciences, another small workforce. Most growth in employment will be in professional, scientific, and technical services and in educational services.

▶ Employment of medical and health services managers is projected to grow by 16 percent from the 283,000 currently employed.

Pathways Beyond the Bachelor's Degree

Of all graduates with a bachelor's degree in health and medical technology, 23 percent proceed to earn a postgraduate degree. Fourteen percent earn a master's degree, 1 percent earn a doctoral degree, and another 8 percent earn a professional degree.

▶ Of those grads whose highest subsequent degree was a master's, only 10 percent earned their master's degrees in health and medical technology.

▶ Sixteen percent earned their master's in business administration.

▶ Of the very small number who went on to a doctoral degree, equal shares (16 percent) earned their Ph.D. in a medical science and in pharmacology. Another 11 percent earned the degree in cell and molecular biology.

▶ Of the grads who proceeded to a professional degree, somewhat more than half earned that degree in a health-care field (medicine, dentistry, optometry, osteopathy, podiatry, or veterinary). Almost one-quarter earned the professional degree in law.

CHAPTER 6

Medical Preparatory Programs

Chiropractors, dentists, optometrists, physicians, podiatrists, and veterinarians all require some undergraduate course work prior to entry into their respective programs. The prerequisites range from 45 semester hours of course work up to a 4-year bachelor's degree. Most minimally require courses in mathematics, biology, organic and inorganic chemistry, and physics. Because medical preparation curricula are competitive and demanding, some people change their original goals.

Becoming a physician takes a long time, usually 11 years: 4 years of undergraduate work, 4 years of medical school, and 3 to 8 years of internship and residency, depending on the specialty selected. Medical education is thus costly, requiring more than 85 percent of students to borrow money to cover expenses. A few medical schools offer 6- or 7-year programs that combine college and professional school. Chiropractic college requires 4 years with at least 2 years of undergraduate college. Most dentists have at least 8 years of education beyond high school. A minimum of 3 years of undergraduate work and 4 years for an optometry degree is required. Ninety percent of podiatrists have an undergraduate degree plus their 4-year program in podiatric medicine.

While a bachelor's degree is not required before the 4-year veterinary medicine program, most students who are admitted possess one.

The practice of medicine has changed substantially in recent years. While the most recent figures show that about two-thirds of physicians are in office-based practices that include clinics and HMOs and about one-quarter are employed in hospitals, the newly trained will more likely take salaried positions in group medical practices, clinics, and HMOs. Pursuing a specialization or establishing a private practice has become too expensive for many doctors.

While 24 specialty boards accommodate a broad spectrum of interests, health cost containment has created a lower demand for some of the specializations. About one-third of physicians are considered to be primary care physicians—that is, internists, pediatricians, and general and family practitioners.

Among other health-care professions, chiropractic treatment of back, neck, extremities, and other joint damage has become more accepted as a result of recent research. Chiropractors do not prescribe drugs or perform surgery, which is appealing to many health-conscious Americans.

Most dentists are general practitioners who run their own practice, often alone or with a small staff. Fluoridation of water supplies has decreased the incidence of tooth decay, but patients have needs for other kinds of dental care, such as esthetic procedures. Ophthalmologists are physicians who perform eye surgery and treat eye diseases and injuries. Dispensing opticians fit and adjust eyeglasses. Optometrists examine eyes to diagnose vision problems and eye diseases. They also provide most of the primary vision care people need—more than half of the individuals in the United States wear glasses or contact lenses. Podiatrists diagnose and treat diseases and injuries of the foot and lower leg by prescribing drugs, ordering physical therapy, setting fractures, and performing surgery. Podiatrists stress the importance of our feet because the 52 bones there make up about one-fourth of all the bones in the human body. Veterinarians are involved in the health care of pets, livestock, and lab animals. Large animal practice is considerably different from small animal practice, which also may determine whether a veterinarian works in an urban or rural setting.

Those in the medical area typically have very good academic ability in the basic sciences, as well as in the humanities and social sciences. They use logic and scientific thinking to make decisive conclusions, often done quickly in emergency situations. They have color perception, spatial ability to use new technologies and X-rays, and finger dexterity to perform clinical work and surgical procedures. Physical stamina is frequently needed. Interpersonal skills are critical when dealing with both patients and families who are in pain or under stress.

The interests of those in health-diagnosing occupations in general are scientific and people oriented. In the specializations, other interests emerge. For example, a surgeon can achieve concrete immediate physical solutions through precise manual dexterity skills, whereas a psychiatrist relies on words to work with the mind of a patient. Chiropractors' involvement in sports injuries of ligaments and muscles is different from a physician treating cancer. A dentist's correction of bad-looking teeth can change a patient's total view of self. And a love for the outdoors and not liking to work indoors can give a large-animal veterinarian personal satisfaction.

Work in the health-care professions is trending away from the long hours that used to be the norm as group practices become more common and emergency-care centers are springing up in many communities. Of course, some loss of autonomy and income accompanies this trend.

Note: People who earn a bachelor's in this field usually intend to earn a professional degree subsequently, and 64 percent do so. Therefore, the figures presented in this chapter are based on *all* graduates with this bachelor's degree, not just those for whom it is the highest degree. In this way, this chapter differs from most other chapters.

Where Do Medical Preparatory Programs Majors Work?

Medical preparatory programs graduates are seeing changes in the sectors that employ them. At the time of the survey, 46 percent worked in their own practice as self-employed workers, and 27 percent worked for businesses and corporations in the private, for-profit sector. The trend has been away from self-employment and toward group practices, HMOs, and other kinds of employers. Sixteen percent worked for educational institutions, and 6 percent worked in the private, nonprofit sector. Less than 5 percent of graduates were employed in government.

Many of the skills and much of the knowledge that medical preparatory programs graduates acquire during their schooling are applicable in the labor market. Therefore, many find jobs that are related to their field. Eighty-two percent are employed in jobs that are closely related to their

Table 1
Percentage Distribution of Employed Persons with at Least a Bachelor's Degree, by the Economic Sector, Size, and New Business Status of the Employer

	Medical Preparatory Programs	All
Economic Sector		
Private for-profit	27.1	47.3
Self-employed	46.2	18.5
Government/Military	4.5	11.0
Education	16.0	15.6
Nonprofit	6.3	7.5
Employer Size		
Small (Fewer than 100 employees)	58.3	28.5
Medium (100–999)	12.7	22.4
Large (1,000–24,999)	18.6	29.6
Very large (25,000 or more)	10.4	19.5
Percent working in new business established within past 5 years	11.8	5.6

undergraduate major field of study. Another 8 percent are employed in jobs that are somewhat related to their major. The remaining 10 percent of medical preparatory graduates work in jobs that are not related to their undergraduate major field of study.

Out of all medical preparatory graduates under the age of 65, 93 percent are employed. Only a little more than 1 percent are officially unemployed; that is, they are not employed and are actively seeking employment. The remaining 5 percent are out of the labor force; that is, they are not employed and are not seeking employment. The main reason underlying the labor force withdrawal of medical preparatory graduates is enrollment in school, accounting for 30 percent of the grads. Most of these are probably working on their professional degrees or are getting additional training to be certified in a specialization. The next most common reason for being out of the workforce is retirement; this is true for 26 percent of those not seeking work. Another 22 percent cite the lack of work in the field.

Occupations

At the time of the survey, a little less than 7 out of 10 graduates of medical preparatory programs were men. The proportion of women enrolled in medical schools has trended upward steadily since 1970 and reached almost 47 percent by the 2010–2011 class.

▶ Male med prep grads are overall more likely than females to choose work as professional health-care practitioners, although in some fields, notably veterinary practice, females outnumber men as new practitioners.

▶ Male med prep grads are also much more likely to opt for teaching medical science, with an insignificant number of female grads in this career at the time of the survey. As the proportion of experienced female medical professionals increases, more are likely to take college faculty jobs.

Table 2
Percentage Distribution of Employed Persons with at Least a Bachelor's Degree in Medical Preparatory Programs, by the Relationship Between Their Job and College Major

Relationship of Job to Major	Percent
Closely related	81.7
Somewhat related	7.8
Not related	10.5

Percent who report the following as the most important reasons for working in a job that was not related to major:

Change in career or professional interests	28.8
Family-related reasons	19.6
Job in highest degree field not available	19.0
Pay, promotion opportunities	18.9
Job location	7.8

▶ Roughly an equal proportion of men and women with degrees in a medical preparatory program are choosing work as medical scientists.

▶ Of the graduates of this major, only a small share of females and an insignificant share of males are opting to work as pharmacists and in health-care occupations that do not require a professional degree.

(At present, pharmacists would not be listed among those other occupations because it now requires a professional degree.)

Work Activities

▶ Eighty-one percent of employed medical preparatory programs graduates regularly engage in providing professional services,

Table 3
Top 5 Occupations Employing Persons with at Least a Bachelor's Degree in Medical Preparatory Programs, by Percentage

Top 5 Occupations	All	Men	Women
Diagnosing and Treating Health Practitioners	69.9	74.6	58.4
Postsecondary Teachers—Medical Science	3.8	4.8	–
Medical Scientists, Except Practitioners	3.2	3.0	3.6
Registered Nurses, Pharmacists, Dietitians, etc.	3.2	–	8.0
Total, Top 4 Occupations	82.2	84.5	76.6
Balance of Employed	17.8	15.5	23.4
All Employed	100.0	100.0	100.0

and 67 percent spend most of their time during a typical week performing these duties.

▶ Management and administration are also important tasks for a significant share of the graduates, 51 percent, but only 8 percent consider these tasks a major part of their job.

▶ Only 4 percent of med prep graduates spend most of their work time teaching, but one-third of them devote significant time to this task.

▶ One-third of the grads engage in employee relations for at least 10 hours of the workweek, but only 2 percent see this as their primary task.

Workplace Training and Other Work-Related Experiences

The career potential of a job is closely associated with the amount of work-related training on the job. Work-related training is regarded as an investment by firms because it makes workers more productive. Sixty-three percent of med prep graduates get work-related training, only slightly higher than the rate among all college graduates with at least a bachelor's (61 percent).

▶ Of those med prep graduates who receive some training during a year, 61 percent receive technical training in the occupation in which they are employed.

▶ Fourteen percent of the training recipients receive management or supervisor training.

▶ Twelve percent receive training to improve their general professional skills, such as public speaking and business writing.

Although medical preparatory graduates decide to participate in work-related training activities, workshops, or seminars for numerous reasons, two reasons stand out as most important to graduates: improving skills and knowledge in the occupational area of their employment (22 percent) and obtaining a professional license or certificate (20 percent). This is not surprising, because medical professions require continuing education as a condition for maintaining licensure. Another 9 percent of the grads cited the need to acquire skills for a new position.

Salaries

The median annual salary of medical preparatory programs graduates with at least a bachelor's degree is an even $100,000, a level that is 43 percent higher than the median annual salary of all employed college graduates with at least a bachelor's. On average, employed medical preparatory programs graduates work for 47 hours per week and for 50 weeks per year, resulting in 2,350 hours of employment per year. The level of work effort among medical preparatory programs graduates is 10 percent higher than the average among all college graduates (which is 43 hours per week and 50 weeks per year, resulting in 2,150 hours per year).

The average annual salary of medical preparatory graduates who work in jobs that are closely related to their undergraduate major field of study is much higher than those who work in somewhat related jobs or jobs that are not related to their major field of study. Closely related jobs pay full-time employed med prep graduates $111,400 annually. Graduates employed in somewhat related jobs earn $37,000 per year, and those whose jobs are unrelated to their undergraduate field of study earn $35,000 per year.

Earning an average salary of $129,00 annually, medical preparatory graduates working for not-for-profit businesses earn a considerably higher salary than those who are employed in other sectors. The remuneration of medical preparatory

Table 4
Annual Salary of Workers with at Least a Bachelor's Degree, Top 5 Occupations (in 2010 Dollars)

Earnings in Top 5 Occupations	All	Medical Preparatory Programs
Total	$100,000	$124,700
Diagnosing/Treating Practitioners (e.g., Dentists, Optometrists, Physicians)	$123,800	$136,200
Registered Nurses, Pharmacists, Dietitians, Therapists, Physician Assistants	$56,800	$37,200
Artists, Broadcasters, Editors, Entertainers, Public Relations Specialists, Writers	$49,500	$41,300
Postsecondary Teachers—Health and related sciences	$67,100	$154,800
Sales/Marketing—Insurance, Securities, Real Estate, and Business Services	$72,200	$41,300

graduates employed in for-profit businesses is $103,200 per year. The same average earnings are reported for those working in their own practice. The government sector pays graduates $85,700 per year. Employment by educational institutions is associated with an average salary of $40,500 per year.

Note: Because of the very small number of survey respondents in some age groups, it was not possible to furnish a useful age/earnings profile graphic for this major.

The average annual salaries of medical preparatory graduates and all college graduates in the top 5 occupations that predominantly employ med prep graduates are presented in Table 4. These figures are based on the earnings of all grads who have at least a bachelor's degree. The degree confers an earnings advantage only in those occupations for which the degree is necessary; in other occupations, a degree in another field can be more lucrative.

Job Satisfaction

The overall level of job satisfaction of medical preparatory programs majors is considerably higher than the average for all graduates.

Table 5
Percentage Distribution of Workers with at Least a Bachelor's Degree, by the Level of Job Satisfaction

Job Satisfaction	Medical Preparatory Programs	All
Very satisfied	58.4	45.4
Somewhat satisfied	35.0	45.0
Somewhat dissatisfied	4.2	7.4
Very dissatisfied	2.4	2.2
Mean Score (4=very satisfied, 1=not satisfied at all)	3.5	3.3

Employment Outlook

According to the projections by the U.S. Bureau of Labor Statistics, employment in occupations that require at least a bachelor's degree is expected to grow faster than employment in other sectors of the American labor market. Between 2008 and 2018, the U.S. workforce is projected to grow by 10.1 percent, creating an average of 15.2 million job openings per year. The jobs requiring at least a bachelor's degree are expected to increase by 15.1 percent over the same time.

The employment growth projections in the top 5 occupations that are most likely to employ medical preparatory graduates are presented in Table 6.

▶ Employment in all health-related professions is projected to increase at much higher rates than the overall job growth in the economy. The demand for practitioners such as dentists, chiropractors, and physicians is projected to increase by almost 23 percent between 2008 and 2018.

▶ Similarly high rates of job growth are projected for therapists, physician assistants, nurses, and pharmacists. Employment in these occupations is projected to increase by 21.5 percent.

▶ Employment of postsecondary teachers of medical specialties will probably grow about 15 percent, the rate projected for all postsecondary teaching occupations.

▶ It is difficult to draw conclusions about the prospects for med prep grads in the highly diverse mix of artistic and communications occupations that together constitute their third-largest employer.

Pathways Beyond the Bachelor's Degree

Postgraduate education is high among medical preparatory graduates. Seventy-eight percent of graduates with a bachelor's degree in a medical preparatory program proceed to earn a postgraduate degree. As you might expect, most of them—64 percent—earn a professional degree. Only 11 percent go no further than a master's degree, and 3 percent earn a doctoral degree.

Table 6

Projected Growth and Job Openings in the Top 5 Occupations Employing Persons with at Least a Bachelor's Degree in Medical Preparatory Programs

Top 5 Occupations	Projected Growth 2008–2018	Projected Annual Job Openings
All top 5	16.5%	377,590
Diagnosing/Treating Practitioners (e.g., Dentists, Optometrists, Physicians)	22.7%	67,000
Registered Nurses, Pharmacists, Dietitians, Therapists, Physician Assistants	21.5%	119,640
Artists, Broadcasters, Editors, Entertainers, Public Relations Specialists, Writers	12.4%	71,740
Postsecondary Teachers—Health and related sciences	15.1%	4,000
Sales/Marketing—Insurance, Securities, Real Estate, and Business Services	11.5%	115,210

▶ Of the professional degrees earned by medical preparatory graduates, 85 percent are in the medical fields—for example, M.D. (physicians), D.D.S. (dentists), and the like.

▶ Of those earning master's degrees, 11 percent specialize in business administration.

▶ Nineteen percent of all doctoral degrees earned by medical preparatory graduates are in the health professions, and 14 percent are earned in biochemistry and biophysics. Eleven percent are in plant sciences.

CHAPTER 7

Nursing

Nursing is a very broad occupational area and accommodates many opportunities for specialization, such as surgery, maternity, pediatrics, emergency room, intensive care, or involvement in specific health areas such as the heart or cancer. Some nurses work in home health agencies, schools, and public health and occupational health settings, with other directions available for nurses who want administrative or nursing education roles. Characteristic of nurses is that they work with people who usually come to hospitals, clinics, and nursing homes with medical problems. They have close prolonged physical contact with people, touching and lifting patients. They also take blood samples, administer injections, apply dressings, and dispense medications. They become accustomed to tolerating conditions associated with mental, emotional, or physical problems or pain. These functions differentiate nursing from many careers, despite its holistic, preventive, and educational focus.

Work environments can be stressful because of the high-level medical knowledge and intensity required in rapidly expanding same-day surgery and treatments such as chemotherapy. Nursing also involves hazards from exposure to diseases such as hepatitis and AIDS, dangers from chemicals, and back injury from moving patients.

High school seniors need to consider their interests and preferences because nursing offers multiple options and career pathways. The three major educational choices are the associate degree (A.D.N.), which takes about 2 years to complete and is offered by community or junior colleges; a bachelor's degree (B.S.N.), which takes

4 to 5 years; and diploma programs offered by local hospitals, which take 2 to 3 years.

The undergraduate pathways to nursing are changing in their popularity, with the bachelor's growing, the associate degree shrinking, and the diploma becoming relatively scarce. All students must graduate from an accredited nursing school and pass a national examination to obtain a nursing license. However, a bachelor's degree is usually necessary for administrative positions in hospitals and for community nursing.

Several abilities are required in nursing: special medical skills, an understanding of technical and pharmaceutical language and information, fast and agile finger dexterity and physical coordination, strength, the ability to change rapidly from one task to another, good communications, record-keeping skills, and a willingness to follow directions exactly. Leadership is important, and this is increasingly evident when nurses must supervise other health-care personnel.

Overall, nurses' interests typically follow their abilities: being social, being good communicators, and being scientifically skilled. Early in life, many entering the nursing field have had opportunities with or volunteered in caring for the elderly or sick relatives or in physical exercises with disabled persons, where they have experienced scientific practices. Newer role models in the health-care field—that is, physician assistants, surgical technicians, and managers in health maintenance organizations—present other examples of high-functioning professionals, which can be attractive career options for

Table 1
Percentage Distribution of Employed Persons with Only a Bachelor's Degree, by Economic Sector, Size, and New Business Status of Employer

	Nursing	All
Economic Sector		
Private for-profit	31.8	47.3
Self-employed	6.8	18.5
Government/Military	12.0	11.0
Education	20.5	15.6
Nonprofit	28.8	7.5
Employer Size		
Small (Fewer than 100 employees)	15.0	35.5
Medium (100–999)	27.1	21.8
Large (1,000–24,999)	45.7	26.0
Very large (25,000 or more)	12.2	16.7
Percent working in new business established within past 5 years	4.9	7.6

people with social and scientific interests. Note that social is the primary interest.

Where Do Nursing Majors Work?

About 32 percent of employed nursing program graduates work as wage and salary workers in private, for-profit organizations, and a slightly smaller share work in the nonprofit sector. One-fifth of nursing graduates work in the educational sector. Twelve percent are employed by government organizations, and only 7 percent are self-employed.

Most employed graduates of undergraduate nursing programs are employed in jobs related to the major. Only 5 percent work in jobs not related to the major field of study.

About 85 percent of those with a bachelor's degree are employed, although one-fifth of these individuals work in part-time positions. Unlike almost all other workers, part-time nurses earn a higher hourly wage than full-time workers, mostly because so many of them work the higher-paid night shift. Among nursing majors who do not work, only 1 percent are officially classified as unemployed—that is, seeking a job but unable to find work. Rather, most nursing program graduates who are not employed have voluntarily chosen not to work. Fourteen percent of the grads have left the workforce, most often because of early retirement (30 percent) or family commitments (29 percent).

Occupations

Graduates with a bachelor's in nursing work overwhelmingly as registered nurses. Very small numbers of the grads work in health-related management. Even smaller numbers work in management or sales. About 8 percent of registered nurses now are male, so the proportion of male grads is now almost certainly higher than the 6 percent found by the survey.

Table 2
Percentage Distribution of Employed Persons with Only a Bachelor's Degree in Nursing, by the Relationship Between Their Job and College Major

Relationship of Job to Major	Percent
Closely related	80.5
Somewhat related	14.2
Not related	5.3

Percent who report the following as the most important reasons for working in a job that was not related to major:	
Family-related reasons	44.4
Working conditions (hours, equipment, environment)	18.2
Change in career or professional interests	17.5
Pay, promotion opportunities	6.5
Other reason	4.6

Work Activities

▶ Eighty-seven percent of employed nursing graduates regularly engage in providing professional services, and 67 percent spend most of their time during a typical week performing these duties.

▶ Fifty-three percent of the graduates spend at least 10 hours of the workweek performing management and administration tasks, and 11 percent consider performing management and administration tasks to be a major part of their job.

▶ Another 57 percent of all employed nursing graduates spend at least 10 hours of the workweek performing teaching duties, and 7 percent report that these duties consume most of their time at work.

▶ Only 2 percent of nursing graduates spend most of their time at work on tasks related to employee relations, but 36 percent engage in these tasks for at least 10 hours out of their typical week.

▶ Twenty-six percent regularly deal with doing sales, purchasing, or marketing, but only 3 percent spend most of their time at work in these activities.

▶ Only 2 percent devote a majority of their typical workweek to providing computer applications, but 95 percent spend significant time at these tasks.

Workplace Training and Other Work-Related Experiences

Work-based learning activities are an important part of the career development of nursing program graduates. Nearly 8 out of 10 employed persons with a degree in nursing participate in a work-based training program during the year, which compares very favorably to the average of 61 percent for graduates of all majors.

Table 3
Top 5 Occupations Employing Persons with Only a Bachelor's Degree in Nursing, by Percentage

Top 5 Occupations	All	Men	Women
Registered Nurses, Pharmacists, Dietitians, Therapists, Physician Assistants	85.9	79.3	86.3
Other Health Occupations	1.6	5.3	1.3
Medical and Health Services Managers	1.4	0.6	1.4
Other Management-Related Occupations	1.0	–	1.1
Sales Occupations—Retail	0.9	–	1.0
Total, Top 5 Occupations	90.8	85.2	91.1
Balance of Employed	9.2	14.8	8.9
All Employed	100.0	100.0	100.0

- Of nursing graduates who receive some training during a year, 73 percent receive technical training in the occupation in which they are employed.

- Twenty percent of the training recipients receive management or supervisor training.

- Eighteen percent receive training to improve their general professional skills, such as public speaking and business writing.

- For 40 percent of the training recipients, the most important reason for getting the training was to improve their general professional skills, such as public speaking and business writing.

- Another 17 percent cite the requirements of licensure or certification as the outstanding reason for getting training. In many states and for many employers, nurses are required to participate in workshops and seminars related to the nursing profession to maintain their certification as professionals in the field.

- Eleven percent seek training primarily because their employer requires it.

Salaries

The median annual salary of nursing graduates with only a bachelor's degree is $50,000, a level that is 3 percent lower than the median annual salary of all employed college graduates. On average, employed nursing graduates work for 36 hours per week for 49 weeks per year, resulting in 1,764 hours of employment each year. Because so many nurses work part-time, the level of work effort among nursing graduates is 18 percent lower than the average among all college graduates (which is 43 hours per week and 50 weeks per year, resulting in 2,150 hours per year).

Unlike graduates of most other fields of study, grads of nursing earn roughly the same average annual pay no matter what sector of the economy employs them, apart from self-employment. In the the nonprofit sector, they average $52,600 per year. In private, for-profit businesses, they earn an average of $51,600. Nursing graduates working in education earn an average salary of $52,800. Those employed in government average $51,300 per year. Persons with a nursing degree who are self-employed have lower average annual earnings than others with a bachelor's degree in the field, $48,500. However, because 44 percent of the self-employed workers are part-timers, their per-hour earnings amount to a higher average rate ($29.60) than that enjoyed by workers for other types of employers ($25.08).

Graduates of nursing programs who work in jobs that are related to their major have much higher annual earnings than those employed in jobs that are not related to the nursing field. Those employed in jobs that are closely related to the field have annual salaries of $51,600. Graduates employed in jobs that are somewhat related to their major earn $51,600 per year. In contrast, the average salary of graduates employed full-time in a job that is not related to their field of study is $41,300.

The earnings of persons with a bachelor's degree in nursing vary considerably by occupation.

Those employed as registered nurses, pharmacists, therapists, and physician assistants earn an average salary of $51,600.

The few graduates working as medical services administrators have salaries that average $82,600 per year, an earnings advantage of about 65 percent compared to the $50,000 average annual salary of all graduates with a nursing degree.

Job Satisfaction

The overall level of job satisfaction of nursing majors is considerably higher than the average for all graduates.

FIGURE 1

Age/Earnings Profile of Persons with Only a Bachelor's Degree in Nursing (Full-Time Workers, in 2010 Dollars)

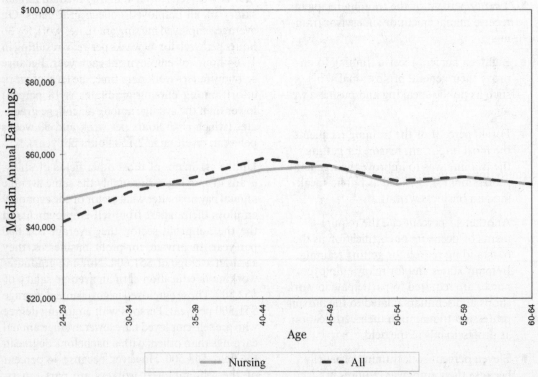

Table 4
Annual Salary of Workers with Only a Bachelor's Degree, Top 5 Occupations (in 2010 Dollars)

Earnings in Top 5 Occupations	All	Nursing
Total	$50,000	$52,700
Registered Nurses, Pharmacists, Dietitians, Therapists, Physician Assistants	$55,700	$51,600
Other Health Occupations	$35,100	$51,600
Medical and Health Services Managers	$74,300	$82,600
Other Management-Related Occupations	$57,800	$85,700
Sales Occupations—Retail	$42,300	$51,600

Employment Outlook

Although overall employment in the U.S. economy is projected to increase by 10.1 percent between 2008 and 2018, the demand for workers with a bachelor's degree is expected to increase 17.7 percent. The rate of job growth for the nursing occupation is projected to be considerably greater than the overall rate of growth in the demand for college graduates. Overall employment among registered nurses is expected to increase from 2,619,000 in 2008 to 3,200,000 by 2018, an increase of 581,000 jobs, or about 22 percent, over the period.

The rising average age of the nation's population, along with new changes in technology and organization of health-care services, is expected to cause this rise in demand. Over the past sev-eral years, shortages of registered nurses have developed across the nation. The number of graduates in the nursing field has not kept pace with the strong demand for skilled nurses. Many health-care organizations have begun relying on graduates of overseas nursing programs to meet their staffing needs. Recent supply-and-demand forecasts suggest continued shortages of nurses in many states as demand rises but growth in supply lags behind need.

Despite slower employment growth in hospitals, job opportunities should still be excellent because of the relatively high turnover of hospital nurses. To attract and retain qualified nurses, hospitals may offer signing bonuses, family-friendly work schedules, or subsidized training. Although faster employment growth is projected in physicians' offices and outpatient care centers, RNs may face

Table 5
Percentage Distribution of Workers with Only a Bachelor's Degree, by Level of Job Satisfaction

Job Satisfaction	Nursing	All
Very satisfied	51.3	45.4
Somewhat satisfied	42.9	45.0
Somewhat dissatisfied	5.0	7.4
Very dissatisfied	0.7	2.2
Mean Score (4=very satisfied, 1=not satisfied at all)	3.5	3.3

Table 6

Projected Growth and Job Openings in the Top 5 Occupations Employing Persons
with Only a Bachelor's Degree in Nursing

Top 5 Occupations	Projected Growth 2008–2018	Projected Annual Job Openings
All top 5	11.8%	404,220
Registered Nurses, Pharmacists, Dietitians, Therapists, Physician Assistants	21.5%	119,640
Other Health Occupations	24.5%	13,920
Medical and Health Services Managers	16.0%	9,940
Other Management-Related Occupations	7.2%	53,020
Sales Occupations—Retail	7.5%	207,700

greater competition for these positions because they generally offer regular working hours and more comfortable work environments.

Employment in the managerial and administrative area, a small source of employment opportunities for nursing majors, is expected to grow more slowly than the overall level of demand for college graduates or for persons with a degree in nursing. Slower growth rates in employment levels in the hospital industry suggest that the demand for managerial and administrative staff in that industry will diminish. However, new opportunities for health professionals are expected in nonhospital health organizations, including skilled nursing facilities and offices of physicians. Strong job growth is expected in health occupations outside the nursing profession, including that of health technician.

Pathways Beyond the Bachelor's Degree

Compared to other major fields of study, persons who earn a bachelor's degree in nursing are somewhat less likely to enroll and complete a graduate program of study. Only one-quarter of all persons with an undergraduate degree in nursing eventually continue their education

and earn an advanced degree. This figure may increase, however, with increased opportunities for advanced practice nurses, who are required to hold the master's degree and have titles such as clinical nurse specialist, nurse anesthetist, nurse-midwife, or nurse practitioner. Advanced practice nurses have considerably more autonomy than registered nurses.

Almost all the advanced degrees earned by nursing grads are at the master's level. Only 2 percent of those who earn a nursing degree at the undergraduate level go on to complete a doctorate or professional degree. This suggests that undergraduate nursing programs are not a good educational pathway to becoming a physician or other medical practitioner with a doctor's degree.

▶ Among those few who do earn a doctorate, most often the degree is in nursing. This is good preparation to be a nursing instructor.

▶ About half of those who earn a master's degree earn it in a nursing specialty. About 9 percent earn their master's degree in health services administration.

▶ Another 8 percent earn a master's in another health or medical science.

CHAPTER 8

Parks, Recreation, Fitness, and Leisure Studies

This field fits in with the current interest in physical fitness, health, and leisure time. Recreation workers are activity leaders, organizers, and facility and equipment managers. By leading activities, they help people in entertainment, self-improvement, and physical fitness. They conduct classes and coach in areas such as drama, arts and crafts, tennis, water sports, gymnastics, and other sports. They plan and organize daily activities, teams, leagues, social functions, and exercise programs, whether at the workplace, a camp, or a recreation center. Work settings include local playgrounds, recreation areas, parks, community centers, health clubs, religious organizations, camps, tourist parks, companies, nursing homes, and park and recreation governmental commissions. Graduates of this major usually have supervisory roles because many workers in this field are part-time, seasonal, or volunteers.

Therapeutic recreation is another related major that prepares graduates to provide treatment services and recreation activities such as games, dance, and arts and crafts for people with illnesses and disabling conditions. The purpose of these activities is to reduce depression, stress, and anxiety. They help individuals to recover basic motor functioning and use resources to become integrated into the community. They work to build individuals' confidence and help them socialize better to foster more independent functioning.

Course work in the recreation field can include community organization, supervision, management, and recreation for the disabled or elderly, plus fieldwork. Specializations are park management, camp management, industrial recreation, and therapeutic recreation. Course work for therapeutic recreation includes human anatomy, physiology, medical terminology, intervention design and evaluation, and study of the characteristics of disabilities.

Attributes for persons with this major include good physical coordination and social, teaching, language, and interpersonal skills to relate to people with a wide range of skills, of different ages, and from diverse backgrounds. Leadership and organization skills are critical for planning and coordinating events, schedules, and programs. Persuasive and motivational abilities are used in instructing beginners, coaching, and in working with the ill and those with disabling conditions.

Recreation workers' interests include strong people and leadership orientations. For example, a team's captain performs a leadership role. Different specializations within the field additionally involve scientific knowledge about the body's anatomical functioning.

Where Do Parks, Recreation, Fitness, and Leisure Studies Majors Work?

Four out of 10 of employed recreation and fitness studies graduates work for businesses and corporations in the private, for-profit sector. However, the government employs a larger share of grads, 24 percent, than it does of most other majors. Educational institutions also employ large numbers of recreation and fitness studies graduates. Almost one-fifth of recreation and

fitness studies graduates work in this sector, primarily as elementary and secondary school teachers. Another 11 percent work as self-employed workers in their own business. Involvement with community fitness programs results in employment of 7 percent of these graduates in the private, nonprofit sector.

About one-third of all recreation and fitness studies graduates are employed in jobs that are closely related to their undergraduate major. Another 13 percent report that their jobs are somewhat related to their undergraduate major. The remaining half of all employed recreation and fitness studies graduates work in jobs that are not at all related to their undergraduate major.

Out of all recreation and fitness studies graduates under the age of 65, 85 percent are employed. Only 1 percent are officially unemployed; that is, they are not employed and are actively seeking employment. The remaining 14 percent are out of the labor force; that is, they are not employed

Table 1
Percentage Distribution of Employed Persons with Only a Bachelor's Degree, by Economic Sector, Size, and New Business Status of Employer

	Parks, Recreation, Fitness, and Leisure Studies	All
Economic Sector		
Private for-profit	39.6	47.3
Self-employed	10.9	18.5
Government/Military	23.8	11.0
Education	18.9	15.6
Nonprofit	6.8	7.5
Employer Size		
Small (Fewer than 100 employees)	34.7	35.5
Medium (100–999)	28.7	21.8
Large (1,000–24,999)	21.8	26.0
Very large (25,000 or more)	14.8	16.7
Percent working in new business established within past 5 years	9.5	7.6

Table 2

Percentage Distribution of Employed Persons with Only a Bachelor's Degree
in Parks, Recreation, Fitness, and Leisure Studies, by the Relationship
Between Their Job and College Major

Relationship of Job to Major	Percent
Closely related	34.2
Somewhat related	13.3
Not related	52.5

Percent who report the following as the most important reasons
for working in a job that was not related to major:

Pay, promotion opportunities	22.7
Change in career or professional interests	22.5
Job in highest degree field not available	18.0
Working conditions (hours, equipment, environment)	13.0
Job location	10.7

and are not seeking employment. When asked what is the most important reason they have withdrawn from the labor force, roughly 3 out of 10 of these grads cite family commitments, and about one-quarter say they have retired. About 15 percent say they have no need to work.

About 9 percent work part-time schedules.

Occupations

With over half of the recreation and fitness studies grads working in fields unrelated to their major, it's not surprising that the occupations they hold are highly diverse and that few patterns emerge. The top 5 occupations employing the grads account for fewer than one-third of

Table 3

Top 5 Occupations Employing Persons with Only a Bachelor's Degree in Parks,
Recreation, Fitness, and Leisure Studies, by Percentage

Top 5 Occupations	All	Men	Women
Other Service Occupations, Except Health	8.3	5.0	10.7
Teachers—Secondary, Other Subjects	5.6	6.3	5.2
Other Marketing and Sales Occupations	5.1	0.5	8.3
Other Administrative Occupations	4.8	6.8	3.4
Sales Occupations—Retail	4.8	10.4	0.8
Total, Top 5 Occupations	28.6	29.0	28.4
Balance of Employed	71.4	71.0	71.6
All Employed	100.0	100.0	100.0

them, and 4 of the 5 occupational titles begin with or include the word "other," indicating diverse groups of jobs.

About 60 percent of the grads are women. The occupational employment patterns of male and female graduates are mostly different, although roughly similar shares of the grads are likely to work as teachers.

Work Activities

▶ One-fifth of the employed graduates spend most of their work time in sales, purchasing, and marketing duties, and 53 percent regularly perform these duties.

▶ For more than half the employed grads, management and administrative duties consume at least 10 hours out of the workweek, and 16 percent see these duties as their primary focus.

▶ About 42 percent of grads regularly perform teaching duties, and 16 percent consider teaching their main function.

▶ Nine out of 10 grads spend a significant amount of time working with computer applications, but only 6 percent do this most of the time.

▶ Forty-five percent regularly deal with employee relations, and another 9 percent spend most of their time at work in these activities.

▶ Accounting, finance, and contracts are significant responsibilities for about one-third of parks, recreation, fitness, and leisure studies graduates, but only 6 percent devote a majority of their typical workweek to these tasks.

Workplace Training and Other Work-Related Experiences

The career potential of a job is closely associated with the amount of work-related training on the job. Work-related training is regarded as an investment by firms because it makes workers more productive. The incidence of work-related training among recreation and fitness studies graduates is signficantly higher than the rate of participation in work-related training among all college graduates: 67 percent, compared to 61 percent.

▶ Of those recreation and fitness studies graduates who receive some training during the year, 57 percent receive technical training in the occupation in which they are employed.

▶ Twenty-three percent of the training recipients receive management or supervisory training.

▶ One-quarter receive training to improve their general professional skills, such as public speaking and business writing.

When asked to identify the most important reason to acquire training, 44 percent of recreation and fitness studies graduates who undergo training identify the need to improve their occupational skills and knowledge. Another 11 percent report mandatory training requirements by the employer as the most important factor underlying their involvement in work-related training. Six percent consider the need to obtain a professional license or certificate as the most important reason influencing their decision to undergo work-related training. Four percent of grads identified qualifying for a salary increase and promotion as the most important reason.

Salaries

The median annual salary of parks, recreation, fitness, and leisure studies graduates with only a bachelor's degree is $37,000, a level that is 39 percent lower than the median annual salary of all employed college graduates. On average, employed parks, recreation, fitness, and leisure studies graduates work for 41 hours per week and for 49 weeks per year, resulting in 2,009 hours of employment per year. The level of work effort among parks, recreation, fitness, and leisure studies graduates is 6 percent lower than the average among all college graduates (which is 43 hours per week and 50 weeks per year, resulting in 2,150 hours per year).

The average annual salary of recreation and fitness studies graduates who work in jobs that are closely related to their major field of study is $39,200. (Many of these grads are employed in teaching occupations.) Those working in jobs that are somewhat related to their major average $41,300, and those doing work not related to their undergraduate major average $36,100.

Self-employed recreation and fitness studies graduates earn the highest average salary, $43,200 per year. Those employed in the government sector average $40,900. Educational institutions pay full-time employed recreation and fitness studies graduates an average salary of $38,700 per year. In the private, for-profit sector, grads average $36,100 annually. Graduates who

FIGURE 1

Age/Earnings Profile of Persons with Only a Bachelor's Degree in Parks, Recreation, Fitness, and Leisure Studies (Full-Time Workers, in 2010 Dollars)

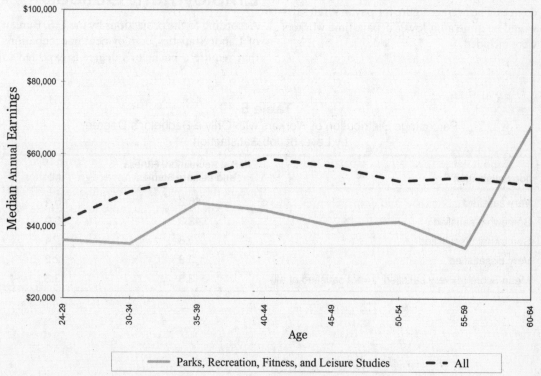

Table 4
Annual Salary of Workers with Only a Bachelor's Degree, Top 5 Occupations (in 2010 Dollars)

Earnings in Top 5 Occupations	All	Parks, Recreation, Fitness, and Leisure Studies
Total	$37,000	$35,800
Other Service Occupations, Except Health	$35,100	$28,900
Teachers—Secondary, Other Subjects	$39,200	$37,200
Other Marketing and Sales Occupations	$54,700	$47,500
Other Administrative Occupations	$38,200	$36,100
Sales Occupations—Retail	$42,300	$35,100

work for nonprofit organizations on a full-time basis earn $34,100 per year.

Of the top 5 occupations employing graduates of this major, the highest earnings are in miscellaneous sales and marketing jobs, but for all 5 occupations the degree confers an earnings disadvantage compared to all other bachelor's degrees. The average figure for pay in retail sales would be quite a bit lower if part-time workers were included.

Job Satisfaction

The overall level of job satisfaction of parks, recreation, fitness, and leisure studies majors is about the same as the average for all graduates.

Employment Outlook

According to the projections by the U.S. Bureau of Labor Statistics, employment in occupations that require a bachelor's degree is expected to

Table 5
Percentage Distribution of Workers with Only a Bachelor's Degree, by Level of Job Satisfaction

Job Satisfaction	Parks, Recreation, Fitness, and Leisure Studies	All
Very satisfied	46.2	45.4
Somewhat satisfied	42.3	45.0
Somewhat dissatisfied	7.8	7.4
Very dissatisfied	3.8	2.2
Mean Score (4=very satisfied, 1=not satisfied at all)	3.3	3.3

Table 6

Projected Growth and Job Openings in the Top 5 Occupations Employing Persons with Only a Bachelor's Degree in Parks, Recreation, Fitness, and Leisure Studies

Top 5 Occupations	Projected Growth 2008–2018	Projected Annual Job Openings
All top 5	9.3%	517,390
Other Service Occupations, Except Health	14.3%	53,570
Teachers—Secondary, Other Subjects	15.3%	25,110
Other Marketing and Sales Occupations	7.3%	64,880
Other Administrative Occupations	10.8%	166,130
Sales Occupations—Retail	7.5%	207,700

grow faster than employment in other sectors of the American labor market. Between 2008 and 2018, the U.S. workforce is projected to grow by 10.1 percent, creating an average of 15.2 million job openings per year. The bachelor's-level jobs are expected to increase by 17.7 percent over the same time.

▶ Employment in the top 2 occupations that are most likely to employ recreation and fitness studies graduates is projected to grow at a rate above the rate of growth of total employment in the U.S. economy. These occupations also will provide numerous job openings, largely caused by employee turnover.

▶ Employment in secondary teaching is projected to increase by 20 percent over the same time period. Job prospects should be better in inner cities and rural areas than in suburban districts.

▶ Jobs for the unspecified service occupations that employ graduates of this program are projected to increase by 14.3 percent between 2008 and 2018. Job turnover will create many openings.

Pathways Beyond the Bachelor's Degree

Among parks, recreation, fitness, and leisure studies graduates with a bachelor's degree, about 3 out of 10 proceed to earn a postgraduate degree: 28 percent earn a master's degree, and doctoral and professional degrees are each earned by 2 percent.

▶ Eleven percent of the master's degrees earned by undergraduate recreation and fitness studies majors are in the field of education administration. Another 11 percent of the master's degrees are in physical therapy and other rehabilitation or therapeutic services. Nine percent of the degrees are in recreation and fitness studies.

▶ Too few doctoral and professional degrees are earned by these grads to suggest any pattern.

CHAPTER 9

Pharmacy

Most people are familiar with the work of pharmacists. Most medicines today are manufactured by pharmaceutical companies in standard dosages and forms. This leaves the pharmacist's role primarily to dispense medications and inform consumers about uses and possible side effects. In community or retail pharmacies, a frequent function is to provide information about over-the-counter drugs and make recommendations after asking the user health-related questions. In hospitals and other health-care settings, pharmacists can become involved in drug therapy programs such as medicines for psychiatric disorders, diagnostic use of radiopharmaceuticals, or intravenous nutrition.

Pharmacists who are trained in the United States must earn a Pharm.D. degree from an accredited college or school of pharmacy. The Pharm.D. degree has replaced the Bachelor of Pharmacy degree, which is no longer being awarded. To be admitted to a Pharm.D. program, an applicant usually must have completed at least 2 years of specific preprofessional study at a college or university. This requirement generally includes courses in mathematics and natural sciences, such as chemistry, biology, and physics, as well as courses in the humanities and social sciences.

Pharm.D. programs generally take 4 years. The courses are designed to teach students about all aspects of drug therapy. In addition, students learn how to communicate with patients and other health-care providers about drug information and patient care. Students also learn professional ethics, concepts of public health, and business management. In addition to receiving classroom instruction, students in Pharm.D. programs spend time working with licensed pharmacists.

Some Pharm.D. graduates obtain further training through 1- or 2-year residency programs or fellowships. Pharmacy residencies are postgraduate training programs in pharmacy practice and usually require the completion of a research project. The programs are often mandatory for pharmacists who wish to work in a clinical setting. Pharmacy fellowships are highly individualized programs that are designed to prepare participants to work in a specialized area of pharmacy, such as clinical practice or research laboratories. Some pharmacists who own their own pharmacy obtain a master's degree in business administration. Others may obtain a degree in public administration or public health.

All colleges of pharmacy offer courses teaching how to dispense prescriptions and manage a practice, leading to preparation for licensure to practice. Other requirements include mathematics, chemistry, biology, and social sciences courses. To be licensed, pharmacy graduates must obtain a degree from an accredited college of pharmacy and pass licensing examinations on pharmacy skills, knowledge, and law. They also must serve an internship under a licensed pharmacist, although this is often done as part of the Pharm.D. program.

Scientific ability, manual and finger dexterity to perform laboratory work, ability to recognize color and texture, and computer skills are important to the performance of pharmacists. Learning interpersonal skills is part of another major trend in pharmacists' training that emphasizes increased direct patient care and consultative services. Increasingly, pharmacists are monitoring a person's reaction to a drug or to multiple prescriptions, so collaborating with physicians requires good communication skills.

Pharmacists' interests vary, depending on whether they follow a hospital and research direction, where scientific activities predominate, or specialize in community pharmacy, which is characterized by a combination of scientific, business, and people orientations. Pharmacists are thorough, very accurate, and orderly. However, the pharmacy field also requires its personnel to be very alert to business changes as well as advances in new available medicines.

Pharmacists value a good income, social interaction, high achievement, research work or at least a knowledge of the results of new drug studies, and the chance to work precisely. In recent years, the fact that about 15 percent of pharmacists work part-time, nights, or weekends may accommodate a better opportunity for work-family balance.

Note: In most other chapters, the discussion and the labels on the charts and tables refer to the kind of degree held by the survey respondents as "only a bachelor's degree." This chapter, however, avoids identifying the degree because the accepted minimal degree for pharmacists has changed. At the time of the survey on which this book is based, a bachelor's degree in pharmacy was acceptable. Only about 10 percent of pharmacy grads held a graduate or professional degree in pharmacy. Now, however, a Pharm.D. is the standard credential for pharmacists. Any references to a bachelor's degree would give the misleading impression that this degree is still acceptable, so these references have been omitted from this chapter.

Where Do Pharmacy Majors Work?

More than half of pharmacy program majors work as employees of private, for-profit corporations and businesses. A substantial proportion

Table 1

Percentage Distribution of Employed Persons, by the Economic Sector, Size, and New Business Status of the Employer

	Pharmacy	All
Economic Sector		
Private for-profit	56.7	47.3
Self-employed	16.8	18.5
Government/Military	5.2	11.0
Education	6.4	15.6
Nonprofit	14.7	7.5
Employer Size		
Small (Fewer than 100 employees)	21.6	35.5
Medium (100–999)	11.0	21.8
Large (1,000–24,999)	35.0	26.0
Very large (25,000 or more)	32.4	16.7
Percent working in a new business established within the past 5 years	6.6	7.6

Table 2
Percentage Distribution of Employed Persons with a Degree in Pharmacy, by the Relationship Between Their Job and College Major

Relationship of Job to Major	Percent
Closely related	87.6
Somewhat related	4.6
Not related	7.8

Percent who report the following as the most important reasons for working in a job that was not related to major:

Family-related reasons	27.3
Working conditions (hours, equipment, environment)	22.8
Job location	14.4
Other reason	13.3
Pay, promotion opportunities	10.6

of those with a pharmacy degree own their own businesses; almost 17 percent of all pharmacy majors are self-employed. Only a small proportion of those with a degree in pharmacy work in educational institutions, nonprofit organizations, or government agencies.

Almost 9 out of 10 pharmacy majors are employed in jobs that are closely related to their major. Only 8 percent are working in jobs that are unrelated to pharmacy.

The employment rate of persons with a degree in pharmacy is very high. Ninety-one percent of all persons under the age of 65 with a degree in pharmacy are employed. Among those not working, less than 1 percent are involuntarily unemployed. Most often those who have decided not to work have taken early retirement. About 15 percent of pharmacy grads work part-time.

Occupations

The vast majority of pharmacy grads who are working are employed in jobs related to health care. They are divided roughly equally between men and women, and so is their employment as pharmacists. However, women made up 61.0 percent of those enrolled in the 2010–2011 class of Pharm.D. programs. The small number of grads who work as health technologists and technicians are almost all female.

Work Activities

▶ Pharmacy majors spend the bulk of their workweek engaged in professional activities related to the major. Two-thirds identify these duties as their primary work function, and 83 percent called them an important function.

▶ Management and administration are also a major part of the job of pharmacists, who often are responsible for the management of the pharmacy (or pharmacy department in a health-care organization) in which they work. About 1 out of 10 grads report that as their primary focus, and 65 consider it important.

Table 3
Top 5 Occupations Employing Persons with a Degree in Pharmacy, by Percentage

Top 5 Occupations	All	Men	Women
Registered Nurses, Pharmacists, Dietitians, Therapists, Physician Assistants	79.5	81.0	77.9
Health Technologists and Technicians	2.9	0.2	5.9
Other Marketing and Sales Occupations	2.7	4.1	1.1
Sales Occupations—Retail	1.5	2.4	0.5
Other Administrative Occupations	1.4	–	2.8
Total, Top 5 Occupations	88.0	87.7	88.2
Balance of Employed	12.0	12.3	11.8
All Employed	100.0	100.0	100.0

▶ Sales is another major activity of pharmacists, reflecting the number who work in community pharmacies. Eight percent say this is their main work role, and almost half say it occupies more than one-tenth of their work time.

▶ More than 9 out of 10 grads work with computer applications at least 10 hours of their workweek, but only 3 percent view this kind of work as their primary role.

Workplace Training and Other Work-Related Experiences

Training workshops and seminars are an important way that persons with a degree in pharmacy stay abreast of developments in the field. The rate of participation in work-related training during a year among employed pharmacy graduates (63 percent) is slightly higher than the training participation rate of all college graduates (61 percent).

▶ Of those pharmacy graduates who receive some training during a year, 57 percent receive technical training in the occupation in which they are employed.

▶ Seventeen percent of the training recipients receive management or supervisor training.

▶ Thirteen percent receive training to improve their general professional skills, such as public speaking and business writing.

▶ In most states, participation in training programs is a requirement for most pharmacists to maintain their license, and this is the reason for training cited by the largest number of grads (35 percent).

▶ Another reason, cited by 15 percent of those getting training, is to learn specific technical skills for the profession.

Salaries

The median annual salary of pharmacy graduates is $84,000, a level that is 39 percent higher than the median annual salary of all employed college graduates. On average, employed pharmacy graduates work for 39 hours per week and for 50 weeks per year, resulting in 1,950 hours of employment per year. The level of work effort among pharmacy graduates is 9 percent lower than the average among all college graduates,

FIGURE 1

Age/Earnings Profile of Persons with a Degree in Pharmacy (Full-Time Workers, in 2010 Dollars)

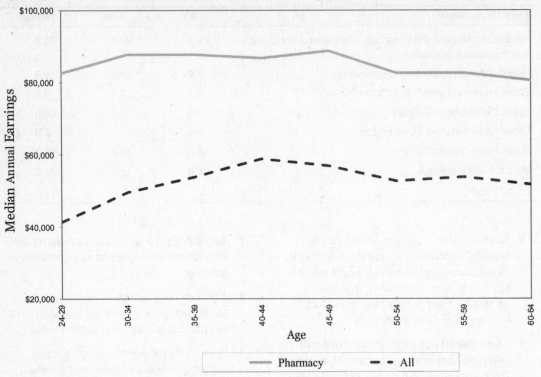

which is 43 hours per week and 50 weeks per year, resulting in 2,150 hours per year.

Pharmacy grads who work as wage and salary workers for private, for-profit corporations have the highest annual earnings, averaging $87,700 per year. Those who are self-employed average $84,600. Grads working in nonprofit organizations earn an average of $82,600 per year. Pharmacy majors employed by educational institutions earn $81,100 per year; those in government organizations average $79,600.

Few graduates of pharmacy programs are employed in positions other than as pharmacists. Those working in jobs that are somewhat related to their major earn $86,700 per year, whereas those working in unrelated jobs average a much lower income, $33,000 per year.

Table 4 shows average earnings of pharmacy graduates and all college graduates. Pharmacy program graduates who work in pharmacy and related health occupations have annual earnings of $87,700 per year. The degree confers an earnings advantage in these occupations and in sales occupations.

Job Satisfaction

The overall level of job satisfaction of pharmacy majors is considerably higher than the average for all graduates.

Table 4
Annual Salary of Workers, Top 5 Occupations (in 2010 Dollars)

Earnings in Top 5 Occupations	All	Pharmacy
Total	$84,000	$84,900
Registered Nurses, Pharmacists, Dietitians, Therapists, Physician Assistants	$55,700	$87,700
Health Technologists and Technicians	$42,300	$38,200
Other Marketing and Sales Occupations	$54,700	$86,700
Sales Occupations—Retail	$42,300	$53,700
Other Administrative Occupations	$38,200	$26,800

Employment Outlook

Employment in the health professions is expected to increase by more than one-fifth between 2008 and 2018 according to the most recent occupational projections produced by the U.S. Bureau of Labor Statistics. The employment level of pharmacists is expected to increase by about 46,000 or 17 percent over the entire projection period. Job prospects are expected to be excellent. Employers in many parts of the country report difficulty in attracting and retaining adequate numbers of pharmacists—primarily the result of the limited training capacity of Pharm.D. programs. In addition, as a larger percentage of pharmacists elects to work part-time, more individuals will be needed to fill the same number of prescriptions. Job openings also will result from faster-than-average employment growth

and from the need to replace workers who retire or leave the occupation for other reasons.

Other occupational areas of projected employment growth are presented in Table 6. Many of them have large workforces and will provide many job openings through turnover, even if the workforce is growing at a slower-than-average rate.

Pathways Beyond the Initial Degree

At the time the survey was conducted, the bachelor's degree in pharmacy was sufficient education for pharmacists, and therefore few grads pursued higher degrees. This probably remains true for graduates who now earn the Pharm.D.

Table 5
Percentage Distribution of Workers, by the Level of Job Satisfaction

Job Satisfaction	Pharmacy	All
Very satisfied	52.4	45.4
Somewhat satisfied	42.7	45.0
Somewhat dissatisfied	3.9	7.4
Very dissatisfied	1.1	2.2
Mean Score (4=very satisfied, 1=not satisfied at all)	3.5	3.3

Table 6

Projected Growth and Job Openings in the Top 5 Occupations Employing Persons with a Degree in Pharmacy

Top 5 Occupations	Projected Growth 2008–2018	Projected Annual Job Openings
All top 5	11.6%	593,420
Registered Nurses, Pharmacists, Dietitians, Therapists, Physician Assistants	21.5%	119,640
Health Technologists and Technicians	20.1%	35,070
Other Marketing and Sales Occupations	7.3%	64,880
Sales Occupations—Retail	7.5%	207,700
Other Administrative Occupations	10.8%	166,130

degree, although those who are interested in research may want to complete a Ph.D. degree.

The most popular graduate degrees at the time of the survey were in pharmacy, which accounted for 32 percent of the master's degrees, 30 percent of the doctorates, and 46 percent of the professional degrees.

Apart from pharmacy, business administration was the most popular master's degree at the time of the survey, attracting about 1 out 5 of those who proceeded to the masters. The degree has obvious value for pharmacists who want to move into management of a retail pharmacy or of the pharmacy department in a health-care facility.

CHAPTER 10

Physical Therapy

In comparison to some of the other majors described in this book, physical therapy program entrants need a good level of self-awareness as well as knowledge of the field before entering this major. High school seniors face one of the stiffest competitions of all collegiate programs with a demanding set of science prerequisites for entry into physical therapy. In addition, the work is physically demanding, requiring strength, the need to touch individuals, and good physical agility. This major also is an emotionally demanding field when physical therapists are working with difficult medical cases.

Physical therapists improve the mobility, relieve pain, and prevent or limit permanent physical disabilities of individuals suffering from injuries or disease. Patients can be accident victims; those with burns, heart disease, head injuries, fractures, or amputations; or people with cerebral palsy, multiple sclerosis, or nerve injuries. Work can be with the elderly, dealing with chronic debilitating conditions and arthritis. Many middle-age persons encounter trauma, strokes, and heart attacks, requiring rehabilitative services. Advances in technology enable more young children to survive birth defects, which also creates a need for care provided by physical therapists.

Before developing a treatment plan for a patient, physical therapists evaluate the patient's medical history to assess strength, range of motion, and functioning. Sometimes physical therapists will implement a physician's orders or delegate to a physical therapy assistant the carrying out of a treatment strategy. Treatment can involve exercise or use of electrical stimulation, hot and cold compresses, or ultrasound to relieve pain, improve the condition of muscles, or reduce swelling. Therapists may use traction or deep-tissue massage to restore function. They teach patients to use crutches, prostheses, and wheelchairs to perform daily activities and home exercises to facilitate recovery.

The specific program that undergraduates study is not important as long as applicants take appropriate courses and do well in them. Among the undergraduate courses that are useful when applying to a graduate program in physical therapy are anatomy, biology, chemistry, physics, social science, mathematics, and statistics. Before granting admission, many programs require volunteer experience in the physical therapy department of a hospital or clinic.

The field's accreditation association and requirements of the state licensure exam determine the postgraduate training physical therapists receive. The program is a combination of academic courses and supervised clinical hospital experience. Course work includes biology, chemistry, physics, biochemistry, neuroanatomy, human growth and development, disease and trauma manifestations, evaluation techniques, and therapeutics procedures.

Physical therapy applicants are excellent students in high school and have demonstrated scientific ability in mathematics and science courses. Classroom work and hands-on clinical applications require manual dexterity and motor coordination skills. Handling immobilized patients and their setup on machines requires mobility and physical stamina. Social and interpersonal skills are critical in motivating people and helping them understand treatments and procedures. These abilities also must be used with family members of patients.

Interests are primarily scientific, followed by social or humanitarian preferences. The scientific interests involve a combination of intellectual understanding with a preference for practical applications and a desire to see concrete results.

A diverse set of benefits can be achieved in physical therapy work. On the personal level, some employers accommodate flexible work schedules, and the pay is good. As well-accepted members of a medical team, physical therapists gain respect, status, and prestige within a community. On the work level, satisfaction can be gained through helping others, working with a variety of patients, and having patients recognize the therapist's use of his or her hands and machines in making them get better or offering them hope.

Note: In most other chapters, the discussion and the labels on the charts and tables refer to the kind of degree held by the survey respondents as "only a bachelor's degree." This chapter, however, avoids identifying the degree because the accepted minimal degree for physical therapists has changed. At the time of the survey on which this book is based, a bachelor's degree in physical therapy was acceptable. Only about 9 percent of the physical therapy grads went on to a graduate or professional degree in physical therapy. Now, however, the doctoral degree has become the standard credential for physical therapists. Any references to a bachelor's degree would give the misleading impression that this degree is still acceptable, so these references have been omitted from this chapter.

Where Do Physical Therapy Majors Work?

Businesses and corporations in the private, for-profit sector employ 45 percent. More than one-fifth are employed in the private, nonprofit sector. Thirteen percent of all employed physical

Table 1

Percentage Distribution of Employed Persons, by the Economic Sector, Size, and New Business Status of the Employer

	Physical Therapy	All
Economic Sector		
Private for-profit	44.9	47.3
Self-employed	13.2	18.5
Government/Military	8.5	11.0
Education	12.4	15.6
Nonprofit	21.1	7.5
Employer Size		
Small (Fewer than 100 employees)	33.3	35.5
Medium (100–999)	33.1	21.8
Large (1,000–24,999)	23.3	26.0
Very large (25,000 or more)	10.2	16.7
Percent working in new business established within past 5 years	6.3	7.6

Table 2
Percentage Distribution of Employed Persons with a Degree in Physical Therapy, by the Relationship Between Their Job and College Major

Relationship of Job to Major	Percent
Closely related	77.4
Somewhat related	9.7
Not related	12.8

Percent who report the following as the most important reasons for working in a job that was not related to major:

Family-related reasons	21.7
Job in highest degree field not available	20.4
Change in career or professional interests	16.8
Pay, promotion opportunities	15.4
Working conditions (hours, equipment, environment)	13.0

therapy graduates are self-employed in their own business or practice, and 12 percent work for educational institutions. The government sector employs less than 8 percent.

The skills and knowledge that physical therapy graduates acquire during their schooling are directly applicable in the labor market. Therefore, many graduates find jobs in their field. Slightly more than three-quarters are employed in jobs that are closely related to their major field of study. Another 10 percent are employed in jobs that are somewhat related to their major. Only 13 percent of physical therapy graduates work in jobs that are not related to their major field of study.

Out of all physical therapy graduates under 65 years old, 83 percent are employed. Of the remaining grads, 17 percent are out of the labor force; that is, they are not employed and are not seeking employment. A bit more than half of these are handling family responsibilities. Almost none (less than 1 percent) of the graduates are officially unemployed; that is, they are not employed and are actively seeking employment.

Occupations

The employment of physical therapy graduates is concentrated in very few occupations. More than 64 percent are employed in the health professions, mostly as therapists but also as nurses and physician assistants. About 5 percent work in other miscellaneous health-care occupations, and another 3 percent work in health technologies.

Work Activities

▶ More than 80 percent of employed physical therapy graduates spend at least 10 hours during a typical workweek providing professional services. About 65 percent report that they spend a majority of their typical workweek in these activities.

▶ Nine percent spend most of their time at work in management and administrative duties, and 55 percent spend a significant amount of time at these tasks.

Table 3
Top 5 Occupations Employing Persons with a Degree in Physical Therapy, by Percentage

Top 5 Occupations	All	Men	Women
Registered Nurses, Pharmacists, Dietitians, Therapists, Physician Assistants	64.4	61.1	65.3
Other Health Occupations	4.9	4.8	4.9
Health Technologists and Technicians	3.5	–	4.4
Personnel, Training, and Labor Relations Specialists	3.1	–	3.9
Sales/Marketing—Insurance, Securities, Real Estate, and Business Services	2.1	2.8	1.9
Total, Top 5 Occupations	78.0	68.7	80.4
Balance of Employed	22.0	31.3	19.6
All Employed	100.0	100.0	100.0

▶ Thirty-seven percent engage in employee relations during a significant portion of their typical workweek, and a similar share spend significant time teaching.

▶ Work with computer applications takes up a significant part of the workweek for 95 percent of physical therapy graduates, but only 2 percent spend most of their work time on these tasks.

▶ Of those physical therapy graduates who receive some training during the year, 82 percent receive technical training in the occupation in which they are employed.

▶ Eighteen percent receive training to improve their general professional skills, such as public speaking and business writing.

▶ Seventeen percent of the training recipients receive management or supervisory training.

Workplace Training and Other Work-Related Experiences

The career potential of a job is closely associated with the amount of work-related training on the job. Work-related training is regarded as an investment by firms because it makes workers more productive. The incidence of work-related training among physical therapy graduates is considerably higher than the rate of participation in work-related training among all college graduates. While 61 percent of all college graduates acquire some kind of work-related training during a year, 85 percent of physical therapy graduates engage in work-related training during a year.

Physical therapy graduates decide to participate in work-related training activities, workshops, or seminars for numerous reasons. When asked to select the one most important reason to acquire training, 52 percent of physical therapy graduates who undergo training identify the need to improve their occupational skills and knowledge. One-quarter report the need to obtain or maintain a professional license or certificate as the most important factor underlying their participation in work-related training. (Many states require continuing professional education for physical therapists.) According to 4 percent of the training participants, the most important reason to participate in training activities is that the employer requires it.

Salaries

The median annual salary of physical therapy graduates with only a bachelor's degree is $53,000, a level that is 3 percent higher than the median annual salary of all employed college graduates. On average, employed physical therapy graduates work for 37 hours per week and for 50 weeks per year, resulting in 1,850 hours of employment per year. The level of work effort among physical therapy graduates is 14 percent lower than the average among all college graduates (which is 43 hours per week and 50 weeks per year, resulting in 2,150 hours per year).

Note: Because of the very small number of survey respondents in some age groups, it was not possible to furnish a useful age/earnings profile graphic for this major.

Physical therapy graduates who work in jobs that are closely related to their undergraduate major earn an average of $56,800 annually. Graduates employed in somewhat related jobs earn $41,300 per year, and those whose jobs are unrelated to their undergraduate field of study average $51,600 per year.

Earning an average salary of $69,500 annually, the physical therapy graduates who are self-employed in their own practice earn a higher salary than those who are employed in other sectors of the economy. The remuneration of physical therapy graduates in the private, non-profit sector is $55,700 per year. The government sector pays physical therapy graduates $52,300 per year. In the private, not-for-profit sector and in educational institutions, graduates who work full-time average $51,600 per year.

The average annual salaries of physical therapy graduates and all college graduates in the top 5 occupations that predominantly employ physical therapy graduates are presented in Table 4.

▶ Nurses, pharmacists, therapists, and physician assistants with a degree in physical therapy earn $56,800 per year. This group of occupations employs 64 percent of graduates.

▶ The average annual salary of graduates employed in other miscellaneous health occupations is only $41,300 per year.

▶ The extremely low earnings figure reported for grads working as health technologists and technicians probably reflects the small (and entirely female) sample and the fact that the great majority of them have been working in that job for less than 3 years.

Table 4
Annual Salary of Workers, Top 5 Occupations (in 2010 Dollars)

Earnings in Top 5 Occupations	All	Physical Therapy
Total	$53,000	$54,000
Registered Nurses, Pharmacists, Dietitians, Therapists, Physician Assistants	$55,700	$56,800
Other Health Occupations	$35,100	$41,300
Health Technologists and Technicians	$42,300	$15,500
Personnel, Training, and Labor Relations Specialists	$53,700	$35,100
Sales/Marketing—Insurance, Securities, Real Estate, and Business Services	$67,100	$72,200

Table 5

Percentage Distribution of Workers with Only a Bachelor's Degree,
by Level of Job Satisfaction

Job Satisfaction	Physical Therapy	All
Very satisfied	54.8	45.4
Somewhat satisfied	41.0	45.0
Somewhat dissatisfied	3.3	7.4
Very dissatisfied	0.8	2.2
Mean Score (4=very satisfied, 1=not satisfied at all)	3.5	3.3

Job Satisfaction

The overall level of job satisfaction of physical therapy majors is considerably higher than the average for all graduates.

Employment Outlook

Employment in the health professions is expected to increase by more than 20 percent between 2008 and 2018 according to the most recent occupational projections produced by the U.S. Bureau of Labor Statistics. Job growth for physical therapists is expected to be even higher: 30 percent. Job opportunities will be good for licensed physical therapists in all settings. Job opportunities should be particularly good in acute hospital, skilled nursing, and orthopedic settings, where the elderly are most often treated. Job prospects should be especially favorable in rural areas, as many physical therapists tend to cluster in highly populated urban and suburban areas.

Other occupational areas of projected employment growth are presented in Table 6.

Pathways Beyond the Initial Degree

At the time the survey was conducted, the bachelor's degree in physical therapy was sufficient

Table 6

Projected Growth and Job Openings in the Top 5 Occupations Employing Persons
with Only a Degree in Physical Therapy

Top 5 Occupations	Projected Growth 2008–2018	Projected Annual Job Openings
All top 5	17.6%	311,830
Registered Nurses, Pharmacists, Dietitians, Therapists, Physician Assistants	21.5%	119,640
Other Health Occupations	24.5%	13,920
Health Technologists and Technicians	20.1%	35,070
Personnel, Training, and Labor Relations Specialists	25.1%	27,990
Sales/Marketing—Insurance, Securities, Real Estate, and Business Services	11.5%	115,210

education for physical therapists, and therefore less than one-quarter of grads pursued higher degrees of any kind. Now that the doctoral degree is becoming the standard credential, grads with this entry-level degree will have little reason to pursue additional higher education, although those who want to focus on managing a physical therapy practice may be interested in a master's in business administration.

CHAPTER 11

Psychology

Psychologists study the human mind and behavior. Research psychologists investigate the physical, cognitive, emotional, or social aspects of human behavior. Psychologists in applied fields, usually requiring post-baccalaureate study, provide mental-health care in hospitals, clinics, schools, or private settings.

Like other social scientists, psychologists formulate hypotheses and collect data to test the validity of the hypotheses. Research methods may vary depending on the topic under study. For example, psychologists sometimes gather information through controlled laboratory experiments, as well as through administering personality, performance, aptitude, and intelligence tests. Other methods include observation, interviews, questionnaires, clinical studies, and surveys.

Psychologists apply their knowledge to a wide range of endeavors, including health and human services, management, education, law, and sports. In addition to a variety of work settings, psychologists with advanced education generally specialize in one of a number of different areas. Clinical psychologists work in counseling centers; independent or group practices; or in health maintenance organizations, hospitals, or clinics. They help mentally or emotionally disturbed clients adjust in life and may help medical and surgical patients deal with their illnesses or injuries. Some work in physical rehabilitation settings, treating patients with spinal cord injuries, chronic pain or illness, stroke, arthritis, and neurologic conditions such as multiple sclerosis. Others help people deal with times of personal crisis, such as divorce or the death of a loved one.

Cognitive psychologists deal with memory, thinking, and perceptions. Some conduct research related to computer programming and artificial intelligence.

Developmental psychologists study the psychological development that takes place throughout life. Some specialize in behavior during infancy, childhood, and adolescence; changes that take place during maturity or old age; or developmental disabilities and their effects. Increasingly, researchers are developing ways to help elderly people stay as independent as possible.

Experimental or research psychologists work in university and private research centers and in business, nonprofit, and governmental organizations. They study behavior processes with human beings and animals such as rats, monkeys, and pigeons. Prominent areas of study in experimental research include motivation, thinking, attention, learning and memory, sensory and perceptual processes, effects of substance abuse, and genetic and neurological factors affecting behavior.

Industrial-organizational (I/O) psychologists apply psychological principles and research methods to the workplace in the interest of improving productivity and the quality of work life. They conduct applicant screening, training and development, counseling, and organizational development and analysis. Industrial psychologists might work with management to reorganize the work setting to improve productivity or quality of life in the workplace.

School psychologists work in elementary and secondary schools or school district offices with students, teachers, parents, and administrators to resolve students' learning and behavior problems. They collaborate with teachers, parents, and school personnel to improve classroom management strategies or parenting skills, counter substance abuse, work with students with disabilities or gifted and talented students, and improve teaching and learning strategies. They test students to measure their educational progress or to determine their career interests.

Social psychologists examine people's interactions with others and with the social environment. They work in organizational consultation, marketing research, systems design in organizational consultation, or other applied psychology fields.

Course work in psychology programs may include learning and motivation, developmental psychology, adult development and aging, social psychology, personality, cognition, industrial/organizational psychology, abnormal psychology, sensation, perception, behavioral theory, psychopharmacology, psychology of women, and child and adolescent psychology. Programs usually include several courses in statistics.

Abilities involved in psychology depend on the specialization. Experimental psychology might be best viewed from a scientist's perspective with quantitative and research methodologies prominent, often similar to those used in biology. Cognitive, developmental, and social psychology may best fit in with a social research grouping, with the social science research methodology predominating. Industrial/organizational psychology with its application emphasis combines the social science research focus with an orientation toward clinical personal

service. Clinical psychology, because of its individual service orientation in which services are mostly covered by health insurance, is a specialization completely different from traditional experimental psychology. The continuum is from experimental psychology, with abilities closer to those of a scientist, to clinical psychology, which uses people-oriented abilities that predominantly represent a practitioner-scientist orientation. Thus, the abilities required in psychology all depend on the area in which one specializes.

The interests of psychologists depend on the specialization. The following three interests predominate, but their order of prominence will vary with a specific specialization. Scientific interests are involved whether the specialization focuses on the physiology of the senses or on the current belief that genetics plays a definite role in mental illness or the intellect. Clinicians rely on linguistics to communicate in their therapy, and other psychological specializations are characterized by their breadth of interests that are typified by a liberal arts education. Lastly, while clinicians may emphasize a social orientation more than most other specialists, even the most scientific of psychologists see their work as having a social application.

The benefits of being a psychologist obviously are broad, depending on a psychologist's orientation. For example, a sampling of psychology majors valued, in descending order, working with people, having variety and diversion in their work, working with their minds, and earning a good salary. However, it is obvious that many human services jobs that psychology majors enter are not high paying. A group of employed clinical psychologists, on the other hand, responded foremost that they valued working with their minds, followed by their sense of independence, creativity, and variety and diversion.

A caution may be that the profile of people in this field can be distorted by the largest grouping of psychologists—clinical psychologists. As a group, they look for new ways of viewing issues or practicing. Personally, they are self-confident and imaginative when it comes to their practice. They seek understanding of the behavior and motives of others. They resist routine activity, which may mean that they do not follow the laboratory-based scientific methodology of their field. Thinking that their work is important and has a greater purpose can drive them; they have a belief in the ideal. They tend to be warm, relate to others easily, are not dependent on facts, and rely on their intuition in relationships. The latter obviously would not be true of many people in other specialties.

Another caution to keep in mind is that a bachelor's degree in psychology, which is the basis for the description of graduates that follows, does not qualify a person to work as a psychologist. A doctoral degree, plus licensure, usually is required for independent practice as a psychologist. People with a master's degree in psychology may work as industrial-organizational psychologists. They also may work as psychological assistants conducting research under the direct supervision of doctoral-level psychologists.

Where Do Psychology Majors Work?

Thirty-nine percent work for businesses and corporations in the private, for-profit sector. The government sector employs 17 percent, and about the same share are self-employed in their own business or practice. Fifteen percent of psychology majors work for educational institutions. The remaining 12 percent work in the private, nonprofit sector for tax-exempt or charitable organizations.

Roughly 30 percent of psychology grads with only a bachelor's work in jobs that are closely related to the field of psychology. This is not a high figure, but that's not surprising, because many jobs that are closely related to psychology require specialized skills such as those possessed by

Table 1

Percentage Distribution of Employed Persons with Only a Bachelor's Degree, by Economic Sector, Size, and New Business Status of Employer

	Psychology	All
Economic Sector		
Private for-profit	39.1	47.3
Self-employed	16.6	18.5
Government/Military	17.1	11.0
Education	15.3	15.6
Nonprofit	11.7	7.5
Employer Size		
Small (Fewer than 100 employees)	34.1	35.5
Medium (100–999)	24.3	21.8
Large (1,000–24,999)	26.3	26.0
Very large (25,000 or more)	15.3	16.7
Percent working in new business established within past 5 years	7.5	7.6

Table 2
Percentage Distribution of Employed Persons with Only a Bachelor's Degree in Psychology, by the Relationship Between Their Job and College Major

Relationship of Job to Major	Percent
Closely related	29.0
Somewhat related	33.0
Not related	38.0

Percent who report the following as the most important reasons for working in a job that was not related to major:

Pay, promotion opportunities	30.4
Change in career or professional interests	20.3
Family-related reasons	14.1
Working conditions (hours, equipment, environment)	11.4
Job in highest degree field not available	9.4

clinical, developmental, cognitive, experimental, or research psychologists with at least a master's degree. A bachelor's degree does not provide these specialized skills in psychology.

Rather, a bachelor's degree in psychology may provide general instruction in the field that can be utilized in marketing research, labor relations, or management and productivity improvement. These skills allow access to jobs that are somewhat related to the field of psychology. Another approximately 30 percent of the psychology grads hold jobs that are somewhat related to their field, and a slightly larger share of the graduates are employed in jobs that are unrelated to the field of psychology.

Out of all psychology graduates under the age of 65, 78 percent are employed. Only 4 percent are officially unemployed; that is, they are not employed and are actively seeking employment. The remaining grads—nearly one-fifth—are out of the labor force; that is, they are not employed and are not seeking employment. About 28 percent of the labor force withdrawals among psychology graduates are attributable to family commitments. Another 24 percent are for the sake of early retirement. Two out of 10 of those who have withdrawn say they have no need for work.

Occupations

The highest concentration of employed psychology gradates is in clerical/administrative occupations, which employ 7 percent of the graduates. Social work accounts for a slightly smaller share of grads. Six percent of psychology majors work in management-related occupations, and an equal share work in marketing and sales occupations. About 5 percent work in a group of health-care jobs.

Female psychology grads outnumber males by roughly two to one, and female grads dominate the top 5 occupations, with the major exception of the miscellaneous management-related jobs.

Table 3
Top 5 Occupations Employing Persons with Only a Bachelor's Degree in Psychology, by Percentage

Top 5 Occupations	All	Men	Women
Other Administrative Occupations	7.3	4.9	8.5
Social Workers	6.6	2.9	8.5
Other Management-Related Occupations	5.5	6.0	5.3
Other Marketing and Sales Occupations	5.3	4.8	5.6
Registered Nurses, Pharmacists, Dietitians, Therapists, Physician Assistants	4.6	1.8	6.0
Total, Top 5 Occupations	29.3	20.4	33.9
Balance of Employed	70.7	79.6	66.1
All Employed	100.0	100.0	100.0

Work Activities

▶ Nearly 56 percent said they regularly spend some time performing management and administrative duties, whereas 19 percent of employed psychology graduates typically spend most of their work time in performing these duties.

▶ While 35 percent of the graduates regularly engage in professional services such as health-care, counseling, and financial services, 18 percent say these duties typically consume most of their time at work.

▶ Fifty-one percent of employed psychology majors regularly engage in sales, purchasing, or marketing, but only 18 percent spend most of their work time at these duties.

▶ Another activity performed by employed psychology majors is teaching. Almost 10 percent of graduates spend a majority of time at work in teaching activities.

▶ Few psychology majors with only a bachelor's are engaged intensively or regularly in basic and applied research, because a graduate degree in the subject is usually required for those activities.

Workplace Training and Other Work-Related Experiences

The career potential of a job is closely associated with the amount of work-related training on the job. Work-related training is regarded as an investment by firms because it makes workers more productive. Sixty-three percent of employed psychology majors participate in work-related training at some time during the year. This is slightly higher than the 61 percent training participation rate among all employed college graduates.

▶ Of those psychology majors who received some training, 57 percent receive technical training in the occupation in which they are employed.

▶ Nineteen percent of the training recipients receive management or supervisor training.

More than one-fifth receive training to improve their general professional skills, such as public speaking and business writing.

When asked to identify the single most important reason to acquire training, 35 percent of psychology majors who undergo training identify the need to improve their occupational skills and knowledge. Another 11 percent report mandatory training requirements by the employer as the most important factor for their involvement in work-related training. Eight percent cite the need to learn skills to obtain a professional license or certificate as the main factor influencing their decision to undergo work-related training. According to 4 percent, the most important factor for their involvement in training is to improve their opportunities for a salary increase and promotion.

Salaries

The median annual salary of psychology graduates with only a bachelor's degree is $42,000, a level that is 23 percent lower than the median annual salary of all employed college graduates. On average, employed psychology graduates work for 40 hours per week and for 48 weeks per year, resulting in 1,920 hours of employment per year. The level of work effort among psychology graduates is 11 percent lower than the average among all college graduates (which is 43 hours per week and 50 weeks per year, resulting in 2,150 hours per year).

FIGURE 1

Age/Earnings Profile of Persons with Only a Bachelor's Degree in Psychology (Full-Time Workers, in 2010 Dollars)

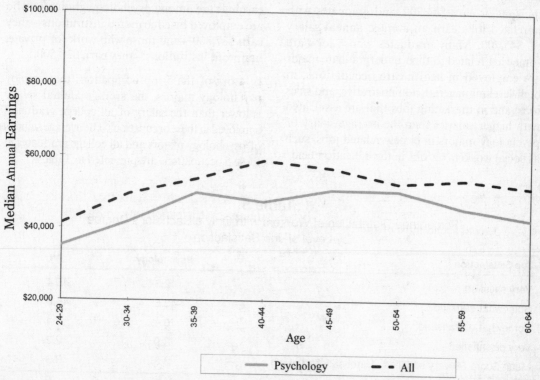

Table 4
Annual Salary of Workers with Only a Bachelor's Degree, Top 5 Occupations (in 2010 Dollars)

Earnings in Top 5 Occupations	All	Psychology
Total	$42,000	$45,800
Other Administrative Occupations	$38,200	$37,900
Social Workers	$36,100	$35,400
Other Management-Related Occupations	$57,800	$52,100
Other Marketing and Sales Occupations	$54,700	$60,100
Registered Nurses, Pharmacists, Dietitians, Therapists, Physician Assistants	$55,700	$54,700

The average annual salary of psychology majors who work in jobs that are closely related to their major field of study is lower than those who are employed in jobs that are somewhat related or not related to their major. Graduates who work in closely related jobs earn $40,100 per year. Those who work in jobs that are somewhat related to their major earn $44,700, and graduates with unrelated jobs earn an average annual salary of $45,700. Many graduates whose jobs are somewhat related to their undergraduate major are employed in health-care occupations; in high-level managerial, administrative, and sales jobs; and in marketing jobs that are associated with higher salaries than the average salary of psychology majors in closely related jobs, such as social workers or jobs in the education field.

The highest average annual salary of psychology majors is for graduates who are self-employed in their own practice or business. They earn $53,600 annually. In the private, for-profit sector they earn an average of $47,600 per year. The average salary of those who work in the government sector is $43,200 per year. The lowest earnings are among psychology graduates who are employed by educational institutions—they earn $37,800—and those who work for private, nonprofit institutions—they earn $36,500.

In 4 out of the 5 top occupations that employ psychology majors, the average annual salary is lower than the salary of all college graduates employed in these occupations. The average salaries of psychology majors and all college graduates in these 5 occupations are presented in Table 4.

Table 5
Percentage Distribution of Workers with Only a Bachelor's Degree, by Level of Job Satisfaction

Job Satisfaction	Psychology	All
Very satisfied	42.3	45.4
Somewhat satisfied	43.5	45.0
Somewhat dissatisfied	10.4	7.4
Very dissatisfied	3.9	2.2
Mean Score (4=very satisfied, 1=not satisfied at all)	3.3	3.3

Job Satisfaction

The overall level of job satisfaction of psychology majors is about the same as the average for all graduates.

Employment Outlook

Although the overall employment in the U.S. economy is projected to increase by 10.1 percent between 2008 and 2018, the demand for workers in occupations that usually require a bachelor's degree is expected to increase 17.0 percent. Growth projections vary widely among the top 5 occupations that are most likely to employ psychology graduates:

▸ The largest area of employment for psychology majors, miscellaneous administrative occupations, is projected to increase by 11 percent between 2008 and 2018 and open 166,000 jobs. This is a very large occupation with a large amount of turnover.

▸ Sixteen percent growth is projected for the second largest area of employment for psychology majors, social workers. Job prospects for social workers are expected to be favorable. Many job openings will stem from growth and the need to replace social workers who leave the occupation. However, competition for social worker jobs is expected in cities where training programs for social workers are prevalent. Opportunities should be good in rural areas, which often find it difficult to attract and retain qualified staff. By specialty, job prospects may be best for those social workers with a background in gerontology and substance abuse treatment. Keep in mind that a master's degree in social work is now expected by some employers.

▸ Employment in the miscellaneous managerial and marketing occupations that employ a large share of psychology grads is projected to grow by 7 percent, creating more than 110,000 job openings.

▸ The collection of health-care occupations that includes many psychology grads is projected to grow by 21 percent and create 119,000 job openings, but this set of occupations is so diverse that it is unclear how much opportunity will be available for psychology grads.

Table 6

Projected Growth and Job Openings in the Top 5 Occupations
Employing Persons with Only a Bachelor's Degree in Psychology

Top 5 Occupations	Projected Growth 2008–2018	Projected Annual Job Openings
All top 5	12.6%	430,130
Other Administrative Occupations	10.8%	166,130
Social Workers	16.1%	26,460
Other Management-Related Occupations	7.2%	53,020
Other Marketing and Sales Occupations	7.3%	64,880
Registered Nurses, Pharmacists, Dietitians, Therapists, Physician Assistants	21.5%	119,640

Pathways Beyond the Bachelor's Degree

An impressive 47 percent of psychology graduates with a bachelor's degree proceed to earn a postgraduate degree: one-third earn a master's degree, but doctoral or professional degrees are earned by only about 7 percent each.

▶ Roughly equal shares of the master's degrees, around 13 percent, are earned in the fields of social work and counseling psychology. The master's is sufficient education for a social worker, but a doctorate is necessary to work independently as a professional counseling psychologist.

▶ Thirty percent of the psych grads who earn the doctorate do so in clinical psychology. This level of education is appropriate for practicing in this field, although it should be understood that preparation includes not just course work but also supervised clinical practice. Another 9 percent of the grads earn their doctorate in each of two other fields: counseling psychology and experimental psychology.

▶ Among the small number of psychology grads who earn a professional degree, 43 percent earn it in law. Another 28 percent earn it in the health professions, such as medicine, dentistry, optometry, osteopathy, podiatry, or veterinary.

PART 3

Business and Administration

CHAPTER 12

Accounting

Accounting is a facet of managerial responsibility. It is the set of rules and methods by which financial and economic data are collected, processed, and summarized into reports that then can be used to make decisions. Accountants measure and communicate information about an organization's operations by recording (although accountants do not perform the clerical and mechanical process of keeping records), classifying data into categories, analyzing, summarizing, and presenting information in financial terms. Accountants examine, deal with, and account for all transactions, which are any business events that are both financial and measurable. Examples of transactions are credit sales, cash receipts, tax payments, buying inventory, selling stocks, financing short- or long-term debt, and writing off uncollectable debt. Accountants touch many aspects of a business or organization, from cost or profit analysis to budgeting to involvement with management information systems.

Unlike teachers and physicians, who work mostly in the education and health-care fields, respectively, accountants can work in all kinds of businesses and industries, accommodating diverse personal interests. Accounting is not a static career. Newly graduated accountants should expect job mobility. For example, beginning management accountants often start as cost accountants, junior internal auditors, or trainees for other accounting jobs before reaching a specific career goal. It is very important that accountants maintain high standards, adhering to regulations, laws, and accepted practices, because of the millions of people who rely on their main work—producing financial statements and monitoring information systems. Some accountants also fulfill multiple work roles, such as financial advising, selling insurance, and working with bankruptcy or financial services such as stocks and bonds. Those involved in preparing taxes must expect to encounter the stress and pressures of working overtime at certain times of the year to produce the figures needed for reports and tax returns.

In general, the level of responsibility that accountants provide is directly related to the amount of their educational experience. The field has a progressive educational system leading to certification or licensure, especially in the field of public accounting. Introductory courses include cost and tax accounting, auditing theory and procedures, finance, economics, and information systems.

Beyond the obvious mathematical skill accountants use, they also need the ability to analyze, compare, and interpret facts and figures quickly and accurately. Good oral and written communication skills are essential, whether it be to prepare financial reports or to convey information to clients and management. They must be skilled with using computers and software packages to incorporate work efficiencies and be capable of the creative thinking needed to design financial or economic systems. An often forgotten skill is that accountants must purge previously learned rules and regulations and learn new and more-complex processes because of changing laws and regulations.

Accountants' interests include working with numbers and being able to categorize tasks in orderly and systematic ways to reach practical fiscal solutions. Accountants play a role in leading or influencing either an individual's or organization's fiscal decisions. They prefer to pay attention to detail and be accurate. Budgeting, financing, monitoring monetary fiscal operations, and making money are interests as well as means to afford accountants a sense of power within organizations and give them a source of satisfaction from the reactions of their clients.

Accountants value work that requires mental stimulation, affording a feeling of high achievement and prestige, which is rewarded with a good salary. Their practical, matter-of-fact orientation and dependability follow from a preference for organizing and running things. Accountants report that important parts of their job are working with people, being involved in a variety of situations to seek fiscal solutions by creating an awareness of financial options, prioritizing choices, and being sensitive to each client's values as they convey their professional analysis of each client's financial situation.

Where Do Accounting Majors Work?

Almost 58 percent of accounting majors work as wage and salary employees in private, for-profit businesses and corporations. Frequently, graduates with degrees in accounting are self-employed; a bit more than one-fifth of graduates in the major own their own businesses or provide consulting services on a self-employed basis. (The work of consultants is described in Chapter 16.) About 10 percent of persons with an accounting degree work in government jobs. Few majors (6 percent) work for nonprofit charities or foundations, and even fewer (4 percent) work in education.

Almost two-thirds of accounting grads work in a job that's closely related to the major. Another 23 percent work in a job that is somewhat related. Only 13 percent of accounting majors are employed in a job not related to the accounting field. Those employed in unrelated jobs earn 30

Table 1
Percentage Distribution of Employed Persons with Only a Bachelor's Degree, by Economic Sector, Size, and New Business Status of Employer

	Accounting	All
Economic Sector		
Private for-profit	57.9	47.3
Self-employed	22.0	18.5
Government/Military	10.2	11.0
Education	3.8	15.6
Nonprofit	5.9	7.5
Employer Size		
Small (Fewer than 100 employees)	40.0	35.5
Medium (100–999)	22.2	21.8
Large (1,000–24,999)	22.4	26.0
Very large (25,000 or more)	15.4	16.7
Percent working in new business established within past 5 years	9.2	7.6

Table 2

Percentage Distribution of Employed Persons with Only a Bachelor's Degree in Accounting, by the Relationship Between Their Job and College Major

Relationship of Job to Major	Percent
Closely related	63.6
Somewhat related	23.4
Not related	13.0

Percent who report the following as the most important reasons for working in a job that was not related to major:

Change in career or professional interests	25.4
Pay, promotion opportunities	18.8
Job in highest degree field not available	15.0
Working conditions (hours, equipment, environment)	11.4
Other reason	11.2

percent less than those employed in jobs that use the skills they developed in their major. Nevertheless, almost one-fifth of these workers took an unrelated job primarily because of opportunities for pay or promotion.

When asked the most important reason they left the field of their major, one-quarter say it was because of a change in their career or professional interests. Another 15 percent were unable to find work in their degree field.

Eighty-six percent of accounting majors under the age of 65 are employed; of those, 92 percent are in full-time positions. Only 3 percent are unemployed and looking for work. Of those 11 percent who are not working and not seeking work, slightly more than one-third have taken early retirement. Another one-quarter are out of the workforce to meet family responsibilities.

Occupations

A very large number of graduates of bachelor's degree programs in accounting are employed as accountants, auditors, and other financial specialists. Almost 46 percent of all accounting graduates are employed in this group of occupations. Additionally, about 12 percent of persons with a bachelor's degree in accounting are employed in management and supervisory occupations, often in a related business area. Thus, well over half of all those with a bachelor's degree in the field work in just two occupational areas. The remaining majors are spread out over a number of occupations, mostly working as accounting and insurance clerks or in other clerical and administrative jobs.

Forty-two percent of the grads are women. The male grads are somewhat more likely to hold managerial positions, and women are more likely to work as accountants or accounting clerks.

Work Activities

▶ Clearly, accounting, contracting, and financial duties play a central role in the jobs of accounting program graduates, with more than half reporting that these are the major duties associated with their positions. More than 8 out of 10 report that these duties consume at least 10 hours out of their typical workweek.

▶ Management and administration are important job responsibilities for many persons who graduate from college with a degree in accounting. For 6 out of 10 grads, these responsibilities are significant, and for 14 percent they are paramount.

▶ Computer skills are another important part of the skills required in these jobs, and a high number of accounting majors either develop or use various computer applications on the job. For 86 percent of grads, these tasks occupy significant work time, but only 7 percent focus mainly on these tasks.

Workplace Training and Other Work-Related Experiences

Those who earn a degree in accounting continue to upgrade and develop work-based skills. About 61 percent of those with a degree in the field participate in some type of work-related training activity over the course of a year, a share that matches the training participation rate of all college graduates.

▶ Much of the training of persons in this field is focused on developing professional skills that enable individuals to keep current with changes in tax codes, rules and regulations, and accounting procedures. Fifty-two percent of those getting training focus on this subject area, and 30 percent said that upgrading these skills is the single most important reason for getting training.

▶ Twenty-three percent receive training to improve their general professional skills, such as public speaking and business writing.

▶ Another 23 percent of the grads get training that focuses on management and supervision, but only about 3 percent sought training primarily to increase their opportunities for promotion or a higher salary.

▶ Roughly 17 percent cite licensure or certification as the most important reason for getting training. Nearly all states require CPAs and other public accountants to complete a certain number of hours of continuing professional education before their licenses can be renewed.

Table 3
Top 5 Occupations Employing Persons with Only a Bachelor's Degree in Accounting, by Percentage

Top 5 Occupations	All	Men	Women
Accountants, Auditors, and Other Financial Specialists	45.8	42.0	51.7
Top-Level Managers, Executives, and Administrators	7.1	9.0	4.0
Other Management-Related Occupations	4.6	5.3	3.5
Accounting Clerks and Bookkeepers	4.1	2.5	6.4
Other Administrative	3.7	3.3	4.3
Total, Top 5 Occupations	65.3	62.2	69.9
Balance of Employed	34.7	37.8	30.1
All Employed	100.0	100.0	100.0

Salaries

The median annual salary of accounting graduates with only a bachelor's degree is $60,000, a level that is 14 percent higher than the median annual salary of all employed college graduates. On average, employed accounting graduates worked for 42 hours per week for 50 weeks per year, resulting in 2,100 hours of employment each year. The level of work effort among accounting graduates is 2 percent lower than the average among all college graduates (which is 43 hours per week and 50 weeks per year, resulting in 2,150 hours per year).

Accounting majors who are self-employed have average annual earnings of $66,100 per year. Those who work as employees of for-profit companies earn an average salary of $61,900 per year. In government organizations, the earnings average $56,700. Employment in the not-for-profit sector brings in a salary that averages $53,700 per year. Lowest earnings are in education, where $42,900 is the annual average.

For graduates of most professional fields of study, access to a job that utilizes the skills acquired in the major while in school results in substantially higher earnings. However, the average annual salary of accounting graduates who work in closely related jobs is $62,900, whereas a higher average is reported for graduates in jobs that are somewhat related to their major: $65,000 per year. It is likely that the higher figure is based largely on the earnings of those grads who have gone into management and therefore

FIGURE 1

Age/Earnings Profile of Persons with Only a Bachelor's Degree in Accounting (Full-Time Workers, in 2010 Dollars)

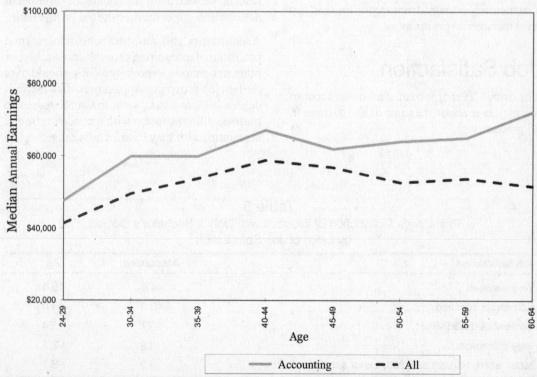

Table 4
Annual Salary of Workers with Only a Bachelor's Degree, Top 5 Occupations (in 2010 Dollars)

Earnings in Top 5 Occupations	All	Accounting
Total	$60,000	$65,700
Accountants, Auditors, and Other Financial Specialists	$59,900	$61,900
Top-Level Managers, Executives, and Administrators	$103,200	$118,700
Accounting Clerks and Bookkeepers	$31,000	$33,000
Other Management-Related Occupations	$57,800	$69,100
Other Administrative Occupations	$38,200	$40,200

are earning more even as their work is less closely related to their major. On the other hand, for those graduates employed full-time in a job that is not related to their field of study, the average salary is only $43,300.

Table 4 shows that an accounting degree produces income advantages in all of the top 5 occupations employing accounting grads, with a particularly strong advantage for those in top-level managerial positions.

Job Satisfaction

The overall level of job satisfaction of accounting majors is about the same as the average for all graduates.

Employment Outlook

Employment levels in the accounting occupation are expected to grow rapidly. Between 2008 and 2018, the demand for accountants, auditors, and other financial specialists is expected to increase by nearly 19 percent, with 127,000 job openings each year. This compares favorably to the 17.7 percent projected for all bachelor's-level occupations. Job opportunities should be favorable.

Accountants and auditors who have earned professional recognition through certification or other designation, especially a CPA, should have the best job prospects. Applicants with a master's degree in accounting or a master's degree in business administration with a concentration in accounting also may have an advantage.

Table 5
Percentage Distribution of Workers with Only a Bachelor's Degree, by Level of Job Satisfaction

Job Satisfaction	Accounting	All
Very satisfied	44.6	45.4
Somewhat satisfied	45.8	45.0
Somewhat dissatisfied	7.7	7.4
Very dissatisfied	1.9	2.2
Mean Score (4=very satisfied, 1=not satisfied at all)	3.3	3.3

Individuals who are proficient in accounting and auditing computer software and information systems or have expertise in specialized areas—such as international business, international financial reporting standards, or current legislation—may have an advantage in getting some accounting and auditing jobs. In addition, employers increasingly seek applicants with strong interpersonal and communication skills. Many accountants work on teams with others who have different backgrounds, so they must be able to communicate accounting and financial information clearly and concisely. Regardless of qualifications, however, competition will remain keen for the most prestigious jobs in major accounting and business firms.

Managerial and administrative occupations (other occupations in which a substantial proportion of accounting majors are employed) are expected to grow more slowly. Top-level management occupations are not expected to grow at all, but they still will create more than 61,000 job openings because of turnover.

Pathways Beyond the Bachelor's Degree

About one-fifth of accounting majors continue their formal education after completing courses for the bachelor's. For CPA candidates, almost all states require an additional 30 semester hours beyond the 120 that are typical for the bachelor's degree, so it's not surprising that 17 percent of accounting grads earn a master's degree. Of these, one-third get the degree in business administration and management, another 27 percent in accounting, and almost 16 percent in financial management.

Very few accounting grads proceed to a doctoral or professional degree. For example, less than 1 percent earn a doctorate in accounting, and only 2 percent earn a law degree.

Table 6
Projected Growth and Job Openings in the Top 5 Occupations
Employing Persons with Only a Bachelor's Degree in Accounting

Top 5 Occupations	Projected Growth 2008–2018	Projected Annual Job Openings
All occupations	10.1%	5,093,000
All top 5	10.6%	410,850
Accountants, Auditors, and Other Financial Specialists	18.9%	127,260
Top-Level Managers, Executives, and Administrators	−0.4%	61,470
Accounting Clerks and Bookkeepers	5.8%	2,970
Other Management-Related Occupations	7.2%	53,020
Other Administrative Occupations	10.8%	166,130

CHAPTER 13

Applied Mathematics, Operations Research, and Statistics

Mathematics can be highly abstract, but the focus of this major is on real-world applications of mathematical ideas. People who use applied mathematics on the job include operations research analysts (sometimes called management science analysts), actuarial scientists, and statisticians. Statisticians apply mathematics to the collection, analysis, interpretation, and presentation of numerical data. They design surveys and experiments; they also collect the data and interpret the results. They can obtain information about a group of people or things by surveying small samples of a larger group, such as to predict the winners in political elections or to determine what television programs people are watching, mostly to set the cost of advertisements. Almost every profession or industry applies statistical techniques for some purpose—for example, to determine how much radiation exposure in a cancer treatment is harmful or to make decisions about the growth or slowdown of the economy.

Operations research analysts are problem solvers who apply mathematical principles to organizational issues such as forecasting, resource allocation, facility layout, inventory control, personnel scheduling, and distribution systems. They use a mathematical model consisting of a set of equations that explain how things work. Use of models enables analysts to break down problems into their component parts, assign numerical values to each, and determine the mathematical relationships between them. Analysts can change values to examine what will happen under different circumstances and arrive at the best course of action. Consider these examples: Hospital staff examine admissions and length of patient stay, assign personnel to shifts, and monitor the use of pharmacy and laboratory services to forecast demand for added hospital services. Airline personnel study the cities served, the amount of fuel required to fly the routes, projected passenger demand, varying ticket and fuel prices, pilot schedules, and maintenance costs to produce the best flight schedules.

Actuarial scientists are involved mostly in work for insurance and investment firms dealing with risk management, pricing decisions, and investment strategies. Actuaries assemble and analyze statistics to calculate the probabilities of death, sickness, injury, retirement income level, property loss, and return on investment. For example, they can calculate the probability of claims due to automobile accidents; these claims can vary depending on the insured's age, sex, driving history, and type of car. These calculations help ensure that the price the company sets for insurance will enable the company to pay the expenses of all claims, while allowing the company to be profitable as well as competitive with other companies selling the same insurance.

Many colleges urge or require mathematics majors to take a course or even a double major in an allied field, such as computer science, engineering, economics, or one of the other sciences. The mathematics courses usually required are calculus, differential equations, and linear and abstract algebra. In the case of actuarial science, more than 100 colleges and universities offer a program, and some companies will hire mathematics grads with probability and statistics course work. The actuarial science curriculum can include accounting, finance, insurance, and economics courses. Two professional societies have examinations leading to full status as actuaries. As actuaries study, pass exams, and upgrade their professional standing, they also increase their salaries.

Table 1

Percentage Distribution of Employed Persons with Only a Bachelor's Degree, by Economic Sector, Size, and New Business Status of Employer

	Applied Mathematics	All
Economic Sector		
Private for-profit	54.8	47.3
Self-employed	16.5	18.5
Government/Military	9.8	11.0
Education	15.3	15.6
Nonprofit	2.7	7.5
Employer Size		
Small (Fewer than 100 employees)	35.8	35.5
Medium (100–999)	17.3	21.8
Large (1,000–24,999)	29.9	26.0
Very large (25,000 or more)	17.0	16.7
Percent working in new business established within past 5 years	6.5	7.6

Where Do Applied Mathematics, Operations Research, and Statistics Majors Work?

Seven out of 10 applied mathematics graduates work in the private, for-profit sector, either for businesses and corporations or as self-employed workers in their own businesses or practices. More than half work for businesses and corporations, and 16 percent are self-employed. (The work of consultants is described in Chapter 16.) About 16 percent of graduates are employed by educational institutions, and another 10 percent work in the government sector. Only 3 percent of all employed applied mathematics graduates work for private, nonprofit organizations.

Applied mathematics includes operations research analysis, actuarial science, and statistics. A number of applied mathematics graduates may not use all of these specific skills on the job but rather use their general aptitude with numbers and ability to perform quantitative analyses.

This fact is evident in the proportion of applied mathematics majors who are working in a job that is closely related to their undergraduate major and the proportion who find their jobs to be only somewhat related to their major. Whereas only about 36 percent of applied mathematics graduates consider their job to be closely related to their major, 41 percent find their job to be somewhat but not closely related to their undergraduate major.

When asked to select the most important reason for employment outside their major field of study, 35 percent of the graduates say the reason is better pay and promotion opportunities. Seventeen percent of applied mathematics graduates who work in unrelated jobs consider the working environment to be the driving force behind their employment choice. Fifteen percent rank a change in their career interests as the number one reason.

Out of all applied math graduates under the age of 65, 84 percent are employed, and 2 percent are officially unemployed; that is, they are not employed and are actively seeking employment. The remaining grads are out of the labor force;

Table 2
Percentage Distribution of Employed Persons with Only a Bachelor's Degree in Applied Mathematics, Operations Research, and Statistics, by the Relationship Between Their Job and College Major

Relationship of Job to Major	Percent
Closely related	35.8
Somewhat related	41.2
Not related	22.9

Percent who report the following as the most important reasons for working in a job that was not related to major:

Pay, promotion opportunities	34.7
Working conditions (hours, equipment, environment)	17.5
Change in career or professional interests	14.7
Job location	11.0
Family-related reasons	9.4

Table 3
Top 5 Occupations Employing Persons with Only a Bachelor's Degree in Applied Mathematics, Operations Research, and Statistics, by Percentage

Top 5 Occupations	All	Men	Women
Actuaries	7.6	7.5	7.7
Other Management-Related Occupations	6.9	6.1	8.3
Computer Engineers—Software	6.3	8.4	2.4
Computer Systems Analysts	5.5	6.0	4.6
Other Administrative Occupations	5.1	3.6	8.1
Total, Top 5 Occupations	31.4	31.6	31.1
Balance of Employed	68.6	68.4	68.9
All Employed	100.0	100.0	100.0

that is, they are not employed and are not seeking employment. One-third of the labor force withdrawals among economics graduates are attributable to early retirement. Another one-fifth happen because of family commitments.

Occupations

Applied mathematics graduates are employed mostly in computer-related and managerial jobs, but within the top 5 occupations, the employment of applied mathematics graduates is quite dispersed. The greatest concentration is in the computer-related occupations, with nearly 12 percent of the graduates employed: 6 percent as software engineers and 5 percent as systems analysts. The second-highest concentration of applied mathematics graduates is in the actuarial field. About 8 percent work as actuaries, a field that is closely related to this major. Miscellaneous management- and administration-related occupations employ 12 percent of applied mathematics graduates.

Men account for about 6 out of 10 applied math grads. Male and female grads are about equally likely to be in jobs as actuaries. Within the computer-related occupations, however, male grads have a much stronger presence, and female grads have a better showing in the managerial and administrative jobs.

Work Activities

▶ Given this field's emphasis on number-crunching, it is hardly surprising to find that 23 percent of grads spend most of their time in computer applications, programming, and systems-development activities. Two-thirds identify these activities as important.

▶ One-fifth say that managerial and administrative duties engage them for the major part of their typical workweek, and 56 percent spend significant time on these tasks.

▶ Employee relations take up a significant part of the workweek for 38 percent of the grads, although less than 1 percent see this as their chief duty.

▶ Accounting, financial, and contractual duties typically consume at least one-tenth of the workweek for 38 percent of all employed applied mathematics graduates, but only 7 percent have these duties as their primary responsibility.

▶ Although only 4 percent of all applied mathematics majors typically spend most of their workweek in design activities, 35 percent spend significant time on these tasks.

Workplace Training and Other Work-Related Experiences

The career potential of a job is closely associated with the amount of work-related training on the job. Work-related training is regarded as an investment by firms because it makes workers more productive. Firms that invest in their workforce are more likely to offer pay increases and promotions to match the increasing productivity of their workers. The incidence of work-related training among applied mathematics graduates is significantly lower than the rate of participation in work-related training among all college graduates. While 61 percent of all college graduates acquire some kind of work-related training during a year, 51 percent of applied mathematics majors engage in work-related training. One reason for this low rate of on-the-job training is that actuaries advance their professional status by studying for and passing exams.

▶ Of those applied mathematics graduates who receive some training, 45 percent receive technical training in the occupation in which they are employed.

▶ Seventeen percent receive training to improve their general professional skills, such as public speaking and business writing.

▶ Sixteen percent of the training recipients participate in management or supervisory training.

When asked to identify the most important reason to acquire training, 30 percent of applied mathematics graduates who undergo training identify the need to improve their occupational skills and knowledge. Another 6 percent report mandatory training requirements by the employer as the most important factor underlying their involvement in work-related training. For the same share, 6 percent, the most important reason for training is to meet the requirements of licensure or certification. Another 4 percent are motivated primarily by the desire to increase opportunities for promotion or higher salary.

Salaries

The median annual salary of applied mathematics, operations research, and statistics graduates with only a bachelor's degree is $62,800, a level that is 18 percent higher than the median annual salary of all employed college graduates. On average, employed applied mathematics, operations research, and statistics graduates worked for 41 hours per week for 50 weeks per year, resulting in 2,050 hours of employment each year. The level of work effort among applied mathematics, operations research, and statistics graduates is 5 percent lower than the average among all college graduates (which is 43 hours per week and 50 weeks per year, resulting in 2,150 hours per year).

Note: Because of the very small number of survey respondents in some age groups, it was not possible to furnish a useful age/learnings profile graphic for this major.

The average annual salary of applied mathematics majors who work in jobs that are closely related to their major is higher than the average salaries of those who are employed in jobs that are somewhat related to their major. Closely related jobs pay full-time employed applied mathematics graduates $67,000 annually. Graduates employed in somewhat related jobs earn $58,900 annually. Those whose jobs are unrelated to applied mathematics earn $66,600 per year, almost as much as the earnings of those in closely related jobs.

Some differences exist in the average annual salaries of applied mathematics majors by the

Table 4
Annual Salary of Workers with Only a Bachelor's Degree, Top 5 Occupations (in 2010 Dollars)

Earnings in Top 5 Occupations	All	Applied Mathematics
Total	$62,800	$75,200
Actuaries	$92,900	$87,800
Other Management-Related Occupations	$57,800	$58,000
Computer Engineers—Software	$82,600	$90,400
Computer Systems Analysts	$72,200	$83,900
Other Administrative Occupations	$38,200	$51,000

sector in which they are employed. Graduates who work for businesses and corporations in the private, for-profit sector earn $67,000 annually. The second-highest earnings accrue to applied mathematics graduates who are self-employed in their own businesses or practices, with average earnings of $64,300 annually. Grads who work for nonprofit enterprises average $63,900 per year. In the government sector, the average annual salary is $55,400. Educational institutions pay full-time applied mathematics graduates only $36,200 per year on average.

There are sizable variations in the average annual salaries of applied mathematics graduates by the occupation in which they are employed:

- Actuaries who are applied mathematics majors earn $87,800 annually.

- Applied mathematics graduates employed as software engineers earn an average annual salary of $90,400.

- Those working in miscellaneous administrative jobs average only $51,000 per year.

Job Satisfaction

The overall level of job satisfaction of applied mathematics, operations research, and statistics majors is about the same as the average for all graduates.

Table 5
Percentage Distribution of Workers with Only a Bachelor's Degree, by Level of Job Satisfaction

Job Satisfaction	Applied Mathematics	All
Very satisfied	41.4	45.4
Somewhat satisfied	49.0	45.0
Somewhat dissatisfied	6.4	7.4
Very dissatisfied	3.1	2.2
Mean Score (4=very satisfied, 1=not satisfied at all)	3.3	3.3

Employment Outlook

According to the projections by the U.S. Bureau of Labor Statistics, employment in occupations that require a bachelor's degree is expected to grow by 17.7 percent between 2008 and 2018, much faster than the 10.1 percent projected for the American labor market as a whole. The employment growth projections for 4 out of the top 5 occupations that are most likely to employ applied mathematics graduates are above the average rate of growth.

▶ The fastest growth in demand is projected for two of the computer-related occupations. The demand for computer software engineers is projected to grow by 32.5 percent between 2008 and 2018, creating 37,000 job openings annually. Job prospects for computer software engineers should be excellent. Those with practical experience and at least a bachelor's degree in a computer-related field should have the best opportunities. Employers will continue to seek computer professionals with strong programming, systems analysis, interpersonal, and business skills.

▶ Computer systems analysts will see employment increase by one-fifth, with 22,000 job openings annually. As with other information technology jobs, employment growth may be tempered somewhat by offshoring. Firms may look to cut costs by shifting operations to foreign countries with lower prevailing wages and highly skilled workers. However, due to the high level of expertise that is required, as well as the frequent need to be near the job site, systems analysts are less likely to be offshored than other IT occupations. On balance, job prospects should be excellent.

▶ Actuaries is a fast-growing occupation, with 21.3 percent growth projected. However, this is a fairly small occupation, with low turnover, so it should account for only 1,000 job openings each year. In addition, job seekers are likely to face competition because the number of job openings is expected to be less than the number of qualified applicants. College graduates who have passed two of the initial exams and completed an internship should enjoy the best prospects. The best employment opportunities should be in consulting firms.

Table 6
Projected Growth and Job Openings in the Top 5 Occupations
Employing Persons with Only a Bachelor's Degree in
Applied Mathematics, Operations Research, and Statistics

Top 5 Occupations	Projected Growth 2008–2018	Projected Annual Job Openings
All occupations	10.1%	5,093,000
All top 5	13.3%	279,610
Actuaries	21.3%	1,000
Other Management-Related Occupations	7.2%	53,020
Computer Engineers—Software	32.5%	37,180
Computer Systems Analysts	20.3%	22,280
Other Administrative Occupations	10.8%	166,130

▶ The miscellaneous management occupations employing applied math grads are projected to grow by only 7.2 percent but will create 53,000 job openings annually.

▶ The miscellaneous administrative occupations will grow only slightly faster than the average for all occupations, but because of a large workforce size and high turnover, they will create 166,000 job openings each year.

Pathways Beyond the Bachelor's Degree

Of all graduates with a bachelor's degree in applied mathematics, 34 percent proceed to earn a postgraduate degree: 26 percent earn a master's degree, 7 percent earn a doctoral degree, but only 2 percent earn a professional degree.

Sixteen percent of all master's degrees earned by undergraduate applied mathematics majors are in the field of business administration and management. The next most popular fields are statistics and computer science, each of which account for 11 percent of the master's degrees earned by applied math grads.

Twenty-three percent of the doctoral degrees earned by applied mathematics grads are in the field of statistics.

CHAPTER 14

Economics

Economics is the study of the allocation of resources and the production, distribution, and consumption of goods and services. Economists examine how societies produce and exchange goods and services to satisfy material needs. They analyze the process of economic growth and change and identify policies that contribute to its success or failure. Most economists are concerned with the applications of economic policy in a particular area such as finance, labor, agriculture, transportation, energy, or health. Others develop theories to explain phenomena such as unemployment or inflation.

Economists conduct research, collect and analyze data, monitor economic trends, and develop forecasts such as energy costs, interest rates, and the amount of imports. They use their understanding of economic relationships to advise businesses and other organizations, including insurance companies, banks, securities firms, industry and trade associations, labor unions, and government agencies. Economists use mathematical models to develop programs predicting answers to questions such as the nature and length of business cycles, the effects of a specific rate of inflation on the economy, or the effects of tax legislation on unemployment levels.

Economists devise methods and procedures for obtaining the data they need. For example, they may use sampling techniques to design a survey and various mathematical modeling techniques to develop forecasts. Preparing reports on the results of their research is an important part of the economist's job. Relevant data must be reviewed and analyzed, applicable tables and charts prepared, and the results presented in clear, concise language that can be understood by noneconomists. Presenting economic and statistical concepts in a meaningful way is particularly important for economists whose research is directed toward making policies for an organization. For example, an economist working in state or local government might analyze data on the growth of school-aged populations, prison growth, and employment and unemployment rates to project spending needs for future years.

College course work may include macroeconomics, microeconomics, medical economics, economics of crime, labor economics, women in the labor market, income inequalities and discrimination, environmental economics, comparative economics, government finance, and managerial economics. Quantitative skills are very important, so mathematics, statistics, econometrics, sampling theory, and survey design courses are often taken.

Undergraduate economics students report that they have interpersonal, leadership, mathematical, and computational abilities. Job analyses also mention understanding and use of appropriate theories and methods, as well as accuracy in processing data. Persistence is required because much time is spent independently, and analysis does involve problem solving. Verbal and oral communication skills are necessary so that economists can present findings in a clear and meaningful way.

Quantitative activities dominate economists' interests. Whether it be mathematical modeling or the presentation of research findings numerically, mathematical interests are high. Economists also are noted for their breadth of interests and should not be pigeon-holed as entirely business-oriented. Economics as a discipline fits well within the breadth and diversity of the liberal arts tradition. Economics is a social science that searches for answers to societal issues.

Economists value earning a good salary and gaining a sense of high achievement when they do difficult tasks very well. Job security is a priority; economists want to work where they will not lose their positions. Also, they differentiate themselves from mathematicians by their desire to work on social problems. They value working independently but accept the routine of research and working with numbers.

Where Do Economics Majors Work?

Sixty-one percent of economics graduates are employed by businesses and corporations in the private, for-profit sector, and one-quarter are self-employed. (The work of consultants is described in Chapter 16.) Economics graduates also work in the government sector for various governmental agencies such as the Labor Department, the Commerce Department, the Treasury, federal reserve banks, and the like. More than 6 percent of economics graduates with a bachelor's degree work in the government sector. The education sector employs only 4 percent of these graduates, and 3 percent work in the private, nonprofit sector for tax-exempt or charitable organizations.

Seven out of 10 economics graduates are employed in jobs that are related to their undergraduate major. Thirty percent consider their jobs to be closely related to economics, and 40 percent are employed in jobs that they consider to be somewhat related to their undergraduate major field of study. The latter group of graduates generally work in the business or finance fields performing duties that, although not directly related to their classroom training, do bear some relationship to what they learned in their undergraduate economics curriculum.

Table 1

Percentage Distribution of Employed Persons with Only a Bachelor's Degree, by Economic Sector, Size, and New Business Status of Employer

	Economics	All
Economic Sector		
Private for-profit	60.6	47.3
Self-employed	25.5	18.5
Government/Military	6.5	11.0
Education	4.0	15.6
Nonprofit	3.2	7.5
Employer Size		
Small (Fewer than 100 employees)	42.3	35.5
Medium (100–999)	18.7	21.8
Large (1,000–24,999)	20.5	26.0
Very large (25,000 or more)	18.5	16.7
Percent working in new business established within past 5 years	7.9	7.6

Why do economics graduates work in jobs that are not related to their undergraduate major field of study? When asked to select the one most important factor influencing their choice to work in an unrelated job, one-third of the graduates employed in unrelated jobs cite pay and promotion opportunities, and 19 percent report a change in their career and professional interests. Eleven percent are forced to work outside their field because of a lack of related jobs, 10 percent seek better working conditions, and another 10 percent report that the most important factor that influenced their employment in an unrelated job is family commitments.

Out of all economics graduates under the age of 65, 85 percent are employed. Only 4 percent are officially unemployed; that is, they are not employed and are actively seeking employment. The remaining 11 percent are out of the labor force; that is, they are not employed and are not seeking employment. Of those who have withdrawn from the labor force, 37 percent have taken early retirement. One-fifth are not working because of family commitments.

Occupations

A large number of economics graduates are employed in managerial, finance, insurance, real estate, marketing, and sales sectors. All of the top 5 occupations that predominantly employ economics graduates belong to these sectors. However, less than 46 percent of all employed economics graduates work in the top 5 occupations.

Graduates are most concentrated in financial jobs: accountants, auditors, and financial specialists. Fifteen percent of grads are working in this field. The next largest groups of grads are working in two marketing and sales occupations: the 9 percent who market financial, real estate, and business services and the 8 percent in miscellaneous marketing and sales jobs. Another 13 percent work in management-related occupations, divided roughly equally between top-level managers and various management-related occupations.

Male graduates outnumber females by 71 percent to 29 percent. They also outnumber females

Table 2

Percentage Distribution of Employed Persons with Only a Bachelor's Degree in Economics, by the Relationship Between Their Job and College Major

Relationship of Job to Major	Percent
Closely related	30.0
Somewhat related	39.6
Not related	30.4

Percent who report the following as the most important reasons for working in a job that was not related to major:

Pay, promotion opportunities	33.4
Change in career or professional interests	19.3
Job in highest degree field not available	11.4
Working conditions (hours, equipment, environment)	10.1
Family-related reasons	9.9

Table 3
Top 5 Occupations Employing Persons with Only a Bachelor's Degree in Economics, by Percentage

Top 5 Occupations	All	Men	Women
Accountants, Auditors, and Other Financial Specialists	15.3	13.3	21.2
Sales/Marketing—Insurance, Securities, Real Estate, and Business Services	9.5	10.5	6.4
Other Marketing and Sales Occupations	7.6	7.9	6.6
Top-Level Managers, Executives, and Administrators	6.8	8.6	1.6
Other Management-Related Occupations	6.6	6.8	6.0
Total, Top 5 Occupations	45.8	47.1	41.8
Balance of Employed	54.2	52.9	58.2
All Employed	100.0	100.0	100.0

within the top 5 occupations, with the exception of the accounting and financial jobs, where more women are to be found.

Work Activities

▶ More than 6 out of 10 employed economics graduates regularly engage in sales, purchasing, and marketing activities, and one-quarter spend most of their time during a typical week performing these duties.

▶ A similar share spend significant work time on tasks related to accounting, finance, and contracts, but only 18 percent see these tasks as their main work function. Managerial tasks have a similar level of importance.

▶ Twenty-nine percent of economics grads regularly provide professional services such as financial consulting to their clients, and 9 percent spend most of their workweek providing these services.

▶ Economics graduates are very quantitatively inclined. They use large databases to estimate and test economic theory for its validity in the "real world." Given this quantitative orientation and the use of large databases, computers are widely used by graduates. About 89 percent regularly perform tasks involving computer applications, programming, and systems-development, and 6 percent spend most of their time at work in these activities.

▶ Another 43 percent regularly spend time at work on employee relations activities; however, only 3 percent consider these duties to be a major portion of their job.

Workplace Training and Other Work-Related Experiences

The career potential of a job is closely associated with the amount of work-related training on the job. Work-related training is regarded as an investment by firms because it makes workers more productive. Firms that invest in their workforce are more likely to offer pay increases and promotions to match the increasing productivity of their workers. The rate of participation in work-related training during a year among employed economics graduates is lower, at 55 percent, than the training participation rate of all college graduates (61 percent).

▶ Of those economics graduates who receive some training during a year, 47 percent receive technical training in the occupation in which they are employed.

▶ Twenty-two percent of the training recipients receive managerial or supervisory training.

▶ Seventeen percent receive training to improve their general professional skills, such as public speaking and business writing.

When asked to select the most important reason to acquire training, 28 percent of economics majors who undergo training identify the need to improve their occupational skills and knowledge. Another 9 percent report a mandatory training requirement by employers as the most important factor for their involvement in work-related training. According to 8 percent, the most important factor for their involvement in training is the need to obtain a professional license or certificate. Nearly 5 percent rank an improvement in their opportunities for a salary increase or a promotion as the number one factor in influencing their decision to participate in training.

Salaries

The median annual salary of economics graduates with only a bachelor's degree is $63,300, a level that is 18 percent higher than the median

FIGURE 1

Age/Earnings Profile of Persons with Only a Bachelor's Degree in Economics (Full-Time Workers, in 2010 Dollars)

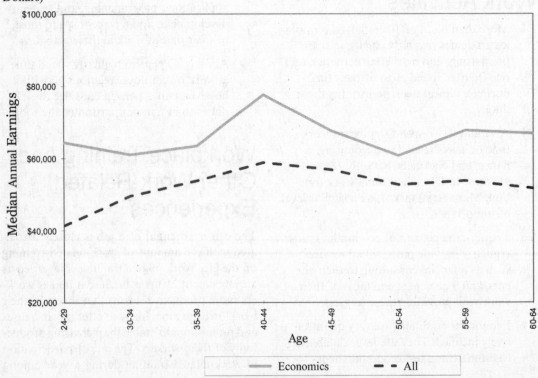

Table 4

Annual Salary of Workers with Only a Bachelor's Degree,
Top 5 Occupations (in 2010 Dollars)

Earnings in Top 5 Occupations	All	Economics
Total	$63,300	$77,300
Accountants, Auditors, and Other Financial Specialists	$59,900	$72,900
Sales/Marketing—Insurance, Securities, Real Estate, and Business Services	$67,100	$81,300
Other Marketing and Sales Occupations	$54,700	$56,800
Top-Level Managers, Executives, and Administrators	$103,200	$114,400
Other Management-Related Occupations	$57,800	$65,100

annual salary of all employed college graduates. On average, employed economics graduates worked for 44 hours per week for 50 weeks per year, resulting in 2,200 hours of employment each year. This level of work effort among economics graduates is 2 percent higher than the average among all college graduates (which is 43 hours per week and 50 weeks per year, resulting in 2,150 hours per year).

The average annual salary of graduates who work in closely related jobs is $71,300. Graduates with employment in jobs that are somewhat related to their major earn $72,700 per year. In contrast, the average salary of graduates employed full-time in a job that is not related to their field of study is $55,500.

Economics graduates who work for businesses and corporations in the private, for-profit sector earn a higher average salary, $70,300, than graduates working in other sectors of the economy. The average annual salary of economics graduates who work in their own businesses or practices is $65,400. Those working in the nonprofit sector average $55,000 per year. The government sector pays an average salary of $54,200 to economics graduates. As it does for most other college majors, the educational sector pays employed economics graduates less than other sectors: $41,500 per year.

In all of the top 5 occupations that predominantly employ economics graduates, economics grads earn considerably higher salaries than the average for all college graduates in those same occupations. The average salaries of economics graduates and all college graduates in each of these 5 occupations are presented in Table 4.

Job Satisfaction

The overall level of job satisfaction of economics majors is about the same as the average for all graduates.

Employment Outlook

According to the projections by the U.S. Bureau of Labor Statistics, employment in occupations that require a bachelor's degree is expected to grow faster than employment in other sectors of the American labor market. Between 2008 and 2018, the U.S. workforce is projected to grow by 10.1 percent, creating an average of 15.2 million job openings per year. The bachelor's-level jobs are expected to increase by 17.7 percent over the same time.

The employment growth projections in the top 5 occupations that are most likely to employ economics graduates are presented in this section.

Table 5
Percentage Distribution of Workers with Only a Bachelor's Degree, by Level of Job Satisfaction

Job Satisfaction	Economics	All
Very satisfied	40.2	45.4
Somewhat satisfied	49.4	45.0
Somewhat dissatisfied	7.7	7.4
Very dissatisfied	2.6	2.2
Mean Score (4=very satisfied, 1=not satisfied at all)	3.3	3.3

▶ The fastest growth in demand is projected for accountants, auditors, and financial specialists occupations. With 127,000 job openings each year between 2008 and 2018, the employment in these occupations is projected to grow by almost 19 percent. This is also the occupation that employs the largest share of economics grads. Accountants and auditors who have earned professional recognition through certification or other designation, especially a CPA, should have the best job prospects. Applicants with a master's degree in accounting or a master's degree in business administration with a concentration in accounting also may have an advantage.

▶ The two sales and marketing occupations that employ large numbers of economics graduates have somewhat different outlooks. For those selling services, 11.5 percent growth and 115,000 annual job openings are projected, whereas for those in miscellaneous other marketing and sales fields, only 7.3 percent growth and 65,000 annual job openings are projected.

▶ There is a similar difference in the outlooks projected for two types of management occupations. The miscellaneous

Table 6
Projected Growth and Job Openings in the Top 5 Occupations Employing Persons with Only a Bachelor's Degree in Economics

Top 5 Occupations	Projected Growth 2008–2018	Projected Annual Job Openings
All occupations	10.1%	5,093,000
All top 5	10.3%	421,840
Accountants, Auditors, and Other Financial Specialists	18.9%	127,260
Sales/Marketing—Insurance, Securities, Real Estate, and Business Services	11.5%	115,210
Other Marketing and Sales Occupations	7.3%	64,880
Top-Level Managers, Executives, and Administrators	−0.4%	61,470
Other Management-Related Occupations	7.2%	53,020

managerial occupations are expected to grow by 7.2 percent, but the workforce of top-level managers is expected to shrink slightly.

Pathways Beyond the Bachelor's Degree

More than 37 percent of economics graduates with a bachelor's degree proceed to earn a postgraduate degree: 26 percent earn a master's degree, 3 percent graduate with a doctorate, and another 8 percent earn a professional degree.

- ▶ About one-quarter earn their master's degree in business management and administration. Twelve percent choose economics as their major for their master's degree. Another 10 percent secure their master's degree in financial management.

- ▶ A bit less than half of all doctoral degrees of economics grads are earned in economics.

- ▶ About 8 out of 10 professional degrees among undergraduate economics majors are earned in law.

CHAPTER 15

Financial Management

Financial managers oversee the flow of cash and financial instruments, monitor the extension of credit, assess the risk of transactions, raise capital, analyze investments, prepare reports to satisfy tax and regulatory requirements, develop information to assess a firm's present and future financial status, and communicate with investors or stockholders. In a small firm, one or two people may do all these functions, but in larger companies, each function may represent an area with a separate manager whose title may be treasurer, controller, cash and credit manager, risk and insurance manager, reserve officer, or financial analyst.

Banks are not the only places where financial managers work. Practically every company employs at least one person with a financial management background. Different industries, such as insurance, securities, and health care, offer a variety of interests to people working in financial management.

This field can be very dynamic, with the expansion of global trade; shifting federal and state laws and regulations; and a proliferation of new, complex financial instruments. Some people enjoy this field because they often work with top management in developing the financial information these executives require in their leadership roles.

A degree in accounting, finance, or business administration is the educational preparation for typical entry into the field of financial management.

Obviously, good computational skills are fundamental, as is facility in the use and understanding of sophisticated computerized software in the financial management field. Key is the ability to make independent analyses of collected quantitative data and to interpret data to make judgments that others might refer to as laden with risks. Financial managers make weighty decisions, often within situations that are well regulated by laws and standard accounting practices. They are both consumers and producers of fiscal reports presented mathematically and diagrammatically. It's important for them to be able to communicate effectively in speaking and in writing.

Financial managers' interests are focused on business, money, numbers, analytical thinking, and a company's or institution's type of organization and operation. Tact is required in dealing with people. Flexibility to both be independent and work on varied projects and in groups will characterize many financial managers. They play influential leadership roles within organizations.

These workers value jobs that can pay a large amount of money and that provide the challenge of giving considerable amounts of thorough, concentrated thought and reasoning to situations. They seek the prestige gained through public recognition of financial success, as well as having others acknowledge their prowess with numbers.

Where Do Financial Management Majors Work?

More than 8 out of 10 persons who graduate in the field of financial management work in the private, for-profit sector, either for businesses and corporations or in their own business or practice as self-employed workers. Sixty-three percent work for businesses and corporations in the private, for-profit sector, and another 21 percent work as self-employed workers in their own businesses or practices. (The work of consultants is described in Chapter 16.) The government sector employs 8 percent of financial management graduates. Only 5 percent work for private, nonprofit organizations, and another 2 percent work for educational institutions.

Financial management graduates possess skills and knowledge that are applicable in a diverse array of industries. In addition to banks, frequent employers of financial management graduates include the health-care, securities, and insurance industries, to name a few. Nearly every firm requires some type of financial management. The extent of practical application of the skills of financial management enables many graduates to find jobs in their field. About 46 percent are employed in jobs that are closely related to their major, and another one-third consider their jobs to be somewhat related to their undergraduate major. Only 21 percent of financial management graduates work in jobs that are not at all related to their undergraduate major.

Why do the latter group of financial management graduates work in unrelated jobs? When asked to pick the most important reason for employment outside their major field of study, 24 percent of the graduates rank a change in career track as the most important factor, and 23 percent point to better pay and promotion opportunities. Nineteen percent consider the general working environment as the top-ranking factor in their employment choice outside the field of financial management. Twelve percent cite the

Table 1

Percentage Distribution of Employed Persons with Only a Bachelor's Degree, by Economic Sector, Size, and New Business Status of Employer

	Financial Management	All
Economic Sector		
Private for-profit	63.5	47.3
Self-employed	21.4	18.5
Government/Military	7.9	11.0
Education	2.0	15.6
Nonprofit	5.2	7.5
Employer Size		
Small (Fewer than 100 employees)	35.4	35.5
Medium (100–999)	18.0	21.8
Large (1,000–24,999)	25.1	26.0
Very large (25,000 or more)	21.5	16.7
Percent working in new business established within past 5 years	14.4	7.6

lack of available related jobs as the number one reason for their employment in an unrelated job. Family-related reasons are the most important factor influencing the employment choice for another 12 percent of the graduates who work in unrelated jobs.

Out of all financial management graduates under the age of 65, 88 percent are employed, and 3 percent are officially unemployed; that is, they are not employed and are actively seeking employment. The remaining grads are out of the labor force; that is, they are not employed and are not seeking employment. Many of the labor force withdrawals among economics graduates are attributable to family responsibilities, early retirement, or the lack of a need to work. Thirty-four percent cite family commitments as the reason for their labor force withdrawal. Retirement has removed 27 percent from the workforce. Thirteen percent of financial management grads say they do not need to work.

Occupations

The employment of financial management graduates is very concentrated in a few occupations. A bit less than half are employed in only 5 occupations. Employment of financial management graduates is mainly concentrated in high-level accounting, managerial, and sales and marketing occupations. Twenty-four percent are employed as accountants, auditors, and financial specialists. Another 16 percent of employed financial management graduates work in marketing and sales occupations, with the greater share in the field of selling insurance, securities, real estate, and business services. Seven percent work in miscellaneous management occupations, and 5 percent are employed in high-level executive, administrative, and managerial positions.

Male grads outnumber females by more than 2 to 1, but grads of both sexes are represented roughly equally within the top 5 occupations employing grads. The notable exception is

Table 2

Percentage Distribution of Employed Persons with Only a Bachelor's Degree in Financial Management, by the Relationship Between Their Job and College Major

Relationship of Job to Major	Percent
Closely related	45.8
Somewhat related	33.6
Not related	20.6

Percent who report the following as the most important reasons for working in a job that was not related to major:

Change in career or professional interests	23.7
Pay, promotion opportunities	23.4
Working conditions (hours, equipment, environment)	18.8
Job in highest degree field not available	12.2
Family-related reasons	12.1

Table 3
Top 5 Occupations Employing Persons with Only a Bachelor's Degree in Financial Management, by Percentage

Top 5 Occupations	All	Men	Women
Accountants, Auditors, and Other Financial Specialists	24.0	23.1	26.4
Sales/Marketing—Insurance, Securities, Real Estate, and Business Services	9.6	9.1	10.9
Other Management-Related Occupations	6.6	6.4	6.9
Other Marketing and Sales Occupations	6.1	6.0	6.3
Top-Level Managers, Executives, and Administrators	4.8	5.3	3.4
Total, Top 5 Occupations	51.0	49.9	54.0
Balance of Employed	49.0	50.1	46.0
All Employed	100.0	100.0	100.0

top-level managers, which has a significantly larger showing of men than women.

Work Activities

▶ Almost 1 out of 3 employed financial management graduates report that they spend at least 10 hours per week in accounting, financial, and contractual duties at work, and 73 percent indicate that they spend a majority of their time at work on these activities. This is not surprising, given the large portion of graduates who are employed as accountants, auditors, and financial specialists.

▶ Sales, marketing, and purchasing activities regularly engage more than half of employed financial management graduates, and more than one-fifth engage in these activities for a major part of their workweek.

▶ About 64 percent regularly perform management and administration duties at work, and 18 percent spend most of their time at work performing these duties. Performance of these duties is related to the high rates of employment in managerial and administrative occupations.

▶ Widespread use of computers in many sectors of the economy, particularly the finance sector, results in a high rate of computer use among financial management graduates. Eighty-eight percent regularly spend time at work in computer applications, programming, and systems-development activities, while 6 percent spend a major part of their typical workweek performing computer application duties.

▶ Professional services, mainly financial services, are regularly provided to clients by 35 percent of employed financial management graduates. About 10 percent spend most of their time during a typical workweek providing these services.

Workplace Training and Other Work-Related Experiences

The career potential of a job is closely associated with the amount of work-related training on the job. Work-related training is regarded as an investment by firms because it makes workers more productive. The incidence of work-related training among financial management graduates (59 percent) is only slightly lower than the rate of participation in work-related training among all college graduates (61 percent).

▶ Of those financial management graduates who receive some training during a year, half receive technical training in the occupation in which they are employed.

▶ Twenty-three percent of the training recipients receive management or supervisor training.

▶ One-fifth receive training to improve their general professional skills, such as public speaking and business writing.

When asked to select the one most important reason to acquire training, 35 percent of financial management graduates who undergo training identify the need to improve their occupational skills and knowledge. Licensure or certification requirements were the motivating factor for another 7 percent. (Salesworkers who handle certain kinds of financial instruments are required to pass a licensing exam.) Six percent report mandatory training requirements by the employer. According to another 5 percent of the training participants, the most important reason is a salary increase or promotion.

Salaries

The median annual salary of financial management graduates with only a bachelor's degree is $63,000, a level that is 18 percent higher than the median annual salary of all employed college graduates. On average, employed financial management graduates worked for 45 hours per week for 50 weeks per year, resulting in 2,250 hours of employment each year. The level of work effort among financial management graduates is 5 percent higher than the average among all college graduates (which is 43 hours per week and 50 weeks per year, resulting in 2,150 hours per year).

The average annual salary of graduates who work in closely related jobs is $73,300. Graduates with employment in jobs that are somewhat related to their major earn $67,100 per year. In contrast, the average salary of graduates employed full-time in a job that is not related to their field of study is only $44,400.

Earning an average salary of $73,300 annually, financial management graduates who work for businesses and corporations in the private, for-profit sector earn a far higher salary than those who are employed in other sectors. The average salary of graduates who are self-employed in their own businesses or practices is $58,600 per year. The average annual pay of financial management graduates employed in the government sector is $52,700, and $47,500 in the not-for-profit sector. The lowest salary among financial management graduates occurs in the education sector, where full-time employed graduates earn $40,900 per year.

In most of the top 5 occupations that predominantly employ financial management graduates, the average annual salaries are higher than the salary of all college graduates employed in those same occupations. There are sizable variations in the average annual salaries of financial management graduates by the occupation in which they are employed. Just within the top 5 occupations, the average annual salaries among full-time workers range from a high of $154,800 to a low of $53,700 among full-time workers.

▶ Financial management graduates employed in top-level executive, administrative, and managerial occupations earn an average annual salary of $154,800.

FIGURE 1

Age/Earnings Profile of Persons with Only a Bachelor's Degree in Financial Management (Full-Time Workers, in 2010 Dollars)

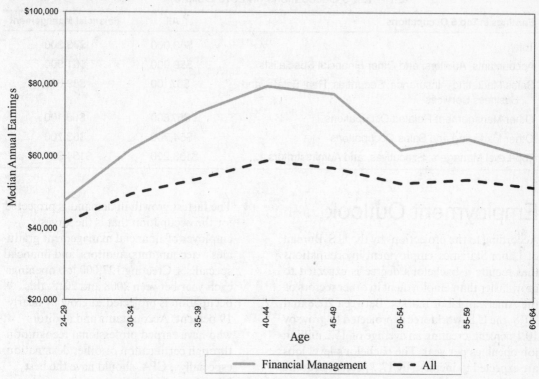

- The average salary in miscellaneous management-related occupations is $68,100 per year.

- Other areas that predominantly employ financial management graduates—selling or marketing insurance, finance, and real estate—pay graduates an average annual salary of $82,600.

- Accounting occupations, which are the top employers of financial management graduates, particularly female graduates, pay graduates an average annual salary of $61,900.

- The miscellaneous sales and marketing occupations that employ financial management grads pay them the lowest salary out of the top 5 occupations, $53,700 per year.

Job Satisfaction

The overall level of job satisfaction of financial management majors is slightly higher than the average for all graduates.

Table 4
Annual Salary of Workers with Only a Bachelor's Degree, Top 5 Occupations (in 2010 Dollars)

Earnings in Top 5 Occupations	All	Financial Management
Total	$63,000	$73,300
Accountants, Auditors, and Other Financial Specialists	$59,900	$61,900
Sales/Marketing—Insurance, Securities, Real Estate, and Business Services	$67,100	$82,600
Other Management-Related Occupations	$57,800	$68,100
Other Marketing and Sales Occupations	$54,700	$53,700
Top-Level Managers, Executives, and Administrators	$103,200	$154,800

Employment Outlook

According to the projections by the U.S. Bureau of Labor Statistics, employment in occupations that require a bachelor's degree is expected to grow faster than employment in other sectors of the American labor market. Between 2008 and 2018, the U.S. workforce is projected to grow by 10.1 percent, creating an average of 15.2 million job openings per year. The bachelor's-level jobs are expected to increase by 17.7 percent over the same time.

Among the top 5 occupations that are most likely to employ financial management graduates, the average rate of growth is slightly higher than the average for all occupations, but outlook varies widely.

▸ The fastest growth in demand is projected for the occupation that is the largest employer of financial management graduates—accountants, auditors, and financial specialists. Creating 127,000 job openings each year between 2008 and 2018, this occupation is projected to grow by nearly 19 percent. Accountants and auditors who have earned professional recognition through certification or other designation, especially a CPA, should have the best job prospects. Applicants with a master's degree in accounting or a master's degree in business administration with a concentration in accounting may have an advantage.

Table 5
Percentage Distribution of Workers with Only a Bachelor's Degree, by Level of Job Satisfaction

Job Satisfaction	Financial Management	All
Very satisfied	44.9	45.4
Somewhat satisfied	45.7	45.0
Somewhat dissatisfied	7.9	7.4
Very dissatisfied	1.5	2.2
Mean Score (4=very satisfied, 1=not satisfied at all)	3.4	3.3

Table 6
Projected Growth and Job Openings in the Top 5 Occupations Employing Persons with Only a Bachelor's Degree in Financial Management

Top 5 Occupations	Projected Growth 2008–2018	Projected Annual Job Openings
All occupations	10.1%	5,093,000
All top 5	10.3%	421,840
Accountants, Auditors, and Other Financial Specialists	18.9%	127,260
Sales/Marketing—Insurance, Securities, Real Estate, and Business Services	11.5%	115,210
Other Management-Related Occupations	7.2%	53,020
Other Marketing and Sales Occupations	7.3%	64,880
Top-Level Managers, Executives, and Administrators	−0.4%	61,470

▶ Employment projections for sellers and marketers of intangibles such as insurance call for growth of about 11.5 percent and 115,000 annual job openings.

▶ The miscellaneous sales and managerial occupations employing financial management grads are each projected to grow by a bit more than 7 percent. The sales and marketing occupations should account for 65,000 job openings each year; and the management occupations, 53,000.

▶ The best-paying job among the top 5, top-level managers, is shrinking slightly but is projected to create 61,000 job openings each year because of turnover.

Pathways Beyond the Bachelor's Degree

Among financial management graduates with a bachelor's degree, 27 percent proceed to earn a postgraduate degree: 23 percent earn a master's degree, less than 1 percent graduate with a doctorate, and another 4 percent earn a professional degree.

▶ Twenty-eight percent of all master's degrees earned by undergraduate financial management majors are in business administration and management, 23 percent are in the field of financial management, and 7 percent are earned in accounting.

▶ The great majority of professional degrees earned by undergraduate financial management majors are in the field of law.

CHAPTER 16

General Business

Business is about making money or achieving the best with given resources. Every enterprise, business, or organization, including nonprofit ones, is administered and managed. Of course, some enterprises, businesses, or organizations are administered and managed better than others. Thus, effective principles and practices of business administration and management are applicable to everyone in business, whatever their self-expressed professional identity.

Because business management is so diverse, college majors have been developed to address specific aspects of business that must be administered, such as finances, marketing, and human resources. But a general management program remains the most popular major in this group, and that is the focus of this chapter.

This major encompasses a very broad field. It involves leading, running things, and supervising people. There are managers in the nonprofit as well as the for-profit sector; business owners, large or small; and administrators, including government administrators. Military officers also administer and manage. Work areas range from construction, engineering and science, health care, advertising, hotels, restaurants, farming, real estate, employment, banking, and industrial production to sales or television program production.

There is a difference between administration and management positions. The U.S. Department of Labor's distinction is that business administrators direct, through lower-level personnel, all or part of the activities in business establishments, government agencies, and labor unions. Administrators set

policies, make important decisions, and determine priorities. Administrators in service areas that provide health care (such as hospitals), safety, recreation, and social services (such as welfare, schools, churches, libraries, and museums) manage, through lower-level personnel, all or part of their activities. Administrators are usually responsible to a board of directors or government agency that sets overall policies and goals for their organization or institution. Within established guidelines, administrators plan and oversee programs and activities that are carried out by others. On the other hand, managers direct the operations of various kinds of establishments such as stores, hotels, food service facilities, distribution warehouses, transportation and airline terminals, and automobile service stations. Managers usually carry out their activities according to policies and procedures determined by owners, administrators, or other persons with higher authority.

Nowadays, much managerial and administrative work is done by consultants rather than by permanent employees of a business. These management consultants, also called management analysts, are brought in to improve an organization's structure, efficiency, or profits. They may be single practitioners or part of large international organizations employing thousands of other consultants. Some analysts and consultants specialize in a specific industry, such as health care or telecommunications, while others specialize by type of business function, such as human resources, marketing, logistics, or information systems. Some projects require a team of consultants, each specializing in one area. In other projects, consultants work independently with the organization's managers. In all cases, consultants collect, review, and analyze information in order to make recommendations to managers.

Educational requirements in a general business major typically include foundational course work in accounting, finance, marketing, economics, management, organizational behavior, business policy, computer-based information systems, and statistics, plus courses in the humanities, mathematics, and social sciences. Most people in the major also choose a concentration area and take advanced courses in accounting, management-information systems, marketing, transportation, international business, human resources, finance and insurance, or small business entrepreneurship.

The ability to recognize and solve business and organizational problems with sound and ethical judgment is critical. Being able to understand the role of a business or organization's social responsibilities within a community or region or around the world can be valuable. Qualities important for success include leadership, self-confidence, motivation, decisiveness, and flexibility. Managers and administrators encounter stress that requires stamina when they are under pressure. The ability to communicate effectively is essential.

Those working in this area like to understand how to function effectively within an organization or group, be involved in interpersonal interactions, and be careful to pay attention to details. While it sounds good to be the boss, it is hard work to take responsibility for something. While interacting with people can be fun socially, getting them to produce efficiently and perform quality work can be difficult. Managers and administrators must accept, at least, that they evaluate performance by the numbers and the results on the bottom line.

High salaries attract people to management and administration positions. There is power also in being boss, especially if one is successful and receives public recognition. As stated earlier, every organization needs to be administered and managed, and often the people in these positions receive public recognition, especially in the small towns across our nation where so many people

Table 1

Percentage Distribution of Employed Persons with Only a Bachelor's Degree, by Economic Sector, Size, and New Business Status of Employer

	General Business	All
Economic Sector		
Private for-profit	56.7	47.3
Self-employed	21.9	18.5
Government/Military	10.5	11.0
Education	5.8	15.6
Nonprofit	4.8	7.5
Employer Size		
Small (Fewer than 100 employees)	36.3	35.5
Medium (100–999)	18.1	21.8
Large (1,000–24,999)	25.5	26.0
Very large (25,000 or more)	20.0	16.7
Percent working in new business established within past 5 years	7.7	7.6

live. Obviously, possessing wisdom and intelligence is viewed as important to having achieved success; however, luck must be acknowledged. Managers and administrators also value having autonomy, being independent, and having diverse opportunities. Those who work as consultants enjoy the variety of business problems they address but must cope with the stresses of constant travel.

Where Do General Business Majors Work?

More than half of all employed general business graduates work for businesses and corporations in the private, for-profit sector. Another one-fifth are self-employed, working in their own businesses or practices. Consultants may be employed in either of these work arrangements. The government sector employs 1 out of 10 general business graduates, and 6 percent work for educational institutions. The remaining 5 percent of employed general business graduates work for private, nonprofit organizations.

General business graduates possess a broad array of skills that are useful in performing management and administrative functions in a variety of industries and occupations. The extent of practical application of general business skills enables many graduates to find jobs in their field. Eight out of 10 general business graduates work in jobs that are related to their undergraduate major. About 35 percent are employed in jobs that are closely related to their major, and another 45 percent consider their jobs to be somewhat related to their undergraduate major.

Why do the latter group of general business graduates work in unrelated jobs? When asked to select the one most important reason for employment outside their major field of study, 27 percent of the graduates point to better pay and promotion opportunities, and 18 percent rank a change in career interests as the number one reason for their employment in unrelated jobs. About 15 percent consider the general working environment as the most important factor to influence their decision to work in unrelated jobs. Roughly equal shares of about 13 percent consider family-rated reasons and the lack of available jobs in the field as the top-ranking factors.

Out of all general business graduates under the age of 65, 87 percent are employed. Only 3 percent are officially unemployed; that is, they are not employed and are actively seeking employment. The remaining grads are out of the labor force; that is, they are not employed and are not seeking employment. Forty-two percent of general business graduates who have withdrawn from the labor force say they have retired early, and 15 percent cite family commitments. Another 13 percent have no need to work.

Occupations

Many general business graduates are employed in managerial, accounting, marketing, and sales sectors. All of the top 5 occupations that predominantly employ general business graduates belong to these sectors. Employment of general business graduates is fairly concentrated. Forty-three percent of employed general business graduates work in the top 5 occupations.

Accounting and other financial management occupations account for 11 percent of the grads. Miscellaneous management and administrative occupations together employ about 17 percent of grads. Marketing and sales occupy about 15 percent, equally divided between those doing miscellaneous kinds of sales and those who focus on insurance, real estate, and intangible products.

Male graduates outnumber females by about 65 to 35 percent, but women are more likely to choose accounting and miscellaneous administrative occupations.

Table 2

Percentage Distribution of Employed Persons with Only a Bachelor's Degree in General Business, by the Relationship Between Their Job and College Major

Relationship of Job to Major	Percent
Closely related	35.1
Somewhat related	45.0
Not related	19.9

Percent who report the following as the most important reasons for working in a job that was not related to major:

Pay, promotion opportunities	27.5
Change in career or professional interests	17.7
Working conditions (hours, equipment, environment)	15.1
Family-related reasons	12.6
Job in highest degree field not available	12.5

Work Activities

- More than 65 percent regularly perform management and administration duties at work, and 21 percent spend most of their time at work performing these duties. Performance of these duties is related to the high proportion of general business graduates employed in managerial and administrative occupations.

- Sales, marketing, and purchasing activities regularly engage 6 out of 10 employed general business graduates, and 21 percent spend a majority of their time at work performing these duties.

- More than 57 percent of employed general business graduates report that they spend at least 10 hours per week in accounting, financial, and contractual duties at work, and 16 percent indicate that they spend a majority of their time at work on these activities.

- Widespread use of computers in almost every sector of the economy results in a high rate of computer use among many college graduates, including general business graduates. Eighty-six percent regularly spend time at work in computer applications, programming, and systems-development activities, although only 6 percent spend a major part of their typical workweek performing these duties.

- Nearly one-half of all employed general business graduates engage in employee-relations activities, including recruiting, personnel development, and training, and 5 percent spend a majority of their workweek in these activities.

- Professional services such as financial and other consulting services are regularly provided to clients by 24 percent of employed general business graduates. About 7 percent spend most of their time during a typical workweek providing these services.

Table 3
Top 5 Occupations Employing Persons with Only a Bachelor's Degree
in General Business, by Percentage

Top 5 Occupations	All	Men	Women
Accountants, Auditors, and Other Financial Specialists	11.2	9.2	15.0
Other Management-Related Occupations	9.3	10.1	7.8
Other Marketing and Sales Occupations	7.7	9.1	5.2
Sales/Marketing—Insurance, Securities, Real Estate, and Business Services	7.6	8.4	6.1
Other Administrative Occupations	7.5	4.8	12.3
Total, Top 5 Occupations	43.3	41.6	46.4
Balance of Employed	56.7	58.4	53.6
All Employed	100.0	100.0	100.0

Workplace Training and Other Work-Related Experiences

The career potential of a job is closely associated with the amount of work-related training on the job. Work-related training is regarded as an investment by firms because it makes workers more productive. Firms that invest in their workforce are more likely to offer pay increases and promotions to match the increasing productivity of their workers. The incidence of work-related training among general business graduates is significantly lower (54 percent) than the rate of participation in work-related training among all college graduates (61 percent).

▶ Of those general business graduates who receive some training during the year, 46 percent receive technical training in the occupation in which they are employed.

▶ Almost one-quarter of the training recipients receive management or supervisory training.

▶ Eighteen percent receive training to improve their general professional skills, such as public speaking and business writing.

When asked to select the one most important reason to acquire training, 29 percent of general business graduates who undergo training identify the need to improve their occupational skills and knowledge. Equal shares, 8 percent each, report mandatory training requirements by the employer and the need to obtain a professional license as the number one reason to acquire training. According to another 5 percent of the training participants, the most important reason is a salary increase and promotion.

Salaries

The median annual salary of general business graduates with only a bachelor's degree is $52,200, a level that is 1 percent higher than the median annual salary of all employed college graduates. On average, employed general business graduates work for 44 hours per week for 50 weeks per year, resulting in 2,200 hours of employment each year. The level of work effort among general business graduates is 2 percent more than the average among all college graduates (which is 43 hours per week and 50 weeks per year, resulting in 2,150 hours per year).

The average annual salary of general business graduates who work in jobs that are related to their major is considerably higher than the salary of graduates who work in jobs that are not related to their undergraduate major. Closely related jobs pay full-time employed general business graduates $61,600 annually. Graduates employed in somewhat related jobs earn $57,800 per year, and those whose jobs are unrelated to their undergraduate field of study earn $42,600 per year.

Earning an average salary of $61,900 annually, general business graduates who work for businesses and corporations in the private, for-profit sector earn a higher salary than those who are employed in other sectors of the economy. The average salary of graduates who are self-employed in their own businesses or practices is $52,300 per year. Those working for nonprofit organizations average $50,000 per year. The pay of general business graduates in the government sector is $49,000 per year. The lowest salary among general business graduates is in

FIGURE 1

Age/Earnings Profile of Persons with Only a Bachelor's Degree in General Business (Full-Time Workers, in 2010 Dollars)

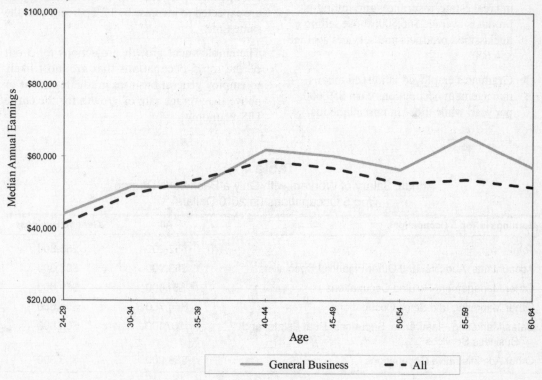

the education sector, where full-time employed graduates earn $40,100 per year.

The average annual salaries in the top 5 occupations that predominantly employ general business graduates are, on average, somewhat higher than the salary of all college graduates employed in those same occupations. There are sizable variations in the average salaries of general business graduates by occupation.

- General business graduates employed in accounting and financial occupations earn an average annual salary of $56,800. Female graduates gravitate toward these occupations more than men do.

- The average annual salary of general business graduates who are employed full-time in marketing and sales occupations depends on the specialization. Those selling real estate, insurance, and intangible products average $66,800; those selling unclassified products and services average $54,600.

- Graduates employed in miscellaneous management occupations earn $59,600 per year, while those in miscellaneous

administrative occupations average only $38,800.

Job Satisfaction

The overall level of job satisfaction of general business majors is slightly higher than the average for all graduates.

Employment Outlook

According to the projections by the U.S. Bureau of Labor Statistics, employment in occupations that require a bachelor's degree is expected to grow faster than employment in other sectors of the American labor market. Between 2008 and 2018, the U.S. workforce is projected to grow by 10.1 percent, creating an average of 15.2 million job openings per year. The bachelor's-level jobs are expected to increase by 17.7 percent over the same time.

The employment growth projections for 3 out of the top 5 occupations that are most likely to employ general business graduates are at or above the average rate of growth for the entire U.S. economy.

Table 4
Annual Salary of Workers with Only a Bachelor's Degree,
Top 5 Occupations (in 2010 Dollars)

Earnings in Top 5 Occupations	All	General Business
Total	$52,200	$55,800
Accountants, Auditors, and Other Financial Specialists	$59,900	$56,800
Other Management-Related Occupations	$57,800	$59,600
Other Marketing and Sales Occupations	$54,700	$54,600
Sales/Marketing—Insurance, Securities, Real Estate, and Business Services	$67,100	$66,800
Other Administrative Occupations	$38,200	$38,800

Table 5
Percentage Distribution of Workers with Only a Bachelor's Degree,
by Level of Job Satisfaction

Job Satisfaction	General Business	All
Very satisfied	45.9	45.4
Somewhat satisfied	45.1	45.0
Somewhat dissatisfied	6.6	7.4
Very dissatisfied	2.4	2.2
Mean Score (4=very satisfied, 1=not satisfied at all)	3.4	3.3

▶ The fastest growth in demand is projected for accountants, auditors, and financial specialists. This group of occupations will grow by almost 19 percent between 2008 and 2018, creating 127,000 job openings annually from growth and turnover. Accountants and auditors who have earned professional recognition through certification or other designation, especially a CPA, should have the best job prospects. Applicants with a master's degree in accounting or a master's degree in business administration with a concentration in accounting also may have an advantage.

▶ Growth of 11.5 percent is projected for those selling insurance, real estate, and other financial products and services, together with 115,000 job openings each year, on average.

▶ Projections for miscellaneous management- and sales-related jobs indicate that employment in these occupations will grow by about 7 percent.

▶ Unclassified administrative occupations are projected to grow by almost 11 percent over the projection period. These jobs, with a large workforce and relatively high turnover, are projected to create 166,000 job openings each year.

Pathways Beyond the Bachelor's Degree

Of all graduates with a bachelor's degree in general business, only one-fifth proceed to earn a postgraduate degree: 17 percent earn a master's degree and most of the remaining 3 percent earn a professional degree.

Table 6

Projected Growth and Job Openings in the Top 5 Occupations Employing Persons with Only a Bachelor's Degree in General Business

Top 5 Occupations	Projected Growth 2008–2018	Projected Annual Job Openings
All occupations	10.1%	5,093,000
All top 5	11.9%	526,500
Accountants, Auditors, and Other Financial Specialists	18.9%	127,260
Other Management-Related Occupations	7.2%	53,020
Other Marketing and Sales Occupations	7.3%	64,880
Sales/Marketing—Insurance, Securities, Real Estate, and Business Services	11.5%	115,210
Other Administrative Occupations	10.8%	166,130

▶ Thirty-nine percent of all master's degrees earned by undergraduate general business majors are in the field of business administration and management.

▶ Another 6 percent of the grads complete a master's degree in financial management.

▶ Almost 80 percent of the professional degrees earned by undergraduate general business majors are in the field of law.

CHAPTER 17

General Mathematics

Mathematics, a basic science, is the foundation upon which many other disciplines are built. The number of workers using mathematical techniques is many times greater than the number of persons called mathematicians. For example, those in engineering, computer science, physics, and economics all use mathematics extensively, but they are not called mathematicians.

Mathematicians speak of their field as being either theoretical or applied, but overlap does exist. Theoretical mathematics concerns developing new principles or new relationships between existing mathematical principles without considering practical uses. Applied mathematicians, on the other hand, use theories and techniques for analyzing such real-world phenomena as the mathematical aspects of computer and communication networks, effects of new drugs on disease, aerodynamic characteristics of aircraft, or distribution costs of businesses.

As a profession, mathematics involves conducting research and testing hypotheses and alternative theories in algebra, geometry, number theory, and logic. It involves performing computations and applying methods of numerical analysis by using computers and plotters in solving problems. Mathematicians use computers extensively to analyze relationships, solve complex problems, develop models, and process large amounts of data. A high degree of proficiency in computer database manipulation and use of sophisticated

software programs is expected. Mathematicians conceive and develop ideas for applying mathematics to other sciences, engineering, defense work, computers, and business.

Most colleges and universities offer a mathematics degree. Common courses offered are calculus, differential equations, linear and abstract algebra, probability theory, numerical analysis, topology, modern algebra, discrete mathematics, mathematical logic, and statistics. Some institutions urge or require mathematics majors to take course work or a double major in an allied field such as computer science, engineering, or economics.

Where Do General Mathematics Majors Work?

Persons who graduate in the field of general mathematics are only slightly less likely than applied mathematics graduates to work in the private, for-profit sector. Seventy percent of general mathematics graduates work in the private, for-profit sector: 53 percent work for businesses and corporations, and 17 percent are self-employed in their own businesses or practices. (The work of consultants is described in Chapter 16.) On the other hand, those who

Table 1

Percentage Distribution of Employed Persons with Only a Bachelor's Degree, by Economic Sector, Size, and New Business Status of Employer

	General Mathematics	All
Economic Sector		
Private for-profit	53.0	47.3
Self-employed	16.9	18.5
Government/Military	7.3	11.0
Education	18.3	15.6
Nonprofit	4.3	7.5
Employer Size		
Small (Fewer than 100 employees)	32.0	35.5
Medium (100–999)	23.6	21.8
Large (1,000–24,999)	25.0	26.0
Very large (25,000 or more)	19.5	16.7
Percent working in new business established within past 5 years	7.7	7.6

major in general mathematics are more likely to enter the field of education than are applied mathematics graduates. Eighteen percent of all employed general mathematics majors are employed by educational institutions, and another 7 percent work for the government sector.

General mathematics graduates may not specifically use their general mathematics skills on the job but rather a whole grouping of skills associated with mathematics. Hence, roughly equal portions consider what they do at work to be closely or only somewhat related to their field of study. Thirty-seven percent of general mathematics graduates work in jobs that are closely related to their undergraduate major. Slightly more consider their jobs to be somewhat related to general mathematics.

When asked to select the most important reason for employment outside their major field of study, 23 percent rank a change in their career interests as the number one reason for their employment in unrelated jobs. Family-related reasons are the most important factor influencing the employment choice in unrelated jobs for 20 percent. A lack of jobs in general math is the most important factor in the decisions of 18 percent of the grads. Sixteen percent of the graduates have chosen work with better pay and promotion opportunities than were available in jobs related to the major.

Out of all general mathematics graduates under the age of 65, 80 percent are employed. Only 4 percent are officially unemployed; that is, they are not employed and are actively seeking employment. The remaining 16 percent are out of the labor force; that is, they are not employed and are not seeking employment. Three main reasons that underlie the labor force withdrawal of general mathematics graduates are retirement, a lack of the need or desire to work, and family responsibilities. Forty-five percent are retired, 19 percent lack the need or desire to work, and 16 percent cite family responsibilities as the reason for labor force withdrawal.

Table 2
Percentage Distribution of Employed Persons with Only a Bachelor's Degree in General Mathematics, by the Relationship Between Their Job and College Major

Relationship of Job to Major	Percent
Closely related	37.5
Somewhat related	38.4
Not related	24.1

Percent who report the following as the most important reasons for working in a job that was not related to major:

Change in career or professional interests	23.4
Family-related reasons	20.4
Job in highest degree field not available	18.3
Pay, promotion opportunities	15.7
Working conditions (hours, equipment, environment)	11.7

Occupations

Most general mathematics graduates are employed in various teaching, computer, and accounting jobs. Only a little more than one-third of all employed general mathematics graduates work in one of the top 5 occupations that employ these graduates. By far, the greatest concentration of grads is in secondary school teaching; nearly 12 percent work in this occupation. Three computer occupations together employ nearly one-fifth of general mathematics graduates. Almost 7 percent work as computer engineers specializing in software, and an equal fraction are employed as computer programmers; another 6 percent work

Table 3
Top 5 Occupations Employing Persons with Only a Bachelor's Degree in General Mathematics, by Percentage

Top 5 Occupations	All	Men	Women
Teachers, Secondary—Computer, Math, or Science	11.6	8.4	16.4
Computer Engineers—Software	6.7	7.9	5.0
Computer Programmers (Business, Scientific, Process Control)	6.7	7.3	5.7
Computer Systems Analysts	5.6	4.8	6.7
Accountants, Auditors, and Other Financial Specialists	5.5	5.6	5.5
Total, Top 5 Occupations	36.1	34.0	39.3
Balance of Employed	63.9	66.0	60.7
All Employed	100.0	100.0	100.0

as computer systems analysts. About 5 percent work in accounting or other financial services.

Men outnumber women among general math grads by about 57 percent to 43 percent. In the workforce, almost twice as many female grads as males choose to teach their specialization in secondary school, and females are also somewhat more likely to become systems analysts. Among the other two computer occupations employing the largest share of grads, men are better represented. The sexes are roughly at par among grads working in accounting.

Work Activities

- One-fifth of all employed graduates spend a majority of their time at work in computer applications, programming, and systems-development activities. With nearly one-fifth of all general mathematics majors employed in computer occupations, it is hardly surprising to find such a prevalence of computer-related activities among general mathematics graduates. Sixty-eight percent of all employed graduates regularly spend at least 10 hours per week in these activities.

- Sixteen percent engage in teaching activities for a major part of their workweek. One-quarter regularly perform some teaching function at work.

- Management and administration activities typically consume most work time among 14 percent of general mathematics graduates. Almost one-half regularly perform these duties at work.

- Sales, purchasing, and marketing duties typically use up most of the workweek among 12 percent of all employed general mathematics graduates, and one-third spend most of their time at work providing financial services to clients.

- More than one-third regularly perform some accounting, financial, and contractual duties at work, and 11 percent spend more hours in that activity than any other activity at work.

Workplace Training and Other Work-Related Experiences

The career potential of a job is closely associated with the amount of work-related training on the job. Work-related training is regarded as an investment by firms because it makes workers more productive. Firms that invest in their workforce are more likely to offer pay increases and promotions to match the increasing productivity of their workers. The incidence of work-related training among general mathematics graduates is significantly lower than the rate of participation in work-related training among all college graduates. While 61 percent of all college graduates acquire some kind of work-related training during a year, only 52 percent of general mathematics majors engage in work-related training.

- Of those general mathematics graduates who receive some training, 46 percent receive technical training in the occupation in which they are employed.

- Fifteen percent of the training recipients participate in management or supervisory training.

- Seventeen percent receive training to improve their general professional skills, such as public speaking and business writing.

When asked to identify the most important reason to acquire training, 3 out of 10 general mathematics graduates who undergo training identify the need to improve their occupational skills and knowledge. Another 10 percent report mandatory training requirements by the employer as the most important factor underlying their involvement in work-related training. Six percent consider the need to obtain a professional license or certificate as the most important reason influencing their decision to undergo work-related training.

Salaries

The median annual salary of general mathematics graduates with only a bachelor's degree is $60,000, a level that is 14 percent higher than the median annual salary of all employed college graduates. On average, employed general mathematics graduates work for 42 hours per week for 50 weeks per year, resulting in 2,100 hours of employment each year. The level of work effort among general mathematics graduates is 2 percent lower than the average among all college graduates (which is 43 hours per week and 50 weeks per year, resulting in 2,150 hours per year).

The average annual salary of general mathematics majors who work in jobs that are closely related to their major is lower than the salary of those who are employed in jobs that are somewhat related to their major. Part of the cause for a lower salary in closely related jobs is attributable to the low salary in teaching positions. Most of the general mathematics graduates in teaching positions consider their jobs to be closely related to their major. Closely related jobs pay full-time employed general mathematics graduates $57,800 annually. Graduates employed in jobs that are somewhat related earn $74,300 annually, and those whose jobs are unrelated to general mathematics earn $43,300 per year.

FIGURE 1

Age/Earnings Profile of Persons with Only a Bachelor's Degree in General Mathematics (Full-Time Workers, in 2010 Dollars)

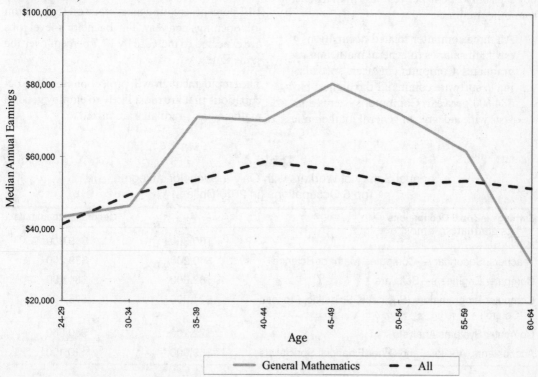

General mathematics graduates working in the private, for-profit sector earn more than their counterparts working in other sectors of the economy. Graduates who work for businesses and corporations in the private, for-profit sector earn $72,200 per year. Self-employed general mathematics graduates earn an average salary of $63,800 annually. Not-for-profit organizations pay grads $45,400 per year. General mathematics graduates in government-sector jobs earn an average salary of $45,300 per year. Educational institutions pay full-time employed general mathematics graduates $42,700 per year.

There are sizable variations in the average annual salaries of general mathematics graduates by the occupations in which they are employed. In 4 out of the top 5 occupations that predominantly employ general mathematics majors, the salaries of general mathematics majors exceed the salary of all college graduates in the same jobs. The exception is secondary school math teachers, and they earn only $1,000 per year less than teachers from other majors.

▶ All three computer-related occupations pay high salaries to general mathematics graduates. Computer engineers specializing in software command the highest pay: $84,600 per year. Computer systems analysts with a degree in general mathematics earn about $4,000 less annually, and programmers earn another $4,000 less.

▶ The lowest-paying of the top 5 occupations, which tends to attract female graduates, is secondary school teaching, with an average salary of $39,200 per year.

Job Satisfaction

The overall level of job satisfaction of general mathematics majors is slightly higher than the average for all graduates.

Employment Outlook

According to the projections by the U.S. Bureau of Labor Statistics, employment in occupations that require a bachelor's degree is expected to grow faster than employment in other sectors of the American labor market. Between 2008 and 2018, the U.S. workforce is projected to grow by 10.1 percent, creating an average of 15.2 million job openings per year. The bachelor's-level jobs are expected to increase by 17.7 percent over the same time.

The employment growth projections for the 5 occupations that are most likely to employ general mathematics graduates are mixed.

Table 4
Annual Salary of Workers with Only a Bachelor's Degree,
Top 5 Occupations (in 2010 Dollars)

Earnings in Top 5 Occupations	All	General Mathematics
Total	$60,000	$65,800
Teachers, Secondary—Computer, Math, or Science	$40,200	$39,200
Computer Engineers—Software	$82,600	$84,600
Computer Programmers (Business, Scientific, Process Control)	$71,200	$76,400
Computer Systems Analysts	$72,200	$80,500
Accountants, Auditors, and Other Financial Specialists	$59,900	$67,100

Table 5
Percentage Distribution of Workers with Only a Bachelor's Degree,
by Level of Job Satisfaction

Job Satisfaction	General Mathematics	All
Very satisfied	41.1	45.4
Somewhat satisfied	51.0	45.0
Somewhat dissatisfied	6.0	7.4
Very dissatisfied	1.9	2.2
Mean Score (4=very satisfied, 1=not satisfied at all)	3.4	3.3

▶ The fastest job growth for mathematics grads is projected for two of the computer-related occupations. Employment of computer software engineers is projected to increase by an impressive 32.5 percent, creating 37,000 annual job openings. Job prospects for computer software engineers should be excellent. Those with practical experience and at least a bachelor's degree in a computer-related field should have the best opportunities. Employers will continue to seek computer professionals with strong programming, systems analysis, interpersonal, and business skills.

▶ Computer systems analysts will see employment increase by one-fifth, with 22,000 job openings annually. As with other information technology jobs, employment growth may be tempered somewhat by offshoring. Firms may look to cut costs by shifting operations to foreign countries with lower prevailing wages and highly skilled workers. However, due to the high level of expertise that is required, as well as the frequent need to be near the job site, systems analysts are less likely to be offshored than other IT occupations. On balance, job prospects should be excellent.

▶ The outlook for computer programmers, however, is much less promising. Increasingly, firms are employing workers in other nations to do routine coding, resulting in the expectation of a diminished American workforce.

▶ Employment of secondary school math teachers, the largest area of employment for general mathematics graduates, is projected to increase by about 9 percent, with 41,000 job openings each year between 2008 and 2018. Opportunities are likely to be better for math teachers than for many other specializations, However, this is the occupation with the lowest salary out of the top 5 employers of general mathematics graduates.

▶ Accounting and financial occupations are projected to grow by almost 19 percent, opening a yearly average of 127,000 jobs. Accountants and auditors who have earned professional recognition through certification or other designation, especially a CPA, should have the best job prospects. Applicants with a master's degree in accounting or a master's degree in business administration with a concentration in accounting also may have an advantage.

Table 6
Projected Growth and Job Openings in the Top 5 Occupations Employing Persons with Only a Bachelor's Degree in General Mathematics

Top 5 Occupations	Projected Growth 2008–2018	Projected Annual Job Openings
All occupations	10.1%	5,093,000
All top 5	17.8%	235,990
Teachers, Secondary—Computer, Math, or Science	8.9%	41,240
Computer Engineers—Software	32.5%	37,180
Computer Programmers (Business, Scientific, Process Control)	−2.9%	8,030
Computer Systems Analysts	20.3%	22,280
Accountants, Auditors, and Other Financial Specialists	18.9%	127,260

Pathways Beyond the Bachelor's Degree

Of all graduates with a bachelor's degree in general mathematics, 45 percent proceed to earn a postgraduate degree: 33 percent earn a master's degree, 8 percent earn a doctoral degree, and the remaining 4 percent earn a professional degree.

▶ Only 16 percent of all master's degrees earned by undergraduate general mathematics majors are in the field of general mathematics. About 9 percent are earned in business administration and management, and 7 percent of the master's degrees are earned in mathematics teacher education.

▶ More than 30 percent of the doctoral degrees earned by undergraduate general mathematics majors are in the field of general mathematics. The next most preferred major in the doctoral degrees of undergraduate general mathematics majors is applied mathematics (11 percent).

▶ Out of the few professional degrees earned by general mathematics bachelor's degree holders, 42 percent are in law and 38 percent in the health professions.

CHAPTER 18

Marketing

Marketing is closely related to advertising and sales. Marketing involves marketing research, marketing strategy, sales, promotions, pricing, product development, and public relations. In small firms, the marketing function may be subsumed by another manager, administrator, or the owner. Because marketing is a specialization within a business administration or management program, the focus here will be on marketing management.

Marketing managers develop the organization's detailed marketing strategy. With the help of subordinates, including product development managers and market research managers, they determine the demand for products and services offered by the firm and its competitors and identify potential consumers—for example, business firms, wholesalers, retailers, government, or the general public. Mass markets are further categorized according to various demographics, such as region, age, income, and lifestyle. Marketing managers develop pricing strategy with an eye toward maximizing the organization's share of the market and its profits while ensuring that the organization's customers are satisfied. In collaboration with managers of sales, product development, and other divisions, marketing managers monitor trends that indicate the need for new products and services and oversee product development. They work with advertising and promotion managers to best promote the organization's products and services and to attract potential purchasers.

Sales managers assign sales territories and goals and establish training programs for their sales representatives. These managers advise their sales representatives on ways to improve their sales performance. In large, multiproduct firms, they oversee regional and local sales managers and their staffs. Sales managers maintain contact with dealers and distributors. They analyze sales statistics gathered by their staffs to determine sales potential and inventory requirements and monitor the preferences of customers. Such information is vital for developing products and maximizing profits.

Except in the largest organizations, advertising and promotion staffs generally are small and serve as liaisons between the organization and the advertising or promotional agency to which many advertising or promotional functions are contracted out. Advertising managers oversee the account services, creative services, and media services departments. The account services department is managed by account executives, who assess the need for advertising and, in advertising agencies, maintain the accounts of clients. The creative services department develops the subject matter and presentation of advertising. A creative director, who oversees the copy chief and art director and their staffs, supervises the department. The media services department is supervised by the media director, who oversees planning groups that select the communication media—for example, radio, television, Web, newspapers, magazines, or outdoor signs—to disseminate the advertising.

Promotion managers supervise staffs of promotion specialists. They direct promotion programs that combine advertising with purchase incentives to increase sales. In an effort to establish closer contact with purchasers—dealers, distributors, or consumers—promotion programs may involve direct mail, e-mail, telemarketing, television or radio advertising, webpage display ads, catalogs, exhibits, inserts in newspapers, Twitter feeds, in-store displays and product endorsements, and special events. Purchase incentives may include discounts, samples, gifts, rebates, coupons, sweepstakes, and contests.

The education of those in marketing and sales is varied, but some of the course work may include marketing, sales, advertising management, retailing, market research, telemarketing, accounting, finance, and statistics. Entrants to the advertising field may take course work in journalism or advertising programs in which courses might include creative and technical writing, communications methods and technology, visual arts, and public relations. Database applications, word processing, search engine optimization, and other computer skills are important.

A key ability in marketing is to create new ways of presenting information that will attract people's attention. This can be related to understanding how people react to words, pictures, and colors. The ability to speak and write clearly and convincingly is part of capturing the minds of all kinds of people and influencing their opinions. People with low energy levels are not found in marketing. Tact and good judgment are necessary.

Marketing personnel like to work in groups, be people-oriented, and be involved in organizational and planning activities. This field requires excellent interpersonal relations to maintain effective relationships with a broad scope of people having different needs. Those in this field tend to like the breadth of learning associated with liberal arts and the opportunity to nurture interests in reading and writing, intellectual topics, and the arts.

Many benefits can be gained in marketing. The field pays well, offers variety, and allows for creative self-expression. There is a mental challenge to promotional work, as well as a competitive mind-set. Major goals are to reach out to persuade and influence other people's decisions.

Table 1

Percentage Distribution of Employed Persons with Only a Bachelor's Degree, by Economic Sector, Size, and New Business Status of Employer

	Marketing	All
Economic Sector		
Private for-profit	63.6	47.3
Self-employed	23.8	18.5
Government/Military	4.3	11.0
Education	5.1	15.6
Nonprofit	3.0	7.5
Employer Size		
Small (Fewer than 100 employees)	40.9	35.5
Medium (100–999)	18.4	21.8
Large (1,000–24,999)	25.8	26.0
Very large (25,000 or more)	14.9	16.7
Percent working in new business established within past 5 years	10.2	7.6

Table 2

Percentage Distribution of Employed Persons with Only a Bachelor's Degree in Marketing, by the Relationship Between Their Job and College Major

Relationship of Job to Major	Percent
Closely related	36.1
Somewhat related	44.2
Not related	19.7

Percent who report the following as the most important reasons for working in a job that was not related to major:

Pay, promotion opportunities	27.5
Change in career or professional interests	21.8
Working conditions (hours, equipment, environment)	14.6
Family-related reasons	14.2
Job in highest degree field not available	7.8

While marketing research is the systematic collection of data, marketing managers usually have public contact where they meet and get firsthand impressions of customers' needs for products and services.

Where Do Marketing Majors Work?

The overwhelming majority of graduates with a bachelor's degree in marketing work in the private, for-profit sector, mostly in sales and marketing positions. More than 6 out of 10 work in businesses and corporations. However, many marketing majors opt to become self-employed. Almost one-quarter of all marketing majors either work as self-employed consultants to other businesses or own and operate companies. (The work of consultants is described in Chapter 16.) Marketing majors rarely work in educational institutions, nonprofit organizations, or government agencies.

Graduates of marketing programs are heavily employed in a few sales, marketing, administrative, and managerial positions and other jobs that are related to the field of study. In fact, more than 80 percent of all marketing majors work in jobs related to their undergraduate major. Fewer than 1 in 5 graduates work in a job unrelated to the major.

Eighty-four percent of all marketing majors under the age of 65 are employed, almost all in full-time jobs. About 4 percent are unemployed and actively seeking a job. Twelve percent have chosen not to work; about one-third of these stay at home to meet family obligations, and about one-fifth have no need to work.

Occupations

More than 45 percent of marketing graduates work in sales, including retail sales jobs, insurance, stocks and bonds, real estate sales, and marketing positions. About 8 percent work in accounting and other financial specializations.

Male graduates outnumber female grads by a small margin. The two sexes have roughly equal

Table 3

Top 5 Occupations Employing Persons with Only a Bachelor's Degree
in Marketing, by Percentage

Top 5 Occupations	All	Men	Women
Other Marketing and Sales Occupations	16.6	16.8	16.3
Sales Occupations—Commodities, Except Retail	12.0	14.9	7.4
Sales/Marketing—Insurance, Securities, Real Estate, and Business Services	8.7	9.0	8.3
Accountants, Auditors, and Other Financial Specialists	6.7	6.1	7.6
Sales Occupations—Retail	6.7	5.3	8.9
Total, Top 5 Occupations	50.7	52.1	48.5
Balance of Employed	49.3	47.9	51.5
All Employed	100.0	100.0	100.0

likelihood to go into the top 5 occupations that employ marketing grads, with the exceptions of commodity sales jobs, which attract more males, and retail sales jobs, the choice of more females.

Work Activities

▶ As you might expect, sales and marketing are the primary activities for 44 percent of marketing graduates, and they are significant activities for 78 percent of the grads.

▶ Management of people or projects is another important duty—the principal focus for 18 percent of grads and an important responsibility for 65 percent.

▶ Accounting, finance, and contracting tasks are a significant part of the work for 56 percent of graduates in the marketing field and the primary duty for 10 percent.

▶ Ninety-one percent of marketing graduates utilize computer applications as a regular part of their work activities, although very few are mainly tasked with this kind of work.

Workplace Training and Other Work-Related Experiences

The development of skills on the job is a critical feature in the career development of marketing majors. While on-the-job learning is an important method of skill development, the majority of marketing majors participate in some type of formal work-based training activity over the course of the year. Fifty-seven percent of majors with a degree in this field participate in workshops or seminars sometime during the year, a rate somewhat lower than the rate for all college grads (61 percent).

▶ Of those marketing graduates who receive some training during a year, 48 percent receive technical training in the occupation in which they are employed.

▶ Twenty-three percent of the training recipients receive management or supervisor training.

▶ Another 23 percent receive training to improve their general professional skills, such as public speaking and business writing.

FIGURE 1

Age/Earnings Profile of Persons with Only a Bachelor's Degree in Marketing (Full-Time Workers, in 2010 Dollars)

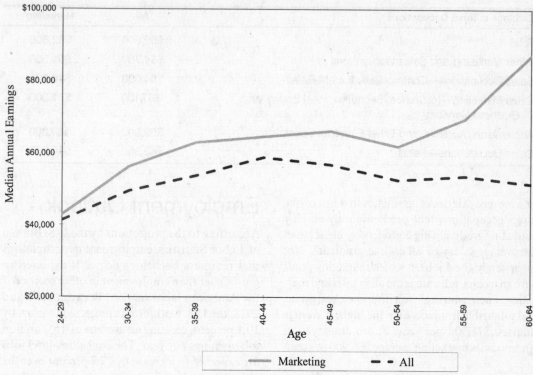

When asked for the most important reason they get training, 3 out of 10 marketing grads say it is to improve their occupational skills and knowledge. About one-tenth say their employer requires it.

Salaries

Marketing graduates employed in full-time jobs have median annual salaries that are about 14 percent higher than the median salary of all college graduates who are employed in full-time jobs. The annual salary for marketing grads is $59,800. On average, employed marketing graduates work for 44 hours per week for 50 weeks per year, resulting in 2,200 hours of employment each year. The level of work effort among marketing graduates is 2 percent higher than the average among all college graduates (which is 43 hours per week and 50 weeks per year, resulting in 2,150 hours per year).

The average annual salary of graduates who work in closely related jobs is $72,600. Graduates with employment in jobs that are somewhat related to their major earn $56,300 per year. In contrast, the average salary of graduates employed full-time in a job that is not related to their field of study is $44,900.

Highest earnings for marketing grads are in for-profit businesses, with an average of $63,800 annually. Self-employed grads average $54,600 per year. Much lower annual earnings are found among those working for nonprofit organizations ($45,900), for the government ($42,600), and in education ($35,400).

Table 4
Annual Salary of Workers with Only a Bachelor's Degree, Top 5 Occupations (in 2010 Dollars)

Earnings in Top 5 Occupations	All	Marketing
Total	$59,800	$62,600
Other Marketing and Sales Occupations	$54,700	$61,500
Sales Occupations—Commodities, Except Retail	$64,000	$66,900
Sales/Marketing—Insurance, Securities, Real Estate, and Business Services	$67,100	$71,300
Accountants, Auditors, and Other Financial Specialists	$59,900	$57,800
Sales Occupations—Retail	$42,300	$50,200

The average salaries of graduates in 4 out of the top 5 occupations that predominantly employ marketing graduates are considerably higher than the average salary of all college graduates. Not surprisingly, the 4 jobs in which marketing grads have an income advantage are all in sales and marketing. Those who deal with insurance, real estate, and intangible products earn the highest average salaries, $71,300 per year. Those employed in commodities marketing average $66,900 per year.

Job Satisfaction

The overall level of job satisfaction of marketing majors is about the same as the average for all graduates.

Employment Outlook

According to the projections by the U.S. Bureau of Labor Statistics, employment in occupations that require a bachelor's degree is expected to grow faster than employment in other sectors of the American labor market. Between 2008 and 2018, the U.S. workforce is projected to grow by 10.1 percent, creating an average of 15.2 million job openings per year. The bachelor's-level jobs are expected to increase by 17.7 percent over the same time.

The demand for many key occupations that employ marketing majors is mixed. Overall demand for salesworkers is expected to increase by about 6 percent between 2008 and 2018, a rate of

Table 5
Percentage Distribution of Workers with Only a Bachelor's Degree, by Level of Job Satisfaction

Job Satisfaction	Marketing	All
Very satisfied	44.1	45.4
Somewhat satisfied	45.3	45.0
Somewhat dissatisfied	8.5	7.4
Very dissatisfied	2.1	2.2
Mean Score (4=very satisfied, 1=not satisfied at all)	3.3	3.3

Table 6

Projected Growth and Job Openings in the Top 5 Occupations
Employing Persons with Only a Bachelor's Degree in Marketing

Top 5 Occupations	Projected Growth 2008–2018	Projected Annual Job Openings
All occupations	10.1%	5,093,000
All top 5	11.0%	515,360
Other Marketing and Sales Occupations	7.3%	64,880
Sales Occupations—Commodities, Except Retail	−1.1%	310
Sales/Marketing—Insurance, Securities, Real Estate, and Business Services	11.5%	115,210
Accountants, Auditors, and Other Financial Specialists	18.9%	127,260
Sales Occupations—Retail	7.5%	207,700

growth well below the average for college graduates. Between the various sales specializations, the outlook varies greatly, with the best outlook for those working with insurance and financial services. Marketing grads who gain experience or an additional degree and move into marketing or sales management have better prospects. The workforce of marketing managers is projected to grow by 12.5 percent; the workforce of sales managers, by 14.9 percent.

Pathways Beyond the Bachelor's Degree

Marketing majors are less likely to complete an advanced degree program than graduates from almost any other undergraduate field of study. Only 15 percent of all those with a bachelor's degree in marketing eventually earn some type of degree beyond the bachelor's. Most who do earn a master's degree.

▶ Thirteen percent of all marketing majors earn a master's degree. Of these about one-quarter specialize in general management and another 16 percent in marketing management.

▶ Almost no marketing degree holders earn a doctoral degree.

▶ About 1 percent of marketing majors go on to earn a law degree.

CHAPTER 19

Public Administration

This field covers government administrators not elected by their constituents. This is a large area because it includes all the managers, except appointees, who are hired to be responsible for running the federal, state, county, city, town, and district government functions.

Public administrators, like business managers, have overall responsibility for the performance of their organizations. Working in conjunction with elected officials, they set goals and then organize programs to attain them. They appoint department heads who oversee the work of the civil servants who, in turn, carry out programs or enforce laws enacted by their legislative bodies. They plan budgets, specify how government funds will be used, and ensure that resources are used properly and programs are carried out as planned.

Because public administrators work for the public, they meet with elected officials and confer with other government leaders and constituents to discuss proposed programs and determine citizens' level of support. They may nominate citizens to boards and commissions, solicit bids from and select contractors to do work for the government, encourage business investment and economic development in their jurisdictions, and seek federal or state funds. The size of the jurisdiction determines how much of the work can be done by aides and assistants and how much by the administrator.

Educational course work may include introduction to politics, public policy analysis, public administration, organization theory, public personnel administration, public budgeting and finance, politics and the mass media, techniques and practices of public management, civil liberties, business and government relations, intergovernmental relations, and legal issues in public administration. Obviously, the work allows many areas for specialization, some of which are finance, personnel matters, legal areas, and civil engineering.

The abilities required in public administration are developing plans, organizing people and their work, and solving problems. Skills for making decisions, sometimes on the basis of limited or contradictory information, are needed. This task can create pressure and stress. Public speaking and communication skills are prerequisites, as well as being able to get along with others. Negotiating and budget skills are critical.

Public administrators like and appreciate the functions of organizations. They are people oriented. They enjoy being in positions of power, control, and status. Because, in the end, they are assessed on their ability to perform, they get satisfaction in being very practical in doing things and delivering services.

The benefits gained in this type of work may vary based on the type and level of government function involved. For example, in rural areas, there may be a lot of public recognition, such as being written up in the newspapers and having public contact, because the issues involved may have a direct impact on people's lives. Some public administrators have a high public profile and thus gain prestige from their leadership. The work of planning, organizing, and budgeting requires working with one's mind and often calls for creative solutions. Public administrators usually are well paid, although they may not make as much money as business managers.

Where Do Public Administration Majors Work?

More than 4 out of 10 employed public administration graduates work in the government sector. However, training in administration, management, organization, and budgeting provides public administration graduates with skills to work in the private sector as managers, administrators, and the like. One-third work in the private, for-profit sector for businesses and corporations. Twelve percent are self-employed in their own professional businesses or practices. (The work of consultants is described in Chapter 16.) Six percent of public administration graduates work for an educational institution, and the remaining 5 percent are employed in the nonprofit sector.

Public administration graduates are divided into three roughly equal shares of those who do work that is closely related to their undergraduate major, somewhat related, or not at all related.

When asked the most important reason they are not working in the field of their major, 39 percent in that situation say they are unable to find work in their degree field. One-quarter report that they choose to work outside their field of study because of better pay and promotion opportunities there. Another 16 percent do so because of a change in their career and professional interests.

Almost 78 percent of all public administration graduates with only a bachelor's degree who are under 65 years old are employed. About 9 percent

Table 1
Percentage Distribution of Employed Persons with Only a Bachelor's Degree, by Economic Sector, Size, and New Business Status of Employer

	Public Administration	All
Economic Sector		
Private for-profit	33.3	47.3
Self-employed	12.3	18.5
Government/Military	43.2	11.0
Education	6.5	15.6
Nonprofit	4.7	7.5
Employer Size		
Small (Fewer than 100 employees)	26.3	35.5
Medium (100–999)	20.2	21.8
Large (1,000–24,999)	32.1	26.0
Very large (25,000 or more)	21.4	16.7
Percent working in new business established within past 5 years	4.3	7.6

Table 2
Percentage Distribution of Employed Persons with Only a Bachelor's Degree in Public Administration, by the Relationship Between Their Job and College Major

Relationship of Job to Major	Percent
Closely related	35.9
Somewhat related	33.0
Not related	31.1

Percent who report the following as the most important reasons for working in a job that was not related to major:

Job in highest degree field not available	38.6
Pay, promotion opportunities	25.2
Change in career or professional interests	16.0
Other reason	9.5
Working conditions (hours, equipment, environment)	8.8

are not employed but looking for employment—a very high figure compared to the other majors in this book. The remaining 13 percent of all public administration graduates are out of the labor force; that is, they are neither working nor looking for work. More than 58 percent of those public administration graduates who withdraw from the labor force do so to take early retirement. (Public-sector jobs traditionally have offered good pension plans.) Nine percent withdraw from the labor force because they do not desire or need to work.

Occupations

The occupational employment of public administration graduates reveals that almost 16 percent work in protective-service occupations, which are concerned with protecting the public against crime, fire, and acts of war. People in these occupations include police officers and detective correction officers, fire department workers, and personnel of the armed forces. A slightly smaller share work in various administrative jobs. Ten percent work in occupations concerned with insurance, real estate, buying and selling securities, and providing

business services such as management, consulting, and public relations. Other predominant occupations of employment for public administration graduates are miscellaneous management occupations such as gaming managers; property, real estate, and community association managers; food service managers; and lodging managers.

Male graduates outnumber female grads by somewhat less than 2 to 1, and their employment patterns are quite different.

Work Activities

▶ Management and administrative functions regularly take up at least 10 hours during a typical workweek of 28 percent of all employed public administration graduates. For almost 8 out of 10 grads, these activities are their primary work role.

▶ One-fifth of public administration graduates perform purchasing, marketing, and sales activities at their jobs on a regular basis, and 57 percent engage in teaching activities.

Table 3
Top 5 Occupations Employing Persons with Only a Bachelor's Degree in Public Administration, by Percentage

Top 5 Occupations	All	Men	Women
Protective Service Workers	15.8	20.2	6.9
Other Administrative Occupations	13.6	5.1	30.7
Sales/Marketing—Insurance, Securities, Real Estate, and Business Services	10.0	10.5	8.8
Other Management-Related Occupations	9.9	14.3	0.9
Mechanics and Repairers	8.9	13.3	–
Total, Top 5 Occupations	58.2	63.4	47.3
Balance of Employed	41.8	36.6	52.7
All Employed	100.0	100.0	100.0

▶ More than 6 out of 10 grads regularly perform employee-relations duties, including recruitment, personnel development, and training. These tasks are the main responsibilities for 14 percent of graduates.

▶ Ninety-four percent regularly engage in computer applications, programming, and systems-development activities, but less than 4 percent pursue these activities most of the time.

▶ More than 43 percent of public administration graduates perform accounting, financial, and contractual duties in a typical workweek as a regular part of their job. For almost 8 percent, these tasks dominate the workweek.

Workplace Training and Other Work-Related Experiences

Work-related training is an important indicator of the long-term career potential of a job. Firms that invest in their workers at high rates are much more likely to offer pay increases and promotions than firms that do not invest in their workers. The rate of participation in work-related training during a year among employed public administration graduates (78 percent) is much higher than the training participation rate of all college graduates (61 percent).

▶ Seventy-one percent of public administration graduates who receive some training are engaged in technical training in their occupations.

▶ Participation in management or supervisor training is reported by 32 percent of those public administration graduates who receive some kind of training.

▶ Thirty-six percent of public administration graduates report receiving training in communication skills, such as public speaking and business writing.

Forty-six percent of employed public administration graduates participate in training primarily to acquire additional skills and to increase their occupational knowledge. According to almost 9 percent of public administration graduates, the most important reason for their participation in work-related training is to increase their salary and to improve their opportunities to secure a promotion. The same share of grads get training chiefly to achieve or maintain licensure or certification. Almost 8 percent are required to participate in work-related training by their employers.

Salaries

The median annual salary of public administration graduates with only a bachelor's degree is $60,000, a level that is 14 percent higher than the median annual salary of all employed college graduates. On average, employed public administration graduates work for 43 hours per week and for 51 weeks per year, resulting in 2,193 hours of employment per year. The level of work effort among public administration graduates is 2 percent higher than the average among all college graduates (which is 43 hours per week and 50 weeks per year, resulting in 2,150 hours per year).

Note: Because of the very small number of survey respondents in some age groups, it was not possible to furnish a useful age/earnings profile graphic for this major.

Of public administration graduates who work full-time, those who are self-employed report the highest average salaries: $121,500 per year. Those who work in the government sector earn an average annual salary of $69,000. The private, for-profit sector pays an average annual salary of $49,500 to public administration graduates. Employment in the education sector secures much lower earnings among public administration majors with only a bachelor's degree. Their average annual salary is $39,200.

Public administration grads earn more when they get to use the skills they learned as undergraduates. The average annual salary of graduates who work full-time in closely related jobs is $75,300. Graduates with employment in jobs that are somewhat related to their major earn $43,300 per year. In contrast, the average salary of graduates employed in a job that is not related to their field of study is $27,900.

There are sizable variations in the average annual salaries of public administration graduates by the occupation in which they are employed. In 4 of the 5 occupations that predominantly employ them, the degree confers an earnings advantage over other bachelor's degrees—in two of the occupations, an impressive difference, indicating a high level of responsibility. Those who are working as mechanics and repairers have an earnings disadvantage because their major does not equip them with job-specific skills.

Table 4
Annual Salary of Workers with Only a Bachelor's Degree, Top 5 Occupations (in 2010 Dollars)

Earnings in Top 5 Occupations	All	Public Administration
Total	$60,000	$75,300
Protective Service Workers	$49,500	$113,500
Other Administrative Occupations	$38,200	$41,300
Sales/Marketing—Insurance, Securities, Real Estate, and Business Services	$67,100	$123,800
Other Management-Related Occupations	$57,800	$64,000
Mechanics and Repairers	$45,400	$27,900

Table 5
Percentage Distribution of Workers with Only a Bachelor's Degree, by Level of Job Satisfaction

Job Satisfaction	Public Administration	All
Very satisfied	44.1	45.4
Somewhat satisfied	47.5	45.0
Somewhat dissatisfied	6.4	7.4
Very dissatisfied	2.1	2.2
Mean Score (4=very satisfied, 1=not satisfied at all)	3.3	3.3

Job Satisfaction

The overall level of job satisfaction of public administration majors is about the same as the average for all graduates.

Employment Outlook

According to the projections by the U.S. Bureau of Labor Statistics, employment in occupations that require a bachelor's degree is expected to grow faster than employment in other sectors of the American labor market. Between 2008 and 2018, the U.S. workforce is projected to grow by 10.1 percent, creating an average of 15.2 million job openings per year. The bachelor's-level jobs are expected to increase by 17.7 percent over the same time. For public administration grads, the outlook is mixed.

▶ Protective-service occupations, which are chosen mainly by male public administration graduates, are expected to grow by 14.1 percent and create 74,000 job openings each year. The level of government spending determines the level of employment in this field. Job opportunities in most local police departments will be favorable for qualified individuals, whereas competition is expected for jobs in state and federal agencies. Prospective fire fighters are expected to face keen competition for available job openings.

▶ Employment in the miscellaneous administrative and sales/marketing occupations is expected to grow faster than average and also create many job openings, largely because of the large workforce of administrative jobs, where much turnover will occur. The same is true for the sales jobs that employ many grads.

▶ The miscellaneous managerial jobs are projected to grow more slowly than average, but there is considerable variation among the specializations. For example, employment of gaming managers is projected to grow by 11.8 percent, whereas the workforce of postmasters and mail superintendents is projected to shrink by 15.1 percent.

▶ The mechanical and repair occupations employing public administration grads are also projected to shrink, but it seems likely that many of the grads working in these jobs are holding them only until a job better suited to the degree becomes available.

Table 6

Projected Growth and Job Openings in the Top 5 Occupations Employing Persons
with Only a Bachelor's Degree in Public Administration

Top 5 Occupations	Projected Growth 2008–2018	Projected Annual Job Openings
All top 5	10.7%	411,290
Protective Service Workers	14.1%	74,300
Other Administrative Occupations	10.8%	166,130
Sales/Marketing—Insurance, Securities, Real Estate, and Business Services	11.5%	115,210
Other Management-Related Occupations	7.2%	53,020
Mechanics and Repairers	−4.4%	2,630

Pathways Beyond the Bachelor's Degree

Nearly 65 percent of all public administration graduates go no further in their education than the bachelor's degree. Of those who do earn higher degrees, a large majority are master's degrees. Only 5 percent earn a doctorate or a professional degree.

▶ Of all public administration graduates who earn a master's degree, 35 percent continue with public administration as their major at the master's level.

▶ Twelve percent choose business management and administration services as their major for the master's.

▶ Another 15 percent earn their master's degree in another business subject.

PART 4

Education

CHAPTER 20

Elementary Teacher Education

Elementary school teachers work in private and public school systems. People entering elementary education know the field well through models they have personally experienced. But what some people considering the field of education may not have experienced is the difficulty in working with unmotivated students, the stress of working with self-doubt, the frustration of working with children with difficulties or from different cultures, and the lack of family or institutional support.

The learning process in schools has become less structured and more group oriented in recent years. For example, to help students understand concepts, educators use problem-solving experiments with apparatus. Distance learning, computers, and visual aids create more realistic situations for teachers to demonstrate applications. While memorization and drill are being downplayed, reading, writing, speaking, and working with mathematics and science problems remain critical. Teachers emphasize development of critical and logical thinking by encouraging students to explore their environment creatively. Reading remains a foundational specialization.

Teachers are licensed in all states, but students considering a teaching career must investigate their state's particular requirements for course work and licensing examinations. The website of the state's Department of Education is a good place to start.

Elementary teachers have a talent for working with children, plus organizational, administrative, and record-keeping abilities. Besides being patient, they can be creative, communicative, influential, and motivational. In addition to language proficiency and leadership skills, they tend to have interests in art and music.

Elementary teachers enjoy young children and must have an idea of the age with which they prefer to work: the primary grades, ages 6 through 8; or 9- to 13-year-olds, who spend more time in subject-oriented lessons. The motivation of working with this latter group may be in seeing students experience the satisfaction of developing new specific content skills. On the other hand, some aspiring to elementary education enjoy a younger age group because they like the independence of working alone with a group in a classroom and the freedom to choose and experiment with different teaching styles and methods. Teaching involves leading and influencing roles.

Elementary teachers and students in training feel that working with people, being creative, working with one's mind, having variety and diversion, and being independent are equally important. Overall, teachers at this level are characterized as friendly, concerned with the feelings of others, and conscientious to fulfill a set of obligations.

Where Do Elementary Teacher Education Majors Work?

Unsurprisingly, the great majority of employed persons with a degree in elementary education work in the education sector. While almost 70 percent of college graduates in this field work in education, private, for-profit firms employ almost 14 percent. About 10 percent are self-employed.

Two-thirds of elementary ed grads work in a job that's closely related to the major. Another 11 percent work in a job that is somewhat related, but more than one-fifth are employed in a job not related to the field of education. Those employed in unrelated jobs earn 16 percent less than those employed in jobs that use the skills they developed in their major. Nevertheless, one-fifth of the workers who took an unrelated job did so primarily because of opportunities for pay or promotion.

Employment rates of elementary education majors are low. Only about three-quarters of all graduates under age 65 are employed. Of this group, 11 percent hold a part-time position. Involuntary unemployment occurs infrequently among graduates in this major; only about 3 percent are jobless and actively seeking work. Almost one-quarter of elementary education graduates choose not to work. Most often these persons say that they have taken early retirement, accounting for 44 percent of those out of the workforce. Another 22 percent do not work to meet family responsibilities. Slightly fewer say they have no need to work.

Occupations

The graduates of this major are overwhelmingly female: more than 92 percent. Male grads are less likely to work in the most popular occupations for female grads. (Twenty-nine percent of males work in unrelated jobs, compared to 21 percent

Table 1

Percentage Distribution of Employed Persons with Only a Bachelor's Degree, by Economic Sector, Size, and New Business Status of Employer

	Elementary Teacher Education	All
Economic Sector		
Private for-profit	13.8	47.3
Self-employed	10.2	18.5
Government/Military	3.9	11.0
Education	68.1	15.6
Nonprofit	3.9	7.5
Employer Size		
Small (Fewer than 100 employees)	36.5	35.5
Medium (100–999)	31.0	21.8
Large (1,000–24,999)	24.8	26.0
Very large (25,000 or more)	7.7	16.7
Percent working in new business established within past 5 years	4.7	7.6

Table 2

Percentage Distribution of Employed Persons with Only a
Bachelor's Degree in Elementary Teacher Education,
by the Relationship Between Their Job and College Major

Relationship of Job to Major	Percent
Closely related	66.7
Somewhat related	11.1
Not related	22.1

Percent who report the following as the most important reasons for
working in a job that was not related to major:

Family-related reasons	27.9
Pay, promotion opportunities	20.2
Change in career or professional interests	16.4
Working conditions (hours, equipment, environment)	14.3
Job in highest degree field not available	8.9

of females.) The only occupation that male grads choose nearly as often as female grads is teaching in elementary school.

Work Activities

▌ Unsurprisingly, teaching comprises the major activity that graduates in this major undertake. Sixty-four percent report it as their chief activity, and it is a significant duty for 74 percent.

▌ About nine-tenths of graduates in the field employ computer applications on their jobs, but only 2 percent see them as the focus of their work.

▌ About 4 out of 10 grads spend significant time managing or supervising people or projects. This is the primary responsibility for only 6 percent of grads.

▌ Only about one-tenth of grads are primarily tasked with sales, purchasing, and marketing activities, but almost one-quarter of grads typically engage in these tasks for at least 10 hours of the workweek.

▌ Employee relations are a regular responsibility for more than one-quarter of elementary education graduates, but hardly any grads see these tasks as their most important function.

Workplace Training and Other Work-Related Experiences

Opportunities for informal on-the-job learning are limited in the teaching profession. However, teachers regularly participate in professional development activities to maintain or improve their teaching skills. About three-quarters of all graduates of elementary education programs participate in training workshops and seminars designed to impart a variety of work-based skills. This rate is much higher than the training participation rate of all college graduates (61 percent).

Table 3
Top 5 Occupations Employing Persons with Only a Bachelor's Degree in Elementary Teacher Education, by Percentage

Top 5 Occupations	All	Men	Women
Teachers—Elementary School	42.7	38.7	43.1
Teachers—Pre-K and Kindergarten	10.2	–	11.3
Teachers—Special Education	4.9	2.4	5.2
Other Administrative Occupations	3.9	2.1	4.1
Teachers—Secondary, Other Subjects	2.8	1.7	3.0
Total, Top 5 Occupations	64.5	44.9	66.7
Balance of Employed	35.5	55.1	33.3
All Employed	100.0	100.0	100.0

▶ Almost 7 out of 10 grads participating in training enroll in workshops and seminars designed to bolster a specific professional skill in teaching or other areas related to their specific job duties.

▶ Only 9 percent of the training recipients receive management or supervisor training.

▶ More than one-fifth participate in training sessions designed to enhance communications skills, including writing and public speaking skills.

Skill-building is the most important reason these grads get training, the reason cited by 46 percent of them. Another one-tenth cite the need to maintain certification, and almost as many note that it is a requirement of their employer.

Salaries

The average annual salary of elementary education majors is quite low compared to other college graduates: $36,000 per year, which is 43 percent lower than the average annual salary of all employed college graduates. Part of this large difference is a result of teachers working fewer hours than the typical college graduate. On average, employed elementary teacher education graduates work for 40 hours per week and for 45 weeks per year, resulting in 1,800 hours of employment per year. The level of work effort among elementary teacher education graduates is 14 percent lower than the average among all college graduates (which is 43 hours per week and 50 weeks per year, resulting in 2,150 hours per year).

Majors who work in education earn $37,100, while those employed by for-profit companies make an average of $36,100. Self-employed graduates average only $25,400 per year.

The earnings of elementary education majors vary somewhat on the type of job in which they are employed. Majors who work as elementary school teachers earn $38,200 per year, while those who work as kindergarten and preschool teachers earn less, averaging $34,100 annually. Majors employed as high school teachers earn $35,100, and special education teachers earn $40,200. Majors who work in administrative occupations (which generally do not require a college degree) have an average annual salary that is significantly lower than the average of graduates in the field.

FIGURE 1

Age/Earnings Profile of Persons with Only a Bachelor's Degree in Elementary Teacher Education (Full-Time Workers, in 2010 Dollars)

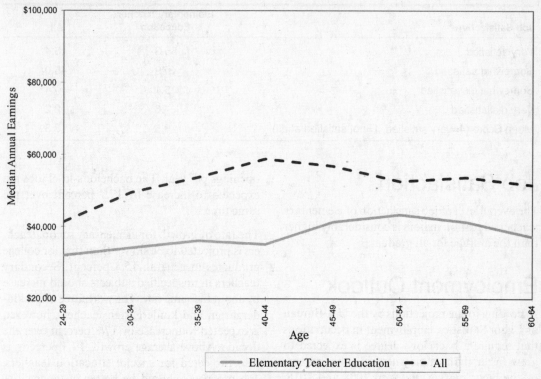

Table 4
Annual Salary of Workers with Only a Bachelor's Degree, Top 5 Occupations (in 2010 Dollars)

Earnings in Top 5 Occupations	All	Elementary Teacher Education
Total	$36,000	$37,300
Teachers—Elementary School	$37,200	$38,200
Teachers—Pre-K and Kindergarten	$33,000	$34,100
Teachers—Special Education	$38,200	$40,200
Other Administrative Occupations	$38,200	$33,000
Teachers—Secondary, Other Subjects	$39,200	$35,100

Table 5
Percentage Distribution of Workers with Only a Bachelor's Degree, by Level of Job Satisfaction

Job Satisfaction	Elementary Teacher Education	All
Very satisfied	55.3	45.4
Somewhat satisfied	37.9	45.0
Somewhat dissatisfied	5.1	7.4
Very dissatisfied	1.6	2.2
Mean Score (4=very satisfied, 1=not satisfied at all)	3.5	3.3

Job Satisfaction

The overall level of job satisfaction of elementary teacher education majors is considerably higher than the average for all graduates.

Employment Outlook

According to the projections by the U.S. Bureau of Labor Statistics, employment in occupations that require a bachelor's degree is expected to grow faster than employment in other sectors of the labor market. Between 2008 and 2018, the U.S. workforce is projected to grow by 10.1 percent, creating an average of 15.2 million job openings per year. The bachelor's-level jobs are expected to increase by 17.7 percent over the same time.

The rate of growth for elementary school teachers is projected to be slower than that for college graduates in general: 15.8 percent. Secondary teachers in unspecified subjects should increase by about the same rate. The workforce of prekindergarten and kindergarten teachers, however, is expected to increase by 17.8 percent over the decade. Above-average growth, 17.3 percent, is also projected for special education teachers. Job prospects should be better in inner cities and rural areas than in suburban districts. Many job openings should occur because of turnover.

Table 6
Projected Growth and Job Openings in the Top 5 Occupations Employing Persons with Only a Bachelor's Degree in Elementary Teacher Education

Top 5 Occupations	Projected Growth 2008–2018	Projected Annual Job Openings
All top 5	13.0%	285,180
Teachers—Elementary School	15.8%	59,650
Teachers—Pre-K and Kindergarten	17.8%	24,130
Teachers—Special Education	17.3%	20,460
Other Administrative Occupations	10.8%	166,130
Teachers—Secondary, Other Subjects	15.3%	25,110

Pathways Beyond the Bachelor's Degree

About 4 out of 10 elementary education majors go on to earn an advanced degree after completing college. Virtually all of those who study at the graduate level earn a master's degree. Only 1 percent continue their education through the completion of a doctorate. Rarely do majors from this field earn a professional degree in law or educational administration.

▶ Most of the master's degrees earned by elementary education majors are in the education field. About 42 percent of them are in elementary education, and another 11 percent are in educational administration.

▶ Most of those who earn a doctorate continue in the education field.

CHAPTER 21

Mathematics and Science Teacher Education

The mathematics and science subject areas traditionally have been separated from general secondary education, receiving specific attention. The practice originally may have arisen because of the belief that a strong knowledge of these content areas was fundamental before one could teach them. In fact, the U.S. Congress set mathematics and science education as a high national priority in post–World War II years, when science and technology were part of the national security race with the Communist bloc. Another reason for focusing on these teacher education areas is that when the interest and personality profiles of teachers were researched, the analysis showed that mathematics and science teachers clustered with scientists, while other teachers clustered primarily with those in social occupations.

As with all education, teaching in these areas increasingly is being geared to having students achieve mastery performance of standards in every subject at each grade level. The aim also is to have students understand abstract concepts, learn problem solving, and develop critical-thinking thought processes. Techniques of evaluating student progress have moved away from total reliance on grades and toward increased use of portfolios. An A grade of performance by one teacher may mean something different from another teacher's assignment of an A grade, but portfolios demonstrate individual mastery by displaying samples of learning results, such as pictures of projects and best examples of writing. Also, new technology, including the use of computers, is improving teaching methodology by offering a more realistic presentation of information.

Each state has its own certification requirements. Those entering teaching need to check out specific state requirements, which can be found on the website of the state's Department of Education. In general, for those working in middle and high schools, course work is required in adolescent development, introduction to special education, the learning process, curriculum theory, methods and materials for instruction, and student practice teaching. In addition, the following kinds of teachers must demonstrate knowledge in these specific areas:

- Mathematics: algebra, geometry, calculus, number theory, probability and statistics, and discrete mathematics

- Biology: botany, zoology, human biology, genetics, ecology, and chemistry

- Chemistry: organic, analytical, and physical chemistry; physics; and related aspects of mathematics

- Earth Sciences: geology; oceanography; astronomy; ecology; meteorology; and related aspects of chemistry, physics, and biology

- Physics: mechanics, heat, light, and sound; modern physics; and related aspects of mathematics

- Also, all mathematics and science teachers must know the modes of inquiry and methods of research and experimentation used in mathematics and science, including laboratory techniques and the use of computers

The interests of mathematics and science teachers are scientific; they like to probe natural phenomena, work with numbers, and solve technical problems. Also, they appreciate the value and role of equipment and machines in the exploration and discovery process. They have a people orientation that serves as the attraction to teaching rather than other applications for their knowledge of mathematics and science.

Those in this major value the opportunity to work with adolescents in a developmental way. The teaching process provides the chance to be creative in motivating youth to learn. Teachers are also leaders and do influence their students about subjects they personally like and value. Also, there is mental stimulation in working with numbers and keeping current with scientific knowledge.

Where Do Mathematics and Science Teacher Education Majors Work?

While the expectation for persons who major in an education field at the undergraduate level is that they will work in some capacity in education, only about one-half of all mathematics and

Table 1
Percentage Distribution of Employed Persons with Only a Bachelor's Degree, by Economic Sector, Size, and New Business Status of Employer

	Mathematics and Science Teacher Education	All
Economic Sector		
Private for-profit	19.4	47.3
Self-employed	13.9	18.5
Government/Military	7.4	11.0
Education	53.2	15.6
Nonprofit	6.1	7.5
Employer Size		
Small (Fewer than 100 employees)	32.4	35.5
Medium (100–999)	32.9	21.8
Large (1,000–24,999)	23.9	26.0
Very large (25,000 or more)	10.8	16.7
Percent working in new business established within past 5 years	3.4	7.6

science teacher education majors end up working in an educational institution. Relatively low pay in the teaching profession and strong demand for persons with technical skills in mathematics-related fields mean that many majors from this area are eventually employed in higher-paying jobs in private, for-profit companies or the government. Private, for-profit firms employ 19 percent of majors from this field, while an additional 14 percent are self-employed either as consultants to other organizations or through their own companies. An additional 7 percent work for a government agency. Only 6 percent of the grads are employed by a nonprofit charity or research foundation.

A substantial number of all majors from this field—54 percent—are employed in jobs that are closely related to the major field of study. About one-quarter work in jobs unrelated to the field, a rate that is higher than for some other educational majors.

The employment rate of persons with bachelor's degrees in the mathematics and science teacher education field is 85 percent. Among the 15 percent not working, only 1 percent are involuntarily unemployed. Most of those not working have chosen not to work. Primarily these are early retirees; this accounts for 55 percent of the grads out of the workforce. Another 16 percent have no need to work, and slightly fewer are out of the workforce to meet family responsibilities.

Occupations

Nearly 40 percent of all graduates with a degree in mathematics and science teacher education are employed as secondary school teachers. An additional 4 percent of all majors in this field work as instructors in noneducational settings—for example, as corporate trainers. About 4 percent of all majors work in accounting, and about 3 percent work in sales- and marketing-related jobs.

Because of the emphasis on science and math in this program, the ratio of women to men among the grads is more balanced than it is in most

Table 2
Percentage Distribution of Employed Persons with Only a Bachelor's Degree in Mathematics and Science Teacher Education, by the Relationship Between Their Job and College Major

Relationship of Job to Major	Percent
Closely related	54.1
Somewhat related	21.8
Not related	24.1

Percent who report the following as the most important reasons for working in a job that was not related to major:

Job in highest degree field not available	25.4
Working conditions (hours, equipment, environment)	20.7
Family-related reasons	14.6
Change in career or professional interests	13.3
Other reason	10.0

Table 3
Top 5 Occupations Employing Persons with Only a Bachelor's Degree in Mathematics and Science Teacher Education, by Percentage

Top 5 Occupations	All	Men	Women
Teachers, Secondary—Computer, Math, or Science	39.3	36.1	42.7
Other Administrative Occupations	5.2	4.1	6.3
Accountants, Auditors, and Other Financial Specialists	4.0	3.5	4.6
Other Teachers and Instructors in Noneducational Institutions	3.8	2.2	5.4
Sales/Marketing—Insurance, Securities, Real Estate, and Business Services	3.0	4.0	1.9
Total, Top 5 Occupations	55.3	49.9	60.9
Balance of Employed	44.7	50.1	39.1
All Employed	100.0	100.0	100.0

teaching programs: 52 percent women, 48 percent men. Among the top 5 jobs employing grads, all have a stronger attraction to female grads, with the exception of the sales occupations.

Work Activities

▶ Sixty-three percent of all graduates in the field engage in teaching activities. For almost half of all graduates in the field, teaching is the predominant job duty.

▶ Ninety-two percent of all majors develop or use computer applications on the job. Four percent of majors say that this is their most important duty.

▶ Managerial and supervisory duties are undertaken by almost half of all majors from the field, but they are the primary responsibility for only 11 percent.

▶ One-quarter of persons with a degree in mathematics and science teacher education have sales, purchasing, or marketing functions as a regular part of their job.

Workplace Training and Other Work-Related Experiences

About 6 out of 10 graduates with a degree in mathematics and science teacher education participate in some type of formal training program related to their job over the course of a year. Those employed as teachers are more likely than those working in other occupations to engage in this type of training. The teaching profession relies heavily on formal classroom training to develop professional skills rather than informal on-the-job learning. Teacher certification requirements often demand regular participation in professional development seminars and workshops.

▶ Fifty-five percent of graduates with degrees in mathematics and science education participate in training designed to enhance specific occupational skills, ranging from teaching methods to computer programming innovations.

▶ Twenty-two percent of the graduates in this major field engage in training designed to enhance their communications skills by participating in public speaking and business writing programs over the course of a year.

▶ About 18 percent of all graduates in the major attend supervisory and management workshops. Most often these sessions are related to personnel, industrial relations, and human resource issues.

Graduates in the field do not participate in training programs because they believe it will help them receive pay increases or promotions. Rather, their participation is chiefly motivated by the need to keep abreast of developments in the field and further sharpen their work-based skills. Thirty percent of the grads who get training cite this as their most important reason. The

only other reasons that come close are employee requirements and licensing or certification requirements, each of which are cited by about one-tenth of the grads receiving training.

Salaries

The average annual salary of mathematics and science teacher education graduates with only a bachelor's degree is $37,800, a level that is 37 percent lower than the average annual salary of all employed college graduates. On average, employed mathematics and science teacher education graduates work for 42 hours per week and for 48 weeks per year, resulting in 2,016 hours of employment per year. The level of work effort among mathematics and science teacher

FIGURE 1

Age/Earnings Profile of Persons with Only a Bachelor's Degree in Mathematics and Science Teacher Education (Full-Time Workers, in 2010 Dollars)

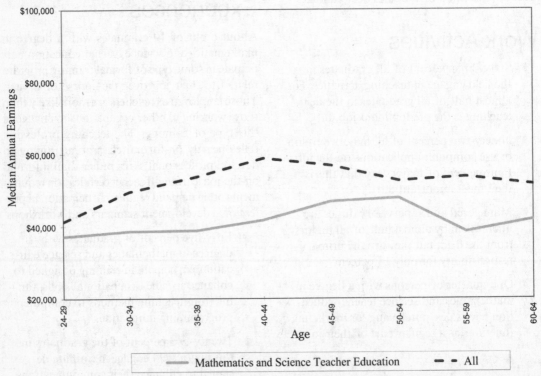

Table 4
Annual Salary of Workers with Only a Bachelor's Degree, Top 5 Occupations (in 2010 Dollars)

Earnings in Top 5 Occupations	All	Mathematics and Science Teacher Education
Total	$37,800	$41,300
Teachers, Secondary—Computer, Math, or Science	$40,200	$38,800
Other Administrative Occupations	$38,200	$51,200
Accountants, Auditors, and Other Financial Specialists	$59,900	$27,400
Other Teachers and Instructors in Noneducational Institutions	$36,100	$70,600
Sales/Marketing—Insurance, Securities, Real Estate, and Business Services	$67,100	$72,200

education graduates is 6 percent lower than the average among all college graduates (which is 43 hours per week and 50 weeks per year, resulting in 2,150 hours per year).

Sharp disparities exist in the earnings of persons with a bachelor's degree on the basis of the sector in which they are employed. Majors who are self-employed earn an average salary of $53,600 per year, a rate of pay 38 percent higher than the $38,900 salary of those who work for an educational institution. Strong demand for consultants and independent salesworkers with mathematics and computer skills contributes substantially to this large earnings differential. Graduates with teaching degrees in these fields also have substantially higher salaries when they work for government organizations. Salaries for those who work in government average $41,600 per year, and those in the for-profit sector average $41,000.

Given the relatively low pay of mathematics and science teacher education majors who work in the education sector, it is not surprising that those majors employed in jobs that are closely related to their undergraduate field of study have annual salaries that are well below those of persons in jobs that are only partially related to the major. Those who report that their work is closely tied to the undergraduate major earn an average of

$39,300, while those who work in somewhat related jobs report an annual salary of $48,800. On the other hand, the skills they learn in their major must create an earnings advantage, because the average salary of graduates employed in a job that is not related to their field of study is only $37,600.

Top-paying jobs are in selling insurance, securities, real estate, and business services, where salaries average $72,200. Mathematics and science teacher education majors who work as instructors in noneducational settings also have high earnings, with an average annual salary of $70,600. Those working as accountants and auditors average $27,400 per year. Majors employed in administrative fields have an average salary of $51,200 per year, dramatically higher than the $38,200 that is the average for all grads working in those fields; the grads of math and science teacher education evidently are working in administrative job specializations employing their technical skills.

Job Satisfaction

The overall level of job satisfaction of mathematics and science teacher education majors is considerably higher than the average for all graduates.

Table 5
Percentage Distribution of Workers with Only a Bachelor's Degree, by Level of Job Satisfaction

Job Satisfaction	Mathematics and Science Teacher Education	All
Very satisfied	53.1	45.4
Somewhat satisfied	41.4	45.0
Somewhat dissatisfied	4.0	7.4
Very dissatisfied	1.4	2.2
Mean Score (4=very satisfied, 1=not satisfied at all)	3.5	3.3

Employment Outlook

According to the projections by the U.S. Bureau of Labor Statistics, employment in occupations that require a bachelor's degree is expected to grow faster than employment in other sectors of the American labor market. Between 2008 and 2018, the U.S. workforce is projected to grow by 10.1 percent, creating an average of 15.2 million job openings per year. The bachelor's-level jobs are expected to increase by 17.7 percent over the same time.

A more mixed picture emerges when one analyzes the demand for workers in the specific occupational areas that are most likely to employ those with a degree in mathematics and science teacher education. Employment levels for secondary school teachers are expected to increase by only 8.9 percent between 2008 and 2018. However, this figure applies to *all* secondary teaching jobs. Although employment-projection figures are not available for subject-matter specializations, such as science and math, school districts have had difficulty finding qualified teachers for these subjects. Graduates of this major should face much less competition for openings compared to other education majors. Job prospects also should be better in inner cities and rural areas than in suburban districts.

Table 6
Projected Growth and Job Openings in the Top 5 Occupations Employing Persons with Only a Bachelor's Degree in Mathematics and Science Teacher Education

Top 5 Occupations	Projected Growth 2008–2018	Projected Annual Job Openings
All top 5	13.9%	499,740
Teachers, Secondary—Computer, Math, or Science	8.9%	41,240
Other Administrative Occupations	10.8%	166,130
Accountants, Auditors, and Other Financial Specialists	18.9%	127,260
Other Teachers and Instructors in Noneducational Institutions	20.8%	49,900
Sales/Marketing—Insurance, Securities, Real Estate, and Business Services	11.5%	115,210

Employment levels in jobs outside the secondary schools are expected to grow faster. Accounting careers are projected to expand by 18.9 percent, creating 127,000 job openings. The workforce of financial salesworkers, another important source of jobs for majors in this field, will likely increase by 11 percent and create 115,000 job openings. Employment of instructors in non-educational settings, although paying well and growing rapidly (at 20.8 percent), will offer fewer job openings than the other top employment options outside the schools because it is a much smaller occupation.

Pathways Beyond the Bachelor's Degree

Like other teacher education majors, those who earn a bachelor's degree in mathematics and science teacher education are more likely to earn an advanced degree compared to other college graduates. More than one-half of all those who earn a degree in this field go on to earn a graduate degree. About 47 percent of all graduates in the field earn a master's degree, while an additional 4 percent earn a doctorate, and 1 percent earn a professional degree.

▶ Among mathematics and science teacher education majors who earn a master's degree, most continue their studies at the graduate level in an education-related field. Seventeen percent of those with a master's earn their degrees in mathematics teacher education, and 12 percent in science teacher education. Sixteen percent earn a master's degree in educational administration.

▶ Of the small number who earn a doctorate, about 6 out of 10 of the degrees are in the education field. The remaining doctorates are mostly awarded in a computer-, mathematics-, or science-related field.

CHAPTER 22

Physical Education and Coaching

Physical education is an attractive major, especially for students who are athletes, enjoy sports, take part in athletic activities, or enjoy teaching people physical activities. For those who major in it, physical education provides the skills to offer others the opportunity to learn physical conditioning, to play a particular sport competently, or to engage in enjoyable activities, including dance.

Physical education teachers plan and conduct activities to build strength, develop coordination, and test physical endurance. They explore with students the concept of wellness and examine behaviors that lead to a high level of physical and emotional well-being. They help people learn techniques to assess health risks, deal with life-cycle issues, and manage stress. They instruct people on proper nutrition, drug use and abuse, and human sexuality.

Coaching is a function many teachers, not just physical education teachers, perform. People with varying levels of skill in a specific sport take part in coaching. Therefore, the level of familiarity with the rules and playing strategies may differ for various coaches, although those from a physical education background are usually expected to have a higher level of skill. Conditioning and motivating athletes are parts of the job, as are planning schedules and activities and arranging for availability of equipment. Coaches usually specialize in specific sports. Modeling activities and practicing plays are typical coaching functions.

Physical education teachers work in elementary schools (grades 1 through 6 or 8), middle schools (grades 5 through 8), or secondary or high schools (grades 7 through 12). While their subject area remains constant, the content and activities are adapted to the developmental levels of students. Generally, the course work of those preparing to work at the elementary level is broader, with more specialized courses in athletic areas and sports being offered for those preparing to work with older students. However, physical education departments have encountered fiscal cutbacks as schools have reduced community educational budgets. Physical education teachers, as a result, often have adapted by covering all grade levels and traveling to various schools on different days of the week. This phenomenon has affected some of the training of physical education teachers. Common courses are anatomy and physiology, motor development, physical conditioning, kinesiology, and theory of coaching.

The abilities of physical education teachers are primarily social and communicative ones. They work to inspire personal confidence and motivate students. They actively participate in the learning process of the unique skills of a specific sport and its rules and strategies of play. They also help students through exercises of physiological development. Leadership and organizational skills are definitely requirements. Obviously, physical education teachers need physical skills, motor coordination, strength, stamina, and physical agility because they typically teach using modeling and one-on-one, hands-on demonstration.

The interests of these majors follow these same abilities. While, in some events, people may compete individually, generally there is a social element to athletics. Planning, organizing, and assuming leadership roles are involved. And, whether or not liking physical involvement is the primary motivation, those in physical education and coaching appreciate activity and action.

Numerous benefits can be derived from physical education teaching and coaching. Competition, public attention, and possibly recognition for successful performance or winning provide one type of satisfaction. Another type of satisfaction is derived from the leadership and authority. Still another area of enjoyment comes from physical activity and an outdoor setting.

Where Do Physical Education and Coaching Majors Work?

You might expect that physical education graduates are employed in some aspect of primary and secondary education, and many are. About 4 out of 10 grads work in education. However, this means that the majority of graduates work in jobs in other sectors. Almost 30 percent of physical education graduates work as employees in private, for-profit businesses and corporations. About 14 percent are self-employed, and 10 percent work for government agencies at the federal, state, and local level.

Forty-three percent of physical education majors work in jobs that are closely related to their field of study, and 16 percent work in fields that are somewhat related. This leaves a full 40 percent working outside their field of study, a rate that is the highest among the education majors covered by this book.

Table 1
Percentage Distribution of Employed Persons with Only a Bachelor's Degree, by Economic Sector, Size, and New Business Status of Employer

	Physical Education and Coaching	All
Economic Sector		
Private for-profit	28.5	47.3
Self-employed	14.1	18.5
Government/Military	10.0	11.0
Education	42.5	15.6
Nonprofit	5.0	7.5
Employer Size		
Small (Fewer than 100 employees)	35.8	35.5
Medium (100–999)	23.2	21.8
Large (1,000–24,999)	29.5	26.0
Very large (25,000 or more)	11.5	16.7
Percent working in new business established within past 5 years	4.0	7.6

Table 2
Percentage Distribution of Employed Persons with Only a
Bachelor's Degree in Physical Education and Coaching,
by the Relationship Between Their Job and College Major

Relationship of Job to Major	Percent
Closely related	43.7
Somewhat related	16.3
Not related	40.0

Percent who report the following as the most important reasons for
working in a job that was not related to major:

Pay, promotion opportunities	38.6
Change in career or professional interests	20.6
Family-related reasons	14.5
Job in highest degree field not available	11.4
Working conditions (hours, equipment, environment)	8.4

Among physical education majors under the age of 65, almost 89 percent are employed, more than 9 out of 10 in full-time positions. Only about 2 percent are jobless and actively seeking work. However, about 9 percent of all majors choose not to work. Most often these individuals have taken an early retirement; this is true for almost 6 out of 10 who have withdrawn from the workforce. Others are out of the workforce to stay at home and better meet family responsibilities (14 percent), or they have no need to work (13 percent).

Occupations

Physical education majors with a bachelor's degree most often work as elementary and secondary school teachers. Almost 30 percent of all graduates do this kind of work. About two-thirds of those employed as teachers work at the high school level, and the rest work in elementary schools. A small number of majors is involved in pre-elementary education activities. Nearly 6 percent of physical education majors are employed in commodities sales positions.

Others work in miscellaneous managerial and administrative occupations.

Men outnumber women slightly among phys ed grads. Male grads are more likely to choose to teach the subject at the secondary level, female grads at the elementary level.

Work Activities

▶ For 38 percent of physical education majors, teaching is the central task they undertake on a daily basis on their job.

▶ Many majors employed outside the teaching profession are engaged in sales and marketing activities as part of their daily job duties. This is an important duty for 39 percent and the key responsibility for 16 percent of grads.

▶ Fifty-five percent of grads manage or supervise people or projects on a regular basis, and for 13 percent of the grads these tasks are paramount.

Table 3
Top 5 Occupations Employing Persons with Only a Bachelor's Degree
in Physical Education and Coaching, by Percentage

Top 5 Occupations	All	Men	Women
Teachers—Secondary, Other Subjects	18.6	19.7	17.0
Teachers—Elementary School	11.2	9.0	14.4
Sales Occupations—Commodities, Except Retail	5.8	8.4	2.1
Other Management-Related Occupations	4.5	4.5	4.5
Other Administrative Occupations	3.4	2.2	5.1
Total, Top 5 Occupations	43.5	43.8	43.1
Balance of Employed	56.5	56.2	56.9
All Employed	100.0	100.0	100.0

▶ Accounting, finance, and contracts are significant elements in the duties of persons employed outside the teaching profession, with 23 percent of the grads devoting at least 10 hours of their workweek to these tasks. Only 6 percent perceive these activities as their main responsibility.

Workplace Training and Other Work-Related Experiences

Among physical education program graduates who become teachers, formal workshops and training seminars are the primary means by which these individuals develop their professional teaching skills. More than 8 out of 10 of the grads who work as teachers participate in these formal work-based training programs. However, among majors employed outside education, on-the-job learning that is informal is a relatively more important method of skills development. Fewer than half of the majors employed in private, for-profit companies participate in formal training activities. Often these individuals engage in training designed to improve their communications skills.

▶ Of those physical education and coaching graduates who receive some training during a year, 58 percent receive technical training in the occupation in which they are employed.

▶ Nineteen percent of the training recipients receive management or supervisor training.

▶ Twenty-six percent receive training to improve their general professional skills, such as public speaking and business writing.

The major motive for participation in these training programs is to further develop professional skills and knowledge. More than one-third cite this as their most important reason. About 14 percent say that their employer requires it, and 8 percent are motivated by the need to obtain or maintain certification or licensure.

Salaries

The average annual salary of physical education and coaching graduates with only a bachelor's degree is $42,000, a level that is 23 percent lower than the average annual salary of all employed college graduates. On average, employed physical

FIGURE 1

Age/Earnings Profile of Persons with Only a Bachelor's Degree in Physical Education and Coaching (Full-Time Workers, in 2010 Dollars)

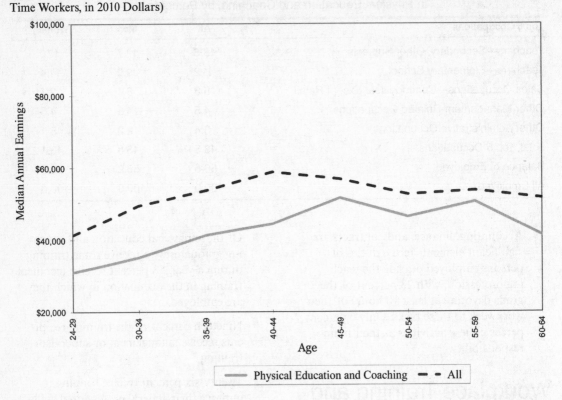

education and coaching graduates work for 44 hours per week and for 47 weeks per year, resulting in 2,068 hours of employment per year. The level of work effort among physical education and coaching graduates is 4 percent lower than the average among all college graduates (which is 43 hours per week and 50 weeks per year, resulting in 2,150 hours per year).

The salaries of physical education majors vary considerably by sector. Those employed in private, for-profit businesses earn an average salary of $55,700 per year. Those employed by educational institutions earn only $41,500. Majors employed in education have lower annual salaries in part because they work substantially fewer weeks over the course of the year than those employed in the private sector.

The earnings of physical education majors vary somewhat by occupation. The best-paying positions among these individuals are found in the high-level sales area, including the sales of real estate, insurance, and stocks and bonds. Earnings of physical education majors employed in these sales areas average $55,700 per year. Majors employed in managerial positions earn $39,200. These managers are largely employed in the education sector and therefore are paid substantially less than other college graduates in similar jobs, most of whom work in the higher-paying private, for-profit sector. Physical education majors who work in jobs closely related to the field of study have salaries that are 13 percent lower than those who are employed in positions that are somewhat related or unrelated to the field—$40,200 per year, compared to $46,400.

Table 4
Annual Salary of Workers with Only a Bachelor's Degree, Top 5 Occupations (in 2010 Dollars)

Earnings in Top 5 Occupations	All	Physical Education and Coaching
Total	$42,000	$42,700
Teachers—Secondary, Other Subjects	$39,200	$44,400
Teachers—Elementary School	$37,200	$34,100
Sales Occupations—Commodities, Except Retail	$64,000	$55,700
Other Management-Related Occupations	$57,800	$39,200
Other Administrative Occupations	$38,200	$41,300

Job Satisfaction

The overall level of job satisfaction of physical education and coaching majors is considerably higher than the average for all graduates.

Employment Outlook

The long-term job prospects for college graduates in the American economy appear to remain strong. U.S. Bureau of Labor Statistics projections of employment suggest that the workforce of those with a bachelor's degree will increase by about 17 percent between 2008 and 2018, a rate of increase that is much more rapid than the expected 10 percent increase in overall employment levels within the economy. The workforce of secondary school teachers is expected to increase by about 9 percent, a rate of change considerably below the average change in the demand for college graduates. The demand for elementary teachers is expected to rise at a faster pace, 16 percent. (Note that employment projections for teaching jobs are not available at the level of subject-matter specializations, such as physical education.) Job prospects for teachers should be better in inner cities and rural areas than in suburban districts.

Most other occupations that employ graduates with a physical education degree are expected to increase demand at a relatively slow rate compared to the change in the level of demand for college graduates overall. However,

Table 5
Percentage Distribution of Workers with Only a Bachelor's Degree, by Level of Job Satisfaction

Job Satisfaction	Physical Education and Coaching	All
Very satisfied	53.5	45.4
Somewhat satisfied	39.6	45.0
Somewhat dissatisfied	5.3	7.4
Very dissatisfied	1.6	2.2
Mean Score (4=very satisfied, 1=not satisfied at all)	3.5	3.3

Table 6

Projected Growth and Job Openings in the Top 5 Occupations Employing Persons
with Only a Bachelor's Degree in Physical Education and Coaching

Top 5 Occupations	Projected Growth 2008–2018	Projected Annual Job Openings
All top 5	11.3%	304,220
Teachers—Secondary, Other Subjects	8.8%	41,240
Teachers—Elementary School	15.8%	59,650
Sales Occupations—Commodities, Except Retail	−1.1%	310
Other Management-Related Occupations	7.2%	53,020
Other Administrative Occupations	10.8%	166,130

the administrative and managerial occupations that employ many phys ed grads have large workforces and should create many job openings through turnover.

Pathways Beyond the Bachelor's Degree

A bit less than 40 percent of all persons who earn a physical education degree at the undergraduate level eventually go on to earn an advanced degree. Virtually all of these degrees are at the master's level. Only infrequently do physical education majors continue their schooling to the doctoral level or earn a professional degree in law or medicine.

▸ About 80 percent of all master's degrees earned by graduates in this field are in physical education or some other education field. Incentives to earn advanced degrees among those working in the educational system are strong because most teacher contracts reward additional degrees earned, along with seniority.

▸ Only rarely does graduate study for these majors deviate from the education field. Those few who earn master's degrees outside education most often study a health- or business-related field.

▸ Only about 3 percent of all those with a bachelor's degree in physical education eventually earn a doctoral degree. Virtually all these doctorates are in the education field.

CHAPTER 23

Preschool/ Kindergarten/ Early Childhood Teacher Education

Early childhood teachers (a term that can cover both preschool and kindergarten teachers) play a vital role in the development of children. They introduce children to reading and writing, expanded vocabulary, creative arts, science, and social studies. They use games, music, art activities, films, books, computers, and other tools to teach concepts and skills.

Preschool teachers nurture, teach, and care for children who have not yet entered kindergarten. They provide early childhood care and education through a variety of teaching strategies. They teach children, usually aged 3 to 5, both in groups and one on one. They do so by planning and implementing a curriculum that covers various areas of a child's development, such as motor skills, social and emotional development, and language development.

Kindergarten teachers use play and hands-on teaching, but academics begin to take priority in kindergarten classrooms. Letter recognition, phonics, numbers, and awareness of nature and science, introduced at the preschool level, are taught primarily in kindergarten.

Young children learn mainly through investigation, play, and formal teaching. Early childhood teachers capitalize on children's play to further language and vocabulary development (using storytelling, rhyming games, and acting games), improve social skills (having the children work together to build a neighborhood in a sandbox), and introduce scientific and mathematical concepts (showing the children how to balance and count blocks when building a bridge or how to mix colors when painting). Thus, an approach that includes small and large group activities, one-on-one instruction, and learning through creative activities such as art, dance, and music, is adopted to teach young children.

Early childhood teachers often work with students from varied ethnic, racial, and religious backgrounds. With growing minority populations in most parts of the country, it is important for teachers to be able to work effectively with a diverse student population. Accordingly, some schools offer training to help teachers enhance their awareness and understanding of different cultures. Teachers may also include multicultural programming in their lesson plans to address the needs of all students, regardless of their cultural background.

Seeing students develop new skills and gain an appreciation of knowledge and learning can be very rewarding. However, teaching may be frustrating when dealing with unmotivated or disrespectful students. Occasionally, teachers must cope with unruly behavior and violence in the schools.

Preschool and kindergarten teachers in private programs and schools generally enjoy smaller class sizes and more control over establishing the curriculum and setting standards for performance and discipline. In public schools, teachers may experience stress in dealing with large classes, heavy workloads, or old schools that are run down and lack modern amenities. Accountability standards also may increase stress levels, with teachers expected to produce students who are able to exhibit a satisfactory performance on standardized tests in core subjects. Many teachers, particularly in public schools, also are frustrated by the lack of control they have over what they are required to teach.

Teachers are sometimes isolated from their colleagues because they work alone in a classroom of students. However, some schools allow teachers to work in teams and with mentors to enhance their professional development.

Part-time schedules are common among preschool teachers, less so among kindergarten teachers. Although most school districts offer all-day kindergartens, some kindergarten teachers still teach two kindergarten classes a day. Among employed grads with a bachelor's degree in this field, only 8 percent work part-time.

Many teachers work the traditional 10-month school year with a 2-month vacation during the summer. During the vacation break, those on the 10-month schedule may teach in summer sessions, take temporary jobs, travel, or pursue personal interests. Many enroll in college courses or workshops to continue their education. Teachers in districts with a year-round schedule typically work 8 weeks, are on vacation for 1 week, and have a 5-week midwinter break. Preschool teachers working in day-care settings often work year round.

Most states have tenure laws that prevent public school teachers from being fired without just cause and due process. Teachers may obtain tenure after they have satisfactorily completed a probationary period of teaching, normally 3 years. Tenure does not absolutely guarantee a job, but it does provide some security.

Early childhood teachers enjoy working with people. The aspects of their job that they value highest are its security, its contribution to society, its fringe benefits, its challenges, and the amount of independence it permits. Like other teachers, they are friendly, concerned with the feelings of others, and conscientious to fulfill a set of obligations.

Where Do Preschool/ Kindergarten/Early Childhood Teacher Education Majors Work?

It's no surprise that almost two-thirds of the grads from early childhood teacher education programs are working for educational institutions. Partly because many preschool teachers work in day-care centers, 14 percent of grads are working at private, for-profit businesses, and an equal share of grads are self-employed.

People with a bachelor's degree in early childhood education tend to follow an all-or-nothing career path. That is, nearly 7 out of 10 work in a field that is closely related to the major and 22 percent work in an unrelated field, but less than 9 percent work in a field that is only somewhat related.

Table 1

Percentage Distribution of Employed Persons with Only a Bachelor's Degree, by Economic Sector, Size, and New Business Status of Employer

	Early Childhood Teacher Education	All
Economic Sector		
Private for-profit	14.1	47.3
Self-employed	14.3	18.5
Government/Military	4.1	11.0
Education	62.9	15.6
Nonprofit	4.6	7.5
Employer Size		
Small (Fewer than 100 employees)	44.3	35.5
Medium (100–999)	24.4	21.8
Large (1,000–24,999)	22.0	26.0
Very large (25,000 or more)	9.3	16.7
Percent working in new business established within past 5 years	5.4	7.6

Table 2

Percentage Distribution of Employed Persons with Only a Bachelor's Degree in Early Childhood Teacher Education, by the Relationship Between Their Job and College Major

Relationship of Job to Major	Percent
Closely related	69.3
Somewhat related	8.6
Not related	22.0

Percent who report the following as the most important reasons for working in a job that was not related to major:

Pay, promotion opportunities	31.9
Change in career or professional interests	26.6
Family-related reasons	17.1
Job in highest degree field not available	12.6
Working conditions (hours, equipment, environment)	4.0

One-quarter of all early childhood education graduates under the age of 65 are out of the labor force; that is, they are not employed and are not seeking employment. This is the highest rate of workforce withdrawal among all the majors in this book. As a result, not quite three-quarters of the grads are employed (the lowest rate of all the majors), yet the unemployment rate for grads is also very low, less than 2 percent.

About one-third of the grads who have left the labor force report doing so for family-related reasons. It seems likely that most of them are staying home with young children; almost 97 percent of the grads are women, and they obviously have a strong interest in young children. They also are about 25 percent younger on average than those not dealing with family commitments. Twenty-seven percent of the grads who are out of the workforce do not need to work, and another 22 percent have taken early retirement.

Occupations

Almost half of the employment of early childhood education graduates is concentrated in educational occupations. One-third teach young children, and another 16 percent teach at the elementary level. Female grads, more than male grads, tend to be attracted to classrooms for younger students. The top 5 jobs for grads are rounded out with an assortment of administrative, sales, and service jobs.

Work Activities

▶ Almost three-quarters of employed grads spend at least 10 hours during a typical workweek in teaching duties, and 57 percent spend most of their time during a typical week performing these tasks.

▶ Forty-five percent of all employed early childhood education graduates spend at least 10 hours of the workweek performing management and administration tasks, but only 6 percent report that these duties consume most of their time at work.

▶ Sales, purchasing, or marketing are signficant activities for 36 percent of the graduates, and 13 percent consider these duties the major part of their job.

Table 3

Top 5 Occupations Employing Persons with Only a Bachelor's Degree
in Early Childhood Teacher Education, by Percentage

Top 5 Occupations	All	Men	Women
Teachers—Pre-K and Kindergarten	33.7	8.2	34.8
Teachers—Elementary School	15.7	19.1	15.6
Other Administrative Occupations	5.5	20.7	4.8
Sales/Marketing—Insurance, Securities, Real Estate, and Business Services	4.9	–	5.1
Other Service Occupations, Except Health	4.8	–	5.1
Total, Top 5 Occupations	64.6	48.0	65.4
Balance of Employed	35.4	52.0	34.6
All Employed	100.0	100.0	100.0

- Education has become high-tech: Ninety-four percent of the grads spend a significant part of the workweek on computer applications, although only 3 percent consider this their major task.

- Twenty-nine percent engage regularly in accounting, finance, or contracts during a major portion of their typical workweek, but less than 7 percent spend most of their time at these tasks.

Workplace Training and Other Work-Related Experiences

Opportunities for informal on-the-job learning are limited in the teaching profession. However, teachers regularly participate in professional development activities to maintain or improve their teaching skills. About three-quarters of all graduates of early childhood education programs participate in training workshops and seminars designed to impart a variety of work-based skills. This rate is much higher than the training participation rate of all college graduates (61 percent).

- Of those early childhood teacher education graduates who receive some training during a year, 70 percent receive technical training in the occupation in which they are employed.

- Twenty-one percent receive training to improve their general professional skills, such as public speaking and business writing.

- Twelve percent of the training recipients receive management or supervisor training.

When asked to select the most important reason to acquire training, 45 percent of graduates who undergo training identify the need to improve their occupational skills and knowledge. Thirteen percent rank the need to obtain or maintain a professional license or certificate as the number one reason to participate in work-related training. Eight percent of grads report mandatory training requirements by the employer as the most important factor underlying their involvement in work-related training.

Salaries

The average annual salary of early childhood teacher education graduates with only a bachelor's degree is $33,000, a level that is 56 percent lower than the average annual salary of all employed college graduates. On average, employed early childhood education graduates work for 40 hours per week and for 45 weeks per year, resulting in 1,800 hours of employment per year. The level of work effort among early childhood education graduates is 16 percent lower than the average among all college graduates (which is 43 hours per week and 50 weeks per year, resulting in 2,150 hours per year).

The average annual salary of graduates who work full-time in jobs that are closely related to their major is $36,100, whereas in unrelated jobs the average is $34,100. Perhaps the relatively low pay in jobs that are somewhat related, an average of $31,000 per year, helps to explain why only a small share of grads are in this category.

Earning an average salary of $40,100 annually, early childhood education graduates who are self-employed earn a higher salary than those who are employed in other sectors. The average pay for graduates in the education sector, where the largest share of the grads work, is $37,100 per year. The private, for-profit sector pays these graduates $31,000 per year.

Among the top 5 occupations employing grads of early childhood teacher education, the highest-paying is elementary school teaching, which pays them an average of $40,200 per year. Preschool and kindergarten teachers average 20 percent less earnings, largely because more of them work in part-time, nonunionized, and private-sector jobs. The same factors help explain the low pay of the grads who sell real estate, insurance, and intangible goods and services.

FIGURE 1

Age/Earnings Profile of Persons with Only a Bachelor's Degree in Preschool/Kindergarten/Early Childhood Teacher Education (Full-Time Workers, in 2010 Dollars)

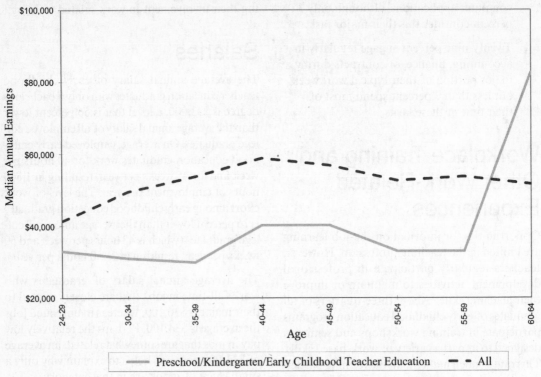

Table 4
Annual Salary of Workers with Only a Bachelor's Degree,
Top 5 Occupations (in 2010 Dollars)

Earnings in Top 5 Occupations	All	Early Childhood Teacher Education
Total	$33,000	$32,600
Teachers—Pre-K and Kindergarten	$33,000	$32,000
Teachers—Elementary School	$37,200	$40,200
Other Administrative Occupations	$38,200	$36,100
Sales/Marketing—Insurance, Securities, Real Estate, and Business Services	$67,100	$18,600
Other Service Occupations, Except Health	$35,100	$20,600

Table 5
Percentage Distribution of Workers with Only a Bachelor's Degree, by Level of Job Satisfaction

Job Satisfaction	Early Childhood Teacher Education	All
Very satisfied	48.7	45.4
Somewhat satisfied	43.3	45.0
Somewhat dissatisfied	6.3	7.4
Very dissatisfied	1.7	2.2
Mean Score (4=very satisfied, 1=not satisfied at all)	3.4	3.3

Job Satisfaction

The overall level of job satisfaction of early childhood teacher education majors is slightly higher than the average for all graduates.

Employment Outlook

According to the projections by the U.S. Bureau of Labor Statistics, employment in occupations that require a bachelor's degree is expected to grow faster than employment in other sectors of the American labor market. Between 2008 and 2018, the U.S. workforce is projected to grow by 10.1 percent, creating an average of 15.2 million job openings per year. The bachelor's-level jobs are expected to increase by 17.7 percent over the same time.

Among the top 5 occupations that employ graduates of early childhood teacher education, the brightest outlook is for preschool and kindergarten teachers, with 17.8 percent projected growth and 24,000 annual job openings. High replacement needs should create good job opportunities for preschool teachers. Qualified persons who are interested in this work should have little trouble

Table 6
Projected Growth and Job Openings in the Top 5 Occupations Employing Persons with Only a Bachelor's Degree in Early Childhood Teacher Education

Top 5 Occupations	Projected Growth 2008–2018	Projected Annual Job Openings
All top 5	12.5%	418,690
Teachers—Pre-K and Kindergarten	17.8%	24,130
Teachers—Elementary School	15.8%	59,650
Other Administrative Occupations	10.8%	166,130
Sales/Marketing—Insurance, Securities, Real Estate, and Business Services	11.5%	115,210
Other Service Occupations, Except Health	14.3%	53,570

finding and keeping a job. Many preschool teachers must be replaced each year as they leave the occupation to fulfill family responsibilities, to study, or for other reasons. Others leave because they are interested in pursuing other occupations or because of low wages.

At 15.8 percent, growth of elementary school teachers is not expected to be as rapid, but it outshines the three nonteaching jobs among the top 5.

Pathways Beyond the Bachelor's Degree

Of all graduates with a bachelor's degree in early childhood teacher education, 3 out of 10 proceed to earn a postgraduate degree, but virtually all of them stop at the master's. Almost all earn their master's in some aspect of education. Thirty-six percent earn the degree in the same field as their bachelor's, early childhood teacher education. Another 17 percent earn the degree in elementary teacher education.

CHAPTER 24

Secondary Teacher Education

Secondary teacher education is one of the broadest majors, covering English to social science, language to geography. People do not enter secondary teaching blindly, because they personally have experienced the field during their own education. What may be novel is the different community support for schools, size, cultural composition, academic rigor, and student commitment to study. Other differences may be the type of school board control. For example, almost all religious groups support and operate schools according to their philosophy of education. Another organizational variation could be working in a middle or junior high school where the grades range from 5 to 9. Some people enjoy working with this volatile developmental age group and feel these students are easier to teach than older students because of their greater motivation to learn.

Teachers prepare group presentations and must adapt to students individually. They assign readings in textbooks, use exercises to develop skill proficiency, listen to oral presentations, and assess students' progress. They must maintain an environment conducive to learning, which means maintaining discipline. They may collaborate with other teachers to articulate a curriculum across grades. Teachers prepare tests, grade papers, assign grades, oversee study halls and homerooms, meet with parents or guardians to discuss achievement and personal development, and may participate in extracurricular activities.

All states license their public school teachers. Those entering teaching need to check out specific state requirements, which can be found on the website of the state Department of Education. For teacher certification, they may need to get a master's degree after first developing competency in an academic discipline.

In general, those who want to teach in middle and high schools need course work in adolescent development, introduction to special education, the learning process, curriculum theory, methods and materials for instruction, and student practice teaching. In addition, the following specific requirements are used as two examples of the knowledge required in specific content areas:

▶ English: History and study of language; English, American, and world literature; theories of language acquisition; written and oral composition; drama; speech communication; literary criticism and techniques of research in the field of English; writing, including techniques for evaluating writing; relationships of English to other fields of knowledge

▶ History: Methods of historical research; physical, economic, political, intellectual, and social forces that shape civilizations, including sex, race, and ethnicity; origin and development of world cultures; the economic, political, social, and cultural history of the United States; relationships between history and related fields such as geography, political science, economics, sociology, anthropology, psychology, literature, and the arts

In addition to the ability to master their specialty area, teachers exhibit language and leadership skills. Critical are interpersonal and communication abilities, both verbal and oral, to convey information and to facilitate expressive language development in students.

Interests universal to all teachers are being social and people-oriented and enjoying communicating and reading. Teaching involves leading and influencing roles. In addition, those who plan to teach need to examine the content of a specialized teaching major, such as foreign languages, for more information about the specific abilities and interests characterizing that career niche. (Science and math teacher education is described in Chapter 21, physical education in Chapter 22, and special education in Chapter 25.)

As a group, secondary teachers value working with their minds, working with people, expressing their creativity, experiencing variety, and having the opportunity for diversion.

Where Do Secondary Teacher Education Majors Work?

Only 38 percent of secondary teacher education graduates work in the education sector. Almost 30 percent work in the private, for-profit sector for businesses and corporations. Sixteen percent are self-employed, and 8 percent of secondary teacher education graduates are employed in the government sector. The remaining 9 percent work for nonprofit organizations.

The distribution of employed secondary teacher education graduates by sector indicates that many graduates are not employed in jobs that

Table 1

Percentage Distribution of Employed Persons with Only a Bachelor's Degree, by Economic Sector, Size, and New Business Status of Employer

	Secondary Teacher Education	All
Economic Sector		
Private for-profit	28.6	47.3
Self-employed	16.2	18.5
Government/Military	7.8	11.0
Education	38.2	15.6
Nonprofit	9.3	7.5
Employer Size		
Small (Fewer than 100 employees)	30.3	35.5
Medium (100–999)	29.4	21.8
Large (1,000–24,999)	26.9	26.0
Very large (25,000 or more)	13.4	16.7
Percent working in new business established within past 5 years	4.8	7.6

Table 2

Percentage Distribution of Employed Persons with Only a
Bachelor's Degree in Secondary Teacher Education,
by the Relationship Between Their Job and College Major

Relationship of Job to Major	Percent
Closely related	42.4
Somewhat related	23.2
Not related	34.4

Percent who report the following as the most important reasons for
working in a job that was not related to major:

Change in career or professional interests	27.9
Pay, promotion opportunities	22.0
Working conditions (hours, equipment, environment)	17.4
Family-related reasons	12.5
Job in highest degree field not available	8.9

are closely related to their undergraduate education. Only 42 percent work in jobs that are closely related to their undergraduate major. Another 23 percent are employed in jobs that are somewhat related to their undergraduate major. The remaining 34 percent of secondary teacher education graduates work in jobs that are not related to their field of study.

Out of all secondary teacher education graduates under the age of 65, 80 percent are employed. Only 1 percent are officially unemployed; that is, they are not employed and are actively seeking employment. The remaining 19 percent are out of the labor force; that is, they are not employed and are not seeking employment. Three main reasons underlie the labor force withdrawal of secondary teacher education graduates: 43 percent have retired early, 21 percent cite family responsibilities as the reason for labor force withdrawal, and 17 percent lack the desire or the need to work.

Occupations

The employment of secondary teacher education graduates is quite dispersed across different occupations. More than one-quarter are employed as secondary school teachers. About 6 percent work in retail sales, and another 5 percent in miscellaneous administrative jobs. Female grads outnumber male grads by about a 60–40 ratio. The two sexes gravitate toward different subject-matter specializations, with men more frequently teaching social sciences, roughly equal shares teaching computers, math, and science, and women more frequently teaching various other subjects.

Work Activities

▶ Teaching activities take up the major portion of the typical workweek of 33 percent of all employed graduates and a significant part of the week for a bit more than half.

Table 3
Top 5 Occupations Employing Persons with Only a Bachelor's Degree
in Secondary Teacher Education, by Percentage

Top 5 Occupations	All	Men	Women
Teachers—Secondary, Other Subjects	17.0	11.1	21.7
Sales Occupations—Retail	6.0	9.8	2.9
Teachers, Secondary—Social Sciences	5.8	8.5	3.7
Teachers, Secondary—Computer, Math, or Science	5.3	5.1	5.5
Other Administrative Occupations	5.2	4.9	5.4
Total, Top 5 Occupations	39.3	39.4	39.2
Balance of Employed	60.7	60.6	60.8
All Employed	100.0	100.0	100.0

▶ Sixteen percent report that sales, purchasing, and marketing duties take up most of their time at work, and another 39 percent spend significant work time at these tasks.

▶ Managerial or supervisory activities consume significant time for a little more than half of the grads, and these are core responsibilities for 13 percent of grads.

▶ Employee relations are frequent duties of 36 percent of grads, although only 3 percent spend most of their time in this job function.

Workplace Training and Other Work-Related Experiences

The career potential of a job is closely associated with the amount of work-related training on the job. Work-related training is regarded as an investment by firms because it makes workers more productive. The incidence of work-related training among secondary teacher education graduates (63 percent) is a bit higher than the training participation rate of all college graduates (61 percent).

▶ Of those secondary teacher education graduates who receive some training during the year, 56 percent participate in technical training in the occupation in which they are employed.

▶ Seventeen percent of the training recipients participate in management or supervisory training.

▶ One-quarter receive training to improve their general professional skills, such as public speaking and business writing.

Although secondary teacher education graduates decide to participate in work-related training activities, workshops, or seminars for numerous reasons, two reasons stand out as most commonly cited by graduates. These are a desire to improve skills and knowledge in the occupational area of their employment and mandatory training requirements of the employer. One-third of graduates who acquire some training consider the desire to improve skills and knowledge in the occupational area of their employment as the most important factor underlying their decision to undergo training. Twelve percent select mandatory requirements of the employer to be the most important factor influencing their participation in training activities.

Among 6 percent of the training recipients, the most important reason to participate in work-related training activities is the need to obtain a professional license or certificate. Only 4 percent of all secondary teacher education graduates who receive training consider the number one reason to be the acquisition of skills for a new position.

Salaries

The median annual salary of secondary teacher education graduates with only a bachelor's degree is $40,000, a level that is 29 percent lower than the median annual salary of all employed college graduates. On average, employed secondary teacher education graduates work for 42 hours per week and for 48 weeks per year, resulting in

2,016 hours of employment per year. The level of work effort among secondary teacher education graduates is 6 percent lower than the average among all college graduates (which is 43 hours per week and 50 weeks per year, resulting in 2,150 hours per year). That difference partly explains the lower level of pay.

Graduates who work in closely related jobs or in unrelated jobs earn the same average salary: $41,300 per year. Graduates with employment in jobs that are somewhat related to their major earn $43,300 per year.

With an average salary of $49,000 annually, secondary teacher education graduates who are self-employed earn a higher salary than those who are employed in other sectors. The average pay for graduates working in the private, for-profit

Age/Earnings Profile of Persons with Only a Bachelor's Degree in Secondary Teacher Education (Full-Time Workers, in 2010 Dollars)

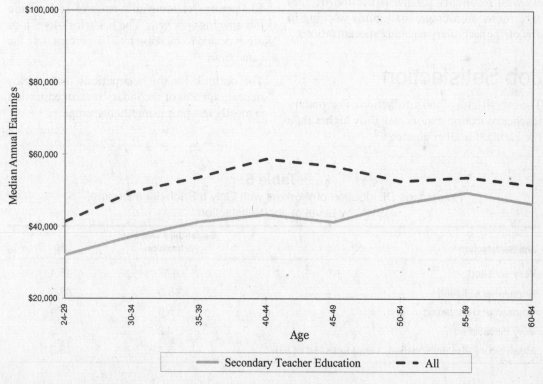

Table 4
Annual Salary of Workers with Only a Bachelor's Degree, Top 5 Occupations (in 2010 Dollars)

Earnings in Top 5 Occupations	All	Secondary Teacher Education
Total	$40,000	$36,600
Teachers—Secondary, Other Subjects	$39,200	$39,200
Sales Occupations—Retail	$42,300	$43,300
Teachers, Secondary—Social Sciences	$40,200	$34,100
Teachers, Secondary—Computer, Math, or Science	$40,200	$38,200
Other Administrative Occupations	$38,200	$23,700

sector is $46,000 per year. The education sector, which employs the largest share of grads, pays an average of $36,600 per year.

Of those grads who teach in secondary schools, the highest earners are those who specialize in teaching computers, math, or science, with average yearly earnings of $38,200. Retail salesworkers with secondary teacher education degrees earn more, on average, than grads working in any of the secondary teaching specializations.

Job Satisfaction

The overall level of job satisfaction of secondary teacher education majors is slightly higher than the average for all graduates.

Employment Outlook

According to the projections by the U.S. Bureau of Labor Statistics, employment in occupations that require a bachelor's degree is expected to grow faster than employment in other sectors of the American labor market. Between 2008 and 2018, the U.S. workforce is projected to grow by 10.1 percent, creating an average of 15.2 million job openings per year. The bachelor's-level jobs are expected to increase by 17.7 percent over the same time.

The outlook for the occupations that employ many graduates of secondary teacher education is mostly less promising than average.

Table 5
Percentage Distribution of Workers with Only a Bachelor's Degree, by Level of Job Satisfaction

Job Satisfaction	Secondary Teacher Education	All
Very satisfied	47.7	45.4
Somewhat satisfied	45.5	45.0
Somewhat dissatisfied	5.6	7.4
Very dissatisfied	1.2	2.2
Mean Score (4=very satisfied, 1=not satisfied at all)	3.4	3.3

Table 6

Projected Growth and Job Openings in the Top 5 Occupations Employing Persons with Only a Bachelor's Degree in Secondary Teacher Education

Top 5 Occupations	Projected Growth 2008–2018	Projected Annual Job Openings
All top 5	9.1%	481,420
Teachers—Secondary, Other Subjects	8.9%	41,240
Sales Occupations—Retail	7.5%	207,700
Teachers, Secondary—Social Sciences	8.9%	41,240
Teachers, Secondary—Computer, Math, or Science	8.9%	41,240
Other Administrative Occupations	10.8%	166,130

▶ Secondary teacher occupations are projected to grow at a rate somewhat below the average rate of all jobs, and considerably below the growth rate for jobs that demand college graduates. The employment in this occupation is projected to increase by 8.9 percent between 2008 and 2018, creating 41,000 job openings shared across three specializations. Job prospects should be better in inner cities and rural areas than in suburban districts.

▶ Employment levels in retail sales occupations are expected to rise by only 7.5 percent between 2008 and 2018, but because these occupations have large workforces and high turnover, they are projected to account for 208,000 job openings each year. In addition, many new jobs will be created for retail salespersons as businesses seek to expand operations and enhance customer service.

▶ The outlook is similar for the miscellaneous administrative occupations that employ about 5 percent of teacher education grads: Growth will be about average, at 10.8 percent, but a very large number of jobs will open each year.

Pathways Beyond the Bachelor's Degree

Postgraduation education is very common among secondary teacher education graduates. Of all graduates with a bachelor's degree in secondary teacher education, 47 percent proceed to earn a postgraduate degree: 42 percent earn a master's degree, 4 percent secure a doctoral degree, and another 1 percent receive a professional degree.

▶ Two-thirds of all master's degrees earned by undergraduate secondary teacher education majors are in the field of education. The rest are spread across an array of majors, including business, psychology, and English language and literature.

▶ A similar distribution of the major fields of study is observed among doctoral degrees earned by undergraduate secondary teacher education majors. Fifty-five percent are earned in the field of education, with educational administration the most popular specialization.

CHAPTER 25

Special Education

The special education major is a subspecialty of early childhood, elementary, or secondary teacher education that prepares the teachers who will work with individuals with special needs. Some special education programs focus on working with learning disabilities, mental retardation, speech or language impairment, emotional disturbance, visual and hearing impairment, orthopedic impairment, autism, brain impairment, multiple disabilities, or the gifted and talented. Special education training helps design learning experiences and modify instruction for these populations among young people.

Working with other educational specialists, special education teachers are legally required to help develop an Individualized Education Program (IEP) for each special education student. The IEP considers the student's ability and learning style in specifying learning objectives and recommending strategies to reach achievement goals. The IEP then becomes a plan that special education teachers follow.

Special education is organized in various ways. Some special education teachers have their own classrooms and teach classes with all special needs students. Others work as resource room teachers, providing individualized help for several hours a day to students in regular education classes. Still others teach along with regular education teachers in classes composed of both general and special education students. There also are residential schools or hospitals that offer educational programs that usually include individuals having more complex and difficult needs.

Requirements for special educators are changing, in that some states and the universities that serve them are requiring a fifth year or post-baccalaureate preparation. In general, special education teachers usually spend longer in preparation than general education teachers. Courses include educational psychology, legal issues of special education, child growth and development, and methodology courses for teaching students with specific disabilities.

Communication ability is a crucial skill because special education teachers work with students and interact frequently with parents, other faculty, and administrators. Language and mathematical skills are needed because they are usually areas that special education instructors teach, especially at the elementary level. Social and persuasive abilities are additional skills that teachers possess and use daily. Knowledge of medical terminology and human anatomy are required in understanding the affected areas of the various disabling conditions.

The interests involved in teaching those with special needs focus on the social area and especially liking to work with children. Often, people entering this field have had direct personal contact with a child with a specific disability. Teaching also involves an organizational approach to learning. This specific field of education calls for paying close attention to details, even following some repetitive and routine activities.

Values satisfied in this career field include creativity, because teachers often can use their imagination and be resourceful. There can be a sense of achievement in performing a difficult and important task. The career offers opportunities for variety and trying out new educational approaches as new specialized equipment is introduced to the field. There is satisfaction in working in close contact with people in a helping relationship. Some teachers enjoy the independence of working with a class of students without someone watching how they do their work.

Where Do Special Education Majors Work?

Special education graduates, regardless of whether they work as special education teachers, most often work in the educational sector. More than three-quarters of those with a bachelor's degree in special education work in some part of the nation's educational system. However, a significant share (almost 6 percent) of graduates of special education programs become self-employed, some providing freelance services to school districts or sometimes to families who want extra help for their children. Ten percent of special education majors are employed in a private, for-profit corporation. Most often these individuals work in jobs that are not closely connected to their undergraduate major.

College graduates with an undergraduate degree in special education are very likely to be employed in a job that is closely related to their undergraduate major. Three-quarters of all employed persons with a bachelor's degree in special education say that their current job is closely related to their college major.

About 15 percent of special education majors are employed in a job that is unrelated to the undergraduate major. Most often these individuals are employed in unrelated jobs because of what they perceive as limited pay and promotion potential in special education teaching.

The employment rate of persons with a special education degree, 75 percent, is below the average of all bachelor's degree holders. However, the

Table 1

Percentage Distribution of Employed Persons with Only a Bachelor's Degree, by Economic Sector, Size, and New Business Status of Employer

	Special Education	All
Economic Sector		
Private for-profit	10.0	47.3
Self-employed	5.8	18.5
Government/Military	5.2	11.0
Education	75.8	15.6
Nonprofit	3.0	7.5
Employer Size		
Small (Fewer than 100 employees)	22.4	35.5
Medium (100–999)	38.0	21.8
Large (1,000–24,999)	30.7	26.0
Very large (25,000 or more)	8.9	16.7
Percent working in new business established within past 5 years	5.6	7.6

Table 2

Percentage Distribution of Employed Persons with Only a Bachelor's Degree in Special Education, by the Relationship Between Their Job and College Major

Relationship of Job to Major	Percent
Closely related	74.8
Somewhat related	10.2
Not related	14.9

Percent who report the following as the most important reasons for working in a job that was not related to major:

Pay, promotion opportunities	30.9
Family-related reasons	26.5
Change in career or professional interests	21.2
Working conditions (hours, equipment, environment)	11.3
Job location	6.9

unemployment rate, under 3 percent, is also lower than the average. Two out of 10 special education majors under the age of 65 are not employed because they are not looking for work. Instead, they have chosen not to work primarily because of family responsibilities (38 percent of those who are not working) or because they have taken early retirement (25 percent).

Occupations

More than half of all special education graduates with only a bachelor's degree are employed as special education teachers. About 9 percent work as elementary school teachers. An additional 6 percent of graduates work in clerical and administrative positions, some within the educational sector.

Women outnumber men among grads by about 9 to 1. Women are somewhat more likely to use their degree to work as special education teachers, men more likely to work as elementary school teachers.

Work Activities

▶ Unsurprisingly, graduates of special education programs spend the greatest amount of time during the workweek engaged in teaching activities. Almost 7 out of 10 grads see this as their main work task, and 85 percent engage in it regularly. Teaching, however, is not the sole task of special education program graduates.

▶ More than 9 out of 10 special education graduates report using some type of computer application while on the job.

▶ Forty-six percent report that they spend at least some part of the workweek engaged in managing or supervising people or projects, although only 7 percent are primarily tasked with this responsibility.

▶ Almost 30 percent of special education graduates with a bachelor's degree are engaged in employee relations activities on the job.

Table 3
Top 5 Occupations Employing Persons with Only a Bachelor's Degree in Special Education, by Percentage

Top 5 Occupations	All	Men	Women
Teachers—Special Education	58.0	50.1	58.9
Teachers—Elementary School	8.8	12.3	8.5
Secretaries, Receptionists, and Typists	3.5	2.7	3.5
Other Administrative Occupations	3.0	–	3.3
Artists, Broadcasters, Editors, Entertainers, Public Relations Specialists, and Writers	2.8	–	3.1
Total, Top 5 Occupations	76.1	65.1	77.3
Balance of Employed	23.9	34.9	22.7
All Employed	100.0	100.0	100.0

Workplace Training and Other Work-Related Experiences

Professional development is an important part of the career development of persons who earn a bachelor's degree in special education. Over the course of a year, 82 percent of all those with a degree in special education participate in some type of work-related professional development activity, including seminars, workshops, and other work-related training activity. This rate is much higher than the training participation rate of all college graduates (61 percent).

▶ About 80 percent of those who participate in a training activity say that they receive training in a specific skill or technique that is related to their immediate job duties.

▶ About 11 percent receive management or supervisor training.

▶ Twenty-three percent receive training to improve their general professional skills, such as public speaking and business writing.

Of those who receive work-related training, 44 percent do so primarily to improve their skills, and 18 percent say the most important reason is to achieve or maintain licensure or certification. All states require special education teachers to be licensed, and continuing education is frequently required.

Salaries

Special education majors have annual salaries that are among the lowest of all college graduates with only a bachelor's degree. The median annual salary of persons with a bachelor's degree in special education is $37,000, 39 percent lower than the median earnings of people with a bachelor's degree. On average, employed special education graduates work for 44 weeks per year, 12 percent less than the average of 50 weeks per year among all college graduates. Most special education majors who work in the educational sector do not work as teachers during the summer and have a number of weeks off during the school year as well. This partly explains the relatively low annual pay of special education majors. Many persons who choose special education as a major do so with the knowledge that while their earnings are lower, they will have much more

FIGURE 1

Age/Earnings Profile of Persons with Only a Bachelor's Degree in Special Education (Full-Time Workers, in 2010 Dollars)

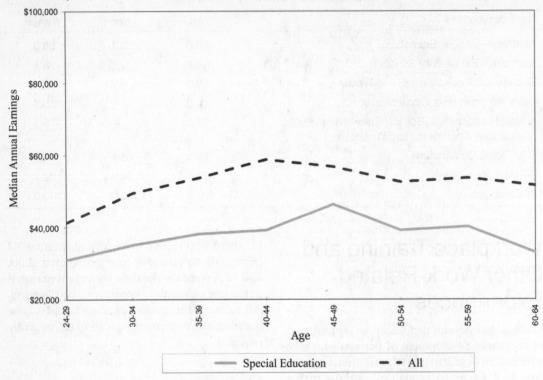

time off than other employed bachelor's degree holders. Thus, special education majors place a premium on this time that is not shared by some other college graduates.

Earnings are highest for special education majors who work in the private, for-profit sector; they report average annual salaries of $43,300. The small portion who are self-employed average $41,700 per year. Those employed in educational institutions earn $38,300 per year.

Special education graduates who work in jobs outside the field have salaries that are well above those working in occupations closely related to their undergraduate major. Those with a bachelor's degree in special education who work outside the field earn almost 20 percent more

per year than those employed in jobs that are closely related ($45,400 compared to $38,200). However, part of this difference is attributable to differences in the number of weeks of work those in education-related jobs actually work over the year relative to those outside the education field. Those who work in jobs that are somewhat related to the major report an average salary of only $35,100.

Special education majors employed as special education teachers earn an average salary of $38,200 per year. Those employed as elementary teachers earn $39,200, which is 5 percent higher than the earnings of those who have graduated from other majors.

Table 4
Annual Salary of Workers with Only a Bachelor's Degree, Top 5 Occupations (in 2010 Dollars)

Earnings in Top 5 Occupations	All	Special Education
Total	$37,000	$38,100
Teachers—Special Education	$38,200	$38,200
Teachers—Elementary School	$37,200	$39,200
Secretaries, Receptionists, and Typists	$31,000	$37,200
Other Administrative Occupations	$38,200	$39,200
Artists, Broadcasters, Editors, Entertainers, Public Relations Specialists, Writers	$49,500	$35,100

Job Satisfaction

The overall level of job satisfaction of special education majors is considerably higher than the average for all graduates.

Employment Outlook

According to the projections by the U.S. Bureau of Labor Statistics, employment in occupations that require a bachelor's degree is expected to grow faster than employment in other sectors of the American labor market. Between 2008 and 2018, the U.S. workforce is projected to grow by 10.1 percent, creating an average of 15.2 million job openings per year. The bachelor's-level jobs are expected to increase by 17.7 percent over the same time.

The workforce of special education teachers is projected to grow at about the same rate as all bachelor's-level occupations, but the growth rate will vary according to the grade level being taught. Like regular classroom teachers, special education teachers will see the most growth at the preschool, kindergarten, and elementary school level (19.6 percent), the least growth at the secondary level (13.3 percent), and intermediate growth at the middle school level (18.1 percent). At all three levels, they are projected to experience more growth than other classroom teachers.

Although most areas of the country report difficulty finding qualified applicants, positions in inner cities and rural areas usually are more plentiful than job openings in suburban or wealthy urban areas. In addition, job opportunities may

Table 5
Percentage Distribution of Workers with Only a Bachelor's Degree, by Level of Job Satisfaction

Job Satisfaction	Special Education	All
Very satisfied	58.1	45.4
Somewhat satisfied	36.6	45.0
Somewhat dissatisfied	3.6	7.4
Very dissatisfied	1.7	2.2
Mean Score (4=very satisfied, 1=not satisfied at all)	3.5	3.3

Table 6

Projected Growth and Job Openings in the Top 5 Occupations Employing Persons
with Only a Bachelor's Degree in Special Education

Top 5 Occupations	Projected Growth 2008–2018	Projected Annual Job Openings
All top 5	12.1%	313,270
Teachers—Special Education	17.3%	20,460
Teachers—Elementary School	15.8%	59,650
Secretaries, Receptionists, and Typists	4.0%	5,590
Other Administrative Occupations	10.8%	166,130
Artists, Broadcasters, Editors, Entertainers, Public Relations Specialists, Writers	12.4%	71,740

be better in certain specialties—for example, teachers who work with children with multiple disabilities or those who work with children with severe disabilities such as autism—because of large increases in the enrollment of special education students classified into those categories. Legislation encouraging early intervention and special education for infants, toddlers, and preschoolers has created a need for early childhood special education teachers. Bilingual special education teachers and those with multicultural experience also are needed to work with an increasingly diverse student population.

Pathways Beyond the Bachelor's Degree

More than half of special education bachelor's degree recipients continue their education and earn an advanced degree of some type. The motivation for obtaining such a degree is closely tied to teachers' compensation systems that offer pay increments partly on the basis of additional degrees earned above the bachelor's level. Almost all the advanced degrees earned are at the master's degree level. Fewer than 2 percent of special education majors go on to earn a doctorate or professional degree.

▶ More than half of those who earn a master's degree continue their studies in the field of special education. An additional 30 percent earn their master's degree in some other education-related graduate field of study.

▶ Few special education majors earn degrees outside the educational field. Those who do so most often earn a master's degree in a social work or counseling field.

PART 5

Engineering

CHAPTER 26

Aerospace, Aeronautical, and Astronautical Engineering

Like all engineering, the aerospace field involves design, development, testing, and involvement in the manufacturing process. Aeronautical engineers develop new technologies for use in commercial aviation, air defense systems, and space exploration. They often specialize in such areas as structural design, guidance navigation and control, instrumentation, communications, or production methods. Or they specialize in such products as commercial planes, helicopters, spacecraft, or rockets. Further specialization can involve aerodynamics, propulsion, thermodynamics, celestial mechanics, or acoustics.

Most jobs for aerospace engineers exist in California, Washington, Texas, and Florida. Defense Department expenditures play a major role in the size of the industry and the availability of work in this highly competitive field. Anyone desiring to enter aerospace needs to seek out institutions with a recognized accredited program and a good placement record for its graduates. A sound academic preparation in the fundamentals is what some employers want because these companies often prefer to give their own specific formal training. Specialized courses are applied aerodynamics, flight vehicle design, trajectory dynamics, and aerospace propulsion systems.

Interests relevant to the field are the enjoyment of science, the conceptualization of design, and the implementation of practical outcomes. As in many fields, some people seek concrete, immediate solutions; some enjoy forming more conceptual and abstract ideas; and others are challenged and respond creatively to brainstorming the solutions for research problems in groups. Teamwork may be a new orientation for some high school students and an important criterion in selecting a college or university where the teaching methodology is oriented toward collective achievement.

Aeronautical engineers value creativity, a good salary, prestige, intellectual stimulation, and opportunities to do research, use mathematics, and encounter varied scientific problems.

Where Do Aerospace, Aeronautical, and Astronautical Engineering Majors Work?

Two-thirds of all employed aerospace engineering majors work for private, for-profit businesses. Another 14 percent are self-employed in their own incorporated or nonincorporated business or practice. The government sector employs 12 percent of all aerospace engineering majors with a bachelor's degree.

Out of all employed aerospace engineering graduates, half work in jobs that are closely related to their undergraduate major, and another 32 percent are employed in jobs that are somewhat related to their field of study. The remaining 17 percent work in jobs that are not related to their undergraduate major.

Out of all aerospace engineering graduates less than 65 years old, 94 percent are employed. Only 3 percent are officially unemployed; that is, they are not employed and are actively seeking employment. The remaining 3 percent are out of the labor force; that is, they are not employed and are not seeking employment. Retirement is the reason for labor force withdrawal among 62 percent of aerospace engineering majors who are out of the labor force; 13 percent withdraw because they have no need to work.

Occupations

Close to half of aerospace engineering graduates are concentrated in 3 occupations. About 24 percent are employed as aeronautical, aerospace, and astronautical engineers. Another 18 percent are employed in transportation occupations, mainly in the air transportation sector. Five percent work as engineering managers. Another 8 percent are employed in either mechanical or miscellaneous managerial occupations. Male grads outnumber female grads by 9 to 1.

Table 1

Percentage Distribution of Employed Persons with Only a Bachelor's Degree, by Economic Sector, Size, and New Business Status of Employer

	Aerospace Engineering	All
Economic Sector		
Private for-profit	66.8	47.3
Self-employed	14.2	18.5
Government/Military	11.9	11.0
Education	3.4	15.6
Nonprofit	3.1	7.5
Employer Size		
Small (Fewer than 100 employees)	23.9	35.5
Medium (100–999)	17.0	21.8
Large (1,000–24,999)	22.8	26.0
Very large (25,000 or more)	36.3	16.7
Percent working in new business established within past 5 years	4.5	7.6

Table 2
Percentage Distribution of Employed Persons with Only a Bachelor's Degree in Aerospace Engineering, by the Relationship Between Their Job and College Major

Relationship of Job to Major	Percent
Closely related	51.0
Somewhat related	32.2
Not related	16.8

Percent who report the following as the most important reasons for working in a job that was not related to major:

Pay, promotion opportunities	30.8
Change in career or professional interests	26.0
Job in highest degree field not available	16.8
Other reason	9.6
Job location	6.5

Work Activities

▶ Two-thirds of all employed aerospace engineering graduates perform managerial and administrative duties as a regular part of their jobs, and these are the primary job focus for one-quarter of grads.

▶ About a half percent performs product development tasks regularly.

▶ Thirty-eight percent are regularly involved in activities related to employee relations, including recruiting, personnel development, and training.

▶ Eighteen percent of the grads are primarily engaged in using computer applications, and another 77 percent devote at least 10 hours out of the workweek to these tasks.

Table 3
Top 5 Occupations Employing Persons with Only a Bachelor's Degree in Aerospace Engineering, by Percentage

Top 5 Occupations	All	Men	Women
Aerospace, Aeronautical, or Astronautical Engineers	24.2	25.6	10.9
Transportation and Material-Moving Occupations	18.5	17.3	29.0
Engineering Managers	5.1	5.5	2.0
Mechanics and Repairers	4.3	4.8	–
Other Management-Related Occupations	3.4	3.8	–
Total, Top 5 Occupations	55.5	57.0	41.9
Balance of Employed	44.5	43.0	58.1
All Employed	100.0	100.0	100.0

◗ More than one-third are engaged in sales, purchasing, and marketing activities as a regular part of their jobs.

Workplace Training and Other Work-Related Experiences

The career potential of a job is closely associated with the amount of work-related training on the job. Work-related training is regarded as an investment by firms because the training makes workers more productive. The rate of participation in work-related training during a year among employed aerospace engineering graduates (59 percent) is about the same as the training participation rate of all college graduates (61 percent).

◗ Of those aerospace engineering majors who receive some training during a year, 45 percent receive technical training in their occupational field.

◗ Twenty-four percent receive training to improve their general professional skills, such as public speaking and business writing.

◗ Only 23 percent of the training recipients receive management or supervisory training.

More than one-quarter of aerospace engineering majors who participate in some work-related training do so to improve their occupational skills and knowledge. About 13 percent are required or expected by their employers to undergo training. Increased opportunity for promotion, advancement, and salary increases is the reason for 9 percent of aerospace engineering majors to participate in work-related training.

Salaries

The median annual salary of aerospace engineering graduates with only a bachelor's degree is $74,000, a level that is 30 percent higher than the median annual salary of all employed college graduates. On average, employed aerospace engineering graduates work for 46 hours per week and for 51 weeks per year, resulting in 2,346 hours of employment per year. The level of work effort among aerospace engineering graduates is 9 percent higher than the average among all college graduates (43 hours per week and 50 weeks per year, resulting in 2,150 hours per year).

The average annual salary of full-time aerospace engineering majors with only a bachelor's degree is $74,000, a level that is 37 percent higher than the average annual salary of all full-time employed college graduates. The average annual salary of aerospace engineering majors who work in jobs that are closely related to their major is $82,600. Graduates whose jobs are somewhat related to their major earn $67,100 per year; the same average is earned by graduates whose jobs are unrelated to the major.

The average annual salary of self-employed aerospace engineering majors is $97,500. Graduates employed in private, for-profit businesses earn an average annual salary of $77,400. Government employees earn an average annual salary of $64,900.

Among the 5 occupations that are predominant employers of aerospace engineering majors, the only one that pays these grads a lower salary than the average for all majors is, ironically, aerospace, aeronautical, and astronautical engineers. (Of the aeronautical engineers surveyed, 93 percent are aeronautical engineering grads; those from other majors must have exceptional skills.) Among the other 4 occupations, the earnings advantages of the engineering degree are sometimes dramatic. For example, aerospace engineering graduates working as mechanics and repairers earn 36 percent more than graduates with other bachelor's degrees. Those working in miscellaneous managerial occupations have a 52 percent salary advantage. The transportation occupations include a broad range of jobs, from pilots to motorboat operators; it seems likely

FIGURE 1

Age/Earnings Profile of Persons with Only a Bachelor's Degree in Aerospace Engineering (Full-Time Workers, in 2010 Dollars)

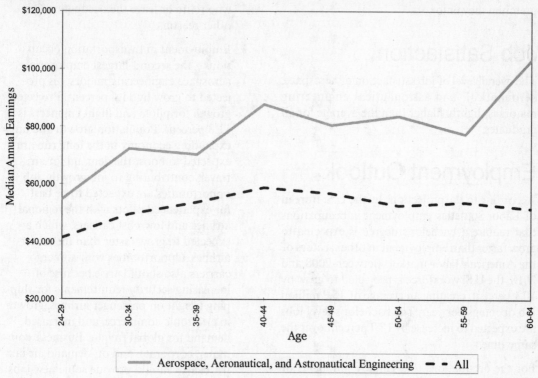

Table 4
Annual Salary of Workers with Only a Bachelor's Degree, Top 5 Occupations (in 2010 Dollars)

Earnings in Top 5 Occupations	All	Aerospace Engineering
Total	$74,000	$81,200
Aerospace, Aeronautical, or Astronautical Engineers	$86,700	$83,600
Transportation and Material-Moving Occupations	$46,400	$74,300
Engineering Managers	$98,000	$103,200
Mechanics and Repairers	$45,400	$61,900
Other Management-Related Occupations	$57,800	$87,700

that, out of this group of jobs, most graduates of aerospace engineering programs are working as pilots, which explains the high earnings premium they enjoy.

Job Satisfaction

The overall level of job satisfaction of aerospace, aeronautical, and astronautical engineering majors is slightly higher than the average for all graduates.

Employment Outlook

According to the projections by the U.S. Bureau of Labor Statistics, employment in occupations that require a bachelor's degree is expected to grow faster than employment in other sectors of the American labor market. Between 2008 and 2018, the U.S. workforce is projected to grow by 10.1 percent, creating an average of 15.2 million job openings per year. The bachelor's-level jobs are expected to increase by 17.7 percent over the same time.

For the occupations that employ graduates of aerospace engineering, the outlook is mixed:

▶ The workforce of aerospace, aeronautical, and astronautical engineers occupations is expected to grow by 10.4 percent between 2008 and 2018. Although the number of degrees granted in aerospace engineering has begun to increase after many years of declines, new graduates continue to be needed to replace aerospace engineers who retire or leave the occupation for other reasons.

▶ Employment in transportation occupations—the second-largest employer of aerospace engineering majors—is projected to grow by 11.4 percent. Projected growth for pilots and flight engineers is 11.8 percent. Population growth and an expanding economy in the long run are expected to boost the demand for air travel, contributing to job growth. Job opportunities are expected to be best for experienced pilots with the regional airlines and low-cost carriers, which are expected to grow faster than the major airlines. Opportunities with air cargo carriers also should arise because of increasing security requirements for shipping freight on passenger airlines, growth in electronic commerce, and increased demand for global freight. Business, commuter, corporate, and on-demand air taxi travel also should provide some new jobs for pilots.

▶ The demand for engineering managers is projected to grow by 6.2 percent, a slower rate than the rate of growth projected for total employment in the U.S. economy between 2008 and 2018.

Table 5
Percentage Distribution of Workers with Only a Bachelor's Degree, by Level of Job Satisfaction

Job Satisfaction	Aerospace Engineering	All
Very satisfied	53.5	45.4
Somewhat satisfied	38.9	45.0
Somewhat dissatisfied	5.7	7.4
Very dissatisfied	1.9	2.2
Mean Score (4=very satisfied, 1=not satisfied at all)	3.4	3.3

Table 6

Projected Growth and Job Openings in the Top 5 Occupations Employing Persons
with Only a Bachelor's Degree in Aerospace Engineering

Top 5 Occupations	Projected Growth 2008–2018	Projected Annual Job Openings
All top 5	7.0%	75,580
Aerospace, Aeronautical, or Astronautical Engineers	10.4%	2,230
Transportation and Material-Moving Occupations	11.4%	12,830
Engineering Managers	6.2%	4,870
Mechanics and Repairers	−4.4%	2,630
Other Management-Related Occupations	7.2%	53,020

(This is an average; growth will vary among the different engineering fields.) Employment growth should be affected by many of the same factors that affect the growth of the engineers that these managers supervise. However, job growth for managers will be somewhat slower than for engineers because the increasing tendency to outsource research and development in specialized engineering and scientific research services firms will lead to some consolidation of management. Opportunities for engineering managers should be better in rapidly growing areas of engineering, such as environmental and biomedical engineering, than in more slowly growing areas, such as electrical and mechanical engineering.

▶ The workforce for all types of mechanics and repairers is projected to shrink by 4.4 percent, partly because many types of machines have been miniaturized and made more reliable. The outlook for aircraft mechanics and service technicians, at 6.4 percent growth, is rosier but still below the average for all occupations. Airlines have discovered that they can save money by having their airplanes serviced in foreign countries, where wages are lower.

Pathways Beyond the Bachelor's Degree

After graduating with a bachelor's degree, 41 percent of aerospace engineering majors proceed to earn a postgraduate degree: 31 percent earn a master's degree, 6 percent graduate with a doctorate, and only 4 percent earn a professional degree.

▶ Twenty-eight percent of all master's degrees are earned in aerospace, aeronautical, and astronautical engineering. Another 17 percent of aerospace engineering graduates earn a master's degree in business management and administration. About 9 percent earn a master's degree in mechanical engineering.

▶ Among those who earn doctoral degrees, 45 percent major in aerospace, aeronautical, and astronautical engineering, and about one-quarter earn their doctoral degrees in other engineering fields.

The survey that provides data for this book does not indicate military service, but a common career path for pilots is to get military flight training after completing a bachelor's in aeronautical engineering.

CHAPTER 27

Architecture and Environmental Design

Architects build ideas. They work in steps. First they consider a client's ideas, requirements, and the budget for what he or she wants to build or develop. Next they produce drawings, a report with environmental impact, and ideas about site selection for their client's review. After discussion with the client, alterations follow. Eventually drawings are developed for construction with details of structural systems that include air conditioning, heating, electricity, and plumbing, as well as site and landscape plans. The plans can specify building materials. Architects follow building codes, zoning laws, fire regulations, and disability-access concerns and requirements. Buildings also must be functional, safe, and economical, and they must meet the needs of the architect's client.

Architects advise the client on building sites and prepare cost analysis and land-use studies. Architects participate in getting construction bids, negotiating the building contract, monitoring the progress of construction to assure specified standards for quality of work, and meeting time schedules.

Training programs are varied. One program is postgraduate. Another combines a pre-professional undergraduate degree with a graduate degree. The quickest and most popular way to get a license is to earn the 5-year bachelor's degree in architecture. However, because courses are specialized, these courses may not transfer easily to other degree programs if a person loses interest in the field. Typical courses include architectural history and theory; building design, including technical and legal aspects; professional practice; mathematics; the physical sciences; and liberal arts.

Although architects design buildings, their duties require engineering, managerial, and supervisory skills. Visual orientation—to conceptualize and understand spatial relationships—is an essential ability. Artistic or drawing ability helps but is not critical. The key is that architects must be able to visually communicate their ideas to clients. Creative as well as written and oral communication abilities are important. Also needed is the flexibility to work independently or as part of a team of engineers, urban planners, interior designers, or landscape architects. Most architects have proficiency and sophistication in computer-aided design and drafting (CADD).

Architecture satisfies a combination of artistic and scientific interests. In addition to creative interests, the field demands specificity, precision, practicality, and application of theory and standards. Highly developed abilities, combined with keen interest in the field, help candidates deal with this competitive field.

Architects thrive on prestige and the recognition by others of their creative efforts. Architects are persuasive and definitely attempt to influence their clients to their own way of thinking. Architects are designers who work with their minds and are seen by others as bright. A high salary, variety, and diversion are important to them.

Where Do Architecture and Environmental Design Majors Work?

Architects are more likely to work in the private, for-profit sector than most other college graduates. They are quite entrepreneurial, with almost 36 percent working in their own business as their primary source of income. About 48 percent of architects work in jobs for private-sector employers, usually in engineering or architectural service firms or in the construction industry. Few opportunities exist for architects in the nonprofit sector. About 9 percent of architects work for a government agency—most often at the local level.

Most graduates with an architecture degree at the bachelor's degree level are employed in jobs that are related to architecture. Sixty-two percent work in closely related jobs, and another one-fifth in jobs that are somewhat related. Only 18 percent of graduates work in jobs unrelated to the field.

About 93 percent of all persons under the age of 65 with a bachelor's degree in architecture are employed, most in full-time jobs. Among those not employed, less than one-quarter are unemployed and actively seeking work. The remaining three-quarters of those architecture majors who are jobless are individuals who are not actively

Table 1
Percentage Distribution of Employed Persons with Only a Bachelor's Degree, by Economic Sector, Size, and New Business Status of Employer

	Architecture and Environmental Design	All
Economic Sector		
Private for-profit	47.8	47.3
Self-employed	35.9	18.5
Government/Military	9.1	11.0
Education	5.6	15.6
Nonprofit	1.6	7.5
Employer Size		
Small (Fewer than 100 employees)	60.8	35.5
Medium (100–999)	15.4	21.8
Large (1,000–24,999)	13.3	26.0
Very large (25,000 or more)	10.5	16.7
Percent working in new business established within past 5 years	12.2	7.6

Table 2
Percentage Distribution of Employed Persons with Only a Bachelor's Degree in Architecture and Environmental Design, by the Relationship Between Their Job and College Major

Relationship of Job to Major	Percent
Closely related	62.2
Somewhat related	20.0
Not related	17.8

Percent who report the following as the most important reasons for working in a job that was not related to major:

Pay, promotion opportunities	28.8
Change in career or professional interests	27.0
Job location	14.9
Job in highest degree field not available	12.3
Family-related reasons	9.0

seeking work. A substantial proportion of these individuals (27 percent) retired from work even though they are under the age of 65. A slightly smaller share withdrew from the workforce because of family commitments.

Occupations

Unlike many other majors at the undergraduate level, most architecture majors can see a clear relationship between their academic program and the labor market. Forty-two percent of all persons who graduate with a bachelor's degree in architecture eventually become employed as architects after college. However, women who earn architecture degrees (about one-quarter of the grads) are somewhat less likely to choose work as professional architects than their male counterparts. Women with an architecture degree are somewhat more likely to choose work as artists and writers or in other creative fields than are their male counterparts. They are less likely to opt for management.

Work Activities

▶ More than 75 percent of these individuals regularly engage in project management and administrative activities during the workweek, and more than one-quarter of grads are primarily responsible for this job function.

▶ Design of buildings and work processes is an important element of the work of architects; design is also important in some other jobs that employ many architecture grads. Fifty-five percent of grads engage in these activities on a weekly basis, and one-fifth focus mainly on these tasks.

▶ More than 9 out of 10 architecture grads spend significant work time using computer applications, although almost none do this work primarily.

▶ About 54 percent of architecture graduates are involved in accounting, finance, and contracting as they oversee design and construction projects.

Table 3
Top 5 Occupations Employing Persons with Only a Bachelor's Degree in Architecture and Environmental Design, by Percentage

Top 5 Occupations	All	Men	Women
Architects	42.5	44.7	34.5
Other Management-Related Occupations	7.1	7.4	6.0
Artists, Broadcasters, Editors, Entertainers, Public Relations Specialists, and Writers	5.0	3.2	11.6
Top-Level Managers, Executives, and Administrators	4.7	5.7	1.2
Other Mid-Level Managers	4.0	4.4	2.5
Total, Top 5 Occupations	63.3	65.4	55.8
Balance of Employed	36.7	34.6	44.2
All Employed	100.0	100.0	100.0

Workplace Training and Other Work-Related Experiences

Degree holders in architecture are slightly less likely than the average college graduate to participate in some type of work-related training during the course of a year. Yet 6 out of 10 persons with a bachelor's degree in the field participate in some type of training activity. Self-employed architects are much less likely to engage in training in the prior year, while those employed by for-profit businesses are much more likely to receive training. Thus, young architects interested in developing skills will find many more training opportunities working for a firm.

▶ Most architects (52 percent) participate in training that is directly related to technical tasks found in their field.

▶ Training in management and supervisory skills is important to architecture graduates, with one-fifth receiving such training in the prior year.

▶ Slightly more architecture majors receive training in communications skills while on the job.

Those who undergo training are motivated most often by a desire to improve their technical skills; 3 out of 10 cite this reason as the most compelling. About half as many get the training primarily to achieve or maintain licensure or certification. (All states require architects to be licensed, and most states also require some form of continuing education to maintain a license.)

Salaries

College graduates with a degree in architecture earn a median salary of $60,000 per year, a rate of pay about 14 percent higher per year than the median pay of all college graduates. On average, employed architecture and environmental design graduates work for 44 hours per week and for 50 weeks per year, resulting in 2,200 hours of employment per year. The level of work effort among architecture graduates is 2 percent higher than the average among all college graduates (43 hours per week and 50 weeks per year, resulting in 2,150 hours per year).

FIGURE 1

Age/Earnings Profile of Persons with Only a Bachelor's Degree in Architecture and Environmental Design (Full-Time Workers, in 2010 Dollars)

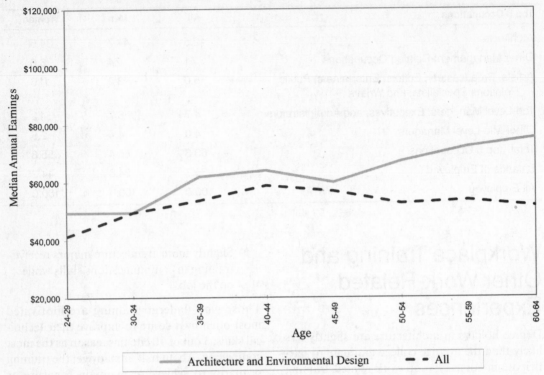

Architects employed in a private, for-profit firm average $65,000 per year, the highest salaries of all architects who work in full-time jobs. Architecture graduates who work in government agencies earn about $57,300 per year. Self-employed architects earn an average of $55,700 per year.

Bachelor's degree holders in architecture who work in jobs unrelated to their undergraduate major have much lower earnings than those who have jobs related to the major. Graduates employed in jobs closely related to the major have annual salaries that average $61,900 per year, compared to the average of $49,500 earned by those who work in jobs that are unrelated to the field. Those working in jobs that are somewhat related average $68,100 per year; some of them have improved their earnings by moving into mid- or top-level management.

The earnings of persons with a bachelor's degree in architecture differ sharply by the occupation in which they are employed. Graduates with a degree in architecture who are employed as architects earn an average of $61,900. Of the architecture majors employed in the top 5 careers, those engaged in top- or mid-level management have the highest average annual salary, $82,600.

Job Satisfaction

The overall level of job satisfaction of architecture and environmental design majors is slightly higher than the average for all graduates.

Table 4
Annual Salary of Workers with Only a Bachelor's Degree, Top 5 Occupations (in 2010 Dollars)

Earnings in Top 5 Occupations	All	Architecture and Environmental Design
Total	$60,000	$63,400
Architects	$59,900	$61,900
Other Management-Related Occupations	$57,800	$56,800
Artists, Broadcasters, Editors, Entertainers, Public Relations Specialists, and Writers	$49,500	$50,600
Top-Level Managers, Executives, and Administrators	$103,200	$82,600
Other Mid-Level Managers	$77,400	$82,600

Employment Outlook

According to the projections by the U.S. Bureau of Labor Statistics, employment in occupations that require a bachelor's degree is expected to grow faster than employment in other sectors of the American labor market. Between 2008 and 2018, the U.S. workforce is projected to grow by 10.1 percent, creating an average of 15.2 million job openings per year. The bachelor's-level jobs are expected to increase by 17.7 percent over the same time.

▶ The job outlook for the architectural profession is strong. Between 2008 and 2018, the number of employed architects is expected to increase by almost 17 percent,

a rate of growth close to that of all college-level occupations. Competition is expected, especially for positions at the most prestigious firms, and opportunities will be best for those architects who are able to distinguish themselves with their creativity. In recent years, some architecture firms have outsourced the drafting of construction documents and basic design for large-scale commercial and residential projects to architecture firms overseas. This trend is expected to continue and may have a negative impact on employment growth for lower-level architects and interns who would normally gain experience by producing these drawings.

Table 5
Percentage Distribution of Workers with Only a Bachelor's Degree, by Level of Job Satisfaction

Job Satisfaction	Architecture and Environmental Design	All
Very satisfied	45.0	45.4
Somewhat satisfied	45.5	45.0
Somewhat dissatisfied	6.4	7.4
Very dissatisfied	3.1	2.2
Mean Score (4=very satisfied, 1=not satisfied at all)	3.4	3.3

Table 6

Projected Growth and Job Openings in the Top 5 Occupations Employing Persons
with Only a Bachelor's Degree in Architecture and Environmental Design

Top 5 Occupations	Projected Growth 2008–2018	Projected Annual Job Openings
All top 5	7.4%	272,540
Architects	16.8%	5,660
Other Management-Related Occupations	7.2%	53,020
Artists, Broadcasters, Editors, Entertainers, Public Relations Specialists, and Writers	12.4%	71,740
Top-Level Managers, Executives, and Administrators	−0.4%	61,470
Other Mid-Level Managers	9.7%	80,650

▸ Creative jobs—such as artists and writers—that employ a substantial number of women architecture graduates are expected to grow at a somewhat slower-than-average rate.

▸ So are the mid-level managerial jobs that tend to employ male graduates. The workforce of top-level managers will actually shrink in size. These managerial occupations will create many job openings because of turnover, but competition for these lucrative jobs will be intense.

Pathways Beyond the Bachelor's Degree

Most persons who earn a bachelor's degree do not go on to earn an advanced degree. Only about one-quarter of all persons who receive a bachelor's degree in architecture earn an advanced degree. Among those who do, most go on to earn a master's degree of some type. Very few architecture majors earn doctoral or professional degrees.

▸ Most who decide to earn a graduate degree continue their education in architecture. About 43 percent of all master's degrees earned by those with a bachelor's degree in architecture are earned in the same field.

▸ An additional 10 percent of master's degrees earned by those with a bachelor's degree in architecture are in business.

CHAPTER 28

Chemical Engineering

Chemical engineering is a relatively small specialization. Its workforce is surpassed by those of electrical, mechanical, civil, industrial, and aeronautical engineering. Chemical engineering combines the knowledge of principles of chemistry with engineering in the production and use of chemicals. The work involves designing and developing manufacturing processes and supervising production. The engineers plan and test new manufacturing processes that increase industrial output and use existing resources safely and efficiently.

Chemistry is a science that applies to every kind of matter, so the products addressed in this discussion cut across numerous industries. Chemicals are used to make paper, fertilizers, PVC pipe for plumbing, and printing ink; they are used to produce crops and process food; and they are used in petroleum refining. Chemical engineers frequently specialize in particular operations, such as polymerization or fermentation, and in areas such as plastics and pharmaceuticals. Chemical engineers also use electrical and mechanical engineering in their work. Sometimes they engage in research and development of new chemicals.

Chemical engineers are involved in biomedicines, agricultural chemicals, fibers, and synthetic fuels. Chemical engineers work on ways to reduce acid rain and smog, to recycle and reduce wastes, and to develop new sources of environmentally clean energy.

Common courses studied are organic and physical chemistry, thermodynamics, kinetics, heat transport, process control, advanced mathematics, and state-of-the-art computer-aided design.

Like other engineers, chemical engineers must be skilled in the basic sciences and high-level mathematics. They must also have good analytical reasoning and technical and spatial abilities. Because chemicals change their form—liquid to gas, for example—and different processes use pressure, heat, and cooling, some engineers find the field difficult because of the level of abstraction and computerized mathematical modeling involved.

Chemical engineers are most interested in scientific data and ideas and in their applications. They enjoy the exploration and the analytical and mechanical facets of their studies and work. Machines and manual activities provide them with opportunities to satisfy their desire to achieve practical results.

Because they are among the best paid of engineers, chemical engineers value income and prestige, but they also enjoy intellectual stimulation, working with numbers, creativity, research, and the opportunity for change and diversity in their work.

Table 1

Percentage Distribution of Employed Persons with Only a Bachelor's Degree, by Economic Sector, Size, and New Business Status of Employer

	Chemical Engineering	All
Economic Sector		
Private for-profit	72.4	47.3
Self-employed	13.2	18.5
Government/Military	8.8	11.0
Education	4.0	15.6
Nonprofit	1.3	7.5
Employer Size		
Small (Fewer than 100 employees)	16.9	35.5
Medium (100–999)	13.5	21.8
Large (1,000–24,999)	40.3	26.0
Very large (25,000 or more)	29.4	16.7
Percent working in new business established within past 5 years	4.8	7.6

Where Do Chemical Engineering Majors Work?

Almost 9 out of 10 employed chemical engineering majors work as wage and salary workers in the private, for-profit sector. Seventy-two percent work at private, for-profit businesses and corporations, and 13 percent are self-employed in their own business or practice. The government sector employs only 9 percent of all chemical engineering majors with only a bachelor's degree. Only 5 percent of employed chemical engineering majors work for educational institutions or for private, nonprofit organizations.

The rate of related employment is high among chemical engineering majors. More than 4 out of 10 employed chemical engineering graduates work in jobs that are closely related to their major. About the same share work in jobs that are somewhat related to their major. Less than 16 percent work in jobs that are not related to their undergraduate major.

Out of all the chemical engineering graduates who are under the age of 65, 89 percent are employed. Only 3 percent are officially unemployed; that is, they are not employed and are actively seeking employment. The remaining 8 percent are out of the labor force; that is, they are not employed and are not seeking employment. Retirement is the reason for labor force withdrawal among 60 percent of nonelderly chemical engineering majors who are out of the labor force. About 10 percent have withdrawn because of family responsibilities, and 7 percent do not want or need to work. About 6 percent have not found available jobs and have given up looking.

Occupations

Chemical engineering majors are concentrated in a few occupational areas; the top 5 occupations employ more than half of all working grads. A large proportion—30 percent—are employed

Table 2

Percentage Distribution of Employed Persons with Only a Bachelor's Degree in Chemical Engineering, by the Relationship Between Their Job and College Major

Relationship of Job to Major	Percent
Closely related	43.3
Somewhat related	41.1
Not related	15.6

Percent who report the following as the most important reasons for working in a job that was not related to major:

Job in highest degree field not available	31.8
Change in career or professional interests	21.8
Pay, promotion opportunities	14.9
Job location	9.0
Working conditions (hours, equipment, environment)	8.9

as chemical engineers. Another 11 percent are employed in managerial jobs, either at the top of the company pyramid or in charge of an engineering department. Sixteen percent of chemical engineering graduates are employed in other engineering occupations. Seven percent are environmental engineers, and industrial engineering and miscellaneous engineering specializations

each employ 2 percent. Only 5 percent of chemical engineering majors are employed in a mix of marketing and sales occupations.

Male grads outnumber females by about 4 to 1, but a somewhat higher percentage of the female grads are drawn to the most popular engineering occupations.

Table 3

Top 5 Occupations Employing Persons with Only a Bachelor's Degree in Chemical Engineering, by Percentage

Top 5 Occupations	All	Men	Women
Chemical Engineers	30.5	29.6	33.7
Environmental Engineers	7.0	6.7	8.0
Top-Level Managers, Executives, and Administrators	6.2	6.0	7.2
Engineering Managers	5.1	6.2	1.5
Other Marketing and Sales Occupations	5.0	5.3	3.9
Total, Top 5 Occupations	53.8	53.8	54.3
Balance of Employed	46.2	46.2	45.7
All Employed	100.0	100.0	100.0

Work Activities

▶ Design is an important task for 46 percent of chemical engineering grads, and it is the chief job function for 12 percent of the grads. Development is a significant task for 41 percent of grads.

▶ Thirty-four percent of grads are engaged in managing quality or productivity, and 11 percent are primarily responsible for these tasks.

▶ One-third are engaged in sales, purchasing, and marketing activities as a regular part of their jobs, and these are the most important tasks for 14 percent of grads.

▶ Nearly 7 out of 10 chemical engineering majors engage in managing people or projects on a regular basis, and nearly one-quarter focus primarily on these duties.

▶ Eighty-eight percent of grads spend significant work time using computer applications.

▶ Thirty-five percent regularly perform accounting, finance, and contractual duties as a part of their jobs.

Workplace Training and Other Work-Related Experiences

The career potential of a job is closely associated with the amount of work-related training on the job. Work-related training is regarded as an investment by firms because it makes workers more productive. The rate of participation in work-related training during a year among employed chemical engineering graduates (63 percent) is somewhat higher than the training participation rate of all college graduates (61 percent).

▶ Of those chemical engineering majors who receive some training, 49 percent receive technical training in their occupational field.

▶ Twenty-seven percent of the training recipients receive management or supervisory training.

▶ One in 5 receive training to improve their general professional skills, such as public speaking and business writing.

One-third of chemical engineering majors who participate in some work-related training do so to primarily improve their occupational skills and knowledge. About 9 percent are required or expected by their employers to undergo training. Increased opportunity for promotion, advancement, and salary increases is the reason for 7 percent of chemical engineering majors to participate in work-related training. Almost 7 percent are engaged in training activities to learn new skills for a recently acquired position.

Salaries

The median annual salary of chemical engineering graduates with only a bachelor's degree is $80,000, a level that is 36 percent higher than the median annual salary of all employed college graduates. On average, employed chemical engineering graduates work for 45 hours per week and for 51 weeks per year, resulting in 2,295 hours of employment per year. The level of work effort among chemical engineering graduates is 7 percent higher than the average among all college graduates (43 hours per week and 50 weeks per year, resulting in 2,150 hours per year).

Access to jobs that are closely related to their undergraduate major is associated with a sizable earnings premium among chemical engineering majors who are employed in full-time jobs. The average annual salary of graduates who work in jobs that are closely related to their major is

FIGURE 1

Age/Earnings Profile of Persons with Only a Bachelor's Degree in Chemical Engineering (Full-Time Workers, in 2010 Dollars)

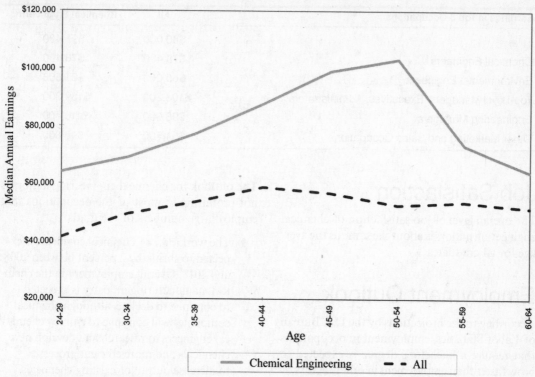

$82,600. An even higher earnings boost is enjoyed by those whose jobs are only somewhat related to the major; their yearly average is $87,700. Doubtless this well-paid group includes many who have moved into managerial positions, a common career path in this field. The average annual salary of chemical engineering graduates whose jobs are unrelated to their major is $54,700, a level that is only two-thirds of the salary of their counterparts with closely related jobs.

The two sectors that are predominant employers of chemical engineering majors also pay them the highest annual salary. Graduates employed by private, for-profit businesses earn $87,700 annually. Self-employed chemical engineering majors have the second-highest salary of all sectors in the economy. Working in their own

incorporated or nonincorporated business or practice results in an average annual salary of $73,400. Government employees earn an average salary of $68,000.

The average annual earnings of chemical engineering majors are much higher than the average earnings of all college graduates in 4 of the 5 occupations that are predominant employers of chemical engineering graduates. Ironically, the only occupation of the top 5 in which their specialized degree does not give them an earnings advantage is chemical engineers, where both majors and nonmajors average $78,400 per year. (Of the chemical engineers surveyed, only 7 percent majored in something other than chemical engineering; those from other majors must have exceptional skills.)

Table 4
Annual Salary of Workers with Only a Bachelor's Degree, Top 5 Occupations (in 2010 Dollars)

Earnings in Top 5 Occupations	All	Chemical Engineering
Total	$80,000	$91,400
Chemical Engineers	$78,400	$78,400
Environmental Engineers	$65,000	$81,500
Top-Level Managers, Executives, Administrators	$103,200	$139,300
Engineering Managers	$98,000	$110,400
Other Marketing and Sales Occupations	$54,700	$96,000

Job Satisfaction

The overall level of job satisfaction of chemical engineering majors is about the same as the average for all graduates.

Employment Outlook

According to the projections by the U.S. Bureau of Labor Statistics, employment in occupations that require a bachelor's degree is expected to grow faster than employment in other sectors of the American labor market. Between 2008 and 2018, the U.S. workforce is projected to grow by 10.1 percent, creating an average of 15.2 million job openings per year. The bachelor's-level jobs are expected to increase by 17.7 percent over the same time.

The outlook for chemical engineering majors is not promising in most of the occupations that employ large numbers of the grads:

▶ The workforce of chemical engineers is expected to shrink by 2 percent between 2008 and 2018. Overall employment in the chemical manufacturing industry is expected to continue to decline, although chemical companies will continue to employ chemical engineers to research and develop new chemicals and more efficient processes to increase output of existing chemicals. However, there will be employment growth for chemical engineers in service-providing industries, such as professional, scientific, and technical services, particularly for research in energy and the developing fields of biotechnology and nanotechnology.

Table 5
Percentage Distribution of Workers with Only a Bachelor's Degree, by Level of Job Satisfaction

Job Satisfaction	Chemical Engineering	All
Very satisfied	38.0	45.4
Somewhat satisfied	51.6	45.0
Somewhat dissatisfied	8.1	7.4
Very dissatisfied	2.3	2.2
Mean Score (4=very satisfied, 1=not satisfied at all)	3.3	3.3

Table 6

Projected Growth and Job Openings in the Top 5 Occupations Employing Persons with Only a Bachelor's Degree in Chemical Engineering

Top 5 Occupations	Projected Growth 2008–2018	Projected Annual Job Openings
All top 5	3.9%	134,790
Chemical Engineers	−2.0%	780
Environmental Engineers	30.6%	2,790
Top-Level Managers, Executives, and Administrators	−0.4%	61,470
Engineering Managers	6.2%	4,870
Other Marketing and Sales Occupations	7.3%	64,880

▶ Environmental engineers are expected to have employment growth of 31 percent over the projections decade, much faster than the average for all occupations. More environmental engineers will be needed to help companies comply with environmental regulations and to develop methods of cleaning up environmental hazards. A shift in emphasis toward preventing problems rather than controlling those which already exist, as well as increasing public health concerns resulting from population growth, also is expected to spur demand for environmental engineers. Because of this employment growth, job opportunities should be favorable.

▶ Employment of top-level managers is projected to shrink slightly, but employment of engineering managers is projected to grow, albeit at the below-average rate of 6.2 percent. (This is an average; growth will vary among the different engineering fields.) Employment growth for engineering managers should be affected by many of the same factors that affect the growth of the engineers that these managers supervise. However, job growth for managers will be somewhat slower than for engineers because the increasing tendency to outsource research and development

in specialized engineering and scientific research services firms will lead to some consolidation of management. Opportunities for engineering managers should be better in rapidly growing areas of engineering, such as environmental and biomedical engineering, than in more slowly growing areas, such as electrical and mechanical engineering. Note that considerably more annual job openings are projected for top-level managers than engineering managers, reflecting a larger workforce with more turnover.

Pathways Beyond the Bachelor's Degree

After graduating with a bachelor's degree, 47 percent of chemical engineering majors proceed to earn a postgraduate degree: About 33 percent earn a master's degree, 11 percent graduate with a doctorate, and 3 percent earn a professional degree.

▶ Of the master's degrees, 29 percent are earned in chemical engineering and 22 percent in business administration and management.

▶ Among those who earn doctoral degrees, 71 percent major in chemical engineering and 4 percent major in chemistry.

CHAPTER 29

Civil Engineering

Civil engineers design and supervise the construction of roads, buildings, bridges, tunnels, airports, water-supply systems, and sewage systems. People can still see the results of the earliest practitioners in this field: the Egyptian pyramids, the Roman Forum, and the Great Wall of China.

Engineers move from place to place as projects begin and end. Many projects are government-sponsored. Specialties include structural, water resources, environmental, construction, transportation, and manufacturing. As civil engineers acquire experience, some assume management functions as top engineers.

Civil engineers analyze reports, maps, drawings, blueprints, tests, and aerial photography on soil composition, terrain, hydrological characteristics, and topographical and geological data to plan and design projects. They calculate costs and determine the feasibility of projects based on analysis of collected data, application of engineering techniques, and mathematical analysis. Civil engineers are involved in preparing modifications to reports and in writing specifications, construction schedules, and environmental impact studies. They make on-site inspections and monitor progress to ensure conformance to plans, specifications, building codes, zoning regulations, and safety standards.

The civil engineering curriculum follows a core of basic sciences and high-level mathematics. The disciplines covered include structural, environmental, transportation planning, and geotechnical engineering. Courses include structural mechanics, fluid mechanics, and environmental science.

The required courses and the solutions to problem-oriented examples used in instruction necessitate analytical reasoning, logical application of theoretical principles, and creativity. Also required is the ability to adapt to new projects, work in groups, communicate, and write reports.

Civil engineers like to study science and mathematics, and they prefer to see concrete manifestations of their work. (Sometimes the results are literally concrete.) They are doers and thinkers with an acute sense of observation. While mechanical and electrical engineers can focus on the project immediately in front of them, civil engineers are not intimidated by the physical size or scope of a project. For example, civil engineers are not afraid of building a bridge across a very broad expanse of water versus working on an electrical switch.

Civil engineers value the use of imagination to discover new ideas, a high income, intellectual thought and reasoning, outside work, status, and variety.

Where Do Civil Engineering Majors Work?

A bit more than half of all employed civil engineering majors work for private, for-profit businesses and corporations. One-fifth of grads are self-employed in their own business or practice. The government sector employs one-quarter of all civil engineering majors with a bachelor's

Table 1
Percentage Distribution of Employed Persons with Only a Bachelor's Degree, by Economic Sector, Size, and New Business Status of Employer

	Civil Engineering	All
Economic Sector		
Private for-profit	52.1	47.3
Self-employed	20.4	18.5
Government/Military	25.3	11.0
Education	1.8	15.6
Nonprofit	0.4	7.5
Employer Size		
Small (Fewer than 100 employees)	36.6	35.5
Medium (100–999)	25.4	21.8
Large (1,000–24,999)	24.5	26.0
Very large (25,000 or more)	13.4	16.7
Percent working in new business established within past 5 years	6.2	7.6

Table 2
Percentage Distribution of Employed Persons with Only a Bachelor's Degree in Civil Engineering, by the Relationship Between Their Job and College Major

Relationship of Job to Major	Percent
Closely related	66.4
Somewhat related	24.6
Not related	9.0

Percent who report the following as the most important reasons for working in a job that was not related to major:

Change in career or professional interests	22.2
Working conditions (hours, equipment, environment)	21.7
Job in highest degree field not available	19.0
Pay, promotion opportunities	12.6
Job location	9.8

degree. The remaining 2 percent work for educational institutions or for private, nonprofit organizations.

The rate of related employment is quite high among civil engineering majors. Two-thirds of all employed civil engineering graduates work in jobs that are closely related to their major. Another one-quarter work in jobs that are somewhat related to their major. Only 9 percent are employed in jobs that are not related to their undergraduate major.

Out of all civil engineering graduates under the age of 65, 92 percent are employed. Only 4 percent are officially unemployed; that is, they are not employed and are actively seeking employment. The remaining 4 percent are out of the labor force; that is, they are not employed and are not seeking employment. Retirement is the reason for labor force withdrawal among 59 percent of civil engineering majors who are out of the labor force. Less than 8 percent withdraw because of family responsibilities.

Occupations

Civil engineering majors are concentrated in very few occupational areas. More than one-half are employed in civil engineering occupations.

Fourteen percent are employed in managerial, executive, and administrative occupations, including engineering management. Another 6 percent are employed in miscellaneous construction and extraction occupations.

Male grads outnumber females by about 9 to 1, but about half of each group are working as civil engineers.

Work Activities

▶ Slightly more than three-quarters of employed civil engineering majors spend part of a typical workweek in managerial and administrative duties. For 41 percent of grads, this is their main responsibility.

▶ More than 44 percent are often engaged in the design of equipment, processes, structures, and models, and 15 percent do this most of the time.

▶ Eighty-seven percent of employed civil engineering majors regularly handle computer applications, programming, and systems development, although only 6 percent see this as their chief work function.

▶ Another 40 percent are regularly involved in sales, purchasing, and marketing.

Table 3
Top 5 Occupations Employing Persons with Only a
Bachelor's Degree in Civil Engineering, by Percentage

Top 5 Occupations	All	Men	Women
Civil, Architectural, or Sanitary Engineers	52.1	51.9	53.5
Top-Level Managers, Executives, and Administrators	7.3	7.9	1.6
Construction and Extraction Occupations	6.1	6.5	2.2
Other Management-Related Occupations	3.5	3.4	3.6
Engineering Managers	3.2	3.3	1.7
Total, Top 5 Occupations	72.2	73.0	62.6
Balance of Employed	27.8	27.0	37.4
All Employed	100.0	100.0	100.0

- Fifty-six percent of grads regularly engage in accounting, finance, and contractual activities.

- Employee-relations activities, including recruiting, personnel development, and training, consume significant work time for 45 percent of grads.

Workplace Training and Other Work-Related Experiences

The career potential of a job is closely associated with the amount of work-related training on the job. Work-related training is regarded as an investment by firms because it makes workers more productive. The rate of participation in work-related training during a year among employed civil engineering graduates (64 percent) is a little higher than the training participation rate of all college graduates (61 percent).

- Of those civil engineering majors who receive training, 56 percent receive technical training in their occupational field.

- One-third of the recipients receive management or supervisory training.

- About one-quarter receive training to improve their general professional skills, such as public speaking and business writing.

FIGURE 1

Age/Earnings Profile of Persons with Only a Bachelor's Degree in Civil Engineering (Full-Time Workers, in 2010 Dollars)

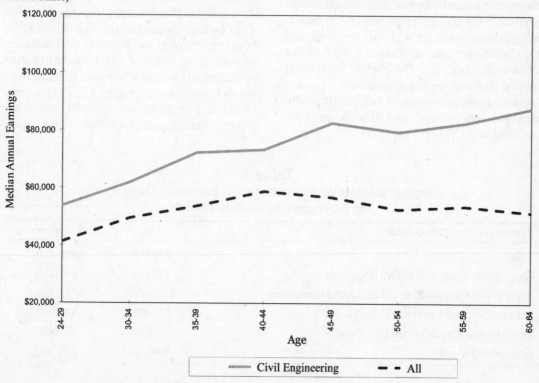

Civil engineering majors cite a variety of reasons for their participation in work-related training activities. When asked to identify the most important reason, 35 percent cite the need to acquire further skills and knowledge in their occupational field. Fourteen percent of all civil engineering majors who received some training cite licensing or certification as one of the reasons they attended training activities during the past year. (Engineers who offer their services to the public must be licensed, and many states require continuing education for relicensure.) About 6 percent state that their employer requires or expects employees to participate in work-related training activities.

Salaries

The median annual salary of civil engineering graduates with only a bachelor's degree is $70,000, a level that is 26 percent higher than the median annual salary of all employed college graduates. On average, employed civil engineering graduates work for 45 hours per week and for 51 weeks per year, resulting in 2,295 hours of employment per year. The level of work effort among civil engineering graduates is 7 percent higher than the average among all college graduates (43 hours per week and 50 weeks per year, resulting in 2,150 hours per year).

The average annual salary of civil engineering majors who work in jobs that are closely related to their major is $72,200. Higher average earnings are reported by graduates with employment in jobs that are somewhat related to their major: $74,300 per year. Many in this well-paid group have advanced to managerial jobs. Civil engineering graduates whose jobs are unrelated to their major earn an annual average salary that is quite a bit lower: $48,500.

Civil engineering graduates who are employed in the private sector by for-profit businesses and corporations earn more than their counterparts employed in other sectors. Their average annual salary is $75,300. Self-employed civil engineering graduates earn an average of $69,600. Government-sector employees with a bachelor's degree in civil engineering earn an average annual salary of $68,800.

The average annual earnings in 3 out of the top 5 occupations that employ civil engineering graduates are higher than the annual average earnings of all college graduates who are employed in those occupations. As it happens, civil engineering itself is the one field where the degree does not impart an earnings advantage, with both majors and nonmajors averaging $72,200 per year. (Of the civil engineers surveyed, 80 percent are civil engineering grads; those from other majors

Table 4
Annual Salary of Workers with Only a Bachelor's Degree,
Top 5 Occupations (in 2010 Dollars)

Earnings in Top 5 Occupations	All	Civil Engineering
Total	$70,000	$78,400
Civil, Architectural, or Sanitary Engineers	$72,200	$72,200
Top-Level Managers, Executives, and Administrators	$103,200	$123,800
Construction and Extraction Occupations	$51,600	$72,200
Other Management-Related Occupations	$57,800	$77,400
Engineering Managers	$98,000	$92,900

Table 5
Percentage Distribution of Workers with Only a Bachelor's Degree,
by Level of Job Satisfaction

Job Satisfaction	Civil Engineering	All
Very satisfied	50.0	45.4
Somewhat satisfied	43.2	45.0
Somewhat dissatisfied	4.4	7.4
Very dissatisfied	2.4	2.2
Mean Score (4=very satisfied, 1=not satisfied at all)	3.4	3.3

must have exceptional skills.) The average annual salary of civil engineering majors employed in top-level management, executive, and administrative occupations is $123,800, which is 20 percent higher than the average earnings of all college graduates employed in that occupation. Those who are employed in other miscellaneous managerial occupations earn $77,400, an earnings advantage of one-third over nonmajors.

Job Satisfaction

The overall level of job satisfaction of civil engineering majors is slightly higher than the average for all graduates.

Employment Outlook

According to the projections by the U.S. Bureau of Labor Statistics, employment in occupations that require a bachelor's degree is expected to grow faster than employment in other sectors of the American labor market. Between 2008 and 2018, the U.S. workforce is projected to grow by 10.1 percent, creating an average of 15.2 million job openings per year. The bachelor's-level jobs are expected to increase by 17.7 percent over the same time. The employment growth projections for the top 5 occupations that are most likely to employ civil engineering graduates are presented in Table 6.

▶ The demand for civil engineering occupations is expected to grow by 24 percent between 2008 and 2018, a rate much faster than the average for all occupations. Decreased environmental regulations at the federal, state, and local levels translate into a smaller need for civil engineers in the planning, execution, and monitoring of requirements of various environmental regulations. Spurred by general population growth and the related need to improve the nation's infrastructure, more civil engineers will be needed to design and construct or expand transportation, water supply, and pollution control systems, and buildings and building complexes. They also will be needed to repair or replace existing roads, bridges, and other public structures. Because construction industries and architectural, engineering, and related services employ many civil engineers, employment opportunities will vary by geographic area and may decrease during economic slowdowns.

▶ Employment in top-level managerial, executive, and administrative occupations—the second-largest employer of civil engineering majors—is projected to shrink slightly, but this group of jobs will account for 61,000 job openings each year because of turnover. Employment in other

Table 6

Projected Growth and Job Openings in the Top 5 Occupations Employing Persons with Only a Bachelor's Degree in Civil Engineering

Top 5 Occupations	Projected Growth 2008–2018	Projected Annual Job Openings
All top 5	4.8%	134,790
Civil, Architectural, or Sanitary Engineers	24.3%	11,460
Top-Level Managers, Executives, and Administrators	–0.4%	61,470
Construction and Extraction Occupations	16.8%	3,970
Other Management-Related Occupations	7.2%	53,020
Engineering Managers	6.2%	4,870

miscellaneous managerial occupations is expected to increase modestly, but this field will also create many job openings.

- The demand for engineering managers is projected to grow by 6.2 percent, a slower rate than the rate of growth projected for total employment in the U.S. economy between 2008 and 2018. (This is an average; growth will vary among the different engineering fields.) Employment growth should be affected by many of the same factors that affect the growth of the engineers that these managers supervise. However, job growth for managers will be somewhat slower than for engineers because the increasing tendency to outsource research and development in specialized engineering and scientific research services firms will lead to some consolidation of management. Opportunities for engineering managers should be better in rapidly growing areas of engineering, such as environmental and biomedical engineering, than in more slowly growing areas, such as electrical and mechanical engineering.

Pathways Beyond the Bachelor's Degree

After graduating with a bachelor's degree, one-third of civil engineering majors proceed to earn a postgraduate degree: 30 percent earn a master's degree, 4 percent graduate with a doctorate, and less than 1 percent earn a professional degree.

- Forty percent of the master's degrees are earned in civil engineering, 18 percent are earned in the field of business administration and management, and 6 percent are earned in environmental engineering.
- Among those few who earn doctoral degrees, half major in civil engineering and most of the rest major in other engineering fields.

CHAPTER 30

Computer Systems Engineering

Computer engineers work with the hardware and software aspects of systems design and development. They tend to focus on the building of prototypes; however, their work overlaps considerably with the work of computer scientists, who focus on both the theoretical realm and also applications of theory. Computer engineering generally applies theories and principles of science and mathematics to the design of hardware, software, networks, and processes to solve technical problems. Computer systems engineers design new computing devices or computer-related equipment, systems, or software. Computer hardware engineers design, develop, test, and supervise the manufacture of chips, device controllers, and storage capacity units.

Both hardware and software engineers may work on hardware device drivers and software packages that act as go-betweens for computer peripherals, such as modems, printers, and the computer itself. However, software engineers usually design and develop software systems for control and automation of manufacturing, business, and management processes. They are also called software developers when they design software applications for customers. Software developers also work on analyzing and solving programming problems.

Course work can include computer architecture, design of digital logic machines and circuits, hardware and software microprocessor interfaces,

robotics, structure of large-scale computer systems, algorithms and data structure, software design and development, operating systems design, computer communication networks, compiler design, calculus, and physics.

The interests of computer systems engineers are heavily influenced by the power and versatility of the computer. Computers have the capacity to empower the creativity of individuals in unique ways. Computer technology even creates a cultural identity of "techies" among those involved. This engineering specialty builds on scientific and technical interests to produce applications. Those involved enjoy being imaginative, independent, and critical. They realize that their work can create a worldwide change in the ways many activities are done. As with all engineering areas, some move on to management positions.

Computer systems engineers value the intellectual stimulation of working with their minds. They achieve success through applying research findings and using mathematics to produce new technology. Developing and designing systems can also challenge theory as one works on the cutting edge in a discovery process. Receiving financial rewards is an important goal, as is enjoying the recognition and prestige of working in the highly visible computer field.

Note that some workers who have the job title of computer engineer come from nonengineering majors—for example, computer science (described in Chapter 57) or physics (Chapter 55). Computer engineers seldom offer their services to the public and therefore do not need to be licensed as engineers; licensure would require a degree in an engineering major.

Where Do Computer Systems Engineering Majors Work?

Most computer systems engineering majors work in the private, for-profit sector for businesses and corporations or in a self-employed position in their own business. More than 70 percent work in the private, for-profit sector for businesses and corporations, and 16 percent of computer systems engineering graduates are self-employed. The government sector employs 5 percent of all computer systems engineering majors with a bachelor's degree. Educational institutions employ 2 percent, and the remaining 2 percent work for private, nonprofit organizations.

Almost all computer systems engineering graduates are employed in jobs that are either closely or somewhat related to their undergraduate major. Sixty-seven percent of all employed computer systems engineering graduates work in jobs that are closely related to their major. Another 25 percent work in jobs that are somewhat related to their major. Only 8 percent are employed in jobs that are not related to their undergraduate major.

Out of all computer systems engineering graduates, 92 percent are employed. Only 4 percent are officially unemployed; that is, they are not employed and are actively seeking employment. The remaining grads, not quite 5 percent, are out of the labor force; that is, they are not employed and are not seeking employment. Seventeen percent of those who have withdrawn from the labor force did so for family-related reasons. An equal share have taken early retirement.

Table 1

Percentage Distribution of Employed Persons with Only a Bachelor's Degree, by Economic Sector, Size, and New Business Status of Employer

	Computer Systems Engineering	All
Economic Sector		
Private for-profit	73.9	47.3
Self-employed	16.5	18.5
Government/Military	4.7	11.0
Education	2.3	15.6
Nonprofit	2.5	7.5
Employer Size		
Small (Fewer than 100 employees)	21.3	35.5
Medium (100–999)	20.7	21.8
Large (1,000–24,999)	24.6	26.0
Very large (25,000 or more)	33.4	16.7
Percent working in new business established within past 5 years	13.4	7.6

Table 2
Percentage Distribution of Employed Persons with Only a Bachelor's Degree in Computer Systems Engineering, by the Relationship Between Their Job and College Major

Relationship of Job to Major	Percent
Closely related	67.0
Somewhat related	24.9
Not related	8.1

Percent who report the following as the most important reasons for working in a job that was not related to major:

Job in highest degree field not available	25.1
Pay, promotion opportunities	22.1
Family-related reasons	19.8
Change in career or professional interests	17.0
Other reason	12.8

Occupations

Computer systems engineering majors are concentrated in very few occupational areas. About 44 percent are employed as computer engineers, with software specialists outnumbering hardware specialists by about 5 to 1. Twelve percent work as computer systems analysts, and another 4 percent are employed as computer programmers. Almost 6 percent are employed in top-level managerial, executive, and administrative occupations. These five occupations employ two-thirds of all employed computer systems engineering graduates.

Table 3
Top 5 Occupations Employing Persons with Only a Bachelor's Degree in Computer Systems Engineering, by Percentage

Top 5 Occupations	All	Men	Women
Computer Engineers—Software	36.8	37.8	31.7
Computer Systems Analysts	12.1	13.8	3.9
Computer Engineer—Hardware	7.2	7.2	7.6
Top-Level Managers, Executives, and Administrators	5.6	5.5	6.0
Computer Programmers (Business, Scientific, and Process Control)	4.3	3.5	7.8
Total, Top 5 Occupations	66.0	67.8	57.0
Balance of Employed	34.0	32.2	43.0
All Employed	100.0	100.0	100.0

Among the graduates, men outnumber women by about 4 to 1. The share of female engineers who specialize in software is somewhat lower than the share of men in that field, but the imbalance in the distribution is reversed among hardware specialists.

Work Activities

▶ Surprisingly, only 48 percent of employed computer systems engineering majors work primarily with computer applications, programming, and systems development. However, almost 40 percent spend significant time on these tasks.

▶ Fifty-six percent spend part of a typical workweek in managerial and administrative duties, and 15 percent of them are chiefly responsible for these duties. This emphasis on management probably explains why the share of grads who are engaged primarily with computer-related tasks is as small as it is.

▶ Forty-five percent of employed computer systems engineering majors are engaged in the design of equipment, processes, and structures on a daily basis, although this is the central task of only 7 percent of grads. Similar shares of workers are involved in developmental tasks.

▶ Thirty-nine percent of all employed computer systems engineering majors regularly undertake applied research activities, and 20 percent utilize findings from research for the production of materials and devices.

Computer systems engineering is a relatively new field and is composed of many younger people. The median age of graduates is 35 years; the average age of all college graduates is 44. In addition to the age difference between computer systems engineering majors and all college graduates, another distinguishing characteristic of this field is the rapidly changing skill requirements. The functions performed by older persons who are employed in the field of computer systems engineering may be different from those performed by their younger counterparts.

Workplace Training and Other Work-Related Experiences

The career potential of a job is closely associated with the amount of work-related training on the job. Work-related training is regarded as an investment by firms because it makes workers more productive. The rapidly evolving field of computer systems engineering requires graduates to be on their toes and engage in work-related training even at a young age. Nevertheless, the rate of participation in work-related training during a year among employed computer systems engineering graduates (55 percent) is somewhat lower than the training participation rate of all college graduates (61 percent). It seems likely that grads are using their time away from the job to keep up to date with developments in their field.

▶ Of those computer systems engineering majors who receive some training, half receive technical training in their occupational field.

▶ Sixteen percent of the training recipients participate in management or supervisory training.

▶ Another 16 percent receive training to improve their general professional skills, such as public speaking and business writing.

When asked to identify the most important reason to participate in work-related training, more than 36 percent cite the need to acquire further skills and knowledge in their occupational field. In addition, 7 percent are required or expected to participate in work-related training activities.

Salaries

The median annual salary of computer systems engineering graduates with only a bachelor's degree is $85,000, a level that is 39 percent higher than the median annual salary of all employed college graduates. On average, employed computer systems engineering graduates work for 47 hours per week and for 51 weeks per year, resulting in 2,397 hours of employment per year. The level of work effort among computer systems engineering graduates is the highest of any major included in this book: 11 percent higher than the average among all college graduates (43 hours per week and 50 weeks per year, resulting in 2,150 hours per year).

The average annual salary of computer systems engineering majors who work in jobs that are closely related to their major is $88,700. Those engineering majors whose jobs are somewhat related to their undergraduate major earn an average annual salary of $87,700. The few computer systems engineering graduates employed in jobs that are not related to their undergraduate major earn an average of $51,600.

The annual average salary of computer systems engineering graduates who are employed in the private sector by for-profit businesses and corporations is $87,700. Self-employed grads average $75,500 per year. Government-sector employees with a bachelor's degree in computer systems engineering earn a slightly lower average annual salary, $71,700.

FIGURE 1

Age/Earnings Profile of Persons with Only a Bachelor's Degree in Computer Systems Engineering (Full-Time Workers, in 2010 Dollars)

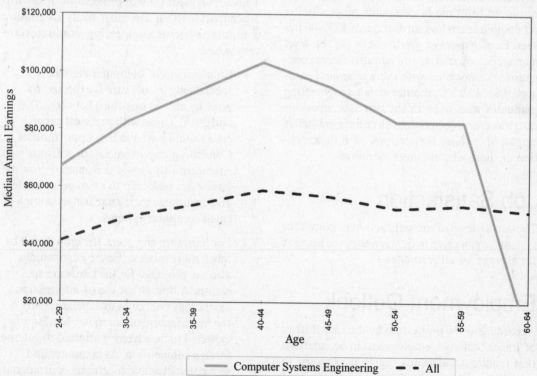

Table 4
Annual Salary of Workers with Only a Bachelor's Degree, Top 5 Occupations (in 2010 Dollars)

Earnings in Top 5 Occupations	All	Computer Systems Engineering
Total	$85,000	$90,600
Computer Engineers—Software	$82,600	$87,700
Computer Systems Analysts	$72,200	$82,600
Computer Engineer—Hardware	$87,700	$72,200
Top-Level Managers, Executives, and Administrators	$103,200	$154,800
Computer Programmers (Business, Scientific, and Process Control)	$71,200	$77,400

The average annual salary of computer systems engineering majors who are employed as computer engineers varies considerably, depending on whether their specialization is software (an average of $87,700) or hardware ($72,200). Graduates who work as computer systems analysts earn an average salary of $82,600. Those employed full-time in computer programming occupations earn less, an average of $77,400 per year. Employment of graduates in the top-level managerial, executive, and administrative occupations is associated with average annual earnings of $154,800. Computer systems engineering graduates who work in the top 5 occupations earn more, on average, than all college graduates employed in those occupations, with the exception of those who engineer hardware.

Job Satisfaction

The overall level of job satisfaction of computer systems engineering majors is about the same as the average for all graduates.

Employment Outlook

According to the projections by the U.S. Bureau of Labor Statistics, employment in occupations that require a bachelor's degree is expected to grow faster than employment in other sectors of the American labor market. Between 2008 and 2018, the U.S. workforce is projected to grow by 10.1 percent, creating an average of 15.2 million job openings per year. The bachelor's-level jobs are expected to increase by 17.7 percent over the same time.

The employment growth projections in the top 5 occupations that are most likely to employ computer systems engineering graduates are very mixed:

▶ Employment of computer engineers specializing in software is expected to grow by almost one-third between 2008 and 2018. Those with practical experience should have the best opportunities. Consulting opportunities for software engineers also should continue to grow as businesses seek help to manage, upgrade, and customize their increasingly complicated computer systems.

▶ For hardware engineers, the growth will be much more modest. Fewer job openings also are projected for the hardware specialists. Although the use of information technology continues to expand rapidly, the manufacture of computer hardware is expected to be adversely affected by intense foreign competition. As computer and semiconductor manufacturers contract out

Table 5

Percentage Distribution of Workers with Only a Bachelor's Degree,
by Level of Job Satisfaction

Job Satisfaction	Computer Systems Engineering	All
Very satisfied	41.3	45.4
Somewhat satisfied	50.7	45.0
Somewhat dissatisfied	7.1	7.4
Very dissatisfied	0.8	2.2
Mean Score (4=very satisfied, 1=not satisfied at all)	3.3	3.3

more of their engineering needs to both domestic and foreign design firms, much of the growth in employment of hardware engineers is expected to take place in the computer systems design and related services industry.

▶ Employment of computer systems analysts—the second-largest employer of computer systems engineering majors—is expected to grow by 20.3 percent from 2008 to 2018, which is much faster than the average for all occupations. Demand for these workers will increase as organizations continue to adopt and integrate increasingly sophisticated technologies and as the need for information security grows.

▶ Although employment of computer programmers is projected to decline, numerous job openings will result from the need to replace workers who leave the labor force or transfer to other occupations. Prospects for these openings should be best for applicants with a bachelor's degree and experience with a variety of programming languages and tools. As technology evolves, however, and newer, more sophisticated tools emerge, programmers will need to update their skills to remain competitive. Obtaining vendor-specific or language-specific certification also can provide a competitive edge.

Table 6

Projected Growth and Job Openings in the Top 5 Occupations Employing Persons
with Only a Bachelor's Degree in Computer Systems Engineering

Top 5 Occupations	Projected Growth 2008–2018	Projected Annual Job Openings
All top 5	9.4%	133,660
Computer Engineers—Software	32.5%	37,180
Computer Systems Analysts	20.3%	22,280
Computer Engineer—Hardware	3.8%	4,700
Top-Level Managers, Executives, and Administrators	−0.4%	61,470
Computer Programmers (Business, Scientific, and Process Control)	−2.9%	8,030

▶ Employment of top-level managers is projected to decrease, but job turnover will generate a large number of openings in this highly lucrative occupation.

Pathways Beyond the Bachelor's Degree

After graduating with a bachelor's degree, 31 percent of computer systems engineering majors proceed to earn a postgraduate degree: 29 percent earn a master's degree, and 2 percent graduate with a doctorate.

▶ A large majority of the master's degrees are earned in fields that are closely related to their undergraduate major: 41 percent of the master's degrees are earned in computer systems engineering, 14 percent in other engineering fields, and another 14 in nonengineering computer fields.

▶ About 23 percent—or most of the remaining master's degrees—are earned in various fields of business administration and management.

▶ Among those who earn doctoral degrees, 45 percent major in computer systems engineering.

CHAPTER 31

Electrical and Electronics Engineering

Electrical and electronics engineers design new technologies and products, write performance requirements, develop maintenance schedules, and supervise the manufacture of electrical and electronics equipment. Like other engineers, they test equipment, solve operating problems, and estimate the time and costs of engineering projects. The major areas in which these engineers work are power generation, transmission, and distribution; communications, including the exploding wireless area; and the manufacture of computer electronics and electrical equipment. Electrical and electronics engineering is foundational to all manufacturing, so it cuts across many areas, such as industrial robotic control systems.

Electrical engineering is the largest engineering specialty. It is a cyclical field affected by the impact of defense spending, such as in aviation electronics. A prime motivating force in the field is industry's drive to remain competitive in the world market. Electrical engineers also want to be involved in research and development, especially with computers and communications equipment. Specific examples of technologies where electrical engineers have had primary roles are integrated circuitry, satellite communications, pacemakers, and microprocessors.

Course work in this field includes circuits and systems, electromagnetic field theory, digital systems, calculus, chemistry, and physics.

Electrical and electronics engineers are interested in both the scientific and technical areas of their field. They need technical and mechanical skills to relate theoretical procedures to practical applications. Some areas of electronics involve higher involvement in scientific interests. In these areas, people often work in technical positions and concentrate on developmental work. Electrical and electronics engineers enjoy being imaginative, independent, and critical. They identify themselves as scientists.

Electrical and electronics engineers value the intellectual stimulation of working with their minds. They achieve this goal through applying research findings and by using numbers to calculate probable outcomes. For some, the opportunity for creative endeavors and varied projects is a motivational tool. Some electrical engineers are content with less diversity in their work and enjoy using their hands in the production phase of this field. Important goals include receiving prestige and financial rewards.

Where Do Electrical and Electronics Engineering Majors Work?

More than 85 percent of all employed electrical and electronics engineering majors work in the private, for-profit sector, either for businesses and corporations (71 percent) or as self-employed workers in their own business (16 percent). The government sector employs 8 percent of all electrical and electronics engineering majors with a bachelor's degree.

The rate of related employment is quite high among electrical and electronics engineering majors. Well over half of all employed electrical and electronics engineering graduates work in jobs that are closely related to their major. Another one-third work in jobs that are somewhat related to their major. Only 13 percent are employed in jobs that are not related to their undergraduate major.

Out of all electrical and electronics engineering graduates under the age of 65, 88 percent are employed. Only 6 percent are officially unemployed; that is, they are not employed and are actively seeking employment. The remaining 6 percent are out of the labor force; that is, they are not employed and are not seeking employment. Retirement is the major reason for labor force withdrawal, accounting for 54 percent of electrical and electronics engineering majors who are out of the labor force. Another 8 percent have withdrawn because of a lack of suitable work.

Occupations

Electrical and electronics engineering majors are concentrated in technical and managerial occupations. More than one-third are employed as electrical or electronics engineers. Almost 10 percent work as computer software engineers. About 7 percent are employed in managerial occupations. Another 3 percent are employed in miscellaneous engineering technology jobs.

Table 1

Percentage Distribution of Employed Persons with Only a Bachelor's Degree, by Economic Sector, Size, and New Business Status of Employer

	Electrical and Electronics Engineering	All
Economic Sector		
Private for-profit	70.9	47.3
Self-employed	16.3	18.5
Government/Military	8.2	11.0
Education	2.9	15.6
Nonprofit	1.6	7.5
Employer Size		
Small (Fewer than 100 employees)	26.3	35.5
Medium (100–999)	19.0	21.8
Large (1,000–24,999)	25.4	26.0
Very large (25,000 or more)	29.2	16.7
Percent working in new business established within past 5 years	9.3	7.6

Table 2
Percentage Distribution of Employed Persons with Only a
Bachelor's Degree in Electrical and Electronics Engineering,
by the Relationship Between Their Job and College Major

Relationship of Job to Major	Percent
Closely related	53.1
Somewhat related	33.8
Not related	13.1

Percent who report the following as the most important reasons for
working in a job that was not related to major:

Job in highest degree field not available	21.5
Pay, promotion opportunities	20.0
Change in career or professional interests	18.7
Job location	12.9
Working conditions (hours, equipment, environment)	10.2

Male grads outnumber females by more than 9 to 1 and are more likely to choose careers as electrical or electronics engineers.

Work Activities

▌ Almost 7 out of 10 employed electrical and electronics engineering majors perform computer applications, programming, and systems-development duties regularly, and for 19 percent of the grads, this is their main job function.

▌ About 60 percent of grads are engaged in managerial and administrative duties at their jobs, and one-fifth of grads see this as their major responsibility.

▌ The design of equipment, processes, structures, and models is a significant task for 55 percent of grads and the central task of 15 percent.

▌ Forty-eight percent of grads spend at least 10 hours of their workweek developing devices or processes.

▌ Applied research is a regular duty of 38 percent of the grads.

▌ One-third regularly engage in sales, purchasing, and marketing.

Workplace Training and Other Work-Related Experiences

The career potential of a job is closely associated with the amount of work-related training on the job. Work-related training is regarded as an investment by firms because it makes workers more productive. Firms that do not invest in their workers are less likely to offer pay increases and promotions. The rate of participation in work-related training during a year among employed electrical and electronics engineering graduates

Table 3
Top 5 Occupations Employing Persons with Only a Bachelor's Degree in Electrical and Electronics Engineering, by Percentage

Top 5 Occupations	All	Men	Women
Electrical and Electronics Engineers	33.7	34.9	21.9
Computer Engineers—Software	9.5	9.4	10.4
Top-Level Managers, Executives, and Administrators	3.9	4.0	2.9
Other Management-Related Occupations	3.2	3.0	5.3
Engineering Technologists/Technicians—Electrical, Industrial, and Mechanical	2.7	2.8	2.0
Total, Top 5 Occupations	53.0	54.1	42.5
Balance of Employed	47.0	45.9	57.5
All Employed	100.0	100.0	100.0

(56 percent) is somewhat lower than the training participation rate of all college graduates (61 percent).

▶ Of those electrical and electronics engineering majors who receive some training, 49 percent receive technical training in their occupational field.

▶ Nineteen percent of the training recipients participate in management or supervisory training.

▶ Fifteen percent receive training to improve their general professional skills, such as public speaking and business writing.

Electrical and electronics engineering majors cite a variety of reasons for their participation in work-related training activities. When asked to identify the most important reason, nearly one-third cite the need to acquire further skills and knowledge in their occupational field. And 7 percent state that their employer requires or expects employees to participate in work-related training activities. Licensure requirements are seldom a motivation, because few electrical and electronics engineers need to be licensed.

Salaries

The median annual salary of electrical and electronics engineering graduates with only a bachelor's degree is $75,000, a level that is 31 percent higher than the median annual salary of all employed college graduates. On average, employed electrical and electronics engineering graduates work for 45 hours per week and for 51 weeks per year, resulting in 2,295 hours of employment per year. The level of work effort among electrical and electronics engineering graduates is 7 percent higher than the average among all college graduates (43 hours per week and 50 weeks per year, resulting in 2,150 hours per year).

Access to jobs related to their undergraduate field of study is associated with a sizable earnings premium among electrical and electronics engineering majors. The average annual salary of graduates who work in jobs that are closely related to their major is $81,500. The annual average salary of graduates whose jobs are somewhat related to their undergraduate major is $79,500. Electrical and electronics engineering graduates whose jobs are unrelated to their major earn an annual average salary of $51,600.

Age/Earnings Profile of Persons with Only a Bachelor's Degree in Electrical and Electronics Engineering
(Full-Time Workers, in 2010 Dollars)

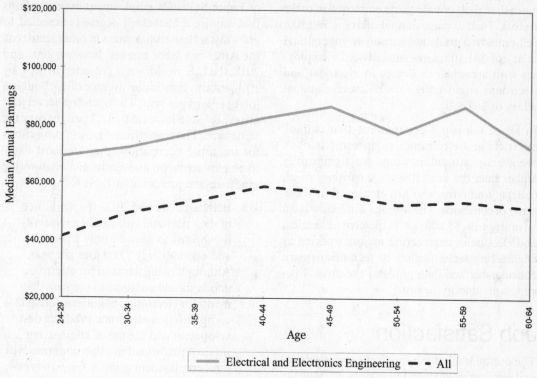

Table 4

Annual Salary of Workers with Only a Bachelor's Degree,
Top 5 Occupations (in 2010 Dollars)

Earnings in Top 5 Occupations	All	Electrical and Electronics Engineering
Total	$75,000	$83,600
Electrical and Electronics Engineers	$78,400	$81,500
Computer Engineers—Software	$82,600	$86,700
Top-Level Managers, Executives, and Administrators	$103,200	$113,500
Other Management-Related Occupations	$57,800	$82,600
Engineering Technologists/Technicians—Electrical, Industrial, and Mechanical	$51,600	$54,700

Electrical and electronics engineering graduates who are employed in the private sector by for-profit businesses and corporations earn more than their counterparts employed in other sectors. Their average annual salary is $80,500. Self-employed graduates earn an average annual salary of $71,100. Government-sector employees with a bachelor's degree in electrical and electronics engineering earn an average annual salary of $69,600.

In all of the top 5 occupations that employ electrical and electronics engineering majors, the average annual earnings are significantly higher than the annual average earnings of all college graduates who are employed in those same occupations. The average difference is an advantage of $8,600, or 11 percent. Electrical and electronics engineering majors working as engineering technologists or technicians earn considerably less than grads in the other 4 occupations among the top 5.

Job Satisfaction

The overall level of job satisfaction of electrical and electronics engineering majors is about the same as the average for all graduates.

Employment Outlook

According to the projections by the U.S. Bureau of Labor Statistics, employment in occupations that require a bachelor's degree is expected to grow faster than employment in other sectors of the American labor market. Between 2008 and 2018, the U.S. workforce is projected to grow by 10.1 percent, creating an average of 15.2 million job openings per year. The bachelor's-level jobs are expected to increase by 17.7 percent over the same time. The employment growth projections for the top 5 occupations that are most likely to employ electrical and electronics engineering graduates are presented in Table 6.

▶ Between 2008 and 2018, the workforce of electrical and electronics engineers is expected to grow by only 1 percent and open up only 7,000 jobs per year. Although rising demand for electronic goods should continue to increase demand for electronics engineers, foreign competition in electronic products development and the use of engineering services performed in other countries will limit employment growth. Growth is expected to be fastest in service-providing industries—particularly in firms that provide engineering and design services.

Table 5
Percentage Distribution of Workers with Only a Bachelor's Degree, by Level of Job Satisfaction

Job Satisfaction	Electrical and Electronics Engineering	All
Very satisfied	41.4	45.4
Somewhat satisfied	48.7	45.0
Somewhat dissatisfied	7.9	7.4
Very dissatisfied	2.0	2.2
Mean Score (4=very satisfied, 1=not satisfied at all)	3.3	3.3

Table 6
Projected Growth and Job Openings in the Top 5 Occupations Employing Persons with Only a Bachelor's Degree in Electrical and Electronics Engineering

Top 5 Occupations	Projected Growth 2008–2018	Projected Annual Job Openings
All top 5	8.1%	174,320
Electrical and Electronics Engineers	1.0%	7,230
Computer Engineers—Software	32.5%	37,180
Top-Level Managers, Executives, and Administrators	−0.4%	61,470
Other Management-Related Occupations	7.2%	53,020
Engineering Technologists/Technicians—Electrical, Industrial, and Mechanical	7.2%	15,420

▶ Although employment of technicians in all engineering fields is projected to grow modestly, the number of technician jobs in electrical and electronic engineering is expected to decline by 2 percent between 2008 and 2018. The same force of foreign competition that is limiting growth of engineers is at work here, together with increased efficiencies in the design process that will reduce demand for these workers.

▶ Computer software engineering occupations—the second-largest employer of electrical and electronics engineering majors—are expected to grow by almost one-third, creating an average of 37,000 job openings each year. Those with practical experience should have the best opportunities. Consulting opportunities for software engineers also should continue to grow as businesses seek help to manage, upgrade, and customize their increasingly complicated computer systems.

▶ Employment of top-level managers is projected to decrease, but job turnover will generate a large number of openings in this highly lucrative occupation.

Pathways Beyond the Bachelor's Degree

After graduating with a bachelor's degree, 40 percent of electrical and electronics engineering majors proceed to earn a postgraduate degree: One-third earn a master's degree, 5 percent graduate with a doctorate, and only 1 percent earn a professional degree.

▶ Almost 40 percent of the master's degrees are earned in electrical and electronics engineering, and 16 percent are earned in the field of business administration and management.

▶ Among those who earn doctoral degrees, almost 60 percent major in electrical and electronics engineering, and equal shares of 5 percent major in computer science and computer engineering.

CHAPTER 32

Industrial Engineering

Industrial engineering determines the most effective ways for an organization to use the basic components of production—people, machines, materials, information, and energy—to make or process a product or service. Industrial engineers link management and operations.

Many people consider the term "industrial" to mean the same thing as "manufacturing," but industrial engineers work in all industries, including health care, mass media, and finance. Their main focus is how to improve quality, efficiency, and safety. They do this by carefully studying the product and its requirements of design, manufacturing, and information systems, and they use mathematical analysis and modeling methods, such as operations research, to seek the best solutions to meet the requirements. They develop management-control systems to aid in financial planning and cost analysis, they design production planning and control systems to coordinate activities and monitor quality control, and they design or improve systems for the physical distribution of goods and services. Industrial engineers conduct surveys to find plant locations with the best combinations of raw materials, transportation, and costs. They also develop wage and salary administration systems and job evaluation programs.

Courses taken by industrial engineers are production engineering, work management, plant layout, work measurement, labor law, cost analysis, and statistics.

Industrial engineers are interested in business first and then in scientific and technical areas, with a hands-on focus on how something is done. By the time they are employed, industrial engineers learn to have a strong business orientation rather than the scientific focus that a mechanical or an electrical engineer would have. As with many engineering specialties, the field demands a skill and interest in knowing how operations are performed.

The priorities of industrial engineers include making a good salary, being recognized in a leadership position, having prestige within the organization, being stimulated by problem solving, and enjoying the variety of different tasks to study and make recommendations about.

Where Do Industrial Engineering Majors Work?

Almost 7 out of 10 employed industrial engineering majors work in the private, for-profit sector as wage and salary workers for businesses and corporations, and 17 percent are self-employed in their own incorporated or nonincorporated business or practice. The government sector

Table 1
Percentage Distribution of Employed Persons with Only a Bachelor's Degree, by Economic Sector, Size, and New Business Status of Employer

	Industrial Engineering	All
Economic Sector		
Private for-profit	69.3	47.3
Self-employed	16.9	18.5
Government/Military	7.9	11.0
Education	1.9	15.6
Nonprofit	3.8	7.5
Employer Size		
Small (Fewer than 100 employees)	29.2	35.5
Medium (100–999)	24.3	21.8
Large (1,000–24,999)	22.4	26.0
Very large (25,000 or more)	24.1	16.7
Percent working in new business established within past 5 years	8.1	7.6

Table 2
Percentage Distribution of Employed Persons with Only a Bachelor's Degree in Industrial Engineering, by the Relationship Between Their Job and College Major

Relationship of Job to Major	Percent
Closely related	37.9
Somewhat related	40.8
Not related	21.3

Percent who report the following as the most important reasons for working in a job that was not related to major:

Pay, promotion opportunities	35.7
Other reason	23.2
Job in highest degree field not available	15.2
Job location	9.0
Working conditions (hours, equipment, environment)	6.0

Table 3
Top 5 Occupations Employing Persons with Only a
Bachelor's Degree in Industrial Engineering, by Percentage

Top 5 Occupations	All	Men	Women
Industrial Engineers	14.5	14.3	15.8
Other Management-Related Occupations	8.3	8.6	6.5
Top-Level Managers, Executives, and Administrators	6.7	7.9	–
Sales Engineers	6.0	7.2	–
Other Administrative Occupations	5.5	4.7	10.1
Total, Top 5 Occupations	41.0	42.7	32.4
Balance of Employed	59.0	57.3	67.6
All Employed	100.0	100.0	100.0

employs 8 percent of all industrial engineering majors with only a bachelor's degree. Nonprofit organizations employ 4 percent of industrial engineering graduates with a bachelor's.

Industrial engineering majors have a strong preference for business and management, and they gravitate toward jobs that are more management oriented. Relative to other engineering graduates, fewer industrial engineering graduates—only 38 percent—are employed in jobs that are closely related to their undergraduate major. A somewhat higher proportion, 41 percent, are employed in jobs that are somewhat related to their undergraduate major. One-fifth are employed in jobs that are not related to their undergraduate major.

Out of all industrial engineering graduates under the age of 65, 83 percent are employed. Only 5 percent are officially unemployed; that is, they are not employed and are actively seeking employment. The remaining 12 percent are out of the labor force; that is, they are not employed and are not seeking employment. Retirement is the reason for labor force withdrawal among 55 percent of industrial engineering majors who are out of the labor force. Only 12 percent withdraw because of family responsibilities, and 8 percent do not want or need to work.

Occupations

Industrial engineering majors, unlike graduates from other engineering fields, are concerned with increasing productivity through the management of people, organizational policies, procedures, and technology. In contrast, engineers in other specialties generally work more with products or processes. This difference is manifested in the occupations where industrial engineering grads work. Fifteen percent of them are employed in managerial, executive, and administrative occupations. Fourteen percent are employed as industrial engineers and 6 percent as sales engineers.

The ratio of male to female grads is about 4 to 1, but female grads are slightly more likely to opt for jobs as industrial engineers. They are also more likely to work in administration, but less likely to work in management or as sales engineers.

Work Activities

▶ Three-quarters of employed grads engage regularly in managing or supervising people or projects, and 27 percent of them see this task as their primary responsibility.

- Sales, purchasing, and marketing occupy at least 10 of the weekly working hours of almost half the grads. For one-fifth of the grads, these activities are their main job function.

- Almost half of the grads spend significant time overseeing the quality and efficiency of production processes, and this is the primary focus of 6 percent of the grads.

- More than 8 out of 10 employed industrial engineering majors regularly use computer applications, do programming, or develop computer systems.

- Half of the grads regularly engage in the design of equipment, processes, structures, and models.

- A little more than 44 percent of industrial engineering graduates spend significant time on accounting, finance, and contractual duties.

Workplace Training and Other Work-Related Experiences

The career potential of a job is closely associated with the amount of work-related training on the job. Work-related training is regarded as an investment by firms because it makes workers more productive. The rate of participation in work-related training during a year among employed industrial engineering graduates (57 percent) is somewhat lower than the training participation rate of all college graduates (61 percent).

- Of those industrial engineering majors who participate in workplace training activities, 47 percent receive technical training in their occupational field.

- Twenty-six percent of the recipients receive management or supervisory training.

- Seventeen percent receive training to improve their general professional skills, such as public speaking and business writing.

Although a variety of reasons motivate industrial engineering graduates to undergo training, the most important reason for their decision to go through work-related training is to sharpen their occupational skills and knowledge. More than one-quarter cite this as the main reason to acquire work-related training. One in 10 consider their employer's requirement to be the main reason for their involvement in work-related training activities.

Salaries

The median annual salary of industrial engineering graduates with only a bachelor's degree is $73,000, a level that is 29 percent higher than the median annual salary of all employed college graduates. On average, employed industrial engineering graduates work for 46 hours per week and for 51 weeks per year, resulting in 2,346 hours of employment per year. The level of work effort among industrial engineering graduates is 9 percent higher than the average among all college graduates (43 hours per week and 50 weeks per year, resulting in 2,150 hours per year).

The average annual salary of industrial engineering majors who work in jobs that are closely related to their major is $75,300. Those graduates whose jobs are somewhat related to their undergraduate major command the somewhat higher average salary of $82,600 per year. (Eleven percent of these workers are top-level managers, executives, or administrators.) The one-fifth of industrial engineering majors who are employed in jobs that are unrelated to their major earn an annual average salary of $57,800.

Self-employed industrial engineering graduates who work full-time earn an average annual salary of $85,500. Most of these high salaries are associated with self-employed graduates with an incorporated business or practice. In the

FIGURE 1

Age/Earnings Profile of Persons with Only a Bachelor's Degree in Industrial Engineering (Full-Time Workers, in 2010 Dollars)

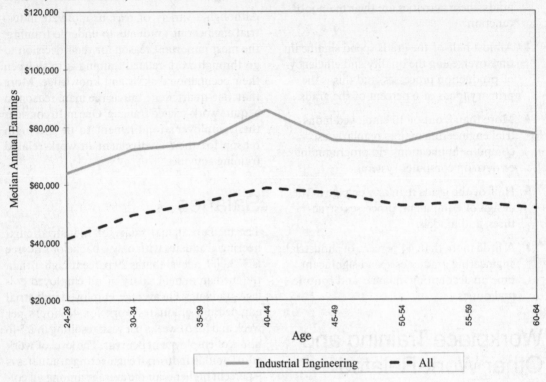

nonprofit sector, the average is slightly higher at $85,700. The annual average salary of industrial engineering graduates who are employed in the private sector by for-profit businesses and corporations is $77,400 per year. Government-sector employees with a bachelor's degree in industrial engineering earn an average of $49,700.

The average annual earnings of industrial engineering majors in 4 of the 5 occupations that are predominant employers of graduates are higher than the annual average earnings of all college graduates who are employed in those same occupations. The average annual salary of industrial engineering majors employed in top-level management, executive, and admin-

istrative occupations is $129,000, which is 25 percent higher than the average earnings of all college graduates employed in that occupation. Sales engineering is another occupation in which industrial engineering grads command a sizable earnings advantage. The annual average salary of industrial engineering graduates employed as industrial engineers, $69,100, is much lower than the pay for these managerial or sales occupations. The extremely low pay earned in administrative jobs suggests that most workers thus employed are holding these jobs only temporarily, until more appropriate employment becomes available.

Table 4
Annual Salary of Workers with Only a Bachelor's Degree,
Top 5 Occupations (in 2010 Dollars)

Earnings in Top 5 Occupations	All	Industrial Engineering
Total	$73,000	$78,800
Industrial Engineers	$67,100	$69,100
Other Management-Related Occupations	$57,800	$71,200
Top-Level Managers, Executives, Administrators	$103,200	$129,000
Sales Engineers	$82,600	$103,200
Other Administrative Occupations	$38,200	$17,500

Job Satisfaction

The overall level of job satisfaction of industrial engineering majors is about the same as the average for all graduates.

Employment Outlook

According to the projections by the U.S. Bureau of Labor Statistics, employment in occupations that require a bachelor's degree is expected to grow faster than employment in other sectors of the American labor market. Between 2008 and 2018, the U.S. workforce is projected to grow by 10.1 percent, creating an average of 15.2 million job openings per year. The bachelor's-level jobs are expected to increase by 17.7 percent over the same time. The employment growth projections

for the 5 occupations that are most likely to employ industrial engineering graduates are presented in Table 6.

▶ The workforce of industrial engineers is projected to increase by 14.2 percent. As firms look for new ways to reduce costs and raise productivity, they increasingly will turn to industrial engineers to develop more efficient processes and reduce costs, delays, and waste. This focus should lead to job growth for these engineers, even in some manufacturing industries with declining employment overall. Because their work is similar to that done in management occupations, many industrial engineers leave the occupation to become managers. Numerous openings will be created by the need to replace

Table 5
Percentage Distribution of Workers with Only a Bachelor's Degree,
by Level of Job Satisfaction

Job Satisfaction	Industrial Engineering	All
Very satisfied	40.4	45.4
Somewhat satisfied	48.1	45.0
Somewhat dissatisfied	6.6	7.4
Very dissatisfied	5.0	2.2
Mean Score (4=very satisfied, 1=not satisfied at all)	3.3	3.3

Table 6
Projected Growth and Job Openings in the Top 5 Occupations Employing Persons with Only a Bachelor's Degree in Industrial Engineering

Top 5 Occupations	Projected Growth 2008–2018	Projected Annual Job Openings
All top 5	7.2%	292,660
Industrial Engineers	14.2%	8,540
Other Management-Related Occupations	7.2%	53,020
Top-Level Managers, Executives, and Administrators	–0.4%	61,470
Sales Engineers	8.8%	3,500
Other Administrative Occupations	10.8%	166,130

industrial engineers who transfer to other occupations or leave the labor force.

- The workforce of miscellaneous management-related occupations—the second-largest employer of industrial engineering majors—is projected to increase by 7.2 percent. This rate is slower than the growth of total employment in the U.S. economy, but these occupations will create many job openings because of turnover.

- The same is true for jobs as top-level managerial, executive, and administrative occupations, even though the workforce is projected to shrink slightly. The high income in these jobs, however, will stoke competition for openings.

- The modest job growth of sales engineers will stem from the increasing variety and technical nature of the goods and services to be sold. Competitive pressures and advancing technology will force companies to improve and update product designs more frequently and to optimize their manufacturing, sales processes, and general business processes, thus requiring the services of sales engineers. Growth will be fastest in technology companies, such as software publishers and computer systems design firms.

Pathways Beyond the Bachelor's Degree

After graduating with a bachelor's degree, almost one-third of industrial engineering majors proceed to earn a master's degree. Very few grads proceed to a doctoral or professional degree.

- Three out of 10 master's degrees are earned in business administration and management.

- One-fifth of master's degrees are earned in industrial engineering.

CHAPTER 33

Mechanical Engineering

Mechanical engineers design and develop power-producing machines, such as internal combustion engines, steam and gas turbines, and jet and rocket engines. They use computers not only to form preliminary designs for systems or devices but also to perform calculations that will predict the behavior of the design and to collect and analyze performance data. They also design and develop power-using machines, such as refrigeration and air-conditioning equipment, robots, machine tools, material handling systems, and industrial production equipment. They can specialize in applied mechanics, design engineering, heat transfer, power plant engineering, pressure vessels and piping, plant maintenance, construction, and underwater technology.

Mechanical engineering is one of the broadest specializations within the engineering field. It cuts across many interdependent concentrations, such as electrical and aeronautical engineering. Mechanical engineers design the tools needed by other engineers to do their work. Mechanical engineers also are involved in developing new technologies. This collaboration requires them to work as part of a team. Most are employed in manufacturing, including defense work, which can create boom-and-bust cycles in job availability. Mechanical engineers can spend considerable time in factories or production areas outside—not in clean, quiet offices.

Beyond the general engineering foundation courses taken by all engineers, special courses in mechanical engineering include machine design, mechanical vibration, power engineering, kinematics, physical metallurgy, and mechanics.

Mechanical engineers combine practical and technical skills with analytical and intellectual pursuits. The particular balance between these two realms may determine whether the individual works primarily as an engineer or as a technologist. The engineer is required to be more involved than the technologist in mental and analytical questions and to be more broadly focused in seeking solutions that cut across other disciplines. Those who aim at a career as a technologist may major instead in mechanical engineering technology, which is described in Chapter 61.

Mechanical engineers value work that requires research and a high level of creativity. They like using their imagination, being inventive, and being well paid for their efforts. They desire to be recognized as having attained high achievement. They enjoy being independent as well as being in situations where they experience variety and diversity by doing different things. They enjoy mental challenges.

Technical, mechanical, and manual skills are involved in mechanical engineering. Mechanical engineers are precise and methodical, and they

Table 1

Percentage Distribution of Employed Persons with Only a Bachelor's Degree,
by Economic Sector, Size, and New Business Status of Employer

	Mechanical Engineering	All
Economic Sector		
Private for-profit	69.7	47.3
Self-employed	17.0	18.5
Government/Military	8.7	11.0
Education	2.3	15.6
Nonprofit	2.1	7.5
Employer Size		
Small (Fewer than 100 employees)	27.6	35.5
Medium (100–999)	16.5	21.8
Large (1,000–24,999)	28.7	26.0
Very large (25,000 or more)	27.2	16.7
Percent working in new business established within past 5 years	6.9	7.6

follow rational principles. They are goal oriented, not easily distracted, and well organized, and they prefer to assume responsibility and control.

Where Do Mechanical Engineering Majors Work?

Seven out of 10 employed mechanical engineering graduates are wage and salary workers at businesses and corporations in the private, for-profit sector. Another 17 percent work in the private, for-profit sector as self-employed workers in their own business or practice. The government sector employs almost 9 percent of all mechanical engineering majors with only a bachelor's degree.

About one-half of employed mechanical engineering majors work in jobs that are closely related to their undergraduate major. Thirty-seven percent are employed in jobs that are somewhat related to their major, and the remaining 12 percent work in jobs that are not related to their major.

Out of all mechanical engineering graduates under the age of 65, 90 percent are employed. Only 4 percent are officially unemployed; that is, they are not employed and are actively seeking employment. The remaining 6 percent are out of the labor force; that is, they are not employed and are not seeking employment. Retirement is the reason for labor force withdrawal among two-thirds of mechanical engineering majors who are out of the labor force. Seven percent do not need or want to work.

Occupations

Like most engineering majors, mechanical engineering graduates are concentrated in a few occupations. Nearly 35 percent are employed as mechanical engineers, the occupation for which they were trained in their undergraduate education. Like graduates of other engineering majors, a significant

Table 2
Percentage Distribution of Employed Persons with Only a Bachelor's Degree in Mechanical Engineering, by the Relationship Between Their Job and College Major

Relationship of Job to Major	Percent
Closely related	51.0
Somewhat related	37.3
Not related	11.7

Percent who report the following as the most important reasons for working in a job that was not related to major:

Pay, promotion opportunities	23.6
Job in highest degree field not available	22.8
Change in career or professional interests	15.7
Other reason	11.1
Working conditions (hours, equipment, environment)	9.7

share (7 percent) of mechanical engineering grads are employed in top- to mid-level managerial, executive, and administrative occupations. Four percent are employed in precision/production occupations in various industries, with the largest concentrations in furniture manufacturing; metal forgings and stampings; machine shops; commercial and industrial machinery and equipment repair and maintenance; and metalworking machinery manufacturing. Another 4 percent manage engineering departments and the projects they undertake.

Male grads outnumber female grads by about 9 to 1, and female grads are less likely to choose employment as mechanical engineers.

Table 3
Top 5 Occupations Employing Persons with Only a Bachelor's Degree in Mechanical Engineering, by Percentage

Top 5 Occupations	All	Men	Women
Mechanical Engineers	34.8	35.5	26.1
Precision/Production Occupations	4.2	4.2	5.0
Top-Level Managers, Executives, and Administrators	3.7	4.0	0.3
Other Mid-Level Managers	3.7	3.5	5.7
Engineering Managers	3.6	3.8	1.1
Total, Top 5 Occupations	50.0	51.0	38.2
Balance of Employed	50.0	49.0	61.8
All Employed	100.0	100.0	100.0

Work Activities

▶ Given their high rates of employment in mechanical and other engineering occupations, it is not surprising that 57 percent of grads are regularly engaged in the design of equipment, processes, structures, and models at their jobs. Ten percent see this as their primary job function.

▶ Almost three-quarters of the graduates spend significant time in managerial and administrative duties. Accounting, finance, and contractual duties are performed regularly by 39 percent of employed mechanical engineering graduates.

▶ Eighty-eight percent of employed mechanical engineering graduates are engaged in computer applications, programming, and systems-development duties.

▶ Forty-three percent of grads regularly engage in developing products or processes, and 39 percent devote significant time to quality or productivity management.

Workplace Training and Other Work-Related Experiences

The career potential of a job is closely associated with the amount of work-related training on the job. Work-related training is regarded as an investment by firms because it makes workers more productive. Firms that do not invest in their workers are less likely to offer pay increases and promotions. The rate of participation in work-related training during a year among employed mechanical engineering graduates (56 percent) is lower than the training participation rate of all college graduates (61 percent).

▶ Of those mechanical engineering majors who receive some training, 45 percent receive technical training in their occupational field.

▶ Twenty-four percent of the training recipients receive management or supervisory training.

▶ Twenty percent receive training to improve their general professional skills, such as public speaking and business writing.

Mechanical engineering majors offer numerous reasons for participating in work-related training activities. Three out of 10 consider improvement of occupational skills and knowledge to be the most important reason for engaging in training. The main reason for 9 percent of employed mechanical engineering graduates is that the training is required by their employer. Five percent report increased pay and promotion opportunities as their motivating force to acquire training, and an equal share cited the need to achieve or maintain licensure or certification. Engineers who offer their services to the public must be licensed, and many states require continuing education for license renewal.

Salaries

The median annual salary of mechanical engineering graduates with only a bachelor's degree is $75,000, a level that is 31 percent higher than the median annual salary of all employed college graduates. On average, employed mechanical engineering graduates work for 46 hours per week and for 51 weeks per year, resulting in 2,346 hours of employment per year. The level of work effort among mechanical engineering graduates is 9 percent higher than the average among all college graduates (43 hours per week and 50 weeks per year, resulting in 2,150 hours per year).

FIGURE 1

Age/Earnings Profile of Persons with Only a Bachelor's Degree in Mechanical Engineering (Full-Time Workers, in 2010 Dollars)

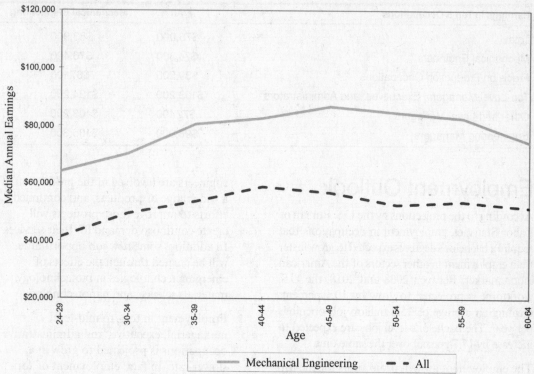

The average annual salary of mechanical engineering majors who work in jobs that are closely related to their major is $80,500. In jobs that are somewhat related to their undergraduate major, the average annual salary is slightly lower: $79,500. Employment in jobs that are not related to their undergraduate major results in a sizable reduction in earnings. Those who are employed in unrelated jobs average $51,600 per year.

The annual average salary of mechanical engineering graduates who are employed in the private sector by for-profit businesses and corporations is $81,500 per year. Self-employed mechanical engineering graduates who work full-time earn an average of $64,000. Government-sector employees with a bachelor's degree in mechanical engineering earn an average annual salary of $79,500. Earnings at nonprofit organizations average $77,400 per year.

In all of the top 5 occupations that predominantly employ mechanical engineering graduates, the average salaries of these grads are considerably higher than the average salaries of all college graduates. The difference in earnings is most stark in the precision/production occupations, where the mechanical engineering degree represents a 71 percent advantage. For mid- and top-level managers, the advantage is about 30 percent.

Job Satisfaction

The overall level of job satisfaction of mechanical engineering majors is about the same as the average for all graduates.

Table 4
Annual Salary of Workers with Only a Bachelor's Degree, Top 5 Occupations (in 2010 Dollars)

Earnings in Top 5 Occupations	All	Mechanical Engineering
Total	$75,000	$83,900
Mechanical Engineers	$74,300	$76,400
Precision/Production Occupations	$39,200	$67,100
Top-Level Managers, Executives, and Administrators	$103,200	$134,200
Other Mid-Level Managers	$77,400	$103,200
Engineering Managers	$98,000	$105,300

Employment Outlook

According to the projections by the U.S. Bureau of Labor Statistics, employment in occupations that require a bachelor's degree is expected to grow faster than employment in other sectors of the American labor market. Between 2008 and 2018, the U.S. workforce is projected to grow by 10.1 percent, creating an average of 15.2 million job openings per year. The bachelor's-level jobs are expected to increase by 17.7 percent over the same time.

The employment growth projections for the top 5 occupations that are most likely to employ mechanical engineering graduates are presented in Table 6.

▶ The mechanical engineering occupation is projected to grow by 6 percent and create 7,500 job openings each year. Mechanical engineers are involved in the production of a wide range of products, and continued efforts to improve those products will create continued demand for their services. In addition, some new job opportunities will be created through the effects of emerging technologies in biotechnology, materials science, and nanotechnology.

▶ Employment in top- to mid-level managerial, executive, and administrative occupations is projected to grow at a slower rate. In fact, employment of top-level managers actually will diminish. However, these occupations have large workforces and will create many job openings because of turnover. The higher the level of management, the higher are the average earnings, resulting in a higher level of competition for job openings.

Table 5
Percentage Distribution of Workers with Only a Bachelor's Degree, by Level of Job Satisfaction

Job Satisfaction	Mechanical Engineering	All
Very satisfied	43.5	45.4
Somewhat satisfied	48.0	45.0
Somewhat dissatisfied	7.0	7.4
Very dissatisfied	1.5	2.2
Mean Score (4=very satisfied, 1=not satisfied at all)	3.3	3.3

▶ Projections for precision/production occupations are mixed because it is a large and diverse collection of jobs. Employment declines are projected for all of the manufacturing industries that employ the largest share of mechanical engineering grads, with the exception of furniture manufacturing, which is projected to grow by about 6 percent. However, these industrywide projections represent the average for all workers; the outlook is much better for highly skilled workers. For example, employment of computer-controlled machine tool operators, metal and plastic, is expected to increase by 7 percent, which is about as fast as the average for all occupations. These workers may face competition for jobs, as many workers currently operating manually controlled machines will be retrained to operate computer-controlled machines and programming activities are increasingly done by these operators; however, workers with the ability to operate multiple CNC machine types should have better opportunities, as companies are increasingly demanding more versatile workers. Graduates of mechanical engineering programs probably have an advantage in competing for jobs in this occupation, just as they have an earnings advantage, the twin results of a high level of skills.

▶ The demand for engineering managers is projected to grow by 6.2 percent, a slower rate than the rate of growth projected for total employment in the U.S. economy between 2008 and 2018. (This is an average; growth will vary among the different engineering fields.) Employment growth should be affected by many of the same factors that affect the growth of the engineers that these managers supervise. Opportunities for engineering managers should be better in rapidly growing areas of engineering, such as environmental and biomedical engineering, than in more slowly growing areas, such as mechanical and electrical engineering. Engineers with advanced technical knowledge and strong communication skills will be in the best position to become managers. Because engineering managers are involved in the financial, production, and marketing activities of their firms, business management skills are also advantageous for those seeking management positions.

Table 6
Projected Growth and Job Openings in the Top 5 Occupations Employing Persons with Only a Bachelor's Degree in Mechanical Engineering

Top 5 Occupations	Projected Growth 2008–2018	Projected Annual Job Openings
All top 5	0.2%	329,980
Mechanical Engineers	6.0%	7,570
Precision/Production Occupations	−3.0%	175,420
Top-Level Managers, Executives, and Administrators	−0.4%	61,470
Other Mid-Level Managers	9.7%	80,650
Engineering Managers	6.2%	4,870

Pathways Beyond the Bachelor's Degree

After graduating with a bachelor's degree, 37 percent of mechanical engineering majors proceed to earn a postgraduate degree: 32 percent earn a master's degree; 4 percent earn a doctoral degree; and 2 percent earn a professional degree.

▶ Three out of 10 master's degrees are earned in the field of mechanical engineering. One-quarter are earned in business management and administration.

▶ Among the few who earn a doctoral degree, 70 percent major in an engineering field: 45 percent choose mechanical engineering, and the remaining 25 percent choose other engineering fields.

PART 6

Humanities and Social Sciences

CHAPTER 34

Anthropology and Archaeology

Anthropology and archaeology are social sciences with a historical focus. People working in both areas have similar abilities, interests, values, and personality patterns.

Anthropology

Anthropology is the study of the origin and behavior of humans and their physical, social, and cultural development. Anthropologists study the way of life, remains, language, or physical characteristics of people in various parts of the world.

Some anthropologists compare the customs, values, and social patterns of different cultures. This kind of specialist usually focuses on one region of the world and some aspect of culture. Sociocultural anthropologists do comparative studies and examine the evolution of customs, cultures, and social lives of groups in settings from nonindustrialized societies to those of modern urban areas. Linguistic anthropologists study the role of language in various cultures.

Physical anthropology is the study of the meanings and causes of human physical differences and their effects on culture, heredity, and environment. Physical anthropologists observe and measure bodily variations and physical attributes of existing human types, often using skeletal remains in museums. These anthropologists study physical and physiological adaptations to differing environments, hereditary characteristics of living populations, and nutrition. They also examine growth patterns, sexual differences, and aging phenomena of human groups. Some examine human remains found at archaeological sites to understand population demographics and factors, such as nutrition and disease, that affected past populations. A related kind of specialist, the biological anthropologist, researches the evolution of the human body, looks for the earliest evidences of human life, and analyzes how culture and biology influence one another.

Anthropologists gather and analyze data on the human physique; social customs; and artifacts, such as weapons, tools, pottery, and clothing. They apply anthropological data and techniques to the solution of problems in industrial relations, race and ethnic relations, social work, political administration, education, and public health. Some work with market researchers to understand the behavior of consumers.

Courses in the major may include peoples and cultures; cultures of the world; language and communication; stones and bones; prehistory of the New World; individual and culture; human origins; cultural survival; and myth and religion.

Table 1

Percentage Distribution of Employed Persons with Only a Bachelor's Degree, by Economic Sector, Size, and New Business Status of Employer

	Anthropology and Archaeology	All
Economic Sector		
Private for-profit	42.5	47.3
Self-employed	19.7	18.5
Government/Military	10.1	11.0
Education	15.2	15.6
Nonprofit	12.2	7.5
Employer Size		
Small (Fewer than 100 employees)	42.0	35.5
Medium (100–999)	21.5	21.8
Large (1,000–24,999)	20.9	26.0
Very large (25,000 or more)	15.6	16.7
Percent working in new business established within past 5 years	5.2	7.6

Archaeology

Archaeology involves the systematic recovery and examination of material evidence, such as tools and pottery remaining from past human cultures, to determine the history, customs, and living habits of earlier civilizations. Archaeologists reconstruct a record of extinct cultures, especially preliterate ones. To determine age and cultural identity, archaeologists study, classify, and interpret artifacts, architectural features, and types of structures recovered by excavation. Archaeologists establish the chronological sequence of development of each culture from simpler to more advanced levels. A person usually specializes in a specific civilization, such as Egyptian or the pre-Columbian history of the Americas. Archaeologists study the material evidence left behind by humans rather than human remains, which are the province of biological or physical anthropologists.

Course work may include archaeological science, archaeological recording, illustration and publication, archaeometry, archaeological method and theory, osteoarchaeology, zooarchaeology, geoarchaeology, biblical archaeology, history and archaeology of the ancient Near East, Syro-Palestinian pottery, problems in the archaeology of Bronze and Iron Age Levant, Greek art and archaeology, coinage, politics and economy in the Greek World, and archaeology of ancient China and South America.

Anthropologists and archaeologists use a high degree of abstract conceptualization in their work. Good reading and language skills are prerequisites. Because this field predominantly deals with data and (in the case of archaeology) doesn't have much involvement with people, it relies on scientific theories to solve problems. Numerical skills are less important than the logical and reasoning abilities that are associated with statistics and that enhance scientific ability. Well-developed spatial skills are required, especially for archaeology.

People considering anthropology and archaeology may at first be confused by their inclusion in the broad category of social sciences. These majors usually do not attract people with high social interests. Anthropologists and archaeologists are researchers and, in fact, share similar interests with people who work in labs or engineering. Although anthropologists and archaeologists deal with ideas, their work is also concrete, meticulous, and manual, as in the case of reconstructing artifacts such as pottery. They also need organizational skills that are used in planning a search or dig.

Values supported by these fields include independence and variety, as well as the obvious ones of the search to discover new facts or hypotheses, intellectual stimulation, and creative insight. Anthropologists and archaeologists decide for themselves what areas to pursue, what their goals are, and how they plan to achieve their goals. Since the social sciences are multidisciplinary, these workers can also choose those with whom they want to work. The nature of the field is expansive, so the work offers the opportunity for a great deal of variety.

Where Do Anthropology and Archaeology Majors Work?

Anthropology and archaeology graduates are employed in all five sectors of the economy. About 42 percent work in the private, for-profit sector for businesses and corporations, and 20 percent are self-employed. Anthropology and archaeology graduates are fond of teaching; educational institutions employ 15 percent, often as teachers in elementary or secondary schools and as postsecondary teachers. The government sector employs 10 percent of anthropology and archaeology graduates, and 12 percent find employment in the nonprofit sector.

At the bachelor's level, the skills that anthropology and archaeology graduates have learned in the classroom cannot readily be applied in the labor market. A graduate degree in the field can sharpen their skills and increase the likelihood of finding jobs in their major. Even then, jobs that utilize the

Table 2
Percentage Distribution of Employed Persons with Only a Bachelor's Degree in Anthropology and Archaeology, by the Relationship Between Their Job and College Major

Relationship of Job to Major	Percent
Closely related	15.5
Somewhat related	32.1
Not related	52.5

Percent who report the following as the most important reasons for working in a job that was not related to major:

Pay, promotion opportunities	31.9
Working conditions (hours, equipment, environment)	16.0
Change in career or professional interests	15.9
Job in highest degree field not available	13.8
Family-related reasons	10.4

skills of anthropology and archaeology are not numerous. Those who have just a bachelor's degree in the field frequently find employment in jobs that are not related to their undergraduate field of study. In fact, 52 percent of all employed anthropology and archaeology graduates holding only a bachelor's degree work in jobs that are not related to their major, while 32 percent consider their jobs to be only somewhat related to their undergraduate field of study. Less than 16 percent report that their employment is closely related to their major.

Of all anthropology and archaeology graduates under the age of 65, 81 percent are employed. About 2 percent are officially unemployed; in other words, they are not employed and are actively seeking employment. The remaining 16 percent are out of the labor force; that is, they are not employed and are not seeking employment. Thirty-seven percent of those out of the workforce cite family responsibilities as the main reason, and 23 percent lack the desire or the need to work.

Occupations

The employment of anthropology and archaeology graduates is spread across many different occupations. No single occupation employs a majority of graduates. Only a little more than

one-third are employed in the top 5 occupations that are predominant employers of these graduates. It's significant that 4 of these top 5 occupations are grab-bag collections of job titles. Note also that the occupations span several industries, from business to health care to services other than health care. Graduates of anthropology and archaeology majors possess good reading and language skills as well as quantitative skills, which they can and must apply to many different career fields.

Female graduates outnumber males by about 2 to 1, but both sexes are equally likely to choose work in marketing or sales.

Work Activities

▸ Three out of 10 grads say that management and administrative duties take up most of their time at work, and nearly 7 out of 10 are primarily responsible for these job functions.

▸ One-fifth spend most of their workweek in sales, purchasing, and marketing activities, and well over half spend significant time on these tasks. As noted earlier, sales and marketing occupations employ nearly 12 percent of the graduates.

Table 3
Top 5 Occupations Employing Persons with Only a
Bachelor's Degree in Anthropology and Archaeology, by Percentage

Top 5 Occupations	All	Men	Women
Other Marketing and Sales Occupations	11.7	11.2	12.1
Other Administrative Occupations	7.4	0.4	12.5
Other Service Occupations, Except Health	7.2	11.5	4.1
Other Mid-Level Managers	5.9	13.5	0.3
Registered Nurses, Pharmacists, Dietitians, Therapists, and Physician Assistants	4.5	6.0	3.4
Total, Top 5 Occupations	36.7	42.6	32.4
Balance of Employed	63.3	57.4	67.6
All Employed	100.0	100.0	100.0

▶ Thirteen percent report that they spend most hours during a typical workweek providing professional services such as consulting services, and one-quarter see these tasks as their primary job duty.

▶ Almost 8 percent of employed anthropology and archaeology graduates work as teachers. About 30 percent state that they regularly spend at least 10 hours per week in teaching activities.

▶ Computer applications regularly occupy the time of 9 out of 10 graduates.

Workplace Training and Other Work-Related Experiences

The career potential of a job is closely associated with the amount of work-related training on the job. Firms that invest in their workforce are more likely to offer pay increases and promotions to match the increasing productivity of their workers. The rate of participation in work-related training during a year among employed anthropology and archaeology graduates (60 percent) is about the same as the training participation rate of all college graduates (61 percent).

▶ Of those anthropology and archaeology graduates who receive some work-related training during the year, 55 percent receive technical training in the occupations in which they are employed.

▶ Twenty percent of the training recipients participate in management or supervisory training.

▶ Twenty-eight percent receive training to improve their general professional skills, such as public speaking and business writing.

When asked to identify the most important reason to acquire training, 39 percent of anthropology and archaeology graduates who undergo training identify the need to improve their occupational skills and knowledge. According to another 7 percent of the training participants, the most important reason to acquire work-related training is to secure a salary increase and a promotion. Only 7 percent cite the necessity to obtain a professional license or certificate as the number one reason for their participation in work-related training activities.

Salaries

The median annual salary of anthropology and archaeology graduates who have only a bachelor's degree and are employed full-time is $42,000, a level that is 23 percent lower than the median annual salary of all full-time employed college graduates. On average, employed anthropology and archaeology graduates work for 42 hours per week and for 51 weeks per year, resulting in 2,142 hours of employment per year. The level of work effort among anthropology and archaeology graduates is about the same as the average among all college graduates (43 hours per week and 50 weeks per year, resulting in 2,150 hours per year).

Note: Because of the very small number of survey respondents in some age groups, it was not possible to furnish a useful age/earnings profile graphic for this major.

The small number of graduates who work in closely related jobs command a higher average annual salary than those in jobs less closely related: $67,100. Graduates with employment in jobs that are somewhat related to their major earn $43,300 per year. In contrast, the average salary of graduates employed full-time in a job that is not related to their field of study is $36,100 per year.

Anthropology and archaeology graduates who are employed by businesses and corporations in the private, for-profit sector earn more than those employed in other sectors. The annual average salary of full-time employed anthropology and archaeology graduates in this sector is $46,400.

Table 4
Annual Salary of Workers with Only a Bachelor's Degree, Top 5 Occupations (in 2010 Dollars)

Earnings in Top 5 Occupations	All	Anthropology and Archaeology
Total	$42,000	$37,600
Other Marketing and Sales Occupations	$54,700	$37,200
Other Administrative Occupations	$38,200	$31,000
Other Service Occupations, Except Health	$35,100	$31,000
Other Mid-Level Managers	$77,400	$61,900
Registered Nurses, Pharmacists, Dietitians, Therapists, and Physician Assistants	$55,700	$18,600

Those who work in the government sector earn an average of $41,900. Employment of graduates in full-time jobs in the education sector yields an average annual salary of $37,400. The private, nonprofit sector pays full-time employed anthropology and archaeology graduates an average salary of $37,200 per year. Self-employed anthropology and archaeology graduates earn $37,100 per year.

Table 4 shows the average salary of anthropology and archaeology graduates in the top 5 occupations that are predominant employers of these graduates. The diverse nature of these occupations is matched by the wide variations in the salaries that they pay. In all 5 jobs, graduates of anthropology and archaeology earn lower wages, on average, than the graduates of all bachelor's programs. This difference suggests that these careers may be more welcoming to graduates of majors that are more directly linked to them. It reinforces the previous statement that anthropology and archaeology grads earn more when they hold jobs related to their major, and yet only a small portion of grads at the bachelor's level are willing or able to do so.

Job Satisfaction

The overall level of job satisfaction of anthropology and archaeology majors is slightly higher than the average for all graduates.

Table 5
Percentage Distribution of Workers with Only a Bachelor's Degree, by Level of Job Satisfaction

Job Satisfaction	Anthropology and Archaeology	All
Very satisfied	45.4	45.4
Somewhat satisfied	44.7	45.0
Somewhat dissatisfied	9.3	7.4
Very dissatisfied	0.5	2.2
Mean Score (4=very satisfied, 1=not satisfied at all)	3.4	3.3

Table 6

Projected Growth and Job Openings in the Top 5 Occupations Employing Persons
with Only a Bachelor's Degree in Anthropology and Archaeology

Top 5 Occupations	Projected Growth 2008–2018	Projected Annual Job Openings
All top 5	12.7%	484,870
Other Marketing and Sales Occupations	7.3%	64,880
Other Administrative Occupations	10.8%	166,130
Other Service Occupations, Except Health	14.3%	53,570
Other Mid-Level Managers	9.7%	80,650
Registered Nurses, Pharmacists, Dietitians, Therapists, and Physician Assistants	21.5%	119,640

Employment Outlook

According to the projections by the U.S. Bureau of Labor Statistics, employment in occupations that require a bachelor's degree is expected to grow faster than employment in other sectors of the American labor market. Between 2008 and 2018, the U.S. workforce is projected to grow by 10.1 percent, creating an average of 15.2 million job openings per year. The bachelor's-level jobs are expected to increase by 17.7 percent over the same time.

Table 6 shows the employment growth projections in the top 5 occupations that are most likely to employ anthropology and archaeology graduates. As with the salary figures, these outlook figures apply to large groups of occupations, and the job specializations within them have widely varying outlooks. Also note that because these are large collections of jobs, they have large workforces that create many job openings because of turnover. In fact, the top 5 occupations are projected to offer a total of almost one-half million job openings each year. However, many of these job openings may not be attractive or inviting to graduates of anthropology or archaeology.

Pathways Beyond the Bachelor's Degree

Postgraduate schooling is widespread among anthropology and archaeology graduates. Of all graduates with a bachelor's degree in anthropology and archaeology, 47 percent proceed to earn a postgraduate degree: one-third earn a master's degree, 7 percent earn a doctoral degree, and 7 percent earn a professional degree.

▶ Seventeen percent of all master's degrees earned by undergraduate anthropology and archaeology majors are in the field of anthropology and archaeology. Eighteen percent are in some field of education. Ten percent are in library science.

▶ A little more than 60 percent of the doctoral degrees earned by anthropology and archaeology undergraduate majors are earned in the field of anthropology and archaeology. The rest are spread across various fields of study, including education, health, social sciences, physical sciences, and business.

▶ Just under half of the professional degrees of undergraduate anthropology and archaeology majors are concentrated in the field of law, and another 41 percent of the degrees are earned in the health professions.

CHAPTER 35

Communications

This major prepares people to write, edit, translate, and report factual information. Graduates of the major use their language skills and knowledge of special writing techniques to communicate facts. Those in communications find employment with radio and television stations, newspapers, and publishing firms and in organizations where they work as public relations specialists.

People in communications have similar abilities and interests. Their talents include the effective use of oral and written language and the simple and clear expression of content. Although speech writing may be referred to as ghost writing, most people in communications are not secretive introverts. They enjoy assuming a promoting and influencing role, they like projecting themselves in front of others, and they feel comfortable in public. They also enjoy working with people.

A communications major satisfies several values. One is the enjoyment of dealing creatively with diverse activities, which provide intellectual challenges and the opportunity to use one's mind. Another value is the prestige that comes with public recognition and personal contact. A third value may be the desire for fame and riches; if riches do not come, the experience of seeking fame may be sufficiently satisfying.

Public relations specialists prepare and disseminate information that keeps targeted groups informed about policies, activities, and accomplishments; the information may be directed to the public, private-interest groups such as employees or consumers, or stockholders of organizations. Public relations specialists also keep management aware of feedback about the public's attitudes and concerns. Some specialists are very involved with political campaigns.

This field requires the preparation of press releases and communication with people in the media who might print or broadcast these materials. Social networks and other Web-based media are emerging as important forms of communication. Public relations specialists set up, plan, and attend speaking engagements as well as represent organizations at community meetings. They also present films or deliver presentations to interested parties who may or may not be part of a public relations program. Their work involves doing research, writing, preparing and distributing materials, maintaining contacts, and responding to inquiries. In government, this person may be referred to as a press secretary, information officer, or public affairs specialist. Most often these specialists work in large cities.

A common public relations sequence of courses includes public relations principles and techniques; public relations management and administration, including organizational development; writing that emphasizes news releases, proposals, annual reports, scripts, speeches, and related items; visual communications, including desktop publishing, computer graphics, and animation; and research, emphasizing social science research and survey design and implementation. Courses in advertising, sociology, and creative writing also are helpful, as is familiarity with word processing and other computer applications. Specialties are offered in public relations for business, government, or nonprofit organizations.

The ability to write and speak well is essential for public relations specialists. They must have research skills and then express the important thoughts clearly and simply. They are doers who possess a creative flair. Good judgment, problem solving, and decision making are part of their job. The abilities to lead and to persuade (to influence others' thinking) are skills that they use to get the intended results and outcomes.

Television newscasters and radio announcers, who often are called disc jockeys, are part of the communications field. Beginners usually start at small stations and move up as they prove themselves. Announcers at small stations may be called on to do all of the following: select and introduce recorded music; present news, sports, weather, and commercials, often chitchatting with their audience to fill time blocks; research and prepare written scripts; write news reports and commercials; and operate control boards. Large stations permit specialization: News anchors introduce videotaped news segments or live reports from reporters in the field; weathercasters or meteorologists report information they have gathered from weather services; and sportscasters select the coverage, write, and report sporting news and events. Podcasts have emerged as a new form of communication, similar in many ways to radio but more targeted at narrowly defined audiences.

Educational courses may include radio news gathering and writing; television newswriting; television news production; fundamentals of sports reporting; advertising; copywriting; sound recording; listening to music; history of music; and history of jazz.

Where Do Communications Majors Work?

Graduates with bachelor's degrees in communications are most likely to work as employees in private, for-profit firms; 6 out of 10 grads do this. Almost 10 percent work in education. Only a

Table 1

Percentage Distribution of Employed Persons with Only a Bachelor's Degree, by Economic Sector, Size, and New Business Status of Employer

	Communications	All
Economic Sector		
Private for-profit	60.5	47.3
Self-employed	17.0	18.5
Government/Military	5.3	11.0
Education	9.7	15.6
Nonprofit	7.5	7.5
Employer Size		
Small (Fewer than 100 employees)	33.2	35.5
Medium (100–999)	25.9	21.8
Large (1,000–24,999)	25.0	26.0
Very large (25,000 or more)	15.8	16.7
Percent working in new business established within past 5 years	9.8	7.6

Table 2

Percentage Distribution of Employed Persons with Only a Bachelor's Degree in Communications, by the Relationship Between Their Job and College Major

Relationship of Job to Major	Percent
Closely related	31.0
Somewhat related	37.8
Not related	31.2

Percent who report the following as the most important reasons for working in a job that was not related to major:

Pay, promotion opportunities	32.4
Change in career or professional interests	23.4
Working conditions (hours, equipment, environment)	13.6
Family-related reasons	13.6
Job in highest degree field not available	10.0

small proportion, 7 percent, work in the nonprofit area for charities, foundations, and nonprofit interest groups. Seventeen percent of the graduates of communications programs are self-employed. This statistic reflects a growing trend in the communications field: Producers, directors, writers, and on-air personalities are hired on a temporary contract basis to complete particular assignments and then move on to complete other work at entirely different organizations. This industry is among the largest employers of these so-called contingent workers, who are contracted to engage in specific tasks, usually for short periods. Educational institutions, particularly colleges and universities, also employ communications graduates in the public relations and marketing departments to support various college publications, such as alumni magazines. Government agencies, along with elected officials, employ communications majors to provide public relations and speech-writing support.

Access to jobs that are closely related to the communications degree is somewhat limited in this highly competitive field. Less than one-third of those with a degree in the communications field report that they work in a job closely tied to their undergraduate degree; just as many have jobs unrelated to their major. However, more than one-third of graduates report that they work in jobs that are somewhat related to the field.

The employment rate of persons with a bachelor's degree in communications is 86 percent. About 11 percent have left the workforce. Of these, about two-fifths are more concerned with family responsibilities, and another one-fifth have no need or desire to work. About 3 percent of all communications majors are classified as unemployed.

Occupations

Only about 16 percent of communications majors report that they work as broadcasters, writers, or public relations specialists or in similar types of creative positions in the field. About one-fifth are involved in sales and marketing positions, whereas about 6 percent have managerial positions, often in the communications sector. Another 5 percent hold administrative jobs.

Table 3
Top 5 Occupations Employing Persons with Only a Bachelor's Degree in Communications, by Percentage

Top 5 Occupations	All	Men	Women
Artists, Broadcasters, Editors, Entertainers, Public Relations Specialists, and Writers	16.2	19.3	13.1
Other Marketing and Sales Occupations	13.0	14.5	11.4
Sales/Marketing—Insurance, Securities, Real Estate, and Business Services	7.6	8.4	6.8
Other Management-Related Occupations	6.1	6.7	5.5
Other Administrative Occupations	5.2	1.3	9.2
Total, Top 5 Occupations	48.1	50.2	46.0
Balance of Employed	51.9	49.8	54.0
All Employed	100.0	100.0	100.0

Slightly more women than men earn this bachelor's degree, but a larger portion of the male grads have chosen jobs that are closely or somewhat related to their major.

Work Activities

▶ Persons with a bachelor's in communications are most likely to spend a good part of their workweek engaged in a marketing or sales activity. Seven out of 10 grads report these tasks as a significant responsibility, and this is the primary work role for one-third of the grads.

▶ Managerial and administrative tasks also are important duties for almost two-thirds of persons with a bachelor's in communication, and employee-relations tasks occupy almost half of the grads on a regular basis.

▶ Computer skills, including the development of computer applications, are an important activity regularly undertaken by 88 percent of communications program graduates.

▶ Forty-three percent of graduates spend significant time working on accounting, finance, and contracts.

Workplace Training and Other Work-Related Experiences

Many skills used by graduates of communications programs are learned through informal, on-the-job training. However, over the course of a year, only 52 percent of all employed persons with a bachelor's in communications engage in some type of formal workplace training activity to improve their job-related skills. This rate of participation is significantly lower than the training participation rate of all college graduates (61 percent).

▶ Forty-six percent of communications grads participate in workplace training to enhance a specific professional skill, such as writing copy, marketing, or art.

▶ Fifteen percent of the training recipients are given management or supervisor training.

▶ Eighteen percent receive training to improve their general professional skills, such as public speaking and business writing.

When asked why they receive this training, almost 3 out of 10 communications majors who get training say they are motivated by a desire to increase their professional skills. Another 6 percent want to achieve or maintain licensure or certification. (Some technical jobs in media require a license from the Federal Communications Commission.)

Salaries

The median annual salary of communications graduates with only a bachelor's degree is $48,000, a level that is 7 percent lower than the median annual salary of all employed college graduates. On average, employed communications graduates work for 42 hours per week and for 50 weeks per year, resulting in 2,100 hours of employment per year. The level of work effort among communications graduates is 2 percent lower than the average among all college graduates (43 hours per week and 50 weeks per year, resulting in 2,150 hours per year).

Communications grads working for businesses in the private, for-profit sector average $52,600 per year. Government-employed grads earn an annual average of $46,500. Those working at nonprofit organizations average $45,400. Self-employed communications majors earn an average of $42,800. Graduates of communications programs who work in educational institutions have earnings of only $39,600 annually.

FIGURE 1

Age/Earnings Profile of Persons with Only a Bachelor's Degree in Communications (Full-Time Workers, in 2010 Dollars)

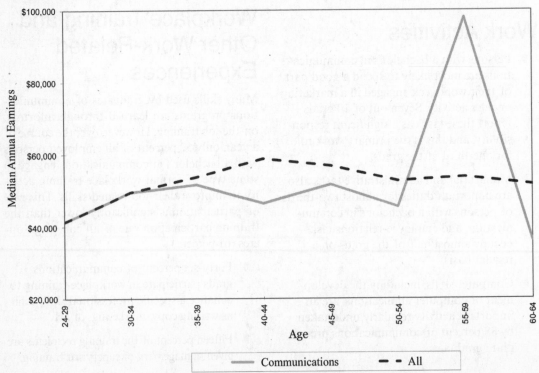

Table 4
Annual Salary of Workers with Only a Bachelor's Degree, Top 5 Occupations (in 2010 Dollars)

Earnings in Top 5 Occupations	All	Communications
Total	$48,000	$49,000
Artists, Broadcasters, Editors, Entertainers, Public Relations Specialists, and Writers	$49,500	$51,600
Other Marketing and Sales Occupations	$54,700	$41,300
Sales/Marketing—Insurance, Securities, Real Estate, and Business Services	$67,100	$61,900
Other Management-Related Occupations	$57,800	$49,500
Other Administrative Occupations	$38,200	$39,200

Graduates of communications programs who are employed in jobs that are closely related to their field of study have substantially higher earnings than other communications graduates. They earn an average of $51,600 per year, compared to an average of $48,500 in jobs that are somewhat related to their field of study and $43,300 in jobs that are not related.

The earnings of persons with a bachelor's degree in communications vary considerably by occupation. Those employed in creative occupations such as writer, artist, and public relations specialist have above-average salaries, earning $51,600 per year. Among the top 5 occupations employing grads, the highest annual pay, $61,900, is found among those communications majors who are employed in sales and marketing positions.

The annual salaries of communications majors employed in occupations that don't generally require a college degree, such as administrative positions, are considerably lower.

Job Satisfaction

The overall level of job satisfaction of communications majors is slightly higher than the average for all graduates.

Employment Outlook

According to the projections by the U.S. Bureau of Labor Statistics, employment in occupations that require a bachelor's degree is expected to

Table 5
Percentage Distribution of Workers with Only a Bachelor's Degree, by Level of Job Satisfaction

Job Satisfaction	Communications	All
Very satisfied	48.5	45.4
Somewhat satisfied	42.6	45.0
Somewhat dissatisfied	7.3	7.4
Very dissatisfied	1.6	2.2
Mean Score (4=very satisfied, 1=not satisfied at all)	3.4	3.3

grow faster than employment in other sectors of the American labor market. Between 2008 and 2018, the U.S. workforce is projected to grow by 10.1 percent, creating an average of 15.2 million job openings per year. The bachelor's-level jobs are expected to increase by 17.7 percent over the same time.

Communications majors are employed in a set of occupations that present a mixed picture of future job prospects.

▶ Employment for communications majors in the creative occupations of artist, broadcaster, writer, and public relations specialist is expected to increase by 12.4 percent through 2018, representing the highest rate of increase among the top 5 occupations that employ communications majors. The outlook is especially good for public relation specialists; job growth of 24.0 percent is projected for this occupation, and it will account for more than 13,000 job openings each year. However, applicants will face keen competition for those jobs. Opportunities should be best for college graduates who combine a degree in journalism, public relations, or another communications-related field with a public relations internship or other related work experience.

▶ The outlook for sales and marketing occupations depends on the nature of the products and services being sold or marketed. Prospects are better for those who work with insurance, securities, real estate, and business services.

▶ Job growth in the miscellaneous administrative occupations that employ communications grads will be close to the average for all occupations. The large workforce of these mostly clerical occupations will create more than 166,000 job openings, largely through turnover.

Pathways Beyond the Bachelor's Degree

Most individuals who earn a degree in communications do not go on to an advanced degree. Only about 22 percent of communications majors eventually earn a graduate degree: 17 percent earn a master's degree, about 2 percent earn a doctorate, and 3 percent earn a professional degree.

Table 6

Projected Growth and Job Openings in the Top 5 Occupations Employing Persons with Only a Bachelor's Degree in Communications

Top 5 Occupations	Projected Growth 2008–2018	Projected Annual Job Openings
All top 5	10.1%	470,980
Artists, Broadcasters, Editors, Entertainers, Public Relations Specialists, and Writers	12.4%	71,740
Other Marketing and Sales Occupations	7.3%	64,880
Sales/Marketing—Insurance, Securities, Real Estate, and Business Services	11.5%	115,210
Other Management-Related Occupations	7.2%	53,020
Other Administrative Occupations	10.8%	166,130

- Only 11 percent of individuals with a bachelor's degree in communications who complete a master's program specialize in the communications field. Another 2 percent focus on journalism. Taken together, various business subjects account for 16 percent of the master's degrees.

- While relatively few communications majors go on to earn a doctorate, about one-fifth of those who do complete their studies in the communications field. Almost one-third of those getting doctorates earn them in education.

- Most of those who earn a professional degree earn it in the field of law.

CHAPTER 36

Dramatic Arts

This broad entertainment field covers majors in theater, the arts, drama, and drama literature. Individuals studying in these majors may aspire to be an actor or actress, comedian, stage director, news or sports announcer, director, production assistant, or producer. The performance media are likewise diversified, including theater, film, television, and radio. Two interests commonly shared among members of this group are expressing ideas and creating images for audiences. Actors and actresses entertain and communicate with people through their portrayal and interpretation of roles. Although some people may never have seen a play on stage, everyone has watched actors and actresses performing in movies or on television.

The business management side of dramatic arts is the focus of directors and producers. Directors interpret plays or scripts. They audition and select cast and crew members. Directors use their knowledge of acting, voice, and movement to achieve the best possible performance. They typically approve the scenery, costumes, choreography, and music. Producers are entrepreneurs. They select scripts of playwrights or scriptwriters, arrange financing, and decide on the size and content of the production and its budget. They hire directors, principal cast members, and key production staff. They negotiate contracts with artistic personnel's booking managers. Producers coordinate activities for writers, directors, and managers.

The field of dramatic arts involves experiential learning, and it is possible to prepare for the field without a college degree. However, most people enter drama curricula to enhance their chances in this highly competitive field and to develop skills that may be useful if a full-time career in the field proves unattainable. Courses include communications, stage speech and movement, directing, playwriting, play production, set design, history of drama, and acting. Opportunities for participating in dramatic productions, announcing, and being in front of audiences are constantly sought after. No specific training requirements are necessary for directors and producers, but course work in drama literature and the technical aspects of production are helpful.

Several abilities are needed in dramatic arts: being able to perform before an audience with poise and self-confidence; interpreting roles and expressing ideas and emotions through gestures, facial expressions, and voice inflections; understanding the script author's ideas and demonstrating to others methods of moving or speaking to convey these ideas to an audience; speaking clearly and loudly; memorizing dialogue; and responding to cues promptly. Although not an ability, physical appearance is often a factor in being accepted for certain roles.

The interests of those in dramatic arts are definitely in the entertainment field and typically include a liking for literary, artistic, and musical activities. Outgoing and extroverted, those in dramatic arts want to work with or in front of people.

Creativity and imagination are hallmark values of those in the dramatic arts. A cluster of rewards—prestige, public attention, and recognition—go along with this field. Those who succeed are recognized and noticed by the public. Because of this field's glamorous image, even an association with it brings prestige. Directors and producers value leadership and, when successful, are rewarded with generous salaries. Actors, however, have the reputation of accepting sporadic work and varied roles, often resulting in the perception that they lead independent lifestyles.

Where Do Dramatic Arts Majors Work?

Finding a job closely related to the field of dramatic arts is difficult. Graduates of dramatic arts programs at the undergraduate level don't generally work in jobs in the field, instead finding employment across key segments of the economy. Half of persons with a bachelor's degree in dramatic arts work in for-profit businesses and corporations. Often dramatic arts graduates are self-employed, usually as consultants rather than as small business owners. Of those with an undergraduate degree in dramatic arts, 14 percent work in an educational institution, frequently as elementary or secondary school teachers. The same share of grads work for nonprofit charitable foundations.

Most dramatic arts majors work in jobs that are not closely related to their undergraduate fields of study. Those who work in jobs related to the field are most often employed in creative occupations such as artist, entertainer, writer, and broadcaster. Still, only one-quarter of dramatic arts majors work in closely related positions. Thirty-five percent work in jobs that are somewhat related to the major, and 40 percent work in unrelated jobs.

A very large share, 19 percent, work part-time. This rate of part-time employment is almost double that of the average college graduate. Some of these are avoiding full-time work to allow time for auditioning or performing.

Table 1

Percentage Distribution of Employed Persons with Only a Bachelor's Degree, by Economic Sector, Size, and New Business Status of Employer

	Dramatic Arts	All
Economic Sector		
Private for-profit	51.1	47.3
Self-employed	16.5	18.5
Government/Military	4.0	11.0
Education	14.3	15.6
Nonprofit	14.0	7.5
Employer Size		
Small (Fewer than 100 employees)	43.4	35.5
Medium (100–999)	27.7	21.8
Large (1,000–24,999)	22.4	26.0
Very large (25,000 or more)	6.5	16.7
Percent working in new business established within past 5 years	8.4	7.6

Table 2
Percentage Distribution of Employed Persons with Only a Bachelor's Degree in Dramatic Arts, by the Relationship Between Their Job and College Major

Relationship of Job to Major	Percent
Closely related	24.6
Somewhat related	35.1
Not related	40.3

Percent who report the following as the most important reasons for working in a job that was not related to major:

Change in career or professional interests	29.9
Family-related reasons	21.6
Job in highest degree field not available	20.6
Pay, promotion opportunities	11.6
Working conditions (hours, equipment, environment)	9.5

About 8 of 10 dramatic arts majors under age 65 are employed. Almost 9 percent are unemployed and looking for work. Another 9 percent have left the workforce. Of these, one-fifth have taken early retirement. Eighteen percent have given up looking because of the lack of available jobs. Fifteen percent are staying at home to handle family responsibilities.

Occupations

A major problem for graduates of dramatic arts programs is that not only are they frequently employed in jobs outside their major, but also they often work in positions that do not require a college degree of any type. A look at the data in Table 3 reveals that 8 percent of all majors in this field work in miscellaneous administrative occupations. Typically these jobs do not require a college degree and generally have salaries that are well below the average of all bachelor's degree holders. On the other hand, almost one-quarter of grads are employed in creative occupations, and the top 5 occupations are rounded out with various managerial and sales jobs in which a bachelor's degree is often helpful, even if it is in an unrelated subject. About half of those involved in sales work in jobs related to insurance, securities, real estate, and business services. Female grads outnumber males by a little less than 2 to 1.

Work Activities

- Almost 6 out of 10 dramatic arts grads spend significant work time managing or supervising people or projects, and almost one-quarter of grads see these duties as their primary role.

- Almost half of grads find that sales, purchasing, and marketing consume at least 10 hours of the typical workweek. These are the main job responsibilities for 17 percent of grads.

- Eighty-eight percent of dramatic arts grads use computer applications for a significant fraction of their work time.

Table 3
Top 5 Occupations Employing Persons with Only a
Bachelor's Degree in Dramatic Arts, by Percentage

Top 5 Occupations	All	Men	Women
Artists, Broadcasters, Editors, Entertainers, Public Relations Specialists, and Writers	24.5	26.0	23.5
Other Administrative Occupations	8.1	1.6	12.3
Other Management-Related Occupations	6.6	7.8	5.7
Other Marketing and Sales Occupations	5.7	9.6	3.2
Sales/Marketing—Insurance, Securities, Real Estate, and Business Services	5.1	3.2	6.3
Total, Top 5 Occupations	50.0	48.2	51.0
Balance of Employed	50.0	51.8	49.0
All Employed	100.0	100.0	100.0

▶ The job duties of one-quarter of grads include routine administrative tasks related to accounting, finance, and contracts.

▶ Teaching duties are a major part of the job responsibilities for 28 percent of graduates from this field. This includes not only those involved in secondary education, but also many of those employed in the creative fields of art, writing, and entertainment.

Workplace Training and Other Work-Related Experiences

Informal on-the-job learning is critical to the long-term career development of persons who earn degrees in dramatic arts. Access to jobs in which employers invest in general skills and in job-specific skills is essential to long-term labor market success for majors in this field. The likelihood of participating in work-based training activities varies considerably among dramatic arts majors, depending on the occupation in which they are employed. For example, about 60 percent of those primarily engaged in sales participate in work-based training seminars and workshops, compared to only 36 percent of those whose primary duty is management. The overall average is 50 percent, which is considerably lower than the average for grads of all majors (61 percent).

▶ Most often (for 44 percent) the training received by graduates in dramatic arts is related to the development of specific occupational skills.

▶ Development of writing and public speaking skills is also an important part of the work-based training activities of 19 percent of grads.

▶ Although many grads do managerial work, only 9 percent of them receive formal on-the-job training in this area.

Three out of 10 of those who participate in training say their most important motivation is the desire to acquire job-specific skills.

Salaries

The median salaries of those employed in full-time jobs with a bachelor's degree in dramatic arts are quite low compared to the earnings of graduates with undergraduate degrees in other major fields of study. Dramatic arts majors earn a median salary of $35,000 per year, a level that is 47 percent lower than the median annual salary of all employed college graduates. On average, employed dramatic arts graduates work for 37 hours per week and for 48 weeks per year, resulting in 1,776 hours of employment per year. The level of work effort among dramatic arts graduates is 17 percent lower than the average among all college graduates (43 hours per week and 50 weeks per year, resulting in 2,150 hours per year).

This difference in work time partly explains the lower wages.

The earnings of majors vary somewhat based on the sector in which they are employed. Earnings are highest for self-employed grads: $48,400 per year. Those working in private, for-profit businesses and corporations average $40,200. Those working in other sectors earn considerably less. Grads employed by educational institutions average only $29,800, a low rate of pay even by that industry's standards. At not-for-profit organizations, the average is $27,900 per year.

It is not easy to find a high-paying job in the arts. It's significant that graduates with employment in jobs that are somewhat related to their major earn a higher average salary ($45,400 per year) than those who work in closely related jobs

FIGURE 1

Age/Earnings Profile of Persons with Only a Bachelor's Degree in Dramatic Arts (Full-Time Workers, in 2010 Dollars)

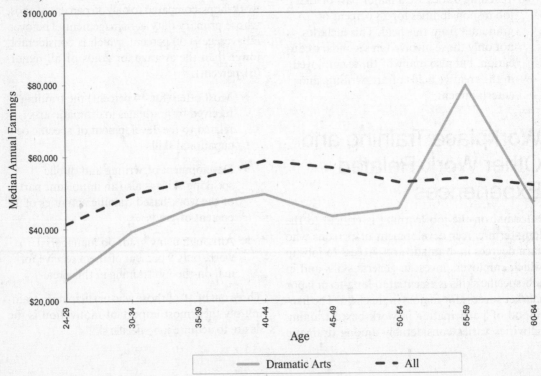

Table 4
Annual Salary of Workers with Only a Bachelor's Degree,
Top 5 Occupations (in 2010 Dollars)

Earnings in Top 5 Occupations	All	Dramatic Arts
Total	$35,000	$41,800
Artists, Broadcasters, Editors, Entertainers, Public Relations Specialists, and Writers	$49,500	$27,900
Other Administrative Occupations	$38,200	$32,000
Other Management-Related Occupations	$57,800	$49,500
Other Marketing and Sales Occupations	$54,700	$87,700
Sales/Marketing—Insurance, Securities, Real Estate, and Business Services	$67,100	$35,100

($33,000). The average salary is $35,100 per year for graduates employed full-time in a job that is not related to their field of study.

As Table 4 shows, the highest earnings among the top 5 occupations employing grads are for miscellaneous sales and marketing occupations and miscellaneous managerial jobs.

Job Satisfaction

Despite their lower average pay, the overall level of job satisfaction of dramatic arts majors is slightly lower than the average for all graduates.

Employment Outlook

According to the projections by the U.S. Bureau of Labor Statistics, employment in occupations that require a bachelor's degree is expected to grow faster than employment in other sectors of the American labor market. Between 2008 and 2018, the U.S. workforce is projected to grow by 10.1 percent, creating an average of 15.2 million job openings per year. This is the exact same rate of job growth that is projected for the top 5 occupations employing dramatic arts grads and is considerably lower than the 17.7 rate that is projected for the bachelor's-level jobs.

Table 5
Percentage Distribution of Workers with Only a
Bachelor's Degree, by Level of Job Satisfaction

Job Satisfaction	Dramatic Arts	All
Very satisfied	38.2	45.4
Somewhat satisfied	49.7	45.0
Somewhat dissatisfied	9.8	7.4
Very dissatisfied	2.2	2.2
Mean Score (4=very satisfied, 1=not satisfied at all)	3.2	3.3

Table 6
Projected Growth and Job Openings in the Top 5 Occupations
Employing Persons with Only a Bachelor's Degree in Dramatic Arts

Top 5 Occupations	Projected Growth 2008–2018	Projected Annual Job Openings
All top 5	10.1%	470,980
Artists, Broadcasters, Editors, Entertainers, Public Relations Specialists, and Writers	12.4%	71,740
Other Administrative Occupations	10.8%	166,130
Other Management-Related Occupations	7.2%	53,020
Other Marketing and Sales Occupations	7.3%	64,880
Sales/Marketing—Insurance, Securities, Real Estate, and Business Services	11.5%	115,210

The job outlook for graduates of dramatic arts programs is mixed:

▶ Employment for artists, entertainers, and others in creative occupations is expected to increase by 12.4 percent between 2008 and 2018. Although the occupations are projected to offer almost 72,000 job openings each year, competition will be stiff, especially for jobs closely related to the dramatic arts.

▶ Most of the other occupations that employ the most majors from this field are expected to have average or slower rates of employment growth through 2018.

▶ On the other hand, many of these occupations have large workforces and therefore will provide numerous job openings because of turnover.

Pathways Beyond the Bachelor's Degree

About 30 percent of all dramatic arts majors who complete an undergraduate program of study go on to eventually earn an advanced degree. Almost all of these individuals decide to earn no more than a master's degree. Only about 2 percent earn a doctorate, and an additional 2 percent earn a professional degree.

▶ Among those who earn a master's degree, almost 40 percent continue their studies in the dramatic arts field. About 1 out of 10 earn a master's degree in education.

▶ Those who earn a doctorate major in dramatic arts about 45 percent of the time.

▶ While only a small number of dramatic arts majors earn a professional degree, most who do earn a professional degree study law.

CHAPTER 37

English Language, Literature, and Letters

As a course of study, English does not convert directly to an occupation, as do most other majors, such as accounting for accountants and art for artists. English is a language and, like other languages, is a foundational ability.

The study of English also involves literature. The study of literature typically is divided by country, such as English or American literature; by time period; or by type of literature, such as poetry or the novel. Some people study literature to critically examine authors' expressive styles or they study, as models, the great works of accepted masters to develop their own creative writing. Others view creative writing as a more unique individualistic expression.

Many English majors continue their appreciation for this field by becoming teachers; these individuals should also explore the education majors. Others studying English use it as a preparatory step to writing. The occupations of writer and editor are described here. For other writing occupations, the journalism major may be an appropriate preparation; it is described in Chapter 41. Another option is the communications major, described in Chapter 35.

Writers and Editors

Writers develop original fiction and nonfiction for books, magazines, trade journals, newspapers, websites, technical reports, company newsletters, radio and television broadcasts, movies, and advertisements. The following are illustrative writing and editing occupations.

Newswriters prepare news items for newspapers, news broadcasts, or news websites using information supplied by reporters or wire services. Columnists analyze news and write commentaries based on personal knowledge and experience. Editorial writers publish comments to stimulate public opinion in accordance with their publication's viewpoint. Bloggers also frequently voice their opinions but usually have more independence to freely express their own point of view. Copywriters write advertising for promotional purposes to sell products or services. Technical writers take technical and scientific information and make it understandable to nontechnical audiences; this information may be presented as assembly instructions, operating manuals, catalogs, and parts lists. Unlike other writers whose work may be assigned by an editor, novelists have freedom in what they write and where they work, such as at home. But writers in general follow a process of collecting information, either by interview or research, and then organizing, writing, rewriting, and shaping the information for the best delivery or organization for a specific purpose or publication.

Editors select and prepare material for publication or broadcast and supervise writers. They review, rewrite, and edit writers' work. The duties of an editor include planning the content of books, magazines, newspapers, or websites and supervising their preparation. Editors decide what will appeal to readers. They hire and assign staff, plan budgets, and negotiate contracts—in other words, they are managers. In a broadcasting firm this person is called a program director.

New recruits to editorial jobs often have titles such as editorial assistant, copy assistant, or production assistant. They review copy for errors in grammar, punctuation, and spelling. They check manuscripts for readability, style, and agreement with editorial policy. They add and rearrange sentences to improve clarity, and they delete incorrect and unnecessary material. Editorial assistants do research for writers and verify facts, dates, and statistics. Assistants also may arrange page layouts of articles, photographs, and advertising. They may compose headlines, prepare copy for printing, and proofread printer's galleys. Some editorial assistants read and evaluate manuscripts submitted by freelance writers or answer letters about published or broadcast material. Production assistants on small newspapers or in radio stations clip stories that come from wire services, answer phones, and make photocopies.

Abilities include good, clear writing and using correct grammar. But writers have visions they want to share. They perceive themselves to have teaching and social abilities. They work well with people and have a goal to keep people well informed. Editors have definite leadership qualities, which they execute when deciding which areas to highlight and what to provide readers.

Table 1
Percentage Distribution of Employed Persons with Only a Bachelor's Degree, by Economic Sector, Size, and New Business Status of Employer

	English Language, Literature, and Letters	All
Economic Sector		
Private for-profit	45.8	47.3
Self-employed	20.1	18.5
Government/Military	6.7	11.0
Education	19.1	15.6
Nonprofit	7.7	7.5
Employer Size		
Small (Fewer than 100 employees)	42.5	35.5
Medium (100–999)	23.4	21.8
Large (1,000–24,999)	22.7	26.0
Very large (25,000 or more)	11.5	16.7
Percent working in new business established within past 5 years	9.2	7.6

Computer proficiency and familiarity with electronic publishing have become basic skills.

Writers and editors have artistic interests such as art, music, and drama in addition to literary interests. The literary interests are closely related to an interest in analyzing, examining, and researching material. In general, writers have social interests. Editors also have a liking for business activities.

Benefits include working with the mind, creativity, variety and diversion, and a good income, which some do not get. Identifying topics and issues, researching them, and then seeking the best way to write them up are a mental challenge. Imagination is needed to discover new untold stories. And, following the saying "old news is stale news," writers and editors are constantly searching for material. In the discovery process they have all their sensory capacities functioning and thus know when it is time to delve further or move on.

Where Do English Language, Literature, and Letters Majors Work?

The employment of English majors is spread across the five sectors of the economy. Less than one-half work in the private, for-profit sector for businesses and corporations. Another one-fifth work in the private, for-profit sector as self-employed workers in their own business or practice. Nearly one-fifth of English majors work in the education sector, hired mainly as teachers. Another 8 percent work in the nonprofit sector for tax-exempt or charitable organizations, and 7 percent work in the government sector.

Not many English majors (28 percent) work in jobs that are closely related to their major. The reason is that English is not an occupation but an ability that provides a foundation on which other occupational skills can be developed. Thirty-two

Table 2
Percentage Distribution of Employed Persons with Only a Bachelor's Degree in English Language, Literature, and Letters, by the Relationship Between Their Job and College Major

Relationship of Job to Major	Percent
Closely related	28.3
Somewhat related	32.0
Not related	39.7

Percent who report the following as the most important reasons for working in a job that was not related to major:

Pay, promotion opportunities	29.6
Change in career or professional interests	19.0
Working conditions (hours, equipment, environment)	12.8
Family-related reasons	12.7
Job in highest degree field not available	12.1

percent say their jobs are somewhat related to their major. The remaining 40 percent work in jobs that are not related to their undergraduate major.

Of all English graduates under the age of 65, 77 percent are employed. A little more than 3 percent are officially unemployed; in other words, they are not employed and are actively seeking employment. The remaining 19 percent are out of the labor force; that is, they are not employed and are not seeking employment. Twenty-eight percent of these English graduates have taken early retirement. Family responsibilities are cited as the reason for labor force withdrawal among 27 percent of this group, and another 23 percent have voluntarily withdrawn from the labor force because they do not want or need to work.

Occupations

Employment among English majors is dispersed across a variety of occupations; less than 40 percent of their jobs are accounted for by the top 5 occupations. Artists, broadcasters, writers, editors, entertainers, and public relations specialist occupations employ 15 percent of all employed English majors. Although women outnumber men among English graduates by a bit more

than 2 to 1, equal proportions of each sex are in this type of job. Eight percent are employed in administrative occupations, and 6 percent are employed as teachers in secondary schools. English majors also are employed selling insurance, stocks and bonds, real estate, and business services, and in miscellaneous managerial jobs.

Work Activities

▶ Although 4 out of 10 of all employed English graduates perform accounting, finance, and contractual duties as a regular part of their jobs, only 8 percent spend most of their time in a typical workweek performing these duties.

▶ Fifty-seven percent of employed English majors perform management and administrative duties regularly, and 14 percent spend most of their time during a typical workweek performing these duties.

▶ Twenty-seven percent of all employed English majors engage in teaching activities, and 14 percent spend more time teaching than in any other activity.

Table 3
Top 5 Occupations Employing Persons with Only a
Bachelor's Degree in English Language, Literature, and Letters, by Percentage

Top 5 Occupations	All	Men	Women
Artists, Broadcasters, Editors, Entertainers, Public Relations Specialists, and Writers	15.4	15.8	15.2
Other Administrative Occupations	7.6	5.2	9.1
Teachers, Secondary—Other Subjects	6.2	5.2	6.8
Sales/Marketing—Insurance, Securities, Real Estate, and Business Services	5.7	6.9	4.9
Other Management-Related Occupations	5.0	4.5	5.3
Total, Top 5 Occupations	39.9	37.6	41.3
Balance of Employed	60.1	62.4	58.7
All Employed	100.0	100.0	100.0

▶ More than half of employed English majors perform sales, purchasing, and marketing duties regularly at their jobs. About 23 percent spend most hours during a week performing these duties.

▶ Engaging in computer applications, programming, and systems-development activities is reported by 88 percent of all employed English graduates. However, only 6 percent spend most of their time on these activities.

▶ Another 34 percent regularly engage in employee-relations activities, including recruiting, personnel development, and training. Only 4 percent conduct these duties during most of their working time.

▶ One-fourth of all employed English majors regularly provide professional services, but only 4 percent of graduates report that they spend most of their time providing professional services.

Workplace Training and Other Work-Related Experiences

The career potential of a job is closely associated with the amount of work-related training on the job. Firms that invest in their workforce are more likely to offer pay increases and promotions to match the increasing productivity of their workers. The percentage of employed English majors who receive work-related training (56 percent) is significantly smaller than the percentage of all employed college graduates (61 percent).

▶ Of those English majors who receive some training, 48 percent receive technical training in their occupational field.

▶ Twenty-three percent receive training to improve their general professional skills, such as public speaking and business writing.

▶ Fifteen percent of recipients who receive training are given managerial or supervisory training.

When asked to identify the most important reason to acquire training, 32 percent of English majors who undergo training choose the need to improve their occupational skills and knowledge. Another 7 percent report mandatory training requirements by the employer as the most important factor for their involvement in work-related training.

Salaries

The median annual salary of English language, literature, and letters graduates with only a bachelor's degree is $44,000, a level that is 17 percent lower than the median annual salary of all employed college graduates. On average, employed English graduates work for 41 hours per week and for 49 weeks per year, resulting in 2,009 hours of employment per year. The level of work effort among English majors is 7 percent lower than the average among all college graduates (43 hours per week and 50 weeks per year, resulting in 2,150 hours per year).

The average annual salary of English majors who work in jobs that are closely related to their major is lower than the average annual salary of those who are employed in jobs that are somewhat related to their major—$44,400 versus $46,400. Graduates whose jobs are closely related tend to be employed in teaching occupations that generally pay lower salaries than some of the jobs in the communications field and in managerial and sales jobs that are somewhat related to the undergraduate major. Many English majors who are employed in unrelated jobs work in clerical and low-end sales and service-sector jobs. The average salary of graduates employed full-time in a job that is not related to their field of study is $45,400.

English graduates who work in the private, for-profit sector for corporations and businesses earn an average salary of $51,600. The government

FIGURE 1

Age/Earnings Profile of Persons with Only a Bachelor's Degree in English Language, Literature, and Letters (Full-Time Workers, in 2010 Dollars)

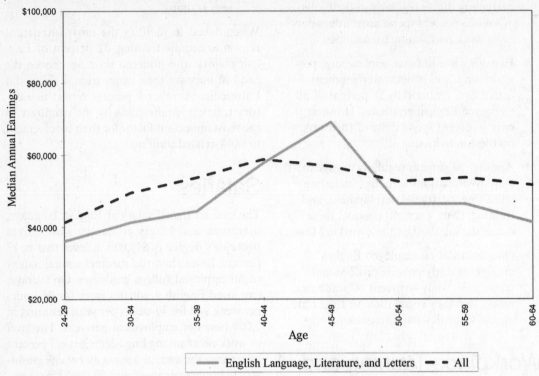

sector pays English graduates who are employed full-time an average annual salary of $44,300. Self-employed English graduates operating their own business earn an average annual salary of $41,800. The annual average remuneration of English graduates with full-time jobs in the private, nonprofit sector is $39,200. English majors who are employed by educational institutions earn only $37,800 per year, a level that is lower than the average salary of English majors employed in all other sectors.

There are sizable variations in the average annual salary of English graduates depending on the occupation in which they are employed. In 3 of the top 5 occupations that are predominant employers of English majors, the salary of all college graduates exceeds that of English majors. Grads who work in the creative occupations have no earnings advantage over those from other majors. Among the top 5 occupations, the best salaries for English majors are in selling business services, insurance, securities, and real estate, with an average of $77,400 per year.

Job Satisfaction

Despite their lower average pay, the overall level of job satisfaction of English majors is about the same as the average for all graduates.

Employment Outlook

According to the projections by the U.S. Bureau of Labor Statistics, employment in occupations that require a bachelor's degree is expected to grow faster than employment in other sectors of the American labor market. Between 2008 and 2018, the U.S.

Table 4
Annual Salary of Workers with Only a Bachelor's Degree, Top 5 Occupations (in 2010 Dollars)

Earnings in Top 5 Occupations	All	English Language, Literature, and Letters
Total	$44,000	$48,200
Artists, Broadcasters, Editors, Entertainers, Public Relations Specialists, and Writers	$49,500	$49,500
Other Administrative Occupations	$38,200	$37,200
Teachers, Secondary—Other Subjects	$39,200	$38,200
Sales/Marketing—Insurance, Securities, Real Estate, and Business Services	$67,100	$77,400
Other Management-Related Occupations	$57,800	$41,300

workforce is projected to grow by 10.1 percent, creating an average of 15.2 million job openings per year. The bachelor's-level jobs are expected to increase by 17.7 percent over the same time.

The employment growth projections for the top 5 occupations that are most likely to employ English graduates are mixed, but none has an outlook as good as the average for all bachelor's-level jobs.

▶ The employment of artists, broadcasters, entertainers, and public relations specialists is expected to grow by 12.4 percent and create almost 72,000 job openings. Among the specializations within this family of occupations that tend to attract English

graduates, the outlook varies from the 18.1 percent growth projected for technical writers to the slight shrinkage projected for editors. Growth of 14.8 percent is projected for writers and authors. Online publications and services are growing in number and sophistication, and these will probably create many jobs for authors, writers, and editors, especially those with Web or multimedia experience. Competition is expected for writing and editing jobs as many people are attracted to this occupation. Competition for jobs with established newspapers and magazines will be keen as many organizations move their publication focus from a

Table 5
Percentage Distribution of Workers with Only a Bachelor's Degree, by Level of Job Satisfaction

Job Satisfaction	English Language, Literature, and Letters	All
Very satisfied	37.3	45.4
Somewhat satisfied	50.4	45.0
Somewhat dissatisfied	8.8	7.4
Very dissatisfied	3.5	2.2
Mean Score (4=very satisfied, 1=not satisfied at all)	3.3	3.3

Table 6

Projected Growth and Job Openings in the Top 5 Occupations Employing Persons with Only a Bachelor's Degree in English Language, Literature, and Letters

Top 5 Occupations	Projected Growth 2008–2018	Projected Annual Job Openings
All top 5	11.0%	431,210
Artists, Broadcasters, Editors, Entertainers, Public Relations Specialists, and Writers	12.4%	71,740
Other Administrative Occupations	10.8%	166,130
Teachers, Secondary—Other Subjects	15.3%	25,110
Sales/Marketing—Insurance, Securities, Real Estate, and Business Services	11.5%	115,210
Other Management-Related Occupations	7.2%	53,020

print to an online presence and as the publishing industry continues to contract. Job prospects for technical writers, especially for applicants with solid communication and technical skills, are expected to be good. However, competition will exist for technical writing positions with more desirable companies and for workers who are new to the occupation.

▶ Secondary school teaching occupations together employ 6 percent of all English majors. The number of teachers employed is dependent on state and local expenditures for education and on the enactment of legislation to increase the quality and scope of public education. Teachers who are geographically mobile and who obtain licensure in more than one subject are likely to have a distinct advantage in finding a job. Most job openings will result from the need to replace the large number of teachers who are expected to retire over the 2008–2018 period.

▶ Employment in administrative and insurance/securities sales occupations, which employ many English majors, is projected to increase at about the average rate for all occupations. These occupations will create numerous job openings because of turnover.

Pathways Beyond the Bachelor's Degree

More than 46 percent of English graduates with a bachelor's degree proceed to earn a postgraduate degree: 33 percent earn a master's degree, 5 percent graduate with a doctorate, and fewer than 8 percent earn a professional degree.

▶ Only 18 percent of the master's degrees are earned in English. Education is the major field of choice among 20 percent of master's degree earners, and another 6 percent of English graduates earn a master's degree in a business field. Master's degrees earned by English majors also include majors in educational administration (4 percent) and psychology (3 percent).

▶ Doctoral degrees among English majors are, for the most part, concentrated in English and education: 42 percent of the doctoral degrees are earned in English, 8 percent in educational administration, and 6 percent in education.

▶ Seven out of 10 professional degrees of English majors are in the field of law. Most of the remaining professional degrees are earned in the health professions.

CHAPTER 38

Foreign Languages and Literature

This is not one major, but many—such as Arabic, Chinese, French, German, Italian, Portuguese, Russian, and Spanish, as well as the classics. The study of language is about communication and includes the knowledge of a language's culture, history, and literature. The purpose of studying a language is more than to foster communication. Today, as great cities of the world become small villages because of telecommunication and satellites, language is an aid to international relations and a foundation for business.

The course work in a foreign language major focuses on proficiency in using the language, reading its literature, and studying its history and geography.

Although proficiency in speaking, reading, and writing a language is basic, context is equally important to the linguist. Similar to the liberal arts orientation, the study of each language involves an examination of the people who speak the language, their way of communicating, and the culture of the countries in which the language is spoken. Just as women's studies often uses significant female innovators and leaders to help convey modern-day perspectives and changes, the study of the literary masterpieces of a language gives insights into historic periods of development.

Linguistics is a specialization that takes a more technical look at the evolution of a language, its relation to other languages, and the structures by which it creates meaning. This focus may be a pathway to understanding how people learn their native tongue or a second language.

Linguistic ability involves memory and visual and auditory discrimination skills. Some people learn certain languages in a more visual manner that requires precise sight memory. For example, learning-disabled students frequently have difficulty in discriminating between *d* and *b* and between *p* and *q*; this difficulty would give them trouble in learning a foreign language because its instruction emphasizes reading. Auditory discrimination of sounds is another important ability, and inflection in tonal sound is also helpful. As in any language, the use of accurate grammar, punctuation, spelling, and sentence structure is important, as is reading ability. The selection of the correct word is important to convey accurately the correct message.

Language majors have literary interests, including both reading and speaking. The focus of oral communication is on the people who are communicating. Because the context in which a person communicates is important to a full understanding of the meaning of a message, appreciation of varying situations is essential.

People who study and use foreign languages value intellectual pursuits, because oral and written communication involve working with the mind. Language also serves as a means of self-expression. With various ways and styles of communicating, people with strong communication skills have the means to influence others.

Where Do Foreign Languages and Literature Majors Work?

The employment of graduates of foreign languages and literature programs is mainly concentrated in the private, for-profit sector and the education sector. Businesses and corporations in the private, for-profit sector employ 36 percent of foreign languages and literature graduates, and 21 percent are self-employed, bringing the total private, for-profit sector employment to 57 percent. Almost 30 percent of foreign languages and literature graduates work in the education sector, hired mostly as secondary school teachers. The nonprofit sector employs almost 7 percent of grads, and the government sector employs a slightly smaller share.

Only 3 out of 10 foreign languages and literature grads work in jobs that are closely related to their major, although this share has grown slightly in recent years along with immigration and global trade. Most jobs that place a preference on or require the knowledge of a foreign language also require the prospective employee to perform tasks that require additional skills and abilities. About one-fifth of the graduates work in jobs that are somewhat related to their undergraduate major, and half work in jobs that are not related to their undergraduate major.

Of all foreign languages and literature graduates under the age of 65, three-quarters are employed—one of the lowest rates among the majors included in this book. Five percent are officially unemployed; in other words, they are not employed and are actively seeking employment. The remaining 20 percent are out of the labor force; that is, they are not employed and are not seeking employment. This is a very high percentage compared to other majors. Family

Table 1

Percentage Distribution of Employed Persons with Only a Bachelor's Degree, by Economic Sector, Size, and New Business Status of Employer

	Foreign Languages and Literature	All
Economic Sector		
Private for-profit	36.5	47.3
Self-employed	20.6	18.5
Government/Military	6.5	11.0
Education	29.7	15.6
Nonprofit	6.6	7.5
Employer Size		
Small (Fewer than 100 employees)	40.3	35.5
Medium (100–999)	24.6	21.8
Large (1,000–24,999)	22.2	26.0
Very large (25,000 or more)	12.8	16.7
Percent working in new business established within past 5 years	9.3	7.6

Table 2
Percentage Distribution of Employed Persons with Only a Bachelor's Degree in Foreign Languages and Literature, by the Relationship Between Their Job and College Major

Relationship of Job to Major	Percent
Closely related	30.3
Somewhat related	19.5
Not related	50.2

Percent who report the following as the most important reasons for working in a job that was not related to major:

Pay, promotion opportunities	27.7
Change in career or professional interests	18.3
Working conditions (hours, equipment, environment)	17.2
Job in highest degree field not available	12.4
Family-related reasons	11.9

responsibilities are most often cited as the chief reason these grads have withdrawn from the labor force. This is a common occurrence among female-dominated majors, and female grads of foreign languages and literature outnumber male grads by about 3 to 1. More than one-quarter of the graduates who are out of the workforce cite this reason. Almost as large a share are not working because they have no need or desire to work. One-fifth cited another, unspecified reason. Only 9 percent said they were unable to find work in their field.

Occupations

Employment among foreign languages and literature majors is dispersed across a variety of occupations, but teaching jobs dominate, accounting for almost one-quarter of the grads who are employed. The second largest employer, with 7 percent of grads, is a group of creative occupations that includes writers, editors, and translators. A slightly smaller fraction of grads sell real estate and intangible goods and services. Less than 5 percent are employed in clerical and other administrative jobs.

Work Activities

- One-quarter of grads list teaching as their primary work activity, and 36 percent of grads spend significant work time teaching.

- One-fifth of grads are mainly tasked with sales, purchasing, and marketing, and this responsibility occupies at least 10 hours a week for 4 out of 10 grads.

- Almost 90 percent of workers regularly work with computer applications, but less than 5 percent see these activities as their primary focus.

- Accounting, finance, and contracts are regular responsibilites for one-third of grads. Almost 8 percent consider this central to their job.

Table 3
Top 5 Occupations Employing Persons with Only a
Bachelor's Degree in Foreign Languages and Literature, by Percentage

Top 5 Occupations	All	Men	Women
Teachers, Secondary—Other Subjects	14.0	18.0	12.4
Artists, Broadcasters, Editors, Entertainers, Public Relations Specialists, and Writers	7.3	3.5	8.9
Sales/Marketing—Insurance, Securities, Real Estate, and Business Services	6.6	4.3	7.6
Teachers—Elementary School	5.0	0.6	6.8
Other Administrative Occupations	4.7	5.2	4.5
Total, Top 5 Occupations	37.6	31.6	40.2
Balance of Employed	62.4	68.4	59.8
All Employed	100.0	100.0	100.0

▌ Fifty-four percent of grads spend significant time managing or supervising people or projects, and 13 percent work primarily as managers.

Workplace Training and Other Work-Related Experiences

The career potential of a job is closely associated with the amount of work-related training on the job. Firms that invest in their workforce are more likely to offer pay increases and promotions to match the increasing productivity of their workers. Employed foreign languages and literature majors are about as likely as grads of any other major to receive work-related training.

▌ Of those foreign languages and literature majors who receive some work-related training, 59 percent are given technical training in their occupational field.

▌ Twenty-one percent receive training to improve their general professional skills, such as public speaking and business writing.

▌ Another 21 percent of the training recipients are given management or supervisor training.

When asked to identify the most important reason to acquire training, 33 percent of foreign languages and literature majors who undergo training cite the need to improve their occupational skills and knowledge. About 1 out of 10 report a mandatory training requirement by their employer, and 8 percent consider better pay and promotion opportunities as the most important factor for their involvement in work-related training. Seven percent get training to achieve or maintain licensure or certification; most states require teachers to get continuing education, which often takes the form of in-service training.

Salaries

The median annual salary of foreign languages and literature graduates who have only a bachelor's degree and are employed full-time is $43,700, a level that is 18 percent lower than the median annual salary of all full-time employed college graduates. On average, employed foreign languages and literature graduates work for 41 hours per week and for 50 weeks per year, resulting in 2,050 hours of employment per year. The level of work effort among foreign languages and literature graduates is 5 percent lower than the average among all college graduates (43 hours per week and 50 weeks per year, resulting in 2,150 hours per year). The difference in work time partly explains the lower average earnings.

The average annual earnings of foreign languages and literature majors who work in jobs that are either closely related or not related to their major are lower than the earnings of those who are employed in jobs that are somewhat related to their undergraduate major. Graduates whose jobs are closely related earn $46,400 annually, and those whose jobs are not related earn $43,600 per year. A number of graduates with closely related jobs are employed in teaching occupations that gener-

ally pay lower salaries. Foreign language grads whose jobs are somewhat related to their major earn an average salary of $59,500 per year.

Foreign language graduates who work in the private, for-profit sector for corporations and businesses earn higher salaries than their counterparts employed in other sectors. These graduates earn an average salary of $49,800 per year. In the government sector, employment results in an average annual salary of $48,400. Self-employed graduates average $45,100 per year. Full-time employment in the education sector among foreign language grads yields an annual salary of $41,700, a level that is substantially higher than the annual average remuneration of graduates with full-time jobs in the private, nonprofit sector, which is $36,400.

FIGURE 1

Age/Earnings Profile of Persons with Only a Bachelor's Degree in Foreign Languages and Literature (Full-Time Workers, in 2010 Dollars)

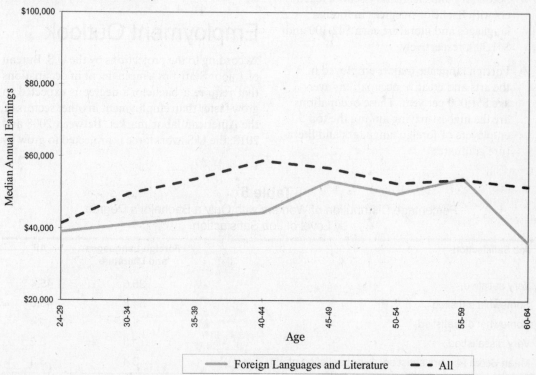

Table 4
Annual Salary of Workers with Only a Bachelor's Degree, Top 5 Occupations (in 2010 Dollars)

Earnings in Top 5 Occupations	All	Foreign Languages and Literature
Total	$43,700	$48,300
Teachers, Secondary—Other Subjects	$39,200	$42,400
Artists, Broadcasters, Editors, Entertainers, Public Relations Specialists, and Writers	$49,500	$51,000
Sales/Marketing—Insurance, Securities, Real Estate, and Business Services	$67,100	$47,500
Teachers—Elementary School	$37,200	$41,300
Other Administrative Occupations	$38,200	$42,300

In 4 of the top 5 occupations that are predominant employers of foreign languages and literature majors, the salary of foreign languages and literature majors exceeds the salary of all college graduates.

▶ Secondary and elementary school teachers with bachelor's degrees in foreign languages and literature earn $42,400 and $41,300, respectively.

▶ Foreign language majors employed in the arts and creative occupations average $51,000 per year. These occupations are the highest-paying among the top 5 employers of foreign languages and literature graduates.

Job Satisfaction

The overall level of job satisfaction of foreign languages and literature majors is slightly higher than the average for all graduates.

Employment Outlook

According to the projections by the U.S. Bureau of Labor Statistics, employment in occupations that require a bachelor's degree is expected to grow faster than employment in other sectors of the American labor market. Between 2008 and 2018, the U.S. workforce is projected to grow by

Table 5
Percentage Distribution of Workers with Only a Bachelor's Degree, by Level of Job Satisfaction

Job Satisfaction	Foreign Languages and Literature	All
Very satisfied	38.0	45.4
Somewhat satisfied	54.8	45.0
Somewhat dissatisfied	5.9	7.4
Very dissatisfied	1.3	2.2
Mean Score (4=very satisfied, 1=not satisfied at all)	3.4	3.3

10.1 percent, creating an average of 15.2 million job openings per year. The bachelor's-level jobs are expected to increase by 17.7 percent over the same time.

There is not a great amount of variation in the employment growth projections for the top 5 occupations that are most likely to employ foreign languages and literature graduates. Most of these occupations are expected to grow faster than the average for all jobs but slower than the rate of the bachelor's-level jobs.

▶ Elementary and secondary school teaching occupations, which together employ 19 percent of all foreign languages and literature majors, are projected to expand by 15.8 percent and 8.9 percent, respectively. The number of teachers employed is mostly dependent on state and local expenditures for education and on the enactment of legislation to increase the quality and scope of public education. Most job openings will result from the need to replace the large number of teachers who are expected to retire over the 2008–2018 period. Also, many beginning teachers—especially those employed in poor, urban schools—decide to leave teaching for other careers after a year or two, creating additional job openings for teachers.

▶ Employment in the creative occupations that employ 7 percent of grads is projected to expand by 12.4 percent. Within this family of occupations, many foreign language grads probably are working as interpreters and translators. The outlook is very good for this occupation, with 22.1 percent growth projected and 23,000 job openings per year. Higher demand for interpreters and translators results directly from the broadening of international ties and the large increases in the number of non-English-speaking people in the United States. Both of these trends are expected to continue throughout the projection period, contributing to relatively rapid growth in the number of jobs for interpreters and translators across all industries in the economy. Urban areas, especially Washington, New York, and cities in California, provide the largest numbers of employment possibilities, especially for interpreters; however, as the immigrant population spreads into more rural areas, jobs in smaller communities will become more widely available.

▶ The sales and administrative occupations that employ many foreign languages and literature graduates are each projected to

Table 6

Projected Growth and Job Openings in the Top 5 Occupations Employing Persons with Only a Bachelor's Degree in Foreign Languages and Literature

Top 5 Occupations	Projected Growth 2008–2018	Projected Annual Job Openings
All top 5	11.7%	453,970
Teachers, Secondary—Other Subjects	8.9%	41,240
Artists, Broadcasters, Editors, Entertainers, Public Relations Specialists, and Writers	12.4%	71,740
Sales/Marketing—Insurance, Securities, Real Estate, and Business Services	11.5%	115,210
Teachers—Elementary School	15.8%	59,650
Other Administrative Occupations	10.8%	166,130

grow by about 11 percent, and they will also create a very large number of job openings through turnover.

Pathways Beyond the Bachelor's Degree

Of those foreign languages and literature graduates with a bachelor's degree, 47 percent proceed to earn a postgraduate degree: 34 percent earn a master's degree, 6 percent graduate with a doctorate, and 7 percent earn a professional degree.

▶ Eighteen percent of the master's degrees are earned in foreign languages and literature. Another 18 percent choose education as the major field of choice for their master's degree. About 11 percent of the master's degrees are earned in business management and administration services, and 7 percent are earned in library science.

▶ Doctoral degrees among foreign language majors are for the most part concentrated in foreign languages and education. One-half of the doctoral degrees are earned in foreign languages, literature, and linguistics. Nine percent are earned in education.

▶ Almost 70 percent of all professional degrees of undergraduate foreign languages and literature majors are in the field of law. Most of the remaining professional degrees are earned in health-related fields.

CHAPTER 39

Geography

Geography is the analysis of distributions of physical and cultural phenomena on local, regional, continental, and global scales. Geography can be viewed as either a physical science or a social science, depending on an institution's or faculty's orientation.

In addition to these two large divisions, the discipline offers several specializations. Economic geographers study the distribution of resources and economic activities. Political geographers are concerned with the relationship of geography to political phenomena, and cultural geographers study the geography of cultural phenomena. Physical geographers study the variations in climates, vegetation, soil, and landforms, along with their implications for human activity. Urban and transportation geographers study cities and metropolitan areas. Regional geographers study the physical, economic, political, and cultural characteristics of regions, ranging in size from a congressional district to entire continents. Medical geographers study health-care delivery systems, epidemiology (the study of the causes and control of epidemics), and the effect of the environment on health.

In schools geography is taught as a social science. The emphasis is on the comparative location of different countries and the relation of their people to those from another country. Oftentimes a descriptive approach is used to understand various cultures, including ethnic distributions, political organizations, and economic activities. Geographers can also consult with governments or international organizations on economic exploitation of regions and on determinations of ethnic and natural boundaries between nations.

Geographers who take the physical science perspective conduct research on physical and climatic aspects of regions and landforms; they survey soils, plants, and animals within an area. These geographers integrate their findings with other specialties such as geology, oceanography, meteorology, and biology. Some geographers construct and draw maps.

Course work may include economic geography; resource management; cultural and political geography; cartography and air photos; environmental issues, such as ecosystems, resources, and energy; air and water quality engineering; various regional geography courses; computer skills; and mathematical and quantitative research methods.

Abilities vary depending on the specialization. For a physical science orientation, individuals need advanced mathematics and science courses requiring a physics background; therefore, understanding technical and scientific information and using numbers to solve problems are required. Those who specialize in mapmaking or photo interpretation need the abilities to understand spatial relations and recognize shapes and sizes. Language skills and making judgments from data are required for decision making. Thinking from a global perspective, instead of analyzing from concrete evidence that is immediately available, is a skill that some individuals may not yet have developed.

The interests of geographers, especially those with a physical science perspective, are scientific, involving the exploration and analysis of natural and social phenomena. Geographers have a technical and practical orientation. After they have

Table 1
Percentage Distribution of Employed Persons with Only a Bachelor's Degree, by Economic Sector, Size, and New Business Status of Employer

	Geography	All
Economic Sector		
Private for-profit	42.9	47.3
Self-employed	19.6	18.5
Government/Military	22.6	11.0
Education	10.5	15.6
Nonprofit	4.4	7.5
Employer Size		
Small (Fewer than 100 employees)	36.1	35.5
Medium (100–999)	19.4	21.8
Large (1,000–24,999)	23.7	26.0
Very large (25,000 or more)	20.9	16.7
Percent working in new business established within past 5 years	6.3	7.6

studied and organized their data, they like to become confident and feel comfortable defending their opinions. Geographers have interests similar to those of civil engineers, who also are able to see the big picture and often work at field sites.

The values of geographers include a research orientation, working with one's mind, and possibly analyzing computer data. They enjoy the variety that the field offers and the possible creative explanations and solutions they devise. Geographers value the prestige afforded by the types of problems they work with or bestowed by the organization for which they work.

Where Do Geography Majors Work?

Geography majors have an above-average likelihood of being employed in the government sector. Nearly one-quarter work for the government. In contrast, 11 percent of all college graduates are government employees. About 43 percent

of geography majors work for businesses and corporations in the private, for-profit sector. One-fifth are self-employed in their own business or practice. Educational institutions employ 1 out of 10 geography graduates, and the remaining 4 percent work for the private, nonprofit sector.

Only 23 percent of geography majors work in jobs that are closely related to their undergraduate major. Another 28 percent are employed in jobs that are somewhat related to their major. The remaining share, almost 50 percent, report that their jobs are not at all related to their undergraduate major.

Of all geography graduates under the age of 65, 86 percent are employed. Only 5 percent are officially unemployed; in other words, they are not employed and are actively seeking employment. The remaining 9 percent are out of the labor force; that is, they are not employed and are not seeking employment. More than 40 percent of the labor force withdrawals among geography majors are attributable to early retirement. Fifteen percent of geography graduates who are

Table 2
Percentage Distribution of Employed Persons with Only a Bachelor's Degree in Geography, by the Relationship Between Their Job and College Major

Relationship of Job to Major	Percent
Closely related	23.0
Somewhat related	27.6
Not related	49.4

Percent who report the following as the most important reasons for working in a job that was not related to major:

Pay, promotion opportunities	40.5
Family-related reasons	13.9
Change in career or professional interests	13.7
Job in highest degree field not available	10.5
Job location	8.8

out of the labor force cite family responsibilities as the main reason for their withdrawal. Twelve percent are unable to participate in the labor force because of a chronic illness or disability.

Occupations

Geography majors are employed in a wide variety of occupations. The top 5 occupations account for less than 40 percent of all employed graduates. More than 13 percent of all employed geography graduates work in miscellaneous administrative occupations. Another 12 percent work in sales. About 7 percent teach in elementary school. Almost 6 percent work in accounting. If this seems like a very mixed group, consider that almost half of the grads say they work in a field unrelated to their major.

Male grads outnumber females by about 2 to 1. A greater percentage of female grads go into teaching careers; among sales and accounting careers, the proportions are reversed.

Work Activities

▶ Although 36 percent of all employed geography graduates perform accounting, finance, and contractual duties as a regular part of their jobs, only 8 percent spend most of their time in a typical workweek performing these duties.

▶ Computer applications, programming, and systems-development duties are regularly performed by 88 percent of employed geography majors. For 5 percent of the graduates, these duties take up most of their time during a typical workweek.

▶ The top employer of geography majors is administrative occupations. Hence, it is not surprising to find that 58 percent of employed geography majors perform management and administrative duties regularly, and 21 percent spend most of their time during a typical workweek performing these duties.

Table 3
Top 5 Occupations Employing Persons with Only a Bachelor's Degree
in Geography, by Percentage

Top 5 Occupations	All	Men	Women
Other Administrative Occupations	13.4	12.5	15.4
Teachers—Elementary School	7.3	1.4	20.2
Other Marketing and Sales Occupations	6.4	7.4	4.3
Accountants, Auditors, and Other Financial Specialists	5.9	7.9	1.3
Sales Occupations—Commodities, Except Retail	5.7	8.3	–
Total, Top 5 Occupations	38.7	37.5	41.2
Balance of Employed	61.3	62.5	58.8
All Employed	100.0	100.0	100.0

▶ More than half of the graduates regularly engage in sales, purchasing, and marketing activities, and 20 percent consider these duties to be a major part of their job.

▶ Another 36 percent of employed geography majors perform accounting, finance, and contractual duties, but only 8 percent spend a major part of their workweek in these activities.

▶ Twenty-eight percent regularly engage in managerial duties to oversee the quality and efficiency of the production process, but less than 1 percent consider those duties to be the main part of their job.

Workplace Training and Other Work-Related Experiences

The career potential of a job is closely associated with the amount of work-related training on the job. Firms that invest in their workforce are more likely to offer pay increases and promotions to match the increasing productivity of their workers. Employed geography majors are substantially less likely to participate in work-related training than all employed college graduates. About half of geography majors receive training, compared to 61 percent of all employed college graduates.

▶ Of those geography majors who receive training, 51 percent are given technical training in the occupation in which they are employed.

▶ Fifteen percent of the training recipients get management or supervisor training.

▶ Thirteen percent receive training to improve their general professional skills, such as public speaking and business writing.

When asked to identify the most important reason to acquire training, 36 percent of geography majors who undergo training identify the need to improve their occupational skills and knowledge. Eight percent consider the need to obtain or maintain a professional license or certificate as the main factor in influencing their decision to undergo work-related training. Another 6 percent report mandatory training requirements by the employer as the most important factor for their involvement in work-related training. For 5 percent, the most important factor is to improve their opportunities for a salary increase and promotion.

Salaries

The median annual salary of geography graduates with only a bachelor's degree is $42,000, a level that is 23 percent lower than the median annual salary of all employed college graduates. On average, employed geography graduates work for 41 hours per week and for 49 weeks per year, resulting in 2,009 hours of employment per year. The level of work effort among geography graduates is 6 percent lower than the average among all college graduates (43 hours per week and 50 weeks per year, resulting in 2,150 hours per year). This difference in work hours partly explains the lower average earnings.

The average annual salary of geography majors who work in jobs that are closely related to their major is much lower than for those who are employed in jobs that are somewhat related or not related to their major. Graduates who work in closely related jobs earn $38,200 per year, whereas those who work in jobs that are somewhat related to their major earn $52,600 per year. Geography graduates with unrelated jobs earn an average annual salary of $41,300. Many graduates whose jobs are somewhat related or unrelated to their undergraduate major are employed in managerial, administrative, and sales jobs that are associated with higher salaries than the average salary of geography majors in elementary school teaching or surveying occupations. Other college graduates (mainly civil engineering majors) who work in civil engineering occupations earn a much higher salary than geography majors employed in this field.

FIGURE 1

Age/Earnings Profile of Persons with Only a Bachelor's Degree in Geography (Full-Time Workers, in 2010 Dollars)

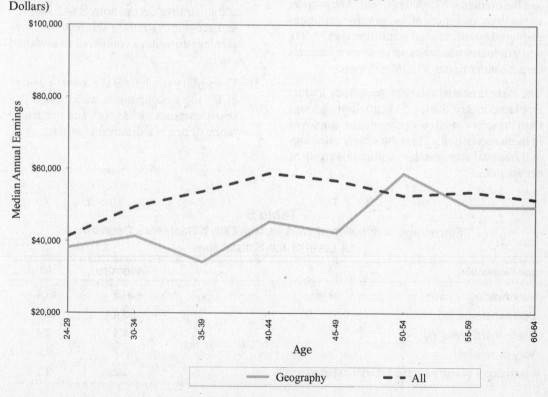

Table 4
Annual Salary of Workers with Only a Bachelor's Degree, Top 5 Occupations (in 2010 Dollars)

Earnings in Top 5 Occupations	All	Geography
Total	$42,000	$46,400
Other Administrative Occupations	$38,200	$42,300
Teachers—Elementary School	$37,200	$33,000
Other Marketing and Sales Occupations	$54,700	$72,200
Accountants, Auditors, and Other Financial Specialists	$59,900	$56,800
Sales Occupations—Commodities, Except Retail	$64,000	$41,300

Geography majors who work for businesses and corporations in the private, for-profit sector earn $51,600 per year. This salary is higher than salaries of geography majors employed in other sectors. The government sector pays geography graduates who are employed full-time an average annual salary of $40,400. In the nonprofit sector, the average is $35,000 per year. The average annual remuneration of geography graduates employed by educational institutions is $33,600, and graduates who work in their own business earn a similar figure, $33,100 per year.

The average annual salary of geography majors employed in 3 of the top 5 occupations is lower than the salary of all college graduates employed in those occupations. There are sizable variations in the annual average salary within this group of occupations.

▶ The highest annual earnings are among geography graduates employed in miscellaneous marketing and sales jobs—an average of $72,200 annually. Employment in commodity sales pays a much lower average annual salary, $41,300.

▶ The annual average remuneration in administrative occupations is $42,300, and geography grads in this field have an earnings advantage compared to all other grads.

▶ Elementary teaching is the lowest-paying of the top 5 occupations, with average yearly earnings of $33,000, and the geography degree is a disadvantage here.

Table 5
Percentage Distribution of Workers with Only a Bachelor's Degree, by Level of Job Satisfaction

Job Satisfaction	Geography	All
Very satisfied	31.5	45.4
Somewhat satisfied	53.4	45.0
Somewhat dissatisfied	14.4	7.4
Very dissatisfied	0.7	2.2
Mean Score (4=very satisfied, 1=not satisfied at all)	3.2	3.3

▶ Accounting is one of the higher-paying career options, with an average of $56,800 per year.

Job Satisfaction

The overall level of job satisfaction of geography majors is slightly lower than the average for all graduates.

Employment Outlook

According to the projections by the U.S. Bureau of Labor Statistics, employment in occupations that require a bachelor's degree is expected to grow faster than employment in other sectors of the American labor market. Between 2008 and 2018, the U.S. workforce is projected to grow by 10.1 percent, creating an average of 15.2 million job openings per year. The bachelor's-level jobs are expected to increase by 17.7 percent over the same time.

Employment projections are very mixed for the top 5 occupations that are most likely to employ geography graduates.

▶ The largest employer of geography majors, a group of administrative occupations, is projected to grow by 10.8 percent

between 2008 and 2018, yielding an average of 166,000 job openings each year. This is a very large occupation, with a lot of job turnover.

▶ Employment projections differ widely between the two sales occupations among the top 5. Opportunities will be much better in the miscellaneous sales occupations than in commodities sales.

▶ Employment of elementary school teachers is projected to grow by almost 16 percent and create almost 60,000 job openings each year. Most of these openings will result from the need to replace the large number of teachers who are expected to retire over the 2008–2018 period. Also, many beginning teachers—especially those employed in poor, urban schools—decide to leave teaching for other careers after a year or two, creating additional job openings for teachers.

▶ Accounting and financial occupations are projected to grow at above-average rates. An increase in the number of businesses, changing financial laws and corporate governance regulations, and increased accountability for protecting an organization's stakeholders will drive job growth.

Table 6
Projected Growth and Job Openings in the Top 5 Occupations Employing Persons with Only a Bachelor's Degree in Geography

Top 5 Occupations	Projected Growth 2008–2018	Projected Annual Job Openings
All top 5	13.3%	418,230
Other Administrative Occupations	10.8%	166,130
Teachers—Elementary School	15.8%	59,650
Other Marketing and Sales Occupations	7.3%	64,880
Accountants, Auditors, and Other Financial Specialists	18.9%	127,260
Sales Occupations—Commodities, Except Retail	−1.1%	310

Accountants and auditors who have earned professional recognition through certification or other designation, especially a CPA, should have the best job prospects.

Pathways Beyond the Bachelor's Degree

Three out of 10 geography graduates with a bachelor's degree proceed to earn a postgraduate degree: 24 percent earn a master's degree, 4 percent graduate with a doctorate, and 2 percent earn a professional degree.

▶ One-fifth of master's degree recipients choose geography as their major. One in 10 get their master's in another social science; the same share focus on a business subject. About 11 percent study education.

▶ Almost half of the doctoral degrees among undergraduate geography majors are in geography. No other subject comes close.

▶ Almost 7 out of 10 of the professional degrees earned by undergraduate geography graduates are in law, and 19 percent are in medicine.

CHAPTER 40

History

Historians are social scientists who study all aspects of human society. They use research as a basic activity to provide insights that help others understand the different ways in which individuals and groups make decisions, exercise power, and respond to change. History develops a greater understanding and appreciation of today's cultures and civilizations. Social sciences are interdisciplinary in nature. Specialists in one discipline often find that their research overlaps with work being done in another field.

Historians research, analyze, and interpret the past. They use many sources of information in their research, including government and institutional records, newspapers and other periodicals, photographs, interviews, films, and unpublished manuscripts such as personal diaries and letters. Historians usually specialize in a specific country or region; a particular time period; or a particular field, such as social, intellectual, political, or diplomatic history. Biographers collect detailed information on individuals. Genealogists trace family histories. Other historians help study and preserve archival materials, artifacts, and historic buildings and sites.

History majors have the opportunity to specialize, and typically a wide range of course work is offered. Courses may include Western civilization; African civilization; and Asian, Middle Eastern, Latin American, European, or United States history (all with designated time periods). Focus can be on specific countries such as China, Japan, or Southeast Asia; Third World countries; the history of religion; or women.

Language, social, and teaching abilities characterize historians. They tend to be excellent readers and possess good memories. Intellectual curiosity and creativity are fundamental personal traits for historians as they seek new information about people, things, and ideas. They think logically and, when writing, work methodically and systematically.

Historians primarily have social interests along with organizational and scientific interests—that is, seeking more definitive understandings through research. Many historians prefer teaching as a field, because it allows them to arrange, construct, and interpret events for others as they imagine them to have occurred. They enjoy reading and appreciate the fact that their field permits use of diverse methodologies to collect and assemble data.

Historians value organization and working independently. Variety and diversion are important to them. They prefer to entertain different perspectives of events while committed to objectivity and open-mindedness. They gain satisfaction by working with their minds and through their appreciation for researching topics.

Where Do History Majors Work?

History majors with a bachelor's degree are employed across the spectrum of the American economy. They are more likely than many other college graduates with degrees in other fields

Table 1
Percentage Distribution of Employed Persons with Only a Bachelor's Degree, by Economic Sector, Size, and New Business Status of Employer

	History	All
Economic Sector		
Private for-profit	43.8	47.3
Self-employed	17.0	18.5
Government/Military	15.1	11.0
Education	16.7	15.6
Nonprofit	7.3	7.5
Employer Size		
Small (Fewer than 100 employees)	33.1	35.5
Medium (100–999)	21.8	21.8
Large (1,000–24,999)	22.5	26.0
Very large (25,000 or more)	22.6	16.7
Percent working in new business established within past 5 years	7.3	7.6

to work in private, for-profit firms, with more than 4 of 10 working for private businesses and corporations. History majors in this sector have the highest earnings of all graduates from this field of study. Frequently history majors work in the education sector; 17 percent are employed there, mostly as teachers. About the same share of grads are self-employed, either operating their own business or serving in a consulting capacity. About 15 percent are employed by a federal, state, or local government organization.

The overwhelming majority of history majors are employed in jobs that are not closely related to their undergraduate field of study. Of those history majors who report that they are employed in jobs related to their major, many work as either secondary or elementary school teachers.

About 82 percent of persons with a bachelor's degree in history are employed, usually in full-time positions. Only 4 percent of history majors are involuntarily unemployed. Most of those who are jobless do not work because they have taken early retirement, they need to devote most of their time to family responsibilities, or they simply have no need or desire for a job.

Occupations

More than 18 percent of employed persons with only a bachelor's degree in history work in various sales and marketing jobs, of which the largest share are concerned with insurance, securities, and real estate. Less than 7 percent work in various administrative occupations. Almost 5 percent work in accounting and financial occupations.

Male graduates outnumber females by 65 percent to 35 percent. Men with an undergraduate degree in history are much more likely than women to opt for sales-related jobs in insurance, real estate, and securities. They are also somewhat more likely than women to work in other marketing and sales jobs. Women are somewhat more likely than men to choose administrative jobs. The odds for either sex to work in accounting are virtually the same.

Table 2
Percentage Distribution of Employed Persons with Only a Bachelor's Degree in History, by the Relationship Between Their Job and College Major

Relationship of Job to Major	Percent
Closely related	22.0
Somewhat related	17.4
Not related	60.6

Percent who report the following as the most important reasons for working in a job that was not related to major:

Pay, promotion opportunities	33.0
Change in career or professional interests	21.2
Family-related reasons	11.4
Job in highest degree field not available	10.6
Working conditions (hours, equipment, environment)	9.5

Work Activities

▶ Half of grads regularly engage in sales, purchasing, and marketing tasks, and these are the primary responsibilities of more than one-fifth of grads.

▶ More than 6 out of 10 grads have managerial and supervisory duties as a major component of their employment. For 18 percent, this is their main work role.

▶ Accounting, contracting, and finance duties are a part of the job duties of 37 percent of history majors. They are the primary focus of 6 percent of grads.

▶ Ninety-one percent of employed history majors with a bachelor's degree are

Table 3
Top 5 Occupations Employing Persons with Only a Bachelor's Degree in History, by Percentage

Top 5 Occupations	All	Men	Women
Sales/Marketing—Insurance, Securities, Real Estate, and Business Services	7.2	8.3	4.8
Other Administrative Occupations	6.6	6.0	7.9
Other Marketing and Sales Occupations	5.6	6.1	4.5
Sales Occupations—Retail	5.5	5.7	5.0
Accountants, Auditors, and Other Financial Specialists	4.9	4.9	4.8
Total, Top 5 Occupations	29.8	31.0	27.0
Balance of Employed	70.2	69.0	73.0
All Employed	100.0	100.0	100.0

- involved in the development or use of computer applications on the job, but only 4 percent see this as their chief work function.

- Teaching is a significant duty for 3 out of 10 history bachelor's degree holders. Fourteen percent say that teaching is how they spend most of their time.

Workplace Training and Other Work-Related Experiences

Graduates of history programs participate in work-related workshops and seminars slightly less often than majors in other fields, so informal on-the-job learning is an even more important method of skills acquisition for majors in this field. Over the course of a year, about 58 percent of employed history program graduates participate in some type of training activity, compared to 61 percent for graduates of all majors.

- Of those history graduates who receive some training, 51 percent receive technical training in the occupation in which they are employed.

- Twenty percent receive training to improve their general professional skills, such as public speaking and business writing.

- Seventeen percent of the training recipients are given managerial or supervisory training.

When asked to identify the most important reason to acquire training, 27 percent of history majors who undergo training identify the need to improve their occupational skills and knowledge. Eleven percent consider the need to obtain a professional license or certificate as the main factor in influencing their decision to undergo work-related training. The same share report mandatory training requirements by the employer as the most important factor for their involvement in work-related training.

Salaries

The median annual salary of history graduates with only a bachelor's degree is $48,000, a level that is 7 percent lower than the median annual salary of all employed college graduates. On average, employed history graduates work for 45 hours per week and for 49 weeks per year, resulting in 2,205 hours of employment per year. The level of work effort among history graduates is 3 percent higher than the average among all college graduates (43 hours per week and 50 weeks per year, resulting in 2,150 hours per year).

History majors with jobs that are closely related to their undergraduate field earn somewhat less than those who are employed in unrelated jobs—$43,300 per year, compared to $48,500. But the highest annual earnings are made by those grads in jobs somewhat related to their major: $65,000.

History majors who work for private, for-profit firms earn an average of $60,900, and self-employed history majors who run their own businesses earn an average of $55,800 per year. In contrast, majors employed by educational organizations earn on average only $39,000 per year. In government, they average $46,300 per year, and in the nonprofit sector the average is $40,200.

The highest salaries for graduates of history programs go to those who work in insurance, securities, and real estate sales positions: an average of $87,700 per year. Those in miscellaneous sales occupations earn substantially less; those in retail sales, still less.

The earnings of those who go into accounting and other financial occupations are substantially higher than the earnings of grads from other majors.

FIGURE 1

Age/Earnings Profile of Persons with Only a Bachelor's Degree in History (Full-Time Workers, in 2010 Dollars)

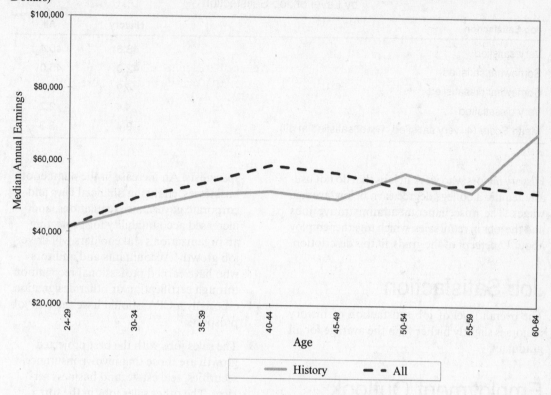

Table 4

Annual Salary of Workers with Only a Bachelor's Degree, Top 5 Occupations (in 2010 Dollars)

Earnings in Top 5 Occupations	All	History
Total	$48,000	$59,200
Sales/Marketing—Insurance, Securities, Real Estate, and Business Services	$67,100	$87,700
Other Administrative Occupations	$38,200	$36,100
Other Marketing and Sales Occupations	$54,700	$59,900
Sales Occupations—Retail	$42,300	$32,000
Accountants, Auditors, and Other Financial Specialists	$59,900	$77,400

Table 5
Percentage Distribution of Workers with Only a Bachelor's Degree, by Level of Job Satisfaction

Job Satisfaction	History	All
Very satisfied	48.6	45.4
Somewhat satisfied	42.0	45.0
Somewhat dissatisfied	7.9	7.4
Very dissatisfied	1.4	2.2
Mean Score (4=very satisfied, 1=not satisfied at all)	3.4	3.3

History majors who work in jobs that do not usually require a college degree earn below-average wages. The miscellaneous administrative jobs and the jobs in retail sales, which together employ about 12 percent of the grads, fit this description.

Job Satisfaction

The overall level of job satisfaction of history majors is slightly higher than the average for all graduates.

Employment Outlook

According to the projections by the U.S. Bureau of Labor Statistics, employment in occupations that require a bachelor's degree is expected to grow faster than employment in other sectors of the American labor market. Between 2008 and 2018, the U.S. workforce is projected to grow by 10.1 percent, creating an average of 15.2 million job openings per year. The bachelor's-level jobs are expected to increase by 17.7 percent over the same time.

The outlook for the top 5 occupations that employ history grads is mixed.

▶ Only one of these top 5 occupations is expected to grow as rapidly as the average of all bachelor's-level jobs: Almost 19 percent growth is projected for employment of accountants and financial specialists. An increase in the number of businesses, changing financial laws and corporate governance regulations, and increased accountability for protecting an organization's stakeholders will drive job growth. Accountants and auditors who have earned professional recognition through certification or other designation, especially a CPA, should have the best job prospects.

▶ The sales jobs with the best projected growth are those that involve insurance, securities, real estate, and business services. The other sales jobs in the top 5 will grow more slowly, but they will create many job openings each year because of their large workforce sizes.

Pathways Beyond the Bachelor's Degree

About one-half of all history majors continue their education beyond the bachelor's degree level and earn an advanced degree. About 28 percent of those with a bachelor's degree complete a master's degree program, and approximately 4 percent earn a doctorate. History is an important educational pathway to the study of law; about 1 out of 8 history majors eventually earn a law degree.

Table 6
Projected Growth and Job Openings in the Top 5 Occupations
Employing Persons with Only a Bachelor's Degree in History

Top 5 Occupations	Projected Growth 2008–2018	Projected Annual Job Openings
All top 5	11.0%	681,180
Sales/Marketing—Insurance, Securities, Real Estate, and Business Services	11.5%	115,210
Other Administrative Occupations	10.8%	166,130
Other Marketing and Sales Occupations	7.3%	64,880
Sales Occupations—Retail	7.5%	207,700
Accountants, Auditors, and Other Financial Specialists	18.9%	127,260

▶ Most history majors who go on to earn a master's degree do not continue their studies in history. Only 14 percent of master's degrees earned by those with a bachelor's degree in history are in history. About 17 percent of all master's degrees earned by history grads are in education, and about 16 percent are in a business subject. Library science is another popular major, pursued by 5 percent of grads who get a master's.

▶ Among history majors who earn a doctorate, about 37 percent are in some type of history specialty. An additional 10 percent earn their degree in educational administration.

CHAPTER 41

Journalism

Journalists gather information and prepare stories that inform the public about local, state, national, and international events. Journalists present points of view on current events, reporting about politics and politicians; businesses and other organizations; and celebrities such as movie, musical, and sports figures. Areas highlighted are foreign affairs, consumer affairs, health, sports, theater, commerce, social events, religion, and science.

Journalists gather information by researching documents, observing, and talking with and interviewing people. Later they organize the material, establish a focus, and write their stories. Reporters take notes and may take photographs or videos. Newswriters write the stories submitted by the reporter. Live stories are reported by radio and TV reporters and through Web-based media. News correspondents operate in large U.S. and foreign cities to report news and interest pieces there. Beginners usually start at small publications, where they cover all the following: take photographs, write headliners, lay out pages (or webpages), edit wire service copy, write editorials, solicit advertisements, and perform general office work. Because most news outlets produce content on a regular schedule, journalists often work against a deadline.

Some journalists move to other communications jobs such as advertising and public relations if journalism proves too hectic or stressful or if the pay is insufficient. Some journalism grads bypass journalism careers entirely and start their careers in other communications roles. (Some communications jobs other than journalist are discussed in Chapter 35.)

About three-fourths of the courses in a typical curriculum are in liberal arts, and the rest are in journalism. Journalism courses include introduction to the mass media, basic reporting, copyediting, history of journalism, and press law and ethics. Broadcasting students take courses in producing newscasts and production. Newspaper- and magazine-oriented students specialize in news-editorial journalism. Liberal arts courses taken are English (especially writing courses), political science, economics, history, psychology, speech, and business. Foreign language and computer courses are key skill courses.

Abilities include writing, speaking, and using correct grammar. Journalists have interpersonal skills and are able to convince and influence others. They also exhibit leadership qualities and are recognized for getting things moving. Word-processing skills are a prerequisite, with computer graphics and desktop publishing skills growing in importance. Recall that most beginning journalists start with small publications, so news photography may be part of the job.

The primary interest of journalists is literary but usually not limited to only one of the arts. A person with artistic interests usually likes art, music, drama, literature, and entertainment. Analytical and research interests are also enjoyed by journalists. They like involvement with people. Journalists enjoy variety in their work because the content shifts daily with the news.

Journalists value doing many different tasks. They seek opportunities to use their imagination, develop new insights, and discover previously unknown information. Journalists enjoy working with their minds and take pride in their intellectual knowledge. Journalists see their work as important, and some achieve public recognition.

Where Do Journalism Majors Work?

A large proportion—56 percent—of journalism graduates work in the private, for-profit sector for businesses and corporations, but another one-fifth are self-employed in their own business or practice. The education sector and the private, nonprofit sector each employ about 8 percent of journalism graduates. The remaining 7 percent work for the government.

Journalism majors have a high likelihood of working in a job that is closely or somewhat related to their undergraduate major. About 4 out of 10 are employed in jobs that are closely related to their major, 26 percent work in jobs that are somewhat related to their major, and the remaining one-third are employed in unrelated jobs.

Of all journalism graduates under the age of 65, 84 percent are employed. Only 1 percent are officially unemployed; in other words, they are not employed and are actively seeking employment. The remaining 15 percent are out of the labor force; that is, they are not employed and are not seeking employment. Family responsibilities are cited as the reason for labor force withdrawal among 39 percent of this group of journalism graduates, and another 26 percent have voluntarily withdrawn from the labor force to take early retirement. Almost 19 percent say they do not want or need to work.

Occupations

Journalism majors are employed in a variety of occupations that prize good communications skills. One-third of them work in a group of

Table 1

Percentage Distribution of Employed Persons with Only a Bachelor's Degree, by Economic Sector, Size, and New Business Status of Employer

	Journalism	All
Economic Sector		
Private for-profit	56.0	47.3
Self-employed	20.1	18.5
Government/Military	7.1	11.0
Education	8.5	15.6
Nonprofit	8.3	7.5
Employer Size		
Small (Fewer than 100 employees)	37.8	35.5
Medium (100–999)	29.1	21.8
Large (1,000–24,999)	21.8	26.0
Very large (25,000 or more)	11.3	16.7
Percent working in new business established within past 5 years	6.4	7.6

Table 2
Percentage Distribution of Employed Persons with Only a Bachelor's Degree in Journalism, by the Relationship Between Their Job and College Major

Relationship of Job to Major	Percent
Closely related	40.5
Somewhat related	25.8
Not related	33.7

Percent who report the following as the most important reasons for working in a job that was not related to major:

Pay, promotion opportunities	29.1
Family-related reasons	15.6
Job in highest degree field not available	15.4
Change in career or professional interests	12.4
Working conditions (hours, equipment, environment)	10.7

creative occupations that includes broadcasters, editors, writers, and public relations specialists. Almost 1 out of 10 grads are involved in miscellaneous marketing and sales jobs. Miscellaneous managerial jobs and accounting jobs each recruit about 6 percent of journalism grads.

Slightly more women than men have a bachelor's in journalism as their highest degree. Similar percentages of each sex go into marketing and accounting, but men are more likely to opt for management and the creative occupations, and women are more likely to take administrative jobs.

Table 3
Top 5 Occupations Employing Persons with Only a Bachelor's Degree in Journalism, by Percentage

Top 5 Occupations	All	Men	Women
Artists, Broadcasters, Editors, Entertainers, Public Relations Specialists, and Writers	33.5	36.0	31.2
Other Marketing and Sales Occupations	9.6	9.4	9.8
Other Management-Related Occupations	5.8	7.4	4.3
Accountants, Auditors, and Other Financial Specialists	5.6	5.6	5.7
Other Administrative Occupations	5.4	1.9	8.5
Total, Top 5 Occupations	59.9	60.3	59.5
Balance of Employed	40.1	39.7	40.5
All Employed	100.0	100.0	100.0

Work Activities

- Close to 3 out of 10 employed journalism graduates spend most of their workweek performing sales, purchasing, and marketing duties. These are significant tasks for almost 6 out of 10.

- Eighteen percent spend most of their time during a typical workweek performing managerial and administrative duties. These are regular duties for 61 percent.

- Engagement in computer applications, programming, and systems-development activities is reported by 88 percent of all employed journalism graduates. However, only 5 percent spend most of their time on these activities.

- Although 37 percent of all employed journalism graduates perform accounting, finance, and contractual duties as a regular part of their jobs, only 6 percent spend most of their time in a typical workweek performing these duties.

- Another 37 percent regularly engage in employee-relations activities, including recruiting, personnel development, and training, but only 3 percent conduct these duties during most of their working time.

Workplace Training and Other Work-Related Experiences

The career potential of a job is closely associated with the amount of work-related training on the job. Firms that invest in their workforce are more likely to offer pay increases and promotions to match the increasing productivity of their workers. The rate of participation in work-related training during a year among employed journalism graduates (54 percent) is significantly lower than the training participation rate of all college graduates (61 percent).

- Of those journalism majors who receive some training, 42 percent receive technical training in their occupational field.

- Twenty-two percent receive training to improve their general professional skills, such as public speaking and business writing.

- Fifteen percent of the training recipients participate in management or supervisor training.

When asked to identify the most important reason to acquire training, 32 percent of journalism graduates who undergo training choose the need to improve their occupational skills and knowledge. Another 8 percent report a mandatory training requirement by the employer as the most important factor for their involvement in work-related training.

Salaries

The median annual salary of journalism graduates who have only a bachelor's degree and are employed full-time is $50,000, a level that is 3 percent lower than the median annual salary of all full-time employed college graduates. On average, employed journalism graduates work for 41 hours per week and for 50 weeks per year, resulting in 2,050 hours of employment per year. The level of work effort among journalism graduates is 5 percent lower than the average among all college graduates (43 hours per week and 50 weeks per year, resulting in 2,150 hours per year).

The average annual salary of journalism majors who work in jobs that are closely related to their major is higher than the average salary of their counterparts who work in jobs that are either somewhat or not related to their undergraduate major. The average annual salary of journalism majors in closely related jobs is $53,700; those employed in jobs that are somewhat related to

FIGURE 1

Age/Earnings Profile of Persons with Only a Bachelor's Degree in Journalism (Full-Time Workers, in 2010 Dollars)

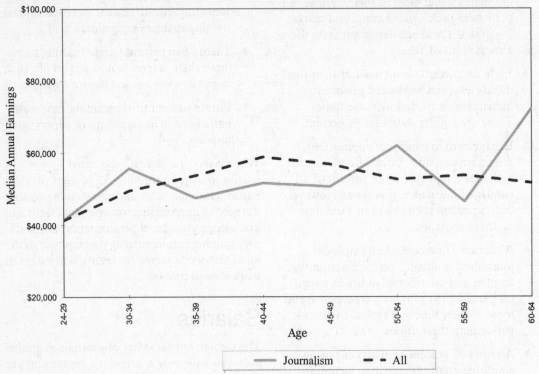

journalism earn $50,600, and employment in unrelated jobs yields an annual salary of only $46,400.

Journalism graduates who work in the private, for-profit sector for corporations and businesses earn an average salary of $53,700. Self-employed journalism graduates operating their own business earn an average annual salary of $53,700. The government sector pays an average annual salary of $49,300. The annual average remuneration of journalism graduates with full-time jobs in the private, nonprofit sector is $46,400, and journalism majors who are employed by educational institutions earn only $44,500 per year.

There are sizable variations in the average annual salary of journalism graduates working in different occupations. In 2 of the top 5 occupations that are predominant employers of journalism majors, the salary of all college graduates exceeds that of journalism majors.

The highest pay among the top 5 occupations is earned by those who work in a miscellaneous collection of management jobs. As broadcasters, writers, editors, and personnel in other entertainment occupations and as public relations specialists, journalism majors earn $10,000 less; so do those in miscellaneous marketing and sales occupations. Accountants and other financial specialists who are history grads average $46,400, which is considerably lower than the earnings of all college grads in those jobs. In administrative jobs, however, history majors outearn other college grads; still, the pay is the lowest among the top 5 jobs employing history grads.

Table 4
Annual Salary of Workers with Only a Bachelor's Degree, Top 5 Occupations (in 2010 Dollars)

Earnings in Top 5 Occupations	All	Journalism
Total	$50,000	$51,700
Artists, Broadcasters, Editors, Entertainers, Public Relations Specialists, and Writers	$49,500	$51,600
Other Marketing and Sales Occupations	$54,700	$51,600
Other Management-Related Occupations	$57,800	$61,900
Accountants, Auditors, and Other Financial Specialists	$59,900	$46,400
Other Administrative Occupations	$38,200	$45,400

Job Satisfaction

The overall level of job satisfaction of journalism majors is slightly lower than the average for all graduates.

Employment Outlook

According to the projections by the U.S. Bureau of Labor Statistics, employment in occupations that require a bachelor's degree is expected to grow faster than employment in other sectors of the American labor market. Between 2008 and 2018, the U.S. workforce is projected to grow by 10.1 percent, creating an average of 15.2 million job openings per year. The bachelor's-level jobs are expected to increase by 17.7 percent over the same time. The jobs that tend to employ journalism majors have mixed prospects.

▶ Among the top 5 occupations employing journalism grads, the best prospects are for accountants, auditors, and other financial specialists. An increase in the number of businesses, changing financial laws and corporate governance regulations, and increased accountability for protecting an organization's stakeholders will drive job growth. Accountants and auditors who have earned professional recognition through certification or other designation, especially a CPA, should have the best job prospects.

Table 5
Percentage Distribution of Workers with Only a Bachelor's Degree, by Level of Job Satisfaction

Job Satisfaction	Journalism	All
Very satisfied	42.3	45.4
Somewhat satisfied	44.4	45.0
Somewhat dissatisfied	9.2	7.4
Very dissatisfied	4.1	2.2
Mean Score (4=very satisfied, 1=not satisfied at all)	3.2	3.3

Table 6

Projected Growth and Job Openings in the Top 5 Occupations
Employing Persons with Only a Bachelor's Degree in Journalism

Top 5 Occupations	Projected Growth 2008–2018	Projected Annual Job Openings
All top 5	12.1%	483,030
Artists, Broadcasters, Editors, Entertainers, Public Relations Specialists, Writers	12.4%	71,740
Other Marketing and Sales Occupations	7.3%	64,880
Other Management-Related Occupations	7.2%	53,020
Accountants, Auditors, and Other Financial Specialists	18.9%	127,260
Other Administrative Occupations	10.8%	166,130

▶ The creative occupations that employ one-third of journalism grads are projected to grow at an above-average rate, but this is a very mixed group of jobs. Employment of broadcast news analysts is projected to grow by 4.1 percent, but the workforce of reporters and correspondents (a much larger occupation) is expected to shrink by 7.6 percent. Competition will be keen for jobs at large metropolitan and national newspapers, broadcast stations and networks, and magazines. Job opportunities will be best for applicants in the expanding world of new media, such as online newspapers or magazines. Employment of public relations specialists is projected to grow by 24.0 percent, but competition is expected to be keen for entry-level jobs, as the projected number of qualified applicants will exceed the number of job openings.

▶ The miscellaneous marketing and managerial jobs that employ many journalism majors are projected to have slower-than-average growth, but these are large occupations that will create many job openings through turnover.

▶ Job growth in the administrative occupations is projected to be about average, but job turnover should help in creating more than 166,000 openings each year.

Pathways Beyond the Bachelor's Degree

Twenty-two percent of journalism graduates with a bachelor's degree proceed to earn a postgraduate degree: 16 percent earn a master's degree, only 1 percent earn a doctorate, and 5 percent earn a professional degree.

▶ Twelve percent of the master's degrees are earned in journalism. About 16 percent earn a master's degree in a business subject. Education is the major field of choice among 11 percent of master's degree earners.

▶ Communications is the most popular major among the few grads who earn a doctorate.

▶ Most of the professional degrees earned by journalism majors are in the field of law.

CHAPTER 42

Legal Studies and Pre-Law

The education of most lawyers takes 7 years of full-time study after high school graduation. The typical pattern is to take 4 years of undergraduate study in a pre-law major and then 3 years in law school. While there is no recommended pre-law major, commonly taken courses are English, foreign language, public speaking or communications, government, philosophy, history, political science, economics, business, mathematics, and computer science. The purpose of these courses is to help a person communicate, define problems, collect information, establish facts, and draw valid conclusions. These skills are useful and are valued in many careers besides legal practice.

All lawyers, also called attorneys, interpret the law and apply it to specific situations. In the United States, attorneys act as both advocates and advisors. As advocates, they represent one of the opposing parties as either the prosecutor or the defense attorney in criminal or civil trials by presenting evidence that supports their position or client in court. As advisors, lawyers counsel their clients about their legal rights and obligations and suggest particular courses of action in business and personal matters.

The legal specialization determines the detailed aspects of a lawyer's job; the amount of time spent in court also depends on the specialization. In criminal law, defense attorneys represent individuals who have been charged with crimes, arguing their cases in law courts. Prosecutors work for various levels of federal or state government, upholding laws

against those who violate them. In civil law, lawyers assist clients with litigation, wills, trusts, contracts, mortgages, real estate titles, and property leases.

Many legal specializations exist, such as bankruptcy, probate, international and intellectual property, and copyright law. Some lawyers work on business activities for corporations (for example, developing contracts), others work in many capacities for the government, and still others function as attorneys general or district attorneys.

In the practice of law, an important skill is to influence the opinions and decisions of others. Lawyers need to win others' respect and confidence to convince them to take certain actions. Using the imagination and being able to demonstrate new ways to do or say something are helpful skills. The ability to search for and discover new facts and develop ways to apply them is required. The need to use computer software packages to research the legal literature is increasing. To reach conclusions, lawyers use perseverance and logical reasoning in their analysis of complex legal issues. During undergraduate education, a person develops skills in analytical thinking, communication and public speaking, and relationships (understanding and working with all kinds of people). Lawyers must be able to read and listen carefully to identify important details that could help a client win a case. Specialized courses require judgment in knowing how to conduct a case or deal with a problem in different areas of law. Contracts, real estate, probate, and tax work require additional numerical skills and the ability to think with numbers to reach solutions.

Lawyers like to be involved in business and organizational pursuits. Being verbally persuasive, they like having the opportunity to lead. Lawyers have concerns about the well-being of others. They have a breadth of interests.

Practicing lawyers value work that requires a high level of mental activity. They enjoy doing many tasks that offer diversion, doing something of perceived importance, and succeeding at something they view as difficult. They also enjoy being paid well for their efforts.

Note: Many people who earn a bachelor's in this field intend to earn a professional degree subsequently. Therefore, the figures presented in this chapter are based on *all* graduates with this bachelor's degree, not just those for whom it is the highest degree. In this way, this chapter differs from most other chapters.

Where Do Legal Studies and Pre-Law Majors Work?

A large share of employed legal studies/pre-law graduates with only a bachelor's degree—45 percent—work in private, for-profit businesses and corporations. Nineteen percent are self-employed in their own for-profit businesses. Another 21 percent work for the government. Less than 8 percent are employed by educational institutions, and only 6 percent by nonprofit organizations.

Forty-five percent of legal studies/pre-law graduates work in jobs that are closely related to their major. Another 22 percent report working in jobs that are somewhat related to their major. The remaining graduates, one-third, work in jobs that are unrelated to their major.

About 83 percent of legal studies/pre-law graduates who are under the age of 65 are employed.

Table 1

Percentage Distribution of Employed Persons with at Least a Bachelor's Degree, by Economic Sector, Size, and New Business Status of Employer

	Legal Studies and Pre-Law	All
Economic Sector		
Private for-profit	44.9	47.3
Self-employed	19.4	18.5
Government/Military	21.4	11.0
Education	7.7	15.6
Nonprofit	6.0	7.5
Employer Size		
Small (Fewer than 100 employees)	28.8	28.5
Medium (100–999)	17.3	22.4
Large (1,000–24,999)	32.3	29.6
Very large (25,000 or more)	21.6	19.5
Percent working in new business established within past 5 years	8.4	5.6

Table 2

Percentage Distribution of Employed Persons with at Least a Bachelor's Degree in Legal Studies and Pre-Law, by the Relationship Between Their Job and College Major

Relationship of Job to Major	Percent
Closely related	44.9
Somewhat related	22.0
Not related	33.1

Percent who report the following as the most important reasons for working in a job that was not related to major:

Change in career or professional interests	28.8
Family-related reasons	19.6
Job in highest degree field not available	19.0
Pay, promotion opportunities	18.9
Job location	7.8

About 5 percent are not employed but are seeking employment, and the remaining 12 percent are neither working nor looking for work. One-quarter of the latter group have chosen to withdraw from the labor force to take early retirement, and another 18 percent have no need or desire to work. Fourteen percent of those out of the labor market say that work in their field is not available, and 13 percent are staying home to take care of family responsibilities.

Occupations

Legal studies/pre-law graduates work in a variety of occupations. The breadth of their undergraduate course work is reflected in the variety of occupations in which they are employed. Only one-fifth are working as lawyers or judges. Nearly an equal share are employed in miscellaneous administrative or managerial occupations. Many of the 7 percent who work in protective services probably majored in a curriculum that was closer to law enforcement than pre-law.

Male grads outnumber female grads by about 3 to 2. Female enrollment in law schools has declined steadily since 2002, when the sexes had almost equal enrollments. Women made up 47.2 percent of the 2009–2010 law school class. The two sexes are equally likely to have chosen a career as lawyers, but because fewer females emerged from law school in the past, women now make up about 32 percent of lawyers. Legal studies/pre-law graduates differ greatly in their odds of pursuing many other career paths.

Work Activities

▶ Professional services, such as giving legal advice, are a significant duty for more than half of grads and the primary work function of one-third.

▶ Managerial and administrative duties are regularly performed by more than 65 percent of graduates and are the chief responsibility of 11 percent.

Table 3
Top 5 Occupations Employing Persons with at Least a Bachelor's Degree
in Legal Studies and Pre-Law, by Percentage

Top 5 Occupations	All	Men	Women
Lawyers and Judges	21.0	21.2	20.8
Other Administrative Occupations	11.8	8.6	16.7
Other Management-Related Occupations	8.0	12.0	2.0
Protective Service Workers	6.8	11.3	–
Teachers—Elementary School	4.2	4.7	3.6
Total, Top 5 Occupations	51.8	57.7	43.0
Balance of Employed	48.2	42.3	57.0
All Employed	100.0	100.0	100.0

▶ More than 57 percent spend significant work time on accounting, finance, and contractual duties; for 5 percent, these are their main job focus.

▶ About 57 percent of graduates are regularly engaged in an assortment of computer applications, including programming and information processing. Only 4 percent are mainly assigned to this work function.

▶ Slightly more than half report that their daily job duties include employee-relations and personnel matters. A similar share is regularly involved in sales, purchasing, and marketing activities.

▶ About one-quarter of all legal studies/pre-law graduates regularly engage in product development activities, teaching, or applied research.

Workplace Training and Other Work-Related Experiences

Work-related training is an important indicator of long-term career potential in a job. Firms that invest in their workers at high rates are much more likely to offer pay increases and promotions than firms that do not invest in their workers. The rate of participation in work-related training during a year among employed legal studies and pre-law graduates (55 percent) is significantly lower than the training participation rate of all college graduates (61 percent).

▶ Half of legal studies/pre-law graduates who receive some training are engaged in technical training in their occupation.

▶ One-fifth receive general professional training to improve their communication skills in public speaking and general writing.

▶ One-fifth receive training to sharpen their managerial and supervisory skills.

When asked for the main reason they attend training activity, 3 out of 10 who engage in a work-related training activity say that it is to increase their occupational skills and knowledge. Ten percent say they need to get training to obtain or maintain licensure or certification.

Salaries

The median annual salary of legal studies and pre-law graduates with at least a bachelor's degree is $56,800, a level that is 9 percent higher than the median annual salary of all employed college graduates with at least a bachelor's de-

gree. On average, employed legal studies and pre-law graduates work for 40 hours per week and for 52 weeks per year, resulting in 2,080 hours of employment per year. The level of work effort among legal studies and pre-law graduates is 3 percent lower than the average among all college graduates (43 hours per week and 50 weeks per year, resulting in 2,150 hours per year).

Legal studies/pre-law graduates who are employed in full-time jobs that are closely related to their major earn much more than those who are employed in jobs unrelated to their undergraduate major—$61,900 per year, compared to $41,300. Graduates with employment in jobs that are somewhat related to their major average $50,000 per year.

<u>**FIGURE 1**</u>

Age/Earnings Profile of Persons with at Least a Bachelor's Degree in Legal Studies and Pre-Law (Full-Time Workers, in 2010 Dollars)

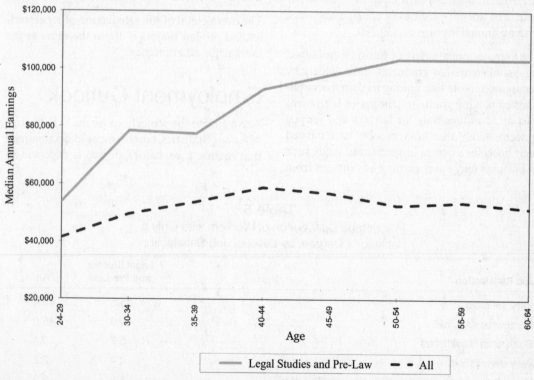

Table 4
Annual Salary of Workers with at Least a Bachelor's Degree, Top 5 Occupations (in 2010 Dollars)

Earnings in Top 5 Occupations	All	Legal Studies and Pre-Law
Total	$49,500	$87,100
Lawyers and Judges	$88,700	$82,600
Other Administrative Occupations	$35,100	$39,200
Other Management-Related Occupations	$55,700	$59,900
Protective Service Workers	$47,500	$59,000
Teachers—Elementary School	$36,100	$45,400

Graduates who are self-employed, operating their own incorporated or nonincorporated business, earn an annual average salary of $76,200, which is higher than the annual average salary of legal studies/pre-law graduates employed in other sectors. Those working at for-profit businesses or government agencies earn close to $52,000 per year. The not-for-profit pays considerably less, with an annual average of $39,200.

The average annual salary of full-time employed legal studies/pre-law graduates varies widely by occupation. Note that among the top 5 occupations employing graduates, the major is an earnings disadvantage only for lawyers and judges. It seems likely that lawyers who have earned their bachelor's degree in specialized fields such as business may enjoy earning advantages from their specialized skills. (About 15 percent of lawyers and judges earned their bachelor's degree in a business subject, compared to only 10 percent whose bachelor's was in legal studies/pre-law.)

Job Satisfaction

The overall level of job satisfaction of legal studies and pre-law majors is about the same as the average for all graduates.

Employment Outlook

According to the projections by the U.S. Bureau of Labor Statistics, employment in occupations that require a bachelor's degree is expected to

Table 5
Percentage Distribution of Workers with Only a Bachelor's Degree, by Level of Job Satisfaction

Job Satisfaction	Legal Studies and Pre-Law	All
Very satisfied	35.6	45.4
Somewhat satisfied	37.6	45.0
Somewhat dissatisfied	5.7	7.4
Very dissatisfied	1.4	2.2
Mean Score (4=very satisfied, 1=not satisfied at all)	3.3	3.3

grow faster than employment in other sectors of the American labor market. Between 2008 and 2018, the U.S. workforce is projected to grow by 10.1 percent, creating an average of 15.2 million job openings per year. The bachelor's-level jobs are expected to increase by 17.7 percent over the same time.

▶ Employment of lawyers and judges is expected to grow by 12.4 percent during the 2008–2018 decade. Growth in the population and in the level of business activity is expected to create more legal transactions, civil disputes, and criminal cases. Job growth among lawyers also will result from increasing demand for legal services. In addition, the wider availability and affordability of legal clinics should result in increased use of legal services by middle-income people. However, growth in demand for lawyers will be constrained as businesses increasingly use large accounting firms and paralegals to perform some of the same functions that lawyers do. Competition for job openings should continue to be keen because of the large number of students graduating from law school each year. Judges and magistrates are expected to encounter competition for jobs because of the prestige associated with serving on the bench.

▶ The fastest employment growth rate of the 5 predominant employers of legal studies/pre-law graduates is among elementary school teachers. The number of teachers employed is dependent on state and local expenditures for education and on the enactment of legislation to increase the quality and scope of public education. Job prospects should be better in inner cities and rural areas than in suburban districts.

▶ Protective service occupations, which are chosen mainly by male legal studies/pre-law graduates, are expected to grow by 14.1 percent and create 74,000 job openings each year. The level of government spending determines the level of employment in this field. Job opportunities in most local police departments will be favorable for qualified individuals, whereas competition is expected for jobs in state and federal agencies. Prospective firefighters are expected to face keen competition for available job openings.

▶ Employment in administrative occupations is expected to grow faster than average and also create many job openings, largely because of the large workforce of administrative jobs, where much turnover will occur.

Table 6

Projected Growth and Job Openings in the Top 5 Occupations
Employing Persons with a Degree in Legal Studies and Pre-Law

Top 5 Occupations	Projected Growth 2008–2018	Projected Annual Job Openings
All top 5	11.6%	378,340
Lawyers and Judges	12.4%	25,240
Other Administrative Occupations	10.8%	166,130
Other Management-Related Occupations	7.2%	53,020
Protective Service Workers	14.1%	74,300
Teachers—Elementary School	15.8%	59,650

Pathways Beyond the Bachelor's Degree

One-fifth of all legal studies/pre-law graduates with a bachelor's degree proceed to earn a professional degree. Another 16 percent earn a master's degree, and 2 percent go on to earn a doctoral degree.

▶ Of all the pre-law/legal graduates who earn a professional degree, 98 percent choose law as their major.

▶ Among those who earn a master's degree, 28 percent study law, 18 percent study business administration, and 13 percent study elementary teacher education.

CHAPTER 43

Liberal Arts and General Studies

For many people this major is what education in general should be: training the individual to have an analytical mind, to be a critical thinker, to communicate orally and in writing, and to be an educated person characterized by breadth of knowledge. Today the support of a liberal arts education is a reaction to college having become vocational training in some people's minds. A liberal arts education upholds the belief in the tradition of obtaining a broad base of knowledge that allows students to develop proficiency in basic skills; to be exposed to methods of inquiry in the various subjects and disciplines in the arts and humanities, social sciences, natural sciences, and mathematics; and to become acquainted with the ideas of Western culture, with the differing views of non-Western cultures, and with the major issues and problems facing contemporary society. Many companies and professional schools, including medicine, value the benefits and problem-solving skills nurtured by a liberal arts tradition—provided a student has taken the prerequisite courses necessary for achieving the particular professional outcome. Some colleges and universities honor this tradition by requiring a core liberal arts curriculum or a general studies component within their programs.

The following is a sample liberal arts curriculum with some illustrative courses. Each student has considerable freedom to choose from among these academic fields.

▌ Basic Skills: English; Mathematics; Foreign Language Proficiency

▌ Methods of Inquiry: Introduction to Science; Introduction to Art; Women's Studies—Images, Myths, and Reality; Culture of the World; Fiction; Drama; Geology of Oceans and Coasts; Principles of Microeconomics

▌ The Western Cultural Heritage: African American History; European Economic Development; Music as Self-Expression; Understanding the Bible

▌ Alternative Cultures and Societies: Rural Workers in the Third World; American Urban History; Eastern Religions; Contemporary Japanese Culture and Society; Economic Issues in Minority Communities; Modern African Civilization

▌ Theoretical Perspectives and Changes: Ethics—East and West; Sociology of the Family; Film Theory; Economics of Developing Nations

▌ Current Issues in Perspective: Philosophical Problems of Law and Justice; Gender Politics; Computers and Society; Science, Technology, and Public Policy; Contemporary Revolutionary Politics; Crisis and Conflict in Black Africa; Water Planning for the Future

The values, interests, and abilities required in a liberal arts education involve exposure to a breadth of knowledge, intellectual stimulation, and the desire to communicate about an inquiry. Individual characteristics follow these personal goals. In addition, it is understood that the student is willing to postpone developing concrete and practical skills for a specific field of concentration. Many liberal arts grads intend to acquire career-focused skills later by means of graduate school, professional school, or on-the-job training.

Where Do Liberal Arts and General Studies Majors Work?

The breadth of the educational experiences of liberal arts/general studies graduates is reflected in the diversity of their employment. Less than one-half of the graduates work for businesses and corporations in the private, for-profit sec-tor, and one-fifth are self-employed in their own business or practice. Almost one-fifth work in the education sector, and 1 out of 10 work in the government sector.

Given the diversity of the educational experiences of these graduates, it naturally follows that most liberal arts/general studies graduates do not work in jobs that are closely related to their undergraduate major. In fact, only 27 percent do so, and another 27 percent work in jobs that are somewhat related to their field. The remaining 45 percent work in jobs that are not at all related to their undergraduate major.

Of all liberal arts/general studies graduates under the age of 65, 77 percent are employed—a low percentage compared to most other majors. A bit more than 4 percent are officially unemployed; in other words, they are not employed and are actively seeking employment. The remaining 18 percent are out of the labor force; that is, they are not employed and are not seeking employment. Of these, equal shares of 28 percent have

Table 1

Percentage Distribution of Employed Persons with Only a Bachelor's Degree, by Economic Sector, Size, and New Business Status of Employer

	Liberal Arts and General Studies	All
Economic Sector		
Private for-profit	42.4	47.3
Self-employed	21.2	18.5
Government/Military	9.6	11.0
Education	18.8	15.6
Nonprofit	7.9	7.5
Employer Size		
Small (Fewer than 100 employees)	39.7	35.5
Medium (100–999)	18.1	21.8
Large (1,000–24,999)	29.2	26.0
Very large (25,000 or more)	13.0	16.7
Percent working in new business established within past 5 years	5.8	7.6

Table 2
Percentage Distribution of Employed Persons with Only a Bachelor's Degree in Liberal Arts and General Studies, by the Relationship Between Their Job and College Major

Relationship of Job to Major	Percent
Closely related	27.1
Somewhat related	27.4
Not related	45.5

Percent who report the following as the most important reasons for working in a job that was not related to major:

Pay, promotion opportunities	37.2
Working conditions (hours, equipment, environment)	16.9
Family-related reasons	12.5
Job in highest degree field not available	11.5
Change in career or professional interests	11.2

taken early retirement or are attending to family responsibilities. Nearly one-quarter say they have no need or desire to work.

Occupations

The education of graduates who major in liberal arts/general studies does not prepare them for any particular profession or vocation. Rather, this education provides exposure to the subject matter of a broad array of disciplines and provides a foundation of critical thinking and problem-solving skills on which the graduates can proceed to build the practical skills needed in specific fields. Consequently, graduates are employed in diverse occupations. The top 5 occupations employing liberal arts graduates account for only one-third of the grads.

The top 5 include occupations in administration, management, sales, marketing, teaching, and accounting. Slightly more women than men earn this degree, and their employment experiences are quite different, as Table 3 shows.

Work Activities

▶ Twenty-three percent of grads spend most of their time at work on sales, purchasing, marketing activities. About twice that share are primarily focused on these duties.

▶ Teaching is the chief responsibility of 14 percent of the grads, and more than one-quarter spend significant work time instructing.

▶ Thirteen percent of employed liberal arts/general studies graduates spend most of their time at work providing professional services, such as counseling, legal services, and health services. One-quarter of the grads devote at least 10 hours per week to these duties.

▶ Almost half of the grads regularly handle management and administrative duties, but only 12 percent of them consider these their main work role.

Table 3
Top 5 Occupations Employing Persons with Only a Bachelor's Degree in Liberal Arts and General Studies, by Percentage

Top 5 Occupations	All	Men	Women
Other Administrative Occupations	7.9	6.1	9.7
Other Marketing and Sales Occupations	7.1	7.9	6.4
Sales/Marketing—Insurance, Securities, Real Estate, and Business Services	6.5	10.3	2.9
Teachers—Elementary School	6.3	1.6	10.7
Accountants, Auditors, and Other Financial Specialists	5.0	7.3	2.9
Total, Top 5 Occupations	32.8	33.2	32.6
Balance of Employed	67.2	66.8	67.4
All Employed	100.0	100.0	100.0

▶ Nine percent of the graduates consider accounting, finance, and contractual duties to consume most of their time at work, and one-third spend significant time at these tasks.

▶ Six percent of employed liberal arts/general studies graduates spend most of their time at work using computer applications, programming, and doing systems-development tasks; 86 percent do these tasks regularly.

Workplace Training and Other Work-Related Experiences

The career potential of a job is closely associated with the amount of work-related training on the job. Firms that invest in their workforce are more likely to offer pay increases and promotions to match the increasing productivity of their workers. The rate of participation in work-related training during a year among employed liberal arts and general studies graduates (56 percent) is significantly lower than the training participation rate of all college graduates (61 percent).

▶ Of those liberal arts graduates who receive some training, 49 percent receive technical training in the occupation in which they are employed.

▶ Eleven percent of the training recipients receive management or supervisor training.

▶ Nineteen percent are given training to improve their general professional skills, such as public speaking and business writing.

When asked to identify the most important reason to acquire training, one-quarter of liberal arts/general studies majors who undergo training identify the need to improve their occupational skills and knowledge. According to 11 percent, the most important factor is to obtain a professional license or certificate. (Many of these may be teachers, who often participate in in-service training as a way of maintaining their licensure.) Another 8 percent report a mandatory training requirement by the employer as the most important factor for involvement in work-related training.

Salaries

The median annual salary of liberal arts and general studies graduates with only a bachelor's degree is $45,000, a level that is 15 percent lower than the median annual salary of all employed college graduates. On average, employed liberal arts and general studies graduates work for 40 hours per week and for 49 weeks per year, resulting in 1,960 hours of employment per year. The level of work effort among liberal arts and general studies graduates is 9 percent lower than the average among all college graduates (43 hours per week and 50 weeks per year, resulting in 2,150 hours per year). The lower level of work engagement partly explains the lower earnings of these grads.

The annual average salary of liberal arts/general studies graduates is affected by whether their jobs are related to their undergraduate major. Jobs that are closely related or somewhat related pay the same average annual salary, $51,600. However, in jobs that are unrelated to their undergraduate major, the average earnings are $40,200. Although liberal arts graduates do not learn profession- or vocation-specific job skills in the classroom, there clearly is an economically significant relationship between their schooling and their earnings on the job.

Self-employed liberal arts/general studies graduates earn a higher average salary than graduates working in other sectors. The annual average salary of self-employed liberal arts/general studies majors who work full-time in their business or practice is $58,800. Those who work for businesses

<u>FIGURE 1</u>

Age/Earnings Profile of Persons with Only a Bachelor's Degree in Liberal Arts and General Studies (Full-Time Workers, in 2010 Dollars)

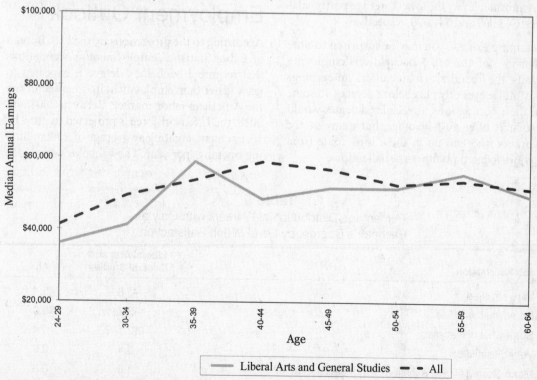

Table 4
Annual Salary of Workers with Only a Bachelor's Degree,
Top 5 Occupations (in 2010 Dollars)

Earnings in Top 5 Occupations	All	Liberal Arts and General Studies
Total	$45,000	$56,400
Other Administrative Occupations	$38,200	$32,000
Other Marketing and Sales Occupations	$54,700	$67,100
Sales/Marketing—Insurance, Securities, Real Estate, and Business Services	$67,100	$82,600
Teachers—Elementary School	$37,200	$47,500
Accountants, Auditors, and Other Financial Specialists	$59,900	$51,600

or corporations in the private, for-profit sector earn an annual average salary of $51,600. Educational institutions pay an annual average salary of $44,500 to liberal arts/general studies graduates who work full-time. The two sectors employing the fewest of these grads, government and nonprofit organizations, pay the lowest average yearly salaries: $43,000 and $41,300, respectively.

Scanning Table 4, you may be surprised to note that in 3 of the top 5 occupations employing grads, the liberal arts major offers an earnings advantage over other bachelor's degrees. In some of these occupations, a specialized degree would probably offer an advantage, but many of the workers who end up in these jobs come from majors focused on other specializations.

Job Satisfaction

The overall level of job satisfaction of liberal arts and general studies majors is about the same as the average for all graduates.

Employment Outlook

According to the projections by the U.S. Bureau of Labor Statistics, employment in occupations that require a bachelor's degree is expected to grow faster than employment in other sectors of the American labor market. Between 2008 and 2018, the U.S. workforce is projected to grow by 10.1 percent, creating an average of 15.2 million job openings per year. The bachelor's-level jobs

Table 5
Percentage Distribution of Workers with Only a
Bachelor's Degree, by Level of Job Satisfaction

Job Satisfaction	Liberal Arts and General Studies	All
Very satisfied	41.8	45.4
Somewhat satisfied	42.7	45.0
Somewhat dissatisfied	12.1	7.4
Very dissatisfied	3.4	2.2
Mean Score (4=very satisfied, 1=not satisfied at all)	3.3	3.3

are expected to increase by 17.7 percent over the same time.

Most of the top jobs employing liberal arts grads are growing at a rate faster than the average for all occupations. They also have very large workforces and therefore will create numerous job openings through turnover.

▶ Job growth in the miscellaneous administrative occupations that employ communications grads will be close to the average for all occupations. The large workforce of these mostly clerical occupations will create more than 166,000 job openings, largely through turnover.

▶ The outlook for sales and marketing occupations depends on the nature of the products and services being sold or marketed. Prospects are better for those who work with insurance, securities, real estate, and business services.

▶ Employment of elementary school teachers is projected to grow by 15.8 percent. This occupation employs mostly female liberal arts/general studies graduates. The number of teachers employed is dependent on state and local expenditures for education and on the enactment of legislation to increase the quality and scope of public education. Job prospects should be better in inner cities and rural areas than in suburban districts.

▶ Accounting and financial occupations are projected to grow at above-average rates. An increase in the number of businesses, changing financial laws and corporate governance regulations, and increased accountability for protecting an organization's stakeholders will drive job growth. Accountants and auditors who have earned professional recognition through certification or other designation, especially a CPA, should have the best job prospects.

Pathways Beyond the Bachelor's Degree

Of those liberal arts/general studies graduates with a bachelor's degree, 39 percent proceed to earn a postgraduate degree: 26 percent earn a master's degree, 4 percent graduate with a doctorate, and another 9 percent earn a professional degree.

Table 6

Projected Growth and Job Openings in the Top 5 Occupations Employing Persons with Only a Bachelor's Degree in Liberal Arts and General Studies

Top 5 Occupations	Projected Growth 2008–2018	Projected Annual Job Openings
All top 5	12.9%	533,130
Other Administrative Occupations	10.8%	166,130
Other Marketing and Sales Occupations	7.3%	64,880
Sales/Marketing—Insurance, Securities, Real Estate, and Business Services	11.5%	115,210
Teachers—Elementary School	15.8%	59,650
Accountants, Auditors, and Other Financial Specialists	18.9%	127,260

- The master's degrees are dispersed across many different major fields. Nine percent earn a master's degree in business management and administrative services. About the same share choose elementary education as the major for their master's degree.

- Of those earning a doctorate, one-fifth study philosophy, religion, or theology. Nine percent study architecture.

- More than half of the professional degrees are earned in law, and one-fifth are earned in the health professions.

CHAPTER 44

Music and Dance

Many people are interested in music and dance for recreational purposes. As a source of employment, however, these fields are very competitive. Musicians play musical instruments, sing, compose, arrange, or conduct groups in instrumental or vocal performances. Dancers perform modern ballet or folk, ethnic, tap, and jazz dances. Many people get involved in music-related occupations, such as music therapists; songwriters; music teachers; booking agents; music store workers; disc jockeys; and, for some with technical knowledge, sound and audio technicians and instrument repairers. Because of the strenuous physical requirements, dancers leave the field at an early age; some become choreographers or dance teachers.

Specialization is common among musicians, such as playing in a band, a rock group, or a jazz group. They typically focus on such specific instruments as string, brass, woodwind, percussion, piano, or electronic synthesizers. Some musicians learn related instruments, such as trombone and trumpet. Singers are classified by the type of music they sing—such as rock, reggae, folk, rap, country and western, or opera—or by their voice range, such as soprano, contralto, tenor, baritone, or bass.

Composers create original music, from popular songs to symphonies and operas. They transcribe their ideas into musical notation using harmony, rhythm, melody, and tonal structure. Use of computers to compose and edit music has become common. Arrangers transcribe and adapt musical compositions to a particular style for bands, choral groups, or individuals. Conductors lead musical groups. They audition and select musicians, choose the music that complements their talents, and direct rehearsals to achieve the desired sound.

Dancers express ideas, stories, rhythm, and sound with their bodies. Most perform as a group. Many dancers sing and act as well as dance; for example, they may work in opera, musicals, television, music videos, and commercials.

Most collegiate dance programs offer courses in ballet and classical techniques, dance composition, dance history, and movement analysis. Dancing and music require instruction, and practice generally begins at an early age. Formal course work includes musical theory, music interpretation, and composition. College programs in music usually require some ability to read and play music on piano, no matter what the instrument specialization is.

Finger and motor coordination are necessary for playing instruments, as well as the ability to recognize music symbols for interpreting music properly. Also important is being able to hear and recognize tonal and harmonic balance, rhythm, and tempo. Singers need to know the qualities of various musical instruments and to understand how they relate in orchestrations and arrangements for desired effects. Performing with poise and self-confidence before an audience is either an innate ability or one to be perfected.

Skill in dancing requires understanding dance steps and memorizing dance routines. Dancers need the ability to move with grace and rhythm and to coordinate body movements to music and to the movements of other dancers. Exercise, practice, and excellent physical condition are necessary. Dancers express such emotions as joy, sorrow, or excitement by the way they move their arms, legs, and body.

Artistic interests characterize those in music and dance. While singers may be more inclined to linguistic expression, dancers express bodily and athletically the flow and rhythm of music. Instrumental musicians can be very involved in technical equipment that enhances the sounds of their instruments. Music and dance are meant to be heard and seen; thus, performers enjoy creatively projecting themselves and their expressions to others.

Opportunities exist for satisfying many values through music and dance. One can get attention and recognition by performing in public, and the work is both varied and creative. Yet differences exist between the two areas of dance and music: Dancing demands physical activity that some enjoy, while music permits an independence that enables the performer to decide how to play or sing a selection.

Where Do Music and Dance Majors Work?

Of employed music and dance majors, one-third hold jobs as wage and salary workers for businesses or corporations in the private, for-profit sector. A fairly large proportion, 28 percent, are self-employed in their own business or professional practice. Educational institutions employ nearly one-fifth of all grads. And 15 percent of music and dance grads are employed in the private, nonprofit sector.

Only 42 percent of music majors work in jobs that are closely related to their major. Another 12 percent report working in jobs that are somewhat related to their major. The remaining 46 percent work in jobs that are not at all related to music.

Of all music and dance graduates under the age of 65, 88 percent are employed. Only 2 percent are officially unemployed; in other words, they are not employed and are actively seeking employment. The remaining 10 percent are out of

Table 1

Percentage Distribution of Employed Persons with Only a Bachelor's Degree, by Economic Sector, Size, and New Business Status of Employer

	Music and Dance	All
Economic Sector		
Private for-profit	33.3	47.3
Self-employed	28.2	18.5
Government/Military	4.1	11.0
Education	19.8	15.6
Nonprofit	14.6	7.5
Employer Size		
Small (Fewer than 100 employees)	58.7	35.5
Medium (100–999)	15.2	21.8
Large (1,000–24,999)	16.2	26.0
Very large (25,000 or more)	9.9	16.7
Percent working in new business established within past 5 years	6.5	7.6

Table 2

Percentage Distribution of Employed Persons with Only a Bachelor's Degree in Music and Dance, by the Relationship Between Their Job and College Major

Relationship of Job to Major	Percent
Closely related	42.1
Somewhat related	11.6
Not related	46.3

Percent who report the following as the most important reasons for working in a job that was not related to major:

	Percent
Pay, promotion opportunities	31.5
Change in career or professional interests	14.2
Job in highest degree field not available	14.0
Other reason	12.6
Working conditions (hours, equipment, environment)	12.4

the labor force; that is, they are not employed and are not seeking employment. Forty-three percent of the labor force withdrawals are attributable to early retirement. One-fifth of the grads are staying at home to deal with family responsibilities.

Occupations

Employed music and dance majors work in a variety of occupations. Almost one-quarter of all employed grads are employed as teachers. One-tenth of grads work as teachers in noneducational institutions; given the large share of self-employed grads, it seems likely that most of these give private music or dance instruction. Seven percent are employed as elementary school teachers and 6 percent as secondary school teachers. About 13 percent are employed as artists, broadcasters, writers, editors, entertainers, and public relations specialists. Another 7 percent are employed in other miscellaneous administrative-related occupations.

Women outnumber men among the graduates slightly and are also considerably more likely to opt for one of the top 5 occupations where these grads work.

Work Activities

▸ Given the high concentration of music and dance majors in teaching occupations, it is hardly surprising to find that almost half are regularly engaged in teaching activities on their jobs. Not only do a large fraction of grads regularly engage in teaching activities on their jobs, but also 28 percent spend most of their typical week in teaching activities.

▸ Although 41 percent of all employed music and dance graduates perform sales, purchasing, and marketing activities as a regular part of their jobs, only 10 percent spend most of their time performing these duties in a typical workweek.

▸ Forty-six percent of music graduates regularly perform managerial and administrative duties as a part of their

Table 3
Top 5 Occupations Employing Persons with Only a
Bachelor's Degree in Music and Dance, by Percentage

Top 5 Occupations	All	Men	Women
Artists, Broadcasters, Editors, Entertainers, Public Relations Specialists, and Writers	12.7	11.6	14.0
Other Teachers and Instructors in Noneducational Institutions	10.4	6.9	14.2
Other Administrative Occupations	7.4	5.6	9.4
Teachers—Elementary School	7.1	3.5	11.0
Teachers, Secondary—Other Subjects	6.3	5.9	6.8
Total, Top 5 Occupations	43.9	33.5	55.4
Balance of Employed	56.1	66.5	44.6
All Employed	100.0	100.0	100.0

employment. Seven percent have these duties as their chief responsibility.

▶ About 3 out of 10 music and dance majors regularly engage in accounting, finance, and contractual duties, but only 10 percent are primarily focused on these tasks.

▶ About 11 percent of all employed music graduates perceive their main work function as falling in an "other" category not specified by the survey, and 14 percent see this as an important work task. It seems likely that many responding this way are engaged in artistic activities, such as rehearsing and performing music.

Workplace Training and Other Work-Related Experiences

The career potential of a job is closely associated with the amount of work-related training on the job. Firms that invest in their workforce are more likely to offer pay increases and promotions to match the increasing productivity of their workers. The rate of participation in work-related training during a year among employed music and dance graduates (52 percent) is significantly lower than the training participation rate of all college graduates (61 percent).

▶ Of those music majors who receive some training, 47 percent receive technical training in their occupational field.

▶ Fifteen percent receive training to improve their general professional skills, such as public speaking and business writing.

▶ Eight percent of the training recipients participate in managerial or supervisor training.

Of those music and dance grads who participate in some work-related training, 40 percent do so to improve their occupational skills and knowledge. About 6 percent are required or expected by their employers to undergo training.

Salaries

The median annual salary of music and dance graduates with only a bachelor's degree is $40,000, a level that is 29 percent lower than the median annual salary of all employed college graduates. On average, employed music and dance graduates work for 37 hours per week and for 49 weeks per year, resulting in 1,813 hours of employment per year. The level of work effort among music and dance graduates is 16 percent lower than the average among all college graduates (43 hours per week and 50 weeks per year, resulting in 2,150 hours per year). The low earnings of the grads are partly explained by this lower level of work engagement.

The average annual salary of music and dance majors who work in jobs that are closely related to their major is only $41,300. Many of the graduates whose jobs are closely related to their majors are employed in teaching occupations. Graduates whose jobs are somewhat related to

their major average only $36,100 per year. The highest earnings go to those whose jobs are unrelated to the major, an average of $45,400 per year.

The average annual salary of music majors who are employed by educational institutions is $40,800, a level that is lower than salaries of music majors in most other sectors. Music and dance graduates employed by businesses in the private sector, whether nonprofit or for-profit, earn the same average yearly salary of $41,300, which is slightly more than what those in education earn. Self-employed music graduates operating their own business earn an average annual salary of $38,300.

FIGURE 1

Age/Earnings Profile of Persons with Only a Bachelor's Degree in Music and Dance (Full-Time Workers, in 2010 Dollars)

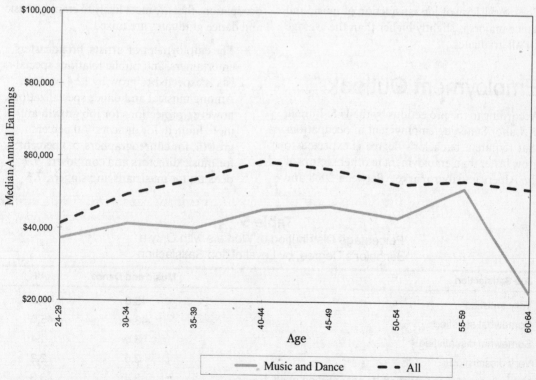

Table 4
Annual Salary of Workers with Only a Bachelor's Degree,
Top 5 Occupations (in 2010 Dollars)

Earnings in Top 5 Occupations	All	Music and Dance
Total	$40,000	$39,800
Artists, Broadcasters, Editors, Entertainers, Public Relations Specialists, and Writers	$49,500	$41,300
Other Teachers and Instructors in Noneducational Institutions	$36,100	$33,000
Other Administrative Occupations	$38,200	$41,300
Teachers—Elementary School	$37,200	$38,200
Teachers, Secondary—Other Subjects	$39,200	$40,200

Among public school teachers, having a degree in this field provides an earnings advantage over majors in other fields.

Job Satisfaction

The overall level of job satisfaction of music and dance majors is slightly higher than the average for all graduates.

Employment Outlook

According to the projections by the U.S. Bureau of Labor Statistics, employment in occupations that require a bachelor's degree is expected to grow faster than employment in other sectors of the American labor market. Between 2008 and 2018, the U.S. workforce is projected to grow by 10.1 percent, creating an average of 15.2 million job openings per year. The bachelor's-level jobs are expected to increase by 17.7 percent over the same time.

The employment growth projections for the top 5 occupations that are most likely to employ music and dance graduates are mixed.

▶ The employment of artists, broadcasters, entertainers, and public relations specialists is expected to grow by 12.4 percent. Among musical and dance specializations, however, projections for job growth are more limited: for dancers, 7.0 percent growth; for choreographers, 5.3 percent; for music directors and composers, 9.9 percent; for musicians and singers, 7.6

Table 5
Percentage Distribution of Workers with Only a
Bachelor's Degree, by Level of Job Satisfaction

Job Satisfaction	Music and Dance	All
Very satisfied	45.6	45.4
Somewhat satisfied	43.4	45.0
Somewhat dissatisfied	8.0	7.4
Very dissatisfied	3.0	2.2
Mean Score (4=very satisfied, 1=not satisfied at all)	3.4	3.3

Table 6
Projected Growth and Job Openings in the Top 5 Occupations
Employing Persons with Only a Bachelor's Degree in Music and Dance

Top 5 Occupations	Projected Growth 2008–2018	Projected Annual Job Openings
All top 5	13.6%	372,530
Artists, Broadcasters, Editors, Entertainers, Public Relations Specialists, and Writers	12.4%	71,740
Other Teachers and Instructors in Noneducational Institutions	20.8%	49,900
Other Administrative Occupations	10.8%	166,130
Teachers—Elementary School	15.8%	59,650
Teachers, Secondary—Other Subjects	15.3%	25,110

percent. Competition for jobs as musicians, singers, and dancers—especially full-time jobs—is expected to be keen. The vast number of people with the desire to perform will continue to greatly exceed the number of openings. New musicians, singers, or dancers will have their best chance of landing a job with smaller, community-based performing arts groups or as freelance artists.

▶ Employment of teachers is projected to grow faster than the average for all occupations. The number of teachers employed is dependent on state and local expenditures for education and on the enactment of legislation to increase the quality and scope of public education. Job prospects should be better in inner cities and rural areas than in suburban districts.

▶ Employment growth should be even better for teachers in noneducational institutions. This group of occupations includes some specializations under which music and dance tutors can be categorized: self-enrichment education teachers (with 32.0 percent growth projected); and a catch-all title, teachers and instructors, all other (with 14.7 percent growth

projected). Between them, these two specializations are projected to offer more than 30,000 job openings each year.

Pathways Beyond the Bachelor's Degree

Nearly 43 percent of music graduates with a bachelor's degree proceed to earn a postgraduate degree. Of those with a bachelor's degree, 36 percent earn a master's degree, 5 percent graduate with a doctorate, and fewer than 2 percent earn a professional degree.

▶ More than half of master's degrees are earned in music; 41 percent of the degrees are earned in education.

▶ A similar choice of majors is observed among music majors who earn doctoral degrees. Two-thirds of the doctoral degrees are earned in the field of music. About 8 percent graduate with doctoral degrees in education or educational administration.

▶ Among the few music majors who earn professional degrees, three-quarters choose law as their major; 11 percent earn their professional degrees in health-related fields.

CHAPTER 45

Philosophy and Religion

Philosophy is speculation about existence and the inquiry, analysis, and interpretation of reality. Philosophy is described as the search to know and to understand what is of basic value and importance in life. The scope of philosophy includes the relationship between humanity and nature and between the individual and society.

Religion is often considered a related discipline, as it is on the survey questionnaire on which this book is based. Religion is the study of organized systems of beliefs, worship, practices, rituals, and ethical values that center on a way of life. Religious beliefs—not limited to Buddhist, Christian, Jewish, or Moslem—usually focus on a divine, superhuman power or powers to be obeyed and worshipped as the creator(s) and ruler(s) of the universe.

Theology is technically the study and description of God, but theology can also be the study of religious doctrines expounded by a particular religion or denomination.

While there are philosophers and teachers of religion and theology, the most common occupation associated with religion is member of the clergy or imam. As religious and spiritual leaders, clergy are teachers and interpreters of their traditions and faith. They organize and lead regular religious services and officiate at special ceremonies, including confirmations, weddings, and funerals. Clergy may lead worshipers in prayer; administer sacraments; deliver sermons; and read from sacred texts such as the Bible or Koran. When not conducting worship services, clergy organize, supervise, and lead religious education programs for their congregations. Clergy often visit the sick or bereaved to provide comfort. They also counsel persons who are seeking religious or moral guidance and those who are troubled by family or personal problems. Clergy may work to expand the membership of their congregations and solicit donations to support their congregations' activities and facilities.

Many of these same functions are performed by laity—that is, members of a religious group other than clergy. For example, some lay graduates of a major in religion work as educators in religious schools.

The educational requirements for philosophy may include ancient philosophy, history of modern philosophy, introduction to logic, symbolic logic, theory of knowledge, metaphysics, moral philosophy, existentialism, Chinese and Indian philosophy, aesthetics, and philosophy of science.

The educational requirements for entry into a professional divinities program and a religious vocation vary greatly, requiring specific information from a particular denomination. Course work for Protestant ministers, Jewish rabbis, and Catholic priests have similarities and focus on the Bible or sacred scripture; dogma and canon law; theology; church history or Jewish history; public speaking or preaching; community services; and religious education.

Clergy members have social, language, and teaching abilities. These are used for religious education, proselytizing, and motivating people to remain committed to religion (persuasive ability also helps for this last purpose). While different leadership styles exist, clergy members direct, manage, and supervise many activities associated with their ministries. Most obvious to many members of religious communities are the skills in providing social services and often the zealous belief or passion an individual expresses on behalf of his or her religious convictions.

Of foremost importance to clergy members of most religions is their selection of a way of life. A commitment is expected about how one leads his or her personal life beyond the more visual aspects of the career, such as preaching. Interests for clergy members are primarily social, followed by what may be described as enjoying the breadth of focus afforded by a liberal arts education. Organizational and persuasive interests are also important.

Clergy members and imams value working with people, working with one's mind, and having variety and diversion. Limitless are the issues and practical problems that community members bring to their clerical leaders to solve; thus, having a creative mind is helpful. Leadership and a sense of achievement are also afforded to religious leaders.

Where Do Philosophy and Religion Majors Work?

More than one-quarter of all employed philosophy and religion graduates work in the private, nonprofit sector, mostly as clergy and other religious workers in churches, synagogues, mosques, and temples. Another 36 percent of employed philosophy and religion majors are employed as wage and salary workers for businesses and corporations operating in the private, for-profit sector. About 17 percent work in the for-profit

Table 1

Percentage Distribution of Employed Persons with Only a Bachelor's Degree, by Economic Sector, Size, and New Business Status of Employer

	Philosophy and Religion	All
Economic Sector		
Private for-profit	35.9	47.3
Self-employed	17.3	18.5
Government/Military	9.4	11.0
Education	11.2	15.6
Nonprofit	26.2	7.5
Employer Size		
Small (Fewer than 100 employees)	53.2	35.5
Medium (100–999)	15.3	21.8
Large (1,000–24,999)	18.0	26.0
Very large (25,000 or more)	13.4	16.7
Percent working in new business established within past 5 years	6.9	7.6

Table 2

Percentage Distribution of Employed Persons with Only a Bachelor's Degree in Philosophy and Religion, by the Relationship Between Their Job and College Major

Relationship of Job to Major	Percent
Closely related	33.1
Somewhat related	19.4
Not related	47.5

Percent who report the following as the most important reasons for working in a job that was not related to major:

Change in career or professional interests	23.8
Pay, promotion opportunities	22.1
Job in highest degree field not available	18.8
Working conditions (hours, equipment, environment)	11.9
Family-related reasons	9.7

sector as self-employed workers in their own business or practice. Educational institutions employ 11 percent of all employed philosophy and religion majors. The remaining 9 percent work in the government sector.

Only one-third of philosophy and religion majors work in jobs that are closely related to their major. A little less than one-fifth report working in jobs that are somewhat related to their major. The remaining 47 percent work in jobs that are not at all related to the field of philosophy and religion.

Of all philosophy and religion graduates under the age of 65, 86 percent are employed. Only 1 percent are officially unemployed; in other words, they are not employed and are actively seeking employment. The remaining 12 percent are out of the labor force; that is, they are not employed and are not seeking employment. Of these, 45 percent have taken early retirement. Family responsibilities are the reason for labor force withdrawal among 17 percent of this group of philosophy and religion graduates, and 14 percent are out of the labor force because they do not need or want to work.

Occupations

Employed philosophy and religion majors work in a variety of occupations, although they are fairly concentrated in religious occupations. Almost one-quarter of employed philosophy and religion graduates with only a bachelor's degree work as clergy and as other religious workers. (When grads with degrees beyond the bachelor's are included, the share rises to 29 percent.) These jobs are closely related to the undergraduate education of philosophy and religion majors. Another 10 percent of philosophy and religion graduates are employed in a managerial or administrative position. Many of these jobs are within the field of philosophy and religion; they are administrative jobs within religious or educational institutions. More than 4 percent work as writers, editors, broadcasters, and public relations specialists. As noted, numerous reasons such as pay and promotion opportunities, as well as a change in career interests, motivate philosophy and religion majors to accept jobs that are unrelated to their undergraduate major. The fifth of the 5 predominant occupations that employ philosophy and religion

Table 3

Top 5 Occupations Employing Persons with Only a Bachelor's Degree in Philosophy and Religion, by Percentage

Top 5 Occupations	All	Men	Women
Clergy and Other Religious Workers	23.0	28.6	5.7
Other Management-Related Occupations	5.0	4.1	7.7
Other Administrative Occupations	4.8	2.4	12.3
Artists, Broadcasters, Editors, Entertainers, Public Relations Specialists, and Writers	4.3	3.3	7.3
Food Preparation and Service Workers	3.6	4.8	–
Total, Top 5 Occupations	40.7	43.2	33.0
Balance of Employed	59.3	56.8	67.0
All Employed	100.0	100.0	100.0

graduates, food preparation and service workers, probably includes mostly workers who are temporarily unable to find work in their undergraduate field, plus some engaged in the ritually prescribed preparation of food.

Male graduates outnumber females by about 2 to 1, and among those who decide to become clergy the imbalance is even higher, although this varies greatly between religious groups.

Work Activities

▶ More than 56 percent of employed philosophy and religion graduates are regularly engaged in managerial and administrative duties at work. About 17 percent spend most of their time at work performing these duties. These activities follow from their concentration in the clergy and in religious, administrative, and managerial occupations. Administrative duties are quite common among clergy members.

▶ About 4 of 10 philosophy and religion graduates regularly engage in teaching duties, and 13 percent spend most of their time performing these duties. This

is another work activity closely identified with clergy.

▶ Clergy also provide professional services, mainly in the form of counseling and guidance services for marital, health, financial, and religious problems. About 12 percent of employed philosophy and religion graduates spend most of their time providing professional services at work, and one-third spend significant time doing this.

▶ Forty-two percent regularly engage in marketing and sales activities, and more than 15 percent spend most of their workweek performing these duties.

▶ Employee-relations activities such as recruiting, training, and labor relations regularly engage 42 percent of all employed philosophy and religion graduates; 5 percent consider these duties to be the major part of their jobs.

▶ Computer applications, programming, and systems-development activities are performed regularly by 88 percent of all employed philosophy and religion graduates, and 6 percent consider these activities to be their chief responsibility.

Workplace Training and Other Work-Related Experiences

The career potential of a job is closely associated with the amount of work-related training on the job. Firms that invest in their workforce are more likely to offer pay increases and promotions to match the increasing productivity of their workers. The rate of participation in work-related training during a year among employed philosophy and religion graduates (60 percent) is about the same as the training participation rate of all college graduates (61 percent).

▶ Of those philosophy and religion majors who receive some training, 55 percent receive technical training in their occupational field.

▶ One-fifth receive training to improve their general professional skills, such as public speaking and business writing.

▶ Nineteen percent of the training recipients participate in management or supervisor training.

When asked to identify the most important factor influencing the decision to participate in work-related training, 39 percent want to improve skills and knowledge in their current occupation, and 8 percent are required by their employer to undergo training.

Salaries

The median annual salary of philosophy and religion graduates with only a bachelor's degree is $35,700, a level that is 45 percent lower than the median annual salary of all employed college graduates. On average, employed philosophy and religion graduates work for 44 hours per week and for 50 weeks per year, resulting in 2,200 hours of employment per year. The level of work effort among philosophy and religion graduates

is 2 percent higher than the average among all college graduates (43 hours per week and 50 weeks per year, resulting in 2,150 hours per year).

The average annual salary of philosophy and religion graduates who work in jobs that are closely related to their major, $35,000 per year, is lower than the salary of their counterparts who work in jobs that are somewhat related or not related to their undergraduate major. Closely related jobs tend to be religious worker and clergy, which are generally associated with lower salaries compared to occupations in which philosophy and religion graduates use just some of their major-related skills on the job. These less closely related occupations pay an average of $36,500 and include managerial and administrative occupations in religious organizations or educational institutions as well as broadcasting and writing occupations.

Occupations that typically are reported by philosophy and religion graduates as unrelated to their major pay either very high or very low salaries. On the high salary end are sales jobs that handle insurance, stocks and bonds, real estate, and other financial services. At the other end of the salary spectrum are clerical and secretarial jobs. The net effect is an average annual salary of $38,300 among graduates who work in unrelated jobs. This salary is higher than the salary in jobs that are closely or somewhat related to their major.

The private, for-profit sector pays a higher average salary to philosophy and religion majors than other sectors (apart from government, which employs very few). Those who are employed by businesses and corporations in the private, for-profit sector earn $37,400 per year. The self-employment segment of the private, for-profit sector pays an average salary of $34,800 per year. Graduates employed by educational institutions earn $35,500 annually.

The not-for-profit sector, where most clergy work, pays an average annual salary of $33,400. This sector also employs many of the grads who work in managerial jobs, which may help to explain why workers in this group of occupations earn

FIGURE 1

Age/Earnings Profile of Persons with Only a Bachelor's Degree in Philosophy and Religion (Full-Time Workers, in 2010 Dollars)

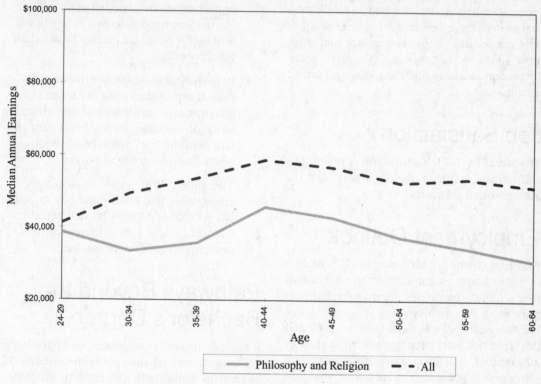

Table 4

Annual Salary of Workers with Only a Bachelor's Degree,
Top 5 Occupations (in 2010 Dollars)

Earnings in Top 5 Occupations	All	Philosophy and Religion
Total	$35,700	$34,900
Clergy and Other Religious Workers	$35,100	$33,000
Other Management-Related Occupations	$57,800	$54,500
Other Administrative Occupations	$38,200	$38,800
Artists, Broadcasters, Editors, Entertainers, Public Relations Specialists, and Writers	$49,500	$36,100
Food Preparation and Service Workers	$35,100	$14,400

higher salaries, on average, if they are graduates of other majors. The extremely low average salary of philosophy and religion grads working in food preparation and service is probably an indication that most of these workers are holding these jobs only temporarily, while they cannot find work more suited to their training. (However, about 10 percent consider this job closely related to their major.)

Job Satisfaction

The overall level of job satisfaction of philosophy and religion majors is slightly higher than the average for all graduates.

Employment Outlook

According to the projections by the U.S. Bureau of Labor Statistics, employment in occupations that require a bachelor's degree is expected to grow faster than employment in other sectors of the American labor market. Between 2008 and 2018, the U.S. workforce is projected to grow by 10.1 percent, creating an average of 15.2 million job openings per year. The bachelor's-level jobs are expected to increase by 17.7 percent over the same time.

Mixed employment growth is projected for the top 5 occupations that are most likely to employ philosophy and religion graduates.

▶ Clergy and other religious occupations are projected to add enough employees to grow by almost 13 percent. Many job opportunities are expected in all faiths, but in some denominations competition is likely for positions leading large urban worship groups.

▶ Employment in administrative occupations is expected to grow faster than in managerial occupations and also create more job openings, largely because of the large workforce of administrative jobs, where much turnover will occur.

▶ The workforce of artists, broadcasters, entertainers, and public relations specialists is expected to grow by 12.4 percent. Competition for jobs in these creative occupations tends to be intense.

Pathways Beyond the Bachelor's Degree

Postgraduation schooling rates are high among philosophy and religion graduates. Nearly 47 percent of philosophy and religion graduates with a bachelor's degree proceed to earn a postgraduate degree. Thirty-one percent earn a master's degree, 8 percent graduate with a doctorate, and another 8 percent earn a professional degree.

Table 5

Percentage Distribution of Workers with Only a Bachelor's Degree, by Level of Job Satisfaction

Job Satisfaction	Philosophy and Religion	All
Very satisfied	46.0	45.4
Somewhat satisfied	46.6	45.0
Somewhat dissatisfied	5.0	7.4
Very dissatisfied	2.4	2.2
Mean Score (4=very satisfied, 1=not satisfied at all)	3.4	3.3

Table 6

Projected Growth and Job Openings in the Top 5 Occupations Employing Persons with Only a Bachelor's Degree in Philosophy and Religion

Top 5 Occupations	Projected Growth 2008–2018	Projected Annual Job Openings
All top 5	9.6%	795,740
Clergy and Other Religious Workers	12.7%	25,220
Other Management-Related Occupations	7.2%	53,020
Other Administrative Occupations	10.8%	166,130
Artists, Broadcasters, Editors, Entertainers, Public Relations Specialists, and Writers	12.4%	71,740
Food Preparation and Service Workers	8.8%	479,630

▸ Thirty-nine percent of the master's degrees are earned in philosophy or religion. Counseling psychology and social work each account for a little more than 4 percent of the master's degrees.

▸ More than half of the doctoral degrees of undergraduate philosophy and religion majors are earned in philosophy or religion.

▸ Forty-six percent of the professional degrees of undergraduate philosophy and religion majors are earned in law. Seventeen percent of professional degrees are earned in philosophy or religion; probably most of these are the Doctor of Divinity or a comparable degree.

CHAPTER 46

Political Science, Government, and International Relations

Three interconnected fields are offered in some institutions as three distinct majors: political science, government, and international relations. In some colleges they may be combined and called political science. (This chapter frequently uses that name for the sake of abbreviation.) Some colleges consider this field as composed of four distinct subfields: political philosophy and theory, American government, comparative politics, and international relations.

Political science is the study of the origin, development, and operation of political systems and public policy. Political scientists conduct research on a wide range of subjects, such as relations between the United States and other countries, the institutions and political life of nations, the politics of small towns or a major metropolis, and the decisions of the U.S. Supreme Court. In studying such topics as public opinion, political decision making, ideology, and public policy, political scientists analyze the structure and operation of governments and various political entities. Depending on the topic under study, a political scientist may conduct a public opinion survey, analyze election results, analyze public documents, or interview public officials.

A person majoring in American government studies the components of the federal government—the presidency, the Congress, and the judicial system—as well as state, county, and local governments. Politics, the election process, political parties, interest groups, think tanks, and the media are analyzed. This field includes domestic and foreign affairs, as well as varied areas such as transportation, civil rights, education, energy, and the environment.

International relations or international affairs may have a perspective that fits a specific institution's goals or the unique expertise of its faculty. This major introduces a variety of theoretical approaches to international politics and economics. In addition to studying comparative politics, international economics, and American foreign policy, students examine major issues such as international war and peace, change and continuity, balance of power assessment, the political utility of military force, regional governmental differences, and issues that foster international cooperation and conflict. The primary objective of the field is to develop an understanding of international affairs and economics, issues and dilemmas facing countries, foreign policy instruments, and processes by which countries make policy decisions to reconcile disparate and incompatible goals.

Course work for political science may include introduction to politics, American ideology, interest groups and public policy, technology and public policy, religion and politics, modern political thought, civil liberties, legislative politics, urban politics, and American social welfare policy.

Course work in government may include introduction to American government, intergovernmental relations, American national security policy, United States foreign policy, American constitutional law, the American presidency, parties and elections, the legislative process, and state and local government. Many political science and government students intern with a member of Congress, an elected public servant, or a federal or state government agency.

Course work in international relations may include politics and government, international relations, comparative political systems, geopolitical issues, bureaucratic and organizational politics, comparative modern economic systems, American foreign policy, international relations theories, international economics, and international security issues.

One of the abilities required in these fields is quickly understanding and analyzing connections and associations between diverse material and information. For example, political scientists compare the merits of various forms of government, and a government major analyzes large amounts of data on the federal budget. There is fluidity to the field, so adaptability is needed as new laws or different interpretations of existing legislation appear; different elected officials push for new policies; and local, state, national, or international events occur that bring about the need for change. So a continuous need exists for critical thinking to make decisions based on

Table 1
Percentage Distribution of Employed Persons with Only a Bachelor's Degree, by Economic Sector, Size, and New Business Status of Employer

	Political Science	All
Economic Sector		
Private for-profit	50.3	47.3
Self-employed	17.2	18.5
Government/Military	16.7	11.0
Education	8.3	15.6
Nonprofit	7.3	7.5
Employer Size		
Small (Fewer than 100 employees)	30.0	35.5
Medium (100–999)	20.4	21.8
Large (1,000–24,999)	26.8	26.0
Very large (25,000 or more)	22.8	16.7
Percent working in new business established within past 5 years	9.1	7.6

new facts and figures. Communication skills are essential, as is the ability to speak authoritatively.

Those who work in these fields are people-oriented. Their interests, however, are more focused on leading and influencing others than on humanitarian concerns. These workers appreciate and understand the value of bureaucracy and organization. While they have good interpersonal skills, they realize that results will come from group activities that involve convincing, negotiating, and compromising. Political science, government, and international relations offer a context for intellectual pursuit in which the scientific method of analysis and inquiry plays a major role.

The values associated with these fields are primarily intellectual, with a research orientation. People in these fields enjoy working with their minds to seek new or creative analyses of situations, problems, or issues. There is opportunity for variety, as the topics and public priorities change. Because individuals often work closely with a policymaker or person with political power, prestige is associated with the work.

Where Do Political Science, Government, and International Relations Majors Work?

While a major in political science is commonly thought of as a means to prepare for a career in government, the majority of political science graduates with a bachelor's degree work in the for-profit sector. More than half of political science majors with a bachelor's degree work as wage and salary employees in private, for-profit businesses. An additional 17 percent are self-employed, owning businesses and consulting services. Almost 17 percent of political science majors work in federal, state, or local government organizations, including legislative and judicial bodies; in the executive agencies such as federal and state departments of labor and justice; and in local government. Eight percent of political science majors work in the education sector, most often as elementary or secondary school teachers. Relatively few graduates with a

Table 2
Percentage Distribution of Employed Persons with Only a Bachelor's Degree in Political Science, by the Relationship Between Their Job and College Major

Relationship of Job to Major	Percent
Closely related	20.5
Somewhat related	31.4
Not related	48.2

Percent who report the following as the most important reasons for working in a job that was not related to major:	
Pay, promotion opportunities	44.7
Change in career or professional interests	19.2
Working conditions (hours, equipment, environment)	8.6
Job in highest degree field not available	7.8
Other reason	7.2

bachelor's degree in political science are employed in nonprofit charities and research foundations.

Political science majors with a bachelor's degree are seldom employed in jobs that are closely related to their field. Only one-fifth of grads say that this describes their job. Instead, almost half of grads work in jobs that are unrelated to political science, and 3 out of 10 work in jobs that are only somewhat related.

Unlike some other majors, most political science majors who are employed in a job unrelated to their field of study are still employed in a job that generally requires a college degree, although not in a specific major. Access to college labor market jobs is a key element to the long-term labor market success of graduates from this major. Those majors who fail to become employed in a job that requires a college degree have much lower earnings.

The employment rate of those with an under-graduate degree in political science is about 83 percent, most of them in full-time positions. Another 4 percent are involuntarily unemployed. The remaining 13 percent are not actively seek-ing employment. When those in this last group are asked why they have withdrawn from the workforce, 3 out of 10 say they have retired early.

Almost one-quarter have family responsibilities that are keeping them out of the job market. Thirteen percent have no need or desire to work.

Occupations

A high proportion of political science majors become employed in sales, marketing, manage-ment, and administration. More than 15 percent of majors at the bachelor's degree level work in sales or marketing. Various managerial or ad-ministrative jobs are also important sources of employment for majors from this field of study. Almost 6 percent of political science grads work in a group of creative occupations that includes writers and editors.

The ratio of male to female grads is a bit less than 2 to 1, and their employment experiences are quite different, as Table 3 shows.

Work Activities

▶ Managerial and administrative tasks are among the most important job duties undertaken by majors from this field of study. They are significant tasks for almost

Table 3
Top 5 Occupations Employing Persons with Only a Bachelor's Degree in Political Science, by Percentage

Top 5 Occupations	All	Men	Women
Sales/Marketing—Insurance, Securities, Real Estate, and Business Services	8.5	9.7	6.1
Other Marketing and Sales Occupations	7.3	6.8	8.4
Other Management-Related Occupations	6.4	5.7	7.6
Artists, Broadcasters, Editors, Entertainers, Public Relations Specialists, and Writers	5.8	5.3	6.8
Top-Level Managers, Executives, and Administrators	5.4	7.5	1.2
Total, Top 5 Occupations	33.4	35.0	30.1
Balance of Employed	66.6	65.0	69.9
All Employed	100.0	100.0	100.0

two-thirds of grads and the primary duty of almost one-fifth.

▶ Sales and marketing activities are also an important job duty for graduates with a political science degree, occupying significant work time for almost 6 out of 10 grads. One-quarter of grads see these activities as their main work role.

▶ Forty-seven percent of political science grads spend at least 10 hours out of the workweek on accounting, finance, and contracts. Nine percent are engaged in these tasks most of the time.

▶ About 89 percent of all political science majors report that they are regularly involved in the development and/or use of computer applications.

▶ One-fifth of political science majors at the bachelor's degree level spend much of their workweek on teaching, but only 6 percent work mainly as teachers.

Workplace Training and Other Work-Related Experiences

Political science majors enter the labor market with few occupationally specific skills, so on-the-job learning is essential for long-term advancement. Many of the skills used on the job are developed simply by observing or learning by doing. However, participation in work-based training programs such as seminars and workshops is also an important way that political science majors develop occupational skills. The rate of participation in work-related training during a year among employed political science, government, and international relations graduates (60 percent) is about the same as the training participation rate of all college graduates (61 percent).

▶ Of those political science, government, and international relations graduates who receive some training during a year, 51 percent receive technical training in the occupation in which they are employed.

▶ Management and supervisory training is an important element of training received by 22 percent of majors who got training.

▶ Developing communication skills such as writing and public speaking are a key goal for 26 percent of those from this field of study who participate in training.

Among those political science grads who receive work-related training, one-third perceive a skill upgrade as the major reason for getting the training. More than 7 percent say they are required by their employer to get this training.

Salaries

College degrees in the social science fields are generally thought to lead to jobs that pay below-average salaries, yet the median annual salaries of political science majors are actually 11 percent higher than the median for all college graduates. The median annual salary of political science, government, and international relations graduates with only a bachelor's degree is $57,800. On average, employed political science graduates work for 46 hours per week and for 49 weeks per year, resulting in 2,254 hours of employment per year. This level of work effort is 5 percent higher than the average among all college graduates (43 hours per week and 50 weeks per year, resulting in 2,150 hours per year).

Those political science majors who work in the private, for-profit sector or in government have much higher earnings than those employed in education or nonprofit organizations. Those working for private firms and corporations earn an average of $68,300, while self-employed political science graduates earn an average of $55,200. Political science majors who work for government

FIGURE 1

Age/Earnings Profile of Persons with Only a Bachelor's Degree in Political Science (Full-Time Workers, in 2010 Dollars)

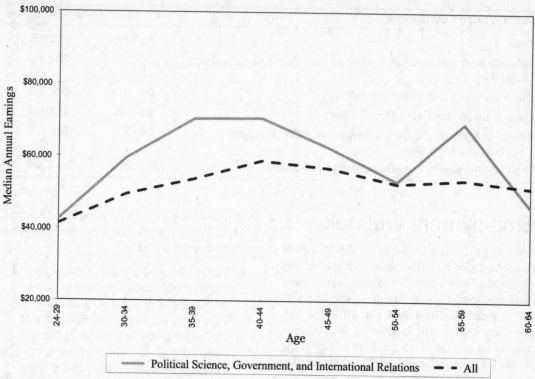

agencies earn about $55,400 per year. In the not-for-profit sector, the average is $43,000 per year, and $40,600 in education.

There is little connection between the earnings of political science majors and the degree to which their job is related to their undergraduate major. Those working in a job related to the political science field average $60,700 per year, compared to $57,400 in unrelated jobs and $62,600 in jobs that are somewhat related. Access to a job that requires a college degree is the key to high earnings for graduates from this field of study.

The highest-paying jobs for majors are for top-level managers, where the annual salary averages $102,300 per year. High annual salaries are also earned by those majors who have jobs related to the sale of insurance, stocks and bonds, and other financial instruments and real estate. Among those grads who work in marketing and sales jobs or as editors, writers, or public relations specialists, the political science degree confers a significant earnings advantage over other bachelor's degrees.

Job Satisfaction

The overall level of job satisfaction of political science, government, and international relations majors is slightly higher than the average for all graduates.

Table 4
Annual Salary of Workers with Only a Bachelor's Degree, Top 5 Occupations (in 2010 Dollars)

Earnings in Top 5 Occupations	All	Political Science
Total	$57,800	$75,200
Sales/Marketing—Insurance, Securities, Real Estate, and Business Services	$67,100	$87,700
Other Marketing and Sales Occupations	$54,700	$68,000
Other Management-Related Occupations	$57,800	$52,000
Artists, Broadcasters, Editors, Entertainers, Public Relations Specialists, and Writers	$49,500	$66,100
Top-Level Managers, Executives, and Administrators	$103,200	$102,300

Employment Outlook

According to the projections by the U.S. Bureau of Labor Statistics, employment in occupations that require a bachelor's degree is expected to grow faster than employment in other sectors of the American labor market. Between 2008 and 2018, the U.S. workforce is projected to grow by 10.1 percent, creating an average of 15.2 million job openings per year. The bachelor's-level jobs are expected to increase by 17.7 percent over the same time.

Opportunities are mixed in occupations that employ a substantial number of political science majors at the bachelor's degree level. Some will grow at a pace above the average for the economy as a whole, but below the average rate of growth in demand for persons with a bachelor's degree; some will grow at a rate below the economy-wide average or even shrink.

▶ The workforce for most of the sales and managerial occupations that are large employers of political science grads will increase at rates near or below the rate for the economy as a whole. However, these occupations will offer numerous job openings because they have very large workforces that create many jobs through turnover.

▶ The exception to this managerial growth is the top-level jobs, which are projected to shrink slightly. In addition, keen competition is expected for top executive positions

Table 5
Percentage Distribution of Workers with Only a Bachelor's Degree, by Level of Job Satisfaction

Job Satisfaction	Political Science	All
Very satisfied	45.0	45.4
Somewhat satisfied	45.0	45.0
Somewhat dissatisfied	7.6	7.4
Very dissatisfied	2.4	2.2
Mean Score (4=very satisfied, 1=not satisfied at all)	3.4	3.3

Table 6

Projected Growth and Job Openings in the Top 5 Occupations
Employing Persons with Only a Bachelor's Degree in Political Science

Top 5 Occupations	Projected Growth 2008–2018	Projected Annual Job Openings
All top 5	7.9%	366,320
Sales/Marketing—Insurance, Securities, Real Estate, and Business Services	11.5%	115,210
Other Marketing and Sales Occupations	7.3%	64,880
Other Management-Related Occupations	7.2%	53,020
Artists, Broadcasters, Editors, Entertainers, Public Relations Specialists, Writers	12.4%	71,740
Top-Level Managers, Executives, Administrators	−0.4%	61,470

because the prestige and high pay attract a substantial number of qualified applicants.

▶ Growth in the high-level sales occupations in insurance and securities is projected to increase by 11.5 percent. Competition for jobs will continue to be keen, with more applicants than available openings. Additionally, the financial crisis has resulted in mass consolidation in the financial industry, a scenario that will likely result in fewer positions as companies attempt to streamline operations by eliminating duplicate tasks.

▶ Creative jobs such as broadcaster and writer that substantial numbers of political science majors hold will grow at a pace well above the overall rate of new job creation for the economy as a whole. However, these occupations also attract more applicants than can be placed in available jobs.

Pathways Beyond the Bachelor's Degree

Political science majors are very likely to earn a graduate degree at some point after graduation from college. Almost one-quarter of all political science majors go on to earn a master's degree. Another 3 percent earn a doctorate. A major pathway to law school and the legal profession is through the undergraduate political science major. Almost one-fifth of all those with a bachelor's degree in the field earn a law degree.

▶ The most popular master's-level field of study for political science majors is business; one-quarter of master's degrees are earned in the business area.

▶ Many undergraduates continue their education in political science or the related field of public administration. About 19 percent of those who earn a master's degree complete their studies in some aspect of political science, while an additional 9 percent earn this degree in public administration.

▶ More than 30 percent of those who earn doctorates continue their studies in political science. About 7 percent earn a doctorate in education or educational administration.

CHAPTER 47

Sociology

One of the most recognized social sciences is sociology. Sociologists study human society and social behavior by examining the groups and social institutions that people form, as well as various social, religious, political, and business organizations. Sociologists also study the behavior and interaction of groups, trace their origin and growth, and analyze the influence of group activities on individual members. These professionals are concerned with the characteristics of social groups, organizations, and institutions; the ways that individuals are affected by each other and by the groups to which they belong; and the effects of social traits such as sex, age, and race on a person's daily life. The results of sociological research aid educators, lawmakers, administrators, and others interested in resolving social problems and formulating public policy.

Specializations in the field are quite varied. Criminologists research the relationship between criminal law and social order to understand the causes of crime and the behavior of criminals. Penologists study the punishment for crime, the control and prevention of crime, the management of penal institutions, and the rehabilitation of criminal offenders. Rural sociologists study rural communities in contrast with urban communities, as well as problems brought about by the impact of scientific and industrial revolutions on the rural way of life. Social ecologists research the effects of physical environments and technology on the distribution of people and their activities. Urban sociologists study the origin, growth, structure, and demographic characteristics of cities and their social patterns, along with the distinctive problems that result from the urban environment, such as social problems and racial discrimination rooted in the failure of society to achieve its collective purposes. Medical sociologists research social factors affecting health care, including the definition of illness, patient and practitioner behavior, social epidemiology, and the delivery of health care. Demographers conduct surveys and experiments to study human populations and trends.

Course work may include American society, social inequality, urban social problems, violence in the family, sociology of prejudice, gender in a changing society, sociology of work, sociology of poverty, aging and society, sociology of health, race and ethnic relations, community analysis, social deviance, social policy, and interventions.

The abilities of sociologists include understanding and using the theories and research methods of social sciences. Being able to analyze and interpret information is an important skill. An expectation is to be able to collect and organize detailed research notes into a logical presentation, as the outcome of sociologists' work is written reports of findings. Good written and oral communication skills are needed, especially the latter for conducting interviews. Computer skills for data processing and analysis are expected.

Like all scientists, sociologists have analytical and problem-solving interests. Because the focus of the field is mostly on formal organizations and families, sociologists enjoy studying group behavior. Their people orientation reflects a concern for the welfare of others, but through indirect contacts such as policies and ideas instead of working in direct service relations such as teaching or counseling.

Sociologists have intellectual and research values. In social research, the topics examined usually are quite varied, and the field allows for use of novel methods of analysis. However, the issues studied require a considerable amount of thought and reasoning, along with searching for new approaches to analyze and interpret information.

Where Do Sociology Majors Work?

Sociology majors at the bachelor's degree level are employed across all the major sectors of the American economy. However, relative to college graduates in other fields, they are much more likely to work in government organizations or nonprofit foundations. About 36 percent of sociology majors are employed by private, for-profit organizations, largely in jobs unconnected to their major. While only about 11 percent of all college graduates work in a government job, almost one-quarter of those with a bachelor's degree in sociology are employed by a federal, state, or local government agency. About 14 percent of sociology majors work for a charitable or nonprofit research organization, almost double the rate of all college grads. Sociology majors are less likely than the average college graduate to be self-employed; those who have this work arrangement usually are engaged as self-employed consultants rather than as the owners of companies.

For undergraduates with a degree in sociology, the rate of employment in jobs related to the major is low at 27 percent. Almost 4 out of 10 work in jobs that are only somewhat related to their degree field. One-third work in unrelated jobs.

The employment rate of sociology graduates is relatively low. Only 77 percent of all majors under the age of 65 are employed. About 4 percent of all sociology majors are involuntarily unemployed

Table 1
Percentage Distribution of Employed Persons with Only a Bachelor's Degree, by Economic Sector, Size, and New Business Status of Employer

	Sociology	All
Economic Sector		
Private for-profit	35.7	47.3
Self-employed	13.0	18.5
Government/Military	22.5	11.0
Education	14.5	15.6
Nonprofit	14.1	7.5
Employer Size		
Small (Fewer than 100 employees)	32.4	35.5
Medium (100–999)	22.7	21.8
Large (1,000–24,999)	28.0	26.0
Very large (25,000 or more)	17.0	16.7
Percent working in new business established within past 5 years	4.8	7.6

Table 2
Percentage Distribution of Employed Persons with Only a Bachelor's Degree in Sociology, by the Relationship Between Their Job and College Major

Relationship of Job to Major	Percent
Closely related	27.2
Somewhat related	39.6
Not related	33.2

Percent who report the following as the most important reasons for working in a job that was not related to major:

Pay, promotion opportunities	33.1
Change in career or professional interests	16.5
Job in highest degree field not available	15.1
Working conditions (hours, equipment, environment)	14.0
Family-related reasons	11.9

and actively seeking work. About 19 percent of sociology majors are not seeking a job. The most frequent reason for withdrawal from the workforce is family responsibilities, accounting for more than one-quarter of those not seeking work. Slightly smaller shares have taken early retirement or have no need or desire to work.

Occupations

Sociology majors with only a bachelor's degree work in a variety of occupations; the top 5 occupations employing them account for less than one-third of the grads. About 8 percent are employed in some aspect of social work. Note that the master's degree (MSW) is typically required for social work positions in health and school settings and is required for clinical work as well. About 12 percent work in miscellaneous administrative or managerial positions; many of these work in public administration. Six percent are employed in various service occupations outside the health-care field. Five percent work as police, firefighters, or other protective service workers.

The ratio of female to male grads is a bit more than 2 to 1, and their employment experiences tend to be quite different, as Table 3 indicates.

Work Activities

▶ Management and supervisory activities are a significant part of the work of 55 percent of the graduates of this major; for 18 percent, these tasks are their main job function.

▶ Almost one-fifth of sociology majors are primarily engaged in sales and marketing activities; almost half say that these tasks occupy at least 10 hours of the typical workweek.

▶ Accounting, finance, and contracts are significant duties for 35 percent of sociology grads and the primary duty of 7 percent.

▶ Eighty-eight percent of grads regularly use computer applications, but only 5 percent are mainly assigned to this task.

Table 3
Top 5 Occupations Employing Persons with Only a Bachelor's Degree in Sociology, by Percentage

Top 5 Occupations	All	Men	Women
Social Workers	8.0	6.1	9.1
Other Administrative Occupations	7.1	4.4	8.6
Other Service Occupations, Except Health	6.0	3.1	7.6
Protective Service Workers	5.2	11.5	1.7
Other Management-Related Occupations	5.0	3.0	6.1
Total, Top 5 Occupations	31.3	28.1	33.1
Balance of Employed	68.7	71.9	66.9
All Employed	100.0	100.0	100.0

▶ Teaching is also an important function for one-third of graduates of this major, but only one-tenth work mainly as teachers.

Workplace Training and Other Work-Related Experiences

Developing skills on the job is an important part of the long-term career development of graduates of sociology programs. Most of this skill development is accomplished through informal on-the-job learning. But formal work-based classroom training is an equally important way that majors from this field acquire skills valued at work. The rate of participation in work-related training during a year among employed sociology graduates (63 percent) is somewhat higher than the training participation rate of all college graduates (61 percent).

▶ Management and supervisory training is a key training activity undertaken by 19 percent of graduates in this field who receive training.

▶ Fifty-six percent of all those who participate in training are involved in developing an occupational skill that is related to their jobs, which may be in sales, marketing, or social services.

▶ Twenty-one percent receive training to improve their general professional skills, such as public speaking and business writing.

When asked to identify the most important reason they receive training, one-third of the grads point to skill enhancement. Almost 13 percent say their employer requires the training.

Salaries

The median annual salary of sociology graduates with only a bachelor's degree is $41,000, a level that is 26 percent lower than the median annual salary of all employed college graduates. On average, employed sociology graduates work for 40 hours per week and for 50 weeks per year, resulting in 2,000 hours of employment per year. The level of work effort among sociology graduates is 7 percent lower than the average among all college graduates (43 hours per week and 50 weeks per year, resulting in 2,150 hours per year).

The earnings of sociology majors vary somewhat by where they work. Those employed in private, for-profit businesses earn an average salary of $45,400, while those working in a government

FIGURE 1

Age/Earnings Profile of Persons with Only a Bachelor's Degree in Sociology (Full-Time Workers, in 2010 Dollars)

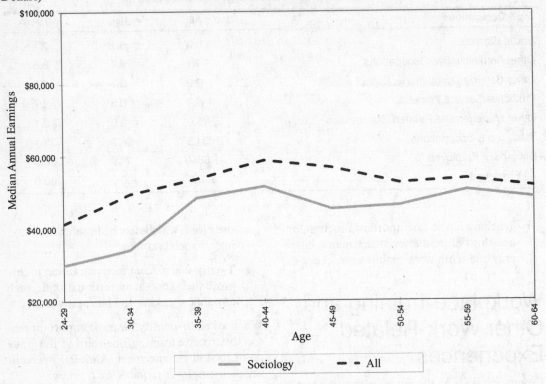

job earn $43,700. Sociology majors employed in educational and nonprofit organizations have average earnings of only $33,600 and $32,000 per year, respectively.

The average annual salary of graduates who work in closely related jobs is $44,400. Graduates with employment in jobs that are somewhat related to their major earn $43,300 per year. In contrast, the average salary of graduates employed full-time in a job that is not related to their field of study is $41,300.

Sociology majors make the highest earnings in service occupations outside the health-care field; probably many of these high earners are working in the insurance industry, which employs 4 percent of grads. Because many social workers learn most of their work-related skills in a master's de-

gree program, an undergraduate degree in sociology does not confer an earnings advantage in that occupation. Neither does it for protective service workers, such as police and firefighters, who usually learn their work-related skills through service academies and on-the-job training.

Job Satisfaction

The overall level of job satisfaction of sociology majors is slightly higher than the average for all graduates.

Employment Outlook

According to the projections by the U.S. Bureau of Labor Statistics, employment in occupations

Table 4
Annual Salary of Workers with Only a Bachelor's Degree, Top 5 Occupations (in 2010 Dollars)

Earnings in Top 5 Occupations	All	Sociology
Total	$41,000	$38,900
Social Workers	$36,100	$33,000
Other Administrative Occupations	$38,200	$33,000
Other Service Occupations, Except Health	$35,100	$52,600
Protective Service Workers	$49,500	$39,200
Other Management-Related Occupations	$57,800	$43,300

that require a bachelor's degree is expected to grow faster than employment in other sectors of the American labor market. Between 2008 and 2018, the U.S. workforce is projected to grow by 10.1 percent, creating an average of 15.2 million job openings per year. The bachelor's-level jobs are expected to increase by 17.7 percent over the same time.

For the occupations that employ large shares of sociology grads, the outlook is not as good as it is for all bachelor's-level occupations, but it is better than the outlook for the economy as a whole.

▶ The occupation with the rosiest outlook is the social work field. The growing elderly population and the aging baby boom generation will create greater demand for health and social services, resulting in rapid job growth among gerontologi-

cal social workers. Employment of social workers in private social service agencies also will increase. Many job openings will stem from growth and the need to replace social workers who leave the occupation. However, competition for social worker jobs is expected in cities where training programs for social workers are prevalent. Opportunities should be good in rural areas, which often find it difficult to attract and retain qualified staff. By specialty, job prospects may be best for social workers with a background in gerontology and substance abuse treatment. Keep in mind, however, that opportunities for those with only a bachelor's degree are highly limited.

▶ Job growth in the miscellaneous administrative occupations that employ

Table 5
Percentage Distribution of Workers with Only a Bachelor's Degree, by Level of Job Satisfaction

Job Satisfaction	Sociology	All
Very satisfied	44.4	45.4
Somewhat satisfied	44.9	45.0
Somewhat dissatisfied	9.2	7.4
Very dissatisfied	1.5	2.2
Mean Score (4=very satisfied, 1=not satisfied at all)	3.4	3.3

Table 6
Projected Growth and Job Openings in the Top 5 Occupations
Employing Persons with Only a Bachelor's Degree in Sociology

Top 5 Occupations	Projected Growth 2008–2018	Projected Annual Job Openings
All top 5	11.5%	373,480
Social Workers	16.1%	26,460
Other Administrative Occupations	10.8%	166,130
Other Service Occupations, Except Health	14.3%	53,570
Protective Service Workers	14.1%	74,300
Other Management-Related Occupations	7.2%	53,020

many sociology grads will be close to the average for all occupations. The large workforce of these mostly clerical occupations will create more than 166,000 job openings, largely through turnover.

▶ Protective service occupations, which are chosen mainly by male sociology graduates, are expected to grow by 14.1 percent and create 74,000 job openings each year. The level of government spending determines the level of employment in this field. Job opportunities in most local police departments will be favorable for qualified individuals, whereas competition is expected for jobs in state and federal agencies. Prospective firefighters are expected to face keen competition for available job openings.

▶ Only a small proportion, 6 percent, of those who earn an undergraduate degree in sociology continue study in this field at the master's degree level. Nearly 18 percent earn a master's degree in social work. Substantial numbers also earn master's degrees in psychology and business fields.

▶ One-third of all doctorates awarded to those with an undergraduate degree in sociology are in sociology. Education and psychology together account for about 30 percent of the doctorates awarded to undergraduates from this field.

▶ About half of those who earn a professional degree study law, and one-seventh earn a degree in a health-care profession.

Pathways Beyond the Bachelor's Degree

About one-third of all sociology majors continue their education beyond the bachelor's degree level and earn graduate or professional degrees of some type. About 27 percent of sociology graduates earn a master's degree, and about 3 percent go on to earn a doctorate. Four percent earn a professional degree after graduation from college.

CHAPTER 48

Visual Arts

Depending on the purpose for creating the art, visual arts can be categorized as either graphic arts or fine arts. Graphic artists use their skills and ideas in commercial interests, as in advertising and design or in working for corporations, retail stores, or publishing companies. Fine artists typically create art to satisfy their own need for self-expression; they may display their art in museums and art galleries, with some of their work sold to private collectors. Most individuals in the visual arts are unable to earn a full-time living unless they are exceptional.

Graphic arts are used in creating packaging, promotional displays, and sales brochures; visual designs for corporate reports and literature; and distinctive logos for products or companies. Graphic artists are responsible for the layout and design of magazines, newspapers, and journals, as well as graphics for television and the Internet.

Fine arts involve different forms. Painters generally work in two dimensions. Painters depict real objects or project varied feelings or thoughts through color, perspective, and shading techniques. Sculptors design in three dimensions. They mold or join materials such as clay, glass, plastic, or metal, or they cut and carve forms from plaster, wood, or stone. Printmakers create printed images from designs cut into wood, stone, or metal. Designs can be engraved in wood or metal, etched in metal by acid, or made as inkjet or laser prints from computers.

Many people work in a variety of visual art professions. Some of these are described here.

Illustrators paint or draw pictures for books, magazines, films, and such paper products as greeting cards, wrapping paper, stationery, and calendars. Illustrators also create story boards used in the making of television commercials and movies.

Art directors or visual journalists decide how to present text in an eye-appealing and organized manner, using photographs or other artwork, such as cartoons, in magazines and newspapers.

Photographers work with stills (portraits), videos of special events such as weddings, or photojournalism. News photographers demonstrate the role that technology plays in the visual arts; for example, digital cameras use electronic memory rather than a film negative to record an image, which then can be transmitted immediately to a computer. Visual communication is entrenched in our society, as we experience it daily.

Designers make up another large group of visual artists. They may specialize in such areas as industrial equipment and products (industrial designers); automobiles; clothing (fashion designers); furniture (furniture designers); fabrics, upholstery, and rugs (textile designers); and interiors of homes, restaurants, retail stores, office space, and buildings (interior designers). After hearing a client's needs, designers first communicate their ideas by sketches and then make models, prototypes, or detailed illustrations drawn to scale. These models, typically developed with computer-aided industrial design, enable decision makers to have a clear idea of the final product. Design is not a static field. Fashion trends are constantly

413

changing. Knowledge of new products, textiles, and fabrics creates demands to keep abreast of many different manufacturers' products and consumers' acceptance of these newer developments.

Most programs in art and design provide training in computer design techniques; this training is especially critical for those entering commercial art. The course work tends to be very practical and, of course, corresponds to the specializations described here.

Artistic ability varies, whether it be the talent to draw, paint, photograph, or sculpt. A person's skills are assessed, captured, and displayed by a portfolio, a collection of samples of one's work. Instructors and potential employers examine the portfolio to evaluate a person's ability. Such samples show ability and technique in eye-hand precision; color usage; vision; and the use of oils, watercolors, acrylics, pastels, pen, and pencil. Artistic ability must be combined with planning and organization to deliver and communicate ideas and feelings. Some might claim the creative and expressive skills to be a persuasive intent.

Additional abilities are spatial—to see differences in size, shape, and form and to visualize relationships; mechanical—to work with equipment and to understand how things come together to produce the best images; and manual—to coordinate use of the hands with creative intellectual thought.

The interests of artists vary depending on the areas in which they work. Besides a predominant liking for art, those in commercial fields like the applications of business, which can offer a hectic and challenging pace that coincides with creative interests. Graphic artists are technologically oriented. Fine artists, however, have a more focused interest in art and a more intellectual approach to the field without the business and technological interests.

Visual artists obviously value creative imagination and the logical correlate of independence, which permits self-expression. Variety and diversion are sought, with routine generally not tolerated. The visual arts offer opportunities for both expressions of feelings and a high level of mental activity. There is also appreciation for

Table 1

Percentage Distribution of Employed Persons with Only a Bachelor's Degree, by Economic Sector, Size, and New Business Status of Employer

	Visual Arts	All
Economic Sector		
Private for-profit	40.3	47.3
Self-employed	32.8	18.5
Government/Military	6.2	11.0
Education	14.6	15.6
Nonprofit	6.0	7.5
Employer Size		
Small (Fewer than 100 employees)	51.4	35.5
Medium (100–999)	20.3	21.8
Large (1,000–24,999)	17.9	26.0
Very large (25,000 or more)	10.4	16.7
Percent working in new business established within past 5 years	10.9	7.6

concrete creations. Opportunities for recognition and high achievement are available and pursued. Artists are accepting of flexible work schedules.

Where Do Visual Arts Majors Work?

The employment of visual arts graduates is spread across the five sectors of the economy. Only 40 percent work in the private, for-profit sector for businesses and corporations. Self-employment is common among arts majors who value independence so that they can maximize individual expression; almost one-third are self-employed in their own business or practice. Another 15 percent of arts graduates find employment in educational institutions, working as elementary or secondary school teachers. About 6 percent work in the government sector, and another 6 percent find employment in the nonprofit sector.

Arts majors have to be exceptionally good at what they do to be able to earn a full-time living with a job in their field. Therefore, it is not surprising that many arts majors work in jobs that are unrelated to their major. Roughly equal shares of 38 percent of the graduates work in jobs that are closely related and unrelated to the visual arts. Another 23 percent say that their jobs are somewhat related to their major.

Fifteen percent work part-time. For some, this allows them free time to pursue their artistic interests; others need the time for family responsibilities.

Of all visual arts graduates under the age of 65, 77 percent are employed, a low number compared to most of the majors in this book. Only 4 percent are officially unemployed; in other words, they are not employed and are actively seeking employment. The remaining 18 percent are out of the labor force; that is, they are not employed and are not seeking employment. Three main reasons underlie the labor force withdrawal of visual arts graduates: 30 percent cite family responsibilities as the most important reason for labor force withdrawal; 22 percent lack the desire or the need to work; and 21 percent are retired. Only 6 percent have given up looking for work because no suitable jobs are available.

Table 2

Percentage Distribution of Employed Persons with Only a Bachelor's Degree in Visual Arts, by the Relationship Between Their Job and College Major

Relationship of Job to Major	Percent
Closely related	38.5
Somewhat related	23.4
Not related	38.1

Percent who report the following as the most important reasons for working in a job that was not related to major:

Pay, promotion opportunities	33.7
Change in career or professional interests	14.7
Family-related reasons	14.5
Working conditions (hours, equipment, environment)	12.8
Job in highest degree field not available	12.3

Occupations

One-quarter of grads work in one of the creative fields that include artists and designers. More than 11 percent work in sales or marketing. Those working in precision/production occupations are primarily engaged in personal and household goods manufacturing, most likely as industrial designers.

Female grads outnumber male grads by 2 to 1 but are somewhat less likely to choose work in a creative occupation and more likely to choose work in a business function.

Work Activities

▶ About half spend most of their workweek in sales, purchasing, and marketing activities. As noted, sales and marketing occupations employ 11 percent of the graduates. More than one-fifth of the grads devote at least 10 hours of the workweek to these duties.

▶ About 14 percent of all employed graduates spend most of their time at work in teaching activities. About 31 percent state that they regularly spend at least some time in teaching activities.

▶ Management and supervisory duties take up most of the time at work among 13 percent of employed arts graduates, and they are a regular activity for 55 percent.

▶ Most arts programs provide training in computer design techniques. Various forms of fine art such as art, design, illustration, sculpting, and even painting require or permit the use of computers. Therefore, it is not surprising to find that 88 percent of employed arts graduates regularly engage in computer applications, programming, and systems-development activities; 7 percent spend most of their time at work in these activities.

▶ Only 5 percent spend most of their typical workweek in accounting, finance, and contractual duties, but 31 percent regularly engage in these tasks.

Table 3
Top 5 Occupations Employing Persons with Only a Bachelor's Degree in Visual Arts, by Percentage

Top 5 Occupations	All	Men	Women
Artists, Broadcasters, Editors, Entertainers, Public Relations Specialists, and Writers	24.9	31.7	20.5
Sales Occupations—Retail	6.4	5.4	7.0
Other Marketing and Sales Occupations	4.8	3.1	5.9
Other Administrative Occupations	4.0	4.1	3.9
Precision/Production Occupations	3.8	3.8	3.8
Total, Top 5 Occupations	43.9	48.1	41.1
Balance of Employed	56.1	51.9	58.9
All Employed	100.0	100.0	100.0

Workplace Training and Other Work-Related Experiences

The career potential of a job is closely associated with the amount of work-related training on the job. Firms that invest in their workforce are more likely to offer pay increases and promotions to match the increasing productivity of their workers. The incidence of work-related training among visual arts graduates is much lower than the rate of participation in work-related training among all college graduates. While 61 percent of all college graduates acquire some kind of work-related training during a year, only 43 percent of arts majors annually engage in work-related training.

▶ Of those arts graduates who receive some work-related training, 38 percent receive technical training in the occupation in which they are employed.

▶ Only 8 percent of the training recipients receive management or supervisory training.

▶ Nine percent receive training to improve their general professional skills, such as public speaking and business writing.

When asked to identify the most important reason to acquire training, one-quarter of visual arts graduates who undergo training identify the need to improve their occupational skills and knowledge. Another 6 percent report a mandatory training requirement by the employer as the most important factor underlying their involvement in work-related training. Another 5 percent rank the need to obtain or maintain a professional license or certificate as the number one reason for participation in work-related training activities. Probably some of these are teachers.

Salaries

The median annual salary of visual arts graduates with only a bachelor's degree is $40,000, a level that is 29 percent lower than the median annual salary of all employed college graduates. On average, employed visual arts graduates work for 38 hours per week and for 48 weeks per year, resulting in 1,824 hours of employment per year. The level of work effort among visual arts graduates is 15 percent lower than the average among all college graduates (43 hours per week and 50 weeks per year, resulting in 2,150 hours per year). This lower level of work engagement probably explains much of the difference in earnings compared to graduates of other majors.

The average annual salary of arts majors who work in jobs that are somewhat related to their major, $47,500, is higher than the salary of those who are employed in jobs that are closely related or unrelated to their major. Closely related jobs pay full-time employed arts graduates an average of $41,300 annually. Graduates whose jobs are unrelated to their undergraduate major earn an average annual salary of $37,200.

Arts graduates working in the private, for-profit sector for businesses and corporations earn an average of $46,400 per year, which is more than their counterparts employed in other sectors. The average annual salary of graduates who work in the government sector is $42,400. Private, non-profit, full-time jobs pay arts graduates $40,200 per year. Self-employed visual arts graduates earn $35,500 per year. The average salary of visual arts graduates working in educational institutions is $34,100 per year.

Visual arts graduates possess skills that are directly relevant to only a limited set of occupations. Therefore, they often find employment in jobs that are unrelated to their field, and these jobs are

FIGURE 1

Age/Earnings Profile of Persons with Only a Bachelor's Degree in Visual Arts (Full-Time Workers, in 2010 Dollars)

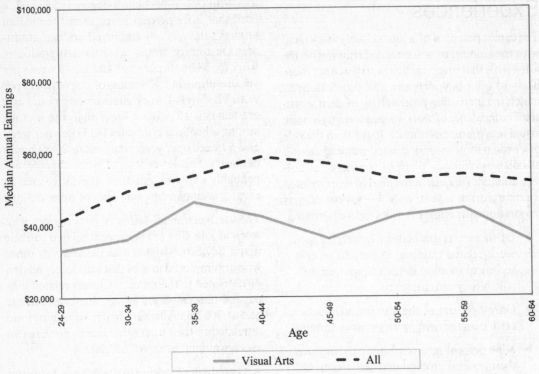

frequently low-paying. Except for those working the retail sales occupations, the average salary of arts graduates in the top 5 occupations is lower than the salary of all college graduates employed in those occupations. The average salary of all college graduates and visual arts graduates in the top 5 occupations that are predominant employers of visual arts graduates is presented in Table 4.

▶ The highest average salary of visual arts graduates in the 5 occupations is in miscellaneous marketing and sales occupations. Graduates employed in these occupations earn $51,600 per year. These occupations are more likely to employ female than male graduates.

▶ The visual arts bachelor's does not confer an earnings advantage in the large group of creative occupations, but it is likely to be advantageous in specific occupations such as artist or industrial designer.

Job Satisfaction

The overall level of job satisfaction of visual arts majors is about the same as the average for all graduates.

Employment Outlook

According to the projections by the U.S. Bureau of Labor Statistics, employment in occupations that require a bachelor's degree is expected to grow faster than employment in other sectors of the American labor market. Between 2008 and

Table 4
Annual Salary of Workers with Only a Bachelor's Degree, Top 5 Occupations (in 2010 Dollars)

Earnings in Top 5 Occupations	All	Visual Arts
Total	$40,000	$40,400
Artists, Broadcasters, Editors, Entertainers, Public Relations Specialists, and Writers	$49,500	$40,200
Sales Occupations—Retail	$42,300	$46,400
Other Marketing and Sales Occupations	$54,700	$51,600
Other Administrative Occupations	$38,200	$34,100
Precision/Production Occupations	$39,200	$28,900

2018, the U.S. workforce is projected to grow by 10.1 percent, creating an average of 15.2 million job openings per year. The bachelor's-level jobs are expected to increase by 17.7 percent over the same time. The employment growth projections for the top 5 occupations that are most likely to employ visual arts graduates are presented in Table 6.

▶ The fastest growth in demand is projected in the arts and entertainment occupations. However, competition for jobs is expected to be keen for both salaried and freelance jobs in all specialties because the number of people with creative ability and an interest in these careers is expected to continue to exceed the number of available openings. Despite the competition, employers and individual clients are always on the lookout for talented and creative artists and designers. For graphic designers, almost 13 percent growth is projected; individuals with website design and animation experience will have the best opportunities. For fashion designers, less than 1 percent growth is projected; the best job opportunities will be in design firms that design mass-market clothing sold in department stores and retail chain stores, such as apparel wholesale firms. Interior designers are projected to grow by 19.4 percent; those with formal training or experience in green or energy-efficient design in particular are expected to have better job

Table 5
Percentage Distribution of Workers with Only a Bachelor's Degree, by Level of Job Satisfaction

Job Satisfaction	Visual Arts	All
Very satisfied	43.7	45.4
Somewhat satisfied	44.0	45.0
Somewhat dissatisfied	9.3	7.4
Very dissatisfied	3.1	2.2
Mean Score (4=very satisfied, 1=not satisfied at all)	3.3	3.3

Table 6

Projected Growth and Job Openings in the Top 5 Occupations
Employing Persons with Only a Bachelor's Degree in Visual Arts

Top 5 Occupations	Projected Growth 2008–2018	Projected Annual Job Openings
All top 5	4.6%	685,870
Artists, Broadcasters, Editors, Entertainers, Public Relations Specialists, and Writers	12.4%	71,740
Sales Occupations—Retail	7.5%	207,700
Other Marketing and Sales Occupations	7.3%	64,880
Other Administrative Occupations	10.8%	166,130
Precision/Production Occupations	−3.0%	175,420

prospects than most due to increased interest in this area.

▶ For industrial designers (the most likely livelihood of those working in precision/production occupations), almost 9 percent growth is projected; the best job opportunities will be in specialized design firms that are used by manufacturers to design products or parts of products.

▶ The miscellaneous marketing and sales occupations that employ many visual arts majors are projected to have slower-than-average growth, but these are large occupations that will create many job openings through turnover.

▶ Job growth in the administrative occupations is projected to be about average, but job turnover should help in creating more than 166,000 openings each year.

Pathways Beyond the Bachelor's Degree

Of all graduates with a bachelor's degree in visual arts, 29 percent proceed to earn a postgraduate degree: 26 percent earn a master's degree, but only 1 percent earn a doctoral degree, and less than 2 percent earn a professional degree.

▶ Well over one-third of all master's degrees earned by undergraduate visual arts majors are in the field of visual arts. Another 4 are in architecture or environmental design.

▶ Almost half the master's degrees earned by visual arts grads are in education or educational administration, with elementary education the most popular specialization.

PART 7

Natural Sciences

CHAPTER 49

Animal Science

Animal scientists develop better, more efficient ways of producing and processing meat, poultry, eggs, and milk. Specialists such as dairy scientists, poultry scientists, and animal breeders study genetics, nutrition, reproduction, growth, and development of domestic farm animals. Some animal scientists inspect and grade livestock, purchase livestock, or work in technical sales or marketing. Others work as extension agents for government agencies, performing educational and consultative roles in bringing farmers and ranchers the latest research and new developments to assist in addressing local problems. This educational outreach system has helped the United States secure preeminence worldwide in the field of agriculture.

While dairy scientists conduct research in selecting, breeding, feeding, and managing cattle, the poultry scientist does the same with poultry. The latter additionally focuses on increasing the efficiency of production and improving the quality of poultry products. These goals are achieved by developing improved practices in incubation, brooding, feeding, rearing, housing, artificial insemination, and disease and parasite prevention and control. Similarly, dairy scientists carry out experiments to determine the effects of different kinds of feed on the quantity, quality, and nutritive value of milk; dairy scientists also study the physiology of reproduction and lactation.

Although this field is relatively small in terms of employment, each state has a land-grant college that offers agricultural science degrees, which include animal science. The curriculum covers communications, economics, business, and physical and life sciences courses. Specific courses may include animal breeding, reproductive physiology, nutrition, and meat and muscle biology.

The abilities required for animal science include scientific, mathematical, and mechanical skills, as well as a business sense. Animal scientists use manual dexterity, whether for working with animals or machinery. A salient feature of graduates is their leadership and interpersonal skills. As noted earlier, they can be disseminators of information, and they need to be constantly involved in new learning as knowledge of their field expands.

A combination of interests can be observed, with animal scientists primarily enjoying science but also liking applications and technology. A people and business orientation also fits those who work in this field.

Animal scientists value the opportunity to have diversity in their work, be independent and do what they want, seek high achievement, and expect to receive a good salary.

Where Do Animal Science Majors Work?

Most animal science majors work in the private, for-profit sector. A large proportion of graduates of animal science programs become self-employed; more than 3 out of 10 animal science majors operate their own businesses after graduation. Many of these self-employed individuals operate their own farms or their own wholesaling or retailing organizations. Only 42 percent of animal

Table 1

Percentage Distribution of Employed Persons with Only a Bachelor's Degree, by Economic Sector, Size, and New Business Status of Employer

	Animal Science	All
Economic Sector		
Private for-profit	42.0	47.3
Self-employed	31.0	18.5
Government/Military	10.6	11.0
Education	11.5	15.6
Nonprofit	4.9	7.5
Employer Size		
Small (Fewer than 100 employees)	44.8	35.5
Medium (100–999)	16.8	21.8
Large (1,000–24,999)	20.1	26.0
Very large (25,000 or more)	18.2	16.7
Percent working in new business established within past 5 years	5.2	7.6

science majors work for a business or corporation. Of the 11 percent who work in government, some are inspectors or agricultural extension agents. A similar share work in education.

More than two-thirds of animal science majors work in jobs that are related in some way to their undergraduate field of study. Less than one-third work in jobs that are unrelated to animal science studies.

About 90 percent of persons with only a bachelor's degree in animal science are employed, a high number among the majors profiled in this book. Among those not working, less than half (3 percent of all grads) are still actively looking for work. The remaining 7 percent of grads have decided not to participate in the labor market. The largest fraction of this group, 38 percent, indicate that they do not want to work because they have retired, even though they have not yet reached 65. Twenty-three percent consider family responsibilities more important than employment. Almost 1 in 10 are not working because they are students.

Occupations

About twice as many men as women graduate from this major. The men are quite likely to be employed in agriculture-related occupations; about one-quarter of men with a college degree in this field work in an agricultural occupation. Women are more likely to work in a managerial or administrative job; many work in segments of the agricultural industry other than production.

Work Activities

▶ Almost two-thirds of grads devote significant work time to management or supervision of people or projects, and it is the main work role for almost 1 in 5.

▶ Sales, purchasing, and marketing are the main activities of 22 percent of animal science majors, and 6 out of 10 grads perform these tasks regularly.

Table 2
Percentage Distribution of Employed Persons with Only a Bachelor's Degree in Animal Science, by the Relationship Between Their Job and College Major

Relationship of Job to Major	Percent
Closely related	45.1
Somewhat related	24.2
Not related	30.6

Percent who report the following as the most important reasons for working in a job that was not related to major:

Family-related reasons	34.2
Pay, promotion opportunities	27.1
Job location	11.3
Working conditions (hours, equipment, environment)	8.0
Change in career or professional interests	7.7

▶ Providing professional services in the occupation in which the graduate is employed, such as a position in health or agricultural science, is also a major activity that for almost one-quarter of grads consumes a substantial number of hours during the workweek. However, only 8 percent are primarily focused on these services.

▶ About 93 percent of graduates of this field regularly use computer applications of some type, although less than 4 percent see this as their main responsibility.

▶ Four out of 10 graduates engage in production- and operations-related activities, and more than one-fifth devote most of their time to these tasks.

Table 3
Top 5 Occupations Employing Persons with Only a Bachelor's Degree in Animal Science, by Percentage

Top 5 Occupations	All	Men	Women
Farmers, Foresters, and Fishermen	19.2	24.8	7.7
Other Management-Related Occupations	7.4	3.7	15.0
Other Marketing and Sales Occupations	5.7	7.8	1.3
Other Administrative Occupations	5.2	2.1	11.5
Other Service Occupations, Except Health	5.0	4.7	5.6
Total, Top 5 Occupations	42.5	43.1	41.1
Balance of Employed	57.5	56.9	58.9
All Employed	100.0	100.0	100.0

▶ More than 4 out of 10 grads regularly handle accounting, financial, and contractual tasks, although only 3 percent perceive these tasks as their chief responsibility.

Workplace Training and Other Work-Related Experiences

The career potential of a job is closely associated with the amount of work-related training on the job. Work-related training is regarded as an investment by firms because it makes workers more productive. Firms that invest in their workforce are more likely to offer pay increases and promotions to match the increasing productivity of their workers. The incidence of work-related training among animal science graduates (58 percent) is slightly lower than the participation rate in work-related training among all college graduates (61 percent).

▶ More than half of animal science majors who participate in some type of training report that the training is designed to improve some specific skill related to their current job.

▶ Unlike majors in other fields of study, few of these majors are trained in the communications area. Fewer than 1 out of 5 majors say they received any training in business writing or public speaking.

▶ Managerial and supervisory training is received by 1 out of 5 graduates with degrees in this field who get training.

When asked the most important reason they get training, almost one-third of those who participate say they want to enhance their work-related skills. About 1 out of 8 are required by their employer to get training.

Salaries

The median annual salary of animal science graduates with only a bachelor's degree is $38,000, a level that is 36 percent lower than the median annual salary of all employed college graduates. On average, employed animal science graduates work for 47 hours per week and for 49 weeks per year, resulting in 2,303 hours of employment per year. The level of work effort among animal science graduates is 7 percent higher than the average among all college graduates (43 hours per week and 50 weeks per year, resulting in 2,150 hours per year).

Graduates who work in educational institutions have earnings that are the highest earnings of all graduates with degrees in this field: $61,300 per year. Animal science majors employed in government average $56,800 per year. Grads working in private-sector jobs earn an average of $45,400. Self-employed graduates earn considerably less than the average for graduates within the field: $34,300.

Animal science majors employed in jobs closely related to their field have higher annual salaries than those who work in jobs that are less related to the field. The average annual salary of graduates who work in closely related jobs is $45,400. Graduates with employment in jobs that are somewhat related to their major earn $33,000 per year. In contrast, the average salary of graduates employed full-time in a job that is not related to their field of study is $41,300.

The earnings advantage of working in a closely related job may seem to conflict with the information in Table 4, where you can see that the grads working in agricultural production earn lower wages than in 3 of the other top 5 occupations employing grads. However, many of those working in the more lucrative occupations, such as marketing or administration, are holding jobs in the agriculture industry and are finding ways to use their education for high earnings.

<u>**FIGURE 1**</u>

Age/Earnings Profile of Persons with Only a Bachelor's Degree in Animal Science (Full-Time Workers, in 2010 Dollars)

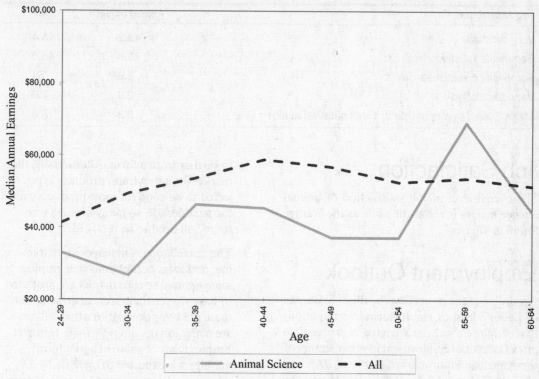

Table 4

Annual Salary of Workers with Only a Bachelor's Degree,
Top 5 Occupations (in 2010 Dollars)

Earnings in Top 5 Occupations	All	Animal Science
Total	$38,000	$39,600
Farmers, Foresters, and Fishermen	$36,100	$36,100
Other Management-Related Occupations	$57,800	$36,100
Other Marketing and Sales Occupations	$54,700	$50,600
Other Administrative Occupations	$38,200	$46,400
Other Service Occupations, Except Health	$35,100	$39,200

Table 5
Percentage Distribution of Workers with Only a Bachelor's Degree, by Level of Job Satisfaction

Job Satisfaction	Animal Science	All
Very satisfied	43.2	45.4
Somewhat satisfied	45.6	45.0
Somewhat dissatisfied	8.3	7.4
Very dissatisfied	2.9	2.2
Mean Score (4=very satisfied, 1=not satisfied at all)	3.3	3.3

Job Satisfaction

The overall level of job satisfaction of animal science majors is about the same as the average for all graduates.

Employment Outlook

According to the projections by the U.S. Bureau of Labor Statistics, employment in occupations that require a bachelor's degree is expected to grow faster than employment in other sectors of the American labor market. Between 2008 and 2018, the U.S. workforce is projected to grow by 10.1 percent, creating an average of 15.2 million job openings per year. The bachelor's-level jobs are expected to increase by 17.7 percent over the same time. The outlook for the dominant occupations employing animal science grads varies but is mostly below average.

▶ Bureau of Labor Statistics projections suggest that overall employment in agricultural production will grow by less than the average for the economy as a whole, reflecting the decline of self-employed farmers because of the consolidation of farms and increasing productivity. With fewer people wanting to become farmers and a large number of farmers expected to retire or give up their farms in the next decade, there will be some opportunities to own or lease a farm. Additionally, the market for agricultural products is projected to be good for most products over the next decade, so many farmers who retire will need to be replaced.

▶ The miscellaneous managerial, marketing, and sales occupations that employ many animal science majors are projected to have slower-than-average growth, but these are large occupations that will create many job openings through turnover. Employment of salaried agricultural managers is expected to increase by 5.9 percent and create about 15,000 job openings each year.

▶ Job growth in the administrative occupations is projected to be about average, but job turnover should help in creating more than 166,000 openings each year.

Pathways Beyond the Bachelor's Degree

About 3 out of 10 animal science majors go on to complete a graduate degree. Nearly 12 percent eventually earn a master's, and 6 percent earn a doctorate. An impressive 12 percent of bachelor's degree holders in animal science earn a professional degree of some type.

Table 6
Projected Growth and Job Openings in the Top 5 Occupations Employing Persons with Only a Bachelor's Degree in Animal Science

Top 5 Occupations	Projected Growth 2008–2018	Projected Annual Job Openings
All top 5	9.7%	340,060
Farmers, Foresters, and Fishermen	9.3%	2,460
Other Management-Related Occupations	7.2%	53,020
Other Marketing and Sales Occupations	7.3%	64,880
Other Administrative Occupations	10.8%	166,130
Other Service Occupations, Except Health	14.3%	53,570

▶ Of those who earn a master's degree, almost 10 percent earn one in animal science. An additional 27 percent earn a master's degree in another area of agricultural science or marketing.

▶ Educational administration is also a major area in which a number of animal science majors earn a master's degree. Twelve percent of master's degrees earned by animal science majors are in this field, often as a stairway to a position in agricultural extension.

▶ Among those who earn a doctorate, almost one-third continue their studies in animal science, and many of the others focus on some other aspect of biological science.

▶ More than three-quarters of the animal science majors who earn a professional degree earn it in the health field, either in medicine or veterinary medicine.

CHAPTER 50

Biology and Life Sciences

Advances in the knowledge of basic life processes, especially at the genetic and molecular levels, are the driving forces in the field of biotechnology. Such specializations as microbiology and biophysics have become large enough to be separate majors. (Microbiology is profiled in Chapter 54.) This development has blurred classifications in the study of biology, but often majors continue to use traditional names of concentration areas. For example, biological scientists who do biomedical research typically are referred to as medical scientists.

Aquatic biologists examine various types of water life, such as plankton, clams, fish, or lobsters. Specialization in saltwater species is designated as marine biology. Aquatic biologists investigate the conditions of water—its salinity, temperature, acidity, light, and oxygen content—to determine its relationship with aquatic life.

Botanists study the development, physiology, heredity, environment, distribution, anatomy, and economic value of plants for application to forestry, horticulture, and pharmacology. Botany also includes the study of chromosomes and reproduction and of the biochemistry of plants and plant cells. Botanists investigate environments and plant communities and the effects of rainfall, temperature, climate, soil, and elevation on plant growth from seed to mature plants.

Physiologists research the cellular structure and organ systems of plants and animals. Physiologists study growth, respiration, and glands and their relationship to bodily functions, excretion, movement, and reproduction under normal and abnormal conditions.

Zoology is the study of reptiles, amphibians, fish, sponges, birds, and mammals. Zoologists also examine these creatures' habits, diseases, relationship to the environment, genetics, growth, and development.

Most colleges and universities offer programs in biological sciences, which are sometimes called life sciences. These institutions approach course work in general biology from a research and development perspective. Specialization often occurs in advanced degrees. Typical courses may include principles of biology, environmental and population biology, genetics, cell physiology, biochemistry, and general microbiology, as well as mathematics, physics, and chemistry.

Biology requires good academic ability to handle the heavy load of science and mathematics courses. Biologists use logic and scientific thinking in their analyses, and they apply methodologies to make judgments. Recognition of differences in size, form, color, and texture is important. Finger dexterity, coordinated use of eyes and manual movement, and the ability to use laboratory and scientific equipment are all requirements. The ability to withstand prolonged periods of concentration is often required.

The interests of biologists are predominantly scientific and technological, with some interest in the liberal arts. The scientific interests are greater in the life sciences. The liberal arts interests can include the humanities as well as social sciences, which foster a wide human perspective. Biologists also are interested in laboratory work or field applications. They are interested in scientific applications related to living beings versus the inanimate applications of physics and chemistry.

Where Do Biology and Life Sciences Majors Work?

Persons with a bachelor's degree in biology are employed across key segments of the American economy. Unlike the graduates from many other fields of study, fewer than one-half of all biology bachelor's degree holders work as wage and salary employees at for-profit businesses and corporations. Only 43 percent of grads work in that segment of the economy. Instead, many biology majors (16 percent) work in educational institutions as teachers. About 1 out of 8 biology majors work in a government organization. An additional 10 percent work in nonprofit foundations and research organizations. A surprisingly large number of biology majors are self-employed; about 18 percent operate their own business or consulting service.

Compared to graduates of most other majors, the share of biology and life sciences grads who do work that is closely related to their major is about average. A little more than 4 out of 10 employed graduates work in jobs that are closely related to their major, and an additional 28 percent consider their jobs to be somewhat related. About 3 out of 10 report that their employment is not related to their major.

About 83 percent of those under age 65 with a bachelor's degree are employed, although about

Table 1

Percentage Distribution of Employed Persons with Only a Bachelor's Degree, by Economic Sector, Size, and New Business Status of Employer

	Biology and Life Sciences	All
Economic Sector		
Private for-profit	43.3	47.3
Self-employed	17.8	18.5
Government/Military	12.6	11.0
Education	16.0	15.6
Nonprofit	10.3	7.5
Employer Size		
Small (Fewer than 100 employees)	33.4	35.5
Medium (100–999)	19.1	21.8
Large (1,000–24,999)	32.7	26.0
Very large (25,000 or more)	14.8	16.7
Percent working in new business established within past 5 years	5.9	7.6

Table 2

Percentage Distribution of Employed Persons with Only a
Bachelor's Degree in Biology and Life Sciences, by the
Relationship Between Their Job and College Major

Relationship of Job to Major	Percent
Closely related	41.5
Somewhat related	28.4
Not related	30.2

Percent who report the following as the most important reasons for
working in a job that was not related to major:

Pay, promotion opportunities	29.3
Change in career or professional interests	19.1
Job in highest degree field not available	17.4
Family-related reasons	16.0
Working conditions (hours, equipment, environment)	7.9

9 percent of those working hold part-time positions, usually because they choose to work part-time. Of those who are not employed, almost all have chosen not to work. Fewer than 3 percent of all those with a biology degree are unemployed and actively seeking work. More than 1 in 4 of those not working have taken early retirement. A slightly smaller share choose not to work to meet family responsibilities. Eighteen percent have no need or desire to hold a job.

Table 3

Top 5 Occupations Employing Persons with Only a
Bachelor's Degree in Biology and Life Sciences, by Percentage

Top 5 Occupations	All	Men	Women
Health Technologists and Technicians	8.6	5.8	12.3
Registered Nurses, Pharmacists, Dietitians, Therapists, and Physician Assistants	6.5	3.4	10.4
Farmers, Foresters, and Fishermen	4.3	6.7	1.1
Sales Occupations—Commodities, Except Retail	4.2	5.7	2.4
Accountants, Auditors, and Other Financial Specialists	4.0	4.4	3.6
Total, Top 5 Occupations	27.6	26.0	29.8
Balance of Employed	72.4	74.0	70.2
All Employed	100.0	100.0	100.0

Occupations

A degree in biology or life science is the gateway to many different kinds of careers. The top 5 occupations employing grads account for barely more than one-quarter of the grads. About 15 percent of the grads are working in the health-care field, either as technologists, technicians, or direct providers. Although the major turns out male and female graduates in roughly equal proportions, the women are more likely to choose these health-related fields. The male grads are more likely to go into agriculture or business.

Work Activities

▶ Biology majors spend the greatest part of their workweek delivering a set of professional services that characterize their current jobs. Such services may include the delivery of laboratory analysis of biological substances or the provision of various health-care services. Seventeen percent of grads see these activities as their main job function, and 3 out of 10 engage regularly in these activities.

▶ Administrative duties also are an important part of the tasks undertaken by biology graduates. These duties include employee relations, purchasing, accounting, finance, and record-keeping activities. About one-third of graduates devote at least 10 hours out of the average workweek to these tasks.

▶ Somewhat more than half of grads spend significant work time managing or supervising people or projects, and this is the primary role for 15 percent of grads.

▶ Teaching is an important part of the job for 29 percent of biology graduates and the chief focus of the job for 9 percent. Teaching can include peer education and training activities or teaching at the elementary or secondary school level.

▶ Production, operations, and maintenance are regular responsibilities for one-quarter of grads. About one-tenth of grads focus on these tasks to the exclusion of most others.

Workplace Training and Other Work-Related Experiences

The career potential of a job is closely associated with the amount of work-related training on the job. Work-related training is regarded as an investment by firms because it makes workers more productive. Firms that invest in their workforce are more likely to offer pay increases and promotions to match the increasing productivity of their workers. The incidence of work-related training among biology graduates is about the same as the participation rate in work-related training among all college graduates. While 61 percent of all college graduates acquire some kind of work-related training during a year, 62 percent of employed biology graduates engage in a job-oriented training program.

▶ Fifty-five percent of the grads say their training is associated with the development of specific professional skills related to the job, such as learning new lab techniques or procedures or learning new methods of conducting treatments or therapies.

▶ About 18 percent of the training participants receive instruction in managerial or supervisory areas.

▶ The same fraction of participants receive training designed to improve communications skills.

More than one-third of life sciences grads who get training report that the most important reason for getting training is to learn new skills. Almost 1 out of 10 need to train to obtain or maintain licensure or certification; this is a requirement in many health-care occupations. More than 8 percent are required by their employers to get on-the-job training.

Salaries

The median annual salary of biology and life sciences graduates with only a bachelor's degree is $46,400, a level that is 11 percent lower than the median annual salary of all employed college graduates. On average, employed biology and life sciences graduates work for 42 hours per week and for 50 weeks per year, resulting in 2,100 hours of employment per year. The level of work effort among biology and life sciences graduates is 2 percent lower than the average among all college graduates (43 hours per week and 50 weeks per year, resulting in 2,150 hours per year).

Biology graduates who work for private, for-profit companies have average salaries of $52,000 per year. Those graduates who are self-employed have annual earnings that average $48,700. Those who work in government and in nonprofit organizations earn slightly less, $47,500 and $47,100 per year, respectively. Educational institutions pay the lowest average salary to biology grads, $40,100.

In many fields of study, access to jobs that are closely related to the undergraduate major leads to higher earnings after graduation. However, this is not the case for biology majors. Those majors employed in jobs that are not related to their major have annual salaries ($48,900) that

FIGURE 1

Age/Earnings Profile of Persons with Only a Bachelor's Degree in Biology and Life Sciences (Full-Time Workers, in 2010 Dollars)

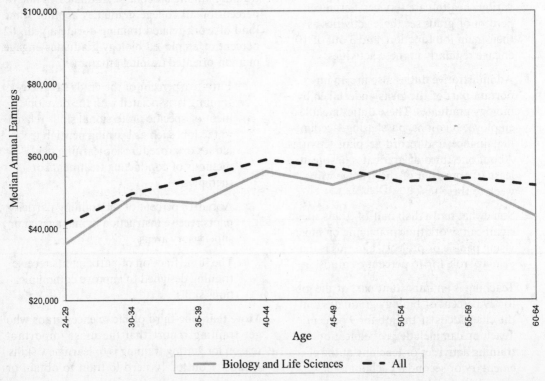

Table 4
Annual Salary of Workers with Only a Bachelor's Degree, Top 5 Occupations (in 2010 Dollars)

Earnings in Top 5 Occupations	All	Biology and Life Sciences
Total	$46,400	$49,300
Health Technologists and Technicians	$42,300	$47,300
Registered Nurses, Pharmacists, Dietitians, Therapists, and Physician Assistants	$55,700	$57,700
Farmers, Foresters, and Fishermen	$36,100	$27,500
Sales Occupations—Commodities, Except Retail	$64,000	$66,600
Accountants, Auditors, and Other Financial Specialists	$59,900	$50,800

are roughly the same as those working in jobs that are closely related to the field ($48,300). Graduates with employment in jobs that are somewhat related to the major earn $46,600.

The earnings of employed biology majors vary sharply by occupation. Those employed as health technologists and technicians—the single largest occupation in which majors find work—earn about $47,300 per year. Direct-care workers earn more. Among the top 5 occupations employing jobs, agricultural production pays the lowest and sales jobs the highest. The degree provides an earnings advantage in 3 of the top 5 jobs, but not in agricultural production or accounting, where a more targeted major is better rewarded.

Job Satisfaction

The overall level of job satisfaction of biology and life sciences majors is slightly higher than the average for all graduates.

Employment Outlook

According to the projections by the U.S. Bureau of Labor Statistics, employment in occupations that require a bachelor's degree is expected to grow faster than employment in other sectors of the American labor market. Between 2008 and 2018, the U.S. workforce is projected to grow by 10.1 percent, creating an average of 15.2 million

Table 5
Percentage Distribution of Workers with Only a Bachelor's Degree, by Level of Job Satisfaction

Job Satisfaction	Biology and Life Sciences	All
Very satisfied	43.5	45.4
Somewhat satisfied	47.4	45.0
Somewhat dissatisfied	7.1	7.4
Very dissatisfied	2.0	2.2
Mean Score (4=very satisfied, 1=not satisfied at all)	3.4	3.3

job openings per year. The bachelor's-level jobs are expected to increase by 17.7 percent over the same time.

The outlook for jobs employing biology grads is highly mixed.

▶ Employment in the health technologists field is expected to grow by one-fifth through 2018, a rate of growth well above the average for all bachelor's-level occupations. Similarly high rates of employment growth are projected for direct-care workers such as nurses, therapists, and physician assistants. In addition, these occupations are expected to create numerous job openings.

▶ Employment in agricultural production will grow by less than the average for the economy as a whole, reflecting the decline of self-employed farmers because of the consolidation of farms and increasing productivity. With fewer people wanting to become farmers and a large number of farmers expected to retire or give up their farms in the next decade, there will be some opportunities to own or lease a farm. Additionally, the market for agricultural

products is projected to be good for most products over the next decade, so many farmers who retire will need to be replaced. In addition, employment of salaried agricultural managers is expected to increase.

▶ The commodities sales occupation is expected to shrink over the projection decade. In addition, the workforce is very small, so it will offer few jobs to compete for. Entry-level sales agents, particularly those with previous sales experience, should face better prospects in smaller firms, as opposed to larger firms, where many positions have been eliminated.

▶ Accounting and financial occupations are projected to grow at above-average rates. An increase in the number of businesses, changing financial laws and corporate governance regulations, and increased accountability for protecting an organization's stakeholders will drive job growth. Accountants and auditors who have earned professional recognition through certification or other designation, especially a CPA, should have the best job prospects.

Table 6
Projected Growth and Job Openings in the Top 5 Occupations Employing Persons with Only a Bachelor's Degree in Biology and Life Sciences

Top 5 Occupations	Projected Growth 2008–2018	Projected Annual Job Openings
All top 5	20.0%	284,740
Health Technologists and Technicians	20.1%	35,070
Registered Nurses, Pharmacists, Dietitians, Therapists, and Physician Assistants	21.5%	119,640
Farmers, Foresters, and Fishermen	9.3%	2,460
Sales Occupations—Commodities, Except Retail	−1.1%	310
Accountants, Auditors, and Other Financial Specialists	18.9%	127,260

Pathways Beyond the Bachelor's Degree

The majority (54 percent) of biology majors earn some type of advanced degree after completing their undergraduate education. More than 1 in 5 biology bachelor's degree holders eventually earn a master's degree. About 8 percent earn a doctorate, and 25 percent earn a professional degree.

▶ Among those who earn a master's degree, more than 1 out 10 choose to study education in preparation for a teaching career, while about the same share earn a master's degree in a health-related field. About 27 percent earn a master's degree in biology or a related life sciences field.

▶ Almost two-thirds of biology majors who earn a doctorate study some life sciences discipline. Health and education are also popular areas in which those with biology undergraduate degrees eventually earn doctoral degrees.

▶ At the professional level, 7 out of 10 of those who earn a degree study a health profession: medicine, dentistry, optometry, osteopathy, podiatry, or veterinary.

CHAPTER 51

Chemistry

All physical things, whether occurring naturally or artificially, are composed of chemicals. Chemists in basic research and development investigate the properties, composition, and structure of matter and the laws that govern the combination of elements and reactions of substances. In applied work, chemists create new products and processes or they improve existing ones, such as plastics. In manufacturing, chemists specify the ingredients, mixing times, and temperatures for each stage in a production process. They monitor automated processes in the production of paint, and they conduct tests to assure that products meet prescribed standards.

Chemists often specialize in a subfield. Analytical chemists determine the structure, composition, and nature of substances, and they develop analytical techniques. For example, they identify the presence and concentration of chemical pollutants in air, water, and soil. Organic chemists study the chemistry of the vast number of carbon compounds. They have developed many commercial products, such as drugs and plastics. Inorganic chemists study compounds consisting mainly of elements other than carbon, such as those in electronics components. Physical chemists study the physical characteristics of atoms and molecules and investigate how chemical reactions work. Their research may result in new and better energy sources.

A chemistry curriculum includes biology, mathematics, and physics courses, as well as analytical, organic, inorganic, and physical chemistry. Computer skills that enable modeling and simulations are necessary to operate computerized laboratory equipment.

Scientific, mathematical, and analytical thinking are critical abilities for chemists. Also, technical and manual skills are required to work in labs and with laboratory equipment. Because chemists often work on interdisciplinary teams, understanding the language and terminology of other disciplines is essential and so is having knowledge of business, marketing, and economics. Leadership ability is important in situations that require chemists to supervise other staff. Good oral and written communication is necessary for report writing.

Beyond enjoying science and mathematics, chemists must like to work with their hands while building apparatus and performing scientific experiments. They enjoy mental challenges, working independently, and the satisfaction of developing practical solutions. Outcomes are achieved by perseverance, curiosity, and the ability to concentrate on detail.

Chemists value intellectual stimulation, where they expend a considerable amount of thought and reasoning. They search for new facts and ways to apply them. The use of mathematics is an integral part of this research. Chemists view themselves as creative in their work. The prestige of the field is a motivational force. The work and projects they are given are varied. Chemists expect to be paid well.

Table 1
Percentage Distribution of Employed Persons with Only a Bachelor's Degree,
by Economic Sector, Size, and New Business Status of Employer

	Chemistry	All
Economic Sector		
Private for-profit	55.5	47.3
Self-employed	16.2	18.5
Government/Military	9.5	11.0
Education	12.7	15.6
Nonprofit	5.9	7.5
Employer Size		
Small (Fewer than 100 employees)	27.0	35.5
Medium (100–999)	24.6	21.8
Large (1,000–24,999)	28.1	26.0
Very large (25,000 or more)	20.2	16.7
Percent working in new business established within past 5 years	7.5	7.6

Where Do Chemistry Majors Work?

More than 55 percent of persons who hold a bachelor's degree in chemistry work for private, for-profit businesses. About 16 percent are self-employed as consultants to other organizations or as independent business owners. The educational sector employs 13 percent of chemistry majors, and almost 10 percent work in the government. Few chemistry majors are employed in nonprofit charities or research foundations.

Graduates of chemistry programs at the undergraduate level are generally employed in jobs that are connected to the major field of study. Nearly half work in jobs closely related to the field of chemistry. Three out of 10 work in jobs that are somewhat related. Less than one-quarter work in unrelated jobs.

About 83 percent of persons with only a bachelor's degree are employed, mostly in full-time positions. This is about average for the majors covered by this book. About 2 percent of chemistry degree holders are officially unemployed; that is, they are not employed and are actively seeking work. Thirteen percent of chemistry majors have decided that they do not want to work. A substantial proportion, 44 percent, have taken early retirement, while 1 out of 5 remain at home to meet family responsibilities.

Occupations

About one-fifth of all persons who earn a degree in chemistry are employed as chemists. However, most of those who are not employed as chemists do not work in a scientific occupation. Approximately 1 out of 8 chemistry majors work in high-level managerial positions that are often related in some degree to the undergraduate field of study. Some chemistry majors are employed in marketing and sales occupations, and others as health technologists and technicians.

Somewhat more than half as many women as men major in chemistry, but a greater share of the female grads find work as scientists or technicians.

Table 2

Percentage Distribution of Employed Persons with Only a Bachelor's Degree in Chemistry, by the Relationship Between Their Job and College Major

Relationship of Job to Major	Percent
Closely related	47.6
Somewhat related	29.9
Not related	22.5

Percent who report the following as the most important reasons for working in a job that was not related to major:

Change in career or professional interests	31.4
Pay, promotion opportunities	24.8
Job in highest degree field not available	15.1
Working conditions (hours, equipment, environment)	7.9
Other reason	7.7

Work Activities

▶ Unlike most other employed persons with only a bachelor's degree, chemistry program graduates often consider applied research an important part of their work. More than 4 out of 10 grads spend at least 10 hours in a typical workweek on these tasks, and for 9 percent applied research is their central job function. Similar shares of chemistry grads do development work.

▶ More than 6 out of 10 chemistry degree holders engage regularly in overall managerial responsibilities. Seventeen percent of grads are primarily engaged in these tasks.

Table 3

Top 5 Occupations Employing Persons with Only a Bachelor's Degree in Chemistry, by Percentage

Top 5 Occupations	All	Men	Women
Chemists, Except Biochemists	19.6	17.6	23.3
Other Management-Related Occupations	7.6	9.0	5.0
Other Marketing and Sales Occupations	4.9	7.1	0.9
Top-Level Managers, Executives, and Administrators	4.7	6.1	2.1
Health Technologists and Technicians	4.5	1.8	9.4
Total, Top 5 Occupations	41.3	41.6	40.7
Balance of Employed	58.7	58.4	59.3
All Employed	100.0	100.0	100.0

- More than one-third of the grads spend significant work time on employee relations, but less than 2 percent spend most of their time on this activity.

- Nine out of 10 of those who hold a degree in chemistry develop or utilize computer applications on the job, but only 6 percent work mainly with these applications.

- One-third of chemistry grads regularly engage in sales, purchasing, marketing, production, operations, or maintenance. These tasks are the main job function of about 10 percent of grads.

Workplace Training and Other Work-Related Experiences

The career potential of a job is closely associated with the amount of work-related training on the job. Work-related training is regarded as an investment by firms because it makes workers more productive. Firms that invest in their workforce are more likely to offer pay increases and promotions to match the increasing productivity of their workers. The rate of participation in work-related training during a year among employed chemistry graduates (57 percent) is slightly lower than the training participation rate of all college graduates (61 percent). (The identical percentage of chemistry grads get postgraduate degrees.)

- Almost half of those who participate in training are developing additional professional skills related to the job in which they are employed.

- Twenty percent receive training in employee supervision or related management-skills areas.

- Almost as many chemistry majors participate in training to improve their general professional skills, such as public speaking and business writing.

When asked to identify the most important reason for getting training, one-third of those who get training do so to improve their work-related skills. Eight percent need training to maintain an occupational license or certification. Often employers require or expect staff to participate in training; 6 percent of chemistry grads get training for this reason.

Salaries

The median annual salary of chemistry graduates with only a bachelor's degree is $56,000, a level that is 8 percent higher than the median annual salary of all employed college graduates. On average, employed chemistry graduates work for 44 hours per week and for 50 weeks per year, resulting in 2,200 hours of employment per year. The level of work effort among chemistry graduates is 2 percent higher than the average among all college graduates (43 hours per week and 50 weeks per year, resulting in 2,150 hours per year).

Chemistry graduates who work as employees of private, for-profit corporations have annual salaries of $64,000. Those employed by other types of employers earn much less. Self-employed chemistry grads average $55,800 per year. In government, average annual earnings are $51,600. At educational institutions, their annual salaries average only $40,800.

Graduates employed in jobs that are closely related to the field of study have a moderate earnings advantage compared to those who work in jobs that are unrelated to the field. The average annual salary of graduates who work in closely related jobs is $59,900. Graduates with employment in jobs that are somewhat related to their major earn $53,700 per year. In contrast, the average annual salary of graduates employed full-time in a job that is not related to their field of study is $54,700.

FIGURE 1

Age/Earnings Profile of Persons with Only a Bachelor's Degree in Chemistry (Full-Time Workers, in 2010 Dollars)

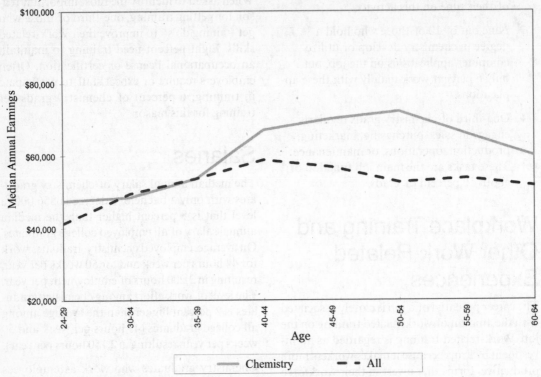

The annual salary of persons with a degree in chemistry varies considerably by the occupation in which they work. However, in the top 5 jobs employing a large number of chemistry grads, the degree brings earnings that are as high as or higher than the average earnings of all grads in the same occupations. Majors who proceed to top-level managerial positions earn more than $100,000 per year, well above the average rate of pay for chemistry majors employed full-time. Those working in marketing and sales come close to that average. Those employed as chemists have annual salaries of $55,700 per year. Chemistry majors who are employed in health technology fields have earnings that are well below the average for the major.

Job Satisfaction

The overall level of job satisfaction of chemistry majors is slightly higher than the average for all graduates.

Employment Outlook

According to the projections by the U.S. Bureau of Labor Statistics, employment in occupations that require a bachelor's degree is expected to grow faster than employment in other sectors of the American labor market. Between 2008 and 2018, the U.S. workforce is projected to grow by 10.1 percent, creating an average of 15.2 million job openings per year. The bachelor's-level jobs are expected to increase by 17.7 percent over the same time.

Table 4
Annual Salary of Workers with Only a Bachelor's Degree, Top 5 Occupations (in 2010 Dollars)

Earnings in Top 5 Occupations	All	Chemistry
Total	$56,000	$65,000
Chemists, Except Biochemists	$52,600	$55,700
Other Management-Related Occupations	$57,800	$59,900
Other Marketing and Sales Occupations	$54,700	$98,000
Top-Level Managers, Executives, Administrators	$103,200	$103,200
Health Technologists and Technicians	$42,300	$41,300

Chemistry majors can expect an outlook that is either better or worse than the average depending on their career choice.

▶ Job growth for chemists is expected to be slower than the average for all occupations. New chemists at all levels may experience competition for jobs, particularly in the declining chemical manufacturing industry. Graduates with a master's degree or a Ph.D. will enjoy better opportunities, especially at larger pharmaceutical and biotechnology firms.

▶ The miscellaneous managerial, marketing, and sales occupations that employ many animal science majors are projected to have slower-than-average growth, but these are large occupations that will create many job openings through turnover.

Employment of salaried agricultural managers is expected to increase by 5.9 percent and create about 15,000 job openings each year.

▶ Marketing, sales, and mid-level management occupations that employ a substantial share of college graduates with degrees in chemistry are expected to grow at a rate that is slower than the overall projected growth in employment. But these are large occupations, so they will create many job openings through turnover.

▶ The exception to this managerial growth is the top-level jobs, which are projected to shrink slightly. In addition, keen competition is expected for top executive positions because the prestige and high

Table 5
Percentage Distribution of Workers with Only a Bachelor's Degree, by Level of Job Satisfaction

Job Satisfaction	Chemistry	All
Very satisfied	49.8	45.4
Somewhat satisfied	40.9	45.0
Somewhat dissatisfied	8.1	7.4
Very dissatisfied	1.2	2.2
Mean Score (4=very satisfied, 1=not satisfied at all)	3.4	3.3

Table 6
Projected Growth and Job Openings in the Top 5 Occupations Employing Persons with Only a Bachelor's Degree in Chemistry

Top 5 Occupations	Projected Growth 2008–2018	Projected Annual Job Openings
All top 5	6.6%	217,880
Chemists, Except Biochemists	3.5%	3,440
Other Management-Related Occupations	7.2%	53,020
Other Marketing and Sales Occupations	7.3%	64,880
Top-Level Managers, Executives, and Administrators	−0.4%	61,470
Health Technologists and Technicians	20.1%	35,070

pay attract a substantial number of qualified applicants.

▶ Jobs in the health technologies will grow rapidly and offer many job openings. The graying of the American population will increase demand for these workers.

Pathways Beyond the Bachelor's Degree

Relatively high proportions of chemistry majors—57 percent—continue their formal education after college and earn an advanced degree of some type. One-fifth earn a master's, almost as many go on to a doctorate, and an impressive 17 percent earn a professional degree.

▶ Three out of 10 degree holders who earn a master's degree continue their studies in chemistry. Almost one-fifth earn their master's degree in business, and an additional 8 percent earn their master's degree in education or educational administration. About 7 percent branch out into engineering at the master's degree level.

▶ Two-thirds of the doctoral degrees earned are in the field of chemistry, biochemistry, or biophysics, and an additional 10 percent are in other biological sciences.

▶ Almost two-thirds of all chemistry grads who earn a professional degree study health care: medicine, dentistry, optometry, osteopathy, podiatry, or veterinary. Chemistry at the undergraduate level is an important pathway to the professional practice of health care.

CHAPTER 52

Forestry and Environmental Science

Currently most foresters and conservationists work for state and federal governments, managing public forests and parks. On the other hand, private industry's role in lumber and paper production is growing and also will be highlighted in this discussion of forestry and environmental science.

Some primary duties of foresters include drawing up plans to regenerate forested lands, monitoring the progress of those lands, and supervising harvests. Land management foresters choose and direct the preparation of sites on which trees will be planted. They oversee controlled burning and the use of bulldozers or herbicides to clear weeds, brush, and logging debris. They advise on the type, number, and placement of trees to be planted. Foresters then monitor the seedlings to ensure healthy growth and to determine the best time for harvesting. If they detect signs of disease or harmful insects, they consult with specialists in forest pest management to decide on the best treatment. When the trees reach a certain size, foresters decide which trees should be harvested and sold to sawmills.

Procurement foresters work with local forest owners (whether public or private) and inventory the type, amount, and location of the timber. They develop an appraisal of the timber's value, ne-

gotiate the purchase, and write a contract for the sale. Afterward, they subcontract with loggers or pulpwood cutters for tree removal, aid in road layout, and monitor the contract's specifications and environmental requirements. Foresters balance the concerns of business economics with the environmental impact on natural resources ecosystems.

Range managers (also called range conservationists, range ecologists, or range scientists) manage, improve, and protect rangelands to maximize their use without damaging the environment. Rangelands contain many natural resources, including grass and shrubs for animal grazing, wildlife habitats, water from vast watersheds, recreation facilities, and valuable mineral and energy resources. Range managers help ranchers attain optimum livestock production by determining the number and kinds of animals to graze, the grazing system to use, and the best season for grazing. At the same time, however, range managers work to maintain soil stability and vegetation for other uses, such as wildlife habitats and outdoor recreation.

Soil conservationists provide technical assistance to farmers and ranchers concerned with the conservation of soil, water, and related natural resources. They develop programs designed to get the most productive use from land without damaging it. Conservationists visit areas with erosion problems, find the source of the problem, and help landowners and managers develop management practices to combat the problem and implement revegetation of disturbed sites.

Foresters and conservation scientists often specialize in one area, such as forest resource management, urban forestry, wood technology, or forest economics.

A forestry curriculum stresses science, mathematics, communications, computer science, forest economics, business administration, wetland analysis, water and soil quality, and wildlife conservation. An experiential component may be required. Range management course work combines plant, animal, and soil sciences with ecology and resource management. Additional courses are in economics, computer science, forestry, hydrology, agronomy, and wildlife and recreation. Few colleges offer programs in soil conservation.

Science, mathematics, and computer skills are required in forestry and conservation work. Increasingly, technology is being applied as aerial and satellite photographs are used for mapping large forest areas and land use, which requires spatial ability. Much of the business practice of a company is learned on the job. Interpersonal skills are needed, whether for use in timber sales or in providing consultation to forest owners, farmers, or ranchers. And specific skills are required in applying scientific principles in practical ways, such as rotating crops so that farm soil remains fertile, treating trees with the proper chemicals to prevent the spread of disease, or obtaining good pasturage for cattle to produce prime quality beef.

The interests of foresters and conservation scientists follow an applied scientific orientation, stressing practical uses of natural resources. These professionals enjoy the outdoors, are mechanically inclined and physically strong, are willing to walk long distances in densely wooded areas to carry out their work, and work long

Table 1

Percentage Distribution of Employed Persons with Only a Bachelor's Degree, by Economic Sector, Size, and New Business Status of Employer

	Forestry and Environmental Science	All
Economic Sector		
Private for-profit	40.0	47.3
Self-employed	18.7	18.5
Government/Military	25.6	11.0
Education	12.4	15.6
Nonprofit	3.3	7.5
Employer Size		
Small (Fewer than 100 employees)	31.4	35.5
Medium (100–999)	25.6	21.8
Large (1,000–24,999)	25.4	26.0
Very large (25,000 or more)	17.6	16.7
Percent working in new business established within past 5 years	5.1	7.6

hours to put out fires. Most work in southeastern and western states and Alaska.

As a group, they value the independence of making decisions on their own, variety, working with their minds, status gained within their community, outdoors work, and high achievement.

Where Do Forestry and Environmental Science Majors Work?

The employment of a majority of environmental science graduates is split between the government sector and the private, for-profit sector. Forty percent of the graduates work for businesses and corporations in the private, for-profit sector, particularly in the timber and paper industry and with farmers and ranchers. About one-quarter of the graduates find employment in the government sector, frequently managing public parks and forests. Only 19 percent of environmental science graduates are self-employed in their own

business or practice, and 12 percent work in the education sector.

Almost 7 out of 10 forestry and environmental science graduates work in a job that is closely related or somewhat related to their undergraduate major. Forty percent are employed in jobs that are closely related to their major field, and 28 percent say their job is somewhat related to environmental science. The remaining graduates consider the duties that they perform at work to be unrelated to their major.

Of all forestry and environmental science graduates under the age of 65, 88 percent are employed. Only 3 percent are officially unemployed; in other words, they are not employed and are actively seeking employment. The remaining 8 percent are out of the labor force; that is, they are not employed and are not seeking employment. The main reason for the labor force withdrawal of environmental science graduates is early retirement, which accounts for 37 percent of those out of the workforce. Additionally, 15 percent cite family responsibilities, and 13 percent do not have the need or desire to work.

Table 2
Percentage Distribution of Employed Persons with Only a Bachelor's Degree in Forestry and Environmental Science, by the Relationship Between Their Job and College Major

Relationship of Job to Major	Percent
Closely related	40.0
Somewhat related	28.1
Not related	31.9

Percent who report the following as the most important reasons for working in a job that was not related to major:

Pay, promotion opportunities	32.5
Job in highest degree field not available	30.2
Change in career or professional interests	16.7
Working conditions (hours, equipment, environment)	8.2
Family-related reasons	6.4

Table 3
Top 5 Occupations Employing Persons with Only a Bachelor's Degree in Forestry and Environmental Science, by Percentage

Top 5 Occupations	All	Men	Women
Forestry and Conservation Scientists	8.5	11.7	0.9
Precision/Production Occupations	4.6	4.6	4.7
Other Administrative Occupations	4.1	1.8	9.6
Biological Scientists	3.7	3.0	5.4
Teachers, Secondary—Computer, Math, or Science	3.3	1.8	7.0
Total, Top 5 Occupations	24.2	22.9	27.6
Balance of Employed	75.8	77.1	72.4
All Employed	100.0	100.0	100.0

Occupations

Forestry and environmental science graduates are employed in diverse occupations. Less than one-quarter are concentrated in the top 5 occupations that are predominant employers of these graduates. About 8 percent are employed as forestry and conservation scientists, and another 4 percent as biological scientists. Almost 9 percent administer timber-producing forests and other natural lands; these workers classify themselves as working either in precision/production occupations or in miscellaneous administrative occupations. Another 3 percent are secondary school teachers.

The ratio of male to female grads is about 2 to 1. Of those who go on to be scientists, the males are more likely to opt for forestry and conservation, while the females are more likely to opt for other biological specializations.

Work Activities

▌ Management and administrative duties dominate. Almost one-quarter of grads spend most of their typical workweek in these tasks, and almost 65 percent spend at least 10 hours per week performing these duties at work.

▌ Twelve percent spend most of their time at work in teaching activities. About one-quarter of all employed graduates state that they regularly spend at least some time in teaching activities.

▌ Fourteen percent of employed environmental science graduates spend most of their typical workweek in sales, purchasing, and marketing activities. Almost half of these graduates regularly engage in these activities.

▌ One-fifth of grads are regularly engaged in providing professional services such as managerial or consulting services. Only 5 percent spend a major part of their typical workweek on these tasks.

▌ Only 8 percent perform computer applications, programming, and systems-development activities most of the time at their job, but 85 percent spend significant time on these activities.

▌ Applied research activities take up most of the time at work among 5 percent of employed forestry and environmental science graduates, and one-third regularly do this kind of work.

Workplace Training and Other Work-Related Experiences

The career potential of a job is closely associated with the amount of work-related training on the job. Work-related training is regarded as an investment by firms because it makes workers more productive. Firms that invest in their workforce are more likely to offer pay increases and promotions to match the increasing productivity of their workers. The incidence of work-related training among forestry and environmental science graduates (60 percent) is about the same as the participation rate in work-related training among all college graduates (61 percent).

▶ Of those environmental science graduates who receive some work-related training, 55 percent receive technical training in the occupation in which they are employed.

▶ Nineteen percent of the training recipients participate in management or supervisor training.

▶ Twenty-two percent receive training to improve their general professional skills, such as public speaking and business writing.

When asked to identify the most important reason to acquire training, 31 percent of environmental science graduates who undergo training identify the need to improve their occupational skills and knowledge. Another 10 percent report a mandatory training requirement by the employer as the most important factor underlying their involvement in work-related training. According to 9 percent of the training participants, the most important reason is the need to obtain a professional license or certificate, and 6 percent rank pay and promotion opportunities as the number one reason for their participation in work-related training.

Salaries

The median annual salary of forestry and environmental science graduates who have only a bachelor's degree and are employed full-time is $47,200, a level that is 9 percent lower than the median annual salary of all full-time employed college graduates. On average, employed forestry and environmental science graduates work for 44 hours per week and for 50 weeks per year, resulting in 2,200 hours of employment per year. The level of work effort among forestry and environmental science graduates is 2 percent higher than the average among all college graduates (43 hours per week and 50 weeks per year, resulting in 2,150 hours per year).

The average annual salary of environmental science graduates who work in jobs that are closely related to their major is $50,200. Graduates employed in jobs that are somewhat related to their undergraduate major earn $51,300 per year, and those whose jobs are unrelated to their undergraduate major earn an average annual salary of $45,700.

Self-employed graduates of forestry and environmental science earn more than their counterparts employed in other sectors: an average salary of $56,800 per year. Graduates who are employed by businesses and corporations in the private, for-profit sector earn an average annual salary of $52,900. Environmental science graduates who work in the education sector earn an average salary of $48,400 per year, and the government sector pays these graduates an average annual salary of $47,600.

Among the top 5 occupations employing forestry and environmental science majors, the best-paying is working as a scientist in this field. More general biological scientists earn less. In 4 of the top 5 occupations, the major confers an earnings advantage.

FIGURE 1

Age/Earnings Profile of Persons with Only a Bachelor's Degree in Forestry and Environmental Science (Full-Time Workers, in 2010 Dollars)

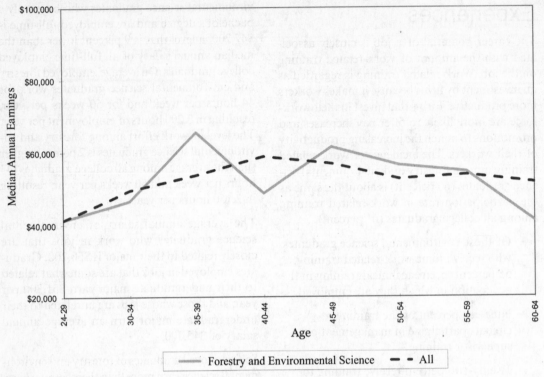

Job Satisfaction

The overall level of job satisfaction of forestry and environmental science majors is slightly higher than the average for all graduates.

Employment Outlook

According to the projections by the U.S. Bureau of Labor Statistics, employment in occupations that require a bachelor's degree is expected to grow faster than employment in other sectors of the American labor market. Between 2008 and 2018, the U.S. workforce is projected to grow by 10.1 percent, creating an average of 15.2 million job openings per year. Of the 5 top occupations employing graduates of the forestry and environmental science major, 3 are projected to have growth that is faster than the average for the economy as a whole; only one of those is growing faster than the average for all bachelor's-level occupations (17.7 percent).

▶ The workforce of forestry and conservation scientists is projected to grow by a healthy 11.9 percent. The federal government and some state governments expect a large number of their workers to retire over the next decade. As a result, there is likely to be a large number of job openings for foresters and conservation scientists in government. In general, workers with a 4-year degree from an accredited university program, along with good technical and communication skills,

Table 4
Annual Salary of Workers with Only a Bachelor's Degree, Top 5 Occupations (in 2010 Dollars)

Earnings in Top 5 Occupations	All	Forestry and Environmental Science
Total	$47,200	$47,700
Forestry and Conservation Scientists	$52,600	$57,600
Precision/Production Occupations	$39,200	$48,200
Other Administrative Occupations	$38,200	$33,800
Biological Scientists	$46,400	$46,700
Teachers, Secondary—Computer, Math, or Science	$40,200	$40,500

should have the best opportunities for entry-level work.

▶ Employment of biological scientists is projected to increase very rapidly (by 21.0 percent), and it is a larger occupation and therefore will create many more job openings through turnover. Doctoral degree holders are expected to face competition for basic research positions in academia. Furthermore, should the number of advanced degrees awarded continue to grow, applicants for research grants are likely to face even more competition. In general, applied research positions in private industry are somewhat easier to obtain, but may become more competitive if increasing numbers of scientists seek jobs in private industry because of the difficulty finding positions in colleges and universities.

▶ Job growth in the production and administrative occupations that employ environmental science grads will probably be better than Table 6 suggests. For management, business, and financial occupations, an impressive 35.8 percent growth is projected in the forestry industry. For precision and production workers in the same industry, 3.8 percent growth is projected.

▶ The number of secondary school teachers employed is dependent on state and local expenditures for education and on

Table 5
Percentage Distribution of Workers with Only a Bachelor's Degree, by Level of Job Satisfaction

Job Satisfaction	Forestry and Environmental Science	All
Very satisfied	47.1	45.4
Somewhat satisfied	41.0	45.0
Somewhat dissatisfied	9.4	7.4
Very dissatisfied	2.5	2.2
Mean Score (4=very satisfied, 1=not satisfied at all)	3.4	3.3

Table 6
Projected Growth and Job Openings in the Top 5 Occupations Employing Persons with Only a Bachelor's Degree in Forestry and Environmental Science

Top 5 Occupations	Projected Growth 2008–2018	Projected Annual Job Openings
All top 5	2.3%	388,050
Forestry and Conservation Scientists	11.9%	410
Precision/Production Occupations	−3.0%	175,420
Other Administrative Occupations	10.8%	166,130
Biological Scientists	21.0%	4,850
Teachers, Secondary—Computer, Math, or Science	8.9%	41,240

the enactment of legislation to increase the quality and scope of public education. Teachers who are geographically mobile and who obtain licensure in more than one subject are likely to have a distinct advantage in finding a job. Most job openings will result from the need to replace the large number of teachers who are expected to retire over the 2008–2018 period.

Pathways Beyond the Bachelor's Degree

Of all graduates with a bachelor's degree in environmental science, one-third proceed to earn a postgraduate degree: 1 out of 5 earn a master's degree, 5 percent earn a doctoral degree, and 8 percent earn a professional degree.

▶ Thirteen percent of all master's degrees earned by undergraduate environmental science majors are in the field of forestry and environmental science. About 17 percent of the degrees are earned in a business subject, and 9 percent graduate with a master's degree in education.

▶ Twenty-one percent of the doctoral degrees are earned in forestry and environmental science and 42 percent in life sciences.

▶ Of the professional degrees earned by graduates who were environmental science majors, 61 percent are earned in a health-care field (medicine, dentistry, optometry, osteopathy, podiatry, or veterinary) and most of the rest in law.

CHAPTER 53

Geology and Geophysics

Geology and geophysics are closely related fields, but there are many differences. Graduates of these programs are often known as geoscientists. Geologists study the composition, structure, and history of the earth's crust. They seek to find out how rocks are formed and what has happened to them since their formation. Geophysicists use the principles of physics and mathematics to study not only the earth's surface but also its internal composition; ground and surface waters; atmosphere; oceans; and magnetic, electrical, and gravitational forces. Both fields are applied to the exploration of natural resources and include such specific activities as designing landfill sites, preserving water supplies, and approving hazardous waste disposal.

The subdisciplines help differentiate the varied types of work that geoscientists perform. Petroleum geologists explore for oil and gas deposits by studying and mapping the subsurfaces of oceans and land. Mineralogists analyze and classify minerals and precious stones according to composition and structure. Paleontologists study fossils found in geological formations to trace the evolution of plant and animal life and the geologic history of the earth. Oceanographers study and map the ocean flow by using sensing devices aboard ships or underwater research craft. Hydrologists examine the distribution, circulation, and physical properties of underground and surface water. They study the form and intensity of precipitation, its rate of infiltration into the soil and movement through the earth, and its return to the ocean and atmosphere.

The curriculum for all geoscientists covers mineralogy, paleontology, stratigraphy, structural geology, and geologic methods. When the goal of employment is environmental or regulatory work, course work includes hydrology, hazardous waste management, environmental legislation, chemistry, fluid mechanics, or geologic logging (data collection during drilling).

Scientific and technical abilities are essential to obtain knowledge of the field and to use the specialized equipment. Spatial skill is needed for comprehending maps, geologic structures, and the layout of sites. Computer skills are necessary for data processing and for constructing models. Oral and written proficiency is needed in report writing and communicating findings. Traits that characterize many workers are general memory, paying attention to detail, and working independently.

Geologists have scientific interests, which include analytical thinking and a research orientation in traditional core subjects such as chemistry, mathematics, and physics. A technical orientation will fit the laboratory and field exploration aspects of this field.

Table 1
Percentage Distribution of Employed Persons with Only a Bachelor's Degree, by Economic Sector, Size, and New Business Status of Employer

	Geology and Geophysics	All
Economic Sector		
Private for-profit	42.9	47.3
Self-employed	25.1	18.5
Government/Military	21.1	11.0
Education	8.4	15.6
Nonprofit	1.6	7.5
Employer Size		
Small (Fewer than 100 employees)	45.4	35.5
Medium (100–999)	18.5	21.8
Large (1,000–24,999)	24.1	26.0
Very large (25,000 or more)	12.1	16.7
Percent working in new business established within past 5 years	9.0	7.6

Where Do Geology and Geophysics Majors Work?

More than 4 out of 10 employed geology graduates work for businesses and corporations in the private, for-profit sector. Another one-quarter work as self-employed workers in their own business or practice. More than one-fifth of all employed geology majors are employed by the government. Another 8 percent are employed by educational institutions.

Equal shares of geology majors work in jobs that are closely related and unrelated to their major. These two extremes account for almost three-quarters of all grads. The remaining one-quarter work in jobs that are somewhat related to their undergraduate major. The undergraduate curriculum of geology majors includes instruction in various scientific fields, particularly physics, mathematics, and chemistry. These skills enable geologists to get jobs in scientific fields that may not be closely related to their major.

Out of all geology graduates under the age of 65, 86 percent are employed. Only 3 percent are officially unemployed; that is, they are not employed and are actively seeking employment. The remaining 11 percent are out of the labor force; that is, they are not employed and are not seeking employment. About 63 percent of geology majors who have withdrawn from the labor force are retired. Another 12 percent withdraw due to family responsibilities.

Occupations

Geology majors are employed in a variety of occupations that span the scientific, technical, and business fields. More than 1 in 5 are employed as geologists and earth scientists. Environmental engineering and extraction-related jobs

Table 2
Percentage Distribution of Employed Persons with Only a Bachelor's Degree in Geology and Geophysics, by the Relationship Between Their Job and College Major

Relationship of Job to Major	Percent
Closely related	36.3
Somewhat related	27.3
Not related	36.4

Percent who report the following as the most important reasons for working in a job that was not related to major:

Job in highest degree field not available	25.9
Change in career or professional interests	21.9
Pay, promotion opportunities	16.7
Job location	11.1
Family-related reasons	10.8

each employ about 7 percent of grads, often using skills related to the major. The top 5 list is rounded out with mid- to high-level managerial and executive occupations; many of these workers are employed in the extractive industries. Male graduates outnumber female graduates by about 4 to 1, but equal shares of the grads find work as geologists.

Work Activities

▶ One of the major employers of geology majors is mid- to high-level managerial and administrative occupations. Hence, it is not surprising to find that 63 percent of employed geology majors perform management and administrative duties on a

Table 3
Top 5 Occupations Employing Persons with Only a Bachelor's Degree in Geology and Geophysics, by Percentage

Top 5 Occupations	All	Men	Women
Geologists, Including Earth Scientists	20.9	21.0	20.4
Environmental Engineers	7.5	8.9	2.1
Construction and Extraction Occupations	7.3	9.2	–
Other Management-Related Occupations	5.5	5.3	6.2
Top-Level Managers, Executives, and Administrators	4.3	5.4	–
Total, Top 5 Occupations	45.5	49.8	28.7
Balance of Employed	54.5	50.2	71.3
All Employed	100.0	100.0	100.0

regular basis, and more than one-quarter spend a majority of their time during a typical week performing these duties.

▶ Thirty-seven percent of employed geology graduates engage intensively in applied research activities, and 11 percent regularly handle these activities.

▶ Computer applications, programming, and systems development are performed by 87 percent of employed geology majors on a regular basis. Seven percent report that these duties take up a majority of their time during a typical week.

▶ Twenty-four percent of employed geology majors regularly perform managerial duties to oversee the quality and efficiency of the production process (often involving extraction of petroleum or minerals), and 10 percent consider these duties a major part of their jobs.

▶ Although 42 percent of all employed geology graduates perform accounting, finance, and contractual duties as a regular part of their jobs, only 9 percent spend most of their time in a typical week performing these duties.

▶ Sales, purchasing, and marketing duties are regularly performed by 42 percent, and 9 percent spend most of their time performing these duties.

▶ Although one-quarter regularly engage in providing professional services (such as financial, legal, and health services), only 9 percent spend most of their time at work in these activities.

Workplace Training and Other Work-Related Experiences

The career potential of a job is closely associated with the amount of work-related training on the job. Work-related training is regarded as an investment by firms because it makes workers more productive. Firms that invest in their workforce are more likely to offer pay increases and promotions to match the increasing productivity of their workers. The rate of participation in work-related training during a year among employed geology and geophysics graduates (55 percent) is significantly lower than the training participation rate of all college graduates (61 percent).

▶ Of those geology majors who receive some training, 46 percent receive technical training in their occupational field.

▶ Sixteen percent of the training recipients participate in management or supervisory training.

▶ The same fraction, 16 percent, receive training to improve their general professional skills, such as public speaking and business writing.

When asked to identify the most important reason to acquire training, 29 percent of geology majors who undergo training identify the need to improve their occupational skills and knowledge. Another 9 percent consider the need to obtain a professional license or certificate as the main factor to influence their decision to undergo work-related training. (A number of states require geoscientists who offer their services directly to the public to obtain a license from a state licensing board.) A slightly smaller fraction report mandatory training requirements by the employer as the most important factor for their involvement in work-related training.

Salaries

The median annual salary of geology and geophysics graduates with only a bachelor's degree is $51,600, a level that is about the same as the median annual salary of all employed college graduates. On average, employed geology and geophysics graduates work for 44 hours per week and for 50 weeks per year, resulting in 2,200 hours of employment per year. The level of work effort among geology and geophysics graduates is 2 percent higher than the average among all college graduates (43 hours per week and 50 weeks per year, resulting in 2,150 hours per year).

The average annual salary of geology majors differs only slightly on the basis of how closely their jobs are related to their major. The average

annual salary of graduates who work in closely related jobs is $53,900. Graduates with employment in jobs that are somewhat related to their major earn $54,900 per year. The average salary of graduates employed full-time in a job that is not related to their field of study is $51,600.

Geology majors working at for-profit businesses earn higher salaries than their counterparts employed in other sectors. Their annual average salary is $67,400. The full-time, self-employed geology majors who work in their own businesses, many as geologists, average $55,100. The government sector pays geology graduates who are employed full-time an average annual salary of $46,400. The average annual salary of geology graduates employed by educational institutions is $37,400.

Age/Earnings Profile of Persons with Only a Bachelor's Degree in Geology and Geophysics (Full-Time Workers, in 2010 Dollars)

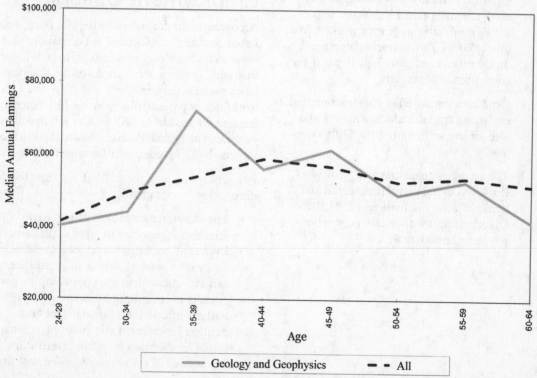

Table 4
Annual Salary of Workers with Only a Bachelor's Degree, Top 5 Occupations (in 2010 Dollars)

Earnings in Top 5 Occupations	All	Geology and Geophysics
Total	$51,600	$58,400
Geologists, Including Earth Scientists	$54,700	$56,900
Environmental Engineers	$65,000	$55,300
Construction and Extraction Occupations	$51,600	$49,500
Other Management-Related Occupations	$57,800	$52,200
Top-Level Managers, Executives, and Administrators	$103,200	$93,300

Within the group of geology majors, there are sizable variations in their average annual salary by the occupation in which they are employed. In 4 out of 5 top occupations that employ geology graduates, their average annual salary is lower than the salary of all college graduates.

▶ Graduates employed as geologists and earth scientists earn $56,900 per year, with a small advantage over workers from other majors. Environmental engineers, on the other hand, earn higher pay if they come from other majors.

▶ Graduates employed in construction and extraction trades, including miners and well drillers, earn more than $49,500 annually.

▶ The average annual salary of geologists employed in high-level managerial and administrative occupations is $93,300. Other management-related occupations pay them considerably less.

Job Satisfaction

The overall level of job satisfaction of geology and geophysics majors is slightly higher than the average for all graduates.

Employment Outlook

According to the projections by the U.S. Bureau of Labor Statistics, employment in occupations that require a bachelor's degree is expected to grow faster than employment in other sectors of the American labor market. Between 2008 and 2018, the U.S. workforce is projected to grow by 10.1 percent, creating an average of 15.2 million job openings per year. The bachelor's-level jobs are expected to increase by 17.7 percent over the same time.

For geology majors, the outlook for their top 5 occupations varies greatly.

▶ The workforce of geologists and earth scientists is expected to grow at the same level as all bachelor's-level jobs. Graduates with a master's degree in geoscience can expect excellent job opportunities, especially in consulting firms and in the oil and gas industry. Ph.D.s may face competition for research and college teaching jobs. Geoscientists may face layoffs during periods of economic recession, but the

Table 5
Percentage Distribution of Workers with Only a Bachelor's Degree, by Level of Job Satisfaction

Job Satisfaction	Geology and Geophysics	All
Very satisfied	45.1	45.4
Somewhat satisfied	41.4	45.0
Somewhat dissatisfied	9.6	7.4
Very dissatisfied	3.9	2.2
Mean Score (4=very satisfied, 1=not satisfied at all)	3.4	3.3

prices of commodities are a much more important source of volatility; for those working in the oil and gas or mining industries, the cyclical nature of commodity prices determines demand. When prices are high, jobs are plentiful, but when prices fall, positions become scarce.

▸ Similarly, the job outlook in the construction and extraction occupations that hire geology grads is sensitive to the ups and downs of commodity prices.

▸ Environmental engineers are expected to have employment growth of 30.6 percent over the projection decade, much faster than the average for all occupations. More environmental engineers will be needed to

help companies comply with environmental regulations and to develop methods of cleaning up environmental hazards. A shift in emphasis toward preventing problems rather than controlling those that already exist, as well as increasing public health concerns resulting from population growth, also is expected to spur demand for environmental engineers. Because of this employment growth, job opportunities should be favorable.

▸ Mid-level management occupations that employ a substantial share of college graduates with degrees in geology are expected to grow at a rate that is slower than the overall projected growth in employment. However, this is a large group

Table 6
Projected Growth and Job Openings in the Top 5 Occupations Employing Persons with Only a Bachelor's Degree in Geology and Geophysics

Top 5 Occupations	Projected Growth 2008–2018	Projected Annual Job Openings
All top 5	3.9%	123,170
Geologists, Including Earth Scientists	17.7%	1,920
Environmental Engineers	30.6%	2,790
Construction and Extraction Occupations	16.8%	3,970
Other Management-Related Occupations	7.2%	53,020
Top-Level Managers, Executives, and Administrators	−0.4%	61,470

of occupations that should create many job openings through turnover. On the other hand, the top-level managerial jobs are projected to shrink slightly. In addition, keen competition is expected for top executive positions because the prestige and high pay attract a substantial number of qualified applicants.

Pathways Beyond the Bachelor's Degree

Forty-six percent of geology graduates with a bachelor's degree proceed to earn a postgraduate degree: 35 percent earn a master's degree, 9 percent graduate with a doctorate, and less than 2 percent earn a professional degree.

▶ More than 38 percent of the master's degrees are earned in geology and earth sciences, and 14 percent are earned in a business subject. About 9 percent of master's degrees earned by geology majors are in the field of education.

▶ More than 60 percent of the doctoral degrees among undergraduate geology majors are earned in geology and earth sciences. Six percent are earned in environmental science or engineering.

CHAPTER 54

Microbiology and Biochemistry

This chapter covers a group of majors that focus on the basic building blocks of life. Microbiologists, biochemists, biophysicists, and others who work in the life sciences have a preference for practicality, and they possess a matter-of-fact thinking style. They are dependable doers who often achieve by overcoming distractions. They are seen by others as intelligent, well informed, skilled at reasoning, and quick at reaching solutions.

Microbiology

Microbiologists investigate the growth and characteristics of microscopic organisms, such as bacteria, algae, or fungi. Medical microbiologists study the relationships between organisms and disease or the effect of antibiotics on microorganisms. Other microbiologists specialize in the environment; food; agriculture; virology, which is the study of viruses; or immunology, which is the study of mechanisms that fight infections. Many microbiologists use biotechnology to study cell production and human disease.

Microbiologists conduct bench research by using cellular, biochemical, or molecular techniques. Their efforts may be directed at discovering therapeutic agents, such as those that prevent or reverse insulin resistance in noninsulin-dependent diabetics. Microbiologists develop cell-based assays that may be aimed at assessing the effects of lead compounds on life processes.

Cell/molecular biology is a sub-specialty of microbiology. Cell/molecular biologists participate in research such as discovering new molecules that inhibit growth or metastasis of tumors, and they may clone cells with suspected molecules to study results.

Scientific, computer, and mathematical skills are essential in this field, as is critical thinking. For bench scientists, manual ability is also critical in the performance of the laboratory work involved. Leadership ability is necessary because teams work on these projects. The scientist must be able to get projects started and to be organized so that goals are reached. Lastly, having well-developed language skills to communicate findings and write reports is highly rated.

A microbiologist's interests are that of a serious laboratory scientist. Microbiologists enjoy ideas, but they also have a wide range of interests. People in this major nurture these diverse preferences through liberal arts courses in the humanities and social sciences.

Microbiologists value creativity—the search to find new ways to do something. They have great confidence in their own minds, and they have the knowledge to accomplish their goals. They are motivated by the self-perceived importance of their work, which they know is difficult, and they seek success and the recognition of high achievement.

Biochemistry

Biochemists study the chemical composition of living things and the complex chemical combinations and reactions involved in metabolism, reproduction, growth, and heredity. Much of the work in biotechnology is done by biochemists and molecular biologists because this technology involves understanding the complex chemistry of life.

Biochemists perform laboratory assays. With an advanced degree or under the supervision of someone at that level, they develop protocols that use well-controlled and reproducible procedures for optimizing cell-culture processes. Biochemists analyze, evaluate, and interpret test results. Documentation is critical, especially for validation purposes; thus, biochemists use mathematics and statistics. Their work can involve modern synthetic methods and techniques.

Biochemists need to be capable in science and mathematics, as well as with computer skills. Communicating well with assistants is important, and so is possessing language skills to write reports that include observations and documentation. Biochemists have good laboratory skills to design experiments, and they are detailed record keepers and accurate data-entry keyers. Their work demands sophistication in statistics. In research and development work, they need to develop goals with a team and work toward the objectives developed.

Biochemists' interests are more like those of chemists, but in the biological area; thus, their scientific interests are more technologically focused. Biochemists enjoy working with things and ideas, but they gain satisfaction from the humanitarian involvement of their work, which improves the health of others.

Biochemists value high achievement and success in doing something of importance. They enjoy the mental stimulation of working with their minds. They look for variety and diversion to satisfy their creative bent. Their laboratory and research work fits with their preference for independence.

Biophysics

Biophysicists study the physical principles of living cells and organisms and their electrical and mechanical energy. Biophysicists investigate the dynamics of seeing and hearing, the transmission of electrical impulses along nerves and muscles, and the damage to cells and tissues caused by X-rays and nuclear particles. They may examine the manner in which characteristics of plants and animals are carried forward through successive generations. They may also examine the absorption of light by chlorophyll in photosynthesis or by pigments of the eye involved in vision. Biophysicists compare the functions of electronics with the functions of the human brain. They also study the spatial configuration of submicroscopic molecules, such as those that form proteins, by using an X-ray or electron microscope. Specializations within this major may include the use of radiation and nuclear particles for cancer treatment or the use of atomic isotopes to discover transformation of substances in cells.

Course work may include molecular biophysics and biophysical chemistry, membrane function, cell biology, function of neural systems, chemical biology, molecular and cellular immunology, population genetics, principles of genetic analysis, structure and function of proteins, nucleic acids, molecular mechanisms of gene control, and microbiology. Prerequisite courses would be in chemistry, biochemistry, physics, advanced mathematics, and biology.

Biophysics is a very demanding academic field. Students entering the program usually are excellent students and are equally proficient at the highest levels in language, mathematics, and science. People in the field are quick to figure things out. They are well read as well as being very capable in mathematics, statistics, and computer usage. They have excellent spatial ability and are proficient in their fine motor skills so that they can use the equipment required by the laboratory work.

Biophysicists are interested in scientific, technical, and mechanical matters. They also are good organizers and planners. Biophysicists must be good at conceptualizing, processing sophisticated data, and operating high-technology equipment. A person entering this major should like laboratory work.

Where Do Microbiology and Biochemistry Majors Work?

Bachelor's degree holders in microbiology/biochemistry are likely to find employment across all major sectors of the American economy. About 4 out of 10 graduates in these fields work in wage and salary jobs for private, for-profit businesses. Another one-fifth are self-employed, many as consultants. Sixteen percent of microbiology/biochemistry majors who earned a bachelor's degree work for educational institutions at the primary, secondary, and university levels. Eleven percent of graduates from this major work in not-for-profit organizations, such as charities or research organizations, and a similar share work for the government.

About 46 percent of microbiology/biochemistry majors with a bachelor's degree are employed in jobs that are closely related to their undergraduate field of study, an above-average representation compared to other majors in this book. About one-fifth work in jobs that are somewhat related to the undergraduate major, and 3 out of 10 work in unrelated jobs.

About 84 percent of microbiology/biochemistry majors under the age of 65 are employed, and 93 percent of these individuals work in full-time jobs. Among those not working, only 4 percent are officially classified as unemployed; that is, they are not employed and are actively seeking employment. Of the 12 percent who have voluntarily chosen not to work, the largest share (26 percent) have taken early retirement. Seventeen

Table 1

Percentage Distribution of Employed Persons with Only a Bachelor's Degree, by Economic Sector, Size, and New Business Status of Employer

	Microbiology and Biochemistry	All
Economic Sector		
Private for-profit	40.8	47.3
Self-employed	20.9	18.5
Government/Military	11.3	11.0
Education	15.9	15.6
Nonprofit	11.1	7.5
Employer Size		
Small (Fewer than 100 employees)	26.3	35.5
Medium (100–999)	22.2	21.8
Large (1,000–24,999)	29.6	26.0
Very large (25,000 or more)	21.9	16.7
Percent working in new business established within past 5 years	6.6	7.6

Table 2

Percentage Distribution of Employed Persons with Only a Bachelor's Degree in Microbiology and Biochemistry, by the Relationship Between Their Job and College Major

Relationship of Job to Major	Percent
Closely related	46.5
Somewhat related	22.8
Not related	30.7

Percent who report the following as the most important reasons for working in a job that was not related to major:

Pay, promotion opportunities	27.8
Job location	16.1
Job in highest degree field not available	13.8
Family-related reasons	13.0
Change in career or professional interests	12.3

percent have chosen to stay at home to meet family responsibilities. Fourteen percent are out of the workforce because they are back in school. (Compared to grads of other majors, a very high proportion of microbiology/biochemistry grads get advanced degrees.)

Occupations

A wide variety of occupations employ those who hold a bachelor's degree in microbiology or biochemistry; the top 5 occupations account for less than one-third of the grads.

Persons with a bachelor's in microbiology/biochemistry are most likely to be employed in the health technologist and technician areas. About 13 percent of all employed microbiology/biochemistry bachelor's degree holders work in this occupational field. Although men and women graduate with this degree in roughly equal numbers, female grads are much more likely to work in this group of occupations. Men, on the other hand, more often find work in direct health-care occupations. About 5 percent of the

grads work in various managerial roles, often in the field of biological research. The same share of grads work in precision/production occupations, primarily employed in beverage manufacturing (most likely brewing) and in sugar and confectionery manufacturing.

Work Activities

▶ Microbiology/biochemistry bachelor's degree holders spend a substantial amount of time engaged in providing the professional services for which they were trained in the biological sciences. These professional services include many activities associated with the delivery of health care and support. Almost 1 out of 3 grads acquit these tasks regularly, and 16 percent are primarily focused on these tasks.

▶ As in many professional jobs, a large share of workers (6 out of 10) engages in managing or supervising people or projects on a weekly basis. Twelve percent of grads are primarily managers.

Table 3
Top 5 Occupations Employing Persons with Only a Bachelor's Degree in Microbiology and Biochemistry, by Percentage

Top 5 Occupations	All	Men	Women
Health Technologists and Technicians	13.1	6.2	20.6
Registered Nurses, Pharmacists, Dietitians, Therapists, and Physician Assistants	5.3	7.5	2.8
Other Management-Related Occupations	4.6	5.1	4.1
Precision/Production Occupations	4.6	6.8	2.2
Other Service Occupations, Except Health	4.2	6.0	2.2
Total, Top 5 Occupations	31.8	31.6	31.9
Balance of Employed	68.2	68.4	68.1
All Employed	100.0	100.0	100.0

▸ Microbiology and biochemistry skills are often applied to quality or productivity management, in industries ranging from biotechnology to food processing to brewing. Thirty-eight percent of grads regularly handle these duties, and almost 11 percent say that these activities dominate their job.

▸ Sales, purchasing, and marketing are significant duties of 36 percent of grads and the chief responsibility of 12 percent.

▸ Applied research is an important component of the jobs of many bachelor's degree holders in the microbiology/biochemistry fields. Thirty-five percent of the grads devote at least 10 hours out of an average workweek to these activities; 9 percent consider applied research their central job function.

▸ About 84 percent of bachelor's degree holders in this field are involved regularly in the development and use of various types of computer applications, but only 7 percent are primarily focused on these activities.

Workplace Training and Other Work-Related Experiences

The career potential of a job is closely associated with the amount of work-related training on the job. Work-related training is regarded as an investment by firms because it makes workers more productive. Firms that invest in their workforce are more likely to offer pay increases and promotions to match the increasing productivity of their workers. The rate of participation in work-related training during a year among employed microbiology and biochemistry graduates (54 percent) is significantly lower than the training participation rate of all college graduates (61 percent). In this field, as in many sciences, formal higher education is almost as common a route to advancement.

▸ Technical training directly related to the professional activities of microbiology/biochemistry majors is the predominant form of training received by these majors; 48 percent of grads receive this kind of training.

▶ Management and supervisory training is also a major training activity undertaken by graduates from these majors and is reported by 19 percent of them.

▶ Sixteen percent receive training to improve their general professional skills, such as public speaking and business writing.

When asked to explain their motivation, about one-third of those who undergo some type of training say they do so simply to expand their skills and abilities. Six percent do so to meet occupational license or certification requirements. (This is an issue for many medical technologists and technicians.) Equal shares of about 5 percent say they are motivated by an employer's requirement or by the desire to qualify for better pay or a promotion.

Salaries

The median annual salary of microbiology and biochemistry graduates with only a bachelor's degree is $45,600, a level that is 13 percent lower than the median annual salary of all employed college graduates. On average, employed microbiology and biochemistry graduates work for 44 hours per week and for 50 weeks per year, resulting in 2,200 hours of employment per year.

The level of work effort among microbiology and biochemistry graduates is 2 percent higher than the average among all college graduates (43 hours per week and 50 weeks per year, resulting in 2,150 hours per year).

Note: Because of the very small number of survey respondents in some age groups, it was not possible to furnish a useful age/earnings profile graphic for this major.

Working in a job related to the major can be rewarding for microbiology and biochemistry graduates. The same average annual salary is reported by graduates who work in closely related jobs or somewhat related jobs: $50,600. In contrast, the average salary of graduates employed full-time in a job that is not related to their field of study is $41,300.

The highest full-time earnings for microbiology and biochemistry majors are won by those who are self-employed: an average of $69,300 per year. Those working in government average an even $50,000 per year. Private businesses pay grads an annual average of $47,100, while nonprofits pay $44,500. In the education sector, grads' earnings are relatively low: $35,800.

The bachelor's degree in microbiology or biochemistry has mixed earnings effects compared to other majors, but it is mostly an advantage. The majors who work as health technologists and

Table 4
Annual Salary of Workers with Only a Bachelor's Degree, Top 5 Occupations (in 2010 Dollars)

Earnings in Top 5 Occupations	All	Microbiology and Biochemistry
Total	$45,600	$48,100
Health Technologists and Technicians	$42,300	$41,600
Registered Nurses, Pharmacists, Dietitians, Therapists, and Physician Assistants	$55,700	$61,000
Other Management-Related Occupations	$57,800	$71,100
Precision/Production Occupations	$39,200	$57,200
Other Service Occupations, Except Health	$35,100	$27,200

Table 5
Percentage Distribution of Workers with Only a Bachelor's Degree, by Level of Job Satisfaction

Job Satisfaction	Microbiology and Biochemistry	All
Very satisfied	40.7	45.4
Somewhat satisfied	50.8	45.0
Somewhat dissatisfied	6.4	7.4
Very dissatisfied	2.0	2.2
Mean Score (4=very satisfied, 1=not satisfied at all)	3.4	3.3

technicians earn slightly less than those who have completed other majors, largely because many of their colleagues have studied more occupation-specific subjects. On the other hand, those working in direct-care medical occupations (such as medical physicist) earn substantially more than the average bachelor's recipient in those careers. The earnings differences are even better for those who go into management or precision/production occupations.

Job Satisfaction

The overall level of job satisfaction of microbiology and biochemistry majors is slightly higher than the average for all graduates.

Employment Outlook

According to the projections by the U.S. Bureau of Labor Statistics, employment in occupations that require a bachelor's degree is expected to grow faster than employment in other sectors of the American labor market. Between 2008 and 2018, the U.S. workforce is projected to grow by 10.1 percent, creating an average of 15.2 million job openings per year. The bachelor's-level jobs are expected to increase by 17.7 percent over the same time.

For the top 5 occupations employing graduates from microbiology/biochemistry, the outlook is mixed.

▶ The health technologist and technician occupations employ a substantial proportion of all graduates from this major. Employment in these occupations is expected to grow rapidly, and the occupations should create numerous job openings.

▶ Rapid employment growth is also projected for direct-care workers such as nurses, therapists, and physician assistants, thanks to the graying of the nation's population. In addition, these occupations are expected to create numerous job openings.

▶ Employment in service-related jobs other than health will grow more slowly than that of other bachelor's-level jobs, but faster than the workforce overall.

▶ Employment in miscellaneous managerial jobs will grow more slowly, but the workforces of these jobs are large, creating many job openings.

▶ The outlook for the precision/production occupations employing microbiology/biochemistry grads is difficult to gauge. Employment of the full range of production workers is projected to decline by

Table 6

Projected Growth and Job Openings in the Top 5 Occupations Employing Persons
with Only a Bachelor's Degree in Microbiology and Biochemistry

Top 5 Occupations	Projected Growth 2008–2018	Projected Annual Job Openings
All top 5	5.8%	436,720
Health Technologists and Technicians	20.1%	35,070
Registered Nurses, Pharmacists, Dietitians, Therapists, and Physician Assistants	21.5%	119,640
Other Management-Related Occupations	7.2%	53,020
Precision/Production Occupations	–3.0%	175,420
Other Service Occupations, Except Health	14.3%	53,570

about 3 percent in the beverage manufacturing industry and by about 7 percent in the sugar and confectionery product manufacturing industry. However, the same high skills that give microbiology/biochemistry grads a substantial earnings advantage in these jobs are likely give them much better chances for employment than lower-skilled production workers.

Pathways Beyond the Bachelor's Degree

Graduate education is an important long-term career pathway for persons who earn an undergraduate degree in either microbiology or biochemistry. More than half of all persons who earn a degree in either of these fields go on to earn an advanced degree of some type. Graduates with degrees in this field are more likely to earn an advanced degree than almost any other undergraduate major. More than one-sixth earn a master's degree, 15 percent earn a doctoral degree, and one-fifth earn a professional degree.

▶ One out of 5 of those who earn a master's degree continue in the fields of microbiology, biochemistry, or biophysics.

▶ One-eighth earn their master's degree in a health-related field. An additional 10 percent earn a master's degree in business administration.

▶ More than 65 percent of those who go on to earn a Ph.D. continue their studies in microbiology, biochemistry, biophysics, immunology, or cell and molecular biology.

▶ Among those who earn a professional degree, almost three-quarters pursue a medical degree, although a few choose to earn a pharmacy or law degree.

CHAPTER 55

Physics and Astronomy

Physics is the exploration and identification of the basic principles governing the structure and behavior of matter, the generation and transfer of energy, and the interaction of matter and energy. Physicists design and perform experiments with lasers, telescopes, and mass spectrometers. They attempt, through observation and analysis, to discover the laws that describe the forces of nature such as gravity, electromagnetism, and nuclear interactions. In laboratories they seek ways to apply physical laws and theories to problems in nuclear energy, electronics, optics, materials, communications, aerospace technology, navigation equipment, and medical instrumentation. Applied research builds on basic research; for example, solid-state physics led to the development of transistors and integrated circuits used in computers. Physicists also design research equipment. This equipment, too, has well-recognized uses. Lasers are used in surgery, CD players, and bar code scanners. Microwaves are used to cook food, and high-tech measuring devices analyze blood or the chemical content of food.

Astronomy is a subfield of physics. Astronomers use the methods of physics and mathematics to learn about the fundamental nature of the universe, including the sun, moon, planets, stars, and galaxies. Astronomers are researchers who analyze large quantities of data from observatories and satellites. These professionals spend only a few weeks each year making observations of the heavens with optical or radio telescopes.

Typical courses in the physics curriculum include mechanics, electromagnetics, optics, thermodynamics, atomic physics, and quantum mechanics. Social science courses such as economics and skill with computer technology are typically required. Some universities may recommend engineering course work to prepare bachelor's degree candidates for entry-level positions such as technicians in laboratories.

In physics and astronomy, scientific, mathematical, and computer abilities are important. The field requires an imaginative mind. The abilities to plan, record, analyze, and produce oral and written reports are requirements that are often provided to others with nonphysics backgrounds. Manual, technical, and spatial skills are used in performing research. Many of these professionals work in teams; thus, interpersonal skills are helpful.

The interests of physicists focus on ideas and data. They like science, research, and probing the unknown. They enjoy laboratory work. Some laboratory work does not allow for a great deal of socialization; however, interpersonal skills are needed if any activity involves teamwork.

People in this field value research, working with their minds, and variety. They enjoy solving practical problems by using their analytical skills.

Where Do Physics and Astronomy Majors Work?

More than half of employed physics graduates work for businesses and corporations in the private, for-profit sector. Another 18 percent who work in the private, for-profit sector are self-employed in their own business or practice. The government sector employs 8 percent of physics graduates, and 17 percent work for educational institutions. Only 2 percent work in the private, nonprofit sector for tax-exempt or charitable organizations.

Nearly three-quarters of all employed physics graduates work in jobs that are either closely related or somewhat related to their major. Only 31 percent consider their employment to be closely related to their major, whereas 42 percent state that their employment is somewhat related to their major. The rest of all employed physics graduates—27 percent—work in jobs that are not at all related to their undergraduate major. The undergraduate curriculum of physics majors includes instruction in other scientific fields, particularly in computer technology and engineering. These skills enable physics graduates to secure employment in fields that may not be closely related to their undergraduate major.

Of all physics graduates under the age of 65, 89 percent are employed. Only 5 percent are officially unemployed; in other words, they are not employed and are actively seeking employment. The remaining 6 percent are out of the labor force; that is, they are not employed and are not seeking employment. Two-thirds of physics graduates under the age of 65 who have withdrawn from the labor force report that they are retired. Eight percent report that suitable jobs are not available, and 7 percent have no desire or need to work.

Table 1
Percentage Distribution of Employed Persons with Only a Bachelor's Degree, by Economic Sector, Size, and New Business Status of Employer

	Physics and Astronomy	All
Economic Sector		
Private for-profit	53.6	47.3
Self-employed	18.5	18.5
Government/Military	8.0	11.0
Education	17.1	15.6
Nonprofit	2.1	7.5
Employer Size		
Small (Fewer than 100 employees)	34.7	35.5
Medium (100–999)	16.2	21.8
Large (1,000–24,999)	24.6	26.0
Very large (25,000 or more)	24.4	16.7
Percent working in new business established within past 5 years	14.9	7.6

Table 2
Percentage Distribution of Employed Persons with Only a Bachelor's Degree in Physics and Astronomy, by the Relationship Between Their Job and College Major

Relationship of Job to Major	Percent
Closely related	30.9
Somewhat related	41.7
Not related	27.4

Percent who report the following as the most important reasons for working in a job that was not related to major:

Job in highest degree field not available	32.0
Pay, promotion opportunities	21.4
Change in career or professional interests	14.1
Other reason	12.9
Job location	9.3

Occupations

The employment of physics graduates is scattered among many occupations; the top 5 occupations employ only 27 percent of physics graduates. Some of these are highly technical: the two computer occupations that employ 11 percent of the grads, plus electrical and electronics engineering, which employs 6 percent. Many of the 5 percent working in miscellaneous administrative occupations are likely to be working in high-tech industries. However, the early childhood teaching that occupies one-quarter of the female graduates appears to have little if any connection to the skills learned in the undergraduate major.

Female grads make up less than one-fifth of those receiving the degree. Besides their attraction to teaching, they are more likely than the

Table 3
Top 5 Occupations Employing Persons with Only a Bachelor's Degree in Physics and Astronomy, by Percentage

Top 5 Occupations	All	Men	Women
Computer Engineers—Software	6.6	6.4	7.3
Electrical and Electronics Engineers	6.2	7.4	0.8
Other Administrative Occupations	5.1	4.6	7.6
Teachers—Pre-K and Kindergarten	4.8	–	25.7
Computer Systems Analysts	4.8	4.7	5.2
Total, Top 5 Occupations	27.5	23.1	46.6
Balance of Employed	72.5	76.9	53.4
All Employed	100.0	100.0	100.0

males to opt for administrative careers. The men, on the other hand, are much more likely to work as engineers.

Note that engineers who offer their services to the public need to be licensed, and one of the requirements for licensure is graduation from an approved engineering program rather than from a science major such as physics. However, most electrical and electronics engineers do not work directly for the public.

Work Activities

▸ Two-thirds of all employed physics graduates perform computer applications, programming, and systems-development duties as a regular part of their jobs, and 22 percent spend most of their time in a typical workweek performing these duties. In addition to the two computer occupations listed among the top 5 jobs, some of the occupations that employ many physics graduates are network and computer systems administrators, database administrators, and computer and information systems managers.

▸ Another major employer of physics majors is administrative and managerial occupations. Hence, it is not surprising to find that 52 percent of employed physics majors regularly perform management and administrative duties, and 18 percent spend most of their time during a typical workweek performing these duties. A much higher proportion of physics majors perform managerial and administrative functions than those doing accounting, finance, and contractual duties as a major part of their jobs.

▸ About one-quarter of all employed physics graduates regularly perform sales, purchasing, and marketing duties, and 7 percent consider these tasks a major part of their jobs.

▸ Physics graduates also design and develop products and equipment. Almost 47 percent of employed physics majors regularly engage in designing equipment and processes. Another 37 percent regularly use research findings to produce materials and devices in their jobs.

▸ Almost one-fifth of employed physics graduates regularly engage in applied research, and 4 percent spend a major part of their time at work in this activity.

Workplace Training and Other Work-Related Experiences

The career potential of a job is closely associated with the amount of work-related training on the job. Work-related training is regarded as an investment by firms because it makes workers more productive. Firms that invest in their workforce are more likely to offer pay increases and promotions to match the increasing productivity of their workers. The rate of participation in work-related training during a year among employed physics and astronomy graduates (52 percent) is significantly lower than the training participation rate of all college graduates (61 percent). Among physics grads, a postgraduate degree is a more common route for advancement.

▸ Of those physics majors who receive some training during a year, 44 percent receive technical training in their occupational field.

▸ One-fifth of the training recipients participate in management or supervisor training.

▸ Twelve percent receive training to improve their general professional skills, such as public speaking and business writing.

Physics majors who receive work-related training offer numerous reasons for acquiring training. When asked to identify the most important reason to acquire training, 27 percent of physics majors who undergo training identify the need to improve their occupational skills and knowledge. Increased opportunity for a promotion and a higher salary is the most important factor influencing training decisions among 8 percent of employed graduates who acquire training. Six percent consider license or certification requirements the most important reason for their participation in work-related training. Another 6 percent report a mandatory training requirement by the employer as the most important factor for their involvement in work-related training.

Salaries

The median annual salary of physics and astronomy graduates with only a bachelor's degree is $72,200, a level that is 29 percent higher than the median annual salary of all employed college graduates. On average, employed physics and astronomy graduates engage in the same level of work as the average for all college grads: 43 hours per week and for 50 weeks per year, resulting in 2,150 hours of employment per year.

Note: Because of the very small number of survey respondents in some age groups, it was not possible to furnish a useful agelearnings profile graphic for this major.

The average annual salary of physics majors who work in jobs that are closely related to their major is significantly higher than the salary of those who are employed in jobs that are somewhat related to their major—$82,200 versus $73,400. For those who work in unrelated jobs, average earnings fall between these two: $76,300.

Physics graduates who are employed in the private, for-profit sector for businesses and corporations, or as self-employed workers in their own business or practice, earn higher salaries than those employed in the government or education sectors. The average annual salary of physics graduates who work for businesses and corporations in the private, for-profit sector is $82,000. Full-time self-employed physics graduates earn $86,600 per year. The government sector pays physics graduates who are employed full-time an average annual salary of only $43,400. The average annual remuneration of physics graduates employed by educational institutions is still lower: $27,500.

Among the top 5 top occupations that employ physics graduates, technology determines the difference between the average annual salary of physics grads and the salary of all college graduates. In the occupations that use a lot of technology, physics majors earn more than the average for all majors, and where technology plays a small role, they earn less. The highest pay

Table 4
Annual Salary of Workers with Only a Bachelor's Degree,
Top 5 Occupations (in 2010 Dollars)

Earnings in Top 5 Occupations	All	Physics and Astronomy
Total	$72,200	$64,100
Computer Engineers—Software	$82,600	$87,700
Electrical and Electronics Engineers	$78,400	$96,000
Other Administrative Occupations	$38,200	$39,200
Teachers—Pre-K and Kindergarten	$33,000	$15,500
Computer Systems Analysts	$72,200	$86,300

Table 5
Percentage Distribution of Workers with Only a Bachelor's Degree,
by Level of Job Satisfaction

Job Satisfaction	Physics and Astronomy	All
Very satisfied	40.7	45.4
Somewhat satisfied	43.8	45.0
Somewhat dissatisfied	12.4	7.4
Very dissatisfied	3.1	2.2
Mean Score (4=very satisfied, 1=not satisfied at all)	3.3	3.3

and the largest income advantage are enjoyed by those working in the engineering and computer occupations.

Job Satisfaction

The overall level of job satisfaction of physics and astronomy majors is about the same as the average for all graduates.

Employment Outlook

According to the projections by the U.S. Bureau of Labor Statistics, employment in occupations that require a bachelor's degree is expected to grow faster than employment in other sectors of the American labor market. Between 2008 and 2018, the U.S. workforce is projected to grow by 10.1 percent, creating an average of 15.2 million job openings per year. The bachelor's-level jobs are expected to increase by 17.7 percent over the same time.

Among the top 5 occupations employing physics grads, the outlook is mostly very favorable.

▶ Employment of computer software engineers is expected to increase by 32.5 percent, which is much faster than the average for all occupations. In addition, this occupation will see a large number of new jobs, with more than 37,000 created over the projection decade. Demand for computer software engineers will increase as computer networking continues to grow. Implementing, safeguarding, and updating computer systems and resolving problems will fuel the demand for growing numbers of systems software engineers. New growth areas will also continue to arise from rapidly evolving technologies. Job prospects for computer software engineers should be excellent. Those with practical experience and at least a bachelor's degree in a computer-related field should have the best opportunities.

▶ Employment of computer systems analysts is expected to grow by 20.3 percent, which is much faster than the average for all occupations. Demand for these workers will increase as organizations continue to adopt and integrate increasingly sophisticated technologies and as the need for information security grows. Job prospects should be excellent. Job openings will occur as a result of strong job growth and from the need to replace workers who move into other occupations or who leave the labor force.

▶ On the other hand, the demand for electrical and electronics engineers is projected to grow barely at all. Although

Table 6

Projected Growth and Job Openings in the Top 5 Occupations Employing Persons
with Only a Bachelor's Degree in Physics and Astronomy

Top 5 Occupations	Projected Growth 2008–2018	Projected Annual Job Openings
All top 5	14.8%	256,950
Computer Engineers—Software	32.5%	37,180
Electrical and Electronics Engineers	1.0%	7,230
Other Administrative Occupations	10.8%	166,130
Teachers—Pre-K and Kindergarten	17.8%	24,130
Computer Systems Analysts	20.3%	22,280

strong demand for electrical and electronic devices should spur job growth, international competition and the use of engineering services performed in other countries will limit employment growth. Electrical and electronics engineers working in firms providing engineering expertise and design services to manufacturers should have better job prospects.

▶ The miscellaneous administrative occupations that employ many physics grads are projected to grow about as fast as the economy as a whole, but the large workforce employed in these occupations will create numerous jobs from turnover.

▶ The number of teachers employed is dependent on state and local expenditures for education and on the enactment of legislation to increase the quality and scope of public education. Teachers who are geographically mobile and who obtain licensure in more than one subject are likely to have an advantage in finding a job. Most job openings will result from the need to replace the large number of teachers who are expected to retire over the 2008–2018 period.

Pathways Beyond the Bachelor's Degree

Almost 64 percent of physics graduates with a bachelor's degree proceed to earn a postgraduate degree: one-third earn a master's degree, one-quarter earn a doctorate, and 4 percent earn a professional degree.

▶ Twenty-two percent of the master's degrees are earned in physics and astronomy, a similar share in engineering fields, 5 percent in the field of business management and administrative services, and 3 percent in education.

▶ More than 62 percent of the doctoral degrees among undergraduate physics majors are earned in physics and astronomy, 8 percent in engineering, and 6 percent in biology and other life sciences.

▶ More than half of the professional degrees earned by undergraduate physics graduates are in health-care professions, and 42 percent are in the field of law.

CHAPTER 56

Plant Science

Agricultural scientists work with biological scientists and researchers in the application of biotechnological advances to agriculture. Agricultural scientists work in three general areas: basic or applied research; management or administration of marketing or production operations in companies that produce food products or agricultural chemicals, supplies, and machinery; and consulting for business firms or government. This chapter includes three specialized majors that are offered at many colleges and universities: food science, plant science, and soil science. For the sake of brevity, "plant science" is used here to refer to all three specialized majors.

Food science or technology helps meet consumer demand for healthful, safe, palatable, and convenient food products. Scientists trained in this field use their knowledge of chemistry and microbiology to develop new or better ways of preserving, processing, packaging, storing, and delivering foods. Some scientists are involved in researching new food sources; analyzing food content to determine levels of vitamins, fats, sugar, or protein; or discovering substitutes for harmful or undesirable additives. In private industry, the scientists may work in test kitchens to investigate new processing techniques. In government, the scientists enforce regulations, inspect food processing, and ensure that sanitation, safety, quality, and waste-management standards are met.

Several specialized fields of science focus on plants from an agricultural perspective. Agronomy is the study of crop production. Agronomists want to discover the best methods of planting, cultivating, and harvesting to get the most efficient yields and quality. Agronomists examine the effects of various climates and soils on such crops as cotton, tobacco, vegetables, or cereal grains. Plant breeders develop and select varieties through crossbreeding, mutating, and hybridization to improve crop yield; size; nutritional quality; maturity; and resistance to frost, drought, disease, and insects. Plant breeders use principles of genetics and knowledge of plant growth. The study of entomology aids in the control and elimination of agricultural and forest pests. Entomologists develop new and improved pesticides and biological methods, which include the use of natural enemies to control pests. Entomologists are involved in preventing importation and spread of injurious insects.

Soil scientists study the best soil types for growing different plants. These scientists conduct clinical analyses of the microorganism content of soil to determine microbial reactions and chemical and mineralogical relationships to plant growth. The scientists investigate responses of specific soil types to tillage; fertilization; nutrient transformations; crop rotation; environmental consequences; gas, water, or heat flow; and industrial-waste control practices.

Every state has a land-grant college that offers agricultural science degrees. All the agricultural majors include communications, economics, business, physical science, and life science courses. In addition, students studying food science take such courses as food chemistry, food analysis, food microbiology, and food-processing operations. Students in plant and soil science take courses in plant pathology, soil chemistry, entomology, plant physiology, biochemistry, and molecular biology.

Those interested in this field need scientific and mathematical abilities as well as business sense. Agricultural scientists use logic and scientific thinking in their analyses, and they apply methodologies to make judgments. The ability to recognize differences in size, form, color, and texture is important. Finger dexterity, eye-hand coordination, and the ability to use laboratory and scientific equipment are requirements. Those involved in management or administration are expected to develop budgets, to communicate orally and in writing, and to lead others.

People in this field should like science. Food technologists—similar to biologists—have more of a people orientation than a technical focus. Agronomists, plant breeders, entomologists, and soil scientists are more technologically oriented and have more similarities with those in the physical sciences than those in the life sciences.

Agricultural scientists value the opportunity to be independent, have variety, work with their mind, gain high achievement, and earn a good salary. These scientists value being practical and view themselves as doers.

Where Do Plant Science Majors Work?

More than 4 out of 10 plant science graduates with only a bachelor's degree are employed in the private, for-profit sector. An additional one-third of plant science majors are self-employed; they operate their own for-profit businesses. Fifteen percent work in government. The remaining plant science graduates are employed by educational and nonprofit organizations.

Although many plant science majors work in jobs with titles that don't readily identify them as plant scientists, most graduates in this field report that they work in jobs related to plant science, sometimes in managerial or sales positions. Forty-three percent consider their job closely related to the major, and another one-quarter see a partial relationship. Less than one-third of all

Table 1

Percentage Distribution of Employed Persons with Only a Bachelor's Degree, by Economic Sector, Size, and New Business Status of Employer

	Plant Science	All
Economic Sector		
Private for-profit	42.5	47.3
Self-employed	33.1	18.5
Government/Military	15.2	11.0
Education	5.0	15.6
Nonprofit	4.2	7.5
Employer Size		
Small (Fewer than 100 employees)	57.4	35.5
Medium (100–999)	12.4	21.8
Large (1,000–24,999)	9.4	26.0
Very large (25,000 or more)	20.8	16.7
Percent working in new business established within past 5 years	5.4	7.6

Table 2
Percentage Distribution of Employed Persons with Only a Bachelor's Degree in Plant Science, by the Relationship Between Their Job and College Major

Relationship of Job to Major	Percent
Closely related	43.3
Somewhat related	26.0
Not related	30.7

Percent who report the following as the most important reasons for working in a job that was not related to major:

Job in highest degree field not available	31.2
Pay, promotion opportunities	21.5
Working conditions (hours, equipment, environment)	20.1
Change in career or professional interests	11.3
Family-related reasons	8.9

plant science graduates work in jobs that are not related to their undergraduate major.

About 93 percent of plant science majors under age 65 are employed. A rather large share, almost 13 percent, work part-time. Less than 1 percent are officially classified as unemployed; in other words, they are not employed and are actively seeking employment. Among the remainder, less than 7 percent, most people have chosen to withdraw voluntarily from the workforce. About one-half of those not participating in the labor force have taken early retirement. Another 15 percent have no need or desire to work.

Occupations

It's not surprising that the occupation employing the greatest share of plant science grads is farmers and that agricultural and food scientists are in second place. In addition, some of the other occupations employing large numbers of plant science grads are linked to agriculture one way or another. For example, many of the grads working in administrative occupations are employed by agricultural or agribusiness companies. Likewise, the industry employing the greatest share of the precision/production workers is wood pulp, paper, and paperboard mills, and a large share of the mechanics and repairers work for landscaping services.

Male grads of this major outnumber females by a little less than 2 to 1, and virtually all those who go into farming are male. Female grads are much more likely than males to choose administrative careers.

Work Activities

▶ One-quarter of the grads say their main work tasks are production, operations, and maintenance, and one-third of the grads regularly engage in these activities.

▶ Two-thirds are involved in managing or supervising people or projects during a typical workweek. For 18 percent, this is the primary work role.

Table 3
Top 5 Occupations Employing Persons with Only a
Bachelor's Degree in Plant Science, by Percentage

Top 5 Occupations	All	Men	Women
Farmers, Foresters, and Fishermen	13.9	21.6	–
Agricultural and Food Scientists	7.3	8.9	4.6
Other Administrative Occupations	7.2	3.3	14.2
Precision/Production Occupations	6.7	7.7	5.0
Mechanics and Repairers	6.2	4.0	10.2
Total, Top 5 Occupations	41.3	45.5	34.0
Balance of Employed	58.7	54.5	66.0
All Employed	100.0	100.0	100.0

- Computer applications, programming, and systems-development activities are a regular part of work for 91 percent of employed majors in this field. However, less than 3 percent of grads spend most of their time on these tasks.

- Sales, purchasing, and marketing are frequent activities for 46 percent of plant science majors. Fourteen percent of grads are mainly focused on these activities.

- More than 4 out of 10 grads regularly are engaged in employee relations activities, but almost none do these tasks most of the time.

- Almost one-third are involved in accounting, contractual, or financial issues as a regular part of their weekly work activities. About 9 percent spend most of their time on these tasks.

- One-quarter spend significant time teaching.

Workplace Training and Other Work-Related Experiences

On-the-job learning is an important indicator of the long-term career potential of a job. Firms that invest in their workers at high rates are much more likely to offer pay increases and promotions than firms that fail to make such investments. The rate of participation in work-related training during a year among employed plant science graduates (59 percent) is only slightly less than the training participation rate of all college graduates (61 percent).

- A little more than half the time, the training received by plant science majors is related to a specific technical aspect of their current job.

- Managerial and supervisory training is also a major training investment. One-quarter of plant science majors had this type of training in the past year.

- Firms also make substantial investments in the communications skills of plant science majors. Seventeen percent of these majors have been to training that has developed either public speaking or writing skills.

When asked the most important reason they get training, 3 out of 10 grads who get training say they are motivated to develop and maintain skills that are needed for their current job. Twelve percent of those who receive training do so to achieve or maintain licensure or certification. Six percent are required by their employer to get workplace training.

Salaries

The median annual salary of plant science graduates with only a bachelor's degree is $44,000, a level that is 17 percent lower than the median annual salary of all employed college graduates. On average, employed plant science graduates work for 45 hours per week and for 49 weeks per year, resulting in 2,205 hours of employment per year. The level of work effort among plant science graduates is 3 percent higher than the average among all college graduates (43 hours per week and 50 weeks per year, resulting in 2,150 hours per year).

Earnings of plant science majors are higher when their jobs are more closely related to their undergraduate major field. The average annual salary of plant science graduates who work in closely related jobs is $51,600. Graduates with employment in jobs that are somewhat related to their major earn $47,500 per year. In contrast, the average salary of graduates employed full-time in a job that is not related to their field of study is $37,200.

<u>**FIGURE 1**</u>

Age/Earnings Profile of Persons with Only a Bachelor's Degree in Plant Science (Full-Time Workers, in 2010 Dollars)

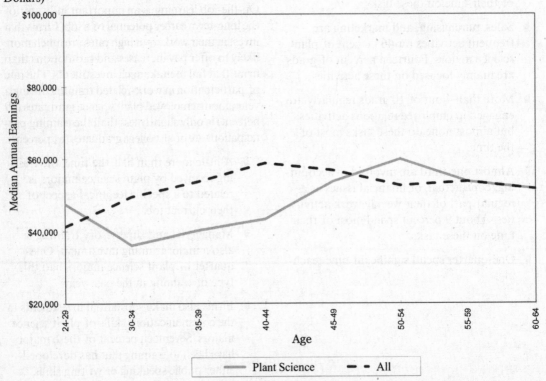

Table 4
Annual Salary of Workers with Only a Bachelor's Degree, Top 5 Occupations (in 2010 Dollars)

Earnings in Top 5 Occupations	All	Plant Science
Total	$44,000	$36,400
Farmers, Foresters, and Fishermen	$36,100	$37,200
Agricultural and Food Scientists	$47,500	$40,200
Other Administrative Occupations	$38,200	$43,300
Precision/Production Occupations	$39,200	$33,000
Mechanics and Repairers	$45,400	$25,800

Plant science graduates who work in government have annual salaries that are higher than those in other sectors: an average of $56,500. Those employed by for-profit businesses average $45,400 per year. Self-employed grads earn an average of $42,000 annually.

Within 3 of the top 5 occupations employing plant science graduates, the grads have lower salaries than the average college graduate employed in that occupation. Exceptions to this observation include farmers and miscellaneous administrative occupations. The particularly low earnings of mechanics and repairers suggest that most of the grads in these positions are holding these jobs (many of them for landscaping services) only temporarily until more appropriate work is available.

Job Satisfaction

The overall level of job satisfaction of plant science majors is considerably higher than the average for all graduates.

Employment Outlook

According to the projections by the U.S. Bureau of Labor Statistics, employment in occupations that require a bachelor's degree is expected to grow faster than employment in other sectors of the American labor market. Between 2008 and 2018, the U.S. workforce is projected to grow by 10.1 percent, creating an average of 15.2 million job openings per year. The bachelor's-level jobs are expected to increase by 17.7 percent over the same time.

Table 5
Percentage Distribution of Workers with Only a Bachelor's Degree, by Level of Job Satisfaction

Job Satisfaction	Plant Science	All
Very satisfied	61.1	45.4
Somewhat satisfied	31.6	45.0
Somewhat dissatisfied	5.1	7.4
Very dissatisfied	2.2	2.2
Mean Score (4=very satisfied, 1=not satisfied at all)	3.5	3.3

The outlook varies widely among the top 5 occupations employing plant science grads.

▶ Bureau of Labor Statistics projections suggest that overall employment in agricultural production will grow by less than the average for the economy as a whole, reflecting the decline of self-employed farmers because of the consolidation of farms and increasing productivity. With fewer people wanting to become farmers and a large number of farmers expected to retire or give up their farms in the next decade, there will be some opportunities to own or lease a farm. Additionally, the market for agricultural products is projected to be good for most products over the next decade, so many farmers who retire will need to be replaced. In addition, employment of salaried agricultural managers is expected to increase.

▶ The demand for agricultural and food scientists will grow at an above-average rate for all jobs in the economy. Job growth will stem primarily from efforts to increase the quantity and quality of food produced for a growing population. Additionally, an increasing awareness about the health effects of certain types of foods and the effects of food production on the environment will give rise to research into the best methods of food production. Opportunities should be good for agricultural and food scientists in almost all fields. Those with a bachelor's degree should experience very good opportunities in food science and technology and in agronomy. Those with a master's or Ph.D. degree in agricultural and food science will also experience good opportunities, although positions in basic research and teaching at colleges and universities are limited.

▶ Job growth in the administrative occupations is projected to be about average, but job turnover should help in creating more than 166,000 openings each year.

▶ The outlook for precision/production workers and for mechanics and repairers who are employed in the field of agriculture probably depends on the workers' specialization. Those who work with agricultural and food scientists probably have better prospects than those who work in agricultural production. The paper manufacturing industry, which employs the largest share of production workers with this degree, is expected to decline in size.

Table 6
Projected Growth and Job Openings in the Top 5 Occupations Employing Persons with Only a Bachelor's Degree in Plant Science

Top 5 Occupations	Projected Growth 2008–2018	Projected Annual Job Openings
All top 5	1.6%	347,330
Farmers, Foresters, and Fishermen	9.3%	2,460
Agricultural and Food Scientists	16.3%	690
Other Administrative Occupations	10.8%	166,130
Precision/Production Occupations	–3.0%	175,420
Mechanics and Repairers	–4.4%	2,630

Pathways Beyond the Bachelor's Degree

About one-third of all persons who earn an undergraduate degree in plant science go on to earn an advanced degree of some type. About one-quarter earn a master's degree, and 9 percent earn a doctorate. Very few plant science majors go on to earn a professional degree in law or medicine.

▶ Of those plant science majors who earn a master's degree, about 1 out of 3 receive their advanced degree in the plant science field. Fourteen percent earn the degree in education. Business is the focus for 11 percent of those earning the master's. Eight percent study agricultural economics.

▶ More than one-half of all plant science majors who earn a doctoral degree continue to specialize in plant science. Most others who earn a doctorate do so in the life or health sciences.

PART 8

Technology

CHAPTER 57

Computer Science

Computer science prepares students for the broad career title of computer scientist. This career consists of a wide range of professionals who design computers and the software that runs them. Computer scientists develop information technologies and develop and adapt principles for applying computers to new uses. At a less-theoretical level of expertise, they engage in computer programming. Programming involves writing, testing, and maintaining the detailed directions and steps computers must execute to perform their functions.

Computer science is distinguished by the higher level of theoretical expertise and innovation applied to complex problems, as well as the creation or application of new technology. Computer scientists can be theorists, researchers, or inventors. Some work at an academic institution on theory, hardware, or language design. Others work in industry, typically applying theory, developing specialized languages or information technologies, or designing programming tools and knowledge-based systems.

A related occupation is systems analysts, who enable computer technology to solve and meet an organization's needs. They often specialize—for example, in financial or engineering organizations. These analysts study the goals of managers to understand the steps involved in the task and break down a process into programmable procedures. Solutions may include planning and developing new computer systems or devising ways to apply existing systems to additional operations. Analysts specify the information to be entered into the system, design the processing steps, and format the output to meet the users' needs. Analysts prepare specifications for hardware and software, flowchart diagrams, and structure charts for computer programmers to follow in implementing the system. (For more discussion of this occupation and a major that often prepares for it, see Chapter 60.)

Programmers often are categorized differently within organizations from the personnel who specialize in more theoretical applications. Computer programs direct the computer on what to do, what information to identify and access, how to process it, and what equipment to use. Programs can be of different complexity, depending on whether a program is a simple accounting function or one for building a complex mathematical model. Programs are written in different languages, and most programmers know more than one programming language. Programmers' skills also vary depending on the systems on which they work, such as the Web or a smart phone. Some programmers have much wider responsibilities than those described here and are programmer-analysts, performing a combined role that integrates a systems analyst's functions.

The educational pathway in this field is varied. In general, present entrants into computer and information sciences are different from many veteran workers because they have more classroom training. Course work focuses on learning programming skills, usually in more than one language, and using common software packages and information systems. Systems analysts can come either from computer science programs or, for example, from information systems, accounting, finance, or engineering programs. This is a skills-based field, so the programming and language experience, the technology one has experienced, and the practical applications one has worked with can come from various sources and are all considered factors by an employer who is judging a person's training and background.

The abilities of computer scientists involve thinking logically and making constant decisions. They often must deal with a number of tasks simultaneously and be able to concentrate and pay close attention to detail. Although many work independently, they often work in teams on large projects. These professionals must be able to communicate effectively with computer personnel such as programmers and managers, as well as with users or other staff who have no technical computer background. The field has experienced tremendous growth; thus, many individuals have been promoted to leadership positions requiring these abilities as well as organizational skills. Most difficult in this fast-growing field is the dual need to perform one's work while simultaneously

doing the continuous study necessary to keep up-to-date with new technology.

Foremost among the interests of computer and information scientists are science and technology. This field is generally an applied one. Satisfaction can be gained from concrete applications and uses, whether in technology, business, or engineering. A systems orientation involves liking interaction with people, observing operations, and possessing knowledge of available hardware and software. Interpersonal skills are needed to fully understand the goals, processes, and desired outcomes of users to deliver a satisfactory systems solution. Programmers are involved in work that demands thoroughness and attention to detail.

Computer scientists enjoy working with their minds and having opportunities to be creative. Computer science is a high-paying field, which is attractive to many. Having challenging work and doing something that is important are also valued. Some view the opportunity for variety and diversity within the field as desirable.

Table 1

Percentage Distribution of Employed Persons with Only a Bachelor's Degree, by Economic Sector, Size, and New Business Status of Employer

	Computer Science	All
Economic Sector		
Private for-profit	71.1	47.3
Self-employed	12.0	18.5
Government/Military	8.1	11.0
Education	5.4	15.6
Nonprofit	3.2	7.5
Employer Size		
Small (Fewer than 100 employees)	23.1	35.5
Medium (100–999)	17.6	21.8
Large (1,000–24,999)	30.8	26.0
Very large (25,000 or more)	28.5	16.7
Percent working in new business established within past 5 years	9.8	7.6

Where Do Computer Science Majors Work?

A large majority of computer science graduates work in the private, for-profit sector for businesses and corporations or are self-employed in their own business or consulting practice. Businesses and corporations in the private, for-profit sector employ about 71 percent, and 12 percent are self-employed. Eight percent of employed computer science graduates work in the government sector. The education sector employs only 5 percent of these graduates, and 3 percent work in the private, nonprofit sector.

Classroom training in the field of computer science is more applicable in the labor market than the classroom instruction in many other fields. Widespread and increasing use of computers in every sector provides computer science graduates many employment opportunities within their field of expertise. As a result, more than 7 out of 10 employed graduates work in jobs that are closely related to their field, and another one-fifth are employed in jobs that are somewhat related

to their undergraduate major. Only 8 percent of computer science graduates are employed in jobs that are not related to their field of study.

Of all computer science graduates under the age of 65, 89 percent are employed. Only 4 percent are officially unemployed; in other words, they are not employed and are actively seeking employment. The remaining 7 percent are out of the labor force; that is, they are not employed and are not seeking employment. Almost one-quarter of the labor force withdrawals among computer science graduates are attributable to family responsibilities. Another 14 percent cite a lack of the need or desire to work as the reason for their labor force withdrawal. A slightly smaller share say that suitable jobs are not available.

Occupations

The employment of computer science graduates is very concentrated in a few occupations. The top-listed occupation employs almost one-quarter of graduates; the top 2 employ more than 4 out of 10 of the graduates. Every one of the

Table 2
Percentage Distribution of Employed Persons with Only a Bachelor's Degree in Computer Science, by the Relationship Between Their Job and College Major

Relationship of Job to Major	Percent
Closely related	71.0
Somewhat related	20.6
Not related	8.4

Percent who report the following as the most important reasons for working in a job that was not related to major:

Job in highest degree field not available	28.2
Change in career or professional interests	19.1
Pay, promotion opportunities	17.6
Family-related reasons	16.3
Working conditions (hours, equipment, environment)	13.4

top 5 occupations employing computer science graduates is computer-related.

It's important to understand that many workers who have the job title "computer engineer" or "software engineer" do not have engineering degrees and come from a major such as computer science. (The computer systems engineering major is described in Chapter 30.) Workers in this field rarely need to offer their services to the public, and therefore they do not need to be licensed as engineers, which would require a degree in some engineering field rather than in computer science.

This major produces about twice as many male as female graduates, and the men are more likely than the women to choose all of the top 5 occupations, especially software engineering.

Work Activities

▶ More than 84 percent of employed computer science graduates devote time at work to computer applications, programming, and systems-development duties. For almost half of all employed grads, these tasks are their primary work function. For

another 36 percent, these tasks occupy at least 10 hours out of the typical workweek. These findings are to be expected given the heavy concentration of their employment in computer-related occupations.

▶ Fifty-five percent of the graduates spend at least 10 hours during the workweek performing management and administrative tasks, and 16 percent spend most of their time at work performing these duties.

▶ Six percent of grads spend most of their workweek designing processes and equipment, but 43 percent do this work regularly.

▶ One-third of computer science majors engage in employee relations, but only 1 percent see this as their chief job function.

▶ More than 3 out of 10 grads regularly develop products from results of applied research, but only 2 percent are primarily engaged in this activity.

Table 3

Top 5 Occupations Employing Persons with Only a
Bachelor's Degree in Computer Science, by Percentage

Top 5 Occupations	All	Men	Women
Computer Engineers—Software	23.9	27.3	16.2
Computer Systems Analysts	19.7	19.7	19.5
Network and Computer Systems Administrators	5.0	6.0	2.9
Computer Support Specialists	4.8	5.1	4.2
Computer Programmers (Business, Scientific, Process Control)	4.6	5.4	3.0
Total, Top 5 Occupations	58.0	63.5	45.8
Balance of Employed	42.0	36.5	54.2
All Employed	100.0	100.0	100.0

▶ Almost one-quarter of employed computer science graduates regularly engage in sales, purchasing, and marketing activities; 6 percent spend most of their time performing these duties.

Workplace Training and Other Work-Related Experiences

The career potential of a job is closely associated with the amount of work-related training on the job. Work-related training is regarded as an investment by firms because it makes workers more productive. Firms that invest in their workforce are more likely to offer pay increases and promotions to match the increasing productivity of their workers. The rate of participation in work-related training during a year among employed computer science graduates (56 percent) is somewhat lower than the training participation rate of all college graduates (61 percent). Because this field requires workers to keep abreast of evolving technology, it seems likely that many workers are undergoing training on their own time.

▶ Of those computer science graduates who receive some workplace training during the year, 51 percent receive technical training in the occupation in which they are employed.

▶ Nineteen percent of the training recipients participate in management or supervisor training.

▶ Fifteen percent receive training to improve their general professional skills, such as public speaking and business writing.

When asked to select the most important reason to acquire training, one-third of computer science majors who undergo training identify the need to improve their occupational skills and knowledge. About 7 percent report a mandatory training requirement by the employer as the most important factor for their involvement in work-related training. Another 5 percent rank improvement in their opportunities for a salary increase and promotion as the number one factor in influencing their decision to participate in training. According to slightly less than 5 percent, the most important factor for their involvement in training is the need to learn skills for a recently acquired position.

Salaries

The median annual salary of computer science graduates with only a bachelor's degree is $73,400, a level that is 30 percent higher than the median annual salary of all employed college graduates. On average, employed computer science graduates work for 43 hours per week and for 51 weeks per year, resulting in 2,193 hours of employment per year. The level of work effort among computer science graduates is 2 percent higher than the average among all college graduates (43 hours per week and 50 weeks per year, resulting in 2,150 hours per year).

Securing employment in a job that is closely related or somewhat related to their undergraduate major is associated with sizable salary advantages among computer science graduates. The average annual salary of graduates who work in closely related jobs is $77,700. Graduates with employment in jobs that are somewhat related to their major average $71,500 per year. In contrast, the average salary of graduates employed full-time in a job that is not related to their field of study is only $40,100.

Graduates who work for businesses and corporations in the private, for-profit sector earn a higher average salary—$78,200—than graduates working in other sectors of the economy. Computer science graduates who are self-employed in their own business or practice earn $75,400 per year. The government sector pays computer science graduates an average annual salary of $56,900. As for most other majors, the educational sector

FIGURE 1

Age/Earnings Profile of Persons with Only a Bachelor's Degree in Computer Science (Full-Time Workers, in 2010 Dollars)

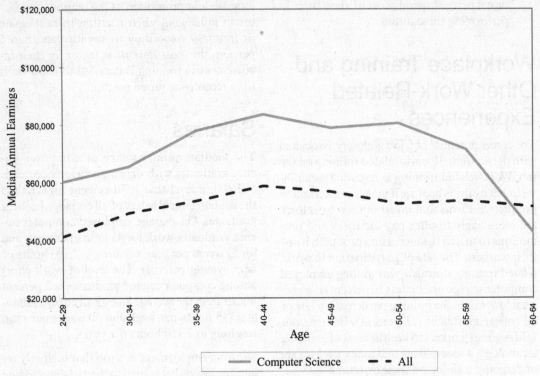

pays computer science grads less than do other employment sectors: $46,500 per year.

The average salary of computer science graduates and all college graduates in each of the top 5 occupations is presented in Table 4. Compared to bachelor's degrees from other majors, the computer science degree provides an earnings boost (or at least parity) in 4 of the top 5 occupations. The one occupation where earnings are lower is computer programmers; skills for this occupation are lower than for the other 4 jobs, so it's likely that computer science grads in these positions are holding the jobs only temporarily until they can find work more closely aligned with their skills.

Job Satisfaction

The overall level of job satisfaction of computer science majors is slightly lower than the average for all graduates.

Employment Outlook

According to the projections by the U.S. Bureau of Labor Statistics, employment in occupations that require a bachelor's degree is expected to grow faster than employment in other sectors of the American labor market. Between 2008 and 2018, the U.S. workforce is projected to grow by 10.1 percent, creating an average of 15.2 million

Table 4
Annual Salary of Workers with Only a Bachelor's Degree, Top 5 Occupations (in 2010 Dollars)

Earnings in Top 5 Occupations	All	Computer Science
Total	$73,400	$75,000
Computer Engineers—Software	$82,600	$82,600
Computer Systems Analysts	$72,200	$73,200
Network and Computer Systems Administrators	$69,100	$74,600
Computer Support Specialists	$50,600	$53,400
Computer Programmers (Business, Scientific, Process Control)	$71,200	$67,400

job openings per year. The bachelor's-level jobs are expected to increase by 17.7 percent over the same time.

The outlook for the top 5 occupations employing computer science grads is uniformly very good to excellent, with the notable exception of computer programmers.

▶ Employment of computer software engineers is expected to increase by 32.5 percent, which is much faster than the average for all occupations. In addition, this occupation will see a large number of new jobs, with more than 37,000 created over the projection decade. Demand for computer software engineers will increase as computer networking continues to grow. Implementing, safeguarding, and updating computer systems and resolving problems will fuel the demand for growing numbers of systems software engineers. New growth areas will also continue to arise from rapidly evolving technologies. Job prospects for computer software engineers should be excellent. Those with practical experience and at least a bachelor's degree in a computer-related field should have the best opportunities.

▶ Employment of computer systems analysts is expected to grow by 20.3 percent, which is much faster than the average for all occupations. Demand for these workers will increase as organizations continue to adopt and integrate increasingly sophisticated technologies and as the need for information security grows. Job prospects

Table 5
Percentage Distribution of Workers with Only a Bachelor's Degree, by Level of Job Satisfaction

Job Satisfaction	Computer Science	All
Very satisfied	37.0	45.4
Somewhat satisfied	52.1	45.0
Somewhat dissatisfied	9.2	7.4
Very dissatisfied	1.7	2.2
Mean Score (4=very satisfied, 1=not satisfied at all)	3.2	3.3

Table 6
Projected Growth and Job Openings in the Top 5 Occupations Employing Persons with Only a Bachelor's Degree in Computer Science

Top 5 Occupations	Projected Growth 2008–2018	Projected Annual Job Openings
All top 5	19.8%	104,500
Computer Engineers—Software	32.5%	37,180
Computer Systems Analysts	20.3%	22,280
Network and Computer Systems Administrators	23.2%	13,550
Computer Support Specialists	13.8%	23,460
Computer Programmers (Business, Scientific, Process Control)	−2.9%	8,030

should be excellent. Job openings will occur as a result of strong job growth and from the need to replace workers who move into other occupations or who leave the labor force.

▶ Employment of network and computer systems administrators is expected to increase by 23.2 percent, much faster than the average for all occupations. Computer networks are an integral part of business, and demand for these workers will increase as firms continue to invest in new technologies. The increasing adoption of mobile technologies means that more establishments will use the Internet to conduct business online. This growth translates into a need for systems administrators who can help organizations use technology to communicate with employees, clients, and consumers. Growth will also be driven by the increasing need for information security. As cyber attacks become more sophisticated, demand will increase for workers with security skills. Job prospects should be excellent. In general, applicants with a college degree and certification will have the best opportunities.

▶ Employment of computer support specialists is expected to increase by 13.8 percent, which is faster than the average for all occupations. Demand for these workers will result as organizations and individuals continue to adopt the newest technology. As technology becomes more complex and widespread, support specialists will be needed in greater numbers to resolve the technical problems that arise. Businesses, especially, will demand greater levels of support as information technology has become essential in business. Job prospects are expected to be good; those who possess a bachelor's degree, relevant technical and communication skills, and previous work experience should have even better opportunities than applicants with an associate degree or professional certification.

▶ Employment of computer programmers is expected to decline slowly, decreasing by 2.9 percent. Advances in programming languages and tools, the growing ability of users to write and implement their own programs, and the offshore outsourcing of programming jobs will contribute to this decline. Nevertheless, numerous job openings will result from the need to replace workers who leave the labor force or transfer to other occupations. Prospects for these openings should be best for applicants with a bachelor's degree and experience with a variety of programming languages and tools. As technology evolves, however, and newer, more sophisticated tools emerge, programmers will need to update their skills to remain competitive. Obtaining vendor-specific or language-specific certification also can provide a competitive edge.

Pathways Beyond the Bachelor's Degree

Almost one-quarter of computer science graduates with a bachelor's degree proceed to earn a master's degree, but extremely few proceed to a doctoral or professional degree.

▶ Thirty-six percent earn their master's degree in the field of computer science, and 18 percent earn the degree in another computer-related field.

▶ About 24 percent of all master's degrees of undergraduate computer science majors are earned in a business field.

▶ Five percent of the master's degrees are earned in engineering.

CHAPTER 58

Electrical and Electronics Engineering Technology

Electrical and electronics technology curricula include the design, development, testing, and manufacture of electrical and electronics equipment, such as radios, radar, sonar, television, industrial and medical measuring or control devices, navigational equipment, and computers. Electrical and electronics technicians may work in product evaluation and testing, using measuring and diagnostic devices to adjust, test, and repair equipment.

Electrical and electronics engineering technology is also applied to a variety of systems such as communications and process controls. Electromechanical engineering technicians combine fundamental principles of mechanical engineering technology with knowledge of electrical and electronic circuits to design, develop, test, and manufacture electrical and computer-controlled mechanical systems.

Educational course work may include college algebra, trigonometry, physics, electric circuits, microprocessors, digital electronics, circuit analysis, communication systems, energy conversion, control engineering, power systems, engineering analysis, electricity and electronics, distributed systems, and related laboratory courses.

Where Do Electrical and Electronics Engineering Technology Majors Work?

A large majority of all employed electrical and electronics engineering technology graduates work in the private, for-profit sector. Of employed graduates, more than 6 out of 10 work for businesses and corporations in the private, for-profit sector. Another 16 percent who work in the private, for-profit sector are self-employed in their own business or practice. The government sector employs 12 percent of electrical and electronics engineering technology graduates. Only 5 percent work for educational institutions, and the private, nonprofit sector employs only 3 percent of these graduates.

Table 1
Percentage Distribution of Employed Persons with Only a Bachelor's Degree, by Economic Sector, Size, and New Business Status of Employer

	Electrical and Electronics Engineering Technology	All
Economic Sector		
Private for-profit	62.4	47.3
Self-employed	16.4	18.5
Government/Military	12.1	11.0
Education	5.5	15.6
Nonprofit	3.3	7.5
Employer Size		
Small (Fewer than 100 employees)	19.1	35.5
Medium (100–999)	22.1	21.8
Large (1,000–24,999)	30.7	26.0
Very large (25,000 or more)	28.2	16.7
Percent working in new business established within past 5 years	9.3	7.6

The applied nature of the classroom training of electrical and electronics engineering technology graduates gives them ready access to jobs that are related to their major. Nearly two-thirds of employed electrical and electronics engineering technology graduates work in jobs that are closely related to their major. Another 23 percent consider their employment to be somewhat related to their major. Only 15 percent of all employed electrical and electronics engineering technology graduates are employed in jobs that are not at all related to their undergraduate major.

Of all electrical and electronics engineering technology graduates under the age of 65, 88 percent are employed. Only 6 percent are officially unemployed; in other words, they are not employed and are actively seeking employment. The remaining 6 percent are out of the labor force; that is, they are not employed and are not seeking employment. Of those who are out of the labor force, more than 58 percent have taken early retirement. About 11 percent have withdrawn from the workforce because they believe that suitable jobs are not available.

Occupations

The employment of electrical and electronics engineering technology graduates is concentrated in a few occupations. These 5 predominant employers of graduates span the engineering, technology, and computer fields.

About 17 percent of the graduates of electrical and electronics engineering technology programs at the bachelor's degree level report that they are employed as electrical or electronics engineers. It is possible for someone with a technology degree, work experience, and further training to advance to an engineering job title, but it is difficult to be licensed as a professional engineer without a degree from an engineering program approved by the Accreditation Board for Engineering and Technology. Electrical and electronics engineers seldom offer their services to the public and

Table 2

Percentage Distribution of Employed Persons with Only a Bachelor's Degree in Electrical and Electronics Engineering Technology, by the Relationship Between Their Job and College Major

Relationship of Job to Major	Percent
Closely related	62.9
Somewhat related	22.7
Not related	14.5

Percent who report the following as the most important reasons for working in a job that was not related to major:	
Change in career or professional interests	34.0
Job in highest degree field not available	24.3
Pay, promotion opportunities	19.5
Job location	11.5
Family-related reasons	10.7

therefore usually do not need to be licensed, so they often can enjoy the title of engineer even though their degree is not in an engineering field.

Computer engineers hold that job title even more often without a degree in engineering or licensure. Fifteen percent of electrical and electronics engineering technology grads work as computer engineers, with software a more popular specialization than hardware. Another 15 percent of grads are working as technicians or repairers.

The ratio of male to female grads is approximately 9 to 1, and the two sexes have very different employment patterns.

Table 3

Top 5 Occupations Employing Persons with Only a Bachelor's Degree in Electrical and Electronics Engineering Technology, by Percentage

Top 5 Occupations	All	Men	Women
Electrical and Electronics Engineers	16.8	17.6	7.3
Computer Engineers—Software	9.3	10.0	2.8
Engineering Technologists/Technicians—Electrical, Industrial, and Mechanical	9.3	10.2	–
Mechanics and Repairers	6.0	6.6	–
Computer Engineer—Hardware	5.8	1.4	53.2
Total, Top 5 Occupations	47.2	45.8	63.3
Balance of Employed	52.8	54.2	36.7
All Employed	100.0	100.0	100.0

Work Activities

- Almost 9 out of 10 employed electrical and electronics engineering technology graduates perform computer applications, programming, and systems-development duties. Seventy-two percent handle these tasks as a regular part of their job; another 16 percent spend most of their time in a typical workweek performing these duties.

- About 4 out of 10 regularly perform managerial duties to oversee the efficiency and quality of the production process, although only half as many spend most of their work time in these activities.

- More than 15 percent of all employed graduates report that they regularly perform management and administrative duties, and 55 percent spend most of their time during a typical workweek performing these duties.

- Electrical and electronics engineering technology graduates also design and develop products and equipment. Forty-seven percent of employed graduates regularly engage in the design of equipment and processes, and 7 percent spend most of their time performing these tasks. Another 41 percent regularly use research findings to produce materials and devices in their jobs, and 6 percent consider these duties to be the main part of their job.

- A little more than one-quarter of all employed electrical and electronics engineering technology graduates regularly perform sales, purchasing, and marketing, and one-tenth consider these duties the major part of their jobs.

Workplace Training and Other Work-Related Experiences

The career potential of a job is closely associated with the amount of work-related training on the job. Work-related training is regarded as an investment by firms because it makes workers more productive. Firms that invest in their workforce are more likely to offer pay increases and promotions to match the increasing productivity of their workers. The rate of participation in work-related training during a year among employed electrical and electronics engineering technology graduates (65 percent) is significantly higher than the training participation rate of all college graduates (61 percent).

- Of those electrical and electronics engineering technology graduates who participate in training, 60 percent receive technical training in their occupational field.

- Nineteen percent of the training recipients participate in management or supervisor training.

- Twenty-three percent receive training to improve their general professional skills, such as public speaking and business writing.

When asked to identify the most important reason to acquire training, 38 percent of electrical and electronics engineering technology graduates who undergo training identify the need to improve their occupational skills and knowledge. Another 11 percent report a mandatory training requirement by the employer as the most important factor for their involvement in work-related training. More opportunity for a promotion and a salary increase is the most important factor influencing the decision to acquire training among 6 percent of employed graduates.

Salaries

The median annual salary of electrical and electronics engineering technology graduates with only a bachelor's degree is $65,000, a level that is 21 percent higher than the median annual salary of all employed college graduates. On average, employed electrical and electronics engineering technology graduates work for 45 hours per week and for 51 weeks per year, resulting in 2,295 hours of employment per year. The level of work effort among electrical and electronics engineering technology graduates is 7 percent higher than the average among all college graduates (43 hours per week and 50 weeks per year, resulting in 2,150 hours per year).

The average annual salary of electrical and electronics engineering technology graduates who work in jobs that are related to their major is considerably higher than the salary of graduates who are employed in jobs that are not related to their major. Graduates working in closely related jobs earn $72,200 per year. The salary of those who are employed in jobs that are somewhat related to their major is $57,800 per year. Only 15 percent of electrical and electronics engineering technology graduates work in jobs that are unrelated to their undergraduate major, and they earn an average annual salary of $48,500.

Working in the private, for-profit sector for businesses and corporations is associated with a higher average annual salary than employment in other sectors among electrical and electronics

<u>**FIGURE 1**</u>

Age/Earnings Profile of Persons with Only a Bachelor's Degree in Electrical and Electronics Engineering Technology (Full-Time Workers, in 2010 Dollars)

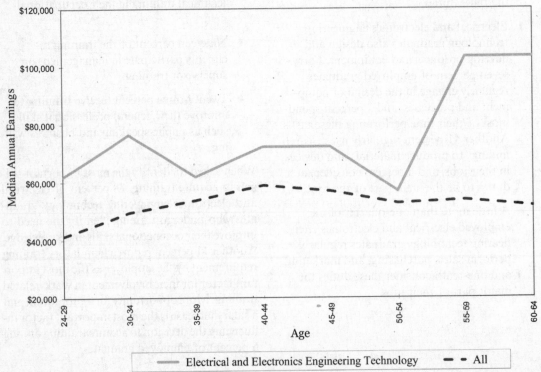

Table 4
Annual Salary of Workers with Only a Bachelor's Degree, Top 5 Occupations (in 2010 Dollars)

Earnings in Top 5 Occupations	All	Electrical and Electronics Engineering Technology
Total	$65,000	$68,400
Electrical and Electronics Engineers	$78,400	$70,200
Computer Engineers—Software	$82,600	$82,600
Engineering Technologists/Technicians—Electrical, Industrial, and Mechanical	$51,600	$51,600
Mechanics and Repairers	$45,400	$36,100
Computer Engineer—Hardware	$87,700	$103,200

engineering technology graduates. Full-time graduates in this setting earn $72,200 per year. Self-employed graduates average $65,200 per year. Government-sector employees with a bachelor's degree in electrical and electronics engineering technology earn $57,700 per year. In the nonprofit sector, the average is $59,900 per year. The average annual remuneration of graduates employed by educational institutions is only $40,500.

Only 2 of the top 5 occupations that employ electrical and electronics engineering technology graduates pay them an average annual salary that is less than the average salary of all college graduates. Those working as electrical and electronics engineers are almost certainly less appropriately trained than workers who hold an engineering degree. The situation is probably similar for graduates working as mechanics and repairers, who are likely to be less well trained than those who have completed an occupation-specific curriculum.

Job Satisfaction

The overall level of job satisfaction of electrical and electronics engineering technology majors is about the same as the average for all graduates.

Table 5
Percentage Distribution of Workers with Only a Bachelor's Degree, by Level of Job Satisfaction

Job Satisfaction	Electrical and Electronics Engineering Technology	All
Very satisfied	36.2	45.4
Somewhat satisfied	55.7	45.0
Somewhat dissatisfied	6.5	7.4
Very dissatisfied	1.6	2.2
Mean Score (4=very satisfied, 1=not satisfied at all)	3.3	3.3

Employment Outlook

According to the projections by the U.S. Bureau of Labor Statistics, employment in occupations that require a bachelor's degree is expected to grow faster than employment in other sectors of the American labor market. Between 2008 and 2018, the U.S. workforce is projected to grow by 10.1 percent, creating an average of 15.2 million job openings per year. The bachelor's-level jobs are expected to increase by 17.7 percent over the same time.

For graduates of electrical and electronics engineering technology, the outlook is highly mixed. Projected losses in the nation's manufacturing sector mean slow growth in many traditional sources of employment for graduates in this field. Demand for workers in this major is more likely to grow rapidly in occupations that apply mathematical skills, such as computer software engineers.

▶ Very slow growth is projected for electrical and electronics engineers between 2008 and 2018. Although strong demand for electrical and electronic devices—including electric power generators, wireless phone transmitters, high-density batteries, defense-related equipment, and navigation systems—should spur job growth, international competition and the use of engineering services performed in other countries will limit employment growth. Electrical and electronics engineers working in firms providing engineering expertise and design services to manufacturers should have better job prospects.

▶ Employment of computer software engineers is expected to increase by 32.5 percent, which is much faster than the average for all occupations. In addition, this occupation will see a large number of new jobs, with more than 37,000 created over the projection decade. Demand for computer software engineers will increase as computer networking continues to grow. Implementing, safeguarding, and updating computer systems and resolving problems will fuel the demand for growing numbers of systems software engineers. New growth areas will also continue to arise from rapidly evolving technologies. Job prospects for computer software engineers should be excellent.

▶ Employment in the electrical and electronics technician and technologist occupations is projected to grow by 7.2 percent. Job prospects will vary by specialty and location, as employment is

Table 6

Projected Growth and Job Openings in the Top 5 Occupations Employing Persons with Only a Bachelor's Degree in Electrical and Electronics Engineering Technology

Top 5 Occupations	Projected Growth 2008–2018	Projected Annual Job Openings
All top 5	16.2%	67,160
Electrical and Electronics Engineers	1.0%	7,230
Computer Engineers—Software	32.5%	37,180
Engineering Technologists/Technicians—Electrical, Industrial, and Mechanical	7.2%	15,420
Mechanics and Repairers	−4.4%	2,630
Computer Engineer—Hardware	3.8%	4,700

influenced by economic conditions similar to those that affect engineers. In general, opportunities will be best for individuals with a bachelor's degree. As technology becomes more sophisticated, employers will continue to look for technologists and technicians who are skilled in new technology and who require little additional training. Even in specialties that are expected to experience job declines, there will still be job openings resulting from the need to replace technologists and technicians who retire or leave the labor force for any other reason.

▸ Computer hardware engineers are expected to have employment growth of less than 4 percent over the projections decade, slower than the average for all occupations. Although the use of information technology continues to expand rapidly, the manufacture of computer hardware is expected to be adversely affected by intense foreign competition. As computer and semiconductor manufacturers contract out more of their engineering needs to both domestic and foreign design firms, much of the growth in employment of hardware engineers is expected to take place in the computer systems design and related services industry.

▸ The demand for mechanics and repairers is projected to shrink between 2008 and 2018. Some specializations are projected to grow at a below-average rate, and some (such as avionics technicians) will grow at an average rate.

Pathways Beyond the Bachelor's Degree

Almost one-fifth of all electrical and electronics engineering technology graduates with a bachelor's degree proceed to earn a postgraduate degree: 16 percent earn a master's degree and 2 percent earn a doctorate. Virtually none earn a professional degree.

▸ Nearly 29 percent of the master's degrees are earned in electrical and electronics engineering technology, and 10 percent are earned in engineering.

▸ Another 22 percent of master's degrees are earned in a business field.

▸ The same share of master's degrees are earned in a computer-related discipline other than engineering.

▸ Electrical and electronics engineering is the field of choice among one-third of the graduates with a doctoral degree. Another 18 percent earn the degree in electrical and electronics technologies.

CHAPTER 59

Industrial Production Technology

This chapter covers academic programs that involve several different facets of production and construction.

Chemical engineering technology prepares people to be employed in industries that produce pharmaceuticals, chemicals, and petroleum products. Chemical engineering technicians work in laboratories as well as processing plants. They help develop new chemical products and processes, test processing equipment and instrumentation, monitor quality, and operate chemical manufacturing facilities.

Civil engineering technology prepares people to help civil engineers plan and build highways, buildings, bridges, dams, and wastewater treatment systems, as well as perform related surveys and studies. Some civil engineering technicians inspect water and wastewater treatment systems to ensure that pollution control requirements are met. Others estimate construction costs and specify materials to be used. Some prepare drawings or perform land-surveying duties.

Industrial engineering technology is the study of the time, motion, methods, and speed involved in the performance of maintenance, production, and clerical operations to establish standard production rates with the goal to improve efficiency,

safety, and quality of output. The engineering technician prepares charts, graphs, and diagrams to illustrate workflow, routing, floor layouts, material handling, and machine utilization. To determine the time involved and fatigue rate, the technician observes workers as they operate equipment or perform tasks. The technician recommends revisions of methods of operation or material handling and suggests alterations in equipment layout to increase production or improve standards. The engineering technician may assist in planning work assignments in accordance with worker performance, machine capacity, production schedules, and anticipated delays.

Courses in these areas may include production planning and control, automated manufacturing and robotics, occupational safety and health, quality control, industrial processes, materials processing, hazardous waste management, cost estimating and bidding, engineering material science, engineering drawing, designing and planning, and computers in industrial technology and industrial electronics. Students also take math, computer, and physics courses.

The study of engineering technology requires knowledge and the use of high-level mathematics. Technologists need eye, hand, and finger

Table 1
Percentage Distribution of Employed Persons with Only a Bachelor's Degree, by Economic Sector, Size, and New Business Status of Employer

	Industrial Production Technology	All
Economic Sector		
Private for-profit	60.4	47.3
Self-employed	24.9	18.5
Government/Military	4.4	11.0
Education	5.2	15.6
Nonprofit	4.8	7.5
Employer Size		
Small (Fewer than 100 employees)	42.4	35.5
Medium (100–999)	19.4	21.8
Large (1,000–24,999)	18.8	26.0
Very large (25,000 or more)	19.3	16.7
Percent working in new business established within past 5 years	6.0	7.6

coordination to operate machines, adjust instruments, and use measuring tools. Drawing and sketching involve finger dexterity. Technicians perform detailed work with great accuracy. Judgment is required in analyzing data to make decisions. The ability to direct the activities of others is called for in setting up equipment such as seismographic recording instruments to gather data about oil-bearing rock layers. Technologists need to be skilled at using computer and software packages and at writing technical reports in clear language.

Where Do Industrial Production Technology Majors Work?

A large majority of all employed industrial production technology graduates work in the private, for-profit sector. Six out of 10 employed graduates work for private, for-profit businesses and corporations; another one-quarter are self-employed in their own business or practice. Educational institutions and the private, nonprofit sector each employ about 5 percent of these graduates. The government sector employs only 4 percent of industrial production technology graduates.

Of all employed industrial production technology graduates, four-fifths work in jobs that are either closely or somewhat related to their major. About 36 percent are employed in jobs that are closely related to their field of study, and about 44 percent consider their employment to be somewhat related to their major. The remaining one-fifth of all employed industrial production technology graduates work in jobs that are not at all related to their major.

Of all industrial production technology graduates under the age of 65, almost 86 percent are employed. About 5 percent are officially unemployed; in other words, they are not employed and are actively seeking employment. The

Table 2

Percentage Distribution of Employed Persons with Only a Bachelor's Degree in Industrial Production Technology, by the Relationship Between Their Job and College Major

Relationship of Job to Major	Percent
Closely related	36.5
Somewhat related	43.6
Not related	19.9

Percent who report the following as the most important reasons for working in a job that was not related to major:

Pay, promotion opportunities	31.7
Job in highest degree field not available	27.3
Change in career or professional interests	13.4
Family-related reasons	12.8
Working conditions (hours, equipment, environment)	9.9

remaining 10 percent are out of the labor force; that is, they are not employed and are not seeking employment. The graduates who are out of the labor force give two main reasons for their labor force withdrawal; nearly 39 percent of this group are retired, and 21 percent are staying home to deal with family responsibilities.

Occupations

Graduates of this major pursue a wide variety of careers. The top 5 occupations employing industrial production technology graduates account for less than 42 percent of the grads. More than 16 percent work in sales occupations, with somewhat more of them selling commodities than retail goods. About 13 percent work in mid-level managerial occupations. Seven percent say they are employed as industrial engineers, although their degree is in engineering technology rather than in engineering. It is possible for someone with a technology degree, work experience, and further training to advance to an engineering job title, but it is difficult to be licensed as a professional engineer without a degree from an engineering program approved by the Accreditation Board for Engineering and Technology. Industrial engineers usually serve businesses rather than public customers and therefore usually do not need to be licensed, so they often can enjoy the title of engineer even though their degree is not in an engineering field.

About 9 out of 10 graduates of this major are male. The female graduates tend not to be attracted to the top 5 occupations; only 14 percent of them hold these jobs, most of them in retail sales.

Work Activities

▶ Eighty-eight percent of all employed industrial production technology graduates perform computer applications, programming, and systems-development duties as a regular part of their jobs, and another 5 percent spend the major part of a typical workweek performing these duties.

▶ Management or supervision of people or projects occupies significant time for

Table 3
Top 5 Occupations Employing Persons with Only a Bachelor's Degree in Industrial Production Technology, by Percentage

Top 5 Occupations	All	Men	Women
Other Management-Related Occupations	12.6	14.0	–
Sales Occupations—Commodities, Except Retail	9.4	10.3	1.3
Sales Occupations—Retail	7.1	6.9	9.4
Industrial Engineers	7.0	7.4	3.4
Precision/Production Occupations	6.5	7.2	–
Total, Top 5 Occupations	42.6	45.8	14.1
Balance of Employed	57.4	54.2	85.9
All Employed	100.0	100.0	100.0

two-thirds of grads. For one-fifth of them, it is their main job function.

▶ Fifty-eight percent of all employed industrial production technology graduates regularly perform sales, purchasing, and marketing duties at work, and one-quarter spend most of their typical workweek performing these tasks.

▶ Industrial production technology graduates also design and develop products and equipment. About 48 percent of employed graduates regularly engage in the design of equipment and processes, and 10 percent spend most of their time performing these tasks.

▶ Thirty-five percent of employed industrial production technology graduates spend at least 10 hours of their workweek in production, operations, and maintenance activities, but only 8 percent are focused mainly on these tasks.

▶ Although 43 percent of the graduates regularly perform accounting, finance, and contractual duties at work, only 9 percent report that these duties take up a major portion of their typical workweek.

Workplace Training and Other Work-Related Experiences

The career potential of a job is closely associated with the amount of work-related training on the job. Work-related training is regarded as an investment by firms because it makes workers more productive. Firms that invest in their workforce are more likely to offer pay increases and promotions to match the increasing productivity of their workers. The rate of participation in work-related training during a year among employed industrial production technology graduates (51 percent) is significantly lower than the training participation rate of all college graduates (61 percent).

▶ Of those industrial production technology graduates who receive some training, 46 percent receive technical training in their occupational field.

▶ Nineteen percent of the training recipients receive management or supervisor training.

▶ Twenty percent receive training to improve their general professional skills, such as public speaking and business writing.

When asked to identify the most important reason to acquire training, about one-third of industrial production technology graduates who undergo training identify the need to improve their skills and knowledge. Another 7 percent report a mandatory training requirement by the employer as the most important factor for their involvement in work-related training. Six percent rank the need to obtain a professional license or certificate as the most important reason for participation in work-related training.

Salaries

The median annual salary of industrial production technology graduates with only a bachelor's degree is $60,000, a level that is 14 percent higher than the median annual salary of all employed college graduates. On average, employed industrial production technology graduates work for 46 hours per week and for 51 weeks per year, resulting in 2,346 hours of employment per year. The level of work effort among industrial production technology graduates is 9 percent higher than the average among all college graduates (43 hours per week and 50 weeks per year, resulting in 2,150 hours per year).

Note: Because of the very small number of survey respondents in some age groups, it was not possible to furnish a useful age/earnings profile graphic for this major.

Industrial production technology graduates lose a lot of earning power when they do work that does not use their skills. They have the same average annual salary whether they work in jobs that are closely related or only somewhat related to their major: $61,900. In contrast, the average salary of graduates employed full-time in a job that is not related to their field of study is only $36,100 per year.

Industrial production technology graduates who work for businesses and corporations in the private, for-profit sector earn more than those who are employed in other sectors of the economy. The average salary of this group of graduates is $61,900 per year. Self-employed graduates who work in their own business or practice earn $53,800 per year. Nonprofit organizations pay slightly less, an average of $53,700 per year. The government sector pays industrial production graduates who work in full-time jobs an average annual salary of $41,200.

In 2 of the top 5 occupations that employ industrial production technology graduates, the average annual salary is noticeably higher than the salary of all college graduates. These include mid-level managerial occupations and commodities sales. For the other 3 occupations, the major appears to be a less appropriate match, at least as reflected in the average income. This is particularly true for those working as industrial

Table 4
Annual Salary of Workers with Only a Bachelor's Degree,
Top 5 Occupations (in 2010 Dollars)

Earnings in Top 5 Occupations	All	Industrial Production Technology
Total	$60,000	$58,600
Other Management-Related Occupations	$57,800	$67,100
Sales Occupations—Commodities, Except Retail	$64,000	$72,200
Sales Occupations—Retail	$42,300	$41,300
Industrial Engineers	$67,100	$61,900
Precision/Production Occupations	$39,200	$37,200

Table 5
Percentage Distribution of Workers with Only a Bachelor's Degree, by Level of Job Satisfaction

Job Satisfaction	Industrial Production Technology	All
Very satisfied	38.3	45.4
Somewhat satisfied	44.5	45.0
Somewhat dissatisfied	15.8	7.4
Very dissatisfied	1.4	2.2
Mean Score (4=very satisfied, 1=not satisfied at all)	3.2	3.3

engineers; they are almost certainly less appropriately trained than workers who hold an engineering degree.

Job Satisfaction

The overall level of job satisfaction of industrial production technology majors is slightly lower than the average for all graduates.

Employment Outlook

According to the projections by the U.S. Bureau of Labor Statistics, employment in occupations that require a bachelor's degree is expected to grow faster than employment in other sectors of the American labor market. Between 2008 and 2018, the U.S. workforce is projected to grow by 10.1 percent, creating an average of 15.2 million job openings per year. The bachelor's-level jobs are expected to increase by 17.7 percent over the same time.

The outlook is mixed for the top 5 jobs employing industrial production technology grads, as Table 6 shows.

▶ The mid-level managerial occupations are projected to have slower than average growth, but because of their very large workforce, they will create numerous job openings through turnover. The same is true for jobs in retail sales.

▶ The workforce of commodities salesworkers is expected to shrink, and competition for jobs will continue to be keen, with more applicants than available openings. Entry-level sales agents, particularly those with previous sales experience, should face better prospects in smaller firms, as opposed to larger firms, where many positions have been eliminated.

▶ Industrial engineers are expected to have employment growth of 14.2 percent over the projections decade, faster than the average for all occupations. As firms look for new ways to reduce costs and raise productivity, they increasingly will turn to industrial engineers to develop more efficient processes and reduce costs, delays, and waste. This focus should lead to job growth for these engineers, even in some manufacturing industries with declining employment overall. Because their work is similar to that done in management occupations, many industrial engineers leave the occupation to become managers. Numerous openings will be created by the need to replace industrial engineers who transfer to other occupations or leave the labor force. However, opportunities for those seeking this job title will be better

Table 6

Projected Growth and Job Openings in the Top 5 Occupations Employing Persons
with Only a Bachelor's Degree in Industrial Production Technology

Top 5 Occupations	Projected Growth 2008–2018	Projected Annual Job Openings
All top 5	7.6%	276,810
Other Management-Related Occupations	7.2%	53,020
Sales Occupations—Commodities, Except Retail	−1.1%	310
Sales Occupations—Retail	7.5%	207,700
Industrial Engineers	14.2%	8,540
Precision/Production Occupations	7.5%	7,240

for those with engineering degrees than for those with degrees in engineering technologies.

▶ The outlook for precision and production workers largely depends on the workers' specialization. Between chemical, civil, and industrial engineering technologies, opportunities should be best in the field of civil engineering technology, moderate in industrial engineering technology, and least favorable in chemical engineering technology, based on the outlook for engineers in these fields.

Pathways Beyond the Bachelor's Degree

Only 18 percent of all industrial production technology graduates with a bachelor's degree proceed to earn a postgraduate degree. Virtually all of the degrees earned by these graduates are at the master's level.

▶ Almost 40 percent of the master's degrees are earned in a business field.

▶ Nearly 16 percent of the master's degrees are earned in industrial production technology.

▶ Education or educational administration is the focus of 12 percent of the master's degrees.

CHAPTER 60

Information Systems

This major lies at the intersection between technology and business. In many colleges it is called management information systems and is taught in the business school with an emphasis on business applications.

Nearly all organizations rely on computer and information technology (IT) to conduct business and operate efficiently. Computer systems analysts use IT tools to help enterprises of all sizes achieve their goals. They may design and develop new computer systems by choosing and configuring hardware and software, or they may devise ways to apply existing systems' resources to additional tasks.

Most systems analysts work with specific types of computer systems—for example, business, accounting, and financial systems or scientific and engineering systems—that vary with the kind of organization. Analysts who specialize in helping an organization select system hardware and software are often called system architects or system designers. Analysts who specialize in developing and fine-tuning systems often have the more general title of systems analysts.

To begin an assignment, systems analysts consult with an organization's managers and users to define the goals of the system and then design a system to meet those goals. They specify the inputs that the system will access, decide how the inputs will be processed, and select and format the output to meet users' needs. Analysts

use techniques such as structured analysis, data modeling, information engineering, mathematical model building, sampling, and a variety of accounting principles to ensure their plans are efficient and complete. They also may prepare cost-benefit and return-on-investment analyses to help management decide whether implementing the proposed technology would be financially feasible.

When a system is approved, systems analysts oversee the implementation of the required hardware and software components. They coordinate tests and observe the initial use of the system to ensure that it performs as planned. They prepare specifications, flow charts, and process diagrams for computer programmers to follow; then they work with programmers to debug the system—that is, to eliminate errors. Systems analysts who do more in-depth testing may be called software quality assurance analysts. In addition to running tests, these workers diagnose problems, recommend solutions, and determine whether program requirements have been met. After the system has been implemented, tested, and debugged, computer systems analysts may train its users and write instruction manuals.

In some organizations, programmer-analysts design and update the software that runs a computer. They also create custom applications tailored to their organization's tasks. Because they are responsible for both programming and systems analysis, these workers must be proficient in both areas. As this dual proficiency becomes more common, analysts are increasingly working with databases, object-oriented programming languages, client-server applications, and multimedia and Internet technology.

One challenge created by expanding computer use is the need for different computer systems to communicate with each other. Many systems analysts are involved with networking—connecting all the computers within an organization or across organizations, as when setting up e-commerce networks to facilitate business between companies.

Employers usually look for people who have broad knowledge and experience related to computer systems and technologies, strong problem-solving and analytical skills, and the ability to think logically. In addition, the ability to concentrate and pay close attention to detail is important because computer systems analysts often deal with many tasks simultaneously. Although these workers sometimes work independently, they frequently work in teams on large projects. Therefore, they must have good interpersonal skills and be able to communicate effectively with computer personnel, users, and other staff who may have no technical background.

Where Do Information Systems Majors Work?

Computer systems analysts work in offices or laboratories. Some analysts telecommute, using computers to work from remote locations. Almost two-thirds of information systems grads work as wage and salary employees at for-profit businesses and corporations. Almost 10 percent of grads work in a government organization. An additional 9 percent are self-employed, often in a consulting service. Educational institutions and not-for-profit organizations each employ roughly 8 percent of grads.

More than three-quarters of information systems majors work in jobs that are related in some way

Table 1

Percentage Distribution of Employed Persons with Only a Bachelor's Degree, by Economic Sector, Size, and New Business Status of Employer

	Information Systems	All
Economic Sector		
Private for-profit	64.5	47.3
Self-employed	9.2	18.5
Government/Military	9.7	11.0
Education	8.5	15.6
Nonprofit	7.9	7.5
Employer Size		
Small (Fewer than 100 employees)	20.9	35.5
Medium (100–999)	18.1	21.8
Large (1,000–24,999)	36.1	26.0
Very large (25,000 or more)	24.9	16.7
Percent working in new business established within past 5 years	6.8	7.6

Table 2
Percentage Distribution of Employed Persons with Only a Bachelor's Degree in Information Systems, by the Relationship Between Their Job and College Major

Relationship of Job to Major	Percent
Closely related	56.5
Somewhat related	26.5
Not related	16.9

Percent who report the following as the most important reasons for working in a job that was not related to major:

Change in career or professional interests	42.0
Job in highest degree field not available	30.8
Family-related reasons	13.3
Pay, promotion opportunities	8.9
Other reason	5.1

to their undergraduate field of study. More than half work in closely related jobs, and more than one-quarter work in jobs that are somewhat related. Less than 17 percent work in jobs that are unrelated to the major.

Almost 90 percent of persons with only a bachelor's degree in information systems are employed. Among those not working, 4 percent of all grads are still actively looking for work. The remaining 7 percent of grads are persons who have decided not to participate actively in the labor market. The largest fraction of this group, 29 percent, consider family responsibilities more important than employment. Another 23 percent have no need or desire to work. Nearly 18 percent are unable to find suitable work.

Occupations

Among the top 5 occupations employing graduates of the information systems major, all but one work directly with computers. Of the 4 computer-related jobs, the one using the lowest level of skill is computer programmers; they tend to focus on writing code rather than on planning

and implementing information systems. Some of the workers who hold administrative jobs may be working in the information technology department of a company, where they can use some of the skills that they developed in this major.

It's important to understand that many workers who have the job title computer engineer or software engineer do not have engineering degrees and instead come from a major such as information systems (or computer science, which is described in Chapter 57). Engineers who offer their services to the public need to be licensed as professional engineers, which requires a degree from an engineering program approved by the Accreditation Board for Engineering and Technology. Those who work with computers, however, usually serve businesses rather than public customers and therefore usually do not need to be licensed. This means they often can enjoy the title of engineer even though their degree is not in an engineering field.

Male grads outnumber female grads slightly and tend to opt for jobs as software engineers and systems administrators more often than the female grads do.

Table 3
Top 5 Occupations Employing Persons with Only a
Bachelor's Degree in Information Systems, by Percentage

Top 5 Occupations	All	Men	Women
Computer Systems Analysts	17.9	17.3	18.8
Computer Engineers—Software	13.1	16.5	7.6
Other Administrative Occupations	7.7	7.6	7.9
Computer Programmers (Business, Scientific, Process Control)	7.1	6.4	8.1
Network and Computer Systems Administrators	6.6	8.2	3.9
Total, Top 5 Occupations	52.4	56.0	46.3
Balance of Employed	47.6	44.0	53.7
All Employed	100.0	100.0	100.0

Work Activities

▎ Unsurprisingly, almost 9 out of 10 information system graduates are responsible for activities involving computer applications, programming, and systems development. About half of the grads engage in these activities more than any other work responsibility, and for another 40 percent these activities are a regular part of the workday.

▎ Fifty-five percent are involved in managing or supervising people or projects over the course of a typical workweek. For 15 percent, this is the primary work role.

▎ One-third of the grads say employee relations tasks occupy at least 10 hours out of each workweek, but only 2 percent are mainly focused on these duties.

▎ Almost one-quarter of grads are involved in accounting, contractual, or financial issues as a regular part of their weekly work activities. About 7 percent spend most of their time on these tasks.

▎ More than 3 out of 10 grads regularly are engaged in design activities, but only 4 percent do these tasks most of the time.

▎ Twenty-eight percent of information systems majors engage in applied research on a regular basis. Only 1 percent are primarily responsible for applied research.

Workplace Training and Other Work-Related Experiences

On-the-job learning is an important indicator of the long-term career potential of a job. The rate of participation in work-related training during a year among employed information systems graduates (58 percent) is slightly lower than the training participation rate of all college graduates (61 percent).

▎ Of those information systems graduates who receive some training, 49 percent receive technical training in the occupation in which they are employed.

▎ About one-quarter of the training recipients receive management or supervisor training.

▶ Nineteen percent receive training to improve their general professional skills, such as public speaking and business writing.

When asked the most important reason they get training, one-third say they are motivated to develop and maintain skills that are needed for their current job. For 6 percent, the key reason is that their employer requires the training. The requirements of licensing or certification and the demands of a new position each serve as the main incentive for about 5 percent of the grads who get training.

Salaries

The median annual salary of information systems graduates with only a bachelor's degree is $62,000, a level that is 17 percent higher than the median annual salary of all employed college graduates. On average, employed information systems graduates work for 44 hours per week and for 50 weeks per year, resulting in 2,200 hours of employment per year. The level of work effort among information systems graduates is 2 percent higher than the average among all college graduates (43 hours per week and 50 weeks per year, resulting in 2,150 hours per year).

Note: Because of the very small number of survey respondents in some age groups, it was not possible to furnish a useful age/earnings profile graphic for this major.

The average annual salary of graduates is influenced greatly by the degree to which their work is related to their schooling. For those who work in closely related jobs, the average salary is $76,400 per year. Graduates with employment in jobs that are somewhat related to their major earn $59,900 per year. In contrast, the average salary of graduates employed full-time in a job that is not related to their field of study is $39,200.

Other dramatic differences in income may be seen when earnings are compared across sectors of the economy. Private, for-profit businesses pay information systems grads an average of $76,400 per year. In government, the annual average is quite a bit lower, $54,800. Self-employed grads earn still lower on average, $44,400 per year.

Among the top 5 occupations employing information systems grads, the major provides an earnings advantage in 3 of the jobs. One occupation that lacks this advantage is computer programmer. The skills for this occupation are lower than for the other 3 computer-related jobs, so it's likely that information systems grads in these positions are holding the jobs only temporarily until they can find work more closely aligned with their skills. The same may be true for those working in the miscellaneous administrative occupations, who also earn less than graduates of other majors.

Table 4
Annual Salary of Workers with Only a Bachelor's Degree, Top 5 Occupations (in 2010 Dollars)

Earnings in Top 5 Occupations	All	Information Systems
Total	$62,000	$73,400
Computer Systems Analysts	$72,200	$78,400
Computer Engineers—Software	$82,600	$96,000
Other Administrative Occupations	$38,200	$34,100
Computer Programmers (Business, Scientific, Process Control)	$71,200	$59,900
Network and Computer Systems Administrators	$69,100	$72,200

Table 5
Percentage Distribution of Workers with Only a Bachelor's Degree, by Level of Job Satisfaction

Job Satisfaction	Information Systems	All
Very satisfied	40.0	45.4
Somewhat satisfied	49.9	45.0
Somewhat dissatisfied	8.2	7.4
Very dissatisfied	1.9	2.2
Mean Score (4=very satisfied, 1=not satisfied at all)	3.3	3.3

Job Satisfaction

The overall level of job satisfaction of information systems majors is about the same as the average for all graduates.

Employment Outlook

According to the projections by the U.S. Bureau of Labor Statistics, employment in occupations that require a bachelor's degree is expected to grow faster than employment in other sectors of the American labor market. Between 2008 and 2018, the U.S. workforce is projected to grow by 10.1 percent, creating an average of 15.2 million job openings per year. The bachelor's-level jobs are expected to increase by 17.7 percent over the same time.

On balance, the outlook for graduates of the information systems major is very good, although some occupations are more promising than others.

▶ Employment of computer systems analysts is expected to grow by 20.3 percent, which is much faster than the average for all occupations. Demand for these workers will increase as organizations continue to adopt and integrate increasingly sophisticated technologies and as the need for information security grows. Job prospects should be excellent. Job openings will occur as a result of strong job growth and from the need to replace workers who move into other occupations or who leave the labor force.

▶ Employment of computer software engineers is expected to increase by 32.5 percent, which is much faster than the average for all occupations. In addition, this occupation will see a large number of new jobs, with more than 37,000 created over the projection decade. Demand for computer software engineers will increase as computer networking continues to grow. Implementing, safeguarding, and updating computer systems and resolving problems will fuel the demand for growing numbers of systems software engineers. New growth areas will also continue to arise from rapidly evolving technologies. Job prospects for computer software engineers should be excellent. Those with practical experience and at least a bachelor's degree in a computer-related field should have the best opportunities.

▶ Job growth in the administrative occupations is projected to be about average, but job turnover should help in creating more than 166,000 openings each year.

▶ Employment of computer programmers is expected to decline slowly, decreasing by 2.9 percent. Advances in programming languages and tools, the growing ability

Table 6
Projected Growth and Job Openings in the Top 5 Occupations Employing Persons with Only a Bachelor's Degree in Information Systems

Top 5 Occupations	Projected Growth 2008–2018	Projected Annual Job Openings
All top 5	14.4%	247,170
Computer Systems Analysts	20.3%	22,280
Computer Engineers—Software	32.5%	37,180
Other Administrative Occupations	10.8%	166,130
Computer Programmers (Business, Scientific, Process Control)	−2.9%	8,030
Network and Computer Systems Administrators	23.2%	13,550

of users to write and implement their own programs, and the offshore outsourcing of programming jobs will contribute to this decline. Nevertheless, numerous job openings will result from the need to replace workers who leave the labor force or transfer to other occupations. Prospects for these openings should be best for applicants with a bachelor's degree and experience with a variety of programming languages and tools. As technology evolves, however, and newer, more sophisticated tools emerge, programmers will need to update their skills to remain competitive. Obtaining vendor-specific or language-specific certification also can provide a competitive edge.

▶ Employment of network and computer systems administrators is expected to increase by 23.2 percent, much faster than the average for all occupations. Computer networks are an integral part of business, and demand for these workers will increase as firms continue to invest in new technologies. The increasing adoption of mobile technologies means that more establishments will use the Internet to conduct business online. This growth translates into a need for systems administrators who can help organizations use technology to communicate with employees, clients, and consumers. Growth will also be driven by the increasing need for information security. As cyber attacks become more sophisticated, demand will increase for workers with security skills. Job prospects should be excellent. In general, applicants with a college degree and certification will have the best opportunities.

Pathways Beyond the Bachelor's Degree

Among information systems graduates with a bachelor's degree, 14 percent proceed to earn a postgraduate degree, of which almost all are at the master's level. The subjects that information systems grads study in graduate school confirm the description of this major as the intersection of technology and business.

▶ A little more than half of the master's degrees are earned in a business subject.

▶ About one-quarter of the master's degrees are in a computer-related subject.

▶ Seven percent of the grads study architecture or environmental design for the master's degree.

CHAPTER 61

Mechanical Engineering Technology

Mechanical engineering technicians work with engineers to design, develop, test, and manufacture industrial machinery, mechanical parts, and other equipment. These technicians may assist in the testing of a guided missile or in the planning and design of an electric power generation plant. They make sketches and rough layouts, record data, make computations, analyze results, and write reports. When planning production, mechanical engineering technicians prepare layouts and drawings of the assembly process and of parts to be manufactured. They estimate labor costs, equipment life, and plant space needed. Some test and inspect machines and equipment in manufacturing departments or work with engineers to eliminate production problems.

Their work may involve the reviewing of project instructions and blueprints. They do this to ascertain test specifications and procedures; the test equipment required; the nature of identified technical problems and possible solutions, such as parts redesign; the substitution of materials or parts; or the rearrangement of parts or subassemblies. They may devise, fabricate, and assemble new or modified mechanical components or assemblies of products. They may set up prototypes and test apparatus such as a control console, recording equipment, and cables in accordance with specifications; they then operate the controls of test apparatus and prototypes to observe and record test results. Afterward, they may recommend design and material changes to reduce costs and production time.

Courses may include mechanics, stress analysis, mechanical design, thermodynamics, materials, measurement and analysis laboratory, heat transfer, refrigeration and air conditioning, fluid dynamics, and related labs. Students also take courses in advanced mathematics, computer science, and physics.

Where Do Mechanical Engineering Technology Majors Work?

About 7 out of 10 graduates of mechanical engineering technology programs at the bachelor's degree level work as wage and salary employees in private, for-profit businesses and corporations. An additional 16 percent are self-employed individuals operating their own businesses or consulting services. Few college graduates with

Table 1

Percentage Distribution of Employed Persons with Only a Bachelor's Degree, by Economic Sector, Size, and New Business Status of Employer

	Mechanical Engineering Technology	All
Economic Sector		
Private for-profit	71.2	47.3
Self-employed	15.9	18.5
Government/Military	7.2	11.0
Education	3.1	15.6
Nonprofit	2.7	7.5
Employer Size		
Small (Fewer than 100 employees)	39.0	35.5
Medium (100–999)	12.7	21.8
Large (1,000–24,999)	24.6	26.0
Very large (25,000 or more)	23.7	16.7
Percent working in new business established within past 5 years	4.8	7.6

a bachelor's degree in mechanical engineering technology are employed in educational or non-profit organizations. About 7 percent work for a government agency.

Nine out of 10 graduates of mechanical engineering technology programs work in jobs that are either closely or somewhat related to their academic training. This large group is divided roughly equally between those who identify their jobs as closely related and those whose jobs are somewhat related. Less than 10 percent of grads say they are working in unrelated jobs.

Of those with a degree in this field, 84 percent of those under the age of 65 are employed, most in full-time jobs. Less than 3 percent are unemployed—that is, out of work but seeking a job. Among the 14 percent who are jobless but not seeking a job, almost half have taken early retirement. Another 22 percent cannot work because of illness or a disability.

Occupations

People holding a bachelor's in mechanical engineering technology work in diverse careers. The top 5 occupations employing them account for about half of the grads.

About 16 percent of the graduates of mechanical engineering technology programs at the bachelor's degree level report that they are employed as mechanical engineers. It is possible for someone with a technology degree, work experience, and further training to advance to an engineering job title, but it is difficult to be licensed as a professional engineer without a degree from an engineering program approved by the Accreditation Board for Engineering and Technology. However, engineers who do not offer their services to the public usually do not need to be licensed. This is the employment situation for many graduates of mechanical engineering technology programs, which is why they are able to enjoy the job title of engineer without an engineering degree.

Table 2
Percentage Distribution of Employed Persons with Only a
Bachelor's Degree in Mechanical Engineering Technology,
by the Relationship Between Their Job and College Major

Relationship of Job to Major	Percent
Closely related	44.8
Somewhat related	45.5
Not related	9.7

Percent who report the following as the most important reasons for
working in a job that was not related to major:

Job in highest degree field not available	33.6
Working conditions (hours, equipment, environment)	27.0
Pay, promotion opportunities	24.7
Change in career or professional interests	10.4
Family-related reasons	2.4

Almost 13 percent work as top-level managers. Probably many of these are employed in firms where their engineering technology skills are highly relevant.

An additional 12 percent are employed in some type of marketing or sales role. Again, their technology skills can work to their advantage if their marketing and sales efforts focus on technical products and services. Almost 11 percent work as mechanics and repairers.

Women account for less than 1 out of 10 graduates from this major and are virtually absent from the top 5 occupations employing graduates. About one-fifth of them are employed as drafters.

Table 3
Top 5 Occupations Employing Persons with Only a Bachelor's Degree in
Mechanical Engineering Technology, by Percentage

Top 5 Occupations	All	Men	Women
Mechanical Engineers	15.7	16.3	–
Top-Level Managers, Executives, and Administrators	12.8	13.3	–
Mechanics and Repairers	10.8	11.3	–
Other Marketing and Sales Occupations	6.9	7.1	–
Sales Occupations—Commodities, Except Retail	5.8	6.0	–
Total, Top 5 Occupations	52.0	54.0	–
Balance of Employed	48.0	46.0	100.0
All Employed	100.0	100.0	100.0

Work Activities

▶ Sales, purchasing, and marketing are the primary activities of 17 percent of the grads. Four out of 10 grads engage in these tasks regularly.

▶ Two-thirds of graduates spend significant work time managing or supervising people or projects. For 16 percent of grads, this is their main job focus.

▶ Half of the grads are responsible for quality or productivity management during at least 10 hours out of the workweek. Sixteen percent consider this their chief responsibility. Grads report the same division of time for tasks related to quality or productivity management.

▶ Computer applications regularly take the time of 82 percent of grads. Another 11 percent work mainly with computer applications.

▶ Design is a significant task for 45 percent of mechanical engineering technology graduates, but only 9 percent regard this as their dominant duty.

Workplace Training and Other Work-Related Experiences

On-the-job learning is an important indicator of the long-term career potential of a job. Firms that invest in their workers at high rates are much more likely to offer pay increases and promotions than firms that fail to make such investments. The rate of participation in work-related training during a year among employed mechanical engineering technology graduates (40 percent) is much lower than the training participation rate of all college graduates (61 percent).

▶ About 36 percent of all those who receive training over the course of the year are trained in some specific activity related to the professional field. Such training can encompass a wide variety of topics, including quality management, training in a specific process of equipment used in production, or training on the use of new materials or production techniques.

▶ About 20 percent of training recipients get training in managerial or supervisory areas, which is consistent with the finding that many graduates in this degree field have supervisory responsibilities as part of their regular job duties.

▶ Only 13 percent receive training to improve their general professional skills, such as public speaking and business writing.

Nearly one-quarter of grads who receive training do so to acquire a specific set of skills or competencies directly related to their job. Almost 7 percent are motivated primarily to advance their career. Only 4 percent get the training to obtain or maintain licensure or certification.

Salaries

The median annual salary of mechanical engineering technology graduates with only a bachelor's degree is $63,000, a level that is 18 percent higher than the median annual salary of all employed college graduates. On average, employed mechanical engineering technology graduates work for 44 hours per week and for 51 weeks per year, resulting in 2,244 hours of employment per year. The level of work effort among mechanical engineering technology graduates is 4 percent higher than the average among all college graduates (43 hours per week and 50 weeks per year, resulting in 2,150 hours per year).

Note: Because of the very small number of survey respondents in some age groups, it was not possible to furnish a useful age/earnings profile graphic for this major.

Table 4
Annual Salary of Workers with Only a Bachelor's Degree, Top 5 Occupations (in 2010 Dollars)

Earnings in Top 5 Occupations	All	Mechanical Engineering Technology
Total	$63,000	$95,500
Mechanical Engineers	$74,300	$72,200
Top-Level Managers, Executives, and Administrators	$103,200	$154,800
Mechanics and Repairers	$45,400	$42,300
Other Marketing and Sales Occupations	$54,700	$109,400
Sales Occupations—Commodities, Except Retail	$64,000	$61,900

The average annual salary of graduates who work in closely related jobs is $67,100. Graduates with employment in jobs that are somewhat related to their major earn $61,900 per year. In contrast, the average salary of graduates employed full-time in a job that is not related to their field of study is $65,000.

Those mechanical engineering technology graduates who work in the private, for-profit sector have annual salaries of about $74,300 per year, a rate of pay that far outstrips the average in all other sectors of the economy that employ large numbers of grads. In government, they average $55,600 per year. Self-employed graduates earn an annual average of $42,200.

Compared to other bachelor's degrees, the degree in mechanical engineering technology provides a substantial earnings advantage in some occupations and a disadvantage in others. Graduates working with the mechanical engineering job title earn about $2,100 less per year than other bachelor's degree holders in the same job; probably many of the others have an engineering degree rather than one in engineering technology and therefore have been trained in more appropriate skills.

In contrast, those working as top-level managers earn half again as much as top-level execs with other bachelor's degrees. Those in marketing and sales command double the pay of those with degrees in other fields. Knowledge of mechanical engineering technology clearly can be highly advantageous for CEOs, marketers, and salesworkers in technology industries.

Those holding jobs as mechanics and repairers are probably a poorer fit for their jobs than people with specialized training; that would explain the slightly lower salaries they receive compared to graduates of all other majors.

Job Satisfaction

The overall level of job satisfaction of mechanical engineering technology majors is about the same as the average for all graduates.

Employment Outlook

According to the projections by the U.S. Bureau of Labor Statistics, employment in occupations that require a bachelor's degree is expected to grow faster than employment in other sectors of the American labor market. Between 2008 and 2018, the U.S. workforce is projected to grow by 10.1 percent, creating an average of 15.2 million job openings per year. The bachelor's-level jobs are expected to increase by 17.7 percent over the same time. For the jobs that employ many graduates

Table 5
Percentage Distribution of Workers with Only a Bachelor's Degree,
by Level of Job Satisfaction

Job Satisfaction	Mechanical Engineering Technology	All
Very satisfied	47.2	45.4
Somewhat satisfied	39.8	45.0
Somewhat dissatisfied	12.5	7.4
Very dissatisfied	0.5	2.2
Mean Score (4=very satisfied, 1=not satisfied at all)	3.3	3.3

of mechanical engineering technology programs, slower-than-average growth is projected.

▮ Mechanical engineers are expected to have employment growth of 6 percent over the projections decade. Mechanical engineers are involved in the production of a wide range of products, and continued efforts to improve those products will create continued demand for their services. In addition, some new job opportunities will be created through emerging technologies in biotechnology, materials science, and nanotechnology. However, job candidates with an engineering degree will probably have an advantage over those with an engineering technology degree.

▮ The highly lucrative jobs in top-level management are projected to shrink slightly. In addition, keen competition is expected for these positions because the prestige and high pay attract many applicants.

▮ The workforce of mechanics and repairers is projected to shrink even more than that of top-level managers, but this is the average across a highly diverse collection of specializations. Some specializations are projected to grow faster than average—for example, avionics technicians, mechanical door repairers, precision instrument and equipment repairers, and medical equipment repairers. However, opportunities will probably be best for those with specialized training in these technologies. A

Table 6
Projected Growth and Job Openings in the Top 5 Occupations Employing Persons
with Only a Bachelor's Degree in Mechanical Engineering Technology

Top 5 Occupations	Projected Growth 2008–2018	Projected Annual Job Openings
All top 5	3.3%	136,860
Mechanical Engineers	6.0%	7,570
Top-Level Managers, Executives, and Administrators	−0.4%	61,470
Mechanics and Repairers	−4.4%	2,630
Other Marketing and Sales Occupations	7.3%	64,880
Sales Occupations—Commodities, Except Retail	−1.1%	310

degree in mechanical engineering technology may not be as good a match.

- ▶ Of the two marketing and sales occupations that round out the top 5 for mechanical engineering technology grads, better prospects can be found in the miscellaneous jobs than in commodities sales. The latter specialization not only is shrinking but has a very small workforce, so it will offer few job openings. Entry-level sales agents, particularly those with sales experience, should face better prospects in smaller firms, as opposed to larger firms, where many positions have been eliminated.

Pathways Beyond the Bachelor's Degree

Of those who earn a degree in mechanical engineering technology, only one-fifth eventually go on to earn an advanced degree of some type. Virtually all these postgraduate degrees are at the master's level.

- ▶ About 48 percent of these individuals earn a master's degree in a business field.

- ▶ A little more than one-quarter earn a master's degree in an engineering technology.

- ▶ A little more than one-fifth of grads go on to earn a master's in computer science or programming.

INDEX

S